Health principles and practice

Fourth edition

Health principles and practice

C. L. Anderson, B.S., M.S., Dr.P.H.

Professor of Hygiene and Health Education and Chairman of Hygiene and Environmental Sanitation, Oregon State University, Corvallis, Oregon; formerly Professor of Biological Science and Health Education, Michigan State University; formerly Head and Professor of Physiology, Hygiene, and Public Health, Utah State University

C. V. Langton, B.S., M.S., Dr.P.H., Ed.D., L.L.D.

Director of Physical Education, Oregon State University, Corvallis, Oregon

Illustrated

The C. V. Mosby Company *Saint Louis 1964*

Preface to
fourth edition

Health, as a branch of knowledge and a field of human concern and action, is both a science and an art. Science, as the process by which knowledge based on natural phenomena becomes organized, provides the procedures for discovering new knowledge in the field of health. It also provides the analysis, organization, interpretation, and evaluation of health knowledge. Art, as skill or the products of skill acquired through practice, furnishes man with the necessary means for applying health knowledge to human needs.

In no field of human discipline are there more misconceptions and more statements made which are not so than in the area of health. As society becomes more complex, it becomes increasingly more important that misconceptions be displaced by established, valid, reliable information on health. If life is becoming more complex, the advance of health knowledge keeps pace with the increasing complexity. The important corollary is to make this knowledge available to those who can understand and utilize knowledge of this kind to improve their present level of health and by its extension can project their life expectancy.

A health-educated student can appraise quite accurately what his health problems are today and what they will be in the years ahead. He can calculate rather accurately what his probable cause of death will be, and thus he will have the necessary knowledge to deal with the probable cause or causes. Today, health as a discipline directs its attention not to generalities but to a specific point, phenomenon, liability, asset, problem, or attainment. Success in health, like success in any other endeavor in life, is a matter of channeling one's efforts to those specific things of greatest importance in which effort will yield the greatest dividends.

The solution of a health problem is always relative, never absolute. Each year the health sciences make advances in the control of infectious diseases and

5

gradually reduce the effects of infection on man. In recent years the health sciences have made significant strides in the control of organic diseases. More than this, these same sciences now place in the hands of citizens measures for the prevention of cardiovascular disease. These are measures which the layman can carry out for his own best interests.

With the continuous parade of new discoveries in health science, there now comes the identification of insults to physical, mental, and emotional health. This is an important milestone for the citizen who seeks to understand this knowledge and who learns to apply it for his betterment.

The student who studies this book will find the basic knowledge he needs as a foundation for his personal health program. This book also will provide the student with procedures and techniques for the practice of the fundamental health principles which are enunciated. A student with a modicum of ingenuity will devise additional procedures of his own for health promotion. Indeed, the primary purpose of any health course in which this text is used is that of providing the student with the fundamentals and the means by which he may continue his own self-directed health education throughout his life. This is in the pattern of higher education in modern America.

C. L. Anderson
C. V. Langton

Contents

Part one

Personal health promotion

Chapter 1 The student and his health, 15

Education as growth, 15
The student and his education, 17
Health education needs of the student, 19
Modern concept of health, 22
Indices of personal health, 24
Levels of health, 26
Health promotion, 29
Extension of the prime of life, 30
Life expectancy, 37
Our aging population, 54
Extent of illness and disability, 56
Impairments, 57
What causes death, 59
Postponing death, 63
Science and health, 65
Interrelationship of personal and community
    health, 67
Using health resources, 68

Chapter 2 Inherited basis of health, 71

Longevity, 79
Inheritance, 80
Eugenics, 95
Nonhereditary disorders at birth, 98

Chapter 3 Daily personal health care, 100

The skin, 100
Oral health, 121

Hearing, 128
Vision, 130
General appraisal, 138

Chapter **4**   Nutrition in health, 139

Energy needs, 140
Building and upkeep needs, 153
Regulation needs, 155
Daily dietary needs, 163
Promotion of the health of digestion, 166
Nutrition as a community problem, 169

Chapter **5**   Exercise, fatigue, and rest, 171

Exercise, 173
Fatigue, 179
Rest, 180
Posture, 185
General considerations, 187

Chapter **6**   Safety for health promotion, 190

Safety councils, 192
Accidents and health, 192
The human factor in accidents, 196
Safety, 198
Emergency medical identification, 222

Chapter **7**   Substances harmful to health, 223

Bacterial poisons, 224
Normal metabolic wastes, 224
Toxins from abnormal growths, 225
Food poisoning, 225
Toxin transfer by food, 227
Drugs, 228
Chemical poisons, 253

Part two

Mental, emotional, and
social health

Chapter **8**   Normal mental and emotional health, 259

Mental health, 259
Mental disorder, 275
Appraisal of mental hygiene, 278

Chapter **9**   Preparation for family living, 279

Marriage in modern America, 279
Maturation for marriage, 283
Dating, 285
Selecting a mate, 287

Engagement, 291
Marital maturity, 292
Marriage as a way of life, 295
Widowhood, 298
Divorce, 298
Preparing for marriage, 299
Sex education, 301
General consideration of sex and
reproduction, 321

Part three

Planning for health protection

Chapter 10 Prevention of disease, 325
The causative agent and its nature, 330
Reservoirs of disease, 334
Exit of organisms from the body, 336
Ways and means of transfer of disease, 339
Blocking routes of transmission, 342
Standardized controls, 344
The disease cycle, 347
Types of individuals who spread disease, 348
Effectiveness of isolation and quarantine, 350
Defense against disease, 350
Infections of the genital system, 355
Fads, fallacies, and quackery, 359
Degenerative diseases, 360
Chronic diseases, 365
The periodic medical examination, 367

Chapter 11 State and local health services, 369
State health services, 369
Local health services, 376

Chapter 12 National and international health
services, 403
Voluntary health agencies, 403
Official national health services, 413
Official international health organizations, 422
Future conservation of human resources, 424

Bibliography, 433

Films and film sources, 443

Health principles and practice

Part one

Personal health promotion

Chapter 1

The student and his health

A college student of today lives in the most fantastic era in all of recorded history. More events and advances have been crowded into the past fifty years than have occurred in any previous five centuries. As knowledge advances at a geometric rate, the social structure becomes more and more complex and makes greater and greater demands in terms of human adaptation. To adjust effectively to the socioeconomic milieu that the student will find himself in after graduation, he must prepare himself in a diversity of fields of knowledge. All are important to his life. His understanding of health is especially important because health is the vehicle on which travels the hopes, the accomplishments, and the joys of life.

Health is one of youth's most valuable possessions, but one which many students do not fully appreciate until it is lost. A person may lose all of his material possessions, but if he still has excellent health he has the prime essential for the reconstruction and enjoyment of life. It is a fortunate student who possesses good health; it is an educated student who understands and practices principles of health protection, maintenance, and promotion.

There is nothing mystical about health science. It is both a collective and an applied discipline which utilizes contributions from several fields. Since responsibility for one's health rests with the individual himself, it is necessary to have a basic understanding of health in order to attain the maximum of one's health potential both today and in the years to come. Education properly must include competence in the area of health knowledge, understanding, and practice.

EDUCATION AS GROWTH

Education is a process of self-growth taking place within an individual. It is growth in one's capacity to understand and adapt to the world in which he lives.

It is a discipline for the adventure of life. Being well informed is an important phase of education, but being well informed is not enough. The importance of knowledge lies in its use. Education implies the ability to utilize knowledge and to apply meaning and value to it. Education is an expression of our capacity to penetrate and deal relevantly with the significant problems of life. It relates what we know to what we need and want. It is represented in our capacity to make valid distinctions and interpretations. It enables us to discriminate, to appraise, and to evaluate. With increased education come wider horizons and the prospect of more fruitful living.

Learning takes place at many levels in many aspects. Some learning, such as simple identification, may be at an extremely low level. Or it may be at a higher level such as learning of an analytical nature. Or it may reach the high level of creativity. A scale of levels of learning from the highest to the lowest will focus attention on those aspects of learning in need of greatest emphasis in the education process.

LEVELS OF LEARNING

Creative	Trial and error
Reflective	Factual
Conceptual	Rote memorization
Interpretive	Simple recall
Analytical	Imitation
Discrimination	Identification
Comprehension	

Teaching directed to the lower levels on the scale is teaching of little value in terms of student self-realization. Too many teachers are doing too much of their teaching on these lower levels of learning.

Education is a product of experience; hence, it may be acquired in all of the channels of life. Yet the college provides a special soil in which human abilities may grow most favorably. Here are assembled the necessary means, the professional supervision, and the proper atmosphere for obtaining the maximum in self-growth during a given period of time. The college illuminates knowledge, and the stimulation and energizing influence of the campus bring ability to greater fruition. A college faculty stimulates and guides students in self-growth.

Properly considered, education means the total unified growth of the individual. Thus education is a garment of seamless whole cloth, the over-all self-growth of the individual. Yet in the college it is recognized that a particular course does not contribute equally to all aspects of the student's education. Some courses serve predominantly to contribute to one phase of a student's education, whereas another course will contribute predominantly to another phase.

Two fundamental phases of college preparation are recognized—general education and vocational or technical preparation. General education encompasses the academic, cultural, and practical education of the student. The academic applies to knowledge for knowledge's sake, the cultural applies to the appre-

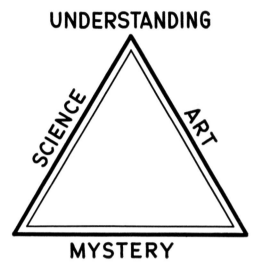

Fig. 1. Science and art—twin disciplines. Each discipline in its own ways seeks to convert the mysteries of the universe to human understanding. Health is based both on science and on art.

ciation of the finer things of human existence which elevate man above the commonplace, and the practical relates to the necessary equipment for adapting effectively to the practicalities of life. Health education is essentially practical education, with some contributions to the student's cultural and academic education.

THE STUDENT AND HIS EDUCATION

Basically students attend college for two purposes—to obtain a broad general or basic education and to acquire the technical preparation necessary to enter a vocation. Health courses available to underclassmen are an integral part of the institution's general educational program designed to meet the basic needs of the student for effective living in college as well as in future years.

General or basic education is designed to provide each student with a sound foundation on which to build an intelligent interest in personal, family, social, and civic problems and with a greater ability to deal with these problems. It encompasses the study of man's relationship to the social, biological, and physical sciences, a comprehensive knowledge of the origins and development of civilization, and enhanced appreciation of cultures expressed in literature, art, and music. It provides students with an opportunity to explore broad areas of knowledge, aids them in the discovery of their own interests and aptitudes, and better equips them to assume their responsibilities as individuals, as parents, and as citizens in a democracy. It will enable them to live more effectively and more enjoyably. It will provide that self-esteem which a broad education engenders. It will be reflected in the respect the individual commands because of a certain nobility which characterizes the well-educated citizen.

A nationally accepted statement of the objectives of general education is contained in a report published by the American Council on Education. The report states:

In the committee's judgment, general education should lead the student:

1. To improve and maintain his own health and take his share of responsibility for protecting the health of others

2. To communicate through his own language in writing and speaking at the level of expression adequate to the needs of educated people

3. To attain a sound emotional and social adjustment through the enjoyment of a wide range of social relationships and the experience of working cooperatively with others

4. To think through the problems and to gain the basic orientation that will better enable him to make satisfactory family and marital adjustment

5. To do his part as an active and intelligent citizen dealing with the interrelated social, economic, and political problems of American life and in solving the problems of postwar international reconstruction

6. To act in the light of and understanding of the natural phenomena in his environment in its implications for human society and human welfare, to use his scientific methods in the solution of his problems, and to employ useful nonverbal methods of thought and communication

7. To find self-expression in literature and to share through literature man's experiences and his motivating ideas and ideals

8. To find a means of self-expression in music and in the various visual arts and crafts, and to understand and appreciate art and music as reflections both of individual experience and of social patterns and movements

9. To practice clear and integrated thinking about the meaning and value of life

10. To choose a vocation that will make optimum use of his talents and enable him to make an appropriate contribution to society*

The ability to think critically and intensely is developed and applied as an inherent aspect of the learning process throughout the educational program. All phases of learning should include the development of mental discipline, which characterizes the well-educated citizen. A college errs in permitting students to get into a mold of slovenly thinking. To acquire a pattern or mode of intensive critical thinking is to be prepared to rise above the commonplace and to live effectively by utilizing the near potential of one's intellectual endowment.

It is noteworthy that the American Council on Education placed the improvement, maintenance, and protection of health as the *first* of the objectives. Even more significant is the Council's further elaboration on the implementation of this first objective of health. In order to accomplish this purpose the student should acquire the following:

A. Knowledge and understanding
  1. Of normal body functions in relation to sound health practice
  2. Of the major health hazards, their prevention and control
  3. Of the interrelation of mental and physical processes in health
  4. Of reliable sources of health information
  5. Of scientific methods in evaluating health concepts

*From American Council on Education: A design for general education, Washington 6, D. C., 1944, The Council.

6. Of the effect of socioeconomic conditions on health
7. Of community health problems, such as problems related to sanitation, industrial hygiene, and school hygiene
8. Of community organization and services for health maintenance and improvement

B. Skills and abilities
1. The ability to organize time to include planning for food, work, recreation, rest, and sleep
2. The ability to improve and maintain good nutrition
3. The ability to attain and maintain good emotional adjustment
4. The ability to select and engage in recreative activities and healthful exercises suitable to individual needs
5. The ability to avoid unnecessary exposure to disease and infection
6. The ability to utilize medical and dental services intelligently
7. The ability to participate in measures for the protection and improvement of community health
8. The ability to evaluate popular beliefs critically

C. Attitudes and appreciations
1. Desire to obtain optimum health
2. Personal satisfaction in carrying out sound health practices
3. Acceptance of responsibility for his own health and for the protection of the health of others
4. Willingness to make personal sacrifices for the health of others
5. Willingness to comply with health regulations and to work for their improvement*

This is an expression, not of health specialists, but of a cross section of citizens who have studied the education needs of American students. It represents a composite evaluation by a group competent to appraise the direction education should take if it is to give the college student the preparation necessary to protect, preserve, and promote his own health and that of his family and community and to make the necessary decisions relating to health which his life's journey will require.

HEALTH EDUCATION NEEDS OF THE STUDENT

Preparation for living requires an intensive and extensive understanding of health. Before the content and scope of health preparation for college students is determined, it is necessary to determine what the health education needs of students actually are. This implies a first step in identifying the actual specific health needs of college students. Many sources have been drawn upon to obtain a true picture of the significant health needs of the student today and in the future years of life. Surveys of students and persons in older age groups on specific health needs and interests, questionnaires on health problems, analysis of morbidity and mortality statistics, analysis of medical reports, study of medical examination findings, and various special studies and reports of health educators have provided a basis on which the core of the college health instruction can properly be based. These health education needs can best be presented in terms

---

*From American Council on Education: A design for general education, Washington 6, D. C., 1944, The Council.

of knowledge, attitudes, and practices as related to the three broad areas of (1) personal health promotion, (2) mental, emotional, and social health, and (3) planning for health protection.

Personal health promotion. Included in this category are the knowledge, attitudes, and practices related to the following:

1. Concept of normal health
2. Indices of optimum health
3. Appraisal of one's health assets and liabilities
4. Demands of college life and orientation to college living
5. Importance and means of attaining balanced living
6. Biological basis of health promotion
7. Role of heredity in health
8. Health aspects of eugenics
9. Fundamentals of nutrition
10. Application of the principles of nutrition to a properly balanced dietary
11. Relationship of activity to health
12. The roles of fatigue, rest, and sleep in health
13. Preservation of vision and hearing
14. Promotion of the health of the teeth and skin
15. Health hazards of stimulants, narcotics, and other poisons
16. Safety as human adjustment
17. Nature, prevention, and control of infectious diseases
18. Nature, prevention, and control of organic disorders
19. Aging as a normal and as a pathological process
20. Extension of the prime of life
21. Causes and postponement of death
22. Factors related to the extension of life expectation
23. Organized plan for health as preparation for living

Mental, emotional, and social health. Included in this area are knowledge, attitudes, and practices related to the following:

1. The nature of personality and mental health
2. The motivation of human conduct
3. Emotional development
4. Attributes of a well-adjusted personality
5. Adjustment to common problems in mental health
6. Disintegration and integration
7. The nature of mental disturbance
8. Procedures for the improvement of personality and the level of mental health
9. Social relationships
10. The nature of love and its fulfillment
11. Male-female relationships
12. Selection of a mate

13. Marriage as adjustment
14. Forms of marriage adjustment
15. Sex adjustment in marriage
16. Function of reproduction
17. Parenthood
18. Harmony in family living

Planning for health protection. This area comprises the knowledge, attitudes, and practices related to the following:

1. Interrelation of personal and community health
2. Community health problems
3. Community health services
4. Official community health agencies
5. Voluntary community health agencies
6. Medical and dental resources
7. Hospital facilities
8. Other community health resources
9. Medical and hospital insurance
10. Use of health resources
11. Community immunization programs
12. Communicable disease control programs
13. Community safety programs
14. Sanitation
15. Citizen participation in community health protection and promotion
16. Health problems, needs, and trends

Health education can be the avenue to a higher level of health, an extension of the prime of life, and an increase in the length of life. Consider the quality of health the nation would possess if all college graduates, the oncoming leaders of our communities, had a health education in these terms. Consider the value of such an education to the health of the student while he is on the campus as well as in the years to come. Consider further the value of such an education to the future family and associates of each of these graduates. All of these student health education needs can be satisfied by the student who applies himself assiduously to his health education opportunities on the campus. Perfection in education is neither expected nor necessary, but a health instruction program should provide each student with a substantial knowledge of fundamental health principles, a positive health awareness, and established health practices.

No instructor could possibly anticipate all of the specific health problems and situations students will encounter in their lifetime. Yet the health class can deal with fundamental health principles and thus provide a foundation on which a student may further build his education in health. Class instruction is designed to develop the student's ability to direct his further independent study of health. Besides the fundamentals of health science, the student will become acquainted with sources of health information and will be able to analyze, interpret, and appraise the merit of what he reads in the health field.

Learning can result only from active participation on the part of the student. An instructor can only help a student to learn. The student can learn entirely under self-direction; yet the guidance and supervision of the learned experienced instructor makes the student's learning more effective and more comprehensive. It further assures the student that his learning is in the pathway recognized by qualified individuals as the true pathway to health understanding.

MODERN CONCEPT OF HEALTH

The contention that health is merely freedom from disease is not adequate in terms of modern needs and present-day understanding of health. True, a person must be free from disease and disabling defects to have an acceptable level of health, but the term *health* encompasses more than this. Today, *health* is conceived of as being *that quality of physical, mental, and emotional well-being which enables one to live effectively and enjoyably*. Disease is a harmful departure from normal health.

Health must be considered in relative terms since the final criteria of effective and enjoyable living are not absolute terms either quantitatively or qualitatively. When any factor or activity is evaluated in terms of possible contribution to health, it is valid to make the evaluation in terms of the following question: What will be the effect on the individual's effectiveness and enjoyment in living? Health, therefore, is a means to an end, a vehicle for more fruitful living. To the normal person physical, mental, and emotional well-being enable him to do the things he wants to do and should do and to achieve life's purposes, with the resulting gratification which is the one true source of personal enjoyment. For a person who suffers from a disease such as tuberculosis or who has a disabling defect such as one of the vertebral column, health becomes an end to be gained if truly effective and enjoyable living is to be attained.

Normal health. In the lexicon of health perhaps no term is used more frequently than the one word *normal*. Usually the term *normal* is used in a rather vague sense without any particular designation. At other times it is used as a synonym for average. Properly normal should be regarded as that which is accepted as the *usual*. What is termed usual is what society has acknowledged as being customary. In reference to health, normal consists of a range rather than a specific entity. It includes the average person as well as many individuals above and below the average level of health. Normal encompasses the health of more than 90% of a typical college student population. All members of the student body are different. No two are alike though both may be in the range of normal health. It is apparent that health is a relative matter, some individuals having a higher level of health than others though all of these individuals may have normal health.

What constitutes normal health must necessarily be set up arbitrarily, based upon the knowledge, experience, and judgment of those who have devoted their talents to a lifelong study of health. In general terms normal health is regarded as that state of well-being in which the individual is free from disabling defects and has sufficient vigor to carry on the usual requirements of life, with social adaptation which produces self-gratification and enjoyment. It is relatively easy to identify the health of most individuals as being within or outside the normal range. Some patients with borderline conditions would require a highly discriminating examination and appraisal by a physician to designate the health category in which the person belongs.

Normal health does not mean perfect health. In this imperfect world every person has his imperfections, but most of these imperfections are of little or no significance in terms of normal health. No person's level of vigor remains uniform but tends to fluctuate or be somewhat cyclic. Although the degree of vigor or zest may decline from time to time, the individual still may be in the normal range of health.

Some students will possess a constitutional makeup which provides almost limitless vitality, endurance, and resurgence, even though they do not practice recognized principles of health promotion. Although young men and women in this category may carry on reasonably successfully during their youth, indiscretions in health care will take their toll in the later years of life, in both premature aging and length of life.

A small percentage of students possess a constitution which is adequate for normal needs only if every principle of health promotion is practiced. An individual with a constitutional makeup on the border of inadequacy can maintain normal health by the proper use of modern health resources and by following a regimen which avoids hazards to health and which promotes the highest possible level of body function. These individuals can truly harvest the fruit of the advances in health science.

Many intergrades are to be found between the extremes of a highly proficient constitution at one pole and the almost inadequate constitution at the other pole. Each individual needs to understand his native endowment so that he can more effectively apply the principles of health promotion to his particular needs if he is to obtain the greatest possible yield in health.

Today health is not appraised in terms of muscular strength or physical size. Obviously a person should have enough strength to carry on the usual demands of life. Perhaps he should have some degree of strength beyond this for special occasions which may arise, but he need not be a circus strong man. Health is an over-all condition of well-being to be evaluated collectively, not a matter of specialized development. As will be pointed out later, massive musculature may be inimical to good health. Likewise a person need not be of large physical stature in order to have a high level of health. Small stature, medium stature, and large stature can all be associated with excellent health. The slender person, the person of stocky build, and the person of moderately broad build can all be extremely healthy. In appraising health it is the over-all quality of physical, mental, and emotional well-being which is evaluated. It is the over-all capacity of the individual to meet the demands of life.

A person with normal health may suffer a transitory illness, such as a cold or appendicitis, or he may suffer a disability, such as a bone fracture, and thus be temporarily outside the range of normal health. Such a person can recover quickly and return to the normal range if his state of well-being has been of a high level generally and if he has followed sound health principles in his day-to-day living.

INDICES OF PERSONAL HEALTH

A thorough inventory of an individual's exact health status would require a clinical examination by a physician, plus a battery of laboratory tests. Such an inventory is made at the time a student enters college and thereafter at regular intervals or for special occasions. However, for practical purposes the student who is obligated to direct his own program of health promotion needs observable health landmarks to guide him. By evaluating these outward characteristics collectively, the student has a day-to-day inventory or templet of his general pattern of health. While of necessity these indices will be interpreted in relative terms, they serve as a sufficient guide in his program of self-improvement and can indicate any significant decline in health status. Most important they point out the significance of physical vitality and social adjustment as attributes of positive health.

Freedom from disease and disabilities. A first essential of normal health is an absence of diseases and defects which hinder effectiveness and enjoyment in living. The presence of even mild illness and a minor defect can have an appreciable adverse effect upon health. Continuing through several years, a minor ailment may have a cumulative effect which will lower the individual's health to a level below normal. Some defects may be nondisabling. Even a loss of hearing in one ear may not be disabling if hearing in the other ear is normal. Or, if a corrective device gives the individual a normal end result, a defect would not be classed as disabling. A remediable defect, however minor, should be corrected. If a defect is nonremediable, the health potential should be weighted accordingly, and due consideration should be given for the degree of compensation which occurs. Conceivably a person with a nonremediable defect, for all practical purposes, might be classed as having normal health.

Lack of consciousness of existence of body. A healthy individual is not aware of his bodily existence unless it is called to his attention. When an organ or any part of the body becomes diseased or disordered, a person is then likely to become aware of the existence of the organ. This holds true whether it is an acute disturbance of the stomach or a chronic inflammation of a joint. More than this, when a general toxic condition exists, the associated fatigue and irritability produce an awareness of the body's existence. A person who has to be reminded that he has a body doubtless possesses a high level of physical well-being.

A feeling of buoyancy. Normal health is characterized by a feeling of lightness or minimum of body weight. In the vernacular it is referred to as bounce. A healthy student feels as though he carries virtually no weight, as though he has little physical restriction. He almost feels as though he were floating. In chronic fatigue or in illness the body feels heavy and is like an anchor. This feeling of weightiness also accompanies the aging process. In contrast normal youth has a pronounced feeling and air of buoyancy.

Adequate vigor. An individual with normal health has sufficient vitality to meet the demands of everyday living. Great muscular strength is not necessary, but a student should have sufficient muscular energy to carry on the customary activities of life. The reserve strength over and above the optimum will depend upon the interests and anticipated activities of the individual.

More important than strength is the physiological condition and endurance of the student. Physiological fitness in which the various body functions are carried on harmoniously and efficiently is far more to be desired than physical fitness expressed merely in terms of strength.

Zest in daily living. A youth with normal health exhibits keen enjoyment in day-to-day activities. Daily physical, mental, and social experiences are more stimulating than fatiguing and provide personal gratification highly enjoyable to the individual. He becomes tired, but he is so engrossed in the activities of the day that he is rarely conscious of fatigue until the day draws to a close. A lack of zest for living is an indication of an inadequate quality of well-being.

General ease and relaxation. To be relaxed and at ease is an indication of wholesome adjustment to the immediate situation and to life in general. In every life there will be occasions when tensions are created, but a healthy individual recovers rather quickly and soon displaces tenseness with ease and relaxation. A student who is unable to relax or is constantly tense is in need of readjustment. Whether the tenseness is due to physical, mental, or emotional factors, the cause must be determined and eliminated if the individual is to attain an acceptable standard of well-being. Your answer to the question "How does your motor idle?" reveals a great deal about your health.

Wholesome appetite. A steady wholesome appetite is customarily an indication of wholesome health. People in poor health usually have a capricious appetite, the poor appetite continuing the downward spiral to an even poorer level of health. Although a wholesome appetite does not assure a balanced diet, nevertheless there is at least a good probability that a person with an adequate appetite will have a reasonably well-balanced diet. At least he will not be one who "picks at his food." Adequate health education plus a wholesome appetite can be the formula for a balanced diet and proper nutrition.

Weight remains stable. Small variations in weight are normal and to be expected, but pronounced fluctuation is abnormal. The normal body tends to attain a balance or homeostasis in all of its functions and conditions, including weight. Stable body weight is an indication of general constitutional stability, a valuable asset. At college age a small gradual increase in weight is quite typical. This gradual slow rate of increase to about thirty years of age may be regarded as normal. At that age the desirable adult weight level should be attained. Pronounced variation in weight is not a normal state and merits the immediate attention of a physician.

Sleeps well and is adequately rested. Regularity in sleep is both an indication of normal health and a factor contributing to normal health. Following the usual night's sleep, the student should be adequately rested to start the day at maximum efficiency. Some individuals have a constitutional makeup which is slow in accelerating in the morning. As will be pointed out in Chapter 5, these individuals have an unusually low temperature upon waking and one which is slow in rising to normal. A hot bath which elevates body temperature will likely speed up general bodily functions.

Any student may show occasional indications of inadequate rest, but chronic fatigue indicates that an individual has an inadequate level of health. A physician should be consulted in an effort to locate the basic causes.

Purposeful and planned daily living. To live effectively and to live enjoyably a student must have a realistic philosophy of the ultimate purpose of life. Further the student needs an orderly organized plan of daily living based upon immediate worthwhile goals. Consistent attainment of these goals yields the personal gratification so essential to a high level of mental and emotional well-being.

Emotional stability. A temperament of congeniality and a poise that can meet the frustrations and crises of life composes a twosome of infinite value in life's adjustment. The well-integrated individual may occasionally experience some disintegration but will mobilize his resources and will recover rather quickly from the disturbing experience.

Social adequacy. No person is as well adjusted as he would want to be, nor is it necessary to be perfectly adjusted socially in order to attain the normal level of health. A sincere interest in people, expressed through an interest in them as personalities and in their abilities and accomplishments, is fundamental to social adjustment. The confidence and ease of the socially well-adjusted individual is the result of applying and expressing this interest in day-to-day social experiences. Just as physical health is improved and maintained through plan and application, so, too, mental health is improved by appraising one's assets and liabilities and pursuing an orderly plan for elevating one's level of mental, emotional, and social well-being.

LEVELS OF HEALTH

Health is relative. The quality of well-being encompasses a range. One individual may have a high quality of well-being, another may possess a somewhat lower quality, and a third may have an even lower quality of health; yet all can be classed as normal. In order to catalog various gradations of health a helpful scale can be devised to rate the various levels of health. Since levels of health are correlated with the energy and vital output individuals possess, for purposes of convenient designation the analogy of octane ratings can be applied to health qualities. As with any other comparative appraisal scale, such a grading does not provide refined discriminations, but it does provide a practical means for evaluating the general quality of an individual's health.

In this scale normal health is represented by the first three levels. This is a recognition that an individual may have normal health without having the high level of health which should be the goal of every student. The fourth and fifth levels on the scale represent two degrees of deviation from the normal. Individuals in these two categories need the services of a professional medical practitioner to restore better health.

90 to 100 octane health. This is the *premium* grade of health, not perfect health but a high level of vigor and buoyancy with an abundance of energy which enables the individual to participate effectively in all of the demands of life. This level of health enables the individual to function at a maximum in the early morning and go through the day with the vigor which effective and enjoyable living requires. This quality of health enables the student to go through a typical day without appreciable fatigue because the individual finds life more stimulating than fatiguing. A student with this level of health is relaxed and at ease and enjoys the gratification of wholesome social adjustment and successful daily accomplishment. Neither physical size nor body type is a factor in classifying a person as possessing this level of health. Such a quality of health obviously means freedom from disease and disabling defects. A person in this top category of health may have an occasional head cold or some mild disturbance, such as a headache or a minor infection, and thus temporarily drop below this level of health. In this situation a wise student will put forth every effort to restore his top-flight premium level of health.

About 30% of all college students possess the 90 to 100 grade of health. In the United States only about 10% of the adult population between the ages of 30 and 70 years maintain this level of health.

80 to 90 octane health. This may be classed as the *regular* grade of health. Absence of disease and disabling defects is characteristic of this level also. People in this category are slightly below the premium grade in terms of vigor, buoyancy, and zest. They live reasonably effectively and enjoyably but at a level about 10% below the premium grade. The difference in these first two levels is essentially one of degree, one of qualitative difference. This is a highly acceptable level of health, but many individuals in this bracket can rise to the premium level of health through the application of recognized principles of health promotion.

About 40% of all college students possess the 80 to 90 grade of health. In the adult population between the ages of 30 and 70 years, about 25% have this quality of health.

60 to 80 octane health. This is the *inferior* grade of health, though still classed within the normal range and having neither disease nor disabling defects.

Individuals in this category pass as well, but lack the necessary vitality and vigor for living in a dynamic society. These individuals are not really sick, but they tend to drag through the day at a low level of function rather than to move along with the vigor that effective living requires. Many of these individuals find the demands of life unduly difficult because they lack the vitality necessary to meet the requirements of modern life. They will feel tired without much reason and will feel unable to do all of the things they want to do and should do. They need more firepower in the form of physical and mental vigor.

No other group of students would benefit so much as this group from an understanding and application of health principles. Most individuals at this level of health have the basic endowment necessary to attain a health status in the next higher category. Some could attain the premium level of health. These individuals should ask themselves, "What is health of that quality worth?" A student with an adequate education in health will answer that question before outright ill health answers it for him. Illness has been labeled the most effective form of health education, but it might be added that it is also the most costly.

About 25% of all college students possess the 60 to 80 grade level of health. In the general adult population between the ages of 30 and 70 years, about 50% are in this category. It is sad to relate that half of the adult population in the United States has an unsatisfactory quality of health.

50 to 60 octane health. In this category are those individuals who are up and around but are not well. These individuals are outside of the normal range of health. They suffer from chronic infection or have an organic disorder which imposes an added burden upon the low level of vitality they have. Most students in this category should not be in school. Exceptions may be made, such as for persons wearing a satisfactory brace for a vertebral disorder. The initial step in reconstruction must be that of identifying the basic pathological condition. This calls for immediate medical service to restore health. This will be followed by a constructive program of health promotion to attain an acceptable level of well-being. Even those students with an extremely low level of vitality, but without specific diseases or defects, should be under medical supervision.

About 3% of the college population is in this classification. About 10% of the adults between the ages of 30 and 70 years are in this category.

Less than 50 octane health. This is the category of recognized disease or disability. Here we find the individuals who are incapacitated by illness or other disorder. It may be a student in the college infirmary with infectious mononucleosis or an individual confined to a wheel chair in his home because of an orthopedic disorder. Obviously individuals in this classification are patients who should be under medical supervision.

About 2% of the college population is in this category. For the 30- to 70-year age group, perhaps 5% are in this category.

Every student should ask two questions: What is health worth, and what level of health do I want? Then the student should organize a life plan for health promotion. It will be an investment in better health, more life in years, and more years in life.

HEALTH PROMOTION

Personal health promotion is expressed in the efforts of an individual to safeguard, maintain, and improve his health status. It encompasses all activities related to the betterment of one's health, including the use of community health resources, but the keystone is the day-to-day application of health principles. Health promotion is not time consuming for the person with a basic understanding of health who has established a regimen of living which incorporates recognized principles of health practice. Such a health promotion plan will be built upon a framework of fundamental needs for healthful living.

1. Taking a regular inventory of the present health status through periodic health examinations
2. Adapting to one's hereditary potential in health through an understanding of one's hereditary endowment and the discharge of responsibilities in matters of heredity and eugenics
3. Caring for body functions, including those factors affecting the skin, teeth, hearing, and vision
4. Avoiding products harmful to health
5. Providing essential nutrition and vitality for the digestive system through scientifically established dietary practices
6. Adapting physical activity to one's capacities and needs in order to obtain maximum physiological and mental benefits
7. Adjusting the pattern of living to avoid extreme fatigue or exhaustion
8. Providing adequate relaxation, rest, and sleep in the daily program for the specific requirements of the individual
9. Adapting to physical hazards through a safety consciousness adequate to anticipate hazardous conditions and practices
10. Preventing infection or immediately attending to infection which does occur
11. Preventing organic disorders and immediately attending to any deviation which does develop
12. Developing a positive mature mental, emotional, and social adjustment
13. Adapting effectively to frustrations
14. Adjusting to the dynamics of group action
15. Using available health resources appropriately and at the proper time

Much of the material in this volume will be devoted to measures for fulfilling these health promotion needs. Although certain general principles, such as moderation, regularity, and balance in living, apply universally in health promotion, specific measures must be applied to certain health factors. These measures will involve an understanding both of basic principles and of the methods of application. Promotion of health is a personal responsibility requiring constant progress in the ability to meet health needs effectively in order to enjoy a high level of health.

EXTENSION OF THE PRIME OF LIFE

Aging is a natural process, but all of us age faster than we should. This accelerated aging is pathological aging, and in this sphere scientists are conducting studies to discover the factors which cause premature aging and to determine what measures can counteract pathological aging. This is not in the realm of theorizing, but is a field of investigation which is both practical and fruitful. Just consider that at least half of a person's liver is replaced every seven days and that the constant changes of the body need not be of a deteriorating nature. The study of the aging process is *gerontology;* the care of the aged is *geriatrics.* Gerontology is of patricular interest to health science, and people in the health field are most interested in the positive aspects of gerontology—the extension of the prime of life.

Aging as a normal process. The distinguishing characteristic of life is that a living organism is capable of autocatalysis, that is, a living organism produces its own enzymes which accelerate the chemical action commonly referred to as living processes. These enzymes are proteins which the various cells synthesize from the amino acids derived from proteins in the diet. It is obvious that physiological aging must be centered in chemical changes associated with the living process. Facility in synthesizing protoplasm is a key factor in retaining the prime of life.

Most of man's knowledge of aging is expressed in descriptive terms, but scientists have discovered some basic biological factors associated with aging. Cellular proteins exhibit changes in aging. Labile proteins are associated with youthfulness of tissues, though even college students will have both stable and labile proteins. Skeletal muscle contains both stable and labile proteins, but with aging stable proteins are increased. There is an associated decline in the solubility of tissue proteins. Folding of the proteins in tissues appears to occur, and this results in a chain effect which typifies aging tissue. The ability of colloids to bind water is decreased in an aging person and accounts for the wrinkled tissue typical of old age. Professor Louis Pillemer and co-workers, at Western Reserve University, have isolated a protein substance *(properdin)* from the blood serum of lower animals and man which is important in maintaining resistance to infectious and noninfectious diseases. The production by the body of this protective substance declines with age. With this decline interference with normal chemical action takes place, with the possible effect of hastening the aging process. Increases in sodium, lipids (fats), and calcium have been reported to be present in aging, and a decline in potassium retention occurs. All of these changes of aging could theoretically be attributed to the loss of the ability of cells to produce the enzymes essential for life processes.

After this consideration of the *why* and *how* of aging, attention should be directed to the descriptive *what* of aging.

In human beings, aging generally sets in between the ages of 25 and 30 years. People who mature late usually have a delayed onset of aging. Although a declining rate of cellular regeneration accompanies the aging process, growth may still continue. Experiments with lower animals indicate that retarding growing by nutritional deficiency will delay aging. Graying of the hair is not a significant index of aging since a lack of pigment and admission of air into the hair shaft are essentially a mechanical or physical phenomenon rather than one of cellular activity. However, general appearance does reflect the aging process because it expresses the loss of elasticity and increased wrinkling of the skin associated with aging of the skin.

Sensory changes. Sensory changes can reflect the aging process. Changes in hearing, which may occur as early as 20 years of age, are not necessarily due to aging. Nerve deafness may be due to aging. Changes in the eyes, such as reduced elasticity of the crystalline lens, generally appear at the age of 40 years. Present evidence does not support the common contention that the state of the crystalline lens reveals a person's true age. It merely reveals the relative aging of the lens.

A decrease in orbital fat causes the eyes to be deeper set in their sockets, thus changing the general facial appearance. Eyelids become thinner and lose their elasticity. Color of the iris fades. Cataracts and glaucoma are associated with the aging process. As will be pointed out later, faulty circulation accounts for many eye disturbances and is obviously related to the rate of aging. At 50 years of age the sense of taste begins to decline, with the number of taste buds reduced from about 208 in the prime of life to about 88 at 85 years of age. Smell begins to be less acute at 60 years of age.

Physical strength. Physical strength changes with the aging process so that at 60 years of age the biceps brachii are about half as strong as they are at 25 years of age and have a decided loss of muscle tone. Part of this decline is due to neurological decay, but the muscles shrink as a result of a loss of water content, fatty infiltration, replacement of muscle fibers by fibrous tissue, and an increase in stable proteins.

Connective tissue. Connective tissue, such as ligaments and tendons, becomes less elastic. Cartilage hardens and contracts, bone becomes demineralized, and the vertebral column bows with a loss in over-all height.

Digestive system. The digestive system usually functions adequately beyond the normal lifetime though the output of saliva, and thus ptyalin, and of hydrochloric acid declines with aging. After the age of 60 years very little hydrochloric acid is produced by the stomach, and there are resulting digestive disorders, such as enteritis and diarrhea. The liver normally has a long life span.

Respiratory system. Changes in the respiratory system associated with aging are not highly important. The reduction of vital capacity and the cellular decline in the covering of mucous tissue still leave respiratory function adequate for normal needs.

Neuron system. Aging of the neuron system involves a multitude of changes which are reflected in the inability of the brain cells to synthesize cellular constituents. Brain weight and size are diminished appreciably, the volume of cerebrospinal fluid is increased, the outer lining *(dura mater)* is thickened and may contain calcium deposits, there is a loss of brain cells due to cellular death *(necrocytosis)*, cerebral blood flow is diminished from 10% to 25%, and the cerebral metabolic rate is diminished by the same amount. The peak of the rate and speed of learning is reached before 30 years of age and shows a slow decline until 40 years of age, when an acceleration of the decline occurs. Speed of the neuron system is an important index of aging, and the speed of simple responses can be useful in assaying the mental status of aging individuals. Experiments reveal that aged animals cannot react quickly under any circumstances.

Endocrine function. Endocrine changes may be the best single index of overall aging, but we lack methods for the precise measurement of all endocrine functions. Thyroxin output declines with age, resulting in a drop of 7% in basal metabolism every ten years after 30 years of age. The thyroid shrinks and atrophies in later years. A decrease in insulin output reveals a decline in pancreatic function. The slow rate of healing and repair in the aged indicates a slowing down of adrenal function with aging.

Reproductive organs. Reproductive organs have a distinctive aging pattern. In a sense in the female the reproductive organs begin wearing out at 14 years of age, and at 50 years of age are not functioning at all. If the endocrine aspect of the reproductive process is considered, aging does not begin to set in until about 40 years of age. In the male, reproductive functioning reaches its peak at about 29 years of age and declines gradually to about 65 years of age, when infertility is reached. Neither a surgical removal of the ovaries (ovariectomy) in the female nor removal of the testes (castration) in the male appears to hasten or retard the aging process.

Circulatory system. Changes in the circulatory system affect all processes of the body since supplying oxygen and nutrients and removing wastes are important to all cell function. With aging the heart gradually shifts from an angular to a more horizontal position. An increase in cardiac bulk is accompanied by an opaqueness of the pericardium. Valves lose their softness. Fat deposits in the walls of the arteries tend to weaken the vessels and may even lead to coronary disturbances. Because of the cardiovascular-kidney relationship, the diminished excretion due to the decline of kidney tissue after the age of 60 years has an adverse effect on circulatory function. The timeworn adage that a person is no older than his arteries is not entirely accurate, but circulation does play an extremely important role in the rate of the aging process.

Aging as a pathological process. Any interference with normal biochemical activity hastens aging. Usually it is not one single major factor but the cumulative effect of several minor factors which hastens aging. If this is recognized, it may well be that what we today think of as normal aging is in reality merely a lesser form of pathological aging. Certainly every adult represents some degree of pathological aging in some aspects, perhaps in most or even all. This is true even of those individuals who have a rate of aging markedly slower than typical. What we today regard as pathological aging is that which is accelerated so markedly that it is generally recognized by the individual's associates.

Premature pathological aging may appear in various guises or combinations of characteristics. A marked slowing down in tempo of all activities, abnormally slow recovery from fatigue, illness, or injury, particularly from wounds, pronounced loss of physical strength and endurance, poor muscle tone, stooped posture, unsteady gait, decline in sensory function, particularly of vision, inability to retain sufficient body heat, leathery appearance of the skin, and changes in life interests are all typical characteristics.

Various factors can contribute to pathological aging, many of which can be identified in a given individual, but others are more subtle and not always recognized.

Heredity. Heredity plays a role. At least well-conducted studies reveal familial tendencies to premature aging. Yet it must be recognized that only physical or physiological factors are inherited. When heredity enters into pathological aging, it must be because a person inherits a certain deficiency, such as an inadequate resistance to disease or a deficient circulatory system. Even such a person could conceivably delay the aging process through the application of knowledge we now have, limited though it is.

Stress syndrome. The stress syndrome, represented in chronic tension, worry, fatigue, and inability to relax, is perhaps the greatest single cause of premature aging in the United States. Relentless pursuit of money, prestige, or power will take its toll in premature aging as well as in other respects. Constant tension may throw the anterior pituitary and adrenal glands out of normal balance, thus upsetting normal biochemical function. In such an intrinsic environment cellular regeneration is disturbed and delayed.

Deteriorating diseases. Deteriorating diseases, such as coronary disorders, hardening of the arteries (arteriosclerosis), high blood pressure (hypertension), stroke (intracranial lesions), cancer, arthritis, and rheumatism, produce premature aging.

Low-grade infection. A low-grade infection which continues over an extended period of time can take a toll in the form of a reduction in the number of prime years of life.

Toxins. Toxins from the intestines, tonsils, and teeth and uremia resulting from malfunction of the kidneys frequently cause premature aging of an extreme form.

Extended critical illness. An extended critical illness which threatens life itself but from which a patient recovers may take a heavy toll which is represented by marked aging.

Prolonged physical near exhaustion. Prolonged physical near exhaustion, such as may be created by a battle situation, can have an unusual aging effect. Even in civilian life repeated extended periods of exhaustion are detrimental to the prime of life.

Lack of rest and sleep. Over an extended period of time lack of rest and sleep may contribute to premature aging. Lack of rest and sleep will usually be associated with marked tension and a continual state of near exhaustion so that the total syndrome must be considered in appraising the effect of lack of rest on the aging process.

Inadequate circulation. Inadequate circulation, which reduces oxygenation of the tissues, can produce rapid aging. Lack of hemoglobin in the blood, lack of permeability of cells, and lack of myoglobin in muscles can all hasten the aging process.

Marked nutritional deficiency. Marked nutritional deficiency, particularly in proteins, vitamins, and minerals, can lead to early aging. The emaciation and run-down condition of markedly malnourished persons, pictured in newspaper and newsreel, is convincing evidence of the ravages of starvation upon youthfulness. To a lesser extent this same effect occurs in those individuals with a less pronounced nutritional deficiency. Indiscreet Spartan dieting to lose weight can have sufficient effect upon the physiological balance of the body to produce rapid aging.

Inactivity. Inactivity can contribute to pathological aging. Too little participation in life's processes can be a rusting out process.

Irregularity. Irregularity in the mode of living may have a deleterious effect upon the prime of life. The human constitution adapts to regularity, with a resulting conservation of vitality. A lack of routine in living appears to be fatiguing and demanding on the delicate function of life processes, doubtless by interfering with biochemical activity. The incidence of pronounced pathological aging is not so high in the United States as in most nations, but even here it is needlessly high. However, the incidence of moderate pathological aging is high despite the progress we have made in the last half century in extending the prime of life. At college age the hurdles to a long prime of life are high blood pressure, heart disorders, arthritis, and tension. Chronic conditions, such as gallstones and peptic ulcers, can be significant hurdles to prolonged youthfulness.

Extension of the prime of life. Life can be divided into two periods—the first, when we want to be older than we are, and the second, when we want to be younger than we are. The wise student begins early in life to preserve his youthfulness becaues he recognizes that the way to keep from getting old is to stay young. It is not just how long one lives, but how well one lives, which is equally important. The productive life of some people is at an end by the age of 40 years. Actually the prime of life should be projected at least to the age of 55 years, and 65 years is not an unrealistic goal for a person who begins by the age of 20 years to extend his viril years of life. The prime of life is represented by the ability of the body to synthesize protoplasm. Just what constitutes the termination of the prime of life is difficult to delineate, but in general terms it is that point at which

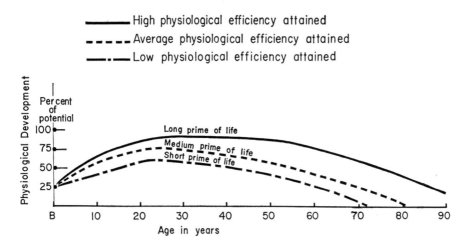

High physiological efficiency attained

Average physiological efficiency attained

Low physiological efficiency attained

Fig. 2. Extension of the prime of life. Three individuals with the same health potential attain different levels of health, length of prime of life, and length of life. The mode of living in the early years affects the quality of health in later years. Proper exercise, nutrition, regularity, moderation, rest, relaxation, prevention of insults to the body, such as disease and harmful substances, and the immediate treatment of disease and defects will extend the prime of life.

there is rather abrupt decline of physical bounce, muscle tone, posture, bounding gait, sensory perception, speed of neuron responses, recovery from fatigue, elasticity of the skin, and the general appearance of virility. In America this turning point occurs between the ages of 45 and 50 years for a vast proportion of citizens. Even this early termination of the prime of life is apparently an improvement since the turn of the century. At least available data indicate that a 50-year-old person today is much younger than a 50-year-old person was in 1900.

There is no single formula or panacea for prolonging the prime of life, but a multiphase program can be designed to contribute to the extension of youthfulness. Such a program should be planned to build up body function to the highest possible level to 30 years of age, to maintain high-level function between 30 and 50 years of age, and to conserve function after the age of 50 years. Use increases and preserves function, but too little use has a deteriorating effect and too much use has a depleting effect.

Inheritance. The inheritance of a constitution which predisposes to an extended prime of life must be acknowledged. An individual cannot alter his inherited makeup, but he can do a great deal to make the most of his genetic endowment.

Health inventory. Inventory of health status by means of a thorough health examination at regular intervals, particularly when deviations are observed, is an important measure for safeguarding and promoting general well-being.

Circulatory efficiency. Circulatory efficiency, which provides the necessary oxygenation of tissues for biochemical cellular activity, is important. All body functions depend upon the circulatory system. Circulatory efficiency is promoted by optimum activity combined with the prevention of circulatory impairment. Up to the age of 30 years this activity must be vigorous enough to bring circulatory capacity to near maximum. From 30 to 50 years of age the vigor of activity must be reduced to a level just necessary to maintain a high level of circulatory efficiency. After 50 years of age the circulatory system is conserved by lighter activity. The same degrees of activity which promote cardiovascular health also promote effectiveness of other body functions.

Relaxation. Relaxation is necessary to permit the human machine to idle at regular intervals during the day and after special demands have been made upon the constitution. Relaxation is somewhat of an art which can be cultivated.

Rest. Rest, which is associated with adequate sleep, is essential for the synthesis of protoplasm.

Regularity. A regulated living routine provides a cycle to which body functions adjust, conserves energy, and permits necessary synthesis of tissue substances. Regularity promotes desirable homeostasis. By regularity is meant a schedule of daily living which provides regular hours for meals, regular hours of sleep, a regular routine of activity, and regular time for relaxation. It is not necessary to become a slave to a schedule in order to live regularly. As conceived here regularity is a relative term.

Oral hygiene. Oral hygiene may appear to be of minor significance in the promotion of youthfulness and the extension of the prime of life, but it can be of marked importance. This is particularly true in terms of the prevention and treatment of abscesses. A good condition of the gums and teeth can be a factor in the promotion of a balanced diet.

Prevention of disease. The prevention of disease extends the prime of life by preventing interference with normal biochemical activity. Preventing even minor diseases can conceivably play a highly important role in promoting youthfulness because the cumulative effect of a series of minor illnesses can affect the aging process.

Treatment of diseases or disabilities. The immediate treatment of diseases or disabilities when they do occur is of obvious value. Not self-medication but the use of the best available medical service can be an investment in the promotion of youthfulness. To this extent the extension of the prime of life is purchasable.

Avoidance of harmful substances. Avoiding harmful substances which interfere with normal processes will conserve efficient biological function. Drugs have a useful purpose when taken upon the prescription of a physician, but indiscriminate use of stimulants and narcotics will have a marked effect on normal biochemical activity. The extent to which the use of tobacco and alcohol hastens the aging process is not too well established, but excessive use of either doubtless does interfere with synthesis of cellular material and will affect the aging process.

Nutrition. A balanced nutrition, both qualitatively and quantitatively, is important. Some evidence exists that certain proteins contribute to the preservation of youthfulness. Lecithin appears to have value in preserving youth. Low fat intake and adequate vitamin B complex to facilitate metabolism of fats and prevent abnormal fat deposits in the walls of arteries have been recommended.

Avoidance of unnecessary exposure. Avoiding unnecessary exposure to weather conditions, such as sun and wind, which may have a harmful effect upon the skin is essential. Exposure to weather extremes can affect the general well-being if continued over a period of time and can thus cause accelerated aging. Prolonged heat has a particularly adverse effect.

Emotional stability. Emotional stability is essential for relieving tensions and for producing the relaxation and ease necessary to permit regeneration of the vitality depleted by the trials of daily living. Emotionally unstable persons wear out prematurely.

Wholesome life interests. Wholesome life interests in the form of gratifying activities and accomplishments promote youthfulness. Vocational pursuits as well as avocational pursuits can be wholesome. The spark of youth and of life itself is expressed in the life interests of the individual. Youthfulness is a psychological state as well as a physiological condition. To continue to learn, to continue to think with the interest and enthusiasm of youth, is to promote the extension of the prime of life.

It will be recognized that the practices which promote the extension of the prime of life are also the practices which promote health. The two are inseparable. Both can be and should be promoted simultaneously. Thus an individual who follows recognized principles of health promotion will reap a double dividend.

LIFE EXPECTANCY

Life span and life expectancy are not the same. Life span is the biological limit of life. For human beings biometrists consider the life span to be 120 years because there are no authentic records of anyone's having lived beyond that age. It is significant that newspaper reports of people living longer than 120 years usually originate from primitive illiterate areas where birth records either do not exist or are unreliable. Because man shortens his life by adverse living practices, we doubtless have some people who should have a life span beyond 120 years. With advances in the health sciences, man's span of life may well extend beyond 120 years in the near future. It must be recognized that not all people have a life span of 120 years. Some segments of the population appear to have a life span considerably below 100 years. Heredity is the significant factor in life span.

Life expectancy refers to the average duration of life that individuals of a given age can expect, based upon the longevity experience of the population. It is the average number of years an individual of a given age can expect to live. Comparative longevity measures must necessarily be based upon the assumption that the longevity experience of the immediate past years will prevail in the future. Actually future years will likely be favorable to an extension of the

Table 1. Expectation of life at birth in selected nations for specific years*

Nation	Male	Female	Nation	Male	Female
Sweden (1959)	71.69	75.24	Czechoslovakia (1958)	67.79	72.3
Norway (1951-55)	71.11	74.7	Australia (1953-55)	67.14	72.75
Netherlands (1952-55)	71.0	73.9	Japan (1959)	65.21	73.47
Israel (1960)	70.67	74.47	West Germany (1959-60)	66.69	71.94
Denmark (1951-55)	69.79	72.60	Switzerland (1948-53)	66.4	71.0
England, Wales (1960)	68.3	74.1	East Germany (1955-58)	66.13	70.68
New Zealand (1955-57)	68.2	73.0	Italy (1954-57)	65.75	70.02
France (1960)	67.2	73.8	Finland (1951-55)	63.4	69.8
Canada (1955-57)	67.1	72.9	Ireland (1950-52)	64.53	67.08
United States (1959)	66.5	73.7	India (1941-50)	32.45	31.66

*From report issued by the United Nations. In Demographic Yearbook, New York, 1961, Publishing Service, United Nations.

longevity, based upon present figures. Again averages apply to the group. Individuals will vary, both above and below the average.

The United Nations report on life expectation at birth in selected nations indicates that the United States ranks well down the list. The life expectancy of American white persons ranks well up with those nations at the top of the list, but the nonwhite persons in America are part of its population and must be considered in any comparison between nations. Indeed the differential between the life expectancy of white persons and nonwhite persons in the United States identifies certain health and related problems in need of increased attention.

Increase in life expectancy. In the United States in the period from 1900 to 1959, the average duration of life from the time of birth has increased by 20 years for white males, 25 years for white females, 28.8 years for nonwhite males, and 32.6 years for nonwhite females.

Improvement in longevity since the beginning of the century has been progressively greater for females than for males, both white and nonwhite.

Much of the increase in the length of life has been due to the prevention of deaths in infancy and childhood. Life expectancy after the age of 30 years had been affected but little until recent years when there has been an appreciable increase in life expectancy in later years of life. Though the improvement in the average remaining lifetime becomes progressively less at older ages, the recent values even at relatively older ages are appreciably above those of earlier periods.

It is of interest that among nonwhite citizens also the female tends to have a more favorable life expectancy than does the male and somewhat in the same degree as among white citizens.

Doubtless of greatest interest to the college student is the present life expectancy at various ages, particularly at the college age. Average remaining lifetime by race, sex, and age in the year 1957 is estimated by the National Office of Vital Statistics.

Table 2. Estimated average length of life in years in United States, 1900 to 1959*

Year	White male	White female	Nonwhite male	Nonwhite female
1900	46.6	48.7	32.5	33.5
1905	47.6	50.6	29.6	33.1
1910	48.6	52.0	33.8	37.5
1915	53.1	57.5	37.5	40.5
1920	54.4	55.6	45.5	45.2
1925	59.3	62.4	44.9	46.7
1930	59.7	63.5	47.3	49.2
1935	61.0	65.0	51.3	55.2
1940	62.1	66.6	51.5	54.9
1945	64.4	69.5	56.1	59.6
1950	66.8	72.4	59.2	63.2
1959	67.3	73.9	60.9	66.2

*From National Vital Statistics Division: Special reports, Life tables, June, 1962.

Table 3. Average future lifetime at selected ages*

Period of data	Age 20 years		Age 35 years		Age 50 years		Age 65 years	
	Male	Female	Male	Female	Male	Female	Male	Female
White								
1900-1902	42.19	43.77	31.29	32.88	20.76	21.89	11.51	12.23
1919-1921	45.6	46.46	33.74	34.86	22.22	23.12	12.21	12.75
1939-1941	47.76	51.38	34.36	37.7	21.96	24.72	12.07	13.56
1959	50.1	56.0	36.1	41.6	23.0	27.8	12.7	15.6
Nonwhite								
1900-1902	33.11	36.89	26.11	27.52	17.34	18.67	10.38	11.38
1919-1921	38.36	37.15	29.54	28.58	20.47	19.76	12.07	12.41
1939-1941	39.74	42.14	28.67	30.83	19.18	21.04	12.18	13.95
1959	45.3	50.0	32.3	36.3	20.9	24.3	12.5	15.2

*From National Vital Statistics Division: Special reports, Life tables, June, 1962.
Figures for nonwhite groups cover only Negroes for 1900 to 1902 and 1919 to 1921.

It is clear from Table 3 that a 20-year-old white male has a life expectation of 49.9 years, whereas a white female of the same age has a life expectation of 55.7 years. Detailed studies reveal that people who attend college have a greater life expectancy than the cross section of the nation's population; therefore college students can expect longevity beyond these figures. Actually by the application of health principles, students can improve considerably beyond the expectation indicated by these figures.

Who lives longest? Longevity is of more than academic interest to the college student. He recognizes that future plans should be geared to the length of life as well as to the prime of life. The inquiring student asks what factors determine how long one lives. In general terms an answer can be given which may serve as a guide.

Race. Race is of significance as revealed by Table 4. At birth the Caucasian male in America has a life expectancy about 6½ years greater than a non-Caucasian, and for females the advantage is almost 8 years. After 65 years of age the non-Caucasian has the greater expectancy. The extent to which these data reveal or conceal biological or economic factors is not definitely established. However, as will be pointed out later economic status is a factor in longevity.

Inheritance. Inheritance has a strong influence on longevity. Chapter 2 will reveal that long-lived parents appear to transmit to offspring the efficient constitutional function, the adequate body structure, and the resistance to disease that are necessary for long life. Offspring from long-lived parents tend to be long-lived.

Sex. The sex of an individual enters into longevity. As revealed in Table 4, white females at birth have an expectancy which is 6½ years greater than the male's. At 20 years of age the advantage is still 5¾ years. Many factors account for the longer life of the female. She inherits a better constitution in terms of life expectancy. Her softer and less bulky musculature and her more resilient

Table 4. Average remaining lifetime by race, sex, and age in United States, 1959*

Age (yr.)	Average number of years of life			
	White male	White female	Nonwhite male	Nonwhite female
At birth	67.3	73.9	60.9	66.2
1	68.2	74.4	63.0	68.0
5	64.4	70.7	59.5	64.4
10	59.6	65.8	54.4	59.6
15	54.7	60.9	49.7	54.7
20	50.1	56.0	45.3	50.0
25	45.5	51.2	40.9	45.3
30	40.8	46.4	36.5	40.7
35	36.1	41.6	32.3	36.3
40	31.5	36.9	28.3	32.1
45	27.2	32.3	24.5	28.1
50	23	27.8	20.9	24.3
55	19.2	23.3	17.6	20.8
60	15.6	19.2	14.9	17.8
65	12.7	15.4	12.5	15.2
70	10.1	12.0	11.2	13.3
75	7.9	9.1	10.4	12.0
80	5.9	6.4	9.4	10.2
85	4.5	4.5	8.3	8.6

*From National Vital Statistics Division: Special repots, Life tables, June, 1962.

connective and other tissues are factors. Her heart and vessels appear to be more adequate. There is less cholesterol deposit in her arteries, which is often the cause of coronary thrombosis. A woman has more white blood cells, which increases her defense against infection, and she has a better internal adaptation environment in terms of constitutional economy. It must be conceded that, also on the credit side, she does not engage in heavy manual labor, at least not after the age of 40 years. She lives under less daily tension and has a lower accidental death rate. However, this is partly offset by the fact that men rarely die of childbirth!

Body build. Doubtless body build represents a certain constitutional capacity to live. However, whatever factors are involved, well-built adults of average height and weight live longer than adults of other body types. Extreme underweight during youth tends to shorten life, and more than 15% of overweight in adulthood tends to be detrimental to longevity. Adults more than 25% overweight have a death rate 75% higher than those of average weight.

Present health. Present health is an indication of possible longevity, particularly if the individual has heart disease, a vascular disorder, disease of the lungs, cancer, or diabetes. Good health today means more years in life as well as more life in years.

Pulse and blood pressure. Pulse and blood pressure are barometers of the life of the human motor as well as of its present performance. A pulse of more than 100 or an irregular pulse is not indicative of long life. The higher the blood pressure, the shorter the life will be because of its association with cardiovascular-renal disorders.

Temperament and habits. Temperament and habits are related to longevity. Easygoing persons outlive fast-paced excitable tense individuals. Manual labor before the age of 40 years does not appear to affect the length of life, but continued hard manual work after 40 years of age shortens life. Tension, overstrain, and overeating also shorten life. Excessive smoking reduces life expectation, but light smoking does not. Heavy alcohol-drinking shortens life, but moderate drinking has no demonstrated effect on longevity—provided that the person continues to drink no more than moderately.

Occupation. Occupation is of significance and of interest. Among males the greatest length of life is among members of the ministry. Other occupations follow in order: lawyers, engineers, teachers, doctors, farmers, business executives, white-collar workers, skilled tradesmen, and unskilled workers. Miners and quarrymen have the shortest expectancy, with granite workers at the bottom of the list.

Income and living conditions. Income and associated favorable living conditions influence longevity. Citizens with a favorable income that is sufficient to provide excellent nutrition, housing, and medical care live longer than those with lesser incomes. High-income cities have a longer average length of human life than do cities with low income. Citizens in the northern and west-coast states live longer than citizens in the southern states. The residents of Nebraska are especially long-lived, and neighboring states have almost as favorable longevity records. Obviously income can include or conceal many factors.

Civil status. Civil status is of interest in terms of longevity. Married men live longer than single men, partially because of the more orderly life of married persons. However, many men in poor health do not marry because of the poor health. Up to 40 years of age married women have a lower death rate than unmarried women, thus a greater life expectation. However, after 40 years of age unmarried women have the same expectancy as their married sisters.

These several factors have significance as a general guide. Combinations of factors are particularly important. For any individual there may be exceptions to the general picture. However, this list of factors has meaning as it is applied to any given individual case.

Degenerative diseases. Degenerative diseases is a general term which has been applied to conditions resulting in the morbid impairment of the heart, arteries, and kidneys. Arteriosclerosis, hypertension, nephritis, and heart disease constitute the degenerative quartet. The cardiovascular-renal relationship is such that a disturbance of one of the three structures usually results in damage to the others. Collectively the heart, blood vessels, and kidneys are often referred to as the *vascular tree.* Although inflammation may initiate the condition, disturbances of these structures usually are in the form of a deterioration in structure and

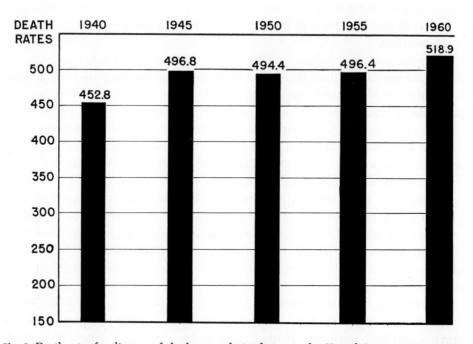

Fig. 3. Death rates for diseases of the heart and circulation in the United States, 1940 to 1960. After a leveling off for ten years at approximately 495 deaths per 100,000 of the population, there has been a rise in the rate of deaths due to diseases of the heart and circulation.

function. The incidence of these disorders has increased progressively since the turn of the present century. This increase is due in part to a greater number of persons living to an age when these disorders begin to occur and is partly caused by a lack of knowledge of how to prevent and treat these conditions. However, if rates are corrected for the aging of the population, death rates for cardiovascular-renal disease have declined as a group. Of the individual disorders heart disease alone has shown an increased death rate. As life expectancy continues to increase, the incidence of degenerative disorders will continue to increase unless new discoveries are made in prevention and treatment. A reciprocal relationship exists between the degenerative disorders and aging. Degenerative disorders are associated with the aging process, and degenerative disorders further hasten aging. A reduction in the incidence of degenerative diseases would effect a proportionate increase in life expectancy.

It should be emphasized that, because of their disabling effects, the degenerative diseases give rise to serious sociological and economic problems. However, this is basically a health problem rather than a welfare problem, and progress in prevention and successful treatment depends upon extensive research.

Diseases of the heart and blood vessels. Diseases of the heart designate a number of different disorders which affect the heart and are the greatest single designated cause of death. This year about 38% of all deaths in the United States will be due to heart disease. It can be predicted that more than two thirds of people past 55 years of age will die of a heart disorder unless improved methods of preventing and treating heart diseases are developed. This year approximately 55% of all deaths in the United States will be caused by cardiovascular-renal disorders.

Congenital heart defects. These defects are those which are present at birth and are the result of disturbances occurring in prenatal life. Some of the defects are so minor they can almost be ignored. Others are so severe that the individual does not even survive to school age. Some congenital heart defects can be benefited by surgery. For others physicians prescribe a routine of living in harmony with the circulatory capacity of the individual.

Rheumatic fever heart. This term is used to designate a condition which has developed as a result of rheumatic fever. In the past, two out of three patients with rheumatic fever suffered a damaged heart, but that incidence is now being reduced. A single attack may cause no harm or only minor damage to the heart. Recurrence of the disease likely will cause recurring damage. Rheumatic fever tends to follow a sore throat caused by either *Streptococcus hemolyticus* or *Streptococcus viridans*. It is possible that a low-level infection continues after the sore throat appears to be cleared up and that toxin produced by the low-level infection causes the damage to heart tissue. Equally plausible is the hypothesis that the antibodies of the streptococcus organisms cause the heart damage. Neither hypothesis has been confirmed.

Today physicians can prevent both rheumatic fever and heart damage from

Fig. 4. Walk-in heart model. Built by the Oregon Heart Association, this gigantic model in a science museum commands the attention of children and adults alike. In terms of health education this novel visual aid motivates an interest in cardiovascular health. (Courtesy Oregon Heart Association.)

rheumatic fever if parents will call a physician immediately when a child complains of a sore throat. By the administration of sulfonamides or antibiotics at that time and subsequent intervals, the physician can prevent the occurrence of rheumatic fever and thus heart damage. Even if a first attack of rheumatic fever should occur, a physician still might prevent heart damage by treating the child at the time of the first rheumatic attack.

During the acute stage of rheumatic fever inflammation of heart muscle (*myocarditis*) may occur. In some cases the outer lining of the heart is inflamed (*pericarditis*). However, in both of these conditions the heart may return to normal after infection is overcome. Permanent injury usually is due to an inflammation of the inner heart lining (*endocarditis*) involving the valves of the left side of the heart. In healing, scar tissue forms, which constricts the valvular opening (*mitral stenosis*) and prevents the valves from opening and closing properly. Surgery may be resorted to in order to open the orifice. An anesthetic is used to induce sleep. With a scalpel attached to his index finger, the surgeon enters the left auricular chamber and incises the scar tissue, thus enlarging the passageway for blood flow. No untoward postoperative effects occur, and there is no effect on the brain.

Arteriosclerosis. This term is used for a variety of chronic pathological conditions affecting primarily the inner lining or the middle layer of arteries and is characterized by thickening, hardening, and loss of elasticity of the blood vessel walls. Whatever the cause, the thickening and rigidity of the walls, together with the reduced lumen of the arteries, produces excessively high blood pressure, with a resulting burden upon the heart and a deleterious effect upon the general circulation. Most arteriosclerosis is associated with the later years of life though doubtless most if not all cases have their genesis in the early or middle adult years.

Atherosclerosis. This disease is a form of arteriosclerosis characterized by areas of thickening of the inner lining of the artery due to localized accumulations of lipids. It is recognized as a metabolic disease and is not necessarily a consequence of aging, though most cases will be discovered after the age of 50 years. It must be recognized that atherosclerosis can have its beginning in poor nutrition, lack of activity, and other poor health practices in the early years of life.

Atherosclerotic plaques are rich in cholesterol esters derived from serum cholesterol. The fatty flecks, which form just behind the innermost lining (intima) of the artery, grow larger and form plaques which reduce the lumen of the artery. These plaques may involve any artery. Centers of the plaques may become dead (necrotic), rupture, and push the material into the bloodstream. A growth (thrombosis) then forms, the plaque obstructing the flow of blood and often causing an occlusion. Atheromas (growths) may extend into the middle layer of the artery and thus weaken the wall. This may lead to the formation of a weak section (aneurysm) of the artery.

Atherosclerosis frequently involves the coronary arteries, particularly the anterior descending branch of the left coronary artery which supplies the muscle of the left ventricle. Atherosclerotic plaques in the coronary arteries are particularly prone to cause ruptures of small vessels within the walls of these arteries. Hemorrhage into these plaques may cause a bulging of the wall and may occlude the artery. Later, cerebral atherosclerosis may occur. An aneurysm of the basilar artery of the brain may result in a rupture of the artery or even the formation of a thrombosis, with serious and even fatal results.

Evidence has been accumulating which suggests that excessive consumption of fat may be involved in the cause (etiology) of atherosclerosis. Surveys have shown that population groups with high serum cholesterol levels have a high incidence of atherosclerosis, and populations with a low serum cholesterol level have a low incidence of atherosclerosis. High cholesteral intake is not correlated with a high blood serum cholesterol level. However, a diet high in cholesterols is also high in fats, and it has been shown that populations with a high fat diet have a high serum cholesterol level. The Europeans in Cape Town, South Africa, whose diet in terms of calories is 40% fat, have an average serum cholesterol level of 241.8 mg. per cent. The Bantus of Cape Town, with a diet of 17%

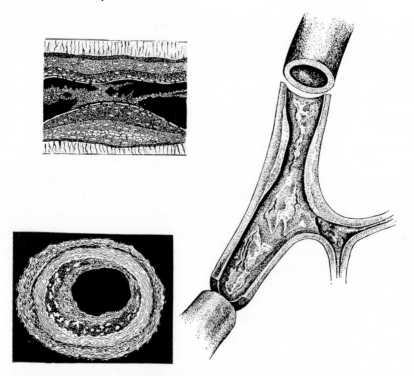

Fig. 5. Atherosclerotic plaques composed of cholesterol. Deposits of cholesterol behind the innermost layer of the artery weakens the wall, narrows the lumen, and increases the likelihood of thrombosis and occlusion of the vessel.

fat, have an average serum cholesterol level of 168.5 mg. per cent. Thus, the relationship exists that people with atherosclerosis have a high serum cholesterol level and people with a high serum cholesterol level are generally people with a high fat diet. However, a closer examination of the dietary factor must be made.

Animals fats and hydrogenated (shortening) vegetable oils tend to raise the serum cholesterol level, whereas marine and fish oils tend to lower the serum level. These latter oils have a high concentration of unsaturated fatty acids, which appears to be a significant factor. Cholesterol from outside (exogenous) sources comes from meats, egg yolk, and milk products. Of itself this source is not significant. Cholesterols produced within (endogenous) the body are synthesized in the liver. A further step in our understanding of the biochemistry involved is that cholesterol plus other lipids combines with proteins to form lipoproteins and that it is the beta fraction of lipoprotein which is usually elevated in atherosclerosis, whereas the alpha fraction is depressed. It is recognized that susceptibility to atherosclerosis and coronary thrombosis varies.

The urgent need for a test to determine those persons prone to these conditions is recognized. However, present knowledge indicates procedures that may be significant in the prevention of atherosclerosis. Reducing animal fats and hydrogenated vegetable oils in the diet and using marine, fish, and vegetable oils in combination with the vitamin B complex may possibly be of value in preventing atherosclerosis. However, care should be taken that the low fat diet is adequate in proteins and vitamins. It is acknowledged that the role of dietary fat in the production of atherosclerosis in man is largely circumstantial, but the case is sufficiently strong to justify the use of the low fat diet as a preventive measure until further discovery produces a better means. It must be pointed out that atherosclerosis likely has its beginning in the early years of life, and measures to prevent atherosclerosis should begin at least in early adulthood.

Angina pectoris. Angina pectoris is a disorder characterized by oppression and distress in the chest resulting from inadequate coronary circulation and often brought on by exercise or an emotional experience. Inadequate blood supply to the muscle layer or myocardium is the underlying factor, and the distress or oppression is probably due to the stimulation of the afferent (sensory) nerve endings in the myocardium by the accumulation of waste products resulting from an oxygen deficiency. Arteriosclerotic coronary narrowing plus an increased oxygen demand on exertion may precipitate the attack. In chronic coronary inefficiency the attack may be brought on simply by physical exertion, excitement, or a heavy meal. However, attacks can occur during rest or sleep.

The oppression and distress is usually located under the breast bone (sternum), but the pain may radiate to the shoulder, to the left arm, to the elbow, and even to the finger tips. Occasionally the sensations may also radiate to the right shoulder and arm. In some individuals dizziness, faintness, and labored breathing may occur. The seizure usually lasts only a few minutes but may be as long as 30 to 60 minutes. Vasodilators, such as nitroglycerin, have been highly effective in relieving the oppression and distress. In recent years these vasodilators have been used as a preventive (prophylactic) measure, and with the regular use of vasodilators prescribed by their physicians some patients have been free from attacks.

Hypertension. Hypertension is a disorder in which the arterioles exhibit abnormal resistance to the flow of blood and is usually associated with an abnormal increase in systolic and diastolic arteriolar pressures. Generally speaking, people with a diastolic pressure above 90 mm. Hg are classified as having hypertension. Thirty-two years is the average age at which the disorder can be detected, and an onset beyond 50 years of age is extremely rare. Approximately ten million adults in the United States are affected. The condition is twice as common among women as among men, and women with the disorder tend to be obese more frequently than is true among men who are affected. A short stocky body configuration and hyperkinetic body reactions appear to be associated with hypertension. Emotional stress and diet do not cause hypertension but may trigger the condition. Doubtless several causes of hypertension exist. Factors in the autonomic nervous system play an important part in producing marked arteriolar constriction. Humoral factors in the kidneys also seem to be related to the disorder. Heredity appears to play a role. Studies indicate that, if one parent has

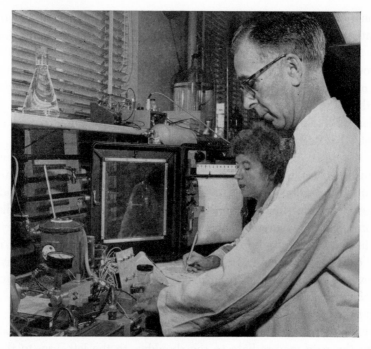

Fig. 6. Research in cardiovascular health. No field of research relating to human health is more demanding and more difficult. Specialized personnel from many backgrounds and precise, complex equipment are usually necessary. (Courtesy Oregon Heart Association.)

hypertension, at least one of a large family will be affected. If both parents have the disorder, a majority of the offspring will exhibit the condition.

Hypertensive vascular disease accelerates the degenerative process. Hypertension seems to provide a fertile soil for the development of atherosclerosis. In addition the high blood pressure may affect the kidneys.

Antihypertensive agents such as some of the derivatives of *Rauwolfia serpentina* have been effective in relieving hypertensive conditions. Unfortunately not all persons with hypertension respond to medication, but sufficient advances have been made in the understanding of the disorder to justify urging all hypertensive persons to have regular medical supervision. Current research justifies the optimistic prediction that within the next few years effective measures will be available for controlling hypertension. The next logical step would be the attempt to discover means for preventing hypertension.

Prevention of cardiovascular diseases. A person is not a helpless victim of cardiovascular diseases. Although not a great deal is known about prevention of these diseases, some things are known, and, if a person uses intelligently what is known, he can do much to prevent cardiovascular disorders. This applies to the college-age person as well as to older citizens, because a positive program for the prevention of cardiovascular disease cannot begin too early in life. The ordinary layman can do much to help himself in this respect.

Intensive and extensive, well-controlled, and well-documented epidemio-logical studies reveal that cardiovascular disorders are lowest among adults (1) who do not smoke cigarettes, (2) who are not obese, (3) who have diets low in saturated fats and cholesterol, and (4) who regularly engage in moderate or more vigorous physical activity.

1. *Not smoking cigarettes* is to refrain from a practice which frequently is injurious to the cardiovascular system. Studies by such authorities as Dr. E.

Are you a candidate for

THE CORONARY CLUB?

1 Your job comes first — personal considerations are secondary.

2 Go to the office evenings, Saturdays, Sundays, and holidays.

3 Take the briefcase home on the evenings that you do not return to the office — this provides an opportunity to review completely all the troubles and worries of the day.

4 Never say NO to a request — always say YES.

5 Accept all invitations to meetings, banquets, committees, etc.

6 Do not eat a restful, relaxing meal — always plan a conference for the meal hour.

7 Fishing and hunting are a waste of time and money — you never bring back enough fish or game to justify the expense.

8 It is a poor policy to take all the vacation time which is provided for you.

9 Golf, bowling, pool, billiards, cards, gardening, etc. are a waste of time.

10 Never delegate responsibility to others — carry the load at all times.

11 If your work calls for traveling, work all day and drive all night to make your appointment for the next day.

Fig. 7. A coronary attack may be hard earned. Tension can build cardiovascular disorders as well as precipitate a cardiac crisis. The ability to relax can be an asset in the prevention of heart disease. (Courtesy Oregon Heart Association.)

Cuyler Hammond, National Cancer Society, and Dr. Jeremiah Stamler, Chicago Board of Health, indicate that among men who smoke two packs or more of cigarettes a day the incidence of cardiovascular disease is from 2½ to six times as high as among nonsmokers. It would be unscientific to conclude that this appalling differential in cardiovascular diseases is due entirely to the cigarette smoking. People indiscreet in smoking are most likely to be indiscreet in other practices affecting health. Yet from present knowledge of the physiological effects of smoking, it is apparent that the cardiovascular system can be directly affected adversely.

2. *Avoiding obesity* can be an effective measure for the prevention of disorders of the heart and vascular tree. Obese people have a high incidence of atherosclerosis and of heart disease. Again it must be recognized that factors related to obesity as well as the actual obesity may be operating to produce the high incidence of cardiovascular diseases among the obese in our population.

3. *Diets low in saturated fats and cholesterol* appear to be of value in the prevention of atherosclerosis. This is especially true for certain people. It is recognized here that differences in susceptibility to atherosclerosis exist. At present no test exists to determine relative predisposition to atherosclerosis. In consequence, the wise course is for all of us to assume we have a high level of susceptibility and to follow diets low in saturated fats and cholesterol. In this way those who do have a high susceptibility level will be benefited, some greatly and some moderately. Others may be benefited very little, but will be thankful that atherosclerosis does not pose a serious threat to them.

4. *Regular moderate physical activity* keeps the cholesterol level of the blood low, aids the circulation of blood in both the veins and the arteries, and appears to be of special value to the coronary arteries. These coronary vessels supply blood to the heart muscle. Their size and general tone are affected favorably by regular exercise. The normal heart muscle does not need special exercise. A college student's heart will contract over 100,000 times in a twenty-four day. No other muscle gets as much exercise. Yet the health of the whole circulatory system does demand regular moderate physical activity.

The segment of our adult population which has the lowest incidence of cardiovascular disease is the one which satisfies this classification:

1. People who do not smoke
2. People who are not obese
3. People who have a diet low in saturated fats and cholesterol
4. People who engage regularly in moderate or more vigorous physical activity.

This is a prescription for cardiovascular health.

Nephritis. Nephritis is a general term applied to many diseases of the kidneys. Two types are common, acute and chronic nephritis. Acute nephritis occurs in children and young adults, usually as a complication from acute infection. Toxins of the infecting agent damage kidney tissue. Symptoms of nephritis often are not so frank as those of the disease which occasioned the damage. Nearly all patients recover, but the kidneys may not return to their normal level of function, and a chronic condition may exist.

Chronic nephritis results from either acute nephritis, arteriosclerosis, or hypertension. When the functioning of the delicate mechanism of the kidneys is disturbed, body wastes are not adequately removed, poisoning results, and excessive fluid is retained in the body tissues, causing edema. Both conditions have a pronounced effect on life expectancy.

Chronic diseases. The word *chronic* is used to describe diseases of long duration that are usually characterized by slowly progressing symptoms.

Cancer. Cancer is a chronic disease which ranks second as a cause of death in the United States.

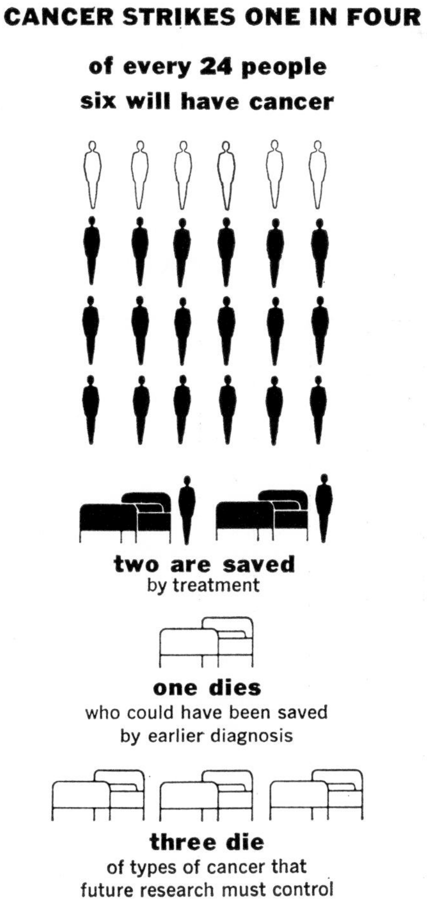

CANCER STRIKES ONE IN FOUR

of every 24 people
six will have cancer

two are saved
by treatment

one dies
who could have been saved
by earlier diagnosis

three die
of types of cancer that
future research must control

Fig. 8. More knowledge means more lives saved. If detected early, half of all cancers could be cured. Two out of every six cancer patients are saved because they go to a doctor in time, and one more out of six could be saved with the medical knowledge available today. (Courtesy American Cancer Society, Inc.)

Cellular growth and cell division in the body normally proceed in an orderly manner. In cancer the multiplication and growth of cells in a localized area become rapid and disorganized, and a tumor forms. The growth and increase of cells serve no useful purpose. Actually cancer cells produce toxins injurious to normal cells. They also rob normal tissue of its blood and thus of its nutrition. If a cancer is unchecked, extension of the growth may take place into adjacent areas. Cancer cells may grow through walls of the blood and lymph vessels and be transported to other portions of the body, where new foci of growth are started. Spread of cancer is virtually certain unless the original growth is destroyed or removed.

Although the cause of cancer has not been established, we do know the factors that incite cancer. Five types of irritation are known to incite cancer: mechanical (friction or rubbing), chemical, thermal (overexposure to heat), actinic (overexposure to the sun's rays), and radioactive (overexposure to roentgen rays, radium, and radioisotopes). All chronic irritation of tissues should obviously be avoided.

Some evidence exists that a high degree of susceptibility or predisposition to cancer may be inherited. A person from a lineage with cancer should give special attention to preventive measures and have a physician diagnose any abnormality

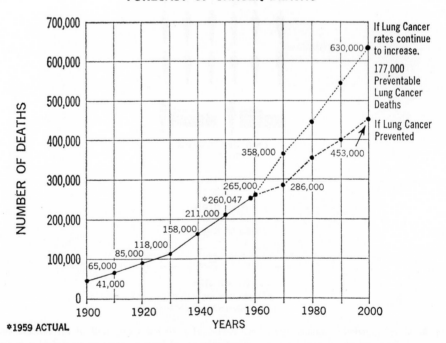

Fig. 9. Alternate routes. The one would result from a resigned acceptance of the present course. The other can be realized by utilizing the knowledge we possess. (Courtesy American Cancer Society, Inc.)

which develops. Sensibly all of us should take every known precaution to prevent cancer since all of us are susceptible.

Only two established means of treatment are available—surgery and irradiation with roentgen rays, radium, or radioisotopes. Current trends in the reduction of deaths from cancer among females indicate the value of early diagnosis and treatment. When males exercise the same alertness as females, a further reduction in the cancer death rate will result.

Diabetes mellitus. Diabetes mellitus is one of the important chronic diseases. In 1900 it was twenty-seventh as a cause of death; today it is eighth. About 1 million persons with known diabetes in the United States and an additional 1 million persons with unrecognized diabetes attest to its importance. About three fifths of the patients are females. The average age of diabetic persons is 55 years, but diabetes can appear in childhood. Its principal cause is malfunction of the islands of Langerhans in the pancreas. The pituitary gland may also be involved. A predisposition to a deficiency of the islands of Langerhans appears to be inherited. Symptoms of diabetes include weakness, excessive thirst, and frequent urination. Laboratory tests reveal sugar in the urine and make diagnosis easy. Most patients with diabetes mellitus can be treated successfully. Early diagnosis and adherence to medical instructions are all-important.

Extending life expectancy. For the community extending life expectation must include research, medical service, hospital and clinical facilities, rehabilitation services, and public health education. For the individual the extension of one's own life expectancy consists essentially in following those principles and practices which promote both a high level of health and extended prime of life.

1. Periodic health examinations can extend the average life expectancy in the United States by at least five years. An annual thorough health examination is particularly important after 30 years of age. Chronic and degenerative diseases are insidious in their development, with symptoms often so imperceptible that only a thorough health examination will reveal the developing condition. Early detection may mean control and even cure. A regular inventory of one's health assets and liabilities is analogous to immunization against infectious diseases. The further assurance that one is in good physical condition is of value to mental health. An investment in a health examination may be an investment in the extension of life.

2. Avoidance of infection by immunization and other known methods is important in extending life expectancy.

3. Immediate treatment of all infections and other disorders is essential for safeguarding life.

4. Regularity and moderation in life's activities conserve one's resources. A slower pace will help many individuals to live longer. Burning the candle at both ends may cast a lovely light, but one of brief duration.

5. Rest and relaxation must be adapted to the demands of life and the con-

stitutional makeup of the individual. In an emergency to have a reserve
may mean the difference between death and survival.

6. Safety practices which avoid injuries as well as death are related to life
   extension. Safety is a matter of human adaptation.
7. Balanced dietary in keeping with modern knowledge of nutrition cannot
   be overemphasized. Doubtless if man had a complete knowledge of nutrition and applied this to his dietary, life expectancy would be extended
   appreciably, perhaps even doubled.
8. Balanced living between work, rest, recreation, and all of the other activities or requirements of human existence is essential to a long life.

Future life expectancy. No one knows with certainty what the future actually holds in the projection of the expectation of life. A decidely conservative
estimate would be that the life expectation of a child born in the United States in
1975 will be four years greater than that of a child born in 1955. A child born
in the year 2000 should have a life expectancy nine years greater than that of a
child born in 1955. Phenomenal discoveries in health science may push these
figures upward appreciably. These same discoveries should also contribute to a
better quality of health and an extension of the prime of life.

OUR AGING POPULATION

Man does not live any longer than he did at the turn of the present century.
It is merely that more people live to attain these top age brackets. In 1900 some
of our citizens attained ages of 100 years and over. According to the 1960 United
States census report, one out of every 17,300 persons in our population was 100
years of age or older. In 1960 of the 10,369 people 100 years of age or older,
7,538 were white and 2,831 were nonwhite. Almost all of the latter were Negroes.
It is of interest that, although the Negroes constitute a little more than 10% of the
general population, they account for almost 30% of those people in the 100 years
and over category.

The postponement of death has changed the composition of our population
so that an increasing percentage of our population is in older age brackets.
Yet we are a relatively young nation. The 1950 census showed the median age

Table 5. Per cent of age distribution according to United States census

Yr.	Under 5 yr.	5-14 yr.	15-24 yr.	25-34 yr.	35-44 yr.	45-54 yr.	55-64 yr.	Over 64 yr.
1880	13.8	24.3	20.2	14.8	10.9	7.9	4.7	3.4
1910	11.6	20.6	19.6	16.5	12.7	9.1	5.5	4.3
1920	11	20.9	17.7	16.2	13.4	10	6.2	4.6
1930	9.3	20.1	18.4	15.4	14	10.6	6.8	5.4
1940	8	17	18.3	16.2	13.9	11.8	8	6.8
1950	10.8	16.3	14.6	15.7	14.1	11.4	8.7	8.2
1960	11.3	19.8	13.6	12.7	13.4	11.4	8.6	9.2

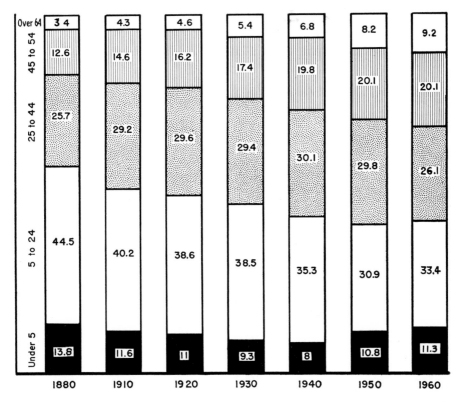

Fig. 10. Percentage distribution of age groups in the United States. Distributions are from United States census data.

in the United States to be 30.1 years. In 1940, 26% of our population were 45 years of age or older. Change in the age distribution of the population indicates the direction of the makeup of our population.

The changing age distribution of the population focuses attention on the problems which must be met. As conquests in the control of infectious disease are made, other causes of death come to the fore. With the changes in the age distribution of the population, certain medical, public health, social, and economic problems take on increased importance. The welfare, care, and security of the aged have become increasingly important, and, as new medical and health discoveries are made, new and more difficult economic and social problems will be created as more people reach the older age brackets. Solving one problem usually creates another.

There is encouragement in recent approaches in mental health which assist people to grow old gracefully, without emotional resistance but with adjustment cultivated during the years leading up to retirement.

Communities must assume responsibility for meeting the needs of our aging population and provide the necessary facilities for an effective program. Hos-

Table 6. Days of disability by condition group in United States, July, 1957, to June, 1958 (number of days in millions)*

Condition group	Restricted activity days	Bed- disability days	Work- loss days†	School- loss days‡
Infectious and parasitic				
Acute	190.3	89.7	19.6	43.1
Chronic	33.3	16.0	4.6	0.8
Circulatory				
Acute	12.8	6.4	2.7	0.6
Chronic	484.2	166.6	69.2	2.1
Respiratory				
Acute	1,172.0	593.1	218.7	195.9
Chronic	144.2	50.0	19.8	11.0
Digestive				
Acute	79.2	33.1	·13.6	8.3
Chronic	217.8	80.2	54.4	0.6
Genitourinary				
Acute	18.0	7.1	3.4	0.5
Chronic	154.2	62.5	25.9	1.5
Arthritis and rheumatism§	255.0	67.2	31.0	—
Injuries				
Acute	246.9	72.2	67.5	12.9
Chronic	39.0	16.0	8.3	0.6
Impairments due to injuries	121.7	21.3	30.9	0.7
Other impairments	228.5	75.7	32.2	2.0
All other conditions				
Acute	203.5	71.3	30.9	11.9
Chronic	648.9	208.3	112.2	12.4
Total person days‖	3,369.6	1,309.9	599.1	291.5

*From U. S. Public Health Service, Washington, D. C., 1959, publication no. 584-B10.
†Persons 17 years of age and over.
‡Children 6 to 16 years of age.
§Chronic.
‖The sum of the condition days is greater than the total person days because a single disability day may be associated with more than one condition.

pitals, nursing homes, recreation programs, and other resources must be provided. The problem is already here and will become greater. There is a continual decline in mortality among older people. For persons in the age group of 45 to 74 years, in the past forty years the death rate has declined about 35%, and in the past forty years the life expectancy for persons 45 years of age has increased five years.

EXTENT OF ILLNESS AND DISABILITY

In the absence of precise figures estimates must be relied upon for an overview of the prevalence of chronic illness and other disabilities. Yet estimates based upon properly conducted surveys are sufficiently accurate to be of practical value for an overview of the extensiveness of the problem and to point up the areas in which special efforts are needed. National health surveys of the incidence of illness and disabilities conducted by the U. S. Public Health Service beginning in 1935 are the most reliable source of such data. In 1957 the U. S. Public Health Service reported the estimated prevalence of illness in the United States.

Respiratory disorders account for more disability than any other condition, but other classifications constitute formidable causes of disability. Even among children, although respiratory disorders account for about two thirds of the disability time, other conditions are of significant importance.

IMPAIRMENTS

Impairments are more widespread than is generally known. The nationwide household interview survey conducted by the U. S. Public Health Service ob-

Table 7. Number of impairments and rate per 1000 persons by type of impairment and sex in United States, July, 1957, to June, 1958*

Type of impairment	Number of impairments in thousands			Rate per 1000 persons		
	Both sexes	Male	Female	Both sexes	Male	Female
Blindness	960	382	578	5.7	4.7	6.7
Other visual impairment	2064	1053	1011	12.3	12.9	11.7
Deafness, total	109	65	44	0.6	0.8	0.5
Other hearing impairment	5714	3211	2503	33.9	39.2	28.9
Speech defects	1098	706	392	6.5	8.6	4.5
Mental retardation	240	133	107	1.4	1.6	1.2
Cerebral palsy	112	64	48	0.7	0.8	0.6
Hemiplegia, paraplegia, and quadriplegia	257	130	127	1.5	1.6	1.5
Other paralysis	570	293	277	3.4	3.6	3.2
Absence, fingers and toes only	1428	1195	233	8.5	14.6	2.7
Absence, major extremities	282	210	72	1.7	2.6	0.8
Absence, other sites and organs	202	65	137	1.2	0.8	1.6
Curvature of spine	329	111	218	2.0	1.4	2.5
Other impairment, back or spine	3608	1794	1815	21.4	21.9	21.0
Flatfoot, weak arches	218	117	100	1.3	1.4	1.2
Clubfoot	104	59	45	0.6	0.7	0.5
Other impairment, feet and legs	2833	1647	1186	16.8	20.1	13.7
Deformity, fingers and thumbs only	243	130	113	1.4	1.6	1.3
Other impairments, hands and arms	1439	893	546	8.5	10.9	6.3
Impairment, hip and pelvis	309	129	181	1.8	1.6	2.1
Impairment, multiple, ill-defined, limbs, back, and trunk	779	400	379	4.6	4.9	4.4
Disfigurement (facial) cleft palate, other dentifacial handicaps	217	122	94	1.3	1.5	1.1
All other impairments	700	262	439	4.2	3.2	5.1
All impairments†	23815	13170	10644	141.4	169.0	123.1

*From U. S. Public Health Service, Washington, D. C., 1959, publication no. 584-B10.
†Detailed figures may not add to totals due to rounding.

tained comprehensive data on the extent of impairments in the over-all population of the nation. It indicated a total of twenty-four million impairments among civilian noninstitutional residents. The data were derived from household interviews obtained in a continuous probability sample of the civilian noninstitutional population of the United States during the period July, 1957, through June, 1958. Interviews were conducted in approximately 36,000 households comprising 115,000 persons. Selected data from the various reports of this survey, adjusted to the total population, indicate the extent to which impairments interfere with effective and enjoyable living in the United States.

When an analysis of these data is made, it must be recognized that one individual with several defects will be included in several categories. Yet even when this factor is considered, more than 20,000,000 Americans have one or more of the classified impairments. The incidence of impairments among males is significantly higher than among females. Accidents account for part of this differential, but not all of it. From these data one might draw the conclusion that the male constitution is inferior to that of the female, that it is more predisposed to impairment. More important, these data also point up the foolhardy tendency of the male to neglect a minor disorder and through this neglect permit the minor condition to culminate in an impairment.

Prevalence of impairments in various age groups is included in the report of the survey, and these data identify both the extent of disabilities at various age levels and the ages at which different impairments tend to appear in the greatest numbers.

In consideration of the prevalence of impairments by age, the cumulative ef-

Table 8. Rate per 1000 persons by type of impairment and age group in United States, July, 1957, to June, 1958*

Type of impairment	All ages	Under 25 yr.	25-44 yr.	45-64 yr.	65-74 yr.	75+ yr.
Blindness	5.7	0.5	1.3	5.9	25.9	83.3
Other visual impairment	12.3	3.6	7.2	18.5	48.8	74.3
Hearing impairments	34.6	7.9	20.6	52.2	129.2	256.4
Speech defects	6.5	9.7	3.5	3.7	6.8	6.1
Paralysis	5.6	2.1	3.4	8.8	15.9	34.4
Absence, fingers and toes only	8.5	1.9	9.7	15.9	22.6	17.4
Absence, major extremities	1.7	0.4	1.5	3.3	4.4	7.0
Impairment, lower extremities	18.7	10.3	20.4	26.5	37.1	39.7
Impairment, upper extremities	10.0	2.9	10.8	17.6	24.6	26.6
Impairment, limbs, back, and trunk, except extremities only	29.9	8.4	42.7	48.7	49.7	61.6
All other impairments	8.1	5.3	9.4	11.2	11.6	8.2
All impairments†	141.4	52.9	130.6	212.4	376.6	615.0

*From U. S. Public Health Service, Washington, D. C., 1959, publication no. 584-B10.
†Detailed figures may not add to totals due to rounding.

fect must be recognized. People who acquire a disability at 20 years of age will some five years later join those who acquire the same impairment during the age span between 25 and 44 years. On the other side of the coin, certain impairments acquired early in life, e.g., hearing, may be corrected before the individual reaches the next age group or classification. Impairments are not the exclusive possession of those in the older age groups. They are the lot of all ages, and for this reason any program for the prevention of disorders and defects must be applied to all age groups.

WHAT CAUSES DEATH

Healthy individuals do not associate death with themselves; yet if each of us knew what our cause of death would be, we would doubtless be in a better posi-

Table 9. Rank and death rates per 100,000 from leading causes in 1962* compared to 1900†

	1900			1962	
Rank	*Cause*	*Rate*	*Rank*	*Cause*	*Rate*
1.	Pneumonia and influenza	202.2	1.	Diseases of heart	368.8
2.	Tuberculosis	194.4	2.	Malignant neoplasms	149.2
3.	Diseases of cardiovascular system	182.3	3.	Vascular lesions affecting central nervous system	106.3
4.	Gastritis, duodenitis, enteritis, and colitis	142.7	4.	Accidents	52.3
			5.	Certain diseases of early infancy	35.3
5.	Symptoms, senility and ill-defined conditions	117.5	6.	Pneumonia and influenza	32.8
			7.	General arteriosclerosis	19.8
6.	Chronic and unspecified nephritis and other renal sclerosis	81.0	8.	Diabetes mellitus	17.0
7.	Accidents	72.3	9.	Symptoms, senility and ill-defined diseases or conditions	12.6
8.	Apoplexy	72.0	10.	Other diseases of circulatory system	11.8
9.	Malignant neoplasms	64.0			
10.	Diseases of early infancy	62.6	11.	Cirrhosis of liver	11.5
11.	Diphtheria	40.3	12.	Congenital malformations	11.3
12.	Typhoid fever	31.3	13.	Suicide	10.9
13.	Deliveries and complications of pregnancy, childbirth, and puerperium	13.4	14.	Hypertension without mention of heart	7.1
14.	Measles	13.3	15.	Chronic and unspecified nephritis	6.4
15.	Cirrhosis of liver	12.5	16.	Ulcers of stomach and duodenum	6.4
16.	Whooping cough	12.2			
17.	Dysentery, all forms	12.0	17.	Hernia and intestinal obstruction	5.4
18.	Syphilis and its sequelae	12.0			
19.	Congenital malformations	12.0	18.	Tuberculosis	5.1
20.	Diabetes mellitus	11.0	19.	Homicide	4.8
21.	Suicide	10.2	20.	Gastritis, duodenitis, enteritis, and colitis	4.5
22.	Acute nephritis and nephritis with edema	7.7	21.	Asthma	2.8
			22.	Bronchitis	2.4

*From National Vital Statistics Division: Vital statistics report, vol. 12, no. 1, March 20, 1963.
†From U. S. Department of Commerce, Bureau of the Census.

tion to postpone death. Statistically we do know what the most likely causes of death will be. We have the benefit of the nation's death rates as a sufficient guide for postponing death. After all, we cannot prevent death. The best we can do is postpone it.

The crude death rate in the United States has declined from 17.2 per 1000 in 1900 to 9.6 per 1000 in 1962. This means that if the death rate we had in 1900 prevailed today, approximately 1,500,000 more deaths would occur this year than actually will occur. This is human conservation of a high order. Equally interesting is the change in the specific causes of death in 1962 as contrasted with 1900. At the turn of the century the infectious diseases were the leading causes of death. Today the chronic degenerative diseases of old age are the leading causes of death. Table 9 shows the leading causes of death in 1962 as contrasted with 1900. Significantly, over 85% of the deaths today are due to ten causes.

In 1962, the death rate from suicide was 10.9 per 100,000, and for tuberculosis the death rate was 5.1, placing these two in ranks eleven and sixteen. This puts tuberculosis outside of the first ten, which is a milestone in the health history of the United States.

A comparison of 1962 death rates for leading causes, by sex, reveals that the male has a higher rate than the female in all but two of the leading causes of death. Table 10 reveals that only for diabetes mellitus, and vascular lesions does

Table 10. Death rates per 100,000 for leading causes by sex and race in United States, 1961*

Cause	White			Nonwhite		
	Both sexes	Male	Female	Both sexes	Male	Female
Diseases of heart	375.3	449.3	303.3	288.2	326.4	252.1
Malignant neoplasms	151.0	164.6	137.7	120.7	136.2	106.1
Vascular lesions affecting central nervous system	103.9	98.5	109.0	114.9	109.6	120.0
Accidents	49.2	68.3	30.7	62.0	87.5	37.9
Diseases of early infancy	31.3	37.7	25.1	76.8	89.1	65.3
Pneumonia and influenza	27.9	31.1	24.7	44.5	55.1	34.5
General arteriosclerosis	19.9	19.4	20.3	12.8	14.0	11.5
Diabetes mellitus	15.8	12.5	19.0	15.7	10.5	20.6
Congenital malformations	11.3	12.8	9.9	12.8	15.8	10.0
Cirrhosis of liver	11.3	15.3	7.5	10.6	12.8	8.6
Suicide	11.3	17.3	5.5	4.1	6.8	1.6
Symptoms of senility and ill-defined conditions	8.3	10.1	6.6	33.2	38.0	28.7
Other diseases of circulatory system	11.5	14.3	8.8	10.2	10.9	9.5
Hypertension without mention of heart	6.1	5.9	6.3	12.4	14.0	10.8
Chronic and unspecified nephritis	5.7	6.2	5.3	11.8	14.0	9.7
All causes†	926.1	1070.3	785.9	926.9	1103.0	830.5

*From U. S. National Vital Statistics Division: Vital statistics report, vol. 10, no. 13, July 31, 1962.
†Average for each classification for both sexes; therefore, detailed figures may not add to totals.

Table 11. Ten leading causes of death by age groups in United States, 1961*

Rank	Cause of death	Rate per 100,000	Rank	Cause of death	Rate per 100,000
	Under 1 year			*25-34 years*	
1.	Certain diseases of early in-fancy	1569.3	1.	Accidents	41.3
2.	Congenital malformations	343.8	2.	Malignant neoplasms	18.7
3.	Pneumonia and influenza	217.1	3.	Diseases of heart	16.3
4.	Accidents	77.2	4.	Suicide	10.7
5.	Gastritis, enteritis, and colitis	57.3	5.	Homicide	8.3
6.	Other bronchial diseases	29.3	6.	Vascular lesions affecting central nervous system	4.3
7.	Hernia and intestinal obstruction	21.1	7.	Pneumonia and influenza	3.3
			8.	Cirrhosis of liver	3.3
8.	Meningitis, except meningococcal and tuberculous	19.7	9.	Chronic nephritis	2.7
9.	Bronchitis	14.3	10.	Deliveries and complications of pregnancies, childbirth and puerperium	2.4
10.	Diseases of heart	8.4			
	1-14 years			*35-44 years*	
1.	Accidents	22.9	1.	Diseases of heart	71.5
2.	Malignant neoplasms	7.7	2.	Malignant neoplasms	60.0
3.	Congenital malformations	5.7	3.	Accidents	39.9
4.	Pneumonia and influenza	5.3	4.	Vascular lesions affecting nervous system	16.3
5.	Diseases of heart	1.4	5.	Suicide	14.2
6.	Gastritis, enteritis, and colitis	1.3	6.	Cirrhosis of liver	12.8
7.	Meningitis	1.1	7.	Pneumonia and influenza	7.9
8.	Anemias	0.8	8.	Homicide	6.7
9.	Bronchitis	0.7	9.	Tuberculosis	5.4
10.	Acute nephritis	0.4	10.	Diabetes mellitus	4.6
	15-24 years			*45-54 years*	
1.	Accidents	54.9	1.	Diseases of heart	269.2
2.	Malignant neoplasms	7.3	2.	Malignant neoplasms	175.5
3.	Homicide	5.8	3.	Accidents	46.4
4.	Suicide	4.4	4.	Vascular lesions affecting the nervous system	46.4
5.	Diseases of heart	3.2	5.	Cirrhosis of liver	27.5
6.	Congenital malformations	3.0	6.	Suicide	20.1
7.	Pneumonia and influenza	2.7	7.	Pneumonia and influenza	12.4
8.	Chronic and unspecified nephritis	1.6	8.	Diabetes mellitus	10.4
			9.	Tuberculosis	9.1
9.	Deliveries and complications of pregnancies, childbirth, and puerperium	1.6	10.	Chronic and unspecified nephritis	7.4
10.	Diabetes mellitus	0.6			

*From National Vital Statistics Division: Vital statistics reports, vol. 10, no. 13, July 31, 1962.

Continued on next page.

Table 11. Ten leading causes of death by age groups in United States, 1961—cont'd

Rank	Cause of death	Rate per 100,000	Rank	Cause of death	Rate per 100,000
	55-64 years			*75-84 years*	
1.	Diseases of heart	720.6	1.	Diseases of heart	3958.8
2.	Malignant neoplasms	386.4	2.	Vascular lesions affecting nervous system	1421.7
3.	Vascular lesions affecting nervous system	136.6	3.	Malignant neoplasms	1079.3
4.	Accidents	58.9	4.	General arteriosclerosis	287.2
5.	Diabetes mellitus	34.3	5.	Pneumonia and influenza	264.9
6.	Cirrhosis of liver	32.3	6.	Accidents	206.4
7.	Pneumonia and influenza	31.4	7.	Diabetes mellitus	163.6
8.	Suicide	25.3	8.	Hypertension without mention of heart	82.0
9.	Ulcer of stomach and duodenum	14.2	9.	Symptoms, senility, and ill-defined conditions	72.8
10.	Tuberculosis	13.8	10.	Chronic and unspecified nephritis	54.1
	65-74 years			*85 years and over*	
1.	Diseases of heart	1708.5	1.	Diseases of heart	9378.9
2.	Malignant neoplasms	721.7	2.	Vascular lesions affecting nervous system	3644.9
3.	Vascular lesions affecting nervous system	453.2	3.	Malignant neoplasms	1412.0
4.	Diabetes mellitus	85.3	4.	General arteriosclerosis	1382.0
5.	Accidents	84.4	5.	Pneumonia and influenza	970.0
6.	Pneumonia and influenza	82.7	6.	Accidents	622.2
7.	General arteriosclerosis	49.4	7.	Symptoms, senility, and ill-defined conditions	281.6
8.	Cirrhosis of liver	36.5	8.	Hypertension without mention of heart	232.9
9.	Ulcer of stomach and duodenum	29.3	9.	Diabetes mellitus	181.2
10.	Symptoms, senility, and ill-defined conditions	27.8	10.	Chronic and unspecified nephritis	121.1

the female have the higher rate. For each of the sexes these data point up the areas in which special emphasis should be placed in further efforts to lower the death rates.

A comparison of specific death rates for white and nonwhite persons is presented clearly in Table 10. Nonwhite persons have a significantly higher death rate for some of the listed causes, with the exceptions, for example, heart disease and arteriosclerosis. A student might profitably consider all of the factors encompassed by these various rates. Heredity, medical services, hospital facilities, public health services, health practices, education, economic conditions, social patterns, and an array of other factors account for the higher death rates in the different groups represented in these tables.

Causes of death in the various age groups reveal the specific hazards to life which exist at the various stages of life. Knowledge of the leading causes of death for one's own age group enables a person to concentrate his preventive efforts more effectively. A person may not know what the specific cause of his own death may be, but, second best, he can know statistically what it is most likely to be. This knowledge can be of importance to the person who uses it wisely.

In planning and pursuing his health program for life, a person might profitably examine death rates for selected causes by sex and by race. In many categories the death rates for the two sexes will not vary appreciably. For other causes the death rates may vary markedly. The same holds true in the death rates by various causes for different races.

POSTPONING DEATH

Some individuals are so overly concerned about even the most trivial pain or disturbance that they dash to a physician on the slightest pretext with apprehension of impending death. This borders on hypochondriasis and is one of the extremes which should be avoided. These individuals should come to realize that normal individuals do not have perfect health. All of us are likely to have a moment of distress or slight pain of a transient nature. Chronic or repeated occurrence of these disturbances would warrant consultation with one's personal physician.

At the other extreme is the individual who recognizes none of the signals which indicate dangers to health. Or, if he does recognize danger signals, he shows no particular concern over the matter. Frequently these individuals do not consult a physician until it is too late for effective treatment or cure.

The sensible course is between these extremes. An individual should not be overly anxious about every symptom, real or imaginary, and worry needlessly. On the other hand, an individual needs to know what common disturbances are not danger symptoms and what symptoms are possible threats to health and even life itself. This does not suggest that the individual should attempt self-diagnosis. It means that he should recognize when he needs the services of a physician to determine whether some abnormality exists. Danger signals which call for the physician's services may be dramatic or decidedly prosaic.

1. Loss of energy for a fairly extended period of time without obvious cause can signal a basic disorder.
2. Sudden change in weight, either rapid weight loss or weight gain, may be an indication of constitutional disturbance.
3. Repeated headaches indicate a possible basic disturbance. Repeated attacks of dizziness likewise can be significant.
4. Severe and definite pain, whether in the pelvic, abdominal, or thoracic region, is a significant signal, especially for a person who has had excellent health and has been free from chronic pain.
5. Shortness of breath deserves attention when it is out of proportion to the

amount of exertion engaged in. After 30 years of age, sharp transient pains in the chest can be highly significant.

6. Any abnormal growth, nonhealing sore, irregular bleeding, or progressive change in any structure should be seen by a physician.

7. Jaundice is a signal of organic disturbance.

8. Distress associated with digestive functions may be significant.

9. Black stool or vomiting of blood obviously are danger signals.

10. Frequent urination or blood in the urine merits the attention of a physician.

11. Vision disturbance or other nerve distress of a somewhat chronic nature should call for a thorough health examination.

12. Depression, confusion, or emotional distress which persists to some degree commands the counsel of a physician.

No attempt has been made to tabulate an extensive list of symptoms. Rather, the more prevalent indications of a disruption in normal health have been presented. It should be apparent that in many instances an individual who heeds these danger signals and seeks the services of a physician will be postponing death itself.

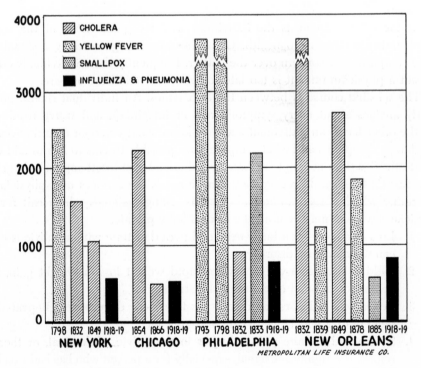

Fig. 11. Death rates per 100,000 of the population during great pandemics. Devastating as the influenza and pneumonia pandemic of 1918 to 1919 was, it was dwarfed by pandemics of other diseases in earlier years. (Courtesy Metropolitan Life Insurance Co.)

SCIENCE AND HEALTH

The dramatic change in the leading causes of death from the respiratory and other infectious diseases to the chronic organic diseases, the striking reduction in the general death rate, and the improved quality of human health are indications of the advances in the health sciences. The death rate of 9.3 in 1955 is but 53% of the death rate of 17.2 in 1900. At the turn of the century deaths from diphtheria and typhoid fever often exceeded 100 per 100,000 of the population, whereas today these diseases cause less than one death per 100,000. Tuberculosis had a death rate of approximately 200 per 100,000 of the population, whereas in 1960 the death rate from tuberculosis was 6 per 100,000 persons in the population. Infant mortality was formerly at such a high rate that three children in every ten live births failed to survive infancy; today nine out of ten children who are born will live to their twenty-fifth birthday anniversary.

As great as the influenza-pneumonia pandemic of 1918 to 1919 was, it was dwarfed by some of the earlier pandemics. The yellow fever pandemic of 1793 took the lives of one eighth of the population of Philadelphia, and the cholera pandemic of 1832 took the lives of one tenth of the people of New Orleans. Pandemics of these proportions will not occur again. Our understanding of the nature

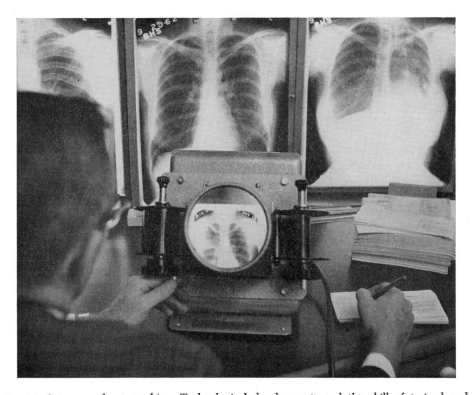

Fig. 12. Science and art combine. Technological developments and the skill of trained and experienced technicians combine to protect human health by the early detection of tuberculosis, cancer, and other diseases. (Courtesy Oregon State Board of Health.)

of communicable diseases and effective measures of control give us this assurance. Although science has not completely conquered infectious disease, reasonably effective control is now exercised. Today health scientists devote their major attention to the chronic organic diseases of later life. This does not mean that attention to acute infectious diseases, to sanitary measures, and to childhood diseases will be relaxed, but rather that greater attention will be focused on those health problems which most urgently need to be solved.

It is of interest to review some of the scientific advances which have had an effect on longevity. Although man's physiological nature, and thus his span of life, has not changed significantly, man's increased control of the environment has extended his life expectancy.

The discovery of the microscope opened up new vistas of exploration. In part

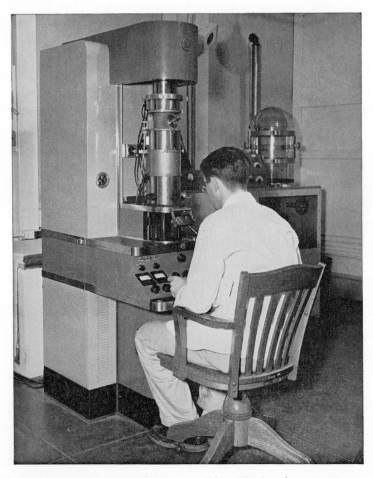

Fig. 13. Electron microscope. New advances possible with the electron microscope are anticipated in bacteriology, cellular biology, chemistry, and other fields. Perhaps the conquest of virus diseases and cancer will be made possible by the use of the electron microscope.

it enabled scientists to establish the germ theory of disease. It laid the foundation for aseptic surgery, pasteurization of milk, and other protective measures.

From the science of microbiology have come momentous developments in immunology, giving man control of diphtheria, smallpox, poliomyelitis, typhoid fever, tetanus, whooping cough, measles, and scarlet fever—to mention some of the past principal causes of death.

Insect-borne diseases can now be attacked successfully through a knowledge of the insect, the pathogen, and the disease. Tangible progress has been made in dealing with the insect-born diseases of malaria, yellow fever, bubonic plague, and typhus fever.

Endocrine disturbances, such as diabetes mellitus, are being controlled through treatment growing out of laboratory research. Advances in biochemistry have brought us nearer to an understanding of the organic diseases. Increased knowledge of nutrition has reduced the incidence of rickets, scurvy, pellagra, xerophthalmia, and other nutritional diseases.

Sanitation science has advanced to a stage at which the application of all that is known in the field would mean almost complete control of the environmental factors affecting health. Control of water supplies, disposal of sewage, protection of foods, and other sanitary measures have reduced the death rate and elevated the standard of personal health.

Special aids in the march of the health sciences include roentgenotherapy, radium, the electron microscope, the electrocardiograph, heliotherapy, hydrotherapy, thermotherapy, and chemotherapy (e.g., sulfonamides). Antibiotics (e.g., penicillin) have opened up new avenues of diagnosis and treatment undreamed of at the turn of the century.

INTERRELATIONSHIP OF PERSONAL AND COMMUNITY HEALTH

How each of us lives affects the community in which we live, and the life of the community has both direct and indirect influences on all who live in the community. Neither the health of the individual nor the health of the community exists isolated and alone. The individual may utilize all known measures for the prevention of disease and the promotion of health, but, if his neighbors disregard measures for preventing diseases, he may find his efforts quite ineffective. An individual who directs efforts toward his own health will also contribute to the health of the community. The collective efforts of all citizens in a community contribute to the welfare of each individual citizen.

Although responsibility for one's health rests with the individual, none of us is totally self-sufficient in dealing with all of the necessary requirements to safeguard, maintain, and promote health. Of necessity in our modern complex society, many things must be done on a cooperative or group basis. Providing a safe water supply, disposing of sewage, protecting milk and other food supplies, erecting hospitals, and providing other health facilities and services must be done on a cooperative or community basis. By safeguarding and providing for the health of individuals, community health is promoted. The ideal is individuals doing everything feasible to promote their own health and a community providing for its citizens those facilities and services which are necessary for health but which can be provided best through community enterprise.

USING HEALTH RESOURCES

Wise use of health resources adds both more life to years and more years to life. A mark of a citizen with an adequate education in health is the use that citizen makes of the health resources available to him. Few citizens make adequate use of available health facilities and services.

Medical services. It is sound health practice to have a personal or family physician to serve as consultant on matters relating to health. When one selects a personal physician, he may ask the county medical society for a listing of medical practitioners in the county. Other sources of information may also be contacted, such as hospials, health departments, and welfare agencies. The physician finally selected should meet several basic requirements:

1. Be a duly registered medical practitioner
2. Be a member of the county medical society
3. Be a member of a hospital staff
4. Be professionally competent
5. Be conveniently available

A general practitioner serves consultant needs admirably, particularly because of his broad over-all interest in health. A general practitioner will treat more than 80% of the ailments which come to his attention. When a specialist is needed, the general practitioner will be best qualified to recommend a specialist. An appealing personality is not a valid basis for the selection of a personal physician because most present-day physicians are prepared primarily as scientists. His professional qualifications are his recommendation.

If he is to obtain the greatest possible value from a physician's services, it is important that the individual provide the physician with all necessary information and implicitly follow the physician's instructions. A busy physician rightly expects the individual to come in for regular examinations, as well as for consultation on special health problems, rather than to wait for the physician to seek out the individual.

College health service. Normally college health service takes the place of a personal physician during student days. The prudent student makes use of this service. Although most college health service is limited to (1) health examinations, (2) consulting service, (3) treatment of minor illness, and (4) emergency care, a national conference on health in colleges* suggested a more extensive service.

---

*National Tuberculosis Association: A health program for colleges, The Association, 1948.

1. A medical examination at time of entrance
2. Follow-up physician-student health conference
3. Additional examinations as deemed necessary by the physician or requested by the student
4. Adjustment of the student's program to his health capacity and needs
5. Special medical examinations for athletes and others in special activities
6. Emergency and ambulatory care during illness
7. Necessary consultation with medical specialists
8. Necessary hospitalization
9. Assistance in providing healthful student living

A student should acquaint himself with the functions of his college health service and cooperate in making the service of greatest possible value to him. If he has a special health problem when he enters college, an explanatory letter from his family physician to the college health service staff will be of value to the college physician in his efforts to serve the student.

Dental services. Every student needs a personal dentist if for no other purpose than that of having a semiannual examination. The county dental society lists all registered dental practitioners, their professional preparation, and experience. A dentist of proved competence, reasonably conveniently available, is not too difficult to locate. A definite appointment for each half of the school year is a recommended procedure even though the student has no known dental defect. Prevention is highly important in dentistry, and retention of the same dentist for several years has merit.

Hospital facilities. Either through tax funds or through private subscriptions or endowments, communities provide hospitals for the needs of their citizens. Construction and operation of a hospital are extremely costly; yet a hospital is one of the most valued assets of the community. A student, like any other citizen, should know about the hospital facilities in the community, use the hospital when his physician so advises, and support it in every possible way.

Hospital and medical insurance. Hospital and medical insurance are not considered typical community health resources, but are means by which the citizen is assured of a full use of the medical and hospital resources in the community. Insurance is merely a device by which average costs are substituted for variable costs. It protects the individual against the possible financial crisis of surgery and extended hospitalization. For the student it can mean security against disruption of his education and assurance of the necessary medical and hospital services.

Local health department. Most communities in the nation now have the benefit of full-time health service. These health departments protect and promote the health of all citizens, but are of greatest service to those who understand the services the health department has to offer. A student should know about the communicable disease control measures of the local health department and the program to promote environmental sanitation. The department issues reports and other information of important health value to the student.

Voluntary health agencies. A number of nonofficial health agencies will likely be available to the college student and may have a service, such as roentgenographic examination or a clinic, which can be of special value to the student. To know about these voluntary health agencies and to use and support them are the marks of a public-spirited informed citizen.

An individual may not be totally able to do for himself everything that must be done in the interest of his health, but all of the necessary services are usually available if the individual has knowledge of the existence of these services and of how to use them. The fruits of health science are more bountiful than ever before. A person with an adequate education in health is prepared to harvest the full benefits of the bumper crop of health science. Whereas the fruits of some phases of education are not harvested until twenty-five years later, the fruits of health education are harvested every day. This is not a profound discovery, just a timely reminder.

Chapter 2

Inherited basis
of health

Nature plus nurture, not nature versus nurture, is the interest of both the health scientist and the college student. A person is born with a certain potential, both physiological and psychological. What potential one has is important, and the origins of this equipment is of equal interest and importance. Knowledge of one's biological inheritance is more than academic. In addition to providing one with an appreciation of one's basic assets, the field of genetics has advanced to a position today where something can be done about genetics as it relates to its actual application to the human. Scientists no longer take the fatalistic view that nothing can be done about human genetics. Although the advances in altering the patterns of human genetics are as yet somewhat limited, progress is being made and the educated citizen keeps abreast of these developments.

The way in which an individual is endowed with certain constitutional factors which contribute to excellent or ill health is of interest to most normal individuals. To have an appreciation of his health potential, one must have an appreciation of the endowment which has been transmitted to him by his parents. The same knowledge of transmission which enables him to evaluate his own health possibilities may also enable him, through reasoned selection of a mate, to perpetuate the best in inherited endowment and to terminate some of the undesirable inherited factors in health.

Heredity. Heredity is the study of the transmission of characteristics from parents to offspring. It deals with the tendency of the offspring to resemble the parents and each other in more respects than they resemble other offspring or other parents. It likewise considers the tendency of offspring to differ from one another despite common parentage. This is of special interest to the hygienist because the causes of variation are both internal and external to the individual.

71

At no time during the life of the individual can one set of factors operate to the complete exclusion of the other.

Inheritance. Inheritance is the transmission of characteristics from parents to offspring. In effect it is the biological element which is transmitted to the offspring. Whatever the trait may be which is inherited—intelligence, motor speed, nearsightedness, or any other characteristic—the basic factor is biological, being represented in protoplasm and its function.

Genetics. Genetics is the study of the mechanism of inheritance. It is concerned with the manner in which traits or characteristics are transmitted from one generation to the next.

The only direct link which connects one human generation with the succeeding one is to be found in the germ, or reproductive, cells. More specifically it is the granular rodlike structures, the *chromosomes,* in the nucleus of the germ cell which contain the inheritable substance. These chromosomes are made up of

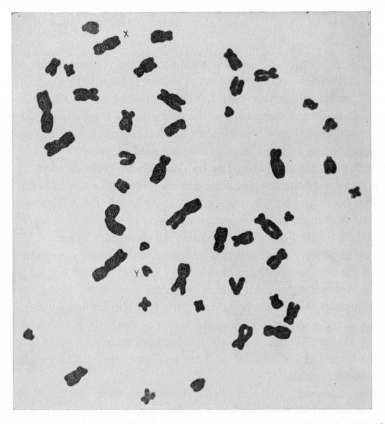

Fig. 14. Photomicrograph of the chromosomes of a male cell in a human being. This preparation from a normal cell was grown in tissue culture and arrested at the metaphase, or middle stage, of cell division. Note the identification of the large X chromosome and the small Y chromosome. (Approximately ×1800.) (Courtesy Dr. J. H. Tjio and Dr. T. T. Puck, Department of Biophysics, University of Colorado Medical Center, Denver, Colo.)

units of length which are called *genes*. Thus regarded, a gene is a minimal part of a chromosome which controls a single specific metabolic reaction in a cell. These units are of different lengths and shapes but are not entirely definable as single objects. Rather, they should be thought of as operational units.

Research indicates that it is the nucleic acid component of nucleoproteins which gives a gene its specific transmissable properties. It has been demonstrated experimentally that it is the *deoxyribonucleic acid* or DNA of nucleoprotein which is of genetic importance in the transmission of traits. The protein fraction of the nucleoprotein has no such effect. Thus, it is the DNA which is capable of initiating the enzyme system that accounts for a particular trait. Different forms of DNA will account for the different traits and combinations of traits. For convenience these particular chemical substances can be referred to as chemical units, molecules, or even particles. The important concept is that it is these specific forms of deoxyribonucleic acid (DNA) within the somewhat linear genes which account for the transmission of specific qualitative traits.

Recent improvements in culturing mammalian cells have made possible a more precise determination of the number and nature of chromosomes in human

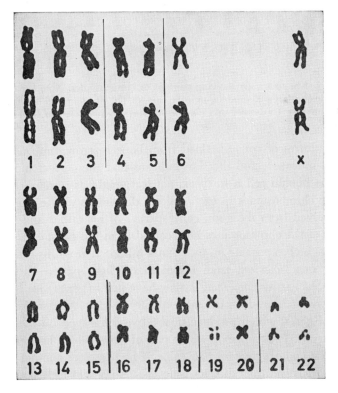

Fig. 15. Idiogram of human female showing pairings of chromosomes. Note the pairing of the X chromosomes. (Courtesy Dr. J. H. Tjio and Dr. T. T. Puck, Department of Biophysics, University of Colorado Medical Center, Denver, Colo.)

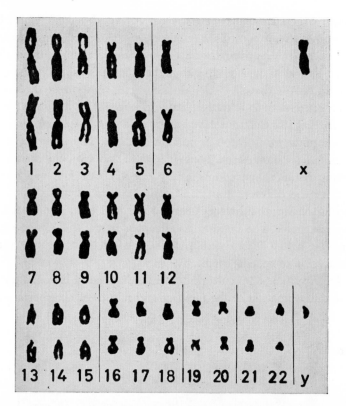

Fig. 16. Idiogram of human male showing pairings of chromosomes. Note the small Y chromosome paired with the large X chromosome. (Courtesy Dr. H. Tjio and Dr. T. T. Puck, Department of Biophysics, University of Colorado Medical Center, Denver, Colo.)

cells. Tissue cultures of cells obtained from bone marrow, mucous tissue of the cheek (buccal mucosa), and the skin indicate that the correct number of chromosomes in the human cell is forty-six, not forty-eight as formerly thought.

Half of the chromosomes in each cell are duplicates of the chromosomes the individual received from the germ cell (sperm) of his father and a like number are duplicates of the chromosomes he received from the germ cell (ovum) of his mother. For each chromosome an individual inherited from his father, there is a corresponding one inherited from his mother. These paired chromosomes are analogous or alike in function. That is, they have units (genes) for the same traits. A pair of genes which produce the same quality of a trait are said to be homozygous. A pair of genes which produce qualitative differences in the trait are said to be heterozygous. Thus a person with a pair of genes which both produce brown hair is said to be *homozygous* for hair color. If he possesses another pair of genes, one for brown eyes and the other for blue eyes, he is said to be *heterozygous* for eye color.

Although ordinary body cells contain twenty-three pairs of chromosomes, the normal germ, or reproductive, cell (ovum or sperm) contains only twenty-three single chromosomes. This occurs because of the special cell division which forms the germ cell. The primary cell from which the germ cell will be formed contains twenty-three pairs of chromosomes. Before its final splitting or division into two cells, the pairs of chromosomes of this primary cell separate. A disjunction or separation occurs. The final mature germ cell contains only one chromosome of each pair of chromosomes. For the person referred to in the previous paragraph, one half of his germ cells will possess the chromosome containing the gene for blue eyes. He will have brown eyes because the gene for brown eyes produces the full development of its trait in the presence of the gene for blue eyes. The gene for brown eyes is said to be *dominant*. Blue eyes occur only in those individuals who possess two genes for blue eyes. Such a gene is termed *recessive*. This person himself will have brown hair since both the genes produce brown hair. It should be observed that hair color and eye color are inherited independently of each other, which indicates that the gene for hair color and the gene for eye color lie on different chromosomes.

To illustrate the transmission of a trait when both parents are heterozygous for the trait, let B represent the gene for brown eyes and b represent the gene for blue eyes. Both individuals would have brown eyes, but since both individuals will produce germ cells, one half having a gene for brown eyes and one half having a gene for blue eyes, four different combinations of the genes are possible in the offspring. Thus it is statistically probable that three of every four offspring will have brown eyes. Of these, one would be homozygous dominant for the brown eye trait, two would be heterozygous, and one would be blue eyed and thus homozygous recessive for that trait.

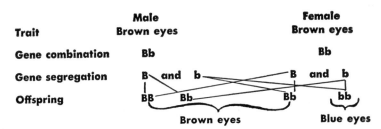

It must be recognized that for this mating and a family of four offspring, the ratio of three brown-eyed children to each blue-eyed child may not prevail. However, a large number of such matings would result in a ratio of three children with brown eyes for each child with blue eyes.

Dominance and recessiveness are not always absolute. *Incomplete dominance* occasionally occurs, in which both traits tend to appear. Thus, a gene for black skin color paired with a gene for white skin color will produce a skin color somewhere between the two extremes. In some instances a gene which acts as a dominant in one individual may act as a recessive in another individual.

In chromosome makeup the female germ cell and male germ cell have one distinguishing difference. All female germ cells contain an X sex chromosome.

Only one half of the male sperm cells contain an X sex chromosome; the remaining half contain a Y sex chromosome. In fertilization a union of an X sperm with a female germ cell produces a female offspring. A union of a Y sperm with a female germ cell results in a male. These sex-determining chromosomes also possess genes which account for other traits.

That children show variations from their parents is a common observation. Why children exhibit physiological characteristics not possessed by their parents is readily answered by the science of genetics. That certain characteristics crop out in different lineages is not something mystical to the geneticist, but a challenge to his application of the known principles of genetics.

An Augustinian monk, Gregor Johann Mendel, was the founder of the science of genetics. Over a period of eight years he conducted experiments in the garden of his monastery at Brünn (now Brno), Austria. Similar studies had been made by previous investigators, but Gregor Mendel succeeded where others had failed. His over-all comprehension of the problem, his precise methods, his painstaking techniques, and his accurate recording of data enabled him to discover basic principles of inheritance. He studied the inheritance of single contrasting characteristics, such as tall versus dwarf plants, yellow versus green color, and smooth versus wrinkled coats in peas. Published in an obscure Austrian journal in 1868, his results aroused little interest until 1900 when, independently, H. de Vries in Holland, E. von Tschermak in Austria, and C. Correns in Germany discovered Mendel's report. In honor of Mendel and his work the two fundamental laws of inheritance are known as Mendel's laws.

Mendel's first law is usually referred to as the principle of gametic (germ cell) purity and states: Inherited pairs of factors segregate at germ cell formation and recombine at fertilization. Thus a germ cell or gamete can carry but one of any two alternative characters.

Mendel's second law states: When two pairs of genes lie on different chromosomes, each pair is inherited independently of the other pair. That is, Mendel showed that the inheritance of green or yellow in peas is entirely independent of smooth or rough coat inheritance.

Gene combinations possible in the human being attest to the vast variation in characteristics we can find even in a given family. Applying the mathematics of combinations, we use the expression two to the nth power. The *two* represents the chromosome pairing and the *n* is twenty-three, representing the number of such pairs. Thus, two to the twenty-third power gives us 8,388,608 possible different kinds of germ cells in terms of chromosome combinations which a given human being can produce. The resulting diversity is apparent. Apply this now to two human beings, a husband and wife, and our expression becomes four to the nth power. This gives us a figure of more than seven billion different possible chromosome combinations which could occur in their zygotes or resulting offspring. Diversity in the offspring is the inevitable end product.

Inherited predisposition. Inherited predisposition (diathesis) is the transmission of a physiological trait which may not express itself except under certain circumstances. In effect it often expresses itself as a weakness or deficiency not apparent until later years. When the level of function has been adequate for childhood needs but inadequate for adult needs, the deficiency does not assert itself until after adulthood has been attained. Although some geneticists will term this type of inheritance a predisposition, perhaps a greater number regard it as basically no different than the mechanism of any other inheritance.

For convenience perhaps more than for basic biological reasons, inherited predisposition is used to denote the condition in which a particular lineage appears to be more susceptible to a particular disorder, infectious or noninfectious, than the general population. If the disease in question is an infectious one, certain extrinsic factors favorable to the causative agent, as well as the presence of the pathogen itself, are necessary for the disease to appear. From the basic genetic standpoint the inheritance must not be considered different from the transmission of any other physiological entity which may be manifest at birth. When inherited predisposition is applied to an organic disorder prevalent in a lineage but not appearing until the later years of life, the genetic basis must be considered in the usual way. The fact that sluggish or submarginal cells of the pancreas are equal to demands made of them in the early years of life, but unequal to the demands of later years, makes the mechanism of inheritance no different than if the defect were apparent at the hour of birth.

Chromosomal abnormalities. Certain inborn errors of metabolism which did not seem to be due to dominant or recessive factors had long been a puzzle to geneticists. Not until a new procedure was developed for layering chromosomes were scientists able to explain why certain disorders occurred without a gene dominance or recessiveness being present.

We have seen that normally, when a primary cell divides to form the mature germ cell, the chromosomes of a pair separate and only one goes into the final mature germ cell. Once in awhile a mishap, atypical alignment, or nondisjunction, of chromosomes occurs. Both chromosomes of a pair remain together, or do not separate. Both of them may be in the final mature germ cell or neither of the two chromosomes may be in the germ cell. Thus when this occurs the germ cell may have one too many chromosomes (twenty-four) or one too few chromosomes (twenty-two). The miracle is that this nondisjunction does not occur more frequently when one considers the complexity of cell division and the great number of germ cell divisions that occur in the lifetime of a human, particularly in the male. Perhaps this nondisjunction of chromosomes occurs fairly frequently, but, since the vast number of germ cells never function in the creation of an offspring, the nondisjunction is never apparent. In addition it well may be that in some nondisjunctions, even though the germ cell does conceive, the extra chromosomes or one chromosome deficiency has no discernible effect on the resulting human being.

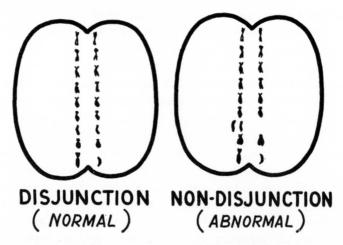

DISJUNCTION NON-DISJUNCTION
(NORMAL) (ABNORMAL)

Fig. 17. Chromosomal abnormality. In normal cell division creating germ cells, paired chromosomes separate to either side of a dividing plane and only one chromosome of a pair is present in the mature germ cell. In nondisjunction, one or more of the paired chromosomes do not separate but remain together. Note that the pair of chromosomes third from the bottom did not separate. One germ cell will have both chromosomes of this pair; the other germ cell will not have one of these chromosomes. (Only ten of the usual twenty-three pairs of chromosomes are shown.)

Mongoloid idiocy. One of the first conditions in which an abnormal chromosome number was found is mongoloid idiocy. This individual has an extra number twenty-one chromosome and thus has forty-seven chromosomes in its body cells instead of the usual forty-six. It appears that the nondisjunction occurs in the production of the ovum of the mother, and the occurence of mongoloid children is most frequent in older mothers. However, factors other than maternal age may be in operation.

About one in every 700 persons in the population is a mongoloid idiot, and about 5% of institutionalized mental defectives are in this group. Mongols are short in stature and limbs, have a small head, short nose, open mouth, and thick tongue, and the small outer fold of the upper eyelid covers the median or inner junction of the lids. This is the root of the term *mongoloid* though the upper lid differs significantly from that of the Oriental. The mongoloid idiot has broad hands and feet, sometimes a webbing of the toes, and marked muscular weakness. Most mongoloids die before the age of 10 years. Heart disease, leukemia, and bronchopneumonia are frequent causes.

*Klinefelter's syndrome.** A condition in which the male has disproportionately long legs, sparse face and body hair, and no temporal hair recession is known as Klinefelter's syndrome. These boys are frequently of low intelligence and constitute about 2% of institutionalized feeble-minded persons.

All patients with Klinefelter's syndrome are sterile including those of normal

---

*Syndrome is an aggregate of symptoms constituting a disease picture.

intelligence. The external genitals are normal except that the testes are very small because they are infantile, fibrous, lacking in tubules, and without germinal cells.

The incidence of Klinefelter's syndrome is about one in every 400 male births. All cases are males, and all have two X chromosomes and one Y chromosome in their body cells instead of the usual complement of one of each sex chromosome. Evidence indicates that the mother's ovum contained two X chromosomes. Like the mongoloid, the male with Klinefelter's syndrome tends to be born most frequently to older mothers.

Turner's syndrome. A certain condition due to a deficiency of the sex chromosomes is known as Turner's syndrome. All persons affected are females and have only one X sex chromosome and thus a total of only forty-five chromosomes in their body cells. The individual is of normal body proportions but is short in stature. She possesses no secondary sex characteristics. Her chest is shieldlike, breasts are underdeveloped, and the nipples are rudimentary and widely spaced. The lower jaw is noticeably small and the neck is webbed with an extremely low hairline. The external genital structure is infantile, and ovaries are absent. In place of the ovaries the woman has fibrous tissue without germinal cells. Thus she does not menstruate and obviously is sterile.

Nondisjunction of the sex chromosomes in the formation of the ovum results in an ovum without an X chromosome to be fertilized by a sperm with an X chromosome. The resulting zygote has only one X chromosome and thus all of the developing child's body cells will have only one X chromosome.

Other nondisjunction disorders. About ten other disorders are suspected of being due to extra, missing, or enlarged chromosomes. Extra chromosomes of number sixteen, seventeen, or eighteen seem to result in brain damage and fatal disorders. Some cancer conditions appear to be associated with a loss of a portion of a chromosome. A chromosome analysis costs about four hundred dollars. Cells are obtained by scraping the inner surface of the cheek or aspirating the red marrow of the sternum and studied under the microscope.

Scientists hope to control factors which produce these disorders and by this means prevent their occurence. In the male this might be done by identifying the abnormal sperms and selecting only normal sperms to fertilize the ova. Solving this problem in the female could be a most formidable task. However, scientists have solved more difficult problems of less importance to mankind. Who solves this puzzling question will truly serve mankind. Perhaps a student or students sitting in our college classrooms today will some day discover the solution to this extremely important problem.

LONGEVITY

In England studying the nobility and upper class families, Beeton and Pearson measured the consistency between length of life of parents and their children.

A low but significant relationship was found. Holmes in a similar study obtained approximately the same findings.

To avoid the faults inherent in genealogy studies, Pearl introduced the method of "total immediate ancestral longevity" (TIAL) which is the sum of the ages at death of both parents and all four grandparents of a given individual. It is unlikely that the TIAL will exceed 600 or fall below 100. For persons 90 years of age or over (longevous group), 45.8% had two long-lived parents, whereas in the unselected (control) group, only 11.9% had two long-lived parents. Admitting biased factors in the study, one must concede the vast difference in the two figures is likely representative of inherited endowment.

A study of insurance records by Dublin and Marks attempted to eliminate all objections to data selected. The study was based on the experience of 118,000 white males, aged 20 to 64 years, who had been insured between 1899 and 1905 and were traced to 1939. At all ages the lowest death rate was recorded for those men whose parents were both living when the insurance was issued. The highest death rate was recorded among those with both parents dead at the time the insurance was issued.

Dublin and Marks also found a high general death rate in the presence of a family history of circulatory and kidney diseases. They also found that, among the individuals whose mother had died from diabetes, the general death rate was considerably above the average.

Appraisal of inheritance in longevity. Although evidence indicates the importance of inheritance in longevity, the relative weighting of inheritance and environment, as well as the mechanism of inheritance itself, is not completely clear. It must be recognized that living in a long-lived family frequently means many environmental advantages—physical, mental, and emotional—all of which could favor longevity. An individual with both parents to look after his welfare is more likely to attain a higher proportion of his potential health and longevity than an individual who, early in his life, loses one or both of his parents. With man's advance in the control and utilization of his physical surroundings, environment must be weighted as more important than formerly in the determination of longevity. Gains in the longevity for the general population must be attributed to environmental change, rather than inherited change. The advantages of better parental longevity still operate in the determination of one's length of life, but doubtless these advantages are relatively less than they were a half century ago.

INHERITANCE

Inheritance of the Rh blood factor. Students as future parents have an understandable interest in the Rh blood factor and the phenomena related to it. Rh incompatibility can produce congenital anemia of the newborn infant (erythroblastosis fetalis), and an understanding of the mechanisms involved is of significance to prospective parents as well as to parents.

Rh refers to a specific group of blood factors. The letters R and h are derived from the first letters in Rhesus, the genus of monkey in whose blood corpuscles the factor first was found. The Rh factor, like all blood factors (twenty-two systems or series now known*), is a mixture of proteins and carbohydrates on the surface of blood corpuscles. The Rh blood factor is antigenic; that is, through chemical, electronic, or mechanical means it can affect the molecules of proteins in the fluid part of the blood of an individual whose blood corpuscles do not have the Rh factor and thereby produce specific isoantibodies. These specific isoantibodies in the blood fluid will have a great affinity or attraction for the specific Rh blood factor, and blood corpuscles containing the Rh factor will at first stick to each other and later dissolve. Thus, if blood corpuscles containing the Rh factor, by transfusion or other means, get into the blood stream of a person who does not have the Rh factor, this person's blood fluid will soon contain isoantibodies which will cause corpuscles with the factor to clump and then dissolve.

There are six known Rh blood factors, but only five anti-Rh isoantibody types have been identified. Rh blood factors are labeled by two classifications—the International Nomenclature (Rh-Hr) and the British Nomenclature (C—D—E). Of the six identified Rh blood factors, only the one labeled Rh_0 or D is significant in the production of erythroblastosis fetalis. Rh positive and Rh negative are terms indicating the presence or absence of this Rh_0 or D factor in the blood corpuscles of individuals. It is this factor which will be considered for purposes of this discussion.

The Rh factor is inherited independently of the inheritance of any other blood factor. Each individual has a pair of genes for the Rh_0 or D factor. If D represents the dominant gene or the one which gives rise to the significant Rh factor in the blood corpuscles, and d represents the recessive gene or the one which does not give rise to the Rh factor, then the following three genotypes are possible:

DD	homozygous dominant	(Rh positive)
Dd	heterozygous	(Rh positive)
dd	homozygous recessive	(Rh negative)

These data can be applied in understanding how incompatibility of the Rh factor might result in erythroblastosis fetalis or congenital anemia.

If both parents are Rh positive, if both are Rh negative, or if the husband is Rh negative and the wife is Rh positive, there is little if any possibility that the offspring will be affected by the Rh factor. However, if the mother is Rh negative and the child she bears is Rh positive (the father also being Rh positive), the newborn child may be affected. In order for erythroblastosis to develop, a series of events must occur.

First, the D factor in the blood corpuscles of the Rh-positive child must get

---

* 1, A—B—O group; 2, Bicker group; 3, Behrens (B. E.); 4, Cavaliere (Ca); 5, Duffy (Fy); 6, Graydon (Gr); 7, Henshaw; 8, Hunter; 9, Jarrell; 10, Jay; 11, Gobbins; 12, Kellcellano group or series; 13, Kidd (JK); 14, Levay; 15, Lewis (Le); 16, Lutheran (Lu); 17, Miltenberger (Mi); 18, M—N; 19, P; 20, Rh—Hr (C—D—E, cde); 21, S–s (Guth); 22, U (10).

past the placenta and into the circulation of the Rh-negative mother. Normally, blood cells and thus the D factor cannot pass through the placental membrane, but damage to the membrane can result in corpuscles from the child passing into the blood stream of the mother. The blood corpuscles with the D factor stimulate the tissues of the mother to produce anti-D antibodies which readily pass through the placenta into the child and cause a clumping (agglutination) and subsequently a dissolving (lysis) of the Rh-positive blood corpuscles of the child. The degree of anemia and damage to the liver and spleen of the child depends upon how great the mother's production of antibodies is.

A child born with erythroblastosis fetalis exhibits such signs as emaciation, anemia, jaundice, and debility. Enlargement of the spleen and liver is quite common. Treatment consists of replacement blood transfusions (sanguination) in which some blood is withdrawn from the newborn infant and replaced with Rh-negative blood. Repeated transfusions will be accompanied by the disappearance of the maternal anti-D antibodies in the infant in four to eight weeks.

In the United States, about 15% of all Caucasions are Rh negative (dd). Thus, theoretically, 12% of all marriages in the United States could have offspring with erythroblastosis. However, this does not occur because some Rh-positive husbands are heterozygous for the Rh factor and half (theoretically) of their children would be Rh negative. Furthermore some women do not produce the anti-D antibodies because the placenta remains intact or their tissues do not produce the antibodies. Surveys indicate that among Caucasions erythroblastosis occurs only in one of each 250 full-term pregnancies. Among Negroes, about 7% are Rh negative, and among Japanese and Chinese less than 1% are Rh negative. Erythroblastosis in these races is rare.

It is apparent that no female, either before or during the childbearing period of life, should receive a transfusion of blood without having been typed for the Rh factor. If she is Rh negative, she should have a donor who is Rh negative, as well as of the same A–B–O type. A transfusion of Rh-positive blood would cause anti-D antibodies to be formed in an Rh-negative woman. If these antibodies remain when she bears an Rh-positive child, the child would likely be affected.

In most marriages in which the wife is Rh negative and the husband is Rh positive, erythroblastosis does not occur. Yet, in such marriages the wise course of action is to seek the advice and guidance of a physician. Present knowledge does not make prevention of erythroblastosis possible; yet a physician has much to offer in addition to the assurance he can give such husbands and wives.

Inheritance of pernicious anemia. Several forms of anemia have been recognized, one of the most dramatic being pernicious anemia. In this form the hemoglobin content of each red corpuscle of the blood may be within the normal range, but a deficiency in red corpuscle production results in a low corpuscle count. Evidence indicates that the basic deficiency lies in the lack of an enzymelike substance secreted by the mucosae of the stomach which governs the rate of production of red corpuscles in the bone marrow.

Most studies reveal that a high percentage of persons with pernicious anemia also have a deficiency of hydrochloric acid in the stomach. Whether the two conditions have a common physiological basis is not known. Likewise, whether a common hereditary basis exists is not known.

Existing evidence indicates that pernicious anemia depends upon an inherited condition which manifests various symptoms and disorders of the digestive and circulatory systems before terminating in pernicious anemia. Doubtless, the basic deficiency in gastric secretory function which reults in pernicious anemia is more frequent than is generally recognized. For this reason many investigators have reported the inheritance to be dominant, with an occasional skip during one generation, when actually the skip does not exist, but merely a mild or forerunner condition. The basic stomach deficiency appears to be a dominant factor although whether one pair of genes produces all of the effects or three independent but closely linked genes produce the effect is a matter of disagreement among geneticists.

Fortunately although at present pernicious anemia cannot be cured, it can be treated successfully with the administration of vitamin B_{12} and protein concentrates.

Inheritance of cardiovascular disorders. It is a common observation that heart and vascular disorders seem to "run in families," but cardiovascular disorders are so common that frequent occurrence in a lineage proves very little so far as inheritance is concerned. So many factors are involved in producing the final picture of cardiovascular disorder that isolation of the genetic factor is often difficult.

If hypertension (high blood pressure) has a true genetic basis, evidence now available indicates it is usually dominant but at times is irregular. That is, in some families it appears as a dominant factor in some persons; in others it appears as a recessive. Arteriosclerosis (hardening of the arteries) appears to be due to a dominant inheritance. Likewise, angina pectoris, a heart condition involving constrictions of the vessels of the heart itself, also appears to have an underlying dominant factor. Probably because of an inherited factor, the Irish are relatively free from angina pectoris.

In all of these conditions the manner of inheritance requires further investigation before valid conclusions can be made. Evidence at present is both too fragmentary and inconclusive for practical application.

Inheritance of certain factors of the nervous system. Intelligence, the ability to adjust to situations in which the central nervous system determines adjustment, is the end result of a physiological process. Thinking is as biological as is digestion. Physiologically intelligence involves the structure of the general nervous system, the structure of nerve cells, the physical and chemical nature of nerve cell substance, enzymes at nerve connections, hormones, body fluids, and a vast number of other factors. Obviously a considerable number of genes must be involved in the transmission of so many and diverse factors.

Normal intelligence. Investigations by various scientists have established the fundamental influence of inheritance upon mental ability. Yet the precise mechanics of the transmission of normal and above normal intelligence remains quite obscure. Like does not always produce like. That parents of normal intellect may have offspring who span the entire range from average to gifted is a common observation. Likewise, parents of high intellect may have children of average intellect. Although statistically it can be demonstrated that parents of high intelligence will have a high percentage of offspring above average in intelligence, the statistical methods are too crude to be of predictive value in specific cases.

In pointing out that intelligence involves the inheritance of certain physiological factors, geneticists do not descredit the influence of environment. That the environment must be satisfactory for the fullest realization of the potentialities of the nervous system is as obvious as the necessity for a satisfactory environment for the effective function of any system or organ. Yet the height of function and its product (intelligence) are limited by the endowment of the nervous system. One could not expect to educate a vacuum, nor has anyone through the educative process been able to cultivate genius from a physiologically defective nervous system. Thyroxin therapy has improved the intellect of children with markedly defective thyroid glands, a ray of hope in a dark field. Yet endocrine therapy has not been effective in altering the level of intellect in persons of normal or above normal intelligence. It is thus apparent that for normal or above normal intelligence the scientist can offer no positive formula either for the production of offspring of high intelligence or for the physiological alteration of the brain to improve the intellect. In most instances a high level of intellect appears to be a fortunate chance combination of genes.

Mental deficiency. Mentally deficient or feeble-minded persons are those with an intelligence quotient below 70. Those with an intelligent quotient between 50 and 70 are classed as morons, those in the 25 to 50 range are classed as imbeciles, and those under 25 are classed as idiots.

The intelligence quotient is the ratio of mental age to the chronological age and multiplied by 100. It is expressed as follows:

$$\text{I.Q.} = \frac{\text{M.A.}}{\text{C.A.}} \times 100$$

Mental age expresses the intelligence level of a given age as indicated by the performance of thousands of individuals on valid intelligence tests. Thus if, in taking an intelligence test, an individual of chronological age 10 years makes a score equal to that of the average 12-year-old child, his intelligence quotient will be 120.

The prevailing notion of the general public that all feeblemindedness is inherited is not supported by the many studies of the problem. Evidence indicates that birth injuries, encephalitis, meningitis, possibly congenital anemia (Rh in-

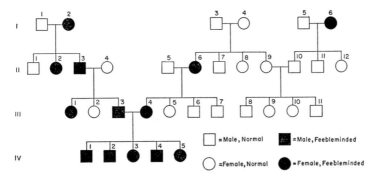

Fig. 18. Pedigree showing inheritance of feeblemindedness. Normal individuals *I-1, I-3,* and *I-4* possess the recessive gene or genes for feeblemindedness; however there is no evidence that *I-5* possesses the gene or genes for feeblemindedness.

compatibility), toxins, and other environmental factors are causes of feeblemindedness. Perhaps in 75% of all persons with feeblemindedness, the condition is basically inherited.

Although independent studies have revealed differing modes of the transmission of feeblemindedness, a general pattern of inheritance is recognized. Since intelligence has been demonstrated to be a multiple gene inheritance, it is not surprising that feeblemindedness involves multiple gene factors. Generally, feeblemindedness is transmitted as a simple recessive. Thus, as shown in Fig. 18, parents of normal intelligence who are heterozygous for intelligence (genes for normal and genes for feeblemindedness) may have offspring who inherit feeblemindedness. By the same token, if both parents have inherited feeblemindedness, all of their children can be expected to be feebleminded. However, if the feeblemindedness of the parents is not hereditary in nature, the offspring may have and likely will have normal intelligence. Thus parents who are feebleminded because of an acquired condition may have offspring with normal intellect.

Prevention of feeblemindedness. An important breakthrough in the urgent need to prevent feeblemindedness has been the prevention of mental retardation in youngsters afflicted with an inherited metabolic disorder which can produce feeblemindedness. This disorder is called phenylketonuria, and the afflicted youngster follows a typical pattern.

At birth the child appears normal but may vomit excessively. Many of these children have blonde hair and a fair skin and are extremely attractive. They soon develop an odor aptly described as "like that of old gym shoes." Between 4 and 24 months of age the child shows a progressive decline in mentality all the way to severe mental retardation. The offending substance is phenylalanine.

In the normal person the blood phenylalanine level is between one and three milligrams per 100 milliliters of serum. In the child with phenylketonuria (PKU) the level is between 20 and 60 milligrams. This high concentration of phenylalanine causes the mental retardation because it is an inhibitor of enzyme systems of the brain.

Fig. 19. Phenylketonuria (PKU) test using filter paper. This simple test for phenylalanine in the blood is highly reliable. (Courtesy Oregon State Board of Health.)

Phenylalanine is an essential amino acid which makes up about 5% of all the protein in a typical American diet. Normally the liver converts it into tyrosine which is metabolized by other enzyme systems and is a precursor of thyroxin from the thyroid gland and epinephrine from the adrenal gland. The child who is unable to convert the phenylalanine to tyrosine acquires a high blood phenyl-alanine level and resulting phenylketonuria (PKU).

The condition is quite easily detected. If one drop of 10% solution of ferric chloride is placed on a freshly wet diaper, the immediate appearance of a dark blue-green to gray-green color indicates the positive reaction of phenylketonuria. Filter paper wet with urine of a child with phenylketonuria will show the same result with the ferric chloride test. A blood test by a physician and other verify-ing tests are available.

Once retardation has occurred, it is irreversible so that as soon as the abnormal condition is discovered, measures are initiated to prevent mental retardation. A phenylalanine-deficient diet is instituted. Commercal protein preparations with minimal phenylalanine, but adequate proteins for growth, are available. These are used with other natural low-protein foods as prescribed by a physician. Usually the diet continues until the child is 5 years old and occasionally longer. By this time the danger of mental retardation is usually past.

Genetically phenylketonuria is inherited as a recessive trait, and the accepted estimate is that one in eighty persons is a carrier of the gene and that in one in 6400 marriages both husband and wife are heterozygous for the trait. Phenylketonuria occurs in one in 25,000 births. There is no test to determine whether a parent carries the gene, but there is a method of treatment to prevent phenylketonuria from producing mental retardation. The need is to make this knowledge available to all parents—present and future—and to put this knowledge to use.

Mental disorder. Whereas feeble-minded persons are lacking in mental equipment, persons with a mental disorder suffer from a disturbance of mentality. Mental disorder itself is not inherited, but the constitutional endowment which predisposes to mental disorder does appear to have a hereditary basis. The specific organic bases of the various psychoses are not completely understood. Yet statistical and pedigree studies reveal the tendency of certain mental disorders to occur with greater frequency in certain families than the nationwide experience would indicate. These studies do not disregard the influence of the environment, but recognize the interaction of environment and constitution. A constitution which may be adequate for one environment may lack the timber to adjust to more complex demands. Many men adequately endowed to meet the strains of civilian life were inadequately equipped for combat life.

Shock therapy and endocrine therapy have indicated glandular imbalances as organic factors in mental disorders. Yet when the inheritance of the physiological factors involved in mental disorders are considered, it must be recognized that many factors, including those of the central nervous system, can predispose to a high degree of susceptibility to mental disorders. When inheritance in relation to mental disorders is considered, an organic predisposition (diathesis) is actually the factor being considered and that factor is not exclusively a nervous disturbance. It must also be recognized that, although a person may inherit a predisposition to mental disorder, he may never exhibit mental disorder in a mode of living which places a minimum of strain and conflict on adjustment.

Schizophrenia. Schizophrenia, literally split personality, consists in four general types. Basic to all types is the tendency for withdrawal from outward contacts and interests to a shut-in lone-wolf type of personality.

Geneticists are generally agreed that schizophrenia has a hereditary basis although the precise manner of transmission has not been finally determined. Studies of various pedigrees reveal several possible modes of transmission.

Maniac depressive psychosis. Maniac depressive psychosis is generally characterized by marked fluctuations in mood although many variations occur.

Evidence indicates that in some families the trait appears as a recessive, and in others it appears as a dominant. In some families irregular dominance seems to be the nature of the inheritance. Some studies indicate that possibly two or more genes are involved in the transmission of the constitutional type or organic deficiency which reflects itself in manic depressive psychosis.

Huntington's chorea. Huntington's chorea, often referred to as adult chorea, is associated with a degeneration of brain tissue, with resulting tremor, incoordination, mental degeneration, and dementia. Although the disorder may appear at any age, the onset usually occurs between the ages of 25 and 55 years.

Huntington's chorea is always transmitted strictly as a dominant factor. Frequently no symptoms appear until the victim is the parent of several children. If it is assumed that the parent is heterozygous (one normal gene and one defective gene) for the trait, the probability that the children will inherit the condition is 50:50. If the afflicted parent is homozygous (both defective genes) for the condition, all of the children will inherit the disorder.

Inheritance of certain neuropathologies. Whereas most nervous disorders have no demonstrated hereditary bases, three which have a genetic background are of special interest and importance.

Friedreich's ataxia. This condition involves a degeneration of the spinal cord and is by no means a rare disease. Mentality remains normal, and no pain is associated with the condition. Symptoms include tremor of the hands and head, incoordination in locomotion characterized by a swaying, jerky gait, and eventually slurred speech. Onset in late childhood is usual. After many years of affliction, muscular weakness may make walking impossible, and a bedridden existence in later years results.

Genetically a few dominant pedigrees have been reported, but the condition is generally inherited as a simple recessive.

Epilepsy. This is a neuropathological entity characterized by convulsive seizures. In the major form, tonic, then clonic, convulsions are followed by prolonged stupor. The minor form is characterized by a transitory loss of consciousness and mild muscular tremors, but without falling or loss of balance.

The machine for recording brain waves (electroencephalograph) reveals that the electrochemical waves emanating from the brain of epileptic persons differ from normal waves. The electroencephalogram (EEG) of the normal brain reveals a marked rhythm in the waves. Practically all epileptic persons reveal dysrhythmia in the waves, and, when the epileptic person has dysrhythmia, at least one of the parents displays dysrhythmia although not necessarily epilepsy. Usually both parents of an epileptic person reveal dysrhythmia.

As shown by studies using the electroencephalograph, dysrhythmia is determined by a dominant gene. Epilepsy may be the homozygous condition, with irregularity in frequency of appearance. If epilepsy occurs in the offspring when one of the parents has a normal EEG, it may be that the afflicted offspring inherits an unstable or susceptible nervous system which predisposes to convulsion when unfavorable constitutional factors (intrinsic environment) are present in the individual.

Although science does not have the total answer on the inheritance of epilepsy, present knowledge dictates that, if an individual comes from a lineage which contains epileptic persons, he should study the EEG of his proposed mate. If both potential marriage partners exhibit dysrhythmia, discretion would suggest reconsideration of plans for marriage.

Color blindness. This disorder is due to a deficiency of the nerve fibers carrying impulses from the cones of the retina of the eye to the brain. Failure of these nerve fibers to function produces an inability to distinguish colors. Most color-blind individuals are red-green deficient although some are blind to all colors. Apparently in place of color these individuals have a concept of gray. At present color blindness is incurable. It is not due to infectious disease or malnutrition. All evidence points to an inherited deficiency. About 5% of white males in the United States are color blind. The male incidence is about twenty-five times greater than that among females.

Red-green color blindness is inherited as a sex-linked recessive. The gene for color vision is present on the X (femaleness) sex chromosome. The gene for normal color vision is dominant; the gene for the defect is recessive. The Y (maleness) sex chromosome lacks a gene for color vision. Thus normal color vision results from two normal X color vision genes, one normal gene and one gene for the defect, and a normal X color vision gene with a Y chromosome without a color vision gene. Fig. 20 diagrammatically illustrates various possibilities in the heredity of color vision and color blindness.

Inheritance of certain eye defects. Geneticists have demonstrated that inherited factors underlie some abnormalities of the eyes.

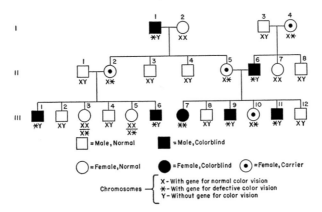

Fig. 20. Pedigree illustrating the inheritance of color blindness. Note the sex-linked nature of the inheritance. Until individuals III-3 and III-5 have offspring, it is not possible to determine their genotype or gene pattern. The pedigree denotes the two possibilities in each case.

Cataract. Cataract is an opacity of the crystalline lens or its enclosing capsule. The turbidity results from a disturbance of the normal chemical state of the lens or capsule. Protein precipitation, cholesterol increase, calcium excess, sugar change, as well as certain deficiencies, have been shown to be present in various forms of cataract. The inherited factor thus lies in the physiology of the lens and capsule.

With some degree of truth it has been stated that, if we only lived long enough, all of us eventually would have cataracts since the lens always undergoes considerable change after 60 years of age. Yet some individuals manifest cataract early. Actually some individuals have cataractous eyes at birth—congenital cataract. It is the early-appearing cataract that has most interested the geneticist.

The inheritance of cataract is usually dominant although at times it is irregular dominance. In some pedigrees the inheritance undoubtedly is recessive. The tendency for cataract to occur at an earlier age in succeeding generations has been reported by some investigators. Neither the genetic mechanism nor the extrinsic factors involved are understood.

Myopia. Myopia (nearsightedness) is primarily due to an elongated bulb or extended axial length of the lens. Whereas a child at birth is hypermetropic (farsighted), the myopia arises surprisingly early in life in some individuals. This factor appears to have a hereditary basis. The usual method of the inheritance of myopia is a simple recessive although irregular dominance occurs in some families. The incidence of this condition tends to be increasing in our population.

Hyperopia. Hyperopia (farsightedness) is less frequent than myopia. The abnormality is the reverse of that for myopia. Generally the inheritance is an irregular dominant although some forms are apparently recessive.

Astigmatism. Astigmatism is an abnormality in which the radius of the curvature of one plane of the cornea or lens is greater or less than the plane at right angles to it. Other irregularities of the cornea may properly be classed as astigmatism. Corneal astigmatism is usually inherited as an irregular dominant although pedigrees have been reported in which the inheritance appears to be recessive.

Lenticular astigmatism (of the lens) is relatively rare and genetically is independent of corneal astigmatism. The few reported studies of lenticular astigmatism indicate the condition is probably inherited as a recessive.

Ptosis. Ptosis, a drooping of the upper eyelid due to a paralysis of its muscles, is often associated with various other minor eye abnormalities. It is not always an inherited condition, but certain families exhibit an inheritance of the condition. Usually the condition is inherited as a dominant whether the condition is bilateral or unilateral.

Glaucoma. Glaucoma, an excessively high pressure of the fluids in the eye, is caused by an obstruction of the lymph drainage, resulting first in reduction of peripheral vision and eventually perhaps in complete blindness. It may be caused by infection, but most cases appear to have a hereditary basis. Practically all studies reveal that when an inherited factor exists, glaucoma occurs as a simple dominant, with variation in the time of life at which the condition manifests itself.

Various other minor abnormalities of the eyes appear to have a genetic basis, but for the practice of hygiene these abnormalities are not sufficiently important for consideration as a general health problem.

Inheritance of allergy. Allergy is a condition of hypersensitivity to a specific foreign substance, usually a protein. Anaphylaxis, the extreme reaction to a foreign substance, results in a condition of shock and even death. However, authorities are not in agreement that anaphylaxis is physiologically the same as allergy. The term *atopy* is sometimes used to indicate inherited hypersensitiveness.

Allergy appears in various forms and at various ages. Yet studies reveal that the allergic condition is neither recessive nor completely dominant but intermediate. At times the gene for allergy appears to act as a simple recessive. Thus an individual who is homozygous for allergy manifests the condition before the onset of maturity (puberty). Heterozygous individuals do not develop allergy until after puberty but transmit the condition according to genetic prediction. Actually fewer than 20% of all heterozygous individuals develop allergy although they may transmit the condition. Based on present knowledge, it would appear that only when both parents show allergic symptoms before puberty will all of their children inherit a hypersensitivity. Further, heterozygous parents who exhibit allergy later in adult life may have children who do not inherit hypersensitivity.

Generally speaking, a family background of allergy is found in 40% to 60% of all asthmatic persons, in 75% to 85% of all migraine patients, in 65% of the people with food allergies, and in 50% of persons who suffer from eczema. The inherited factor physiologically is a cellular protoplasmic makeup which reacts readily to foreign substances. As a consequence a person who inherits allergy may exhibit types of allergies different from those of the parents. Allergy may express itself in the skin as eczema or hives; in the respiratory tract as bronchial asthma, bronchitis, or hay fever; as irritation of the eyes, the eyelids, and even the ears; in the genitourinary tract as irritation of the mucous lining; and even as a disturbance of the heart and blood vessels. A person with allergy choosing a mate from an allergy-free family may as a result have nonallergic offspring.

Inheritance and gastric ulcers. The tendency to have gastric ulcers appears to be inherited although the nature of the inheritance is not certain. Studies of identical twins reveal that, when one twin suffers from peptic ulcer, the other twin is likewise afflicted. Although some studies reveal a lower standard of health associated with gastric ulcer when a hereditary basis appears to exist, a few studies reveal gastric ulcers in families of general good health. Since stomach ulcer appears to result from a series of conditions, it is apparent that marked variations in its mode of inheritance will be found. If gastric ulcer is regarded as merely one manifestation of a deficiently functioning stomach, it will be understood why gastric ulcers do not maintain the genetic regularity theoretically plausible. The trait for a stomach deficiency appears to be recessive, and ulcers appear to occur in the homozygous condition; although apparently the homozygous condition can manifest itself as dyspepsia or some other chronic stomach disorder.

It is doubtful that duodenal ulcers have a hereditary basis. They usually occur in people of good general health and in families without discernible digestive abnormalities.

Inheritance and appendicitis. The vermiform appendix, like any other organ of the body, shows a high degree of variability in susceptibility to infection and inflammation. A tendency in some families toward a high incidence of appendicitis indicates an inherited susceptibility to infection. Inheritance appears to be dominant, with considerable irregularity. Perhaps the irregularity may be accounted for in missed diagnosis, occluded lumen, absence of infective agents, and high general resistance to infection.

Inheritance and diabetes mellitus. The syndrome of diabetes mellitus is loss of strength, general emaciation, excessive thirst, frequent urination, and even coma. It is caused by a disturbance of metabolism that results in a high sugar content in the blood (hyperglycemia).

Diabetes mellitus may result from a deficiency of the cells of the islands of Langerhans in the pancreas. These cells produce a secretion containing insulin. Normally the range of glucose concentration in the blood is between 0.08% and 0.14%. When the glucose level of the blood approaches 0.14% insulin converts glucose to the more stable glycogen, which is stored in the liver. Insufficient insulin results in a blood glucose concentration above 0.14%, which is above the normal threshold of the kidneys, and sugar appears in the urine (glycosuria). Insulin also functions in the utilization by muscle of glucose.

Some individuals exhibit diabetes early in life and others later in life. A young child may have an insulin production at a level sufficient for his needs as a child. Yet, as an adult, diabetes mellitus may appear if the insulin output does not keep pace with the increased needs of the body during growth and development. In some persons an exhaustion of the cells of the islands of Langerhans appears to occur in the later years of life.

Diabetes mellitus is a highly complex disorder and is not necessarily due to a deficient or pathological pancreas. Research indicates that disorders of the anterior pituitary gland, the thyroid, and the adrenal cortex may be associated with diabetes mellitus, which explains why some diabetic persons receive little relief from insulin.

Since the causation of diabetes mellitus is such a complex multifactored one, diversity of results in studies of its heredity is not surprising. In addition perhaps many potential diabetic persons die of some other cause before the symptoms of diabetes are manifest. Although some families may show variation from the usual mode of inheritance, generally it appears that the severe form with onset at an early age is recessive and the mild form with later age of onset is dominant. Environment plays a role in the appearance of diabetes, and thus irregular dominance is often reported by investigators.

Most persons with diabetes mellitus can be treated successfully although not cured. Some observers fear that the discovery of a successful treatment for diabetes will have a dysgenic effect upon our population because many persons who otherwise would have died before maturity now survive to transmit the defect to offspring. Yet at least in women diabetic persons are often infertile or even sterile despite insulin treatment. Assuming that the incidence of diabetes increases, who is to deny a diabetic person his right to a fruitful and enjoyable life? Oddly the death rate from diabetes is increasing despite the wonders of insulin therapy.

Diabetes insipidus. Diabetes insipidus is a disturbance in the salt balance of the body due to malfunction of the pituitary gland. The primary symptom is excessive thirst. The condition is rather rare and is usually dominant in genetic transmission. It can be treated successfully by pituitary therapy.

Inheritance and cancer. Cancer is basically a phenomenon of cell activity. In the transformation of a normal cell to a malignant one, certain protoplasmic changes occur. Research indicates that in some instances there occur both a genetic mutation in the nucleus and a cytoplasmic change not arising from the nucleus. During the precancerous stage these cells acquire an abnormally rapid rate of growth and division. In addition a chemical disturbance of protoplasmic hydrocarbons occurs.

Present knowledge indicates three plausible explanations for the etiology of new abnormal formations (neoplasms)—gene mutations, viruses, and carcinogens (cancer-causing substances)—with the possibility that all three are interrelated or complementary. Marked alteration of the genes may be an expression of a basic cellular deficiency. Susceptibility to virus or carcinogen effects also indicates a cellular endowment of a specific type. That such carcinogens as heat, ultraviolet rays, roentgen rays, and cyclic hydrocarbons will change cells to malignancy in some individuals but not in other individuals suggests inherited cellular differences. It is with these differences that a consideration of inheritance and cancer must concern itself. In effect it is a predisposition (diathesis) to cancer which must be analyzed genetically. It may be a susceptibility to enzymic alteration, which is the basic inherited factor.

In considering the hereditary basis of cancer investigators recognize that both inheritance and environment are operating to produce many irregularities, from the standpoint of genetic study. Thus a person with a high degree of inherited susceptibility, by accident or design, may possess an environment for the susceptible cells which will never disturb the normal pattern of function. In consequence most investigators hesitate to prescribe a particular mode of genetic transmission. They further recognize that varying degrees of susceptibility exist.

Table 12. Some characteristics in man known to be inherited

Dominant	Recessive
Nervous system	
Huntington's chorea	Normal
Migraine (sick headache)	Normal
Paralysis agitans	Normal
Normal	Amaurotic idiocy
Normal	Constitution predisposing to manic depressive psychosis
Normal	Constitution predisposing to schizophrenia
Circulatory system	
Blood types (A, B, and AB)	Blood type O
Rh factor (positive)	Rh negative
Normal	Hemophilia (sex-linked)
Normal	Sickle cell anemia
Hypertension	Normal
Endocrine and metabolic factors	
Normal insulin output	Diabetes mellitus
Normal phenylalanine level	Phenylketonuria
Allergy (incomplete dominance)	Normal
Skeletal and muscular systems	
Short stature (multiple genes)	Tall stature
Progressive muscular atrophy	Normal
Polydactylism (more than 5 digits)	Normal
Brachydactylism (short digits)	Normal
Syndactylism (webbing of digits)	Normal
Eyes	
Color vision	Color blindness (sex-linked)
Astigmatism	Normal vision
Normal vision	Myopia
Hyperopia	Normal vision
Glaucoma	Normal
Cataract	Normal
Displacement of lens	Normal
Brown iris	Blue or gray
Hazel or green iris	Blue or gray
Skin and hair	
Black skin (two pairs of genes, incomplete dominance)	White skin
Pigmented skin and hair	Albinism
Early baldness (dominant in male)	Normal
White forelock	Normal color
Piebald (skin and hair spotted white)	Normal
Ichthyosis (scaly skin)	Normal
Normal	Absence of sweat glands
Features	
High narrow bridge of nose	Low broad nose
Roman nose	Straight nose
Broad nostrils	Narrow nostrils
Broad lips	Thin lips
Large eyes	Small eyes

Some studies reveal a susceptibility to cancer which appears to be a dominant trait, with some cases of irregularity. Other studies indicate that the susceptibility is likely transmitted as a recessive. Most competent investigators recognize a hereditary factor in most patients with cancer and account for the sporadic patient in terms of cell mutations resulting from some unusual environmental factor.

Individuals who come from a family with a high incidence of cancer would wisely be alert for any abnormal growth and would bring it immediately to the attention of a physician. However, the same caution can well apply to an individual who comes from a cancer-free lineage.

EUGENICS

Sir Francis Galton coined the term *eugenics* in 1883. He defined eugenics as the study of agencies under social control that may improve or impair the racial qualities of future generations, either physically or mentally. Today eugenics is defined as race betterment through the study and cultivation of practices and conditions which will improve and not impair the physical and mental qualities of future generations. Essentially it is a practical application of the knowledge of human inheritance in an endeavor to produce improved stock, but it also necessarily has a close relation with sociology, political science, education, medical science, and economics.

Most Americans are aware of the contributions our knowledge of genetics has made to the improvement of domestic plants and animals. Through selective mating is has been possible to produce desired types. Usually the motivating factor has been economic advantage although some selection has been based on less materialistic motives. The methods employed in improving some of the lower forms of life have not been applied to the human species. Biologically the same principles apply equally to the human being, but thus far individuals have been but little interested in a positive improvement of the human species as a whole. The interest almost solely has been in applying knowledge of human heredity to prevent the occurrence of undesirable traits in the coming generation. As such, the interest has been a negative one.

Negative program. As constituted at present, the negative aspect of eugenics in the United States manifests itself in five different approaches: (1) examination of immigrants and investigation of lineage, (2) isolation of certain tainted individuals, usually in public institutions, (3) instruction in contraception methods, (4) surgical sterilization, and (5) prohibition of consanguineous marriage.

Immigration regulations which exclude persons with gross defects, particularly of an inherited form, are accepted and established practices. Whatever the underlying motive, their virtually universal acceptance indicates a nation committed to such a policy, and its continuation is advocated and expected. Yet its effect is small in terms of the total eugenics problem of the nation.

Isolation, particularly of the lowest level of feebleminded persons, while practiced primarily for other social reasons, does incorporate possible eugenic effects. Costly as isolation is, it has proved to be an investment in race improvement. It is recognized that many low-grade feebleminded persons are sterile; nevertheless isolation does reduce the procreation rate among institutionalized defective persons.

Instruction in contraception methods has had negative results in those instances in which contraception has not been practiced by the biologically inferior stock but has been practiced by the better biological stock.

Sterilization has been aggrandized as the one great instrument in eugenics. Yet, as it has operated thus far in the United States, its claims exceed its contributions. There is little doubt that in specific cases sterilization has prevented the procreation of defectives. When the genetic pattern in an individual case is sharply and definitely outlined, sterilization has served its intended purpose.

Yet who is inferior in the light of social, biological, intellectual, and other values?

Twenty-seven states have laws providing for the sterilization of feebleminded or insane persons or both. In practice the law is applied largely to individuals being discharged or furloughed from institutions for feebleminded persons. Sterilization laws make provisions for safeguarding the constitutional rights of the individual. Court hearings with proper announcements and recognized procedures are required in all twenty-seven states. Although sterilization does not alter the individual's sexual responsiveness or otherwise affect his well-being except to prevent procreation, sterilization laws have been challenged in the courts. However, the constitutionality of sterilization laws was upheld in the decision handed down on May 2, 1927, by the United States Supreme Court in the case of Buck versus Bell. In ruling on the questions of whether society had the right to require sterilization and of what constituted proof of inherited feeblemindedness, Justice Oliver Wendell Holmes pronounced the legal classic, "Three generations of imbeciles are enough."

Although the constitutionality of sterilization has been upheld, not often is possible genetic transmission of the disorder the basis of a petition for sterilization. Experience has demonstrated that laymen in our courts do not comprehend the science of genetics. It is difficult to convince some lay people that one member of a family has inherited feeblemindedness if one or more members of his family are of normal intelligence. In addition enforcement is difficult because responsible people are loath to act. Usually economic grounds are used as the basis of a petition for sterilization. The contention is made that a feebleminded person finds it difficult enough to support himself in the complex economic world, but the problem becomes manyfold more complex if he has to support a family. Courts usually understand the socioeconomic implications.

All negative eugenic devices have had a minor effect on the quality of our American population. Based on present genetic knowledge, even the stringent methods of Hitler would take perhaps 1000 years to have a pronounced effect on the health quality of a population. Defects due to a single dominant gene could be virtually eliminated, sex-linked traits likewise could be eliminated, and given several hundred years, single recessive gene traits could be eliminated. However, the multiple gene traits and those which operate irregularly would probably defy the efforts of the most determined programs. Not until science can identify carriers can a real advance be expected in the reduction of hereditary defects. The usual biological forces operating in biotic determination, as in the past, doubtless will continue to play an important role.

Marriage between second cousins is considered consanguineous marriage. Generally the closer in ancestry marriage partners are, the more likely they are to have somewhat the same genetic endowment. Thus a recessive trait is more likely to appear in a consanguinous marriage than in one in which the biological relationship is far removed. In practical terms in consanguineous marriage, if undesirable traits exist in the lineage, these are more likely to appear than is usual. By the same token, if desirable traits exist in the lineage, these preferred traits are more likely to appear than is usual. The general apprehension of the public concerning consanguineous marriage should be replaced by a scientific genetic appraisal of specific cases.

Positive program. A positive program of eugenics is one in which reason in the selection of a mate is primary and the better stock reproduce at a rate more rapid than the poorer stock.

It does not require profound analytical research to determine that the emotions rather than reason usually govern the selection of a mate. Reasoning may be used to justify the emotional choice. It may not be in the scheme of biological existence that reason should completely govern the selection of a mate. Yet a knowledge of genetics coupled with social vision should at least condition emotional responsiveness and lead to some degree of reason. An individual who suffers from lifelong allergic affliction, understanding the genetics of the condition, could be expected to give some thought to future offspring before marrying an individual with a similar affliction and genetic endowment. With a knowledge of genetics an individual from a family exhibiting epilepsy, feeblemindedness, and psychosis may perhaps avail himself of scientic knowledge before being a party to needless perpetuation of inherited disorders.

The selection of a mate based upon the propagation of healthy offspring is as tangible and as attainable an ideal as marriage for beauty, prestige, or other reasons. A goal not yet come of age in the United States, marriage with responsibility for the endowment of one's offspring has been attained by other social orders. Its cultivation would doubtless reward the United States with a potentially healthier nation of citizens. The greatest obstacle to overcome is the glamourizing of superficial social values in marriage. An individual whose genealogy reveals a recessive disorder would wisely seek a mate whose genealogy reveals a total absence of the disorder.

Programs to encourage large families among the better (social, economic, biological, and intellectual) strata of populations generally have been ineffective. Subsidies have not proved catalytic. The recent increase in family size among parents with a college education is not correlated with improved economic status although in individual cases economic factors have contributed. Shifting of social values and goals in certain strata in society in the United States has had an influence. Surveys among mothers who are college graduates reveal that technical advances in obstetrics have been a highly potent factor in the promotion of positive eugenics. Safety and ease of delivery have promoted eugenics by encouraging larger families in the better biological strata.

The home is an important agency in positive eugenics because the standards, ideals, ideas, and attitudes of the home are reflected in the children. The school can influence the best-qualified persons to give their attention to the importance of the selection of a mate and the perpetuation of the best physical and mental qualities. Many college courses contribute to eugenics—social sciences, natural sciences, and psychology, particularly. Physicians, nurses, social workers, clergymen, and others contribute to eugenics. Any program of positive eugenics must include the improvement of the environment through the reduction of poverty, ill health, and ignorance if we are to encourage more births among responsible parents. Because the size of the family is affected by the social factors, attitudes, and values of the society in which we live, education in social science and in human heredity is fundamental to the betterment of the race.

A nationwide program of education in heredity has never been attempted. Yet any positive eugenics program in a democracy must be based upon a nationwide understanding of heredity. Supplemented by competent consultant service, a program of education in heredity can have a discernible effect upon the health level of the nation. No one would expect perfection, but conceivably at least a portion of those persons eligible for marriage would select mates in the light of genetic endowment. Those with an excellent genetic background would be more likely to seek as mates members of the opposite sex who likewise have an excellent background.

NONHEREDITARY DISORDERS AT BIRTH

It has been pointed out that disorders of genetic origin may not be discernible at the time of birth but may manifest themselves later in life. It also should be pointed out that not all disorders present at birth are hereditary in nature. Developmental and congenital disorders are not of hereditary origin but may be present at birth.

Developmental disorders. Developmental disorders are those which result from deviations from the normal pattern of development. When one considers the complex mechanism of development from the single-celled zygote of less than 1/100 inch in diameter to the complex fully formed child at birth, one marvels that developmental anomalies do not occur more frequently. Indeed, that 98% of all births are normal is one of the amazing and fortunate wonders of this universe.

Just why these anomalies occur is not always completely understood, but any factor which interferes with normal cell division and function will interfere with the formation of tissues and organs. Mechanical pressure, malnutrition, disturbance of circulation, toxins, and changes in body fluid are recognized factors.

Although many developmental anomalies have been reported, only some of the more commonly occurring developmental disorders are of interest here. Harelip and cleft palate are classed as developmental disorders by most scientists although in some instances a hereditary factor may appear to operate. Endocrine disturbances resulting in giantism, midgetism, and cretinism are classed as developmental. Spina bifida, a failure of the vertebrae to fuse, is due to incomplete development. Hermaphroditism (dual sexed), as well as displaced heart, stomach, kidneys, and other viscera, are disorders of development.

Congenital defects. Congenital defects are defects due primarily to the maternal environment and occur before or at the time of birth. Clubbed feet, clubbed hands and fingers, and congenital dislocation of the hips or other joints due to pressure in the maternal pelvis are all properly classed as congenital disorders.

Any infection a child may have at birth must be classed as congenital. A child with syphilis at birth acquired the infection from its mother. The condition is classed as congenital syphilis. Likewise a child acquiring gonorrheal infection of the eyes during delivery is congenitally infected by a gonorrheal mother. Occasionally a child is born with smallpox or even with measles. In either case the disease must be classed as congenital.

It is doubtful that congenital tuberculosis exists. All evidence indicates that, if a child acquires tuberculosis from a tuberculous mother, the disease was postnatally acquired. In support of this conclusion are the reports of public health officials that, whenever a child is removed from its tuberculous mother immediately after birth, he shows no indications of tuberculosis.

Maternal impressions. Maternal impressions are those supposed effects upon the unborn child produced by the experiences of the mother while bearing the child. The old superstitions with respect to maternal impressions still influence some segments of our population. Yet since there is no nervous connection between fetus and mother, no psychological experience of the mother could possibly affect the unborn child. Sudden scares, abnormal experiences, dreams, frightening sights, and similar experiences cannot possibly have either a known physiological or psychological effect upon the fetus, despite the "authentic" cases related in every hamlet across the nation.

Fortunately many developmental and congenital defects can be treated successfully and some can be cured. Some congenital conditions, such as syphilis and gonorrhea, can be prevented. Further study of embryology may answer the question of the causes of developmental disorders and their prevention. Until that time, we must rely on corrective measures.

Chapter 3

Daily personal
health care

$\mathbf{P}$romotion of the health of the skin, mouth, hearing, and vision is not primarily a matter of the prevention of death or even of the extension of the prime of life. Its principal emphasis is upon effective and enjoyable living. Indeed many of the recognized practices in the general care of the body are primarily of esthetic value rather than of health value. Yet the esthetic aspects of these practices are of social and mental health significance. They contribute indirectly to effective and enjoyable living.

To many individuals the promotion of general bodily well-being is a relatively simple matter. Even these fortunate individuals can benefit by the application of the principles of health science in promoting a higher level of effective and enjoyable living through the proper application of dental health, conservation of vision and hearing, and skin care. Other individuals encounter special problems in body care which require constant attention and special procedures.

THE SKIN

By far the largest organ of the body, the skin functions in close collaboration with other organs and body systems. It is the contact line between the body and its external environment, but it is more than just a mechanical barrier.

Human skin is an effective thermostat, affording a cooling system in the summer and a heat-conservation mechanism in winter. This function depends upon an efficient circulation, including responsive vessels in the periphery of the body. To eliminate body heat, the blood must carry the heat to the body surface where well-functioning sweat glands will hasten elimination of heat. Evaporation of water from the skin draws heat from the body. To conserve heat in the winter, vessels of the skin constrict, thus reducing the body heat coming to the surface. Cutaneous fat also serves as insulation.

Signal board is an apt designation for the skin since it receives the stimuli which produce the sensations of touch, pain, and temperature.

Protection against infection is made possible by the acidity (pH 6.4 to 6.5) of the skin as well as by exposure to light and drying. At all times millions of bacteria and fungi are present on the skin, but are nonpathogenic or unable to produce infection because of the unfavorable environment. As an indicator of immunity or susceptibility the skin serves for diagnostic and therapeutic purposes.

As an excretory organ the skin eliminates water, salts, fatty acids, and urea and other nitrogen wastes. Except for differences in concentrations, perspiration is similar to urine and will become rancid. The major odor from the skin comes from the secretion of the apocrine glands located in the armpits and the external genital areas. Apocrine secretion normally contains an odor principle, but the odors of certain foods, notably onions and garlic, pass into it.

Factors influencing skin health. In health the skin should be soft, supple and moderately oily, without cracking and scaling, and free from eruptions. Elasticity of the skin declines with age. Lack of skin elasticity is a fairly accurate indicator of physiological age.

General health. General health is reflected in the functioning of the skin. Resiliency and tone as well as clearness of the skin require that the general level of health be high. Basic to the improvement of any skin condition is the elevation of general health.

Circulation. Circulation is of particular importance in promoting skin function because of the intimate relationship of blood to all skin functions. Ruddiness of the skin is not the cardinal index of a healthy skin or of the blood picture of an individual. A person with an olive or even somewhat sallow coloration may have a healthy skin. When the vessels of the skin are extremely near the surface or epidermis, the appearance is ruddy. However, a person whose cutaneous vessels are structurally rather deep in the skin may show little of the ruddiness of other individuals and still have excellent circulation and function in the skin. Dilation of peripheral vessels also varies.

Metabolic rate. Metabolic rate as an expression of thyroid output has a direct relationship to the condition of the skin. A low production of thyroxin is reflected in a dry inelastic dull-appearing skin. Application of oil may compensate for the skin dryness but at best would serve as merely a supplement. Under the direction of a physician the correction of the basic metabolic deficiency could provide the means by which the skin would supply its own products necessary for a soft, supple, and moderately oily condition.

Nutrition. Nutrition affects the function of all body tissues, including those of the skin. Vitamin A is essential to the normal function of the epithelial or lining tissues of the skin. Vitamin C affects the vessels of the skin as well as the other vessels of the body. Vitamin B affects nerves of the skin beneficially as it affects other nerves of the body. The production of vitamin D in the body depends upon an adequate amount of cutaneous fat. Minerals enter into the function of the skin. A balanced dietary for general health includes the needs of the skin.

Cleanliness. Cleanliness is primarily for esthetic reasons rather than for health reasons. Yet cleanliness removes bacteria, detritus, excessive oil and grit as well as other accumulations, and permits unencumbered skin function.

Bathing. One of the most controversial topics in health circles is the value and application of bathing to well-being. Much of the controversy arises from the tendency to generalize about bathing rather than to distinguish the different types of bathing and their specific purposes.

Cleansing baths. Cleansing baths are primarily to remove perspiration, odors, and other objectionable accumulations from the body surface. As such the cleansing bath is of esthetic value though the contribution to mental health is not insignificant. Some protection against infection is inherent in the cleansing bath. Soap alters the permeability of the membrane which encloses a bacterium so that the membrane becomes permeable to water. As a result water diffuses into the bacterium protoplasm in excessive amounts (hydration) and destroys the organism.

Water at body temperature feels warm, but not hot. Water at a temperature between 95° and 100° F. will be adequately warm for cleansing purposes. At this temperature the bath does not unduly disturb circulation or body temperature. It may have some sedative or relaxing effects.

In a cleansing bath, soap should not be rubbed onto the skin, except upon the palms of the hand. Soap rubbed directly upon the skin may close ducts and interfere with normal skin function if the soap is not dissolved. In addition soap will tend to produce an undesirable dryness of the skin. Working up a good lather in the hands and then briskly applying the lather to the skin is the approved method.

Individuals who are allergic to soap constituents or find soap to be irritating can use liquid germicidal detergents, which are as cleansing as soap and serve as satisfactorily. Individuals with unusually dry skins may need to bath less frequently than most individuals and perhaps use olive oil or some other skin lubricant after the bath when no correctable basic factor accounts for the dryness.

Finishing the bath with slightly cooler water can be an aid in adjusting to the coolness of the surrounding atmosphere. It should be emphasized that extremes in hot and cold should be avoided in normal bathing. The practice of athletes of abruptly changing the temperature of the shower from hot to cold is of doubtful benefit and is usually shocking to the constitution. Although the human body has a remarkable ability to adapt to environmental conditions, it cannot make sudden extreme adjustments without some disturbances. From warm to cool is the prescription in changes in the temperature of bath water.

Contrast baths. Contrast baths have therapeutic value and are used regularly in hospitals to stimulate circulation, relax and stimulate muscles, speed up metabolism, and tone up the body generally.

Warm water for three or four minutes followed by cool water for about three minutes is the procedure. Alternating the warm and cool water from three to six times, depending upon the person's needs and condition, should have a beneficial effect. Athletes use a contrast bath to hasten recovery from fatigue.

Sedative baths. Sedative baths are those in which water at a lukewarm temperature has a sedative effect. They also are called tepid baths. An individual who is upset, restless, or irritable will find the effects of a tepid bath comforting and restful. A tendency to have the water too warm defeats the intended purpose of the sedative bath. The water should be just comfortably warm.

Stimulating baths. Stimulating baths are those which are unusually hot or cold. A hot bath elevates body temperature, stimulates the nervous system, and speeds up circulation. It is especially valuable to individuals who have difficulty in functioning at a high level in the morning. Cold water is stimulating to the nervous system, but tends to keep the blood away from the surface of the body. However, body heat increases, and, if the bath is followed by a brisk rub, the total effect is that of a hot bath. If a cold bath tends to produce a shock condition, an individual should experiment with a cool bath or with a hot bath.

Commercial skin preparations. No commercial preparation is nourishing to the skin or serves as a skin food. Neither does any such preparation build tissue. Yet preparations for the skin and its appendages serve accepted purposes.

1. Cold cream usually contains lanolin, almond oil, and beeswax and serves to lubricate the skin which tends to lack oil.
2. Hand lotions usually contain glycerin or other base and tend to retain their moisture as well as to prevent moisture from evaporating from the skin. They are not tonics or skin-nourishing, but they aid the skin in retaining a soft supple condition.
3. Vanishing creams are semiliquid soaps which tend to dry the skin. They may be of value to a person with an exceedingly oily skin, but the tendency of the soap to close ducts makes vanishing cream of doubtful value to most people.
4. Talcum is derived from the mineral substance talc and reduces oily appearance of the skin. In this role it serves an acceptable purpose.
5. Astringents constrict small cutaneous blood vessels and thus may reduce the output of oil by reducing the blood available to the sebaceous glands. Alcohol is the principal constituent of astringents.
6. Deodorants are usually harmless. However, a deodorant may produce a rash in some individuals because of aluminum chloride, zinc sulfate, or tannic acid which may be in the deodorant.
7. Depilatories are of doubtful value since they do not affect the bulb or growing part of a hair. To destroy the hair bulb an electrolytic needle in the hands of an expert technician is most satisfactory. Using a razor to remove superfluous hair does not hasten the regrowth of the hair, nor does

the hair become more coarse. The regrowth resembles stubble, which is perhaps the principal objection to the use of the razor.

8. Nail polish is usually a harmless lacquer with pigment for coloring. Nail polish removers usually contain the solvent acetone which should be harmless to the hands.

Clothing. From the standpoint of health, clothing is selected to aid the body in eliminating or conserving body heat. Loose clothing of loosely woven materials which permits space for heat to leave the body is essential for summer wear. To retain body heat, wool is of special value because its weave creates dead air pockets which serve as insulation. However, a person who spends winter days indoors should wear light underclothing and rely upon heavy outer garments when it is necessary to go outdoors. Wool underclothing worn indoors in the winter causes perspiration to accumulate, and an inevitable chill results if the person should go outdoors.

People vary in their dress requirements because of individual differences in metabolic rate, deposits of subcutaneous fat, and caloric nature of the diet. Each individual needs to find his own requirements. Generally there is a tendency, especially among men, to overdress in winter, and in the summer there is a tendency to overexpose the body to direct sun rays.

Care of the scalp. In childhood the hair is fine, but it tends to become more coarse as adulthood is reached, often becoming less coarse in the later years of life. The typical adult head of brown hair will have about 120,000 hairs. Blonds tend to have about 140,000 hairs, and persons with red hair will have about 90,000 hairs. Normally about 20 hairs a day fall out. However, the hair bulb remains, and a new shaft begins to grow in place of the one which was shed. Growth of the hair occurs at the base, and the rate is determined primarily by the circulation to the hair bulb which, by constant cell division, contributes dead cells to the hair shaft. Cutting or singeing hair does not affect the usual uniform growth of about three to four inches a year.

Baldness results from the failure of the hair bulb to function. Such failure can be due to a general grandular condition or to a disturbance in the circulation to the bulb. Apparently some males inherit bulbs with a short life span. An extended high fever can affect the hair bulb adversely. Some baldness can be checked by a dermatologist or skin specialist.

Gray hair results from an inadequate production of pigment and the admission of air into the spaces of the hair shaft.

Oily hair gets dirty more readily than does other hair and is harder to wash. Exposing the hair and scalp to the air tends to reduce oiliness. On the other hand, a person with a fairly dry hair and scalp should wear a hat or otherwise prevent exposure to the air and sun in order to retain all possible oil.

The scalp should be washed with a good soap lather, with at least two thorough rinsings. People with a dry scalp find liquid detergents or oily shampoos more acceptable than soap.

Only circulation to the hair bulb can provide nourishment for the hair. Thus no legitimate hair tonics exist. Oil may be of benefit in controlling the hair for combing and may supplement an inadequate oiliness of the scalp.

Waving lotions alter the protein chains of the hair shaft and cause the hair to assume a molded linear pattern which will remain "permanent" with the evaporation of the liquid. Except for individual cases of susceptibility, present-day lotions are not harmful although the hair may lose its glossiness and attractiveness from the continual use of lotions and driers.

Dandruff may be physiological or infectious. The physiological type accumulates as a gummy or sticky deposit on the scalp. Perhaps a small amount of this type of dandruff is normal as the result of natural function of the scalp, but an excess collection indicates a need for more frequent cleaning of the scalp. The infectious type of dandruff is due to a virus that infects the sebaceous glands of the hair follicles. At times some inflammation is noticeable, particularly if the eyebrow areas are involved. Infectious dandruff is characterized by dry flaky scales which cause some itching and which are shed rather abundantly. Dermatologists, using different antiseptic ointments, are usually able to clear up infectious dandruff. Although not dangerous, dandruff does present a nuisance problem—itching as well as the undesirable shedding on clothing and elsewhere.

Common skin disorders. Perhaps no organ of the body is subject to such a diversity of diseases and abnormalities. Most of these conditions command the professional services of a dermatologist. However, a number of minor disorders are of such common occurrence that they are of interest and of importance to the citizen who is interested in the promotion of personal health.

Excessive oiliness. An excessively oily skin is due to overactivity of the sebaceous glands, doubtless associated with excellent circulation in the skin. Frequent cleansing baths tend to reduce oiliness. The use of vanishing cream and astringents on the face should be restricted to special occasions and special uses. In some cases a reduction of animal fats in the diet appears to be helpful, but the possible relationship is not clear.

Blackheads are not due to uncleanliness. Indeed, people with blackheads are overly conscientious about cleanliness. A blackhead is due to the oxidation of the sebaceous secretion which has become congested in the narrow tubular follicles. Hot packs on the skin will tend to dissolve the black oxidized oil so that the blackhead can easily be squeezed out with a ring-type tweezer.

Eczema. Eczema is an inflammatory skin condition with various forms of lesions. Some forms are characterized by fluid-filled vesicles and a watery discharge and a subsequent development of scales and crusts. Others may produce a rough cracked surface. The affected areas may appear in patches or over an extended area. Itching and burning are usually present.

Many times eczema is due to an allergy. Most allergic eczema in children is due to a food or several foods. In adults contact of the skin with chemicals, even dust, is frequently the cause. Even with expert medical care, eczema may be difficult to clear up successfully.

Warts. Warts are caused by a virus, but no evidence exists that the virus is communicable from person to person. Warts often disappear as suddenly as they appear. If a wart is troublesome, it should be removed by a physician. Self-medication is an invitation to danger.

Moles. Moles are pigmented spots caused by an overdevelopment of the pigmented deep layer of the skin. Moles may be congenital or acquired postnatally. Although most moles are harmless, special care should be taken to avoid irritation of all moles. If the location is such that clothing or any other object causes frequent or constant irritation, a surgeon should be consulted.

A colored growth on the skin, such as a dark mole, which increases rapidly in size is called a melanoma. This rapid growth may be associated with glandular changes such as occur at puberty and during pregnancy. Specialists usually recommend surgical removal of all pigmented growths on the palms and soles, pigmented lesions which tend to be ulcerated, those with irregular projections, and those subjected to repeated irritation or pressure.

Corns. Corns are horny thickenings of the skin due to friction and pressure. The conical mass descends into the skin proper and causes pain. Because of the dangers of infection, paring corns with a razor or other instrument is ill advised. Medicated corn plasters may be used safely if proper measures are taken to prevent infection. A severe case of corns should be referred to a doctor. Properly fitting shoes are the obvious preventive action. Yet because in a considerable proportion of the population, the left foot is longer and narrower than the right, a good shoe fit for one foot will mean a poor fit for the other. A pair of shoes long enough for the left foot but wide enough for the right may be satisfactory.

Cold sores. Cold sores (herpes simplex) are an irritation, usually of the mucocutaneous line, caused by a virus. A cold sore occasionally occurs before or during an attack of the common cold, but often occurs at other times and is not caused by the virus which causes the common cold. Spirits of camphor hasten the drying and healing of the sore. Precaution should be taken to prevent secondary infection in an open lesion.

Acne. Acne is due to an infection in a hair follicle. From an hour after birth until an hour after death, the human skin is inhabited by living *Staphyloccus albus.* Because of the acid state of the skin, the organisms cannot produce an infection even though they survive. A decline of the skin acidity enables the organisms to increase their activity and set up an infection. Endocrine changes, such as those occurring at puberty, alter the skin so that the *Staphylococcus albus* has a medium suitable for bacterial activity.

Most individuals have an occasional pimple, but the extreme form of acne vulgaris usually covers the face, chest, and shoulders. Large papules develop and have a pustular formation underneath. Bacterial action often corrodes the underlying tissues, with resulting skin faults or blemishes.

A reduction in animal fats in the diet and an increase in the intake of water-soluble vitamin A are helpful in combating acne. Dermatologists have developed effective methods for treating acne, and even a moderate case of acne should be brought to the attention of a dermatologist. Above all, picking at the eruptions, which invites secondary involvement, should be avoided.

Boils. Boils (furuncles) are caused by a staphylococcus that invades the follicles of the skin. A granular layer of tissue surrounds the infectious mass. Squeezing the boil would rupture the granular layer and permit infection to migrate, via areolar connective tissue, to other locations in the skin where another furuncle would develop. Self-reinfection from external sources will result unless aseptic techniques are used in treating the boil.

Neither bad blood nor diet is associated with boils. Diabetic persons are highly susceptible to boils, but in all cases there must be organisms to produce the infection.

Ringworm. Ringworm is caused by a fungus and results in lesions which often are circular, nonpustular, and itching. Foot ringworm, usually between the toes, is more common in adults, whereas ringworm of the body, face, and head is more common among children.

Cleanliness of the body and feet, of clothing, and of floors is helpful in preventing ringworm. In public bathing and swimming facilities, requiring users to walk through a solution of 1% sodium thiosulfate has been of doubtful value as a community preventive measure. Personal cleanliness, thorough drying of the feet after bathing, use of sandals, cleanliness in the gymnasium and shower room, regular inspections, and immediate treatment of infections are effective preventive measures. Advertised "cures for athlete's foot" are of doubtful value and are often irritating.

Impetigo contagiosa. Impetigo contagiosa is an infectious disease that affects the superficial layers of the skin and is characterized by pink-red macules which become fluid-filled, then pustular, and then crust and leave temporary scars. The areas about the mouth and the hands are commonly involved, but other parts of the body may be affected. Ointments containing any of the sulfa compounds are effective in treating impetigo if the ointment is worked under the margin of the crusts or if the crusts are removed by soaking with boric acid.

Scabies. Scabies is caused by a burrowing of the female mite *(Sarcoptes scabiei)* into the superficial layer of the skin. The female dies after laying her eggs, but the larvae hatch in about six days and cause an eruption which produces an unbearable itching. Frequent sites of eruption are the webs between the fingers, the crotch, the waist, the wrists, the armpits, the face, and even the scalp. Sulfur ointment is effective, particularly if there is frequent bathing and subsequent change of underclothing and bedding.

Ultraviolet radiation and the skin. Most of us have observed that the amount of sunshine available to us varies from hour to hour, day to day, season to season, and place to place. Variation in available ultraviolet rays is greater than variation in observed sunshine. Because they absorb ultraviolet rays, smoke, fog, and dust affect ultraviolet radiation adversely, as do ordinary glass and clothes. Reflected ultraviolet rays, such as from water or snow, can be quite effective although not so intense as the direct rays. Ultraviolet radiation can be produced artificially. Ordinary electric light bulbs give off ultraviolet rays but of negligible intensity. However, the air-cooled mercury-vapor lamp and the carbon arc lamp furnish ultraviolet radiation of considerable intensity. The use of artificially produced ultraviolet radiation should always be under the supervision of an expert.

Biological effects of radiation are due to the absorption of radiant energy into the chemical substances of the body. The resulting chemical change may be beneficial or harmful. Intensity of radiation as well as variation in human susceptibility to radiation is the significant factor in the biological effects of ultraviolet rays.

Beneficial effects of ultraviolet rays are important in growth. Ultraviolet radiation is essential in the production of calciferol (vitamin D) and thus affects the metabolism of calcium and phosphorus. Absorption of ultraviolet radiation by cutaneous lipids (sterols) produces the calciferol. In some individuals ultraviolet rays stimulate the production of red blood corpuscles. Moderate intensities of ultraviolet radiation have a beneficial stimulating effect on the skin. Muscles appear to benefit from the radiation.

Tanning of the skin results from radiant stimulation of skin cells that transforms tyrosine into a brown or black pigment (melanin). A light or moderate tan may be beneficial to health, but a dark tan reduces the amount of radiation absorbed by fats and thus reduces the possible benefits of ultraviolet rays. Blonds and people with red hair have a low rate of pigment production and should extend tanning over a prolonged period of time by a considerable number of short exposures to low intensities of radiation.

Harmful effects of ultraviolet rays are due to excessive intensity of radiation. Sunburn redness results from excessive ultraviolet rays that transform histidine into a substance which dilates the blood vessels. Inflammation of the eyelids (conjunctivitis) as well as damage to the eye itself occurs from overexposure to ultraviolet radiation. Snow blindness is due to reflected ultraviolet rays. Irritation of nerve endings is apparent in an irritable restless child who has been in the sun all day or in an adult who is unable to sleep after his first full day outdoors in the spring. The summer vacationer who has "lived in the sun" may find himself highly nervous and irritable for a week or more after returning home. Headache, dizziness, and nausea result from excessive exposure to radiant energy. Evidence indicates that chronic irritation by ultraviolet rays may terminate in skin cancer. Excessive exposure to the sun dries the skin and gives it the leathery inelastic wrinkled appearance of old age.

In the practice of personal health a normal individual is affected beneficially by moderate exposure to the sun's rays. Seasonal variations in the intensity of ultraviolet rays should be expected. In summer the intensity of ultraviolet radiation may be one thousand times that in winter. Midday radiation is more intense than that in early morning and evening. During the summer months overexposure is to be avoided. Sunburn is an indication of overexposure whether it is a sunburn of a blond or a brunette person. Individuals unusually sensitive to sunlight have found short exposure to early morning and evening radiation highly satisfactory in acquiring a gradual healthful tan. During any extended exposure to intense sunlight the head and eyes should be protected from direct rays.

In the winter city dwellers especially get insufficient sunlight for optimum health needs unless special efforts are made to get more exposure to the sun than normal living habits provide. Infants and expectant mothers need calciferol concentrates the year round because of inadequate sunlight.

The use of ultraviolet radiation for the treatment of specific conditions such as acne is the province of the physician and a danger area for the layman.

The bacteriacidal action of ultraviolet rays is due to the resulting oxidation of enzymes within the bacteria. Artificial ultraviolet rays are as effective as those of the sun and have an advantage in that their wave length and intensity can be maintained and the bacteriacidal action can be controlled. Not all ultraviolet rays have a definite bacteriacidal effect. Waves between 2540 and 2800 Å. (Angstroms) have a proved bacteria-killing effect, and a radiation of 2537 Å. is the most effective. An Angstrom is a unit of length equal to 1/10,000 of a micron. Ultraviolet rays do not destroy bacteria within body tissues because bacteriacidal action is restricted to surfaces exposed to the rays.

In practice, ultraviolet rays have been of limited use as a killer of bacteria because the rays are readily absorbed by inorganic and organic particles of all kinds. Bacteria cannot be killed by ultraviolet rays in an opaque substance such as milk or meat. Even in clear water the rays penetrate less than a quarter of an inch beneath the surface. Hospitals use artificially produced ultraviolet radiation to destroy bacteria on surfaces in operating rooms. However, the practical use of ultraviolet rays in sterilizing the air of rooms poses many questions. Sufficient intensity of radiation to destroy bacteria in the air may expose the occupants of a room to excessive ultraviolet radiation. Germicidal vapors, such as triethylene glycol, rather than ultraviolet rays are being adopted more frequently for use as a germicide in public buildings, but are of doubtful value.

The warming effect of sunshine comes from the infrared radiation. When infrared rays are absorbed by a body cell, the light energy is converted to heat in the process. The penetration of the tissues by infrared rays is not very deep, usually less than one quarter of an inch. Short infrared rays such as those from the sun rarely burn human tissues, but the artificially produced longer rays of radiant heaters can burn human tissues. The principal danger in the use of artificial devices for producing infrared rays is the danger of tissue burns.

Infrared radiation normally serves human beings merely through its effect in the maintenance of body temperature. However, for recovery purposes, infrared radiation is used to relieve pain and for the treatment of arthritis, sprains, dislocations, scars, muscle inflammation, and poor circulation in the extremities.

Atmosphere and the skin. Under ordinary conditions the chemical composition of the atmosphere is of little health interest or consequence. However, the physical factors of the atmosphere are of importance to the well-being of persons in their relation to body temperature and comfort. For this reason physical factors of the air are of interest to health scientists.

In its metabolic processes the human body produces heat. The body functions most effectively at about 100° F. If all heat produced in the body were retained, death would occur. However, the body possesses a heat-regulating mechanism which keeps body temperature remarkably uniform by maintaining a balance between the production and elimination of heat. Control is largely effected by dilating and constricting the vessels of the skin. Blood carries heat to the body surface where the heat is emitted by the natural tendency of heat particles to move to a cooler medium. Evaporation of sweat increases the rate of heat elimination.

When heat and moisture elimination are markedly retarded, a person becomes uncomfortable and irritated, due largely to the accumulation of body heat and the resulting temperature rise. If the elimination of body moisture and heat is just slightly retarded, the individual experiences drowsiness, headache, lassitude, depression, and loss of vigor. Thus the physical factors of temperature, humidity, and movement of the atmosphere are important to the well-being of an individual. Air in terms of physical comfort is the hygienist's principal interest in the atmosphere though other factors such as pollution, including radioactivity, are of importance.

Temperature. Man, by the use of clothes, has been able to survive temperatures from −75° to 250° F., a remarkable range. Yet from the standpoint of effective living the optimum temperature range for man is rather narrow.

High temperatures over an extended period of time can cause harmful upsets of normal chemical balances of the human body. Heat exhaustion may occur during continued exposure to heat or some hours later. Consciousness is retained, but the individual experiences dizziness, general weakness, and excessive perspiration while exhibiting the pallor of shock. The body temperature remains above normal. Recovery is rapid if the person rests and is cooled off.

Sunstroke, caused by long exposure to excessive heat, especially exposure to the sun without a cover for the head, is characterized by extremely high body temperature, hot flushed skin, dizziness, severe headache, and even stupor or delirium. Death from sunstroke occurs quite frequently, especially among older persons because of the inability of the constitution of the aged to readjust to salt imbalances. It is for this reason that during heat waves older people are urged to take extra salt in their diet to compensate for the excessive loss of salt through perspiration.

Heat prostration is caused by a combination of excessive heat and excessive fatigue. The victim is usually a manual laborer who works in a furnace room, foundry, or other excessively hot working place. The patient exhibits the symptoms of shock. His temperature is not elevated, but his skin is pale, cold, and clammy. He is weak to a point of prostration and will experience nausea and dizziness.

Any disturbance due to excessive heat merits the services of a physician.

Low temperature over an extended period of time increases metabolism and causes a rise in blood pressure. A decrease in white cells of the blood, together with a drop in body temperature, partially accounts for the susceptibility to respiratory infection during exposure to low temperatures. Cold also reduces the protective functions of the lining of the respiratory tract by reducing protoplasmic activity of ciliated cells.

The relationship of moderate temperatures to human well-being is of positive importance in effective and enjoyable living. Temperatures neither too high to prevent desirable body heat loss nor too low to require marked body adjustments are the ideal. Temperature has its own particular contribution to body comfort, but its effects are related to the factor of humidity. That interwoven relationship can best be understood by a consideration of humidity and its effects as related to temperature.

Humidity. Various amounts of water vapor are present in the atmosphere at all times. The degree of vapor in the atmosphere is termed its humidity. Absolute humidity is the total amount of vapor, expressed in grains per cubic foot, which will cause saturation of the atmosphere. It is the total moisture that air can hold. The amount of vapor that air can hold varies with different temperatures. Universally recognized standards are those of the Royal Observatory, Greenwich, England.

Relative humidity is the percentage of moisture present in the air as compared to the amount necessary for saturation, which is designated 100. Thus, at a temperature of 80° F. a relatively humidity of 50 means that each cubic foot of air holds 5 grains of moisture. Several instruments (hygrometers, psychrometers, etc.) are used for a precise determination of humidity. In the absence of any device to measure relative humidity, a person may suspect a high relative

Table 13. Maximum water content of the air at different temperatures

Temperature (Fahrenheit)	Grains of water vapor per cubic foot of air
10	1.1
20	1.5
30	2.1
40	3.0
50	4.2
60	5.8
70	7.9
80	10.0
90	14.3
100	19.1

humidity when body moisture tends to cling to the skin rather than to evaporate readily as would occur if the relative humidity were low.

Within limits the human body can adjust to variations in humidity and temperature. Yet moisture and heat produce significant effects in the human being. Dry air is stimulating; moist air is depressing and deprives a person of vigor. Cold air is invigorating and speeds up metabolism. Warm air has the reverse effect, producing sluggishness and apathy.

Precisely how damp cold air affects health is not too well known, but it causes a sudden loss of heat, with a chilling of the body. This throws an unusual load on the mechanism of heat regulation. Metabolism, digestion, circulation, kidneys, and nervous system are affected by the unusual adjustment necessary. Persons with a high level of health are but mildly affected. However, infants, the aged, and individuals with a low level of health may suffer serious effects. The respiratory system is particularly vulnerable. However, proper clothing and physical activity are preventive measures.

In practice the health interest of the public is in the temperature-humidity range which promotes comfort and permits greater effectiveness in living. Of special importance is the comfort zone as applied to artificially controllable indoor conditions.

Several investigators, working independently, have discovered that the comfort zone during the summer months ranges between 66° and 71° F.; during the winter months the range extends from 63° to 71° F. The lower temperature effective during winter months is accounted for largely by the type of clothing worn. In the temperature range of 66° to 71° F., any relative humidity between 30 and 70 provides a comfortable effective temperature-humidity range. Not only does the individual feel comfortable because of optimum bodily heat adjustment, but also both physical and mental activity attain a high level of efficiency.

Excessively dry heat causes a rapid loss of body moisture, producing a chilly feeling. Excessive loss of body moisture predisposes to irritation and infection of the mucous lining of the respiratory tract.

Increasing the humidity in large commercial and public buildings has been solved by air-conditioning engineers, but the typical home still seeks an inexpensive method for increasing humidity. Improvised home methods of growing plants, flowers in water, pans of water on radiators, and wet towels near electric fans are helpful but not always adequate.

Excessive humidity interferes with the evaporation of body moisture and decreases the capacity of the air to carry away heat. Excessive humidity thus produces a discomfort because the body moisture clings to the skin. It also makes cold air feel colder and hot air feel hotter. Except when a significant rise in body temperature results, no serious damage to health occurs because of moisture. The principal effect is discomfort, with a decline in mental and physical performance.

The undesirable effects of excessive atmospheric moisture can be reduced by using light clothing. However, under most circumstances an easier and more effective means for relieving bodily discomfort is to lower the room temperature and increase the movement of air.

Air movement. A third atmospheric factor that contributes to bodily comfort and general efficiency is the movement of air. A current of air too slight to be felt by the skin will nevertheless aid in the loss of heat from the body's surface. However, to be appreciably effective a current of air should be perceptible. The least perceptible current is spoken of as the *threshold velocity.* Currents of air may act directly and affect the blood vessels and nerve endings of the skin, causing changes in metabolism, blood distribution, and temperature sensations. Subjectively the effect on the skin is pleasant.

Under ordinary room conditions the movement of air should at least be of threshold velocity to be appreciably effective. However, a current perceptible at one time may not be perceptible a few minutes later. As room temperature declines, the perceptible velocity rises. In practice, since temperature and air movement vary, window ventilation is highly effective because it permits these variations to operate in producing comfortable sensations of the skin. Mechanical ventilation systems do not provide for variations; in this respect they are not so acceptable as the window-gravity method of ventilation.

Ventilation standards. The objective of all ventilation, whatever the situation, is to provide an indoor atmosphere which will be comfortable to the individuals concerned by permitting ready loss of body heat and moisture. Under usual conditions the carbon dioxide and oxygen content of the air are of no concern. The primary emphasis is upon the temperature, humidity, and movement of air as they relate to bodily comfort.

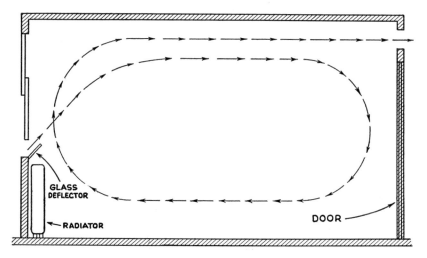

Fig. 21. Gravity ventilation method. Upward draft forces cold air toward the ceiling, but being heavier than warm air, it falls. As the air warms, it rises. Note the importance of the outlet to complete the air circuit.

For the usual conditions in the home, school, office, business place, and commercial establishment, an established standard has the support of scientific investigation and everyday practical experience. The established standard consists of the following: window ventilation with variable currents and without drafts, temperatures 66° to 71° F., and relative humidity 30 to 70.

For sleeping purposes the same basic objective of ventilation still prevails, with the standard being altered merely in temperature range. An accepted standard for the normal individual is a temperature range of 50° to 65° F., window ventilation with variable currents and without drafts, and relative humidity 30 to 70. Outside atmospheric conditions govern modifications of the accepted standard. However, zero or near zero temperatures for sleeping quarters are not conducive to the best sleeping conditions. As has been pointed out, cold air reduces the protective functions of the lining of the respiratory tract, reduces body temperature, and reduces the white cell count of the blood, all of which predispose to infection of the respiratory tract. Cool, not cold, temperatures are the accepted standard for the best sleeping conditions.

Air conditioning. In an effort to control the temperature, humidity, movement, and purity of air, engineers have devised air-conditioning systems which have been highly effective for large buildings. The air is filtered and washed to remove dust, smoke, obnoxious gases, and pollen. Temperature is maintained at 68° to 69° F. in the winter and 70° to 71° F. in the summer. Humidity is held at 40% to 45% in the winter and 45% to 50% in the summer.

For the typical medium-sized home, air conditioning is not yet universally feasible, largely for economic reasons. A satisfactory substitute is to use the warm-air heating system to provide filtered, cool, and dry air in summer and filtered, warm, and moistened air in winter. However, advances in air-conditioning engineering will soon make air conditioning a commonplace commodity for most dwellings in America.

Pollution of air. Pollution of the atmosphere is not a new phenomenon. Natural pollution existed before the advent of man. Natural pollution exists in the form of dust, sea spray, gas from volcanoes, and smoke from forest fires. Even man-made pollution as a community problem dates back to the pre-Christian era. However, never in the history of man has man-made air pollution been the serious problem it is today. Industrial development and the mode of living have produced pollution of the atmosphere of such serious proportions as to pose a major health problem in some communities.

Technically air pollution of a community concerns itself only with man-made pollution. A concise definition will clarify what is meant by air pollution as the term is used at the present time in health circles. Community air pollution is the presence in the surrounding atmosphere of substances put there by the activities of man in concentration sufficient to interfere directly or indirectly with his comfort, safety, or health, or with the full use and enjoyment of his property. In general it does not refer to the atmospheric pollution incident to employment

Fig. 22. Pollution of the air in a modern city. Air pollution is not limited to the large metropolitan areas. Many small industrial towns have serious air pollution problems.

in areas where workers are employed, nor is it concerned with airborne agents of communicable disease nor with overt or covert acts of war. This emphasis upon man-made pollution does not disregard the serious conditions which might result from natural pollution. Both kinds can be serious, but something can be done about man-made pollution. About natural pollution man can usually do very little. Man-made air pollution can come from several sources:

1. Combustion resulting in true smoke, dust, grit, sulfides, carbon monoxide, benzpyrene vapor, hydrochloric acid, and nitrogen wastes.
2. Roasting and heating processes resulting in dust, fumes, sulfides, and fluorides.
3. Mining and quarrying resulting in dust and smoke.
4. Cooking processes resulting in noxious odors.
5. Chemical processes resulting in dust, fumes with toxic substances of arsenic and lead compounds, and gases from chlorine, sulfur, nitrogen, and fluorine.
6. Nuclear processes resulting in radioactive dusts and gases.

Air pollution is a problem for all industrial areas and large cities. Some smaller communities with certain types of industrial plants also find air pollution a community problem. For practical purposes communities may consider air pollutants in two main groups. The first includes smoke, gas, soot, and cinders from fly ash caused by the combustion of fuel in the home and in railroad locomotives as well as in industry. The second is the combustion from a varied group of fumes, mists, gases, and dusts caused by industrial operations and exhausts from motor vehicles. Weather and topography play a large part in the concentration of air pollutants. As an illustration the topography of the area which rings Los Angeles, together with the proximity of the ocean, forms an inversion layer in which the air pollutants are trapped and concentrated just above the ground, with little chance of dispersion because of the overlayer which holds the polluted air near the ground level.

The effects of air pollution may be divided into five aspects: (1) economic, (2) effect on vegetation, (3) effect on animals, (4) nuisance effect, and (5) effect on health. The first three of these do not command the attention of health authorities but the latter two do.

The nuisance aspects of air pollution are recognized, but as yet knowledge and experience do not permit us to state with any degree of certainty at what level the concentration of gases, dust, and other materials in the air is sufficient to be classified a nuisance. Common law pertaining to air pollution holds that the emission of smoke fumes or dust into the atmosphere may constitute a nuisance, whether public or private, depending upon the extent of damage or injury. However, this does not cover the situation when the pollution merely annoys the individual or group without causing damage or injury.

The important problem in air pollution comes in its effect upon health. As would be expected, air pollution has the greatest damaging effect upon the respiratory system. Studies in Great Britain have established that air pollution in communities is directly related to chronic bronchitis. In addition a number of air pollutants are known to produce cancer in experimental animals. Research has established that cancer of the respiratory tract is much higher among people in a community plagued by heavy air pollution than among people living in rural or nonindustrial areas. The same studies also indicate that cigarette smokers in industrial communities have a higher incidence of diseases of the respiratory tract than nonsmokers. This is the basis for the conclusion by some scientists that a combination of extreme air pollution and heavy cigarette smoking constitute an important cause of cancer of the respiratory tract.

Air pollutants have an irritating effect upon the eyes and skin, as well as upon the respiratory tract. During periods of heavy overlays of air pollutants or smog, the pneumonia rate and the rate of other respiratory diseases tend to rise in a community. Apparently a combination of irritants from the atmosphere and a lack of sunlight team up to effect an increase in infectious diseases. Sulfur oxides in the air make breathing more difficult, and ozones can cause scarring of the lung tissues. Doubtless this irritation could serve as a lesion in which pneumonia might develop.

Digestive disturbances are much greater in communities with problems of extreme air pollution. Medical authorities generally agree that swallowing pollutants can produce digestive disturbances.

Control of the causes of air pollution may be accomplished in four ways:

1. Substitution of a material or machine for the one dispersing pollutants
2. Conversion of air pollutants to less irritating forms
3. Retention of the pollutants by not discharging them into the air
4. Disposition of pollutants by reducing the concentrations to a low level, a plan which is especially suitable for gases and smoke.

On July 14, 1955, the President approved Public Law No. 159 of the Eighty-Fourth Congress. This law, known as the Air Pollution Act, authorizes the Surgeon General of the U. S. Public Health Service to conduct a program of research, with technical assistance, relating to air pollution. The law does not provide any method of federal enforcement of air pollution, but enables the Surgeon General to investigate causes, results, and possible methods of control.

An effective program to deal with air pollution must emphasize causes and

Fig. 23. Air quality control. Pollution control requires constant, accurate determinations of changes in the concentrations of foreign substances in the atmosphere. (Courtesy Oregon State Board of Health.)

prevention rather than cure. Actually present laws can be invoked only when a disaster has been declared. Legal control of atmospheric conditions must await clarification of the subject. In the meantime the public must be educated to know the threat of air pollution to health.

The Los Angeles County Air Pollution Control District suggests the following controls for existing sources of air pollution:

1. Rubbish collection and disposal systems must be inaugurated by the cities of the Los Angeles Basin as a basis for an ultimate ban on all single-chamber incineration.
2. Renewed efforts within the automobile industry to secure the development of an effective control device, acceptance by the public of the urgent necessity for installing such a device, and development of alternate methods of transportation, such as an effective rapid transit system.
3. Voluntary acceptance of responsibility for air pollution control by all elements of industry.*

With controls of this type, authorities can prevent further increase in air pollution due to unrestrained growth and can seek extension of controls to presently uncontrolled sources of pollution. Each individual citizen must accept personal responsibility for reducing the amount of pollutants in the atmosphere. This health problem of modern vintage threatens to become more serious unless determined efforts are made to solve it.

Radioactive particles in the air. Man has always been subjected to a certain amount of radiation even though he knew nothing or little about radioactivity. Cosmic radiation as well as radiation from natural sources of chemical activity has always been with man. Today radiation of this type is spoken of as background radiation, and everyone is subjected to about 0.1 r (roentgens) per year. Although the roentgen ray has long been recognized as a potential radiation danger, radioactive particles in the air did not become a concern until scientists began to split the atom, beginning with the first successful attempt by Lord Rutherford in 1919. Man-made radioactive particles in the atmosphere constitute air pollution, but radioactive fallout is of sufficient interest and importance to merit special consideration, especially in view of the known effects of nuclear detonations.

In the development of nuclear weapons and their testing, fission explosions spray radioactive particles into the air. These particles very gradually settle to the earth. Those particles with a short half-life are of little concern to man, but strontium^{90} and cesium^{137}, whose half-lives are about 28 years, can represent a real danger to health and to life itself.

Scientists generally agree that penetration of the body cells by radioactive particles causes ionization of the atoms of the cells, and those cells most likely to ionize are those undergoing cell division. This includes the reproductive cells undergoing miotic division. The extent of the effect depends

---

*From What is being done about smog, published by the Air Pollution Control District, County of Los Angeles, Calif., 1955.

upon the dose received and whether it is received externally or internally.

When doses of radiation are received or applied externally, the unit is called a roentgen, which means radiation that causes two ionizations per cubic micron. An average adult exposed to 1 r would receive about 10^{17} ionizations over the whole body. About 500 r in one dose cause death, but less than 100 r produce no external signs or symptoms. However, as low an exposure as 25 r produces changes in the white cell count of the blood. According to the Atomic Energy Commission, the average dose externally from fallout is 0.001 to 0.005 r per year. This is less than 5% of the background radiation of 0.1 r per year.

To express internal dosage the Sunshine Unit (S.U.) is used, and it is equivalent to 0.003 r per year to bone tissue. Internal doses result from drinking radioactive milk or water and eating other types of foods that are radioactive. The internal effects of radioactivity are now the primary concern of health scientists. Special attention is being given to the effects of cesium[137] and strontium[90]. Cesium[137] forms soluble compounds which act like potassium or sodium in the body and is thus dispersed throughout the body though it is not likely to concentrate in any one area. It is not likely to be dangerous to more than one in 500,000 persons. Strontium[90] is chemically similar to calcium. It follows the course of calcium in the body and is deposited in bone.

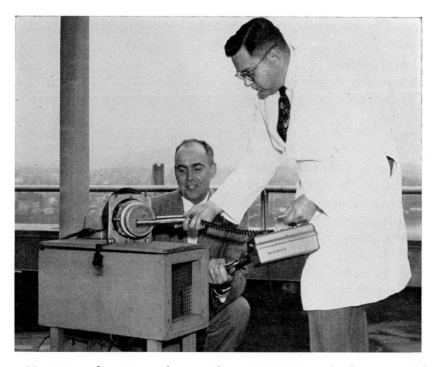

Fig. 24. Monitoring radioactivity in the atmosphere. Concentrations of radioactive particles in the air have become of such importance that health departments have extensive programs for monitoring the changes which occur. (Courtesy Oregon State Board of Health.)

Investigation indicates that strontium[90] is deposited differently in the bones of adults and of children. In adults the cancellous bone, where the blood-forming functions are located, is usually affected, causing hot spots or acute poisoning. Radiation damage to the bone marrow at this site may result in bone cancer or leukemia. In children under 6 years of age strontium[90] poisoning is more evenly distributed throughout the bone because the strontium[90] follows the vast network of bone canals which make up the haversian system. This form of poisoning is not so dangerous as the acute type. Apparently any malignancy is due to localized high doses.

What constitutes a maximum permissable concentration (MPC) has not been established to the satisfaction of all scientists in the field. Dr. Karl Z. Morgan, a physicist at the Oak Ridge National Laboratory and a member of the U. S. Public Health Service Surgeon General's Advisory Committee, contends that there is no such thing as a safe level of radiation internally. The National Academy of Sciences has proposed 50 S.U. as the MPC, but the National Committee on Radiation Protection maintains the MPC can be at a level at least 25% higher than this. Citizens of the United States have a special stake in this matter because fallout is greater in the United States than anywhere else.

By using as their basis the level of strontium[90] in the stratosphere and the anticipated concentrations of strontium[90] in the diets of people in the area of Western culture, Dr. J. L. Kulp and co-workers of the Lamont Geological Observatory, Columbia University, report that the maximum concentration of strontium[90] in the bones of children will occur in 1966.* The report contains other data of interest.

1. Strontium[90] in vegetables varies more than in milk.
2. In rice-diet areas, the strontium[90] is lower than in the northeast United States.
3. High and low concentrations of strontium[90] in plants will not produce equivalent ranges in the human being.
4. Fallout is somewhat proportional to rainfall.

The U. S. Public Health Service is the official federal agency concerned with the problem of radioactivity and its effect upon health. Radium poisoning in watch factories, use of x-ray machines, and use of fluorographic equipment have come under control. However, determination of tolerance levels of radiation exposure is needed.

Health authorities are less concerned with the external effects of radiation than with the internal effects. The nuclear detonations have transmuted elements into strontium[90] which will eventually fall to the earth. If these radioactive particles become part of the food one consumes, the possible consequences are many. One preventive approach being investigated is that of developing sub-

---

*Kulp, J. L., Schulert, A. R., and Hodges, Elizabeth J.: Strontium-90 in man. Part III. Science **129:**1249, 1959.

stances which combine with or trap strontium[90]. Dr. Teiji Ukai, a Japanese biologist, has demonstrated that the tannin of tea combines with strontium[90] to produce an insoluble oxide which can be passed out of the body, leaving little or none to cling to the bone structures.

If man's present understanding of radioactivity is essentially correct, the general public has little cause for alarm. This is based upon the assumption that the concentration of radioactivity in the atmosphere will not be increased by nuclear detonations or other means. The cumulative internal effects of radioactivity is the immediate concern of health scientists, not the acute external effects.

ORAL HEALTH

A healthy oral cavity is one which is free from defects and infection and whose tissues function efficiently. Such a mouth cavity is of esthetic and social importance as well as of health value. Being subjected daily to many hazards, the oral cavity requires constant attention to certain specific factors.

Dental hygiene. Good dental health is a combination of inheritance and care. Individuals vary in their inherited dental endowments. Although inheritance cannot be changed, the wise use of scientific developments can aid each individual in making the most of his dental health potential.

Nutrition. Nutrition is important in tooth formation during the early years of life. Calcium, phosphorus, and vitamins C and D are essentials. Nutrition has no known effect on tooth structure after childhood years. However, for healthy gums vitamin C is important at all ages. Carbohydrates in the mouth provide a necessary medium for bacteria and thus may be regarded as having an established relationship to dental caries for all age groups.

Dental examinations. Dental examinations should be thorough and include the use of the x-ray machine when doubtful conditions exist. An examination at least twice a year should be a minimum. A practical program consists in a family reserving a certain hour of a certain day each month with the family dentist. Thus all members of a family which reserves the four o'clock hour on the first Wednesday of every month can be reasonably certain of having the regular professional service essential to good dental health.

Toothbrushing. If the teeth are brushed immediately after each meal, it will aid in the prevention of caries. Evidence indicates that dental caries is due to a bacterial-chemical process. Bacteria in the presence of carbohydrates on the teeth will produce an acid which dissolves the enamel of teeth. The consumption of sugar in the United States in 1850 was 20 pounds per capita. In 1950 the consumption had increased to 108 pounds per capita. Perhaps this accounts for some of the present tooth decay. Brushing the teeth within ten minutes after a meal will remove virtually all carbohydrates in the mouth. Even a mouthwash with water can be helpful if circumstances prevent brushing the teeth.

The toothbrush of moderately stiff natural bristles should have a small head and a straight handle. Brushing should be from the gums toward the tips of the teeth. Care should be taken to avoid damage to the gums. After each use the brush should be cleaned thoroughly and dried before it is used again. Some dental hygienists advocate that each person should have more than one tooth-brush to assure thorough drying of the brush before it is used again.

A dentifrice serves primarily as a cleanser, but also provides some temporary alkalinity in the mouth. A good lather will have a cleaning effect whether tooth paste or tooth powder is used. A mixture of three parts baking soda and one part table salt is as good as any paste or powder for brushing the teeth.

Fluorine treatment. Fluorine treatment of childrens' teeth reduces caries. Topical application consists in covering the teeth with a 2% solution of sodium fluoride at ages 3, 7, 10, and 12 years although other schedules are used. In each of these years four treatments, two days apart, are given the child. The treatment is given by most dentists and effectively reduces the incidence of dental caries. A more simple and perhaps more effective way of preventing caries is through fluoridation of the public water supply.

Fluoridation of public water supplies promises the best present solution to the problem of preventing or of reducing dental caries. The need for some solution is generally recognized, but the urgency springs from the fact that there is a ratio of one dentist for every 1700 people in the nation. As a result many areas in the nation now have a shortage of dentists, and, with a population increase proportionately more rapid than the increase in dentists, this shortage of dentists will become more severe.

For more than half a century health scientists observed that in certain localized areas the incidence of dental caries was far less than that for the nation as a whole. Scientists hypothesized that some chemical substance was responsible, but pointed out that in some other areas with fluorine people had faulty, even mottled teeth. More critical analysis of the data revealed that in those areas where the fluorine content of the water was approximately one part per million (1 ppm.) the incidence of dental caries was extremely low, whereas in areas where the fluorine content of the water was considerably higher than this many people had mottled or irregular teeth.

It now is clear that fluorine consumed regularly in small amounts while teeth are forming prevents dental caries through three possible means: (1) lowering the solubility of tooth enamel, (2) inhibiting the bacterial processes which dissolve the substance of the enamel, and (3) changing the bacterial flora of the mouth. The first of these seems to be the effective means.

It has further been established that, when fluorine in small amounts is consumed regularly, a balance is established between excretion and storage.

As a result of developments municipalities began adding fluorides to the water supplies as a preventive measure for dental caries. Many of these communities had a small amount of fluorine in the water supply, and the need was to increase the concentration to about 1 ppm. In northern states the concentration is held just above this level, and in southern states the concentration is held just below this level. This is done as an adjustment to the amount of drinking water consumed by the people of these different areas.

In 1963 more than 4,000,000 people in the United States were drinking water with a natural fluorine concentration between 0.7 and 3 ppm. An additional 47,000,000 were drinking water to which fluorine had been added. These 51,000,000 people live in 4,251 communities. Records show that a proportionately greater number of the larger communities fluoridate the water supply than the smaller ones, as the following data indicate:

> Cities of more than 500,000—60% (e.g., Boston, San Francisco, Baltimore, Chicago, Philadelphia, Pittsburgh, Milwaukee, St. Louis, New York City, and Washington, D. C.)
> Cities 10,000 to 500,000—32%
> Cities 2,500 to 10,000—17%
> Communities under 2,500—5%

New York City is the most recent of the large cities to add fluorides to the municipal water supply. There, as elsewhere, this preventive health measure was adopted in the face of bitter opposition.

Sweden, Netherlands, West Germany, Japan, Brazil, Chile, and Colombia are some of the nations in which cities are making fluoridation of water supplies available to their citizens. Fluoridation of water supplies as a preventive measure is rapidly becoming generally accepted.

Adding fluorides to the water supply is relatively simple and precise. At present three fluoride compounds are preferred for fluoridation: sodium fluoride, sodium silicofluoride, and hydrofluosilicic acid. The compounds selected depend on such factors as the facilities of the water plant and the cost and the availability of the compounds.

Machines originally designed for adding other chemicals to water are used as fluoride feeders. Some of these are dry feeders which deliver a predetermined amount of fluoride solution into the water during a given time. In general, dry feeders are used for large water systems, and solution feeders are used for the smaller ones. The original investment in the mechanical equipment for feeding fluorides into the water system is relatively low. A feeder for a small community may cost as little as $500. Feeder equipment for a city of two million people would cost about $15,000. These costs should be thought of in terms of investments extending over ten or more years.

The feeders are simple to operate and highly dependable in terms of maintaining a relatively uniform concentration of fluoride in the water supply. The cost of fluoridation may be less than 15 cents per capita per year and may run as high as 35 cents per year. Many factors enter into the spread of the per capita costs of fluoridation. The biggest factor is a matter of bookkeeping in the allocation of employees and other services to the fluoridation program.

Excessive consumption of fluorides could conceivably be harmful. Some uninformed people have seized upon this as a basis for objecting to fluorides in water. However, water with fluoride concentrations from 0.732 to 2.6 ppm. has

Table 14. Fluorine content of foods (parts per million)

Food	Fluorine	Food	Fluorine
Tea (various brands)	30.00–60.00	Whole wheat flour	1.30
Canned mackerel	26.00	Rice	1.00
Canned salmon	9.00	Corn	1.00
Canned sardines	12.50	Dried beans	0.20
Canned shrimp	4.40	Flour	1.20
Herring (smoked)	3.50	Rye bread	5.30
Frankfurters	1.70	Ginger biscuit	2.00
Liver	1.60	Cocoa	2.00
Round steak	1.30	Milk chocolate	2.00
Chicken	1.40	Chocolate (plain)	0.50
Pork chop	1.00	Spinach	1.00
Pork	0.20	Tomatoes	0.90
Beef	0.20	Lettuce	0.80
Cheese	1.60	Cabbage	0.50
Butter	1.50	Carrots	0.20
Egg yolk	2.00	Potato (white)	0.20
Egg white	0.60	Potato (sweet)	0.20
Milk	0.22	Apples	0.80
Whole buckwheat	1.70	Orange	0.22
Oats	1.30	Pineapple (canned)	0.00

no known effect upon the human body. For more than eighty years, the citizens of El Paso County, Colorado, have used public water supplies containing 2.6 ppm. fluorides. In 1953 the El Paso County Medical Society in a resolution testified that the citizens of the county exhibited no systemic effects other than mottled tooth enamel. In other sections of the nation millions of citizens have been drinking water with a natural fluoride content of 2 ppm. or less. The health histories of these people show no deviation from that of the population at large, except a decreased incidence of dental caries.

Virtually all foods contain traces of fluorine, but in most of them the quantity is negligible. The daily fluorine intake from food is estimated from 0.19 to 0.32 ing. Studies of laboratory animals and human beings indicate that there is no reason to believe that the consumption of fluoride-bearing foods will produce either beneficial or harmful effects on health.

Opposition to new health measures is not new. People in the public health field expect opposition to health innovations. In years past there was vigorous opposition to vaccination, to the installation of indoor plumbing, to chlorination of water supplies, and to the pasteurization of milk. Past history reveals that several types of individuals are most likely to object to health innovations. People with aggressions can find something to oppose, something to vent their aggressions on, in new health measures. These individuals usually lead the "anti" forces. In the ranks of those who object to new health measures, we also find the uninformed, the highly emotional, and the easily frightened persons and those with a high resistance to change or anything which is new. Some individuals review the basis for the new health provisions, but find themselves unable to agree with the conclusions. One of the glories of democracy is that the idea with merit will prevail. Opposition to fluoridation of the public water supply will doubtless delay the inevitable general acceptance of water fluoridation as an effective means for the prevention of dental caries.

Scientific surveys indicate a general decline in dental caries among children who have regularly consumed fluoridated water during their growing years. In general the decline in incidence is from 40% to 60%. Some adults appear to be helped in preventing dental caries by regularly consuming fluoridated water. However, health scientists report that, in general, fluoridation of water supplies is of value primarily during the first sixteen years of life. A summary of dental caries in school children in twenty-one cities is reported by H. T. Dean and co-workers (Table 15).

Fluoridation of public water supplies has been endorsed by many health and parahealth organizations. From a long and formidable list a few might be mentioned: American Dental Association, American Medical Association, State and Territorial Dental Directors, State and Territorial Health Officers, American

Table 15. Summary of dental caries in 7257 school children aged 12 to 14 years in 21 cities*

City and state	No. of children examined	Per cent of children caries free	No. DMF† per child with caries experience	Fluorine concentration (ppm.) public water supply
Galesburg, Ill.	273	27.8	2.36	1.9
Colorado Springs, Colo.	404	28.5	2.46	2.6
Elmhurst, Ill.	170	25.3	2.52	1.8
Maywood, Ill.	171	29.8	2.58	1.2
Aurora, Ill.	633	23.5	2.81	1.2
East Moline, Ill.	152	20.4	3.03	1.2
Joliet, Ill.	447	18.3	3.23	1.3
Kewanee, Ill.	123	17.9	3.43	0.9
Pueblo, Colo.	614	10.6	4.12	0.6
Elgin, Ill.	403	11.4	4.44	0.5
Marion, Ohio	263	5.7	5.56	0.4
Lima, Ohio	454	2.2	6.52	0.3
Evanston, Ill.	256	3.9	6.73	0.0
Middletown, Ohio	370	1.9	7.03	0.2
Quincy, Ill.	330	2.4	7.06	0.1
Oak Park, Ill.	329	4.3	7.22	0.0
Zanesville, Ohio	459	2.6	7.33	0.2
Portsmouth, Ohio	469	1.3	7.72	0.1
Waukegan, Ill.	423	3.1	8.10	0.0
Elkhart, Ind.	278	1.4	8.23	0.1
Michigan City, Ind.	236	0.0	10.37	0.1

*From Dean, H. T., Jay, P., Arnold, F. A., Jr., and Elvove, E.: Pub. Health Rep. 56:761-792, 1941; Dean, H. T., Arnold, F. A., Jr., and Elvove, E.: Pub. Health Rep. 57:1115-1179, 1942.
†D = decayed; M = missing; F = filled.

Public Health Association, American Water Works Association, National Research Council, and United States Public Health Service.

None of these organizations has anything of a personal nature to gain from the fluoridation of water. Actually members of the dental profession would stand to lose some professional practice and income from widespread use of fluoridation. This is well substantiated by a study by the Oregon State Board of Health which shows that children drinking nonfluoridated water had dental bills between $180 and $220 during the first 16 years of life, whereas those drinking fluoridated water had dental bills between $38 and $60 during their first 16 years of life. The dental profession realizes full well that, unless some effective means is used to reduce dental caries in the United States, dentists will not be able to provide the necessary professional services to care for the dental needs of the nation.

It should be re-emphasized that a substance which can be injurious in high concentration is not necessarily harmful in low concentrations. In many instances a substance can be highly beneficial at low concentrations though injurious at higher levels.

Ordinary table salt in small amounts is beneficial to man. In large amounts salt can be injurious, even fatal, as witness the consequences of drinking sea water. Sugar is indispensable to human life, yet too much sugar can be injurious to health by killing cells and causing gangrene. Death due to diabetes mellitus is death due to an excess of sugar.

Even oxygen in excess can be poisonous. When premature babies were placed in incubators with an oxygen content of 40% or higher, the infants developed fibrosis (retrolental fibroplasia) of the optic lenses, resulting in blindness. Not until research workers demonstrated the inability of infant metabolism to utilize oxygen in such high concentrations did we know that oxygen was the poison responsible for the blindness.

This same principle holds in the instance of fluorides. In high concentrations fluoride can be a poison. Concentrations in the order of 1 ppm. fluoride can be beneficial to man if, utilizing this newly gained knowledge, we will use this knowledge to man's own betterment. This is in the tradition of the march of health science and of human progress.

Common mouth disorders. Few deaths occur as a result of mouth disorders; yet many individuals suffer needlessly from mouth disorders, and in many cases the general health is markedly impaired. Most of these conditions are preventable. All can be treated successfully and with negligible damage if they are discovered early.

Dental caries. Dental caries is the process of tooth decay and *cavity* is the end result. The process is initiated by the *Lactobacillus acidophilus* (L.A.) organism and can be represented as follows:

$$L.A. \rightarrow Enzyme + Carbohydrate = acid$$

The acid dissolves the enamel of the teeth. Dental cavity is the most prevalent physical defect in the American population. Of itself a simple cavity may have no effect on health. However, the cavity can be an avenue of invasion for disease-producing organisms which can pass via the pulp cavity to the apex of the tooth root and produce an abscess. Caries which is permitted to progress may also result in the loss of the tooth.

Recent research with germ-free rats at the National Institutes of Health reveals that these animals have no dental caries when they are fed germ-free food and live in a sterile environment. If these germ-free animals reach adulthood and are then exposed to *Lactobacillus acidophilus,* they still do not develop dental caries. However, surprisingly if they are exposed to various streptococcus strains, these rats develop dental caries. These results may indicate that the streptococcus has a possible relationship to dental caries.

Gum abscesses. Gum abscesses may be localized gum infections at the apex of a tooth root. The bacteria may have entered via a tooth cavity. Or the bacteria may have entered directly into the gum along the shaft of the root. At times a gumboil appears, but more often there is no outward symptom except perhaps tenderness. Suspected abscesses should be brought to the attention of a dentist because of the likelihood of focal infection and resulting complications.

Pyorrhea. Pyorrhea is an inflammation of the periodontal membrane which attaches the tooth to the gum and alveolar bone. Pus forms, and a progressive destruction of tissue of the tooth socket causes the tooth to become loose. Brown calcareous matter may form on the root of the tooth. Since these damaged tissues will not repair, it may be necessary to extract the tooth.

Pyorrhea is an infectious condition which usually follows neglect of oral cleanliness and dental care. Neglect of tartar formation may permit an irritation of the gum which provides a suitable site for infection to begin. Tartar is composed of mineral salts from the saliva. Some tartar is formed in every person's mouth, but those people who form more than the usual amount need to take extra precautions to deal with the problem. When first formed, tartar is not hard, but will become hard in about ten hours. Thus brushing the teeth after each meal should be a reasonably successful measure in reducing tartar deposit. During the periodic checkup the dentist will scale off any tartar which has formed and thus remove possible irritation of the gums.

Vincent's infection. Vincent's infection (trench mouth) is an infectious condition which causes an inflammation of the gums, often producing a deep red or purple coloration of the gum margins. A bad odor to the breath is usually present. This infection may involve the throat and has been fatal. A communicable disease, Vincent's infection can be transmitted by such vehicles as unsanitary drinking glasses, spoons, forks, and other objects which reach the mouth. The use of disinfectants after thorough washing of dishes is particularly important when this infectious disease prevails. The condition can be treated successfully by dentists.

Gingivitis. Gingivitis is a localized or general tender irritated inflamed condition of the gums. The irritation may be due to tartar, rough fillings, improper brushing, malocclusion, or factors associated with a deficiency of ascorbic acid and niacin. The marked redness of the gum will not disappear until the cause of the irritation is removed and the nutrition is improved. Because it can be the forerunner of various serious disorders, even the mildest gingivitis should be given immediate care. People in good health rarely have gingivitis.

Malocclusions. Malocclusions, in which the upper and lower teeth are not in reasonable alignment, may cause irritation to the gums and interfere with proper chewing of food. However, the mental hygiene aspect in terms of personal appearance represents a primary consideration in persons with malocclusion. When irregular teeth, a pronounced overbite, or an underbite is present, a child should have the services of the dentist who specializes in orthodontia (*ortho*, straight; *dontia* teeth). Orthodontia is rarely attempted on adults, but for persons between the ages of 12 and 20 years orthodontic work can be highly effective. For the child who needs corrective work, the service of an orthodontist is not a luxury; it is a necessity.

Canker sores. Canker sores are caused by a virus which is present in the mouth much of the time. Normally, the mouth is chemically neutral. In the neutral medium the virus can survive but is relatively inactive. If a temporary mildly acid state exists, the virus can become virulent enough to cause an ulceration known as a canker sore.

Most people have an occasional canker sore. An alkaline mouthwash may help as a preventive for a person who has a canker sore at moderate intervals. The person who is plagued with canker sores should consult a physicial to determine the basic underlying cause of the chronic condition.

Unpleasant breath. Unpleasant breath is generally regarded as a social specter rather than a health hazard. Most individuals have an occasional transitory siege of unpleasant breath. The usual cause is mild sinusitis, infection of tonsil crypts, or other infection of the mucous tissues of the oral passage. An antiseptic mouthwash may be helpful. A soda and salt solution is effective for a short time. However, a mouthwash has no effect on a sinus condition.

Chronic breath of a very foul type is frequently caused by chronic sinusitis. Not until the infection is cleared up can the unpleasant breath be abated. Vincent's infection and uncleanliness of the mouth are possible causes of bad breath. When the mouth is unclean, protein putrefaction and carbohydrate fermentation produce odors. Perhaps the most devastatingly foul breath is due to a unique condition for which little can be done. In some individuals waste substances in the blood volatilize and diffuse through the highly permeable membranes of the lungs. The cause and treatment have not been discovered.

HEARING

Good hearing is an attribute which is rarely appreciated until it becomes defective. Perhaps the complex society of present-day America places a greater value on hearing acuity than ever before. Everyday effectiveness and enjoyment in living are heavily dependent upon efficient function of the auditory apparatus.

Hearing impairments. Studies indicate that more than 12,000,000 people in the United States suffer a hearing loss of at least 6%, which is the accepted landmark of defective hearing. At least 7% of students of junior high school age have hearing impairments. Most of these hearing defects are missed by parents and teachers, but can be identified by modern audiometric techniques. Between junior high school age and adulthood the incidence of hearing impairments increases very little.

Hearing impairments in adulthood increase appreciably with the advance of the years. The accepted incidence of hearing deficiency by age groups indicates this trend.

Table 16. Hearing impairments among adults

Age group	Number with hearing defects (per 1000)
25–44	20
45–64	52
65–75	130
Over 75	250

Specialists in the prevention and treatment of hearing impairments report that 70% of all hearing defects could be prevented if impairments were discovered early and the best of present-day treatment instituted immediately. Fortunately when this has not been done, modern hearing aids can supplement what hearing function one still has and thus, from the practical standpoint, provide satisfactory hearing. This second best measure is a fortunate benefaction, but infinitely better would be the conservation of natural hearing.

Conduction deafness. This type of deafness is most often found in children and is often designated as middle ear deafness. It is due to obstruction of the sound vibrations and may be caused by dirt and wax in the outer canal, a perforation of the drum, adhesions, scar tissue, or an abscess in the middle ear. Or it may be caused by a congestion of the eustachian tube. Many of these conditions result from repeated colds which are neglected, from blowing the nose improperly, from infected tonsils, from chronic sinusitis, or as a complication following measles, scarlet fever, diphtheria, septic throat, or pneumonia. It is apparent that many times conduction deafness is due to neglect of seemingly negligible infections or other disorders. The obvious course of action for the informed person is to regard all infections as important and in need of immediate care.

Individuals with a catarrhal form of involvement of the middle ear do not always recognize the symptoms of head noises, dull pain, and diminished hearing. A medical examination is always advisable when a pain is present in the region of the ear. If a doubtful condition, such as possible fungus growth, exists in the canal, a physician should be consulted. Hearing is too valuable to be entrusted to an amateur.

Perception deafness. Perception deafness or nerve deafness occurs frequently in adults and is caused by some injury or disease in the inner or neuron part of the ear. It may be caused by toxins produced by infected gums or gallbladder or other focal infection. It may result from meningitis or influenza or from drugs, such as quinine and salicylates. Even high body temperature can produce perception deafness.

Some types of hearing loss, in both the child and adult can neither be prevented nor corrected. Fortunately hearing aids can compensate for much of the deficiency in most persons with impaired hearing. It can be predicted with assurance that within the next ten years the use of hearing aids will be as generally accepted as the wearing of glasses is today.

VISION

Truly one of the amazing functions of the amazing human body, vision attains maturity in about one decade of life. Man is able to see a lighted candle a distance of 14 miles. Yet this heritage, even with the best of care, does not retain its peak efficiency. Without proper care vision can be inadequate for effective and enjoyable living, even to the point of a complete loss of the sense of sight.

Normally an infant is farsighted, and his ability to control his visual apparatus is limited. Yet the tears of the infant, like those of the adult, have a protective antiseptic action. Excess lacrimal secretion is drained off by ducts leading from the orbit to the nasal passage. Gradually normal vision is attained so that by school age the visual apparatus and its coordination provide the acuity necessary for reading and other demands normal living makes of the eyes. Not until after the age of 40 years is there normally an organic change in the eye, when the crystalline lens tends to become progressively inelastic. Physiological age cannot be fully determined by the degree of elasticity of the lens.

Blindness. The National Association for the Prevention of Blindness reported that in 1963 the United States had 392,000 blind people and that 30,000 persons become blind each year. The association reported that 8% of the blind are employed and that another 25% could be employed if they were trained for jobs suitable to their capabilities.

At least 50% of blindness is preventable. Infection and injury are leading causes, both of which are preventable. Further, when infection or injury does occur which jeopardizes sight, immediate medical services may save the sight.

Glaucoma, which causes about one eighth of all cases of blindness, usually can be treated successfully if treatment is begun at the early stages of the disorder. Cataract cannot be prevented by means now at our disposal, but surgery combined with proper prescription of glasses can restore sufficient vision for practical needs. Needless delay in obtaining medical service may be the real leading cause of blindness.

Table 17. Causes of blindness in the United States*

Children		Adults	
Cause	*Per cent*	*Cause*	*Per cent*
Unknown	49	Infection	23
Inherited condition	16	Unknown	22
Infection	14	Cataract	17
Injury	7	Glaucoma	12
Other (tumor, poison, etc.)	14	Injury	9
		General disease (diabetes, etc.)	6
		Other	11

*From Britton, R. H.: Pub. Health Rep. **56**:1017, 1941.

Conservation of vision. Effective vision can be conserved by the practice of a few simple principles. This does not imply that the lifelong practice of good visual hygiene will mean that visual acuity at the age of 70 years will be as sharp as at the age of 20 years. It will mean less proneness to visual fatigue and thus greater efficiency and enjoyment through the years, with significantly better vision in later years than otherwise would be likely. As was indicated in the discussion on heredity, people vary in the quality of their visual endowment. Yet basic principles of visual hygiene apply to all individuals within the normal range.

1. Consult a specialist for any abnormal or even questionable condition of the eyes. Undue fatigue of the visual apparatus can be relieved by glasses of proper prescriptions. There may be no improvement in visual acuity, but the muscles of accommodation will be relieved of much of their task by the proper refraction of light rays by the glasses. Ophthalmologists or oculists are medical doctors specializing in all disorders of the visual apparatus. Optometrists are nonmedical practitioners licensed to correct refractive errors and limit their practice to the prescription of glasses. Opticians grind lenses.

2. Refrain from self-medication of the eyes. Normal eyes do not need treatment, and disordered eyes need the services of a specialist. Vision is too valuable an asset to be jeopardized by a nonprofessional person. Even commercial cleverly advertised washes for the eyes should be shunned if for no other reason than that their use may delay the time when a person seeks the professional service of an ophthalmologist. Only medicaments prescribed by a physician should be put into the eye structures.

3. Proper light, whether a person is reading or engaged in other activities, conserves vision and reduces fatigue. In the discussion on sunlight, standard requirements of lighting are presented. Differing situations and needs demand differing lighting requirements; yet a basic measuring stick is the attainment of efficient vision with a minimum of fatigue.

4. Position of the field of vision is important in terms of both distinctive vision and the avoidance of fatigue. When a person is in an upright posture, the

Fig. 25. Natural lighting for reading. Diffused light comes over the left shoulder, the book is at a convenient angle, and glare is absent. Reading surface illumination is between 50 and 100 foot-candles.

Fig. 26. Proper use of artificial light. General overhead lighting is supplemented by well-dispersed local lighting, the lamp is properly located, and the book is held correctly. Background has an illumination of 20 foot-candles and the reading surface an illumination of about 35 foot-candles.

Fig. 27. Vision conservation program. Preservation of vision, restoration of vision loss, and prevention of vision disorders constitute the goal of the present-day vision conservation program. (Courtesy Oregon State Board of Health.)

position of his eyes requires that the field of vision be at an angle between 45 and 60 degrees. The angle at which the book is held is one reason why vision is so quickly fatigued when a person reads while lying down. For most individuals, reading while in a moving vehicle is extremely fatiguing and even distressing. The jolting action of the vehicle abruptly moves the field of vision. Since in reading the eyes move in a series of jumps, rather than along a smooth line, the added strain of a shifting visual field is evident.

5. Rest intervals during reading conserve both time and visual health. Few people can read continuously for more than an hour and a half without beginning to experience a marked loss in retention. The individual may continue to read, but comprehension wanes appreciably. A rest of about twenty minutes will be time well invested. Closing the eyes, looking into the distance, or even going about other activities will be restful to the eyes. The same principle applies to visual fatigue while one is driving a car. Pulling to the side of the road and closing the eyes for twenty minutes will have an amazing recuperative effect.

6. Proper nutrition for effective vision is provided by a balanced diet, particularly one with adequate amounts of vitamin A. Xerophthalmia, the deficiency disease of the eyes, occurs only when there is marked deficiency of vitamin A and is rare in the United States. However, moderate vitamin A deficiency does exist and results in a deficiency in twilight vision.

7. Foreign particles beneath the eyelids cause an increased secretion of lacrimal fluid which tends to flush out the object. The eyelids should remain loosely closed, and the eyes should be kept as stationary as possible. Above all, the lids should not be rubbed. If these procedures do not remove the particle from the lid, a moist cotton swab on the flat end of a toothpick may serve if used with care. If discomfort continues, the services of a physician are needed. If the foreign object is on the eyeball, an amateur should not attempt to remove it but should rush the patient to a physician.

8. Chemical substances in the orbit call for washing the eye with lots of plain tap water. Even if the discomfort is relieved, a physician should be consulted immediately.

9. Protection against ultraviolet rays directly from the sun, reflected from snow, or from a suntan lamp is desirable. Likewise, protection against unavoidable glare may be necessary. Tinted lenses in shades No. 3 or No. 4 (C or D) are satisfactory for most purposes. For some indoor conditions No. 1 and No. 2 (A and B) tinted lenses may be sufficiently dark, but a darker lens should be used outdoors. The particular color is not too important, except that dark green absorbs everything but green, including the red in a stop light. Because they reflect light irregularly, plastic lenses are not recommended. There is no established value in having a light tint in regular prescription lenses.

10. A black eye is ordinarily not serious. Immediate cold compresses may reduce the extent of discoloration. Later the application of heat should be beneficial in removing discoloration. If any injury to the eye or disturbance of vision is even suspected, an examination by an ophthalmologist is the prudent course of action.

Illumination. A consideration of the relationship of visible radiation to human health confines itself essentially to the efficiency and comfort of vision. Present-day civilization makes constant severe demands of man's visual apparatus, and proper light is necessary to meet these demands. Contrary to popular misconceptions, a person does not become blind from reading or working in poor light. Acquired blindness comes from infection, mechanical injury, or abnormal growths and function. Improper light does affect the efficiency of vision, hence is of health importance. Proper light promotes efficient vision, prevents visual fatigue, and thus prevents general fatigue.

The intensity of visible light is measured in foot-candles. A foot-candle is defined as the amount of light received at a point one foot removed from a source of a standard candle power. The universal standard unit of light is in the possession of the U. S. Bureau of Standards in Washington, D. C. Foot-candle meters, adjusted to the standard unit, conveniently measure the intensity of illumination. These instruments are easily read and are usually reliable.

From the standpoint of effective vision and general health, at least three light factors are important—sufficient illumination, proper distribution, and an absence of glare.

On a sunny day the outdoor illumination will be about 1000 foot-candles. Indoors near a window the amount of light may be about 100 foot-candles. Across the room the intensity may be down to 10 foot-candles.

When speed of vision is not a factor, distinctness of vision (visual acuity) reaches its maximum at about 5 foot-candles. Thus, for ordinary purposes about 12 foot-candles may be sufficient light. However, speed of vision reaches its maximum effectiveness at about 20 foot-candles. When speed is a factor, such as in reading, a minimum of 20 foot-candles may be advisable. Many industries with high-speed operations have a minimum of 75 foot-candles of light. A margin of safety is commendable, but doubtless 50 foot-candles would be satisfactory and economical.

Ordinarily natural sunlight is the preferred form of light, but artificial semidirect and indirect lighting units are highly satisfactory from the standpoint of both sufficient light and proper distribution of light.

Proper distribution of light requires that all areas of the field of vision have approximately the same intensity. Contrasts or brightness differences in light fatigue the eye muscles of accommodation which adjust to the different requirements of the field of vision. A brightness difference of 50 foot-candles at the window side of a schoolroom and 20 foot-candles at the opposite side would tend to hasten the fatigue of the visual apparatus, with resulting distress and inefficiency.

Glare is a condition of light of such a nature as to cause annoyance, discomfort, or distress to the eyes. Open direct light, such as when one faces a window or open lamp, is distressing. Contrast in light, the extreme example being automobile headlights at night, is distressing to the eyes. Reflected light from polished surfaces is a common source of glare. Even a small amount of light reflected from a desk top can produce considerable fatigue over an eight-hour period.

In practice sufficient light properly distributed without sharp shadows and an absence of glare should assure a person of visual efficiency and general physical comfort. The visual apparatus of man fatigues readily even under ideal lighting conditions, and visual fatigue tends to produce a feeling of general fatigue. For most adults reading comprehension and speed decline rapidly after one and a half hours of reading because of fatigue of the visual apparatus. Closing the eyes for ten minutes or refraining from reading for twenty minutes provides effective recovery from visual fatigue. Undue tendency to visual fatigue indicates improper lighting conditions or the need for the services of an eye specialist or both. By being conscious of lighting conditions and requiring proper standards, a person can do much to promote his effectiveness and enjoyment in living.

Common disorders of vision. Although the whole list of vision disorders is not the province of this volume, certain common disorders are of interest to the layman, and a fundamental knowledge of these conditions is valuable in the promotion of personal health.

Several disorders have been discussed in Chapter 2. Of special interest at this point is the importance of early recognition of these conditions and the effectiveness of modern methods of treatment.

Myopia. Myopia or nearsightedness is indicated when an individual experiences a blurring of lines beyond arm's length. A careful examination will reveal the extent of the defect. When a young person is examined, atropine or homatropine is used to paralyze the ciliary muscles in order to test the vision while the crystalline lens is in a resting position. A drug is rarely used for older patients. Lenses with concave surfaces are used in correcting myopic vision.

Hyperopia. Hyperopia or farsightedness is often missed in ordinary screening examinations because a youngster will test 20/20. If the test were continued, the youngster would also read the 30 line. Convex lenses correct farsighted vision.

Astigmatism. Astigmatism causes a blur of lines, and some persons can be helped with the usual frame lenses. Contact lenses have special value in the correction of astigmatism by replacing irregular or differing meridian curvatures with an artificial regular curvature of the cornea.

Amblyopia. A reduction in the acuteness of vision, particularly in bright light, can be due to a variety of causes and usually is referred to as amblyopia. It can occur in children and youth as well as in adults. It usually involves both eyes, but occasionally only one eye is affected. Frequently the cause cannot be identified, and the condition clears up spontaneously. However, dimness of vision, even if temporary, is too important to be left to chance. It merits the services of the professional practitioner who will seek out the cause and institute the necessary treatment.

Cataract. Cataract manifests itself as a clouding of vision due to a developing opaqueness of the crystalline lens or its enclosing capsule. Use of the eye does not hasten the formation of cataract. A delicate but not dangerous surgical procedure under local anesthetic can remove the opaque structure. Following surgery, proper correction with glasses will provide good vision. It will not be the sharp vision of youth, but it will be adequate for most needs.

Glaucoma. Glaucoma, which is caused by excessive pressure in the eye, is less well known than cataract, but it is a greater problem. It is a condition of late middle age. The symptoms of chronic glaucoma are quite imperceptible, but are distinguishable by the observant person. Pain in the eyes, a halo around a light, headaches, reduced peripheral vision, rapid loss of ability to do work at close range, and frequent change of glasses are some of the symptoms. If glaucoma is recognized early, blindness can be prevented in 90% of the patients.

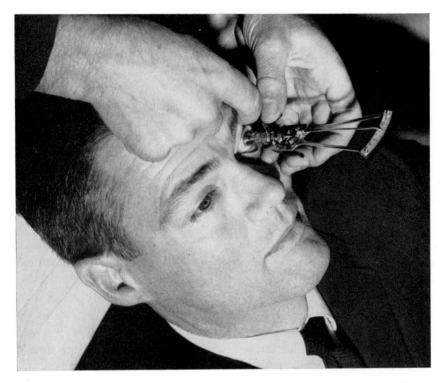

Fig. 28. Glaucoma test. Measuring the pressure exerted against the cornea by the aqueous humor between the cornea and the crystalline lens. This extremely sensitive gauge rests on the cornea and makes an accurate measure of intraocular pressure. (Courtesy Oregon State Board of Health.)

Styes. Styes are caused by an infection of the oil glands of the margins of the eyelids. Of itself eyestrain does not cause a stye, but rubbing the eyes so often associated with eyestrain may transmit organisms to the lid or facilitate the entry of the organisms into the oil glands. A succession of styes should suggest professional consultation. For a single stye, aseptic methods should be followed to prevent the spread of the infection. Hot compresses soften the stye. Incising the core makes control of spread easier.

Blepharitis. Blepharitis usually occurs in poorly nourished persons and is an inflammation of the margins of the eyelids in which small white and gray scales form. Sulfa ointments can be highly effective. Neglect can cause serious damage to the margin of the lids.

Pink eye. Pink eye is a highly communicable inflammation of the lining of the eyelid caused by a bacillus. Common towels and other handled objects are vehicles of transmission. When an endemic of pink eye invades a school, swimming pools are often closed on the assumption that the water in the pool is a vehicle of transmission. No scientific basis supports the assumption. Properly treated water in a swimming pool would be a poor medium for the bacillus.

Exclusion of an infected child from school until the inflammation is cleared is the established procedure

There is no such thing as a cold in the eye. Any inflammation of the eye or its associated structure is due to a specific organism or other irritation.

Trachoma. Trachoma is becoming rare in the United States as sanitation advances. Caused by a virus, trachoma produces granular scales of the upper lid. These hard scales can damage the eye itself, hence the necessity for early diagnosis and treatment. The sulfonamides are highly effective in the treatment of trachoma, but are of little value to an eye which has already been damaged by the hard scales.

GENERAL APPRAISAL

General care of the body rarely yields spectacular returns. Most health benefits are rather inperceptible. Indeed much of the effort in the promotion of general body health appears to be without reward. Yet if even moderate benefits are to be attained, general body care must be a day-to-day routine, each day's efforts contributing a small part to the general well-being. It requires knowledge and vision to have an appreciation of the value of general body care in the prevention of disease and the promotion of positive health. Whether the motive is self-pride in good grooming or a desire to promote health scientifically, adherence to established principles of body care is essential to the highest level of effective and enjoyable living.

Promotion of the health of the skin, mouth, hearing, and vision is a responsibility of the individual himself. He properly will avail himself of professional service for special needs which arise, but he alone has the responsibility for his program of health promotion.

Chapter 4

Nutrition
in health

A widespread interest in nutrition exists in the United States, and the field of nutrition science has much to offer the interested citizen. The existing need is to bring together the knowledge nutrition science has made available and the citizen who needs and can utilize this knowledge. Unfortunately this widespread interest in nutrition in the United States has made possible an exploitation of the public through cults of food fadism. This has been possible through the promulgation of four great food myths, all four patently false. They are stated briefly as follows:

1. All disease is due to faulty diet.
2. Most Americans suffer from hidden nutritional deficiencies and hence must supplement their diets with various "health foods" and other concoctions.
3. Commercial food processing destroys the nutritional value of foods.
4. Soil depletion results in foods that cause malnutrition.

All of these myths have been discredited by scientists, but the myths can be kept alive because anyone can write a book on nutrition and say anything he wishes so long as he does not make a false claim for a special product.

In terms of practical health needs for the individual citizen, all nutrition education should be channeled to practical sensible meal selection based upon the fundamentals of nutrition science. To obtain optimum nutrition through well-balanced meals, the citizen should have realistic easily applied guidelines on meal selection which he can follow in his day-to-day pattern of living. This is the practical answer and antidote of food fadism.

Life is a continuous chemical process going on in the cells of the individual. The sum of all chemical processes in cells is termed *metabolism*. To maintain its life processes, a cell requires materials for energy, materials for building and upkeep, and materials for the regulation of cell function. Any substance not injurious to cells which provides cells with energy or materials for building and upkeep or which regulates functions is classed as a food. Most foods satisfy one of these criteria, but some foods meet two or even three of these requirements.

Nutrition includes all processes by which an organism takes in and utilizes food substances. For a one-cell organism, nutrition is a relatively simple process. Proximity of food to any part of the cell makes diffusion into the cell relatively easy. In addition a small amount of simple energy-yielding food may meet the needs of the cell.

For an organism as complex as the human being, nutrition is an extremely complicated function. The billions of cells of the body depend upon a specialized digestive system to convert certain foods to usable forms. Being far removed from the digestive tract, most cells depend upon specialized systems to transport the food to them. Further the various types of specialized cells in the human body require special building and upkeep materials as well as special regulating substances. Nerve cells require regulating substances different from those required by epithelial (covering) cells. These special needs must be supplied if the particular cells or tissues are to remain healthy and are to function with normal efficiency.

ENERGY NEEDS

Perhaps no one knows precisely what energy is, but scientists generally agree that energy is a force which is capable of producing movement (potential energy) or which is producing movement (kinetic energy). Energy may exist in many forms and can be converted from one form to another.

The ultimate source of all energy is the sun (solar energy). By a process of photosynthesis green plants, containing chlorophyll, transform solar energy to chemical energy which is bound up in sugar (glucose) particles (molecules) produced in the same process of photosynthesis. The process is represented as follows.

$$6CO_2 \quad + \quad 6H_2O \quad + \quad \boxed{S} \quad \longrightarrow \quad \boxed{C_6H_{12}O_6} \quad + \quad 6O_2$$

Carbon dioxide (from the air)	+	Water (from soil)	+	Solar energy converted to (from the sun)		Glucose, (containing chemical energy)	+	Oxygen (into the air)

Glucose molecules are converted quickly to stable more complex starch (glycogen).

Man's cells are incapable of photosynthesis. Since man's cells require chemical energy, man is entirely dependent upon plant life for his energy needs. Man eats the plants containing chemical energy, or he may obtain chemical energy by ingesting the tissues of certain domestic animals which obtained the chemical energy from plants.

Chemical energy is in potential form. Human cellular activity requires heat (thermal) energy in kinetic form. Human body cells are capable of converting chemical energy to thermal energy. This conversion from potential to kinetic form is due to the presence of enzymes within the cells. Enzymes are chemical substances which hasten or alter chemical reactions without entering into or being affected by the reaction.

Energy is required by the human body for two specific needs. First, energy is necessary to carry on the automatic functions indispensable to life. Among these are the contractions of the heart, the maintenance of the walls of the arteries, the secreting by glands, the conduction of nerve impulses, the processes of breathing, and all other processes inherent in the maintenance of life itself. Second, energy is necessary for the voluntary muscular contraction associated with the activities of everyday living.

For convenience the calorie has been designated the unit of energy. A calorie is the amount of heat required to raise the temperature of one kilogram of water one degree centigrade. Thus, if the burning of a certain quantity of food yields ten calories of heat, the food contained ten calories of energy. Likewise, when the human body gives off ten calories of heat, it has burned ten calories of chemical energy. That is, it has converted ten calories of chemical energy to heat energy.

Basic energy needs of a normal healthy person average about one calorie per kilogram (2.2 pounds) of body weight per hour. A man weighing 154 pounds would thus require 1680 calories of energy for basal requirements per day. Activity needs may vary from 500 calories for a person with a sedentary occupation to 5000 calories for a person engaging in heavy manual labor. In unusual cases activity requirements may exceed 5000 calories per day.

Organic foods. Substances containing carbon and derived from living organisms serve as the energy source for man. These substances are termed organic foods and are of three classes—carbohydrates, fats, and proteins.

Carbohydrates. In the human diet carbohydrates are the sugars and starches. Sugar in pure form occurs in a number of foods; cane, beet, corn, and maple sugar are examples. Sugar also occurs in other common items of the diet, such as fruits, vegetables, and milk. Starches compose a considerable portion of plants since the glucose end product of photosynthesis is converted immediately to starch. They occur in the roots, bulbs, tubers, and seeds of plants and to a lesser extent in the leaves and stems. Main starch sources in the human dietary are cereal grains (and flour), mature potatoes, corn, and peas. Unripe bananas and apples contain considerable starch which is converted largely to sugar as the fruit ripens.

In human beings 1 gram (0.035 ounce) of carbohydrates yields an average of 4.1 calories of energy. A pound yields 1860 calories. In the human body carbohydrates may be burned to yield energy for internal activity, for voluntary muscular activity, and for body heat. In addition they may be converted to stable glycogen (animal sugar) and stored, or they may be converted into fat and stored in that form

Fats. Fats may occur in liquid form as oil or in solid form, as in commercial food fats. Dietary fats come from such sources as olives, salad oils, cream, butter, cheese, fatty meat, chocolate, and nuts.

Fats have the highest energy value of any known food. One gram of fat yields an average of 9.3 calories. A pound yields 4210 calories. In the human body fats may be burned to yield energy for internal activity, for muscular activity, and for body heat. Usually the fat is converted to glucose before being burned, but at times fats are burned directly. Fats may be converted to special fats for specialized tissue needs or may be stored. Stored fats serve as an insulating medium against the loss of body heat.

Some foods containing fats contain substances important in the regulation of body functions.

Proteins. Proteins are organic substances which contain about 16% nitrogen and usually some sulfur. The protein molecule or structural unit is relatively large and complex. Amino acids, the basic units of proteins, can be formed only by plant cells although animal cells can rearrange the amino acids and thus form different proteins. Each molecule of protein may contain several hundred basic units (amino acids) of as many as twenty-two different kinds. The unlimited number, complexity, and diversity of proteins is thus understandable.

Proteins of vegetable origin occur in cereal grains, such as wheat, rye, and corn, and in legumes such as peas and beans. Proteins of animal sources come from milk, cheese, eggs, and the meat of hogs, cattle, sheep, and fowl.

One gram of protein yields an average of 4.1 calories of energy. A pound yields 1860 calories. In the human body proteins may furnish heat energy for the various purposes by being converted to carbohydrates in the liver. The subsequent oxidizing or burning of the carbohydrate yields the energy contained in the protein. This conversion of protein to carbohydrate results in nitrogen wastes (e.g., urea) which are excreted by the kidneys.

As will be pointed out later, in addition to yielding energy, proteins may be used in the building and upkeep of tissues as well as in the formation of certain body regulators.

Digestion and absorption. Digestion and absorption of organic foods are necessary if these substances are to be made available to the cells of the body. With the exception of small amounts of simple carbohydrates appearing in such foods as honey and grapes, carbohydrates, fats, and proteins in the diet cannot be absorbed into the blood or lymph and be utilized by the body cells. By the process of digestion these complex substances are broken down into smaller components and converted to a fluid form.

Digestion is a hydrolytic process by which complex substances are converted to simpler substances by the addition of water. This action is facilitated by the presence of enzymes in the digestive canal. These enzymes are chemical substances in the digestive juices that are produced by the cells of the glands of the digestive system. Enzymes are protein substances. They act by contact and hasten chemical action without being affected themselves. Enzymes do not initiate action. They only accelerate it. The end products of digestion—glucose, amino acids, fatty acids, and glycerol—are absorbed into the blood and lymph streams. Changes which these products undergo from this point on are referred to as metabolism. That is, digestion goes on in the stomach and intestines, technically outside of the body; metabolism goes on inside of the body. The transport system (blood and lymph) convey the digestion products about the body where the cells may use these products for fuel or for building and upkeep. The cells can reconstruct some of the digestion products into constituents of their own pattern.

Digestion and absorption are slow processes. The customary American dinner remains in the stomach from three to seven hours. The entire journey through the digestive system will take from twenty-two to thirty-six hours. While the amount of absorption of the materials in the food will vary, depending on the cellulose present, usually about 92 per cent of proteins will be absorbed into the blood stream, about 95% of fats will be absorbed into the lymph, and about 98% of carbohydrates will be absorbed into the blood stream.

Basal metabolism. Even if the body is at rest, a certain amount of chemical change must always be going on in cells to maintain life itself. The lowest rate of chemical change in the waking state is designated as basal metabolism and is expressed as the basal metabolic rate (B.M.R.). The basal metabolic rate is the rate of energy expenditure of an individual when lying down who is well rested, who has a normal body temperature, and who has ingested no food for about twelve hours so that no digestion or absorption is taking place (post-absorptive state). It is necessary that no absorption of food takes place while the basal metabolic rate is being measured because 6% of the dynamic action of food is utilized in digestion and absorption. Thus any test when digestion and absorption take place would not be a test under basal conditions. Because a direct relationship exists between basal metabolism and oxygen utilization, the basal metabolic rate is measured by recording the length of time required to use one liter of oxygen. It is somewhat like measuring fuel consumption when the motor is idling. To measure the rate, a device is used which permits the subject to breathe only a measured amount of pure oxygen. Blood tests can also be used to measure the basal metabolic rate.

Basal metabolism is determined by the total mass of living substance (protoplasm) and the total stimulation of cellular activity. In consequence height, weight, age, and sex are the important factors to be considered in appraising an individual's rate. Up to 10 years of age the difference in the basal metabolism of boys and girls per unit of weight is negligible. In the teen years the dif-

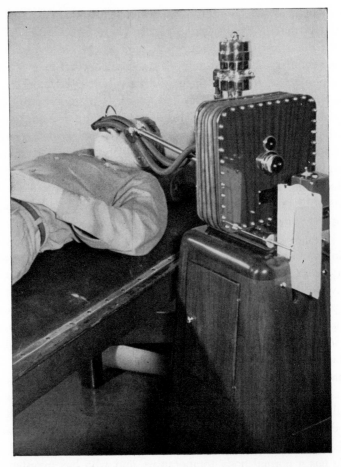

Fig. 29. Basal metabolism test. The machine records the time a person requires to consume a measured liter of pure oxygen. It is a simple yet highly valuable test.

ference is greatest, diminishing until in adulthood the rate is about 6% higher in males.

As a result of measuring the basal metabolic rate of thousands of individuals, standards have been established, based upon height, weight, age, and sex. If a person's utilization of oxygen is precisely the same as the average for his height, weight, age, and sex, he has a B.M.R. of 100. If he uses the oxygen 10% faster than the average for his height, weight, age, and sex, he has a B.M.R. of plus ten. Conversely if his oxygen use is 10% slower than average for his category, he has a B.M.R. of minus ten. The normal range is generally considered to be between plus ten and minus ten.

About 75% of a person's basal metabolic rate is determined by the thyroxin output of the thyroid gland. Other secretions, particularly of anterior pituitary origin, also play a role in determining the rate of chemical change in the tissues. However, studies reveal that the habitual level of food intake can alter the

B.M.R. For example, reducing the caloric intake 10% over several weeks' time may lower basal metabolism by 15%. After 30 years of age, basal metabolic needs for the same body weight decline about 7% every ten years. The individual who continues the same dietary practices and mode of living as he grows older can expect to gain weight.

Weight determination. All the matter which goes to make up an individual's weight has been ingested by the individual. Hence a person's weight is determined by the relationship of his food intake and his food utilization or output. When intake exceeds output, the individual gains weight. When intake and output are equal, weight is maintained. When intake is less than output, there is a resulting loss in weight.

Normally intake is entirely dependent on the food ingested. Output depends upon the basal metabolic rate, plus muscular activity and other activities, such as digestion, which utilize energy. Inherited factors merely operate to govern the capacity for a chemical change, such as thyroxin output, and the disposition of building and upkeep materials.

A college man 20 years of age, weighing 154 pounds and with a B.M.R. of 100, would require about 1680 calories per day for basal needs. If he lives a sedentary existence, he would require another 1000 calories. Moderate activity would require perhaps 1500 calories more. Vigorous activity would require perhaps an additional 2200 calories. Thus, if he is sedentary in habits and consumes over 3000 calories a day, he will gain weight.

Obesity. Obesity is a condition in which excess fat has been stored in the body until body weight is above the normal. About half of a person's fat is subcutaneous. The extent of this layer of fat can be determined by using skin-fold calipers. A simple but fairly good index of obesity consists in grasping the skin on the side of the body just below the ribs between the thumb and index finger. If the thickness of the fold exceeds one inch, a person is obese. Average weight as represented by height, weight, and age tables is of value only as a general guide in determining whether a person is obese. Normal is that which is regarded as the usual and must be considered within a range to allow for differences in general body types. When this criterion for normal is used, studies reveal that 28% of the men and women in the United States are more than 10% overweight. However, there can be a difference between obesity and overweight. A person with firm muscle may be overweight, if the tables on average weight are used as a basis, without being obese. Basically, the important problem is that of obesity.

It must be recognized that some individuals enjoy their best level of health when slightly overweight—perhaps 10% overweight. However, for the best level of health adults generally should establish a weight norm not more than 10% above the average for their sex and stature in the 30- to 35-year age group. This norm should be maintained with little fluctuation for the promotion of a high health level. Uniform weight from year to year is an indication of balanced function of the body and resultant good health. For the normal individual, maintenance of desirable weight over the years is an indication that a proper intake-output caloric balance is being maintained.

As a public health problem obesity has received too little attention; yet it is the most serious nutrition problem in the United States. Obesity over a period of years can have an adverse effect upon the length of life. People markedly overweight (more than 10%) over an extended period of years have a shorter life expectation than those of normal weight. In addition to its effect upon the length of life, obesity is a constant hazard to health.

Obesity has a recognized adverse effect upon heart disorders, kidney disturbances, high blood pressure, arthritis, and varicose veins. People suffering from these disorders merely aggravate the condition by excessive weight. People without organic defects place an added burden on their circulatory and excretory systems by carrying excess fat. The added weight reduces general muscular responsiveness and endurance. To carry a load of thirty pounds would produce fatigue even though it were carried on one's shoulders.

A few misconceptions concerning obesity may be analyzed in the light of scientific knowledge.

"Obesity runs in the family." Only because of common dietary habits (social conditioning) within the family circle will all members of a family tend to be obese. Obesity is not an inherited factor. A tendency toward sluggish function of the thyroid may be inherited, and a hypothyroid individual may become obese from the same diet which maintains average weight in a person with normal thyroid function. Such a person must consume less than the average person if he is to avoid obesity.

"We just grow fatter as we grow older." Properly the weight norm should be established between the ages of 30 and 35 years and be maintained. Dietary practices should be adjusted to the reduced activity of later life.

"Everything I eat turns to fat." Excessive carbohydrate intake will turn to fat. In all instances excessive fat means excessive intake.

"After childbearing a woman becomes obese." More women than men are overweight, but not because of childbearing. A woman needs fewer calories than a man for basal needs and usually fewer calories for muscular activity. Yet she sits down with her husband and eats the same meal and often eats more frequently between regular meals.

"Obesity results from the menopause." The menopause is primarily due to the decline in the function of the ovaries, and the ovaries have no tangible effect on weight. In the male nothing in the functions associated with the climacteric will cause overweight.

"Obesity is due to glands." It is true that the places where fat is deposited in the body is affected by glandular secretions. Thus, when the ankles, lower legs, wrists, and forearms are normal in size, but the thighs, hips, abdominal region, and upper arms are markedly obese, the obesity is classed as pituitary. When the neck and shoulders harbor excessive fat, a thyroid deficiency likely exists. Yet in either case the obesity itself is due simply to the fact that the individual has a higher intake of calories than is burned. Some individuals tend toward obesity more easily than others because of a disturbance in the carbohydrate metabolism. This can be due to a thyroid or pituitary deficiency or other factor which causes carbohydrates to be converted to fats at an abnormally rapid rate. However, even in these individuals the fundamental law of physics holds that the obesity can result only from ingesting more food than is burned.

Obesity is rather insidious in its onset. An individual gradually increases his caloric intake, and the pounds accumulate. The effect is cumulative. As his dietary habits become fixed, he finds it increasingly more difficult to change them. Although hunger is primarily physiological, appetite is primarily psychological, something acquired. In addition many obese people eat as a release from emotional tension. Emotionally this type of overeater may be the prototype of the chain smoker.

Not all excessive eaters are compulsive eaters. Many have a physiological imbalance which accounts for their overeating. The hunger center is located in the thalamus, which is situated near the central portion of the brain. When the blood sugar level gets low, the hunger center is stimulated and the person seeks food. If the individual has an overproduction of insulin (hyperinsulinism), the effect is to reduce the blood sugar level. Such a person may feel hungry in less than two hours after a normal meal. The hunger feeling might be delayed by eating meals high in proteins, which seems to have an effect on retaining the normal blood sugar level and delaying hunger sensations.

The control of body weight is simply a matter of balance between food ingested and food burned in metabolism. The remedy for obesity is to eat less or to burn more food or to do both.

Use of any drug or other stimulant in weight reduction is too dangerous to be undertaken except upon the prescription and supervision of a physician.

Physical activity is the greatest variable on the calorie expenditure side of the ledger in weight control. Contrary to popular belief, the various activities of everyday living do not require great expenditures of energy. This is well illustrated by the values for human energy expenditure obtained through extensive research and reported by Dr. J. V. G. A. Durnin and Dr. R. Passmore, Institute of Physiology, University of Glasgow, in Scotland. The calorie expenditures for various tasks listed in Table 18 are of an adult weighing between 140 and 155 pounds.

From these figures one can calculate the approximate expenditure of energy over a given period of time, such as for a day. Many students are surprised by the small amount of energy they expend during a day. Frequently the energy used in daily physical activity represents far less energy than is utilized in basal metabolism. However, a very active student will burn more fuel in physical activity during the day than will be necessary for basal metabolic needs.

Physical exercise to increase metabolism and thus reduce weight may be ad-

Table 18. Caloric expenditures for various tasks

Activity	Energy cost (calories per minute)	Activity	Energy cost (calories per minute)
Lying at ease	1.4	Walking, 4 mph	5.2
Sitting at ease	1.6	Cyclying, at own pace	6.6
Sitting, writing	1.9	Dancing a rhumba	7.0
Sitting, playing cards	2.4	Gardening, weeding	5.6
Standing at ease	1.8	Gardening, digging	8.6
Standing, drawing	2.3	Gymnastic exercises	
Washing and dressing, man	2.6	Abdominal	3.0
Washing and dressing, woman	3.3	Trunk bending	3.5
Romping with children	3.5	Arms swinging, hopping	6.5
Hand sewing	2.0	Bowling	4.4
Hand washing	3.0	Golf	5.0
Ironing	4.2	Tennis	7.1
Polishing	2.4	Football, soccer	8.9
Peeling potatoes	2.9	Swimming	6.5
Walking, 3 mph	4.0	Back stroke or breast stroke	11.5
		Ski running, moderate speed	10.8

visable for some overweight individuals. However, vigorous activity would be unwise for an obese person with a circulatory or other disorder. Weight reduction through muscular exercise is often both arduous and disappointing. A person weighing 154 pounds, walking over level ground at a customary rate, would have to walk over 30 miles to lose one pound of weight. However, vigorous activities will burn reserve energy at a more rapid rate than will walking. It is important in exercise for reducing that, after a person becomes well warmed up and perspiring, he covers up with blankets for about an hour. The extended perspiration and resulting water balance will have an appreciable weight-reducing effect.

For most obese persons a crash diet is neither necessary nor advisable. The most practical method of weight reduction is to reduce the caloric intake while maintaining the customary routine of physical activity. When the caloric intake is reduced, care should be taken not to sacrifice the natural food values of building and regulating substances. The usual items in reduced portions should be continued in the diet. If eating is a release mechanism, emotional readjustment should complement dietary changes.

A deduction of about 600 calories from the daily diet means that about 400 grams of reserve fat per week will be burned. This will be a loss of one pound of weight—four fifths fat and one fifth water. This rate of weight loss is rapid enough unless the person is under medical supervision.

Fluctuation in weight frequently occurs. Paradoxically a person on a reducing diet may gain weight. On a reduced calorie diet, fat in the tissues is burned. The tissue spaces are filled by water which is heavier than fat. If the person tends to store water, he will gain weight. This persistent water retention may go on for a week or more. When the water balance adjusts, there may be a fairly rapid release of water through the kidneys and a resulting rather rapid loss of weight.

In some individuals, with a loss of about ten pounds in weight the body attains a new equilibrium, and basal metabolic needs become less. These individuals will have to deduct more than the 600 calories from the daily intake if there is to be further weight loss.

A more recent approach to reducing diets has been the virtually complete elimination of fats and most carbohydrates from the diet. These are the low calorie—high protein diets in which grapefruit, eggs, steak, lamb chops, chicken, fish, tomatoes, spinach, lettuce, combination salads, black coffee, and occasional dry toast constitute the essentials. Salt is completely ruled out of the diet. Although the total food mass in the diet will be satisfying, the caloric value will be low, being represented essentially in proteins. The additional energy needs will be drawn from the deposited fat reserves of the body. However, a diet completely free of fat may be harmful if continued for three or four weeks.

Individuals on these diets lose from ten to twenty pounds in two weeks. It is inadvisable to continue this type of diet for more than two weeks. After an interval of a month during which fats and carbohydrates are kept at reduced levels in the diet, the protein diet may be followed safely for another two-week period.

A variety of adequate low-fat high-protein menus can be developed which will

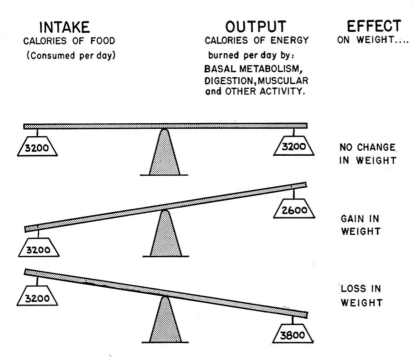

INTAKE
CALORIES OF FOOD
(Consumed per day)

OUTPUT
CALORIES OF ENERGY
burned per day by:
BASAL METABOLISM,
DIGESTION, MUSCULAR
and OTHER ACTIVITY.

EFFECT
ON WEIGHT....

3200 — 3200 NO CHANGE IN WEIGHT

3200 — 2600 GAIN IN WEIGHT

3200 — 3800 LOSS IN WEIGHT

Fig. 30. Relation of energy intake to energy output. A person's body is made up only of those substances which he has ingested. The human machine stores excess fuel and will burn reserve fuel when the present feeding is inadequate.

provide a daily diet of 1600 calories or less. It must be recognized that fats should be avoided for cooking. Eggs should be boiled or poached; meat should be boiled, baked, or grilled.

Breakfast	Lunch	Dinner
½ grapefruit	2 eggs	Steak
2 eggs	Tomato	Tomato
1 slice dry toast	1 slice dry toast	1 slice dry toast
Black coffee or skim milk	Black coffee or skim milk	Black coffee or skim milk
½ cup orange juice	Lettuce and tomato sand-	Ground beef
2 eggs	wich with no butter	Vegetable salad
1 slice dry toast	Slice pineapple	1 slice enriched bread
Black coffee or skim milk	Black coffee or skim milk	2-inch square cake
		Black coffee or skim milk
4 cooked prunes without	Fruit salad	Fish
sugar	2 slices dry toast	Combination salad
2 slices Canadian bacon	Black coffee or skim milk	1 slice dry toast
1 slice dry toast		½ grapefruit
Black coffee or skim milk		Black coffee or skim milk
½ cup tomato juice	Vegetable soup	Chicken
2 small rolls	Egg salad sandwich	Tomato
2 eggs	Black coffee or skim milk	1 slice dry toast
Black coffee or skim milk		½ grapefruit
		Black coffee or skim milk

Snacks can be taken with these representative menus if fats are avoided completely and carbohydrates are consumed sparingly. A slice of toast with a thin layer of jam or jelly and black coffee or skim milk would be acceptable. Many people on a low-calorie diet find that a meal is more satisfying if it is eaten slowly.

Underweight. Underweight is the term used to describe the condition of those individuals who are appreciably below (10% or more) the standard average for their height, age, and sex. These individuals often enjoy passable health. Yet studies reveal that many of them enjoy an even higher level of health with an increase in weight. After gaining weight underweight women who have considered themselves healthy often notice that they are less prone to fatigue and enjoy a more buoyant health.

A moderate amount of body fat is a health asset. Besides serving as reserve fuel, fat in the abdominal cavity serves to support the kidneys and other organs. Fat directly beneath the skin (subcutaneous) conserves body heat and protects skeletal muscles. Maintenance of proper body temperature may be a defense against infectious disease.

Undoubtedly a tendency toward underweight exists. A combination of excessive thyroxin output and poor appetite and eating habits, together with marked physical exertion, combine to produce a tendency toward underweight. Yet if no infectious disease or constitutional abnormality (e.g., overactive thyroid) exists, underweight is basically a nutritional problem although appetite and eating habits must be considered in a program to gain weight.

Stimulation of the appetite may require one half hour of light enjoyable exercise followed by one half hour's rest just before mealtime. Even moderate fatigue should be avoided. Smoking before meals should be stopped. Special efforts should be made to make food attractive. Foods high in caloric value without sacrificing natural nutritional values should be served. Supplementary midmorning, midafternoon, and evening lunches often prove advantageous. One half hour's rest after each meal can be helpful.

For some individuals, gaining weight is a tedious, difficult, and even discouraging task. Gain in weight is usually slow, which is desirable since the entire body adjusts easily to slight changes in attaining an equilibrium between body functions.

Calorie values. The customary foods in the American diet vary so greatly in energy value that a list of the calorie values of representative food portions is helpful in nutritional practice. Although carbohydrates and proteins have the

Table 19. Calorie values of typical food portions

Food material	Weight in grams	Portion	Calories
Almonds (shelled)	15	12	100
Apple (baked)	165	1 large	200
Apple pie	160	4½″ section	300
Apple sauce	125	½ cup	130
Apple (fresh)	125	1 medium	80
Apricots (canned)	100	3 halves, 1½ tbs. juice	80
Bacon (broiled)	15	5 small slices	100
Banana	100	1 medium	100
Beans (baked)	100	½ cup	130
Beans (string, canned)	120	½ cup	40
Beef (lean)	100	¾″ × 2½″ × 2⅛″	150
Bread (rye)	30	1 slice	70
Bread (white)	20	1 slice	50
Butter	12	1 tbs.	100
Buttermilk	240	1 cup	90
Cabbage (new, green)	65	¾ cup	20
Cake (plain)	100	1″ × 4⅛″ × 5″	440
Cake (chocolate)	100	2½″ × 2½″ × 4″	400
Cantaloupe	180	½ melon (5″ dia.)	50
Carrots (fresh)	75	½ cup	30
Carrots (canned)	130	½ cup	35
Cauliflower	100	⅔ cup	30
Celery	35	1 stalk (5″)	7
Cheese (American)	25	1 cube (1⅜″)	100
Cheese (cottage)	100	6 tbs.	110
Cherries (fresh, pitted)	130	20 (⅞″ dia.)	100
Cherries (canned)	110	7, 3 tbs. juice	100
Chicken (broiled)	100	½ medium broiler	100
Cocoa (powder)	8	1 tbs.	40

Continued on next page.

Table 19. Calorie value of typical food portions—cont'd

Food material	Weight in grams	Portion	Calories
Coconut custard pie	230	4½″ section	475
Corn (canned)	125	½ cup	130
Cornflakes	25	¾ cup	100
Cracker (graham)	10	1	40
Cracker (soda)	6	1 (2″ × 2″)	25
Cream (18.5%)	50	¼ cup	100
Egg	50	1 (medium)	75
Fish (fried)	100	¾″ × 2½″ × 3¾″	200
Frankfurt sausage	40	1	100
Fudge, chocolate	25	¾″ × 1″ × 1½″	100
Ginger ale	235	1 cup	75
Grapefruit	200	½ (4″ dia.)	100
Grapefruit	100	1½ cup pieces	50
Grapefruit juice (unsweetened)	240	1 cup	100
Grape juice	100	½ cup	75
Ham (broiled)	50	⅛″ × 5″ × 5″	100
Hamburger steak	100	1 and gravy	160
Ice cream (vanilla)	100	½ cup	220
Jelly (fruit)	20	1 tbs.	60
Lamb	50	⅛″ × 3⅛″ × 4½″	100
Lettuce	60	1/5 large head	10
Liver (veal, fried)	100	⅜″ × 3″ × 5″	250
Macaroni (cooked)	160	¾ cup	100
Maple syrup	35	1½ tbs.	100
Mayonnaise dressing	15	1 tbs.	100
Milk (malted)	10	1 tbs.	35
Milk (whole)	250	1 cup	170
Mutton	35	⅛″ × 3″ × 4″	100
Oats (rolled, cooked)	135	¾ cup	100
Oleomargarine	12	1 tbs.	100
Orange juice	185	¾ cup	100
Orange	150	1 medium	80
Peach (canned)	210	2 large halves, 3 tbs. juice	100
Peach (fresh)	100	1 medium	50
Peanut butter	18	1 tbs.	100
Pear (canned)	100	2 halves, 2 tbs. juice	75
Pear (fresh)	100	1 large	65
Pea soup (cream of)	100	½ cup	65
Peas (canned)	150	½ cup	100
Peas (fresh)	100	¾ cup	100
Pineapple (canned)	50	1 slice, 2 tbs. juice	60
Pineapple juice (canned)	150	⅔ cup	100
Pork chop (lean)	55	1 broiled	200
Pork roast	60	¼″ × 2½″ × 3″	100
Potatoes (french fried)	120	11 pieces, ½″ × ½″ × 4½″	300
Potato (sweet)	160	1 medium	200
Potato (white, baked)	80	1 medium	100
Prunes (dried)	35	4 medium	100
Prunes (canned)	130	½ cup	130
Pumpkin pie	230	4½″ section	370
Rice (cooked)	100	½ cup	90

Table 19. Calorie value of typical food portions—cont'd

Food material	Weight in grams	Portion	Calories
Rolls (cinnamon)	30	1½″ × 2½″ × 2¾″	100
Salmon (fresh steamed)	50	¾″ × 2″ × 3″	100
Salmon (red, canned)	75	⅝ cup	100
Spinach	100	½ cup	20
Squash (Hubbard)	100	½ cup	45
Strawberries	100	½ cup	40
Sugar (granulated)	12	1 tbs.	50
Sundae (with chocolate sauce)	150	½ cup, 3 tbs. sauce	335
Tapioca (uncooked)	28	2 tbs.	100
Tomato catsup	30	2 tbs.	35
Tomato juice (canned)	200	1 cup	55
Tomato soup (cream of)	100	½ cup	110
Tomatoes (canned)	100	⅜ cup	20
Tomatoes (fresh)	100	1 (2½″ dia.)	20
Turkey	50	¼″ × 2½″ × 4″	100
Veal (lean)	80	¼″ × 3″ × 4″	100
Vegetable soup	130	½ cup	55
Wheat (shredded)	28	1 biscuit	100

same average calorie value, fat and water content usually accounts for the marked differences in the energy value of various foods. A tablespoon of butter will have a high calorie value because of its high fat content. A head of lettuce will have a low calorie value largely because of its high water content.

BUILDING AND UPKEEP NEEDS

The living material in human cells is changing constantly. As the cell carries on its processes, materials are being broken down and used up, requiring both building and replacement. The substance essential in the protoplasm of the cell and necessary for the maintenance of the cell is protein.

Water is the most abundant substance in a cell. Other than water, the chief constituent of cells is protein. Without proteins there would be no life. They constitute the structural units of the cell as well as its functioning substances, such as hormones from glands and enzymes. Both the building and upkeep of the cells, hence of life itself, depend upon a supply of proteins for the cells.

Amino acids. As we have seen, proteins are composed of a variety of amino acids in many different combinations. Each plant tissue and each animal tissue has its own specific proteins, the differences being essentially in the content of amino acid. In digestion complex protein molecules are broken down into their simpler constituent amino acids, all chemically different. Scientists have identified twenty-two of them. From the amino acids made available to it, the body forms its proteins. Some of these building blocks the body itself can synthesize (put together), but there are eight amino acids the human body is incapable of

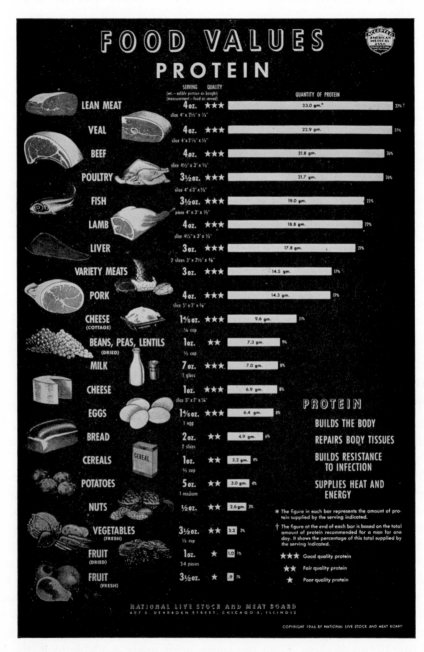

Fig. 31. Protein value of selected foods. Adequacy and variety of proteins are as important in the diet as adequacy and variety of vitamins. (Courtesy National Live Stock and Meat Board.)

synthesizing. Since these amino acids are essential to the body and since the body itself cannot produce them, foods containing these amino acids are termed indispensable or complete proteins. Generally speaking, proteins of animal origin (milk, eggs, beef, pork, mutton, fowl, and fish) contain the essential amino acids and are considered to have high biological value. Proteins of cereals and the seeds of legumes (soybeans excepted) lack the essential amino acids and are classed as incomplete proteins. However, incomplete proteins have a place in the diet in that they supplement the complete proteins. Various studies indicate the advisability of using proteins from both animal and vegetable sources in the diet. If both kinds of proteins are eaten, the mixture derived from the two sources will likely provide the necessary proteins for growth and body upkeep.

It must be recognized that if enough calories from nonprotein sources are not present in the diet, proteins will be used for their energy and thus will not be available for the building of body proteins.

For optimum normal nutritional needs, 1 gram of protein per day per kilogram of weight is usually the recommended standard although a healthy adult doubtless needs only one half of that amount. During old age an individual requires even less than one half of the usual standard. Recommended standards for infants and young children are between 3 and 4 grams per kilogram of body weight daily, which no doubt is in excess of actual needs. During the youth period an increased need for proteins as well as other nutrients indicates the necessity for consuming high quantities of meat, eggs, milk, and other foods rich in proteins. Expectant and nursing mothers are advised to follow diets with twice the normal protein content.

In practice, proteins from a variety of sources would likely supply all of the amino acids essential to the life and proper function of all body cells. Foods high in protein content usually supply other nutrients. Protein-deficient diets are usually deficient in other respects.

Effects of protein deficiency are not easily detected. Muscular weakness, retarded growth, undue fatigue, and depression are early but not easily detected symptoms. This level of deficiency is not disturbing enough to send a person to a physician's office. Only when the bloating or swelling symptomatic of extreme protein deficiency is reached will medical aid be sought. Extreme protein deficiency is rare in the United States although a minor level of deficiency is quite prevalent in some groups.

REGULATION NEEDS

General observation and scientific research have revealed that foods which yield energy and foods which provide materials for building and upkeep are not sufficient for human nutritional needs. Also necessary are certain food substances which have a regulating effect on the cells in the various parts of the body. Many different regulating substances found in natural foods, each with a unique chemical makeup, perform special functions in a variety of ways. These chemical substances stimulate cells, tissues, and organs. They facilitate the complex chemical changes which constitute life processes. They are essential to a high level of health. Deficiencies result in recognized diseases.

Vitamins. Certain organic substances present in natural foods which are essential to the maintenance of the tissues and the regulation of normal functions of the body are classed as vitamins. Chemically these substances have no particular relationship to one another, but they have many functional similarities. In general, vitamins are needed in very small amounts. They are related to the function of most, perhaps all, of the cells of the body. Vitamins are important not only to health, but also to life itself. Generally, excessive amounts beyond optimum needs are not harmful.

Normal healthy individuals should obtain their vitamins from the natural foods in their everyday diet. Drugstore vitamins should be taken under medical supervision for special needs. For example, pregnancy, infancy, or known deficiency of a vitamin requires the administration of supplementary vitamins. As vitamin deficiency is overcome, the natural foods should be relied upon as the vitamin source.

Deficiencies cause specific destructive diseases. The deficiency actually is the disease. Vitamin deficiencies may occur in various degrees. In minor forms symptoms are difficult to recognize, and the results of treatment are hard to determine. Frequently vitamin deficiency will produce no observable specific symptoms, but may have an adverse effect upon general health and efficiency. Most deficiency cases in the United States are of the borderline variety. Unrecognized mild deficiencies can have cumulative effects and terminate in ill-defined poor health. An actual disease due to a lack of vitamins is referred to as a deficiency disease or avitaminosis.

Some of the known vitamins are still of merely research and academic interest. Only those which are apt to be deficient in the American diet are of importance for purposes here, and only these will be discussed. Further, in keeping with current practice, the descriptive chemical names of vitamins will be given primary emphasis.

Carotene. Carotene is the forerunner or provitamin form of what is commonly called vitamin A. The carotene form of the vitamin is present in fruit and vegetables, whereas the complete vitamin is found in animal tissues. Evidence indicates that carotene is converted into the vitamin in the liver of the human being. People with liver disorders show evidence of inadequate conversion.

Vitamin A is soluble (capable of being dissolved) in fat but normally not in water. It is not easily destroyed by boiling but oxidizes easily. In consequence foods containing this vitamin should be kept covered and should be stored in a cool dark place. In frozen food the vitamin is preserved, but defrosting results in extreme reduction in vitamin content. Drying (dehydration) reduces the vitamin A content of foods.

Because of its special importance to covering tissues, vitamin A is frequently described accurately as the epithelium-protective vitamin. It also is referred to as the anti-infection vitamin, which is a misnomer because it is not anti-infectious. Its function in promoting the activity of epithelium cells merely enables the lining tissues to expel invading microorganisms. Vitamin A is also known as the anti-xerophthalmia vitamin because it is specific for the prevention of xerophthalmia. This is a disease characterized by an inflammation of the eyelids, with an abnormally dry and lusterless condition of the eyeballs.

Vitamin A is essential to the healthful function of the eyes, skin, kidneys, respiratory tract, and digestive tract. It stimulates vigor and general health and contributes to the health of the nervous system. It also affects tooth development.

Excellent sources of carotene or vitamin A include fish liver oils, liver, egg yolk, butter, cheese, spinach, parsley, chard and kale, green beans and peas, sweet potatoes, yellow squash, yellow corn, corn meal, and carrots. Good sources include cream, whole milk, red salmon, asparagus, green lettuce, tomatoes, pineapple, oranges, and bananas. Commercial concentrates are derived from pure carotene and from cod, shark, salmon, and halibut liver oils.

A deficiency of this vitamin lowers the function of the respiratory tract. The effect on the digestive tract may result in diarrhea. Dry rough skin and dryness and roughness of the hair can result from vitamin A deficiency. Reduced twilight vision occurs when the intake of vitamin A is inadequate. A lack of vigor and retardation of growth may also occur.

Thiamine. Thiamine (vitamin B_1) is highly soluble in water and is somewhat destroyed by moist heat and by alkalis such as soda. If most of this vitamin is to be saved, vegetables should be cooked in a small amount of water in as short a time as possible and without soda. Water in which the vegetables are cooked can be used to advantage in gravies and soups. Drying has little effect on thiamine.

Thiamine is essential to the function of the nervous system. It is stimulating to the appetite and is important for the normal condition of the muscles of the digestive system. Thiamine is essential for complete carbohydrate metabolism. Alcohol addicts are particularly prone to severe thiamine deficiencies.

Excellent sources of thiamine include liver, kidney, heart, chicken, lean pork, egg yolk, whole grains, germ of grains, brown rice, wheat, oats, navy beans, dried peas, fresh beans, fresh peas, milk, oranges, prunes, pineapple, pears, and nuts. Good sources are spinach, cauliflower, turnips, bananas, cabbage, onions, lettuce, beets, and potatoes. Commercial concentrates are derived from rice polishings, brewer's yeast, and wheat germ.

A deficiency of thiamine results in an inflammation of nerves (polyneuritis). The painful paralytic form is diagnosed as beriberi. Coordination sometimes is affected, and nervousness may appear when a moderate deficiency exists.

Ascorbic acid. Ascorbic acid (vitamin C) is soluble in water. Hence, cooking vegetables in large quantities of water reduces their vitamin content. Drying, storage, and exposure to air destroy the vitamin. Thus highest ascorbic acid value is obtained when the fruit or vegetable is freshly harvested, eaten raw, or prepared with a minimum of exposure to air and heat. An alkali such as soda neutralizes ascorbic acid. Vitamin C is stored in the body for extremely short periods and thus should be in the diet daily.

Ascorbic acid is essential to healthy blood vessels, particularly the capillaries. Its role in maintaining the cement substances between cells is important in maintaining firmness of tissues such as gum tissue. Ascorbic acid is important in calcium metabolism, thus important in bone formation, as well as in the functioning of the blood-forming cells in bone marrow. Tooth development and formation are dependent upon this vitamin.

Excellent sources of ascorbic acid must be led by oranges, grapefruit, lemons, and tomatoes. Vitamin C in milligrams per 100 grams of edible fruit is approximately 55 for oranges, 40 for grapefruit, and 25 for tomatoes. Although citrus fruits are excellent sources of ascorbic acid, other sources of vitamin C should be included in the diet. Evidence indicates that excessive use of citrus fruits predisposes to dental caries because of the acid state the ascorbic acid produces in the mouth. Other excellent sources of ascorbic acid include strawberries, cantaloupe, raw cabbage, green peppers, green peas, raw turnips, and asparagus. Good sources are apples, peaches, bananas, cherries, pineapple, raspberries, cauliflower, and raw carrots. Commercial concentrates are derived from purified ascorbic acid from lemon or orange juice.

A deficiency of ascorbic acid results in fragile capillaries, with a tendency toward undue hemorrhaging, soft gums, and loose teeth. Improper formation of both bones and teeth may occur. Anemia due to disturbances of bone marrow may also be present. In extreme deficiency scurvy may exist and is characterized by generalized tenderness and irritability, chronic pain in the extremities, spongy gums, hemorrhaging in the skin and mucous lining, lack of appetite with weight loss, diarrhea, and vomiting. In the United States scurvy exists although the incidence is low. However, mild and moderate vitamin C deficiency is surprisingly prevalent. An extreme oversupply of vitamin C can be harmful.

Calciferol. Calciferol (vitamin D) is fat soluble, is stable to heat and oxidation, and is formed by the action of ultraviolet radiation on fatlike sterols. Since at least ten different precursor sterols exist, several different forms of vitamin D are indicated. D_2 and D_3 are of greatest importance to health, but other forms of vitamin D are also effective. Calciferol (D_3) is produced in the human body itself by the action of ultraviolet rays on cutaneous sterols.

Calciferol is necessary for the absorption and utilization of calcium and phosphorus. Thus it is of extreme importance in bone formation and growth. It is of special importance to growing children and to expectant mothers.

Excellent sources of calciferol are fish liver oils, irradiated foods (e.g., milk), and liver. Good sources are egg yolk, salmon, sardines, butter (if cow is on green feed), and vegetable greens. Concentrates are obtained from irradiated fish liver oils. In the temperate zone, sunlight is not consistently potent enough to be relied upon for a high production of calciferol. Dietary sources of vitamin D may be sufficient for normal adults, but not for expectant mothers and children. For these individuals it is advisable that the diet be supplemented by commercial concentrates. Since pharmaceutical sources vary in form and potency, the form and amount of the vitamin administered to a child or expectant mother should be prescribed by a physician. Although still a matter of dispute, there is some evidence that an extreme oversupply of calciferol can be harmful.

A deficiency of calciferol results in rickets (rachitis), a condition of retardation of the normal calcification of developing bones. Severe rickets, although not fatal, may indirectly affect the individual's lifelong health. Some of the symptoms are curved bones (tibia and fibula) of the lower leg, large head, protruding forehead, pigeon chest, depressed ribs, curved upper arm and upper leg bones, protruding abdomen, and depressed tip of the breast bone (sternum). The most reliable sign of rickets, however mild, is the depressed tip of the sternum. When this significant index is used as an indication of rickets, public health surveys reveal that there is still a high incidence of rickets in minor form in the United States.

Niacin. Niacin (P.P. factor) formerly was referred to as nicotinic acid. It is a water-soluble, heat-stable vitamin which contributes to the health of the skin, digestive system, nervous system, and mental state. It is important to enzymes which function in tissue oxidation.

Excellent sources of niacin include liver, lean meat, salmon, heart, kidney, wheat germ, dried whey, and yeast. Good sources are eggs, kale, collards, green peas, potatoes, tomatoes, milk, and haddock.

A deficiency of niacin may result in inflammation of the skin (dermatitis), soreness of the mouth, excess salivation, diarrhea, nervous disorders, and mental disturbance (dementia). The extreme condition is known as pellagra, a disease which can be fatal and which is characterized by skin inflammation, diarrhea, and mental disturbance. Sunlight aggravates the inflamed areas, which are usually on the exposed surfaces of the body. Nausea, vomiting, and diarrhea indicate extreme disturbance of the digestive tract. Depression, confusion, and delirium indicate severe mental disturbance.

Riboflavin. Riboflavin (vitamin B_2 or G) is water soluble, is stable to heat and oxidation, and is sensitive to light.

Riboflavin is essential to the growth of the young and the health of people at all ages. Its presence as a part of several enzyme systems in animal tissues indicates its value in the metabolism of amino acids and carbohydrates.

Excellent sources of riboflavin include liver, eggs, pork, beef, wheat germ, kale, broccoli, spinach, cheese, soybeans, strawberries, and dried prunes. Good sources are milk, bacon, chicken, fish, asparagus, corn, lettuce, tomatoes, carrots, apricots, figs, grapefruit, raisins, and oranges. Concentrates are derived from yeast and whey.

The effect of a deficiency of riboflavin is difficult to appraise because riboflavin deficiency generally occurs along with other vitamin B deficiencies and affects many types of tissues. However, present evidence indicates riboflavin deficiency can cause general weakness, lack of vigor, digestive disturbances, loss of weight.

nervousness, roughness of the skin, soreness of the mouth, and disturbances of the eyes. Investigators report that mild to moderate vitamin B_2 deficiency is quite common in all age groups in the United States.

Minerals. A second group of regulating substances consists of the numerous minerals which are constituents of the human body. These elements are supplied to the body chiefly by the mineral salts or ash constituents combined with or mixed with carbohydrates, fats, and proteins in foods as they naturally exist. These mineral elements constitute the ash left after the combustible part of the food is burned up. Certain foods, such as pork, beef, fish, poultry eggs, and cereals, leave an acid ash composed of the minerals, sulfur, phosphorus, and chlorine. Milk, fruit, and vegetables leave an alkaline ash composed of sodium, calcium, potassium, and magnesium. Minerals also exist in natural foods as free mineral salts in combination with some of the organic foods.

Minerals serve as building materials for the bones and teeth, for the skin, hair, and nails, for muscles, for nerves, for blood, and for glandular secretions. As regulators they maintain the oxidation processes, the exchange of body fluids, the neutral state of the body, the clotting of blood, the irritability of nerves, and the contractibility of muscles.

Some minerals are needed in larger amounts than are others, but it would be incorrect to say that one mineral is more important than others. All are essential to life. However, from the standpoint of dietary needs, only four are important—calcium, phosphorus, iron, and iodine.

Calcium. Calcium serves as the principal building material of bone. During the period of growth calcium requirements are relatively great. The body stores surplus calcium in the interwoven framework of the ends of long bones. When a shortage of calcium occurs in the soft tissues, stored calcium in the bones is converted to a form in which it can be transported about the body. This ability to utilize reserve calcium explains why the calcium level of body fluids remains normal even after prolonged periods of inadequate calcium intake. Although calcium is an important constituent of tooth structure, calcium is not stored and then extracted from teeth.

Calcium is normally indispensable for the clotting of blood. It is essential for the responsiveness of nerves and the contraction of muscles, including the rhythmic contractions of the heart. Membrane function is regulated by calcium.

Milk is the most important source of calcium. One quart supplies the daily calcium requirement for most children, and a pint and one half furnishes the daily requirements for an adult. Other good sources of calcium are cheese (cheddar and cottage), eggs, broccoli, kale, lettuce, wheat, and oatmeal.

For its proper utilization calcium requires phosphorus, ascorbic acid, and calciferol. Thus, calcium deficiencies are usually associated with other nutritional deficiencies. It also must be recognized that an inability of the body to utilize calcium may result in a calcium deficiency even though the diet is adeqaute in calcium content.

Extreme calcium deficiency in childhood may result in stunted growth, rickets, soft bones, and malformed teeth. In adults severe calcium deficiency may manifest itself as softening of bones (osteomalacia) and as painful spasms or tremors of the muscles (tetany). Mild calcium deficiency may result in slow clotting of the blood and reduced muscular contractibility and nerve responsiveness. With general reduction in tissue oxidation, the general health level is below normal.

Phosphorus. Phosphorus is an essential substance in every cell and tissue in the human body. Almost 90% of the phosphorus in the body is found in the bones. Body fluids and other tissues contain smaller but equally important amounts of phosphorus. Like protein, phosphorus is indispensible to cell life.

Phosphorus functions in the formation of bones and teeth. It is essential in carbohydrate metabolism and in maintaining the neutrality of the blood.

Phosphorus is more plentiful than calcium in the usual items of food. A diet that supplies protein and calcium usually will be adequate in phosphorus. Cheese (American and cottage), lean meat, eggs, whole-grain bread, cereals, dried beans, nuts, dried apricots, and prunes are dependable sources.

A deficiency of phosphorus in youth adversely affects growth and causes soft structure of bones. Teeth become malformed. A lack of vigor and endurance is usually associated with phosphorus deficiency.

Iron. Iron is usually ingested in organic form although copper and vitamin B enable the body to utilize ingested inorganic iron. Total iron content of the body is small; yet the nucleus of every cell contains some of the mineral. In red corpuscles iron is a constituent of the pigment which combines with protein to form hemoglobin, the principal oxygen-carrying substance of the blood. Thus the formation and function of red corpuscles are dependent upon iron.

Human red corpuscles have a life span between 100 and 120 days. About ten million are formed and about ten million disintegrate each second. Thus, hemoglobin is being formed and iron utilized continually. However, the body recovers most of the iron as the corpuscles disintegrate in the liver and spleen. Iron in the body is used again and again.

At birth a child has enough iron stored to take care of about six months' needs. If the infant's diet is deficient in iron, at about 7 months of age the child will suffer from iron deficiency. Pregnant and nursing women as well as infants and children require considerably more iron than men. A woman normally requires about four times as much iron as a man.

Sources of iron include liver, lean beef, egg yolk, molasses, whole-wheat bread, oatmeal, shredded wheat, dried beans, spinach, kale, dried apricots, prunes, and raisins. Milk is a poor source of iron.

A deficiency of iron causes a deficiency in red corpuscles and in the hemoglobin content of the blood, a condition known as anemia. Not all anemias are nutritional. Several types of anemia are recognized. Even in nutritional anemia the protein, copper, and B-complex contents of the diet as well as the iron factor are important. The inability of the body to utilize iron is a factor in the occurrence of nutritional anemia.

Iodine. Iodine is an important element in the production of thyroxin by the thyroid gland. Circulating through the body, thyroxin regulates the rate of chemical change in the body. Iodine is stored in the thyroid and in other tissues so that a daily supply of this element is not necessary in the diet.

Sea foods serve as the best source of iodine. Halibut, salmon, tuna, sardines, shrimp, clams, and lobsters are excellent sources. In regions where the soil has a moderate iodine content, milk, butter, vegetables, grains, and fresh fruit are acceptable sources. The addition of small amounts of iodine salts in city water supplies and the use of table salt with potassium iodide added are measures taken in areas of iodine-poor soil.

A deficiency of iodine may result in a reduced production of thyroxin, which causes a reduced rate of metabolism. Lowered vitality, mental sluggishness, and an increase in body weight usually occur. When the thyroid functions under difficulty because of insufficient iodine, the gland may enlarge and result in a condition known as simple goiter. Iodine therapy may be an effective method of treatment.

Not all goiter conditions nor all thyroid disorders are due to an iodine deficiency in the diet.

Water. Water constitutes about two-thirds of man's weight. Man is truly an aquatic being. All of his processes take place in water. It is a constituent of all tissues and thus is tissue-building material.

Chemical reactions in the body do not take place unless the reacting substances are in a dissolved state. The role of water in dissolving the cellular substances of life processes is an indispensable one. Water also keeps substances in solution in circulating fluids, in secretions, and in excretions.

Regulation of body temperature is dependent upon water. It carries heat in the body. Its evaporation accelerates heat elimination.

The body's daily loss of two to three quarts of water must be replaced. Water produced by metabolic processes in the body furnishes only a small part of the replacement. Fluids in the diet supplemented by water in solid foods represent the major source of water.

Foods generally regarded as solid contain considerable water, ranging from about 5% to 90%. Bread is about 30% water, and an apple is 85% water. Watermelons and cucumbers are over 90% water. Thus, a person whose diet includes considerable fruit and vegetables will need very little water in the form of beverages or other fluids.

Normally the physiological mechanism of thirst appears to serve as an index of water needs. Adults will consume water to relieve the discomfort of thirst. Children may disregard thirst sensations if fluid is not available. However, under normal conditions, it is doubtful that any harmful effects result. Likewise, within reasonable limits an excess of water intake is not harmful. It may well be beneficial.

Fluids drunk before or with a meal may dilute the acid of the stomach, which may delay digestion. Water helps convert food to a semiliquid state and thus tends to hasten the passage of food from the stomach to the intestine. For most individuals fluids with the meal increase the total food intake. Dry meals tend to be small meals. The use of fluids or no fluids with the meal is largely a social custom or habit. From the health standpoint, there is little scientific basis for or against the practice. Iced beverages may inhibit the function of gastric glands (stomach) and thus retard digestion. However, digestion will go on after the slight delay, and no evidence exists that health is injured. Until better evidence is advanced, fluids with meals will continue to be a matter of table discussion rather than of health importance.

DAILY DIETARY NEEDS

In practice the normal individual is too busy and not sufficiently interested to follow an extensive complicated table translating food requirements into food

Fig. 32. Pathway to an adequate diet. A varied diet which includes these four food groups is based upon established principles of nutrition. (Courtesy American Institute of Baking.)

shares. The individual with a tendency toward obesity may be sufficiently interested in his caloric intake to exhibit an interest in a table of caloric values of
common foods. However, along with his associates he is not sufficiently interested
in the qualitative aspects of his diet to make consistent use of vitamin and mineral
tables.

Although precise detailed tables of food values have been used little by the
general public, the popular dictum, "Eat a varied diet," likewise has been of little
value. A varied diet means many things to many people—not always a balanced
diet.

Several practical plans have been developed to simplify the selection of a
balanced diet. Two which have been adopted widely and have been found to
be highly satisfactory are the Right Food List and the Four Broad Food
Groups.

Right food list. The first plan, the Right Food List, is issued by the Bureau
of Home Economics, U. S. Department of Agriculture, in cooperation with other
federal agencies. In this plan, a person includes the following foods in his meals
every day:

> Milk—for the growing child, ¾ to 1 quart
>> for the expectant or nursing mother, 1 quart
>> for other members of the family, 1 pint or more
> Leafy, green, or yellow vegetables—1 or more servings
> Tomatoes, oranges, grapefruit (any raw fruit or vegetable rich in vitamin C)—1 or more
>> servings
> Potatoes, other vegetables, or fruit—2 or more servings
> Eggs—1 (at least 3 or 4 a week)
> Lean meat, poultry, fish—1 or more servings
> Cereals and bread—at least 2 servings of whole-grain products
> Fats
> Sweets
> Water

Four broad food groups. The second plan, the Four Broad Food Groups,
has been developed by the Bureau of Home Economics, U. S. Department of
Agriculture, to simplify the task of selecting a balanced diet.

> I. Milk group
>> Foods
>>> Milk—fluid whole, skim, evaporated, dry, or buttermilk; part or all of milk may
>>>> be derived from sources other than fluid whole milk
>>> Cheese—cottage, cream, or cheddar type
>>> Ice cream—cheese and ice cream may be replaced by part of milk, amount being
>>>> based on equivalent calcium content
>> Amounts recommended
>>> Daily whole fluid milk (8 ounce portions)
>>>> Children—3 to 4 portions
>>>> Teenagers—4 or more
>>>> Adults—2 or more
>>>> Pregnant women—4 or more
>>>> Nursing mothers—6 or more

Fig. 33. Four broad food groups. This is the foundation for a good diet. Use more of these and other foods as needed for growth, for activity, and for desirable weight. The nutritional statements made in this illustration have been reviewed by the Council on Foods and Nutrition of the American Medical Association and were found consistent with current authoritative medical opinion. (Courtesy National Dairy Council, Chicago.)

II. Meat group
Foods
> Beef, veal, pork, lamb, mutton, liver, heart, kidney, and other variety of meats
> Poultry and eggs
> Fish and shellfish
> Alternates—dry peas, dry beans, lentils, nuts, or peanut butter

Amounts recommended
> Two or more servings daily (standard servings)
>> 3 ounces lean cooked meat, no bone
>> 3 ounces poultry or fish, no bone
>> 2 eggs
>> 1 cup cooked dry beans, dry peas, or lentils
>> 4 tablespoons peanut butter

III. Vegetable-fruit group

Foods

All fruits and vegetables, especially orange, grapefruit, tangerine, cantaloup, honeydew mellon, watermellon, raw strawberries, apricots, tomatoes, asparagus tips, broccoli, Brussels sprouts, raw cabbage, carrots, chard, collards, cress, kale, pumpkin, spinach, sweet potatoes, dark greens, and winter squash

Amounts recommended

Four or more servings daily (standard servings)

½ cup of fruit or vegetables

1 medium apple

1 banana, orange, or potato

½ grapefruit or cantaloup

IV. Bread-cereal group

Foods

All breads and cereals that are whole grained, enriched, or restored, especially breads, cooked cereals, ready-to-eat cereals, corn meal, crackers, grits, macaroni, spaghetti, noodles, rice, rolled oats, and flour

Amounts recommended

Four or more servings daily (standard servings)

1 slice bread

1 ounce ready-to-eat cereal

½ to ¾ cup cooked cereal, corn meal, grits, macaroni, noodles, rice or spaghetti

A balanced diet does not imply an unpalatable and nonsatisfying diet. A person following a nutritionally adequate diet can include his favorite items and need not include a particular food which he dislikes. The primary objective of a properly balanced diet is to include from each group some of those foods necessary to the qualitative and quantitative requirements for good health. For normal individuals natural foods contain the necessary constituents for good health. Infants, growing children, and expectant and nursing mothers require dietary supplements of calciferol and thiamine. In some areas supplemental iodine may be indicated. People with a known vitamin deficiency will be administered concentrated forms of vitamins by their physician. Except for physicians' prescriptions for persons with diagnosed nutritional deficiency, drug store vitamins are neither necessary nor advisable for nutritional needs.

PROMOTION OF THE HEALTH OF DIGESTION

It is recognized that the first requisites of effective digestion is an inherited endowment that provides a digestive system with a potentially high level of efficient function. Yet the extent to which a person realizes that potential depends upon his dietary practices. Not only the present quality of digestion, but also life span of good digestion in the later years of life, is the consequence of good health practices during the early years. Usually a disturbed digestive system in the later years of life is the consequence of poor health practices during the interval between the ages of 20 and 40 years.

It is often difficult to offer precise scientific evidence in support of practices which will promote the best health of the digestive system. Yet there are certain basic practices of health promotion for which there is sufficient evidence to make them highly acceptable as a guide to health. In a field in which so many fads exist, the logical course is to be guided by a few well-supported health practices rather than to attempt to include those of doubtful value.

Balance in the dietary. Proper nutrition and the health of the digestive system are complementary. A balanced diet provides the vitamins and minerals necessary for the effective function of the tissues of the digestive system.

Proper emotional state. Negative emotions, such as anxiety and depression, result in a shift of the blood mass away from the organs of digestion. A retardation in digestive processes occurs although digestion is not suspended totally. An occasional disturbance due to an emotional upset has little effect of a permanent nature. However, continual tension resulting in chronic disturbance of digestion has a harmful effect on the delicate tissues of the digestive tract. Pleasant emotional states, free from tension, permit the digestive system to carry out its functions efficiently and with an ease that conserves the tissues of the entire tract. Appetizing food and pleasant surroundings at mealtime are also helpful in promoting the health of digestion.

Regularity. In dietary habits regularity is highly favorable to good digestion. Eating at the same hour each day is beneficial to health. However, the practice of three meals a day is an adjustment to our workday and not a principle of hygiene. There is no scientific evidence that three meals a day is hygienically the ideal. Many authorities hold that eating oftener but eating less each time promotes the highest level of health. This is particularly true for older people whose digestive processes are not highly responsive to digestive demands. Since the output of digestive secretions of older people is somewhat low, smaller meals which permit the digestive processes to function most of the waking day appear to be the best practice. Five meals a day may be ideal. No evidence exists that the normal stomach needs periods of rest during the day.

The practice of some college students of omitting breakfast is questionable from the health standpoint. Meals should be taken regularly, but, if one is to be missed, it should be the noonday meal rather than breakfast. If breakfast is missed, it means an interval of perhaps eighteen hours from dinner of one day to lunch of the next. The interval from dinner to breakfast would be about thirteen hours. Regularity in dietary practices is essential to vigorous and effective living.

Moderation. It has been pointed out that nutritionally a moderate meal is sufficient for all nutritional requirements. A moderate meal furthermore does not place an undue burden upon the process of digestion. An established habit of overeating may have little harmful effect on those few individuals who are endowed with exceptionally efficient digestive systems. However, for most individuals excessive eating over a period of years tends to predispose to digestive difficulties in the late decades of life. A consistently moderate diet over the years appears to conserve the healthy function of the tissues of the digestive tract.

Relaxation. Both before and after a meal, one half hour of relaxation can facilitate digestion. The most important contribution of such relaxation comes from the beneficial emotional effects produced. After a meal sleep is not necessary to good digestion although the reduced blood flow to the brain may promote drowsiness. Exercise after a meal may retard digestion although evidence is lacking that permanent harm results.

Avoidance of infection. Of special importance is the avoidance of infection of the digestive tract. Mild transient infection generally has little effect upon the lifelong function of digestion. Acute severe infection or chronic moderate infection should receive immediate medical attention. More important, all possible precautions should be taken to prevent infectious agents from entering the digestive tract, by observing standard practices in food sanitation.

Avoidance of self-medication. High-pressure advertising has made the United States a nation of self-appointed specialists in treating ailments of digestion. To the public any distress of the digestive system is "indigestion." The term itself is ill-defined and not in good repute in scientific circles. Yet one glib television announcer after another has the "cure" for all digestion difficulties. A person trying the "cure" may get some temporary relief and thereafter rely on it.

Most individuals experience occasional digestive distress, usually of little consequence. Perhaps no treatment is necessary because the condition clears rather quickly through normal processes. These infrequent transient disturbances do not indicate the need for medical service. However, chronic digestive disturbance or distress is the signal to consult a physician.

A specific digestive disorder requires specific treatment. Thus accurate diagnosis is the first essential and requires the analysis of a highly trained physician, not the guess of a layman. Perhaps unfortunately the early stages of digestive disturbances are not incapacitating. In consequence in the early stages of digestive disorder, only persons who have an understanding of the importance of professional service wisely seek the advice of a physician. At this early stage the medical doctor can usually treat or cure the condition successfully.

The health of the digestive tract is too important to be left to chance or quackery. Chronic constipation, diarrhea, burning sensations, or dull pains are danger signals that abnormalities of the digestive canal exist. All of these call for the expert services of a physician. Self-medication, unsafe at any time, is dangerous when the digestive tract is involved.

Sound general health. The health of the digestive system is not distinct from the health of other systems or of the entire individual. The health of the circulatory system is particularly important to good digestion. In general the health of the entire body is reflected in the function of the organs of digestion. In a reciprocal manner good digestion contributes to good general health.

Special measures. Some individuals require special measures to meet their individual nutritional needs and digestive function. Whereas most normal people benefit by following objectively established nutritional practices, there are individuals for whom deviations in practice are highly beneficial and justified. Mere observation that one particular food is disturbing may justify its elimination from the diet since no one food is indispensable. Beyond such rather unimportant deviations, any special nutritional measures should have the approval if not the recommendation of a qualified physician. Too often self-determined special nutritional measures are merely fads or fancies having neither scientific rhyme nor reason. Special measures can and should be based on a professional diagnosis and prescribed program.

NUTRITION AS A COMMUNITY PROBLEM

Community responsibility for the promotion of better nutrition is accepted by public health officials. Although professional workers provide the essential leadership in community nutrition promotion, many organizations and individuals have made outstanding contributions. To be effective a community nutrition service must utilize all possible agencies which have a contribution to make.

The staff of a present-day city, county, or district health department will include at least one specialist in nutrition. This individual is competent as a consultant and educator in nutrition and is usually the key individual in the community nutrition program. However, the home demonstration agent in the county is also qualified professionally to provide leadership in the nutrition field. Other individuals, e.g., home economics teachers, may serve as specialists in providing the technical services needed in answer to certain nutrition questions and problems. Many interested lay people have an interest in the nutrition program and can be a valuable resource in the promotion of nutrition.

Various agencies have a contribution to make to the promotion of community nutrition. The federal government, the welfare department, service clubs, women's clubs, parent-teacher groups, child study clubs, as well as other organizations have contributed to the organized promotion of better nutrition in communities. Proper use of all possible resources is basic to an effective program.

Community nutrition service. The primary objective of a community nutrition service is the promotion of normal nutrition in the community. This program is not spectacular, nor does it produce immediate tangible results. It must be organized on a long range basis. The attack must be through community education involving the coordinated efforts of all possible individuals and agencies. It must utilize school lunch and health programs, parent-teacher assistance, demonstrations, lectures, radio, newspapers, pamphlets, posters, and other media of communication.

Mass education cannot be effective if some of the needy members of the community are unable to supply themselves with the essential foods. Public welfare agencies contribute directly to the lowest income group, and social workers encourage these families in the best nutritional practices. However, families with a low income but not on the welfare rolls find adequate family nutrition difficult in times of high food costs. Supplementary family income and the enlistment of the aid of voluntary agencies have been instrumental in assuring optimum nutrition for these families. The school lunch program of the federal government, the mid-day lunch, and the supplemental milk programs of some communities contribute to the nutrition of children of practically all economic levels.

The necessity for early recognition of nutritional defects in children is inherent in a well-rounded program of community nutrition. Periodic examination of infants and preschool and school children should single out the children with moderate or severe malnutrition. However, a mild nutritional deficiency is difficult to detect and constitutes the principal problem in malnutrition. Thus a program directed to all segments of a community is essential if deficiency diseases are to be prevented or corrected and positive health is to be promoted.

Chapter 5

Exercise, fatigue, and rest

War and emergencies usually focus attention upon total fitness, and physical fitness in particular. Between these periods little attention is given to enhancing optimum physiological growth and development. During the 1950's and particularly 1955 to 1956 several incidents called attention forcibly to the fact that we as a nation are becoming physically soft and culminated in the 1956 President's National Conference on the Fitness of American Youth. The findings of this conference were such that the President established a Council on Youth Fitness, composed of Cabinet members who head departments with activities in this area. Also a President's Citizens' Advisory Committee on the Fitness of American Youth was established, with the assignment "to examine and explore the facts, and thereafter alert America on what can and should be done to reach the much-desired goal of a happier, healthier, and more totally fit youth in America." President Kennedy gave added impetus to the program and broadened it to include all the population, adult as well as youth. Fitness has been interpreted in many ways, but no concept can be complete without answering the question, "Fitness for what?" The prevailing answer, "Fitness for living," implies a broad definition of fitness. Mental, emotional, and social fitness are involved as well as physical fitness.

The term *exercise* has come to connote more than formal exercise under commands in a gymnasium. It extends to all forms of physical activity, formal and informal, recreational and nonrecreational, vocational and nonvocational. Bodily movement from the mildest form to the most extreme exertion must be regarded as exercise.

Exercise is the oldest single approach to health. At the height of Corinth, the Greeks emphasized exercise as the vehicle for bodily grace and well-being necessary for the glorification of the individual. Doubtless the ancient Greeks attained

171

a high level of physical dexterity, grace, and development, but in terms of modern standards their level of health would hardly serve as a model.

Even today the United States has extremists who view the "body beautiful" as the true index of health. These are the individuals who regard physical strength and muscular development as the sole index of health. At the other extreme are the asthenics who decry exercise as debasing and who hold physical activity and development in low repute. Between the two extremes lies the interpretation of the health scientists.

Interpretation. Just as there is no single index of health, there is no known single road to health. Muscular strength is not the index of health nor is exercise the panacea for all matters in health. Every healthy person should possess sufficient muscular strength to meet the demands of everyday life efficiently and enjoyably. Not all people need the endurance of a cross-country runner nor the strength of a professional weight lifter. Activity and resulting development should be correlated with capacity and needs. Physical fitness does not imply that an individual should attain the fitness level of a combat soldier, but the level of well-being appropriate to his individual needs. Health must be considered in terms of the social, mental, and physical well-being necessary to effective and enjoyable living.

Physical fitness is important not only from a military standpoint, but also because of the physiological effect on the human mechanism. Great strides have been made in the control and prevention of communicable diseases and the extension of the average length of life. The maintenance of an optimum total fitness to meet the complexities of modern civilization has not received the attention it should. Americans may have lost the art of walking, which is indicated by the distaste for walking even the shortest distance. The development of a physical laziness is encouraged by cars, buses, drive-in banks, offices, movies, escalators, elevators, and many other modern conveniences. Growth is dependent upon activity. Activity of the proper kind and amount is required throughout life if we are to live to the fullest extent.

The healthy individual is capable of action and work. He is equipped with normal bodily energy and control. Physical and mental growth are closely related, and both are a continuous process. The bodily functions, both physical and mental, must be developed.

Many disorders have their beginnings in overstrain and wear and tear on the skeletal and muscular systems. These overstrains are often produced by conditions not recognized as overstrain. They often occur in the back, legs, and arms of office workers as a result of overstrained muscles. This may be produced by such things as nervousness, long working hours, cramped working position, static muscular activity, tension caused by pain or long monotonous work, and varied forms of rigidity.

Exercise can tear down as well as build up the human mechanism. Overexertion can be harmful to an individual's well-being. A person with a defective heart or an inefficient circulatory system can do irreparable damage to his health by engaging in activities which overtax his capacities.

Just as overexertion can deplete vitality, underactivity is of little value to health. Except for invalids some measure of activity is desirable in order to build up and keep physiological efficiency at a high or adequate level. Recent recognition of this fact is obvious in the present practice of having convalescents move about as soon as possible. Surgical and obstetrical patients are no longer kept in bed for weeks. Instead they are urged to begin walking a day or two after surgery has been performed. Certain types of cardiac patients, once advised to remain quiet and even to remain in bed, are now placed on a routine of light, then moderate, activity. As will be pointed out later, this practice is based upon sound principles derived from studies of the physiology of activity.

Exercise should be continuous throughout the life span if optimum function is to be maintained. Once muscle potential is lost, restoration is a long laborious process. The older the individual becomes, the longer the period required to restore potential. Often only partial recovery can be obtained.

For individuals with normal health the problem is that of using exercise to the best advantage in building up a level of health which will make possible the highest possible level of effective and enjoyable living. Before the age of 30 years exercise tends to contribute to physiological efficiency, hence to health. Exercise gradually brought to a level of moderate or severe form, depending upon capacities, should develop a high level of effective function of all the systems affected by exercise. The level of bodily function is thus near its inherited and developmental potentiality. From 30 to about 40 years of age a gradual tapering off in exercise will tend to maintain function at a high level, though obviously not at the peak attained before 30 years of age. After 40 years of age most individuals would be benefited by further tapering off of exercise. Graduating from moderate to light activity as the years go by should be the regimen of healthful living. The achievement af maximum physical fitness until 30 years of age and optimum fitness thereafter is hygienically sound.

If exercise is to be physiologically beneficial, it must be dynamic enough to stimulate metabolism, respiration, and circulation as well as other processes. It is well established that a sedentary life contributes to the incidence of atherosclerosis and coronary disease. There must be sufficient strength and physical efficiency to supply a reserve to meet emergencies. Lack of exercise and the large amount of sitting time of the average American predispose to weaknesses in three regions: the upper back and neck, the lower back and abdomen, and the feet.

EXERCISE

Effects of regular exercise. Many of the effects of exercise have very little if any health implications, others are only indirectly of health consequence, whereas others are of significant health value. When activity contributes to health, the effect is a positive or constructive one. Its contribution is mainly in building

Table 20. Activities suitable for men of various levels of physiological capacity

Age 16 to 30 yr. (trained)	Age 16 to 30 yr. (not trained)	Age 30 to 45 yr.	Age 45 to 75 yr.	Cardiac patients
Badminton	Baseball	Cycling	Archery	Archery
Basketball	Boating	Fencing	Ballroom dancing	Billiards
Boxing	Canoeing	Fishing	Billiards	Darts
Crew	Cricket	Folk dancing	Darts	Golf
Cross-country running	Deck tennis	Hiking	Flycasting	Quoits
Diving	Motorcycling	Iceskating	Golf	Shuffleboard
Field hockey	Roller skating	Riding	Horseshoes	Walking
Football	Skiing	Sailing	Quoits	
Gymnastics		Softball	Pistol shooting	
Handball		Swimming	Shuffleboard	
Ice hockey		Table tennis	Skeet	
Mountain climbing			Trapshooting	
Paddleball			Walking	
Snowshoeing				
Soccer				
Speedball				
Tennis				
Track				
Water polo				
Wrestling				

A normal individual in one group can participate in the activities in all lists to the right of his age group.

up and maintaining a high level of well-being. Exercise is necessary for growth and maintenance of optimum physiological function.

Metabolism. Perhaps the greatest physiological value of proper exercise lies in its effects upon the metabolism of tissues. Life processes of body cells are stimulated to a higher level of effective function. Chemical function more nearly equal to the absolute potential of the cells is attained. Overexertion, however, may retard normal metabolic processes.

Regular exercise of proper intensity establishes a better equilibrium between the oxygen required by the tissues, particularly muscle tissues, and the oxygen made available. This increased function in oxygen absorption contributes to better oxygen utilization and thus improves metabolism, including recovery. Best evidence for the improvement in metabolism is in the increased size of the crest load or the greatest load at which recovery (anabolism) and energy expenditure (catabolism) are maintained in equilibrium, thus resulting in work being accomplished with greater efficiency, with less heavy breathing, and with a slower heart rate.

Circulation. The heart cannot be expected to carry the entire load of circulation. Other muscle groups which are supplementary to the heart become activated through exercise. Muscles not only perform work, but also assist in moving fluids through the body. Thus a sedentary existence puts a strain upon the heart. Strengthening of the heart muscle increases the heart output per beat and reduces the frequency of the cardiac rate. The effect on the heart muscle may cause a slight increase in the size of the heart, but the condition will be a normal one. The old concept of athlete's heart has been discarded in the light of scientific investigation. If a youthful person with a sound heart engages in vigorous athletic training, there is no reason to expect a disordered or abnormally sized heart. However, a damaged or defective heart may be injured seriously by vigorous exercise. The advisability of a thorough health examination before engaging in athletic training is evident. Such an examination should include an electrocardiogram as well as a stethoscopic examination of the heart.

A more efficient heart with a greater output per contraction is also a heart which comes back to its normal rate more rapidly after exertion.

Regular exercise tends to reduce the height to which the arterial pressure rises during exertion. It further lessens the time during which pressure remains below normal after severe activity.

Strenuous exercise tends to reduce the red corpuscle count in all individuals, but in a person who exercises regularly the normal count is regained in a few hours. An untrained individual may experience anemia for two or three weeks following strenuous exercise. Regular exercise increases the functional activity of the red bone marrow in the production of red blood cells. This is one of the reasons why people who lead an active life have a higher red corpuscle count than those who lead a sedentary life.

Exercise, much like massage, aids lymphatic circulation as well as the flow in the veins in the blood circulatory system. Blood is returned to the heart through the veins. There are valves in the veins which permit the blood to flow only toward the heart. The pressure on the veins through rhythmic contraction of muscles promotes the flow of blood. When it is contracted, the diaphragm, the large dome-shaped muscle of respiration near the midriff, exerts pressure on some of the large veins of the body and thus enhances the flow of blood toward the heart.

Respiration. Regular training increases the efficiency of the respiratory system. The capillary area of the air pockets (alveoli) of the lungs is increased, thus permitting a greater exchange of gases (oxygen and carbon dioxide) between the lung spaces and the blood stream. This increased capillary area is especially important at the apices of the lungs where infection is most likely to occur. The added capillary area and increased ease of gas exchange result in slower and deeper breathing, which reflects increased efficiency of the lungs.

No reliable evidence exists that regular exercise, of itself, produces immunity to respiratory infection, but resistance to the common infections of the respiratory system may result from a higher level of general body function.

Regular exercise does not predispose to any known infectious conditions.

Muscular action. An increased muscle tonus is the immediate effect on the skeletal muscles which is produced by regular exercise. The feeling of muscular vigor which regular exercise gives a person is a reflection of increased muscle tone. Improved posture and sense of well-being usually result. Increased strength and endurance arise from the increased fuel storage as well as from the amount of oxygen made available to the muscle fibers. Improved coordination arises principally from the metabolic improvement affecting the transmission of nerve impulses as well as from the improved responsiveness of the muscle fibers. The development of neuromuscular coordinations and motor skills is a safety factor in emergencies. Skill increases the efficiency of the individual in producing greater results with less effort.

Strength is not the cardinal index of health. Yet moderate strength somewhat above that demanded by the ordinary routine of life contributes to effectiveness and enjoyment in living.

Flexibility. As we grow older, the effects of sedentary life on the mobility or flexibility of joints is noticeable. When tendons and ligaments are not stretched and actively elongated, they shorten, or, if they sustain a constant load, they thicken. Under these conditions pressure is exerted on nerves, resulting in sensitivity and pain. The endocrine system may be affected by these irritations, with a possible disturbance of the nervous system.

Daily stretching exercises over a period of time—of the neck, shoulder girdle, back, and pelvis—may be beneficial. Most apparent results will be relief from the neck and back pains, headaches, and other pains caused by lack of use of the various joints and muscles of the body.

Chemistry of the body. Regular activity increases the fuel reserves of the body. It also increases the alkaline reserve of the body, which may be of significance in an emergency requiring prolonged effort. The margin of safety provided by the high alkaline reserve of a physiologically fit individual could well be the margin of survival in case of injury or severe extended illness.

That exercise tones up the glandular system has long been recognized. The beneficial effects are reflected in the chemical action of the body. Increased or improved circulation underlies improved glandular function. Noticeably increased output of the thyroid gland is an important factor in the metabolic changes associated with exercise.

General body effects. The margin of safety provided by regular exercise is largely expressed through the general body effects which are attained. Regular exercise creates a greater stability of normal body processes at a high level of efficiency. The efficiency with which energy is utilized may increase from the usual range of 20% to 25% to a range of 25% to 35%. A general feeling of vigor motivates the individual to increased daily output. Flexibility of the skin and general appearance are improved. Digestion and elimination may be improved as a by-product of improved circulation and muscle tonus. Improvement in relaxation and sleep is an indication of beneficial effects upon the nervous system. A better mental performance has resulted for some individuals, with the learning process enhanced. This must not be interpreted to mean that native intelligence is improved by physical exercise.

Many intangible benefits from regular exercise have been reported by various individuals. Although highly subjective factors cannot be accepted as universal in application, these benefits cannot be ignored in those specific individuals who live more enjoyably and perhaps more effectively, at least partially, as a result of physical activity.

Mental health values. In modern industrialized America perhaps the recreational values and resulting mental health effects of activity should be given most emphasis. In the preindustrial era the guild worker took great pride in his product. With this degree of self-expression and self-gratification in his work, the guildsman had little need for recreational outlets. His vocation provided the fruits of recreation. The same is true for many individuals today, but a vast army of workers get little self-expression or self-gratification from their vocational pursuits. Automation and a shortened work week tend to aggravate the situation. These individuals seek an outlet for self-expression in some recreational activity. If they find an activity or activities commensurate with their abilities and capacities, they have a vehicle for the promotion of a high level of mental health.

There exists at birth the physiological organization of activity as an avenue through which the self is expressed. Restrain the infant, and his response will be expressed in the negative emotions of resentment and anger. Permit him unrestrained activity, and the child expresses through his pleasant emotions the self-gratification he experiences. Perhaps all through life the normal healthy individual can find self-expression through activity, particularly if the activity is one in which one's skill provides a high level of self-status. If with this self-status is associated social acceptance, the individual finds a vehicle for effective and enjoyable living and a high level of mental health.

Early in life one should profitably begin to acquire skills in those recreation activities which can be carried on throughout most of life. High school and college athletics as commercial entertainment rather than as lifelong recreational activities hardly serve the purpose. Instead one should look to the activities of moderate and light exertion for lifelong recreational hobbies, not as an escape from the realities of life, but as an entry into a more stimulating and gratifying life.

Social opportunities growing out of physical activities may properly be regarded in the light of mental health values. Social experiences as by-products of physical activities provide individuals with opportunities for identification with groups. To identify the self with common group interests promotes the self-status essential to a high level of health. The wholesome atmosphere which usually surrounds recreational activities promotes a high standard of fellowship beneficial to all participants.

Doubtful effects of exercise. Although regular activity has much to contribute to human well-being, its proponents in their enthusiasm at times are inclined to make claims for exercise which available data do not support. Perhaps further study may support the claims of these enthusiasts, but we must be governed by known data until such data have been refuted.

Length of life. Studies of college athletes and nonathletes reveal that ten or twenty years after graduation there has been no significant difference in their death rates. Admittedly several factors which tend to counterbalance each other may be concealed in the rates. Whether the two groups had inherently equal constitutional endowments in terms of life span is not known. It may well be that, if these studies were extended to fifty years after graduation, a significant difference in life expectancy might be indicated. Significantly these studies reveal that the best scholars have the lowest death rate, thus the best life expectancy. However, the significant correlation doubtless is that between high intellect and high constitutional endowment

If athletics are deleterious to life expectancy, present knowledge points an accusing finger at two offenses. The first is the practice of excessive competitive play for adolescent boys without adequate supervision. In adolescence the skeletal muscles grow and develop at a faster rate than the heart. In effect the curve for circulatory maturity lags behind that for muscular development. Thus a basically immature circulatory system can easily be overtaxed by the extreme and prolonged effort of a more mature musculature. The second offense to life expectation occurs when a boy with an undiscovered heart defect or other abnormality or illness is permitted to continue in vigorous athletics. No athletic contest should be as important as the lifelong well-being of each of its participants, and every effort should be made to discover all possible defects before participation.

In the industrial world, studies reveal that heavy manual labor before the age of 40 years does not seem to affect the length of life, but heavy labor after 40 years of age affects the length of life adversely.

Immunity to disease. Resistance to communicable disease is a speiific factor. The individual who possesses the specific chemical substances which agglutinate typhoid bacilli is immune to typhoid fever regardless of whether he leads an athletic or a sedentary existence. Likewise, without these specific chemical substances the person is susceptible to typhoid fever regardless of athletic conditioning. The same holds true for other diseases to which man may develop immunity. The cause of communicable disease can no longer be thought of as a single entity. A multiplicity of causes is always needed to produce that alteration of tissues creating maladjustment. (See Chapter 10.)

To the extent that training tones up the general function of the body, an individual's general resistance to infection may be improved. Perhaps the margin may be sufficient to avoid illness in some persons in whom otherwise the symptoms of illness would have appeared.

Doubtless a person who exercises regularly may be better able to survive an emergency such as an injury. The better heart condition, better blood supply, more efficient respiration, and enhanced body physiology and chemistry may be the assets that make the difference between survival and death in the event of an auto accident injury, a gunshot wound, or some other traumatic occurrence.

Perhaps even in an infectious disease regular physical conditioning may be a definite asset in survival. Certainly an excellent level of physiological well-being should not be a liability.

FATIGUE

Fatigue is a pressing modern problem brought about in all too many persons by poor physical condition. There is great need for persons of all ages to keep in a physical condition commensurate with their age level. Physiological fatigue in general terms may be spoken of as the loss of irritability and contractility associated with muscular exertion. Associated with the loss of responsiveness is a distress syndrome which may be simulated in various conditions not associated with muscular exertion. What gives rise to the distress is not completely understood, but doubtless various metabolic wastes which affect function of the nervous system are an important factor.

Muscular contraction involves the burning of glucose and the production of lactic acid, carbonic acid, and other wastes which tend to produce a reduced alkalinity of the tissues. Whereas the effects of reduced alkalinity are quickly distributed over the entire body by the body fluids, the tissues overproducing the acid wastes will be most immediately and intensely affected. Body substances requiring an alkalinity approaching that of the normal level tend to be inactivated by the near acid medium. Apparently the distress is associated with the inactivity of some of the chemical substances of the body.

Although the accumulation of waste products is usually the primary and most effective factor in fatigue, a depletion of nutrients available to tissues may be associated with the fatigue condition, indeed may even be a primary factor in fatigue. Records from psychosomatic medicine offer evidence of the role of nutrient deficiency in chronic fatigue. A distinctive symptom of neurasthenia (hypochondriasis) is chronic fatigue. These individuals seem to lack an ability to utilize nutrient material.

Acute fatigue. Acute fatigue of muscular exertion is of paramount importance to an individual with substandard health and to the aged. In these individuals exertion which induces acute fatigue taxes the circulatory mechanism as well as delicate physiological balances to a point of permanent damage or even immediate death. A diseased or defective constitution may fail to respond to the end products of fatigue. Thus the deficient constitution may be taxed further over an extended period of time. Permanent impairment of the body's weakest link, frequently the circulatory system, is the end result.

For an individual with normal health moderate fatigue of muscular exertion is not of great health concern. In a normally healthy person waste products of acute fatigue initiate a series of physiological changes which tend to counteract the fatigue and promote recovery. Carbonic acid stimulates the respiratory centers and increases the frequency and depth of breathing. Acid wastes, acting on the cardiac inhibitory centers in the brain, speed up the heart rate which, together with vascular changes, speeds up circulation, and thus wastes are removed more rapidly than usual.

Even for an individual with normal health extreme acute fatigue from extreme overexertion may require hours or even days for complete recovery. Perhaps no discernible health damage occurs from a single experience of overexertion, but repeated overexertion and overfatigue doubtless may take a toll in terms of physiological efficiency.

Although children fatigue more quickly than adults, their recovery is also more rapid. The circulatory system of a child possesses a wide margin of safety for the function of the body so that it can easily remove the wastes of fatigue and restore the necessary chemical energy to the tissues.

Chronic fatigue. Day-in, day-out chronic fatigue can be expected to affect the protoplasm of the cells of the body. Eventual reduction in the functional efficiency of the tissues is expressed in malfunction, lowered tissue responsiveness, nervous irritability, and a possible adverse effect upon longevity. Chronic fatigue may arise from a number of sources—inadequate rest, focal infection, toxemia, malnutrition, sinusitis, diabetes mellitus, heart deficiency, anemia, tuberculosis, alcoholism, drug addiction, eyestrain, painful feet, poor posture, emotional tension, and a monotonous uninspiring routine of living.

Rest is not a panacea for all forms and aspects of fatigue. The prime requisite is the correction of the basic defect or trouble. Removing infection, relieving eyestrain, reducing stress and strain, or correcting the monotony of an uninteresting job are basic to the relief of fatigue when these factors are the underlying cause. Drugs are only a temporary stopgap, not a solution for chronic fatigue. Not until the removal of the basic cause of fatigue, coupled with proper rest, produces a condition of euphoria in the individual can one assert that normal health has been regained. The end result will be improved effectiveness and enjoyment in living.

REST

Industry has long been aware that work performance lags during the latter part of the morning and latter part of the afternoon. As a solution for this drop in efficiency and output, industry has found that a fifteen-minute rest period in midmorning and a similar rest period in midafternoon are an investment in production. Some firms supplement the rest with a light lunch which apparently yields returns in increased production.

Aside from the psychological factor the recuperative efforts of a brief rest period are understandable in physiological terms. During the period of rest anabolism, the restorative phase of metabolism, exceeds catabolism, the destructive phase. Thus wastes are removed more rapidly than they are being produced. At the same time the nutrient supply of the cells is being replenished. The end result will be improved function of the tissues affected by the recovery process.

Relaxation. A relaxation period of about thirty minutes after the noonday lunch proves highly recuperative. Because eating results in a shift of the blood mass away from the skeletal muscles, the noonday rest is indicated as physiologically consistent. Sleep is not necessary. Indeed sleep is not recommended. Except for the most unusual case, two cycles of sleep do not work out satisfactorily for the normal healthy adult.

Each day provides opportunities for relaxation, but unfortunately too few Americans have cultivated the healthful art of relaxation. The ability to relax is merely the reflection of a cultivated habit that pays off in improved efficiency, increased endurance, added enjoyment, and extended living.

Sleep. Theme of poets and physiologists, sleep is an enigma to artist and scientists alike. No one knows precisely what sleep is, why it is necessary, what causes sleep, or what takes place during sleep that is biologically useful or why some sleep periods appear to be more effective than others in restoring the effects of lack of sleep.

Sleep-deprived persons often feel tired, sleepy, irritable, and confused, but they are able to do well-motivated tasks with their usual strength and skill. They exhibit periodic variations in alertness. Recovery from muscular fatigue occurs in the absence of sleep, and a completely rested person can fall asleep. In fact immediately after sleep most individuals are physiologically at a low level of efficiency. Paradoxically fatigue can be a hindrance to sleep. A thyroid-deficient individual goes to sleep with ease, whereas his counterpart, a hyperthyroid person, finds sleep both a nuisance and a problem. The old hypnotoxin theory of sleep has been discarded in the absence of the discovery of any substances in the blood that may be increased before sleep and decreased after sleep. Yet sleep appears to be a necessary component of health and longevity. It utilizes about one third of our life span and thus is worthy of consideration.

Man, along with almost all other animals, exhibits a sleep cycle. For man the two-cycle pattern of sleep gradually fuses to a single-cycle pattern. Even this single cycle undergoes a variation process. Newborn babes sleep between twenty and twenty-two hours a day. At about 5 years of age the single-sleep cycle has been established, and twelve hours of sleep a night is quite typical. Although individual differences must be recognized, an adequate sleep period for various age levels is given in Table 21.

The sleep cycle of any given individual is the result of constitutional or somatic makeup and socially conditioned practice. A robust athletic individual usually establishes an exceedingly consistent cycle. He gets sleepy at about the same hour each day. He falls asleep quickly, sleeps soundly, and requires less sleep than the average individual of his age. A lean overactive individual frequently has an irregular sleep cycle. He lies awake for long periods before going to sleep and then sleeps very lightly. Yet he may get sufficient sleep for his needs. A pyknic or squat individual sleeps easily and soundly. His sleep period usually extends beyond his actual need. Women generally sleep more than men,

Table 21. Adequate hours of sleep for various age levels

Age (yr.)	Sleep required (hr.)
6- 8	10-11
9-11	9-10
12-14	8- 9
15-17	7- 8
18-25	6- 7
26-35	7- 8
36-55	8- 9
56-70	9-10
Over 70	10 or more

and the sleep is equally as deep as that of men. Manual workers usually require more sleep than do so-called brainworkers.

The demands and practices of society, reflected in the family regimen, will habituate individuals to certain hours of retiring and arising. A farm population has a sleep cycle timed differently from that of its urban neighbors although the number of hours of sleep may be the same for each group. Once a definite sleep cycle is established, any attempted deviation proves to be disturbing; although by applying oneself to the task a new schedule can gradually be attained. The shift plan utilized by industry when the workday is lengthened beyond the usual period is not detrimental when workers are assigned a shift for a long period of time. Shift changes from month to month are not conducive to a proper sleep cycle and rest. As will be pointed out later, various mechanisms, such as temperature control, blood pressure, and heart rate, become adapted to an established cycle, and any change in the cycle is reflected in the effects on these mechanisms.

Physiologically sleep itself involves a chain of events with fluctuations from the onset to the close of the sleep period. These processes which interact in normal human sleep are periodic and nonperiodic. One phase is a cycle of electrical activity in the brain with an eighty-five to ninety minute period. A wide variety of physiological and behavioral phenomena is correlated with the cycle, including respiratory and heart rates. The nonperiodic process modifies or varies the periodic phases. The nonperiodic phase changes continuously from the beginning of sleep, leading to the notion that sleep is deeper at some times than at others and that sleep is less deep near the waking point. Typically the first thirty minutes are characterized simply as generalized muscular relaxation. Then follows a twilight zone, characterized as the hypnagogic state. Although the subject is conscious, general body awareness is absent. The general sensation is one of buoyancy. Next follows a complete loss of consciousness. Gradually blood pressure falls, reaching a low plateau in about three hours, and the heart rate declines during the same period. The resulting reduction in blood flow to the brain reduces the oxygen available for respiration in the brain cells, and loss of consciousness results. Breathing becomes slower and deeper as metabolism slows down. Body temperature drops from one to three degrees. The digestive system may continue activity throughout the sleep period. During a normal eight-hour sleep, the fourth and fifth hours tend to be the deepest. At the sixth hour the rise in blood pressure, heart rate, and metabolism indicates that the sleep is getting lighter. In effect the body gradually moves toward the waking state. From the sixth hour onward short intervals of consciousness occur. However, regardless of the phase, throughout sleep the recovery division of the nervous system and its recovery effects are dominant over any expenditure or activation effects.

Dreams vary from two seconds to thirty minutes in duration and occur only during light sleep. Occasionally the intense emotional excitement during the dream elevates both heart rate and blood pressure. If there is a defective circulatory system, such changes may be serious since the whole body is near its lowest level of function at the time of the onset of the dream. The fact that most deaths occur between midnight and daylight is correlated with the lowest level of function attained by the human mechanism during its daily cycle.

Perhaps all individuals should avoid hopping out of bed the instant they awake. The sudden change of gravitational effect on the circulatory system imposed upon an extremely accelerated demand on the system may be taxing to the whole body. Lying in bed for a minute or two after awakening and then sitting for a minute or two before standing may be beneficial.

Scientifically it is difficult to determine just how much sleep each individual needs. Empirically one might say that, if a person attains an exhilarating feeling of well-being following a period of sleep, he has had sufficient sleep. Yet even here allowances must be made for individual constitutional endowments. One individual will reach the peak of activity a short time after rising. His mornings will be highly productive. Another individual will not function at a maximum until about noon. The afternoon will see his greatest productivity. A third individual, who feels sluggish all morning may not reach his peak of well-being

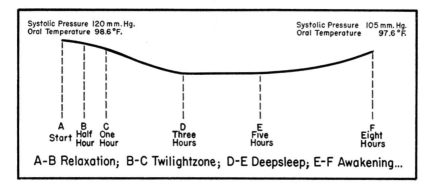

Fig. 34. Systolic pressure and oral temperature during sleep. Although the two curves are not precisely identical, as represented, an exceedingly high correlation exists between blood pressure and temperature during sleep. Both are at their lowest level during deep sleep, and neither tends to be back to normal at the time of awakening.

until late in the day. Perhaps his greatest performance will be in the evening. Bodily temperature is a correlated factor. Thus a person must appraise his feeling of well-being in terms of his cycle. Or he may alter his temperature and sleep cycle by gradually changing the hour at which he goes to bed. Contrary to popular belief, many adults sleep more than is necessary for sound health. The same feeling of well-being and efficiency in performance may be obtained from one or two hours' less sleep each night. It may mean a saving of 10% to 15% in one's waking hours and thus promote effectiveness and enjoyment in living.

Promotion of sleep to most individuals may be as nonessential as the promotion of thirst. Yet some may benefit from certain sleep-promoting practices. Although it may not be possible to set down rules for sleep promotion which are universal in application, many popular misconceptions about sleep make it essential that certain established practices be presented.

1. So far as practical a person should get to bed at the same time each night and get up at the same hour each morning. In the event a person who regularly sleeps seven hours should get but four hours' sleep one night, the next night he needs but his customary seven hours of sleep. Sleep lost in this manner need not be made up so far as the hygienist has been able to interpret the health factor involved. Undersleeping at isolated intervals does not necessarily produce demonstrable physical or mental disturbance or damage.

2. Each person should attempt to establish a cycle with the hours of sleep which appear to produce a desirable feeling of well-being.

3. The practices or habits just before going to bed tend to condition one for sleep. A bedtime routine may promote regularity in sleep routine.

4. The best position in which to sleep is the most comfortable position. Most people shift positions from twenty to forty times during the usual night's sleep. A position which shuts off the blood supply to a muscle causes a tetanus (cramp) of the muscle. The pain rouses the sleeper, and a new position will soon be taken. Likewise, pressure on a nerve tract causing the limb to "go to sleep" results in a change of sleeping position. Some body movement is essential for proper rest.

5. Bed covers, room temperature, and ventilation are individual matters. It is hardly the part of wisdom during subzero weather to throw open all windows and thus necessitate the use of all the bedding and clothes in the house in order to keep comfortable during sleep.

6. A hard or soft mattress, a pillow or no pillow—all are personal preferences, not related to health.

7. Moderate exercise and fatigue before bedtime will usually tend to promote sleep.

8. A lunch before bedtime tends to promote sleep. Solid foods rather than fluids are advisable since a distended bladder tends to disturb sleep.

Whether the meal is hot, warm, or cold seems to be of no particular importance.

9. A tepid or slightly warm bath promotes sleep. A cold bath or a hot bath, both being stimulating, tends to interfere with sleep.
10. Reading while lying down produces eyestrain which is conducive to sleep. Although some individuals use this device regularly to produce sleepiness, the hygienist does not advocate it as a regular practice.
11. Each individual should follow those practices which are giving him adequate sleep, however unique his practices may appear to be.
12. Barbiturates (sleeping pills) should never be taken except upon the prescription of a physician.
13. A person who thinks he is not getting enough sleep because he does not sleep as long as others may be getting all the sleep he needs. Many people in excellent health sleep only five hours a night.
14. Sleep is not necessary for rest. To lie down for several hours without sleeping will produce recovery from fatigue.

POSTURE

Man does not stand in a straight line but in four counterbalancing curves—cervical, thoracic, lumbar, and sacral. These vertebral curves are not in perfect compensating alignment but must be supported by the skeletal muscles. Whether one is standing, walking, or sitting, four criteria can be applied as the index of good posture: (1) head erect, neck back, and chin level, (2) no exaggeration of vertebral curvatures, (3) chest lifted slightly, and (4) shoulders held broad, without tension.

In standing the body weight should be over the center of each foot, and the feet should be toeing straight forward. In walking a rhythmical gait with a free and easy leg swing should be supplemented by a free arm swing. The feet should be nearly parallel. In sitting the hip, knee, and ankle joints should form right angles. The feet should point straight ahead and be flat on the floor.

When posture is properly aligned, a small degree of muscular contraction is necessary to maintain the position of the body. Yet good muscle tone is as essential to the maintenance of good posture as is the proper skeletal alignment. Most poor posture is functional, that is, results from carelessness in habits, and a considerable amount is due to poor muscle tone. Many of these conditions are remediable through indicated exercises. Deformities of the skeleton and joints account for a very small percentage of poor posture.

Which is cause and which is effect, poor posture or pood health? In many persons poor health reflected in poor muscle tone leads to poor posture which leads to further poor health in a downward spiral. In other persons slovenly habits reflected in poor posture have a deleterious effect on health, with a downward spiral of both posture and health.

In specific cases it has been demonstrated that poor posture has affected the circulation, the kidneys, the intestines, and the joints. The disturbances due to poor posture are not pronounced and spectacular, but rather are insidious and chronic, which lowers the general health level and interferes with fully effective and enjoyable living.

Perhaps the greatest contribution of good posture is the mental health attributes of confidence, euphoria, and vitality which proper posture can provide. Good posture is essential to a vigorous state of health.

For those individuals whose faulty posture is due to poor muscle tone, a program designed to improve the health generally and the musculature specifically should be supplemented by intensive attention to standing, walking, and sitting in good posture at all times.

Two common causes of poor posture are round shoulders and a pelvis which is tipped down in front.

Round shoulders. The major problem of most people with poor posture is the condition in which the shoulder blades are pulled forward, with the associated drooping head and depressed chest, termed *round shoulders.* Most occupational and routine daily activities require arm action in front of the body. The inevitable result is that the powerful chest muscles which pull the shoulders forward increase in strength and become shorter. At the same time the light antagonists relax to permit the forward motion produced by the chest muscles. A simple exercise to correct this condition would consist in raising the arms to a side horizontal position; then, keeping the arms at the same level, swinging them forward until the palms touch; then fling the arms forcibly backward as far as possible. Repeat this movement several times. This exercise will stretch the chest muscles and strengthen the antagonistic muscles which hold the shoulders back. This exercise must be repeated daily over a protracted period of time if results are to be obtained.

Visceroptosis. In this condition the abdominal paunch is caused by a weakness of the muscles of the abdominal wall. The position of the pelvis is fundamental in good posture. The pelvis should be tipped up in front. Weak muscles which permit the front of the pelvis to drop down will result in poor posture, the forerunner of low backache. If this condition is to be corrected, the abdominal muscles must be strengthened. This can be done by performing sitting-up exercises. Lying on the back, with the feet secured to the floor, raise the body to a sitting position and then lower it gradually to the starting position. This exercise should be repeated until the abdominal muscles begin to tire. If this exercise is painful, the individual should consult a physician for the possibility that a hernia is present before continuing. At the start the arms may be folded in front of the chest or kept at the sides. As the muscles are strengthened, the arms may be held horizontally or vertically over the head to increase the load.

Trunk-raising exercise should be alternated with leg-raising exercise with knees straight from a prone position. The number of times the exercise is performed should be increased as the muscular tone develops.

Maintaining good posture requires constant vigilance, but the task is much less than that of recovering good posture which has been lost. The correction of posture is usually a matter of self-discipline motivated by the rewards of better health, better appearance, and greater poise.

GENERAL CONSIDERATIONS

The amount and nature of exercise or activity needed to maintain a satisfactory level of well-being vary from individual to individual. What is satisfactory for one person may be excessive for another. A person who engages in vigorous manual labor hardly needs strenuous exercise after working hours as a physical

Fig. 35. Vigorous activity. Basketball is an activity for properly conditioned youth with unimpaired circulatory system. (Photograph by Sam Bess.)

health measure. His recreational needs may well be served best by some sedentary activity. On the other hand an office worker may find moderate recreational activities tuned to his health needs. As the years advance a person might profitably find his recreational needs in activities that do not push him near the limit of his physical capacity. Exercise which is highly profitable to health at one stage of life may be decidedly damaging to health at a later stage. Whereas a near maximum level of physical fitness may be desirable up to 30 years of age, thereafter optimum fitness needs should be the guide.

For people with defects that would be affected by exercise, a physician should prescribe the form and severity of activity. Individuals in the normal range of health can be governed by the feeling of well-being or euphoria experienced in a particular activity. When an activity is more stimulating than distressing, more invigorating than fatiguing, it should be an acceptable one. If in doubt, an individual should incline toward the side of moderation. Above all he should be guided by his capacities, particularly in terms of his physiological age.

Community recreation. It has been pointed out that, if the public schools are to prepare students for effective and enjoyable living, one phase of that preparation must provide these students with skills that will serve their lifelong recreational needs and interests. As the work week becomes ever shorter, the increased leisure time makes it more imperative that citizens in the United States be trained for wholesome use of leisure time. An obvious corollary is that every community has an obligation to provide opportunities for the various recreation needs and interests of its citizens.

Fig. 36. Sanitary and safe recreation facilities. An investment in personal and community health, adequate recreational facilities are as much a part of modern community services as are police and fire protection. (Courtesy Oregon State Board of Health.)

Commercial recreation, including sheer entertainment, has a place in the recreational life of the United States. Radio, television, movies, professional athletics, and other forms of commercial entertainment, while of definite value, do not fulfill the real recreational needs of the community for activities in which citizens get the full benefit of personal participation. It also must be recognized that many individuals are capable of providing their own recreation leadership and facilities. However, not all individuals can belong to golf clubs or own riding horses or yachts, and the necessity for community recreation programs is apparent.

Trained leadership. Fundamental to an effective recreation program is qualified trained leadership capable of appraising and visualizing needs and possibilities and competent to organize and administer an over-all program and, above all, to provide that stimulation needed for enthusiastic participation. Such leadership provides both individual and group activities for adults of various age levels as well as for youth. It also provides recreation of limited physical exertion as well as that of vigorous activity. It coordinates the recreation facilities and resources of all agencies in the community.

Facilities. Ideally a community should provide playgrounds, parks, recreation buildings, shelters, swimming pools, skating rinks, game supplies, equipment, and other facilities. Doubtless many communities have difficulty financially in providing a minimum of facilities. Yet communities with vision have found that an appropriation for recreation is an investment in effective and enjoyable community living. The fruits of recreation are harvested for many years in more wholesome community life.

Chapter 6

Safety
for
health promotion

Health is properly considered in terms of effective and enjoyable living. That the ultimate purpose of safety promotion is effective and enjoyable living is frequently clouded by the negative view that safety is merely accident prevention. A positive approach to safety for health promotion is safety for effective living. It follows neither a course of recklessness nor a "safety at all costs" course which would impede progress, but it follows a course which will yield most effective and enjoyable living.

Safety does not imply the elimination of all risk. It recognizes certain risks as necessary, inevitable, and worthwhile, but it eliminates the needless risk. Conceived as the promotion of effective living, safety extends the scope of human adventure by controlling factors which would limit the extensiveness of human activity.

Accidents are a factor in natural selection or survival among all species in an unorganized uncontrolled environment, but man through his ability to organize and control his environment is able to diminish the factor of accidents. In some phases of the environment man has been able to anticipate and control the factor of safety to a mathematical certainty. He constructs giant bridges and buildings calculated to withstand all strains, expansions, contractions, or other forces that may be brought to bear on these structures. This same precision cannot be applied to all environmental factors related to human safety. In some environmental factors the advancing complexity of our social order has outstripped man's prog-

Unless otherwise noted, all statistics cited in this chapter are from Accident facts, published by the National Safety Council, Chicago, Ill., 1962.

ress in the foresight and knowledge necessary to the creation of a nonhazardous environment.

Man has not been able to create a completely safe environment principally because his environment is not a set or static one. It is dynamic, one of change and action. Since man cannot create an environment without physical hazards, he is obligated to condition himself to the complexities of a fast-moving shifting environment. To promote his well-being through safety, an individual must condition himself in the foresight and awareness necessary to anticipate possible hazards to his physical well-being. He must modify his course of living to the changing patterns of his environment. No accident can occur unless it is preceded by an unsafe act.

Adjustment of the human being to his needs in safety as a part of health promotion has been the most difficult phase of safety promotion. Perhaps some people lack the potential ability to make the necessary adjustment to the complexities of modern civilization. Yet many people who doubtless have sufficient endowment for promoting their own safety suffer injury and even death because of failure to make the necessary adjustments to the environment. Safety in complex American life requires intense study and analysis through formal training and instruction as a supplement to normal life experience. Modifying the responses of the individual to fit the demands of his physical environment is essential to safety as a factor in health promotion.

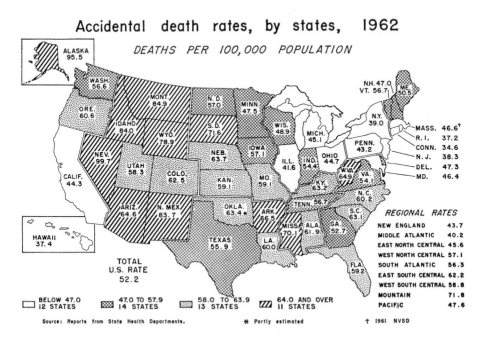

Fig. 37. Accidental death rates by states, 1962, in deaths per 100,000 population, based on reports from state health departments. (From *Accident facts*, published by the National Safety Council, Chicago, Ill., 1963.)

SAFETY COUNCILS

An important step in the reduction of accidents is to stimulate the interest of large numbers of people. This is best accomplished through organization. A safety council of representative citizens is often formed to provide the means for making effective the resources of a community to meet its safety needs.

Such an organization can mobilize all public and private agencies and professional and influential citizens in attacking the accident problem and promoting public support. Attention can be focused on accident problems by publishing local accident facts, insisting on adequate training of police officers, firemen, and other personnel involved in public safety, encouraging employers to promote both on and off the job accident prevention training, and continuously promoting various safety programs.

ACCIDENTS AND HEALTH

In terms of cost, misery, lowered productivity, shortened life, wasted resources, and loss of valuable skills, accidents stand at the top of the list. Their magnitude is evidenced by approximately 91,000 deaths and 46,000,000 injuries a year.

The loss to the nation in manpower due to accidental deaths yearly is estimated to be over 3,000,000 man-years of life annually. In addition one out of four Americans suffers an accident serious enough to require medical care, hospital care, or restricted activity for at least one day. These 46,000,000 accidents result in 424,000,000 days of restrictive activity, 114,000,000 days of bed disability, and 107,000,000 days lost from work. Loss of life and incapacity caused by accidents are greater than from any disease entity.

Accidents are not the result of uncontrollable events, but are caused by what people do and do not do. Accidents do not happen; they are caused.

The three basic groups of human factors in accidents are the physical, the psychological, and the physiological and are listed in Table 22.

The importance of accidents as hazards to life is reflected in a study of the rank and specific rate of accidental deaths in the United States for representative years during the past half century (Table 23).

From the data in Table 23 it is apparent that the accidental death rate in the nation has declined about 35 per 100,000 population during the fifty-eight year span covered by the figures. Yet as a cause of death accidents have risen from a rank of sixth to a new rating in fourth position. The explanation lies in the fact

Table 22. Basic groups of human factors

Physical	*Psychological*	*Physiological*
Defects	Temporary emotional states	Age
Disease processes	Habit patterns	Drugs
	Behavior	Medications
	Judgement	Fatigue

Table 23. Accidental deaths and death rates*

Year (av.)	Rank as cause of death	Number of deaths	Deaths per 100,000 population
1903-1912	6	73,700	85.9
1913-1922	6	78,600	76.8
1923-1932	6	92,100	77.4
1933-1942	5	98,765	76.2
1943-1947	5	97,561	71.4
1948-1952	4	93,280	61.8
1953-1956	4	93,322	57.4
1951-1960	3	92,748	51.6
1961	3	91,500	50.4

*Data for 1903 to 1932 from information on registration states collected by the U. S. National Office of Vital Statistics; data for 1933 to 1961 from national totals compiled by the U. S. National Office of Vital Statistics.

Table 24. Accidental deaths and injuries in the United States, 1961*

Class of accidents	Deaths	Nonfatal injuries	Per cent change in death rate from 1940
Home	26,500	4,000,000	+17
Motor vehicle	38,000	1,400,000	− 9
Work	13,500	1,900,000	+ 4
Public†	16,500	2,100,000	+22
Totals‡	91,500	9,300,000	+5.5

*From Accident facts, published by the National Safety Council, Chicago, Ill., 1962.
†Excludes motor vehicle and work accidents; includes recreational (swimming, hunting, etc.), transportation (except motor vehicle), and public building accidents, etc.
‡Some duplication in motor vehicle accidents occurs in all classes; therefore, columns will not add to true totals.

that there is greater reduction in deaths caused by infectious diseases, such as tuberculosis, pneumonia, gastritis, and enteritis, which were among the leading causes of death at the turn of the last century.

A comparison on an international basis indicates that year after year the United States consistently has one of the highest accidental death rates. Among the major nations of the world the United States has the doubtful honor of having the highest accidental death rate over a span of the past quarter century.

Fatalities and injuries. The 1962 report of the National Safety Council on accidental deaths and injures reveals the importance of accidents in the welfare (Table 24) of the nation.

Principal causes of accidental deaths, excluding motor vehicle accidents in 1961, indicate the nature of the accidents which terminated fatally (Table 25).

The significance of these figures lies in their implications for safety promotion. The national experience is valuable as a general guide, but for specific communi-

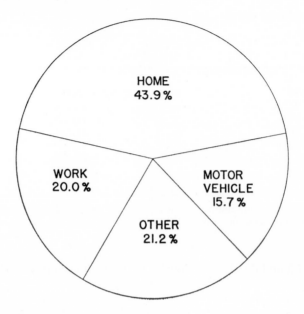

Fig. 38. Where accidents happen—estimates of per cent of injuries by place, United States, 1962. (Based on data from the National Safety Council, 1963; Courtesy Oregon State Board of Health.)

Table 25. Fatal accidents (all ages) in the United States, 1961, excluding motor vehicle accidents*

Nature of accident	Death total	Per cent change in death rate from 1957
Falls	18,400	−10
Drownings	6,550	− 3
Fire burns and other injuries associated with fire	6,900	+ 7
Railroad accidents	2,300	− 4
Firearms	2,300	+ 1
Poison gases	1,050	+10
Poisons (solid or liquid)	1,800	+ 3
All other types	15,400	− 8

*From Accident facts, published by the National Safety Council, Chicago, Ill., 1962.

ties or groups the local experience in terms of various age groups must be analyzed for the organization of effective safety programs on the local level. A study of nonfatal injuries will cast light on the specific needs in safety promotion.

Although deaths from accidents are more easily counted and seem more tragic, injuries can be more costly both in money and in lifelong grief. A person who loses his eyesight or a limb or is paralyzed is a more tragic reminder of the accident-producing situation than a headstone in the cemetery.

The most costly injuries result from falls from one level to another. There were 230,000,000 man-days lost because of work injuries in 1961, costing $4,600-000,000. More injuries occur among workers off the job than on. The accident rate among workers has been decreasing steadily, but more rapidly at work than away from work. It is estimated and studies throughout the country are bearing this out that for every home accident fatality there are 200 injuries that will cause temporary loss of time from ordinary activities and there will be four people who will sustain permanently disabling injuries.

Cost of accidents. Accidental injuries and deaths, together with noninjury motor vehicle and work accidents, and fires cost the staggering sum of at least $14,500,000,000. These costs may be roughly divided into the following categories: wages lost during inability to work, lower wages because of permanent impairment, and value of future earnings lost through death or permanent disability, $4,100,000,000; medical fees and hospital expenses, $1,400,000,000; administrative and claim settlement, $3,200,000,000; property damage in motor vehicle accidents, $2,300,000,000; property destroyed by fire, $1,209,000,000; and property destroyed or production lost due to work accidents, $2,300,000,000.

Age group experience. In the United States, in 1959, accidents were the leading cause of death for persons in the age group 1 to 36 years. How important accidents are as a cause of death in the younger age groups can be more fully appreciated by noting the wide margin between accidental and other causes of death in these younger groups.

In the age group 1 to 4 years accidental deaths are about twice as high as deaths due to pneumonia, the second highest cause, although the rate is about half what it was at the turn of the century. In age group 5 to 14 years, the number

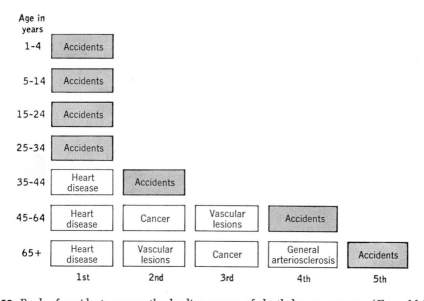

Fig. 39. Rank of accidents among the leading causes of death by age groups. (From McFarland, R. A.: The role of human factors in accident trauma, Am. J. Med. Sc. **234:**1, 1957.)

of deaths due to accidents is twice that of the combined total of the next two causes, cancer and congenital malformations. In the age group 15 to 24 years, accidents account for twice as many deaths as the combined total of the next two causes, cancer and heart trouble. For the age group 25 to 44 years, although heart disease is the principal cause of death, it exceeds accidental deaths by an insignificant amount. In every age group in the United States accidents are one of the five leading causes of death, but in the younger age group they are in a commanding first position. The youth of the United States foolishly and needlessly throw away their lives. Accidents take their greatest toll in the prime of life.

THE HUMAN FACTOR IN ACCIDENTS

Safety is primarily a matter of individual adaptation. Safe effective living requires adaptation not only to the physical environment, but also to other human beings who modify the physical environment. The requirements for living safely in the kaleidoscope of situations in complex modern community living become more exacting year after year. Everyone must learn to recognize situations involving hazards. Each of us must develop orderly patterns of conduct which will enable us to meet situations of daily life with as little hazard as possible to ourselves and to others. Alertness, agility, and coordination are valuable assets when a person is confronted with dangerous situation, but the foresight to anticipate danger is a more valuable and necessary attribute. Established safe practices in the exercise of everyday activities and the safe use of facilities are essential to health and survival. Cooperation with others and consideration for their welfare are contributions to one's own safety. Understanding of safety rules, regulations, and standards and a constant obedience to these safety requirements are invaluable aids in safety promotion. An individual living in a complex social order must acquire wholesome reactions toward organized efforts to assure safety for all. These are the human attributes necessary for maximum safety, the only justifiably acceptable standard.

Whereas individuals vary markedly in physical and mental equipment, the vast majority of people within the normal range have adequate native equipment to acquire a mode of life necessary to safe living. Perhaps some individuals in normal life actually lack the necessary native equipment to adjust to the usual hazards of life. However, scientific data are lacking to confirm the contention. Evidence does indicate that accident repeaters or those who tend to be unduly involved in accidents are those who have failed to develop certain personal qualities essential to safety. In identifying accident repeaters the most common approach is to realize that "a man works or drives as he lives." At the other pole are those safe individuals who rarely suffer accidental injury because they have acquired personal traits which are the true guardians of personal safety. These traits are four: knowledge, practices, skill, and attitudes.

Knowledge. Most individuals have a general knowledge of the cause and nature of accidents in the home, in traffic, in industry, in the school, and in other areas of common experience. Yet more than a generalized knowledge is demanded for maximum or even optimum safety. An individual must have specific knowledge of the likely hazards in the environment in which he lives. More, he must have specific knowledge of his hazardous practices and those of the persons about him. A knowledge of particular hazards must be supplemented by knowledge of definite preventive action and procedures. Whereas knowledge is an essential in the promotion of personal safety, knowledge that is not applied is of little more than academic value.

Practices. All practices in life may be regarded as having hazard and safety implications. Yet certain practices in each person's mode of life are of such great significance as to command special analysis and evaluation in terms of the best accepted safety practices. Habitual conduct particularly should conform to accepted safety practices and be subjected to frequent evaluation and overhauling. The demands of changing life situations require constant modification of habits. New experiences should be approached with considerable critical analysis and studied adjustment in the light of safety requirements. Intense effort is required to establish safe personal and community practices.

Skill. Success in establishing a safe practice depends upon one's proficiency in the performance of the practice. Some avenues of life require a high degree of skill for safe living. Whether it be driving a car on a highway or handling an animal on a farm, skill contributes immeasurably to safety. Acquiring optimum skill may require extensive application. Indeed many individuals may fail to attain optimum skill because of a lack of sufficient effort. In other instances an individual may lack the ability to acquire the necessary skill. Industry has found that unskillful workers are unsafe workers, and, in practice, workers are shifted to jobs in which they have sufficient skill to work safely. The same theory is used in the attempt to deny a driver's license to an unskillful car driver, but the practice here is not so easily applied as in industry. However, lack of skill is a hazard in any walk of life.

Attitudes. One of the basic elements in the causation of accidents is faulty attitudes. By improving attitudes safety behavior can be improved. There appears to be a common pattern of emotional reactions and personalities in accident repeaters. Usually combinations of outside pressure and inner tempest are present. Such things as impulsiveness, concentration on current pleasures to the exclusion of long-range goals, resentment of authority, aggressiveness, insecurity, and emotional instability are common among members of the accident group. The same traits are found in habitual lawbreakers.

An attitude is commonly regarded as a predisposition to react in a certain way in a given situation. That the proper predisposition to react to hazards is important in survival and good health is generally recognized. Yet too little attention is given to the development of desirable safety attitudes.

Most attitudes are specific although some are fairly generalized. Attitudes are basically emotional, a matter of feeling. Pronounced likes or dislikes are not necessarily involved. However, in the development of health attitudes a tangible degree of favorable acceptance, satisfaction, and self-gratification is essential. Attitudes develop largely as by-products of experience rather than by any artificial process of manufacture.

Desirable safety attitudes will be expressed through alertness, observation, precaution, apprehension, thoughtfulness, regard for the safety of others, respect for rules and regulations, orderliness, patience, willingness to accept inconvenience, and pride in safety achievement.

Many avenues of experience may contribute to desirable safety attitudes. Most important is the effect of the practices of others about us, particularly those for whom we have a high regard—parents, brothers and sisters, teachers, city officials, and associates. The old dictum, "Attitudes are more quickly caught than taught," is well supported. Group opinion, special safety experiences, organized safety programs, special appeals, and special responsibility for safety tend to promote a predisposition to react properly in promoting safety in each situation encountered. The caution of later years is largely the cumulative effect of modifying and intensifying attitudes of safety.

SAFETY

Home safety. Even though home accidents cause one third of all accident fatalities and about one half of the injuries, most people are not aware that the home can be a dangerous place, but think of it rather as a safe place. The phrase, "in the safety of your own home," is a myth. Because of this attitude safety practices learned and applied elsewhere are often not carried into the home. For instance, a father learns to wipe up spilled grease, use a well-built and well-supported ladder, and store paints and explosives properly on the job, but does none of these things at home. The problem is to develop a safety awareness which will apply no matter where the individual may be. Promotion of safety in the home requires an analysis of home accident experience as a basis for a well-formulated definite program of accident prevention. Causes of home accidents are almost without number, and each is of significant importance. Yet certain types of accidents occur with such high frequency that they command major attention and are the focus of all efforts for the prevention of home accidents.

Nature of home accidents. New devices in the home are producing an increase in the types of accidents and new accident problems. Among these devices are power tools, power mowers, plastic bags, discarded refrigerators, chemical cleaners, weed killers, and pesticides. Home accidents cause more than one fourth of all accidental deaths. In 1961, there were 26,500 home fatalities and 4,000,000 injuries. This represents a cost of over $1,050,000,000 in lost wages, medical expense, and overhead cost of insurance. This does not include property damage, of which fire losses totaled more than $400,000,000.

Of these 26,500 home fatalities, fire and burns were the major contributors for persons between the ages of 1 and 64 years. Falls were a major cause of death to people over 65 years of age.

Suffocation occurs primarily to infants. Most of these deaths are due probably to an acute upper respiratory illness. Often deaths of this nature are classified as accidental by the coroner, without an autopsy.

Location of home accidents. Studies reveal that about one fourth of all fatal home accidents occur in the bedroom, usually from a fall. Half of all fatal fires start in the bedroom. The principal causes are smoking in bed and defective heaters. Stairs are the location of about one eighth of all fatal home accidents. The largest portion of fatalities on stairways result from the falls of older persons. About one tenth of the accidental home fatalities occur in the kitchen, and a like amount occur in the yard. Contrary to popular belief, less than one twentieth of all fatal home accidents occur in the bathroom, although 5% is not an insignificant portion.

It is in the ordinary activities of the home that accidents occur. Simple as the home environment appears to be, it represents many hazards to health and even to life itself. Very young and very old persons find it particularly difficult to adjust to the physical demands of the home.

Preventing home accidents. The survey method is a practical tangible approach to the prevention of home accidents. Although a survey is a means to an end, it is an effective means to the final goal of safety promotion. Hazards must be discovered if accidents are to be prevented and safety is to be promoted.

The newer survey approach recognizes that *conditions* and *practices* in the home are the two factors which operate in causing accidents and are the two factors by means of which a constructive accident prevention program can be promoted. For this reason home conditions and practices are incorporated into a home safety survey.

A *home safety survey* is based upon home conditions and practices of recognized importance in safety promotion.

Basement and laundry
1. Are all flues, stovepipes, and chimneys clean and tight?
2. Are combustible surfaces near stoves, furnaces, and vents insulated?
3. Is kindling wood stored at a safe distance from the furnace?
4. Are furnace fires started without the use of gasoline, kerosene, or other explosive materials?
5. Are ashes always placed in metal containers?
6. Are old newspapers and other inflammable materials removed promptly from the basement?
7. If the laundry floor tends to be damp, is a rubber mat provided?
8. Are cords that are exposed to water rubber coated?
9. Are the moving parts on the washing machine properly guarded?
10. Does the wringer have a properly operating safety release?
11. Are tubs so placed that little children will not fall into them?
12. Are soap, powder, and other detergents kept off the floor to prevent slipping?
13. When not in use, are electrical appliances disconnected from the wall socket?
14. Are the basement and laundry room adequately lighted?

15. Are all gas connections checked twice a year to detect leaks or defects?
16. Are noninflammable cleaning fluids used and only out of doors?
17. Is a regular place provided for tools?
18. Is an inspection made once a month to check any special hazards peculiar to a particular basement or laundry?

Kitchen

1. Is the floor clean and free from hazards, such as upturned linoleum edges?
2. Are matches in metal containers and out of children's reach?
3. Is a short, sturdy stepladder used for reaching high places?
4. Are electric appliances disconnected from the wall when not in use?
5. Is the electric iron rested on a proper stand when not in use?
6. Are the handles of pots and pans on the range turned out of the reach of children?
7. Are receptacles with water emptied immediately after using?
8. Are all gas connections checked twice a year to detect leaks or defects?
9. Is care taken to prevent gas flames from being extinguished by liquids boiling over or by drafts?
10. Are knives and other sharp instruments kept out of the reach of children?
11. In using a knife, do you always cut away from the body?

Fig. 40. Safety in the kitchen. A strong stool, low-heeled shoes, balanced stance, adequate light, handles turned out of reach of children, and unused appliances disconnected protect the homemaker and others against mishaps.

Living room and dining room

1. Are small rugs anchored so that they do not slip on polished floors?
2. Are the edges of rugs prevented from curling?
3. Is there a storage place for toys, and are they kept there when not in use?
4. Is nonskid wax used on floors?
5. Are chairs and other furniture in good repair?
6. Are scissors kept out of reach of small children?
7. Are pins and razor blades wrapped and disposed of properly?
8. Are extension cords placed where they will not be tripped over?
9. Are open wall sockets plugged?
10. Are all electric fixtures of an approved type and in good condition?
11. Is a sturdy stepladder used in reaching high places?
12. Are cigarette stubs extinguished and placed in convenient noninflammable containers?
13. Is a screen placed in front of a fireplace?

Stairs

1. Are stairs well lighted and unobstructed?
2. Do light switches operate from top and bottom of the stairs?
3. Is carpeting fastened securely to the floor and in good repair?
4. Is there a strong handrail on at least one side of the stair?
5. Are there secure gates at the bottom and top of stairs to protect young children?
6. Are all members of the household careful not to carry heavy loads on stairs?
7. Do the aged live entirely on the first floor and avoid the use of stairs?
8. Is the bottom step on the basement stairs painted a luminous white?

Bathroom

1. Is a rubber mat placed in the tub and a handhold installed on the wall?
2. Are electric fixtures of porcelain or other insulating materials?
3. Are portable appliances and cabinets moved out of the way when not in use?
4. Are medicines and poisonous substances placed in a locked cabinet or other place inaccessible to children?
5. Are all poisons kept in clearly marked containers?
6. Is a pin stuck in the cork of every bottle containing poison and are labels double checked under clear light before the poison is used?
7. Are little children never left alone in the bathroom?
8. Is there an extra key in the event that a child locks himself in?

Bedroom

1. Is the passageway from the bed to the door unobstructed?
2. Are dresser drawers and closet doors always closed when not used?
3. Are window screens securely installed?
4. Are electric heaters disconnected at the wall before the occupant goes to sleep or leaves the room?
5. Is there a convenient light switch for emergency night use?
6. Is it a practice never to smoke in bed?
7. Are safeguards provided to prevent children from falling out of cribs or beds?

Garage, yard, and porch

1. Are garage doors open while the car motor is running?
2. Is there a safe place to store garden equipment?
3. Is rubbish burned in a metal container on windless days and are children kept away?
4. Is the ladder of sound construction and properly anchored when used?
5. Are snow and slush promptly removed from porch and walks?
6. Is ice covered with sand, ashes, or other gritty materials?
7. Do the porch steps have a strong handrail?
8. Are the porch steps and walks unobstructed?

This over-all survey covers the essentials in the prevention of home accidents. The survey is a means to an end. Without a constructive determined program which produces changes in home safety conditions and practices, a home survey is a mere gesture. Translating the results of the survey into a positive way of living is the effective approach to home safety.

Farm safety. On the farm the place of work and the home are one and the same. Promotion of safety on the farm must be based upon an understanding of farm accident experience from which is formulated a definite program of accident prevention. The need for such a program is reflected in the 8700 farm residents who were killed in accidents and the 800,000 who were injured in 1961. The fatalities break down into motor vehicle accidents, 3500; home accidents, 2100; work accidents, 2700; public nonmotor vehicle accidents, 900. The 2700 deaths in farm work are the greatest number in any major industry, and the death rate per 100,-000 workers places farming third, following mining and extraction and construction. During the past five years farm accident rates have remained about the same.

Nature of farm accidents. Half of the fatalities on farm land and around service buildings are caused by machinery and drowning. A large proportion of farm accidents occur among persons in the younger age group (under 25 years of age). A comparison of the causes of accidents between farm and nonfarm groups is given in Table 26.

Location of farm accidents. The surveys of the Bureau of Agricultural Economics reveal the following locations of accidents causing injury to farm residents:

Home	16%	Road or street	11%
Barn	22%	Elsewhere or unkonwn	17%
Elsewhere on farm	34%		

The vast variety of activities of life on a farm poses a special problem of safe living not only for survival, but also for effective and enjoyable living. Accidents in the farm home are comparable to accidents in urban homes, but farm life places the agricultural family in a variety of places having unique safety problems.

Table 26. Fatalities on farm land and around service buildings by cause and comparison with comparable nonfarm fatalities

Cause	Farm (%)	Nonfarm (%)	Cause	Farm (%)	Nonfarm (%)
Machinery	34.1	5.6	Electric current	3.4	3.4
Drowning	15.0	22.3	Lighting	2.5	0.4
Farearms	12.0	3.8	Poisoning	1.7	1.1
Falls	9.1	35.6	Suffocation	1.4	1.0
Blows	5.7	4.7	Other	5.0	17.0
Burns	5.2	5.0	Total	100.0	100.0
Animals	4.9	0.1			

Data for farm accidents are from U. S. Department of Agriculture; data for nonfarm accidents are estimates by the National Safety Council.

Preventing farm accidents. A program for preventing farm accidents will include the prevention of home accidents as well as prevention of accidents in other realms of farm experience. A survey of conditions and practices serves as the basis for constructive preventive action.

A *farm safety survey* includes the home as well as all other aspects of the farm environment

Farmyard

1. Do farmyard driveways provide a clear vision for car drivers and pedestrians who may use them?
2. Are cars driven slowly in the farmyard?
3. Is the parking place provided for cars one which will promote safety in backing out or in driving away?
4. Are unused lumber and other materials piled or properly put away?
5. Are bins, racks, gates, and fences in good repair?
6. Are postholes and other holes properly covered or barricaded?
7. Are highly inflammable materials, sharp objects, and rubbish disposed of properly?

Buildings

1. Are all buildings in good repair?
2. Are stairs and ladders in good condition and free from obstruction?
3. Are all loose boards nailed down?
4. Are slippery floors covered with sand, straw, or other materials to prevent slipping?
5. Do only qualified people climb the silo, windmill, barn, or other high places?
6. Are hayloft and other openings properly covered or barricaded?
7. Is smoking in the hay barn prohibited?
8. Is the hayloft properly ventilated to help prevent combustion?

Equipment, machinery, tools, and supplies

1. Are dangerous tools locked up away from the grasp of children?
2. Are insecticides and other poisons properly locked up?
3. Is gasoline stored separately in a proper tank?
4. Is a definite place assigned for all tools and and equipment?
5. Are handles on tools secure?
6. Are children not allowed on farm machinery while the motor is running or the team is hitched to it?
7. Is the motor shut off when the operator is not in the seat?
8. Are all machines and motors stopped before repairs are attempted?
9. Are all pulleys, hoisting equipment, and parts required to hold heavy loads inspected carefully before being used?
10. Is machinery properly stored and kept in good repair?

Animals

1. Do only qualified people handle livestock?
2. Are dangerous animals properly penned?
3. Is a lead staff always used in handling bulls?
4. Are animals always approached by speaking to them to avoid frightening them?
5. Is special care taken in harnessing, hitching, and unhitching horses to prevent runaways?
6. Are children properly instructed in necessary safety measures to avoid being injured by animals?

Together with the home survey, this farm survey may serve as the basis for a constructive reappraisal of safe living on the farm. As busy as a farm family may be, time is well invested which is used to formulate a safe routine of living. Too often it takes a serious accident to arouse an agricultural family to an awareness of hazards on the farm. Although this is perhaps the most effective form of safety education, it likewise is the most costly. No farm family is too busy to give proper time and attention to safety on the farm.

Occupational safety. With the introduction of Workmen's Compensation laws in 1912, industry began a safety program which effectively reduced the rates of both fatal and nonfatal accidents. The occupational death rate continues to decline, the rate for 1961 being 21 per 100,000 workers. This compares very favorably with the 1951 rate of 28 per 100,000 workers. Yet, during 1961, 13,500 workers were killed as a result of occupational accidents and 1,900,000 were injured. Time lost because of work injuries in 1961 amounted to 230,000,000 mandays. The estimated cost of work accidents was $4,600,000,000. More fatalities occurred in agriculture than in any other industrial classification. However, based on statistics for fatalities and injuries per 100,000 workers, the classification of mining, quarrying, and oil and gas wells was by far the most hazardous. The next most hazardous classification was construction work, followed by farming.

Nature of occupational accidents. Year after year the handling of objects by workers continues to be the principal source of injuries. About 24% of all accidents occur in this activity. About 18% are due to falls, 10% are associated with machinery, and 10% are due to falling objects. Hand tools and vehicles each account for about 7% of the occupational injuries.

In over 80% of all occupational accidents which cause permanent disability or death, an unsafe condition or act or both are important contributing factors. Among unsafe conditions may be listed hazardous arrangement or procedure, improper guarding, defective agencies, unsafe dress or apparel, and improper ventilation. Unsafe acts may be unnecessary exposure to danger, unsafe or improper use of equipment, working on moving or dangerous equipment, nonuse of protective devices, improper starting or stopping, over-loading or poor arranging, making safety devices inoperative, and operating at unsafe speed. It is obvious that many, if not most, of these conditions and acts could be prevented.

The parts of the body most commonly injured are: the trunk, 25%; the fingers, 20%; the legs, 12%; and the arms, 9%. Injuries to the trunk are on the average most costly. Eye injuries are the most costly among the permanent disabilities.

Workers suffer over twice as many deaths and injuries off the job as at work. Off-the-job deaths have decreased, but not as much as on-the-job deaths.

Preventing occupational accidents. Problems in accident prevention vary from industry to industry, from plant to plant, from job to job, and from worker to worker. Yet fundamentally the approach to the prevention of occupational accidents is basically the same. The program is based on eliminating or modifying unsafe conditions and preventing unsafe acts.

Unsafe conditions, being somewhat stable physical factors, are rarely difficult to correct. An ability to foresee physical dangers is essential to safety, and industries engage safety experts to work constantly at accident prevention.

Unsafe acts represent a more difficult problem in prevention largely because of that extreme variable, the human being. Developing in each worker the knowledge, skill, practices, and attitudes necessary for promoting his own safety and the safety of others is a problem in education. Many individuals appear to be incapable of working with reasonable safety in certain jobs. The accident-prone worker is usually in this category. Safety specialists in industrial firms strive to locate the right job for every worker as well as the right worker for every job. Although safety is recognized as an economic asset, industries are sincerely interested in protecting the health and lives of their employees through effective continuous safety programs.

Motor vehicle safety. In 1895, the four motor vehicles in the United States were an oddity and a source of considerable amusement. In 1961 the 76,000,000 registered motor vehicles representing a total of 735,000,000,000 miles and the 90,500,000 licensed drivers in the United States posed a major problem in human health and life conservation. Since the turn of the century, more than 1,000,000 people have lost their lives in motor vehicle accidents in the United States. The cost of these accidents is in excess of $100,000,000,000. During the same period more than 32,000,000 people have suffered nonfatal injuries in motor vehicle accidents. The volume of vehicular accidents a year is about 10,000,000, involving 17,-000,000 cars, or one in four of the 76,000,000 in use. The cost of accidents in 1961 was $14,500,000.

No one would advocate that motor vehicles be abolished. No one acquainted with motor vehicle safety programs would deny that progress is being made in preventing motor vehicle accidents. Yet a survey of motor vehicle accidents in recent years indicates the need for intensified effort to prevent deaths and injuries

Table 27. The motor vehicle problem, 1921 to 1961*

Year	Number of vehicles (millions)	Vehicle miles (billions)	Number of drivers† (millions)	Costs ($ millions)	Deaths	Mileage death rate‡
1921	10.5	55	15		13,900	25.3
1925	19.9	122	30		21,900	18.0
1930	26.5	206	39	1,450	32,900	16.0
1935	26.2	229	39	1,600	36,369	15.9
1940	32.0	302	48	1,600	34,501	11.4
1945	30.6	249	46	1,450	28,076	11.3
1950	48.6	458	62	3,100	34,763	7.6
1955	62.0	595	76	4,500	38,300	6.4
1960	73.9	719	87.9	6,500	38,200	5.3
1961	76.0	735	90.5	6,900	38,000	5.2

*From Accident facts, published by the National Safety Council, Chicago, Ill., 1962.
†Estimated at 1.5 drivers per vehicle prior to 1950.
‡Number of deaths per 100,000,000 vehicle miles.

Table 28. Fatalities due to motor vehicle accidents, 1961*

How fatalities occurred	1961	Change from 1951
Collision between motor vehicles	14,700	+8%
Noncollision in roadway, overturning, running off highway	12,200	+9%
Pedestrian accidents	7,650	−19%
Collisions with railroad trains	1,225	−5%
Collisions with fixed objects	1,650	+1%

*From Accident facts, published by the National Safety Council, Chicago, Ill., 1962.

due to these accidents. Unless the rate is reduced appreciably from the 1961 level, it can be predicted that one out of every three children born in the United States in 1961 will be killed or injured in a motor vehicle accident. Some aspects of the motor vehicle problem are shown in Table 27.

Nature of motor vehicle accidents. Of the 38,000 fatalities due to motor vehicle accidents in 1961, 10,500 occurred in towns and cities and 27,500 occurred in rural areas. Deaths according to type of accident were distributed as shown in Table 28.

From year to year the picture concerning motor vehicle accidents changes somewhat. Yet a composite picture can be drawn from the experience of the past decade. From that composite summary certain factors relating to the driver, pedestrian, vehicle, and physical conditions are of significance in determining the course of action necessary to an effective program of safety promotion. In 1961, 90% of all drivers involved in fatal traffic accidents were violating proper driving procedures.

In approximately one third of all fatal accidents unsafe speed is a contributing or primary cause. In towns and cities violation of the right of way is involved in about 20% of all fatal accidents. In rural areas driving on the wrong side of the road and improper passing are factors in about 17% of all fatal accidents.

Based on mileage driven, drivers under 20 years of age have the highest accident rate. Speeding is a frequent accident factor in this group. Year after year drivers in the age group between 45 and 49 years combine skill and conformity to driving regulations to have the most favorable driver safety record; although in 1961 drivers in the age group between 55 and 59 years had the best record.

More than 21% of all drivers in fatal accidents have been drinking alcohol before the time of the accident. The physical condition of one out of thirteen drivers is a contributing factor in fatal accidents. In about two thirds of these drivers sleep or fatigue was the cause. Other conditions in order of importance were defective eyesight, illness, and defective hearing.

Unsafe condition of the vehicle is a factor in about 6% of all fatal accidents. Usually the unsafe condition of the vehicle is a contributing factor in the accident, but not a primary factor. Nevertheless the condition of the vehicle is of significance in traffic safety.

Motor-vehicle death rates, by states, 1962

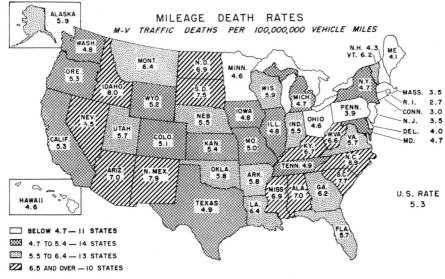

Fig. 41. Mileage death rates for motor vehicle accidents by states in 1962 (motor vehicle traffic deaths per 100,000,000 miles). (From Accident facts, published by the National Safety Council, Chicago, Ill., 1963.)

Motor-vehicle death rates, by states, 1962

POPULATION DEATH RATES
M-V TRAFFIC DEATHS PER 100,000 POPULATION

ALASKA 15.9

WASH. 20.3
ORE. 26.0
IDAHO 39.0
MONT. 36.1
N.D. 27.1
MINN. 20.0
WIS. 23.3
MICH. 19.7
N.H. 17.6
VT. 26.4
ME. 17.6
N.Y. 13.6
MASS. 13.6
R.I. 9.9
CONN. 12.4
N.J. 14.6
DEL. 20.0
MD. 18.4

NEV. 48.4
WYO. 35.3
S.D. 34.1
IOWA 22.3
NEB. 27.0
PENN. 14.3
OHIO 18.3
IND. 26.0
ILL. 18.6
W.VA. 24.1
VA. 23.3

CALIF. 24.3
UTAH 24.1
COLO. 23.6
KAN. 26.9
MO. 23.4
KY. 25.7
N.C. 27.9

ARIZ. 33.7
N. MEX. 42.8
OKLA. 28.9
ARK. 28.3
TENN. 22.3
S.C. 31.1

HAWAII 12.3
TEXAS 23.9
LA. 23.2
MISS. 26.4
ALA. 27.4
GA. 27.1

FLA. 24.7

U.S. RATE 22.0

- [ ] BELOW 19.0 — 13 STATES
- 19.1 TO 24.0 — 12 STATES
- 24.1 TO 28.0 — 15 STATES
- 28.1 AND OVER — 10 STATES

Source: National Safety Council estimates based on data from state traffic authorities. National Vital Statistics Division, and U.S. Bureau of Public Roads.

Fig. 42. Population death rates for motor vehicle accidents by states for 1962, in deaths per 100,000 population. (From Accident facts, published by the National Safety Council, Chicago, Ill., 1963.)

Obstruction to vision is a significant factor in 15% of all fatal motor vehicle accidents. Snow, rain, sleet, fog, trees, bushes, crops, and cars are common obstructions.

Highway defects are a factor in less than 5% of all fatal accidents. Yet the condition of the road is an important factor. About 20% of all fatal motor vehicle accidents occur on wet, muddy, icy, or snowy roads although the condition of the road is not always the primary cause of the accident.

Based on miles driven the accident rate at night is about three times as high as the daylight rate. Twilight hours are hours of high motor vehicle accident rates. Drunk driving accounts for another high rate around the midnight hour.

Pedestrian fatalities are heaviest among persons in the age group 65 years and over. Inability to adjust to the modern tempo of life is characteristic of the aged. In pedestrian fatalities the pedestrian himself is violating the law in approximately 75% of the accidents. About 25% of pedestrians killed by a motor vehicle had been drinking alcohol previous to the time of the fatal accident. It is apparent from these data that the human being himself is the important factor in motor vehicle accidents. Although attention must be given to the vehicle, the highway, and other physical factors, it is the individual driver and pedestrian who command the greatest attention.

Prevention of motor vehicle accidents. Early attempts to deal with the problem of motor vehicle accidents were disorganized unscientific hit-or-miss efforts. By 1925 traffic experience in the United States had provided sufficient data on which to base a tangible objectively planned program of accident prevention. Using surveys, statistics, and special investigations as a basis, various groups, organizations, communities, and states initiated planned controlled traffic safety programs. In 1939 the composite contributions of all of these efforts were unified to produce the Standard Highway Safety Program for States, which serves as the pattern for a broad over-all safety program for motor vehicles.

The present-day traffic safety program has four basic essential phases: legislation, enforcement, engineering, and education. All are essential elements in a complete program. To these may be added research, personnel training, and motor vehicle administration, but these can be incorporated into the four basic phases:

Legislation. Legislation crystallizes the experience of the public into regulations which promote both safety and facility in motor vehicle traffic. Absolute uniformity of traffic regulations in all states may not be desirable, but the wide disparity in regulations from state to state is not conducive to the highest level of traffic safety. Uniformity and coordination of traffic laws, so far as practical, must be obtained in the interest of human survival and welfare. Data are available on which effective uniform traffic regulations can be based. States can work cooperatively on such a subject without any sacrifice of sovereignty or identity.

Enforcement. Enforcement is an essential corollary of legislation and is a highly important phase in the promotion of motor vehicle safety as well as in traffic movement. However, many citizens wrongly assume that enforcement is the only necessary activity for traffic safety. These individuals look upon the enforcement program as a matter of running down law violators. Actually in operation the enforcement program is aimed at guiding the public in safe conduct and resorts to the ultimate in authority only in the extreme situations.

A primary requisite to good enforcement is the licensing of qualified motor vehicle drivers. Although forty-eight states now require a license to drive a car, in most states the requirements for a license are little more than a gesture. A written examination on traffic regulations and driving problems, a test of vision and hearing, and a road test of actual driving skill should be a minimum. Many who can pass this threefold examination may be poor driver risks. A driver may have good vision and hearing, know traffic regulations, and have driving skill, but still be an accident-prone driver. Personality deficiencies account for recklessness, disregard for others, lack of responsibility, and frequent accidents. Histories of accident-prone drivers reveal these individuals to be impulsive, defiant of authority, impatient, excitable, lacking in a concept of responsibility, grossly careless, slow in desirable reactions, unstable, casual in social relations, or even unsocial. Although all accident-prone drivers do not manifest all of these characteristics, they do manifest this general pattern of personality. Although revoking the license of an accident-prone driver is the device used to eliminate him as a public hazard, this action is usually taken after damage has been done. What is needed is a pretest that will locate the accident-prone person before he becomes a driver.

Enforcement officers cannot cover every foot of highway and every action of driver and pedestrian. As a result statistics and past experience indicate where emphasis in enforcement must be placed. Selective enforcement is thus practical enforcement. Special accident investigations are important in giving direction to enforcement efforts.

Warning tickets for erring first-violation drivers have merit because they give an offender an opportunity to demonstrate his willingness and ability to drive within legal regulations. No stigma is attached to the warning. After a third warning ticket, an arrest order should be issued.

The enforcement index is an attempt to measure the quantity of police traffic enforcement by relating the number of violation convictions to the number of accidents reported. The usually accepted standard is ten convictions for moving vehicle violations for every accident resulting in injury or death. Studies reveal this quantity of enforcement is reasonably effective in curbing motor vehicle accidents.

Requiring a traffic law violator to attend a traffic law violator's school has been effective in educating drivers and creating a better relationship between driver and police officer. The success of this program depends largely upon the ability of the individuals conducting the school.

A constructive approach to enforcement has been made by recognizing and rewarding safe and courteous drivers. Giving good drivers something to live up to rather than something to live down tends to make them even better drivers. A special safe-driver sticker on his vehicle motivates the driver to measure up to his reputation.

Effective enforcement cannot rise above the level of the enforcing officers. Competent traffic officials mean competent traffic control and safety promotion. Competent courts with adequate personnel for thorough study of violators are a recognized nationwide need. Traffic violations must be regarded as crimes and are involving an increasing proportion of our total population. The implications are obvious.

Engineering. Engineering and its indispensable role in the promotion of motor vehicle safety are inherent in the nature of motor vehicle operation. Beginning with the design of the car, the automotive engineer incorporates every possible safety factor into the design of the motor vehicle. All-steel bodies, shatter-proof glass, low center of gravity, balance, frame, brakes, lights, steering apparatus, tires, defrosters, seat belts, and all other aspects of the vehicle are designed with safety as a dominant factor. Although motor cars are faster and more powerful, they are safer than ever before.

Highway engineering incorporates all possible safety features into highway construction. Width and curvature of highways, highway locations, highway surfaces, underpasses, overpasses, guide lines, and guardrails are planned primarily in the interest of safety.

In 1925 the new field of traffic engineering was recognized. Traffic engineering concerns itself with problems of effective and safe motor vehicle transportation. Its interest in facilitating traffic is basically an aspect of safety. Traffic engineering deals with highway plans, the flow of traffic, volume of traffic, delays in traffic, traffic diversion, special zones, accident incidence, signs and signals, illumination of highways, driver vision obstruction, pedestrian traffic, and all other traffic problems of an engineering nature.

Motor vehicle accidents could be reduced sharply if the precise methods of the engineer could be utilized to the fullest extent. Cost has been the principal limiting factor to the engineer. Conceivably a national system of highways can be designed in which every physical safeguard would be incorporated to compensate for the imperfect variable, man himself. Completely separated traffic lanes, adequate underpasses and overpasses, proper guardrails and illumination, together with other engineering developments on an extensive scale would be a multibillion dollar project. In effect it would not be an expense but an investment in human life and welfare.

Education. Education and its importance in motor vehicle safety arise from the imperfection and variability of the human being himself. The engineer can employ precise calculations when dealing with the physical factors involved in traffic safety. Our physical environment is consistent and thus amenable to precise measurement and prediction. The human being in relation to traffic problems is highly variable, individualistic, and not definitely predictable. The most difficult factor to deal with in traffic accidents is the human being, and our only method for dealing with him is the slow, tedious, inexact process of education.

Education for traffic safety is directed toward altering the individual himself so that his responses to physical environment and other people are in harmony with recognized safety practices. Any program aimed toward improving an individual's ability to adjust to traffic situations must recognize four major objectives: safety knowledge, safety habits, safety skills, and safety attitudes.

Knowledge of traffic rules and regulations as they pertain to the pedestrian as well as to the car driver and the bicycle rider is a primary essential. Knowledge of both accident hazards and necessary safety procedures is the base of the safety pyramid which each individual can build within himself. Knowledge in itself is not enough. It is a means to an end, but its translation into safety habits, skills, and attitudes will equip the individual to meet the safety demands of modern complex living.

Attitudes of responsibilty for the safety of others and oneself, combined with an awareness of potential hazards, condition an individual to respond to situations with an optimum of safe behavior. Perhaps the ideal is an apprehension of hazardous traffic situations, fortified by a justifiable confidence in one's ability to adjust to these situations.

Education of an adult in the interest of traffic safety is made difficult by his relatively fixed habits and attitudes. It is possible to add to an adult's knowledge through several media, such as pamphlets, leaflets, newspaper articles, radio, television, public addresses, special campaigns, and special classes. Although knowledge can be the avenue through which safety attitudes may be acquired, knowledge of safety gives no assurance of proper safety attitudes. Involvement in a traffic accident is perhaps the most effective single device for inculcating desirable attitudes toward safety, but it is also the most costly method. What is needed is a constructive program in advance to inculcate proper attitudes toward safety without the necessity for tragedy to be the teacher.

Unless safety education is specific enough to cause each individual to identify himself with hazardous situations, it is of little value. The typical response to most safety education is the statement, "Wonderful thing, for the other fellow." To get individuals to grasp the application to themselves is the need and the challenge in safety education.

Public education in traffic safety must be planned, must be definite, continuous, and consistent, and must be undertaken by qualified people. Whatever medium is used, the approach must be directed to the individual, not a broadside effort. Traffic safety slogans are usually delightfully clever but educationally valueless.

Seat belts. Although seat belts do not prevent accidents, they definitely reduce markedly injuries and deaths. The Crash Injury Research Group of Cornell University estimated that, if seat belts were installed and used in all motor vehicles, they would save 5000 lives a year and reduce serious injuries by one third.

Seat belts do have some preventive value in that the act of fastening the belt may create a "safety attitude," and their presence acts as a continuing reminder of attention to safety while driving. In addition they aid in maintaining better posture and reduce fatigue. The need for seat belts is always present since more than half the accidents occur at speeds less than 40 miles per hour and three out of four traffic deaths occur within twenty-five miles of the homes of the victims. These figures correct the false assumption that seat belts are not needed because one drives in his own community at moderate speed.

Driver education. Driver education, adequately administered, can be highly effective in promoting traffic safety education. Driver education is usually the introductory foundation of a systematic driver-training program whether given for students in a high school or for adults. It precedes or accompanies actual road instruction. Or driver education can be given as a separate program for persons who are already licensed to drive. The objectives of driver education indicate the approach and potentialities of the program.

1. To develop an understanding and consequent application of sound principles of traffic efficiency and safety
2. To accept the necessity for laws and regulations as fundamental to safety and to inspire self-disciplined adherence to these laws and regulations
3. To acquire a scientific attitude toward safety and to evaluate critically the justification of existing traffic regulations
4. To accept personal responsibility for the conservation of life and health on the highways
5. To develop a realization of the effect of mental, emotional, and physical characteristics of drivers and pedestrians in prevention and occurrence of accidents
6. To motivate an interest in one's own characteristics affecting safety and in positive action for improvement in terms of accident prevention

Traffic safety education is usually most effective in schools. The program is well organized, students are receptive, and teachers are skilled and experienced in teaching methods. Even in elementary schools pedestrian safety is taught effectively in actual life experiences. The school safety patrol, under supervision, is an effective safety education device.

Driver-training programs can be most effectively organized and administered in the senior high school. Thorough preliminary education with supervised training in driving can turn out skillful and safety-conscious drivers. Interested and competent driver-training instructors in every high school in the nation would pay high dividends in human lives and health.

Whether in the high school or in private promotion, driver-training instruction should be under the supervision of qualified, trained, and interested instructors. Various programs and procedures in driver-training have been used successfully, but the key to success, whatever the method, lies in the competence of the instructor. Adequate time, facilities, and insurance coverage are essentials in the program. A final standard test of competence in both safety knowledge and safety practice should be required of every pupil at the end of the course. The values accruing from skillful and safe driving outweigh manyfold the nominal cost of driver-training programs.

It may not be desirable to have compulsory driver-education training before a driver's license is issued, but it may become a necessity. The ideal is universal voluntary enrollment in driver-education training programs as preparation in qualifying for a driver's license.

Fire safety. Fire has been of tremendous importance in the history of man. Under controlled conditions it has been beneficial. When uncontrolled, it has done and can do untold damage. It is important to recognize that fire is alive; it spreads and grows. A single match carries in it the potentialities of a large conflagration, requiring only inflammable material and an opportunity to reach it.

A casual survey of potential fire hazards which surround us—matches, cigarettes, various types of heating units, candles, trash burners, and sparks from various kinds of appliances and machinery—is evidence of the need for respect for fire and for alertness to its dangers. From the 6,900 deaths and the property damage of $1,209,000,000 annually, not counting forest fires, a loss which is incalculable, it is apparent that we are careless and do not recognize the hazards. Each day fires break out in 800 homes. In 1961, 563,000 urban homes were struck by fire.

In fire safety it is important that proper behavior patterns be developed. The disastrous effect of improper behavior and incorrect practices should be appreciated. Personal responsibility to one's own self and to others should be inculcated in all persons. Acts of carelessness, such as throwing a lighted cigarette from a car window, may create a forest fire and cause great loss not only of timber, but also of wildlife and recreation areas. In many instances lives may be lost. Those who habitually take foolish chances themselves have no right to endanger the well-being and property of others.

Most fires are caused by carelessness. Two of the worst hazards to fire safety are smoking and matches. Careless smoking and the improper use of matches cause 25% of fires. Some faulty habits in smoking include smoking in bed, leaving burning cigarettes on trays where they may fall off or be dumped into a wastepaper basket, and smoking near highly inflammable material.

When matches are used, they should be extinguished and broken before being discarded. Safety matches are preferred, but care should be exercised to close the cover before striking them. Whenever possible, the use of a flashlight for seeing is more effective and much less dangerous. Matches should be stored in metal containers and kept out of the reach of children.

The widespread use of electricity in the home has created many hazards. Perhaps the worst offender is old wiring, poorly installed and insulated, extended by wires hung on nails or nailed to the walls, and new appliances which overload the existing circuits. The usual symptom of the latter condition is a blown fuse.

If this symptom were understood and heeded, the situation might not be so bad. Too often a fuse of larger capacity is used, or a penny is put in place of the fuse. Such action ignores the fact that fuses blow because the wire is not heavy enough to carry the current needed. The larger fuse permits a heavier load, with a consequent heating of the wire which may become intense enough to cause a fire.

The improper use of electrical appliances causes many fires. When not attended or in use, appliances should be turned off. Irons should be set on a metal stand when not in use.

Furnaces and other heating units, if improperly installed and maintained, are a potential hazard. Heating units should be cleaned and adjusted regularly by trained technicians. Inflammable material may come in contact with heating units of kitchen stoves. Spilled grease is a bad offender. Curtains, drying towels, and paper towels should not be so located that they may come in contact with the heating element.

Many of the deaths resulting from fire are caused by improper use of inflammable liquids. Carelessness in use and ignorance of the volatility of liquids such as gasoline, naphtha, benzine, quick-drying paints, paint remover, synthetic thinners, lacquers, and ethyl alcohol are examples. Fumes from some of these liquids will flow 200 feet from their source and explode even when not in contact with a flame. A spark from an electric switch or static electricity may be the exciting cause of an explosion.

Escaping gas is always dangerous. It should never be ignored. When odor of gas is detected, windows should be opened, flames and sparks should be eliminated, and the leak should be sought out; if it is not found, the gas maintenance men should be called. When gas burners are lighted, the match should be ignited before the gas is turned on.

Many fires start in the basements, garages, or attics of homes. This is a matter of poor housekeeping. In the basement and attic are stored or thrown newspapers, cardboard boxes, corrugated paper cartons, excelsior-filled boxes, trunks, clothes, toys, Christmas decorations, and trash of all kinds. These accumulations grow and grow. The carelessly used cigarette or match in proximity to this combustible material can start a fire that will spread rapidly. Much trash, along with paints and oil, is stored in the garage, making it susceptible to fire.

Outdoor fires are always potentially dangerous. If they get out of hand, they may cause millions of dollars of damage and loss of life. Over one third of the forest fires in this country are caused by campers and hunters. Careless smoking habits, use of matches, and improperly attended campfires are responsible in a majority of cases. Campfires should always be kept under control, should not be larger than needed (usually a bed of coals makes the most efficient cooking fire), and must never be left unattended; when left, the fire should be spread out and thoroughly soaked with water, and soil should be thrown over it.

Fires built outdoors to burn leaves or rubbish should be controlled and attended. It is better to burn material in small quantities often than to allow large accumulations that necessitate a large fire which may get out of hand. This is especially true on windy days. After the fire has burned out, the ashes should be spread to discover sparks and then drenched with water.

In case of fire the basic rule is to remain calm. Ideally everyone should have a planned procedure worked out to follow in case of fire. This should prevent panic or ill-considered actions and facilitate the mobilization of all resources available to aid escape. Emergencies may occur in unfamiliar places, but certain fundamental rules will be helpful in most situations.

Be prepared. If you are in a building, check the nearest exit; if you are warned of fire, feel the door to see if it is hot or open it slightly, with a shoulder or a foot firmly placed against the door, to detect pressure from the hall and to prevent smoke and flames from bursting into the room. If it is necessary to leave the room, cover the nose and mouth with a wet towel and crawl on the floor; always close the door behind you to prevent drafts. If it is necessary to escape from a window, jump as a last resort; if it is not too high, knot sheets and other material together to make a rope. The only valid reason to enter a burning building is to save a life.

Recreational safety. Safe adventure or the act of doing things the right way is basic to recreational safety. There has been a tremendous boom in outdoor recreation during the past quarter of a century. Over 70,000,000 people participate yearly in outdoor recreation. A partial list of activities would include swimming, fishing, hunting, boating, golfing, skiing, both water and snow, horseback riding, camping, hiking, and outdoor sports of all kinds. The amount of money spent on outdoor recreation is tremendous, in the tens of billion of dollars annually.

It is recognized that accident hazards are present in many of the activities just enumerated. The key to the prevention of accidents or safety is an understanding of how to do things correctly, instruction and preparation before participation, awareness of one's limitations, and observation of all safety factors of the particular activity.

The number of persons participating in outdoor recreation is increasing year by year, but the number of fatal accidents has not increased. This is excellent testimony to the preparation that most participants make before engaging in outdoor sports, the programs of organizations that sponsor participation, and the engineering and safety devices of physical plants and equipment.

About 16,500 people are killed annually in recreation accidents, and this figure has remained rather constant for the past decade. Unfortunately most of these deaths occur to persons in the prime of life, over half being in the age range from 15 to 64 years. The largest number of deaths, or 43%, are the result of drownings, including boat accidents. Firearms are responsible for 8%.

Water safety. The popularity and growth of such sports as swimming, surfboarding, water skiing, skin diving, boating, canoeing, motorboating, sailing, and skating, while providing excellent recreation, have hazards for careless and unskilled persons. Most fatalities in these sports, some 6500 annually, are drownings. About seven out of eight victims of drowning were unable to swim at all or could swim very little. Intensive campaigns by various organizations in aquatic safety have been beneficial.

The four principal causes of drownings are careless handling of small boats, failure to wear adequate life jackets, children playing alone in the water, and carelessness or showing off in swimming.

Usually water accidents happen rapidly, such as when a boat capsizes or an individual steps into a deep hole. The person is thrown under water quickly, often under adverse conditions; therefore, more than elementary skill in swimming may be necessary. Knowing how to swim may not be enough in an emergency.

Over half of the fatalities in small pleasure boats are caused by negligence of the operator or by capsizing. The next two principal causes are swamping and collision. Fishing and cruising are the two leading activities at the time of the accident. Three quarters of all boats involved in accidents are powered by outboard motors and account for over one half of the accidents.

Millions of Americans participate in recreational activities in which water is a necessary factor. Many nonswimmers participate in these activities, thinking they are safe and that a crisis will not occur. Many times the activity is not recognized as associated with swimming, but rather with hunting, fishing, boating, or wading in which attention is directed toward other goals. Even hiking along river banks presents hazards, such as sloping banks, falling off logs, or tripping and falling. People who frequent the seashore should be familiar with tides, undertow, and high breakers. Logs and large driftwood on beaches are a hazard at high tide.

Some general precautions for avoiding accidents around water include the following:

1. Know your physical capabilities for swimming. When having your periodic physical examination, ask your doctor whether it is safe for you to swim.
2. Do not swim immediately after eating. A two-hour wait is recommended.
3. Never swim alone or when tired, overheated, or chilled. Be particularly careful about diving into water so cold that it may cause numbness, and remember that swimming in cold water exhausts the body more quickly.
4. Know the depth and condition of the bottom before diving into strange water.
5. If you develop a leg cramp, assume a floating position, draw the knees up toward the chest, and massage or move the foot or leg.
6. Do not show off while swimming, and never call for help unless you are really in trouble.
7. While fishing, do not attempt to wade in cold fast water beyond a depth at which you can stand easily. Footwear should provide traction.

8. Never allow children to play unattended near fast water.
9. Never rock a boat. Stay near the center of gravity, particularly in a canoe, and do not stand up unless entering or leaving the boat. In case of trouble stay near the boat until help comes. Boats will usually support your weight even when filled with water.
10. Do not boat in rough water unless thoroughly experienced and always wear an adequate life jacket.
11. In the event of trouble while in the water, try to keep your head. Do not panic.
12. When attempting to rescue a swimmer in distress, approach him from behind. If he attempts to seize you, duck your head, push him away, or turn him around.
13. Do not attempt long swims alone or from overturned boats or canoes.
14. Be familiar with swimming, diving, and boating conditions.
15. Know your limitations. No swimmer is good enough to take a chance.

If water safety is to be achieved, swimming instruction must be provided. Swimming ability is a prerequisite to aquatic sports; safety instruction should be available and routine; instruction and supervision of beginners in the various water sports is valuable; and habits of safety and a desire for sane participation must be inculcated in all who take part in these activities.

Boat safety. The increase in the sale and use of recreational boats has been enormous, increasing from 1,500,000 in 1930 to 8,025,000 in 1960. The number of outboard motors in use has grown from 2,643,000 in 1949 to 6,050,000 in 1960. Fishing and water skiing are the two most popular activities. About 41% of outboard boats are used for fishing and about 20% for water skiing. Deaths of persons engaged in fishing accounted for 54% of boating fatalities, but only 4.5% of deaths occurred to persons skiing. Three fourths of the drownings involved persons in small boats with a capacity of less than ten.

Boats are a necessary adjunct to many recreational activities. Boating and the use of boats in sports are gaining popularity rapidly. Accidents resulting from failure to operate boats according to rules are increasing. Remember, "boats don't tip over . . .; people tip them over." The outboard motor has made motorboating available to large numbers and at the same time has magnified the dangers.

Motorboats should be navigated at all times "in a careful prudent manner and at such a rate of speed as not to endanger the property of another or the life and limb of any person," as an Oregon law expresses it.

The Outboard Motor Club of America suggests a good dose of *Common Sense Afloat.* They find that in the great majority of cases, accidents result from too many people in the boat, failure to keep a sharp outlook, or speeding at the wrong time or place. The following pointers are recommended:

Do not overload your boat's weight capacity.

Do not overpower your boat.

Do not show off.

Fig. 43. Boating hints for safety. (Courtesy Oregon State Game Commission.)

Do not go out in bad weather.

Always carry a buoyant preserver or cushion for each passenger.

Boating in coastal waters presents a different problem from that in inland waters because of varying conditions. In coastal waters the right kind of boat is important. The small boat often used for fishing on an inland lake is not suitable for use in coastal water or at the mouths of many rivers that empty into the ocean because of strong currents and tides.

Listed are some common rules that should be followed for safety:

1. Have an adequate boat and equipment
2. Know your boat, its limitations, and its capabilities

3. Check weather conditions (consult the weather bureau)
4. Familiarize yourself with the area to avoid hazardous spots
5. Observe all safety rules

Hunting and fishing safety. More people engage in hunting and fishing than any other recreative activity. The potential danger in these activities is recognized. Hunting and fishing are open to everyone of legal age in most states for the payment of a small license fee. The astounding fact is that so few deaths occur for the number involved.

Fig. 44. The do's and don't's of gun handling in the field. **A,** At close range a shotgun is even more destructive than a rifle. This type of fence-crossing also asks for disaster. **B,** Fences need not be the invitation to disaster, as shown by the proper method of crossing. **C,** Basic safety rules say to treat every gun as if it were loaded and watch that muzzle. Pictured is a sight unpleasant to any hunter. **D,** "Road hunting" is one of the most dangerous practices engaged in by hunters. A double mortality could result from this situation. **E,** Keeping a gun barrel free of mud and dirt is a good idea, but doing it this way may put an abrupt end to hunting days. **F,** A safe way of removing débris from a gun barrel proves no risk to man or beast. (Courtesy Oregon State Game Commission.)

Despite this, many deaths occur needlessly because of improperly handled firearms, with many accidents affecting persons between the ages of 15 and 24 years. Instructions in the handling of firearms should be available in public schools. A large proportion of accidents occur when loaded guns are handled, when persons move into the line of fire, and when guns are accidentally discharged. Most of these could have been avoided if the gun handlers had had an adequate knowledge of firearms and their use.

Such cautions as (1) unload a gun when not in use, (2) always keep it pointed in a safe direction, and (3) keep it on safety when not pointed at a target should be axiomatic. An excellent statement regarding the proper use of firearms is the *Ten Commandments of Safety.*

1. Treat every gun with the respect due a loaded gun. This is the cardinal rule of gun safety.
2. Carry only empty guns, taken down, or with the action open, into your automobile, camp, or home.
3. Always be sure that the barrel and action are clear of obstructions.
4. Always carry your gun so that you can control the direction of the muzzle, even if you stumble. Keep the safety on until you are ready to shoot.
5. Be sure of your target before you pull the trigger.
6. Never point a gun at anything you do not want to shoot.
7. Never leave your gun unattended unless you unload it first.
8. Never climb a tree or fence with a loaded gun.
9. Never shoot at a flat hard surface or the surface of water.
10. Do not mix gunpowder and alcohol.°

Evaluation of safety programs. In the practice of personal and community health the promotion of safety is as important as the control of communicable diseases or as any other activity related to health. Many widely separate attempts are made to promote safety. In some instances the program is a well-integrated highly organized effort with a fairly uniform method of approach. However, the need still exists for a well-organized nationwide program based upon scientifically determined cause-and-effect relationships and proved solutions. Such an ultimate program will grow out of the varied attempts now being fostered to promote safety in the various areas of American life. In lieu of an existing comprehensive program, individuals and communities must strive to promote safety in relation to their own living problems. Certain basic concepts must be recognized.

The physical environment is amenable to consistent predictable cause-and-effect physical laws. In respect to physical environment man needs first to recognize and anticipate cause-and-effect relationships and second to modify the situation in the light of safety. This requires a safety consciousness in human beings.

The human being himself is the most difficult factor in the problem of safety promotion. Yet man is susceptible to change and in the desired direction. It is

---

°From Watch that muzzle, published by Sporting Arms and Ammunition Manufacturers Institute, New York, 1954.

thus apparent that basically human safety is a problem in changing the human individual and his responses.

Safety consciousness implies that an individual possesses those attitudes of safety necessary to the safe arrangement of the environment and to personal safe conduct. Attitudes are developed for specific needs and situations, such as traffic needs or fire precautions. Constant emphasis on safety in a vast variety of situations eventually develop a generalized trait of safety consciousness which will serve to govern safe conduct in new situations as well as in repetitions of old situations. Safety is a process in people's minds. The problem of establishing the process firmly and universally requires constant and intensive effort.

In the final analysis any localized or even individualized program of safety promotion must be appraised in terms of its effect upon people's attitudes and subsequent responses. The extent to which a safety program modifies an individual in the direction of safety consciousness is the true measure of the value of

Front

Why You Should Carry Emergency Medical Identification

An emergency medical identification card is your protection in an emergency. If you are not able to tell your medical story after an accident or sudden illness, the information entered on this card can save your life.

You may have health problems which can affect your recovery from an emergency. You may have a problem which is no emergency but often is treated as one, such as epilepsy. Even if you do not have a health problem, the information on this card can be of valuable assistance to the first aid attendant.

Why You Should Wear an Emergency Signal Device

In an emergency, you may be separated from your pocket card. Possibly you are one who has a medical problem so critical that it must be immediately known to those who help you. If so, a signal device of some durable material should be worn around your neck, wrist, or ankle in such a way that it can be present at all times --even while swimming.

The device should be fastened to the person wearing it with a strong nonelastic cord or chain so designed that it does not become an accident hazard in itself.

On this device there should be:
A symbol of emergency medical identification
The name of your major health problem
For children, the name and address of parents or guardians and a telephone number, including area code

Carry Your Card and Wear Your Signal Device at All Times!

EMERGENCY MEDICAL IDENTIFICATION

prepared by the
AMERICAN
MEDICAL ASSOCIATION
535 N. Dearborn St.
Chicago 10, Illinois

ATTENTION
In an emergency where I am unconscious or unable to communicate, please read the other side to know the special care I must have.

PERSONAL IDENTIFICATION
Name_____
Address_____
_____
Religion_____

NOTIFY IN EMERGENCY
Name_____
Address_____
_____
Phone_____
Name_____
Address_____
_____
Phone_____
My Doctor is_____
Address_____
Phone_____

Back

MEDICAL INFORMATION
(with date of notation)

Present Medical Problems_____

Medicines Taken Regularly_____

Dangerous Allergies_____

Other Important Information_____

Last Immunization Date
Tetanus Toxoid_____   Polio:Salk_____
Smallpox_____   Sabin_____
Diphtheria_____   Others_____
Typhoid_____
REMEMBER: This is the minimum medical and personal information needed by those who help you in an emergency. It is not designed to be a complete medical record. Check its accuracy with your doctor.

To put your EMERGENCY MEDICAL IDENTIFICATION CARD to work for you, fill in both sides of this card.
For example, under **Present Medical Problems**, include:

Epilepsy .... Tracheotomy (neck breather)
Diabetes .... Pneumothorax
Glaucoma .... Pneumoperitoneum
Hemophilia .... Colostomy
Chorea

Medicines Taken Regularly
Anticoagulants .... When noting drugs, use the
Cortisone or ACTH .... class name because the
Heart drugs such as .... brand names of some drugs
  digitalis or nitrites .... are difficult to identify in an
Thyroid preparation .... emergency.

Dangerous Allergies
Drug allergies .... Feathers (pillows)
Horse serum (as in .... Common foods
  tetanus antitoxin) .... Penicillin sensitivity

Other Information
Deep sea diver .... Speak no English (note the
Recurring unconsciousness .... language you speak)
Hard of hearing .... Wearing contact lenses

Immunizations
The date is important. If you note immunization over three years old, ask your doctor about a booster immunization. For tetanus toxoid, note the date of your first immunization as well as your last.

AMERICAN MEDICAL ASSOCIATION
535 N. Dearborn St. • Chicago 10, Illinois

Fig. 45. Card suggested by the American Medical Association for use as a health record or for identification in case of emergency.

the program. The decrease in injuries and fatalities is the result and indication of the change which has been produced. Like general resistance to disease, safety consciousness is a general resistance to hazards.

EMERGENCY MEDICAL IDENTIFICATION

Many deaths occur needlessly in accident and other critical situations because of lack of information that is needed in emergency treatment of a condition requiring special attention. There are over two hundred such conditions. The most common of these include diabetes, cerebral palsy, heart trouble, epilepsy, and many allergic conditions such as to antibiotics, biologics, drugs, and sulfonamide compounds.

In order to provide information regarding an estimated 40,000,000 Americans having "hidden medical problems," the American Medical Association has developed a symbol which identifies the wearer as having a condition that requires special attention. The symbol may be a wristlet, anklet, medallion, or card. The condition may be indicated on the symbol, or the symbol may indicate that medical facts are on a card in the purse or wallet.

The wearing of such a symbol by persons with special conditions is a prudent precaution that ensures proper treatment in case of an emergency in the shortest time. Both time and correct treatment are of utmost importance.

Chapter 7

Substances harmful to health

Throughout life the level of health is markedly affected by poisons. In addition mild chronic poisoning at various times in one's life has a deleterious effect on the length of life. Except for death by mechanical injury, perhaps all of us eventually will die of a poison.

The word *poison* is a relative term. In one instance a substance may be a poison; yet in another it may be a medicine. Not only the quantity of the substance, but also the sensitivity of the individual will be factors in classifying a substance as poisonous or nonpoisonous. Small amounts of a substance may be highly beneficial, slightly increased amounts may be injurious, and large amounts may be lethal. A bee sting can be fatal to a person highly sensitive to the secretion of the bee. Thus a satisfactory definition of poison must be so broad in scope that perhaps an explanation of the term would be more satisfactory. A poison is any substance which in small amounts is harmful to the body and which in large amount may cause death. Its effect may be narcotizing, stimulating, or destructive to the tissues of the body.

Action of poisons. Except for those poisons which have a corrosive action and destroy tissues, the general action of poisons is to affect cellular enzymes. Since the life processes of a cell are dependent upon enzymic action, the cell cannot function if its enzymes are inactivated. Thus when a neurotoxin, such as snake venom, inactivates the enzymes of nerve cells in vital nerve centers, death will result. By the same token a stimulant seems to have the effect of sensitizing enzymes to greater action. In the nervous system this action appears to be effective for the extracellular enzymes at the nerve connections as well as for the intracellular enzymes.

Individual sensitivity to poisons varies greatly. Generally children are more susceptible to poisons than are adults. Thus stimulants and narcotics tend to have a greater effect upon a child than on a mature individual.

Classification of poisons. Various classifications of poisons are possible. Poisons may be classed according to origin—either mineral or organic. They may be subdivided further into acids and alkalis and regrouped further into various classes. However, for convenience of presentation the health scientist makes a classification which most effectively includes those poisons of greatest health significance in the everyday lives of normal citizens. Such a classification recognizes the general classes of poisons as bacterial poisons, metabolic poisons, drugs, food poisons, and chemical poisons.

BACTERIAL POISONS

A poison produced by a living organism is a toxin. Thus the poisons of bacteria are properly called toxins. Even in small concentrations these toxins may be extremely injurious to certain tissues. Some body cells may be inactivated by the toxin, and others may produce antitoxin which neutralizes the toxin.

Focal infection. A low-grade infection localized in some part of the body is classed a focal infection. Virulent bacteria are able to multiply and produce toxins without greatly disturbing the host. Often the host is not aware of the infection. At such times the infection may persist for several years. In some cases the infection may produce a continuous minor pain with an occasional flare-up which is temporarily moderately painful. Common sites of focal infection include pharyngeal tonsils, teeth, gum abscesses, sinuses, gallbladder, generative tract, and colon. Infection in the crypts of tonsils may not be detected. Likewise, infection underneath a dental filling or at the apex of the root of a tooth may escape detection. Focal infection is difficult to locate. Whereas no general symptoms appear in some instances, many persons exhibit fatigability, irritability, lack of vitality, general sluggishness, and occasional unexplained fever. A thorough health examination may locate the site of infection. Treatment with penicillin and other antibiotics may enable the body to destroy the infection without the site ever being discovered.

The most significant health danger in focal infection lies in possible complications. Toxins from the original infection diffuse into the blood and lymph and thus are circulated about the body. Studies have revealed that complications involve the heart (endocarditis), the joints (arthritis), the blood vessels (hypertension), the urinary tract, muscles, nerves (including chorea), and possibly the over-all aging process. Early discovery and treatment of low-grade infection contributes to effective and enjoyable living and doubtless to the length of life itself.

NORMAL METABOLIC WASTES

Several of the wastes of normal metabolism may be classed as metabolic poisons. As a result of the conversion of proteins to carbohydrates, certain nitrogen wastes are produced. In addition muscle and protein metabolism produce other wastes. Some of these wastes are urea, uric acid, creatin, creatinin, ammonia salts, and a series of acids. All of these wastes can diffuse into the blood stream. The body tolerates a low concentration in the blood and other tissues. Healthy kidneys constantly filter out the wastes, maintaining the waste of the blood at a low level. Deficiency of kidney function often permits the concentration of wastes in the blood to rise to a level which is toxic to the body. Uremia, with bloating and other imbalances, is a typical example of malfunction of the kidneys. The disturbance may translate itself into complications involving the degenerative disease of the vascular tree (heart and vessels). Thus the kidneys are important in the defense of the body against toxins of the body's own making.

TOXINS FROM ABNORMAL GROWTHS

Tumors as well as other abnormal growths that are permitted to continue their course without treatment or cure may eventually begin to produce toxins which are damaging to specific tissues of the body. Many of these toxins dissolve red corpuscles (hemolysins), and technically death is due to toxins; although officially the cause of death may be listed as tumor. Any abnormal growth should be suspected of producing abnormal products toxic to the body.

Autointoxication. At birth the digestive tract is free from microorganisms. Within a few days the large intestine will harbor millions of organisms. Vast numbers are eliminated with the fecal discharges, but millions are retained in the intestine and are always present.

Among the normal bacterial parasites in the intestine of the human being is one group that causes the putrefaction of proteins. This bacterial action results in the production of toxic materials. In constipation the putrefaction continues for a considerable period of time without the discharge of accumulating toxins. Doubtless a small amount of the toxin diffuses into the blood stream, but the liver easily detoxifies these poisons. No reliable evidence exists that any appreciable amounts of putrefaction toxins diffuse into the blood stream to produce toxication in the body. Thus the concept of autointoxication must be rejected as without foundation.

The headache which often accompanies constipation is not due to chemical toxin, but is apparently due to mechanical pressure against the wall of the intestine. Experimentally produced pressure in the rectum by the insertion of cotton quickly creates a headache which is just as quickly relieved by removing the mechanical pressure. It should not be assumed that because autointoxication does not exist that constipation is hygienically unimportant.

FOOD POISONING

In the United States the general term *food poisoning* includes several conditions in which food merely acts as the vehicle for the transfer of organisms or toxins to the human alimentary canal where disturbance results. The list of conditions commonly referred to as food poisoning includes food allergy, ptomaine poisoning, and toxin transfer.

Food allergy. That which is food to one person may in another person incite bodily disturbances ranging from a simple rash to a fatality. Allergy is a condition of altered tissue reaction in which re-exposure to a substance produces disturbing effects. About 30% of the population in the United States exhibit some form of food allergy. The cellular function which results in the biological reaction of allergy appears to be an inherited factor.

The offending substance, usually a protein, is known as an allergen. Its biochemical effect is to cause the metabolic processes of body cells to produce substances irritating to the tissues themselves. These irritants may cause swelling, cellular overactivity, or other abnormal function, with disturbing symptoms.

Wheat causes over 50% of all food allergy. Most cases of wheat allergy occur in adults. Cooking reduces the likelihood of an allergic reaction. Rice, corn, oats, and rye are less frequent offenders.

Eggs are next to wheat in terms of allergic frequency; the albumin is the offending portion and affects children most frequently. Boiling eggs reduces allergic effects in susceptible people.

Milk is highly important in the allergy of infants.

Fruits are offenders more frequently than commonly supposed. Cooking fruit reduces its antigenic action.

Among vegetables legumes, potatoes, cabbage, cauliflower, tomatoes, and peanuts are offenders. Virtually all nuts are capable of producing allergy in man. Some spices and condiments are offenders.

Among the meats pork is the most frequent disturbing substance although some people may react to most meats. Lamb rarely produces allergy. Sea food may cause allergy.

Among beverages chocolate is the most frequent offender. Coffee, tea, and the grains in alcoholic beverages may cause allergies.

Food allergy may cause migraine headache, rhinitis, asthma, gastrointestinal disturbances, such as vomiting, diarrhea, and pain, cardiovascular disturbances, and various skin conditions, such as urticaria and eczema.

Skin tests for food allergies are extremely unreliable. In consequence specific diagnosis must consist of the elimination of suspected reactor foods in the diet. If improvement results, then a large amount of each food article must be eaten separately to see if symptoms return. The elimination diet may have to be repeated for subsequent tests, but, once the offending foods are determined, treatment is simply a matter of excluding reactors from the diet.

It must be recognized that substances other than foods produce allergy in the human being. Drugs (e.g., quinine), pollens, dusts, hair, fabrics, and other substances cause allergy in susceptible people. The reactions can be the same as those resulting in food allergy.

Ptomaine poisoning. The term *ptomaine* is derived from the Greek word *ptomos* meaning dead body. A ptomaine is an intermediate or transient product formed during the putrefaction of certain proteins. Ptomaines extracted from decomposing meat have a highly toxic effect upon experimental animals. From this fact comes the popular assumption that any food poisoning is a ptomaine poisoning. Yet it is doubtful that many, if any, actual cases of ptomaine poisoning occur in the United States. Meat which is so far decomposed that ptomaines are present is too unpalatable for human consumption. Even slightly decomposed meat with a decided odor which is subjected to the usual heat of cooking produces no demonstrated ill effects when consumed by man. It is thus apparent that what may be mistaken for ptomaine poisoning might well be due to organisms or their toxins conveyed to the human alimentary tract via meat or some other food. At least there must be serious doubt that poisoning due to ptomaines actually has occurred.

TOXIN TRANSFER BY FOOD

Although normal cooking processes usually destroy toxins, food occasionally serves as the medium by which toxins produced elsewhere are conveyed to the alimentary canal in man.

Botulism. Botulism is the classical example of a toxin transferred to the alimentary tract in man via the food route. The term *botulism* comes from *botulus* which means sausage and came into general use following a series of European outbreaks of poisoning incriminating sausage as the offender.

Botulism is due to a toxin produced by the organism *Clostridium botulinum*. Soil which is not acid is the reservoir of the organism. Of selected samples of soil from various locations in the northwest section of the United States, over 80% contained the spores of the *Clostridium botulinum*. Other western states report the same results in soil examination. Except for the southeastern part of the United States, apparently spores (latent stage) of this organism are found in the soil in every part of the nation. Under conditions lacking free air, spores germinate, and the vegetative form produces a toxin. Thus raw vegetables (e.g., beans) will contain no botulinus toxin although they will contain the inactive spores of the organism. A human being who eats these raw beans would thus be unaffected. However, improper canning of the beans could lead to botulism. Whereas the spores are destroyed by a temperature of 120° C. (248° F.) maintained for ten minutes, they withstand ordinary boiling.

If the vegetables referred to were heated insufficiently to destroy the spores during canning and then permitted to stand for several weeks or months, the anaerobic conditions in the container would be an ideal medium in which the organism could grow, multiply, and produce toxin. If the vegetables are then eaten without being reboiled, botulism will result. Home-canned peas and occasionally meat are media for the toxin.

From six to forty-eight hours (usually about twenty-four) after the toxin is ingested, the first symptoms of poisoning appear. Gastrointestinal symptoms may or may not be present, the principal effect being that of neurotoxin. Acute poisoning of the central nervous system is apparent, and paralysis of the respiratory system is the usual cause of death although paralysis of the muscles of swallowing can be fatal.

Serum is available for treatment of botulism but must be given before the onset of paralysis, which means within twenty-four hours of the first manifestation of symptoms. A polyvalent antitoxin, types A and B, is given intravenously. Other supplementary medication may be used to deal with various side symptoms.

Since commercial canners have solved the problem completely, prevention is principally a matter of proper home-canning procedures and practices. Because vegetables, particularly green beans, are the most frequent medium, home canners are advised to use pressure cookers. An alternate method is to boil the beans in semisealed jars for one hour on three consecutive days. An added precaution is to reboil the vegetables before they are eaten since boiling will disintegrate the toxin molecules. Home-packed green beans that were used in vegetable salad without having been reboiled have resulted in several reported deaths. Fruits are usually so acid that no problem of botulism is involved.

DRUGS

In its broadest sense a drug is any chemical agent which affects living protoplasm, but in its more practical application the term *drug* refers to any substance of medicinal use. Drugs vary in their effect upon human beings. Some are stimulants in that they speed up or activate function. Others are narcotics in that they produce a narcosis or stuporous effect. Drugs cannot impart new functions to cells and tissues.

With few exceptions drugs are selective in their action, affecting one specific class of tissue. The precise manner and site of action are unknown in many instances. Some drugs have an effect only when they have penetrated the cellular membrane. In others the site of effect appears to be extracellular. Whereas in general the chemical structure of the drug is associated with the action of the drug, in other cases two drugs of vastly different molecular configuration may have the same effect.

Drugs have been of infinite benefit to mankind. Their use has contributed to the effectiveness and enjoyment of life and has prolonged life, allayed pain, and increased the efficiency of bodily function. It is in the abuse of drugs that the problem of poisoning lies, not in the use.

Nature of addiction. A common misconception is that addiction to any drug or substance is entirely a psychological phenomenon. The expression is used that a person has a craving for morphine, or for alcohol, or for a cigarette. For some years scientists have recognized that a psychosomatic pattern is present in all addiction. More recently it has become apparent that, when addiction occurs, there has been a derangement of cellular metabolism in which the drug which caused the derangement is also the one which allays the symptoms or distress of the chemical derangement. More than this, scientists recognize that levels of susceptibility differ from person to person. Indeed some individuals have such a low level of susceptibility to a particular drug that they are virtually immune to addiction to that drug though other individuals may show various levels of susceptibility. On the other hand all individuals seem to be susceptible to addiction to certain drugs if exposed even to a relatively minor extent.

Present evidence does not enable scientists to identify levels of susceptibility to addiction in persons in advance of the individual exposure to a drug. Likewise, data are not sufficient to permit precise assessments of the percentage of people who are susceptible to various addictions. However, from statistics and studies of specific case histories certain conservative estimates can be made which indicate the extent of addiction susceptibility to certain drugs.

If 100 adults each receive an average dose of morphine daily for six months, all of them would likely become addicts. All of them would have experienced a derangement of cellular metabolism which would produce abnormal physiological and psychological effects. If 100 adults each took four ounces of liquor each day for six months, perhaps 20 of them would likely become alcohol addicts or alcoholics. If 100 adults each smoked ten cigarettes a day for six months, perhaps 90 would be addicted to nicotine.

Since susceptibility to addiction cannot be predetermined, the wise course of action is to assume that one is susceptible and that the most effective measure for preventing addiction is not to take the first injection of morphine, or drink the first glass of liquor, or smoke the first cigarette.

Morphine. Morphine is an alkaloid of opium which is obtained from the juice of a poppy *(Papaver somniferum)*. It is by far the most potent of the opium derivatives and may cause death by asphyxiation. Morphine depresses reasoning but exhilarates the imagination and produces pleasurable sensations. Judgment and restraint are reduced. Sleep usually follows the euphoric stage, and wild dreams often characterize the sleep.

The morphine addict is an individual who has come to lean on morphine as a crutch to aid his solution of a problem in personality defect or adjustment. Reliance upon morphine to relieve pain may be the genesis of the addiction. Whatever the initial or exciting cause, morphine addiction is an indication of personality deficiency in which an individual with the deficient personalty relies on morphine to give him a desirable mental state that he otherwise cannot attain or to escape an undesirable mental state. With continued addiction he is unable to face the everyday world without the support of his crutch. Most addicts appear normal physically. The conventional misconception that the addict has a cadaverous appearance may be a reality following withdrawal of the drug.

The withdrawal of morphine does produce some physical symptoms. However, the addict tends to dramatize his situation. Loss of appetite, fear, restlessness, and insomnia are the immediate symptoms. Prolonged sleep follows. Reawakening may be followed by tremors, perspiration, muscular convulsions, gastrointestinal disturbances, and perhaps some sensory disturbance. These symptoms subside in two or three days. It may be several weeks before all symptoms disappear, but a hygienic regimen will hasten complete recovery. Evidence that the personality deficiency inherent in morphine addiction may have a physiological basis lies in the effectiveness of endocrine therapy in hastening recovery from the symptoms of morphine addiction.

Federal and state laws regulate the dispensing of all narcotics, including morphine. The federal provisions are contained in the Federal Narcotic Regulations,* which originated with the Harrison Anti-Narcotic Act. A prescribing physician must be registered with the Collector of Internal Revenue and is bound by fixed regulations governing the prescription of narcotics. Together with the pharmacist, he is responsible for the dispensing of morphine.

In the United States the drug addict must turn to the illegitimate market for his daily supply. On the black market morphine will cost the addict about $35 a day. Few addicts can afford this cost and often resort to crime to obtain money for the purchase of morphine. Theft, embezzlement, swindling, burglary, robbery, and even homicide have been used as means for obtaining the necessary money to buy dope. In many instances the addict himself has been the victim of blackmail.

In England the law grants the addict's private physician the right to issue daily prescriptions so that his patient may obtain morphine from a legal source at a moderate price. This realistic approach has been highly effective in preventing a black market in morphine and in preventing an increase in drug addiction.

Barbiturates (sleeping pills). More than three billion sleeping tablets are consumed in the United States each year. With few exceptions these are barbiturates in some form. Barbiturates are odorless, white, crystalline powders and are marketed in tablet, ampule, capsule, and suppository forms. In medical practice the drug is used for hypnotic (sleeping) or sedative (calming) purposes. As such the barbiturates have been highly beneficial in relieving pain, in controlling convulsions, in treating disease, and for anesthesia.

For the purposes of inducing sleep, the administration of barbiturates is synchronized with the normal sleep cycle. Depending on whether a short-acting or long-acting derivative is used, the amount of drug is adjusted to normal sleeping needs. From fifteen to thirty minutes are required for sleep to be induced. Sometimes two administrations are necessary. Dreamless sleep is followed by a lassitude of two or more hours' duration after the person awakens. Repeated use usually results in habituation.

Indiscriminate use by the public of barbiturates in the form of sleeping pills has resulted in a series of deaths, with a vastly greater number of nonfatal poisonings. An ordinary therapeutic dose is not fatal despite an idiosyncrasy or high

---

*Narcotic-Internal Revenue Regulations, Washington, D. C., 1938, U. S. Government Printing Office.

degree of sensitivity to barbiturates. Poisoning occurs if the dosage is from five to ten times the normal and in isolated cases may be fatal. A dosage fifteen times the normal is usually fatal. Symptoms of poisoning indicate nervous and circulatory effects. Breathing is slow and irregular with an increase in the minute volume. Blood pressure fall and shock symptoms are apparent. Body temperature falls. Death usually results from paralysis of the respiratory center although pneumonia may be a final cause of death.

Many deaths regarded as suicide due to an overdose of sleeping pills are actually accidental deaths rather than intended deaths. In some individuals barbiturates do not produce immediate sleep. Instead they produce a twilight zone during which the individual does not recall having ingested a pill. He takes another which he also forgets about. Thus unwittingly he may take a dozen pills.

The use of any hypnotics, barbiturates as well as others, should be taken under the direction of a physician, not only to prevent accidental death, but also to prevent addiction. Although rigid control of barbiturates is necessary, education of the public is essential to allay this growing blight on the health and welfare of the United States. The psychosomatic approach to problems of insomnia and personality disturbance has made available an avenue through which an informed populace can find its haven of rest.

Alcohol. Alcohol is a general name for a series of alcohols—ethyl, methyl, propyl, butyl, and amyl. Ethel (grain) alcohol is the most common and is produced by the action of yeast plants upon sugar. It is represented as follows.

$$\underset{\text{(glucose)}}{C_6H_{12}O_6} + \underset{\text{(enzymes)}}{\text{yeast}} \longrightarrow \underset{\text{(ethyl alcohol)}}{2C_2H_5OH} + \underset{\text{(carbon dioxide)}}{2CO_2}$$

The fermentation action of yeast upon fruit juices is the basis for the production of alcohol which people drink. Alcohol is not produced in the human body; the fermentation must take place outside of the body.

When the concentration of alcohol reaches 17%, the fermentation process ceases because the yeast plant cannot survive an alcohol concentration beyond this point. Liquors of higher concentration are produced by distillation. Alcohol boils at 176° F. The steam that is given off at about 180° F. is collected and cooled, and liquid alcohol is distilled from the steam. Redistillation produces almost pure alcohol. Whiskey is obtained from distilled malt liquors or potatoes and beets, brandy from fermented fruit juices, gin from grain, and rum from fermented sugar cane juices or molasses. An ounce of 100-proof whiskey (50% alcohol) contains about the same amount of alcohol as three ounces of wine (17% alcohol) or twelve ounces of beer (4% alcohol). Thus one glass of whiskey will have about the same alcoholic content as twelve glasses the same size of beer.

Alcohol is one of man's finest servants, being particularly valuable as a dehydrant and as a solvent, especially as a fat solvent. Some of its more common uses are as a preservative, disinfectant, astringent, antiseptic, fuel, antifreeze fluid, and cleaning preparation.

Absorption and metabolism. The absorption and metabolism of alcohol are rapid. Taken on an empty stomach, alcohol is absorbed from the stomach to the extent of 40%. With food or water two ounces of alcohol (four ounces whiskey) is usually completely absorbed and burned by the body in about seven hours. So readily does alcohol diffuse through membranes that its concentration in the blood may be taken as an index of its concentration in the tissues generally. Four ounces of whiskey would produce a concentration of about 0.08% in a person of about 150 pounds. For medicolegal purposes, less than 0.05% is sobriety; 0.05% to 0.15%, uncertain; 0.15% and over, definite intoxication. Various degrees of alcohol tolerance by individuals account for some being intoxicated in the 0.05% range, whereas others are not. Body concentration can be determined from the blood, urine, or breath.

Alcohol has a food value of 200 calories per ounce. This might be compared with 114 calories per ounce of carbohydrate and 270 calories per ounce of fat. Primary oxidation of alcohol occurs in the liver, and no intermediate product is formed. Alcohol cannot be stored but is oxidized at a fairly uniform rate quite independent of muscular exercise. The peak of alcohol concentration in the body usually occurs about one and one half hours after drinking. The amount eliminated in the urine, breath, and perspiration is small, usually between 2% and 4%. Alcohol does not increase body temperature. Alcohol can produce acidosis by repressing the breathing center in the brain so that the carbon dioxide level rises in the blood by increasing the lactic acid level and by reducing the alkali reserve of the body. The basic physiology of the alcoholic hangover is thus apparent.

The effect of alcohol depends largely on the accumulation in the blood. This depends on the amount taken in, the rate of drinking, the concentration of alcohol in the drink, and the physical size of the drinker. Food in the stomach will delay the absorption of alcohol into the blood stream but will not prevent it. Contrary to popular belief, mixing drinks does not increase the intoxicating effect of the alcohol.

Effects on digestion. The effects on digestion produced by alcohol depend upon the quantity consumed. Small amounts of alcohol produce an increase in gastric secretion and give rise to a sensation interpreted as hunger. For this reason alcoholic beverages have been used to stimulate appetite. However, the increase in gastric juice renders the stomach more acid. For this reason physicians advise against alcoholic beverages for people with gastric ulcer though alcohol does not cause ulcers. Larger amounts of alcohol may inhibit digestion.

Strong alcoholic beverages irritate the digestive tract. Continued use causes an irritated (alcoholic) throat and chronic inflammation (gastritis) of the stomach.

Cirrhosis of the liver is a condition which occurs almost exclusively in chronic alcoholics. The exact cause of cirrhosis is not completely understood, but nutritional deficiencies associated with alcoholism are an ever-present factor. Fat accumulates around liver cells of alcoholics.

Effects on circulation. The effects on circulation produced by alcohol are the result of the narcotic effect of alcohol on the nerves governing circulation. It is common knowledge that the ingestion of alcohol is followed by a flushing of the skin due to a dilation of the vessels near the surface of the body. In itself this dilation of peripheral vessels will cause an acceleration of heart rate. However, the narcotic effect of alcohol on the cardiac inhibitory centers in the brain reduces impulses along the inhibitory nerve fibers to the heart. In effect the braking action on the heart is reduced, and the heart tends to speed up. Thus although the heart itself speeds up, the action of alcohol is narcotic. Its effect on human beings may be considered narcotic at all times.

Under the continued influence of alcohol the heart is markedly irregular. The effect is generally a depressant one, and when a heart is chronically affected by alcohol, venous pressure rises and inherently weak walls of veins may exhibt the strain.

Effects on nerve conduction. The effects on nerve conduction caused by alcohol indicate that different parts of the nervous system are affected by different concentrations of alcohol. Psychological experiments reveal that alcohol is always a depressant and never a stimulant. Its first effect is on the higher voluntary brain areas. Centers such as those affecting the heart and respiration are affected later. The vital nerve centers do not appear to be affected by low concentrations of alcohol. They thus are the last portions of the nervous system to be affected seriously.

Two to four glasses (four to eight ounces) of whiskey will produce marked psychological effects upon a drinker. One hour after drinking, the subject will show reduction in reaction time, reflex time, accuracy, speed, coordination, memory, and learning. The loss in performance will vary from 3% to more than 40%. This decline in performance causes experimental subjects to tend to think that they are doing better than before taking the alcohol. They are extremely uncritical of their performance and exhibit marked relaxation and pleasure.

Alcoholic malnutrition. Alcoholic malnutrition is a more recent concept of the general long-range effects of the chronic use of alcohol. What formerly was diagnosed as alcoholic polyneuritis is now recognized as a series of deficiency diseases due to the substitution of vitamin-free, protein-free alcohol for the normal dietary which includes vitamins and proteins.

A typical American daily diet for adults contains about 2600 calories with 7000 units of thiamine (vitamin B_1). The ratio of thiamine to calories thus is 2.5, which protects against any of the deficiency diseases of the nervous system. A ratio of less than 1.8 results in definite neuropathic conditions. A confirmed alcoholic consuming a pint of whiskey will tend to displace about 1500 calories of his usual food with 1500 calories of alcohol. Since thiamine is not stored in the body, a deficiency soon develops. The same occurs for riboflavin, niacin, and ascorbic acid. The fat-soluble vitamins do not appear to be involved.

Pellagra and beriberi are deficiency diseases prevalent among chronic alcoholics. Central neuritis, involving permanent damage to the brain and a resulting clouding of consciousness occurs in advanced alcoholism. Doubtless, alcohol itself is a contributing factor, but the condition is primarily a vitamin deficiency. Delirium tremens occurs only in excessive drinkers. It is usually accompanied by fever or a head injury. Alcohol must be regarded as a causative factor.

The alcohol drinker. The alcohol drinker merits analysis as an individual and as a problem in the promotion of community hygiene.

Introduction of alcoholic beverages is usually a socially conditioned pattern in which the initiate conforms to group action or even to group pressure. Curiosity and even revolt against social restraint may be motivating factors.

Drinking behavior varies in the various social classes. It runs the entire gamut from mere toleration of drinking, to the cocktail set, to aggressive drinking. However, on an individual basis the motivating factor of drinking follows a discernible pattern.

Most people who drink alcohol regularly do so not for its taste, but for the mental and emotional state it creates. The social drinker imbibes for the effect of social well-being. Drinking may not go beyond the stage of jovial well-being, or it may reach a stage at which normal inhibitions are released. It may even go to a point at which primary impulses of aggression and hostility can lead to social offensiveness.

The chronic, moderate, day-to-day drinker resorts to the sedative effects of alcohol to relieve the tensions of the day. He finds three or four glasses of whiskey, or its equivalent in other beverages to be a relatively easy effective means of resolving the conflicts and anxieties of the day. Thousands of others with tensions of equal intensity are able to adjust to the demands of life without the aid of an artificial crutch. Yet the moderate drinker finds that alcohol makes relaxation both a comfort and a pleasure, without the demands of personality integration. The resultant effect of reduced integration makes reliance on the effects of alcohol altogether more attractive and essential.

Alcoholism. Alcoholism represents one of the five most important health problems in the United States and one which becomes progressively worse with the passage of time. The Report of the Twenty-Fourth International Congress Against Alcoholism in 1952 indicates the extent of alcoholism in the United States as well as in some other nations. As reported by the Congress the number of alcoholic persons per 1000 of the population was France, 22; Switzerland, 16; Chile, 15; United States, 10; and Great Britain, 3.

This means that the United States has more than 1,900,000 alcoholic persons, a figure higher than is generally acknowledged. However, whether the data of the Congress or those of some other reliable agency are accepted will depend upon one's concept of what constitutes alcoholism. Basically a person is an alcoholic when alcohol, and not the person, is the master. The true alcoholic, often spoken of as a polydipsiac (many drinks), is the slave of alcohol. His cellular metabolism has undergone such a derangement that he suffers both physiological and psychological tensions which he finds alcohol can relieve. The pathway to alcoholism is well marked with well-established classical landmarks.

1. The person drinks socially occasionally.
2. He drinks to relieve severe anxiety and tension.
3. He drinks to relieve minor tensions.
4. He drinks more than he intended.
5. He starts taking eye openers as soon as he wakes in the morning. This is the best single index that alcohol is now the master and the person is an alcoholic.
6. He prefers to drink alone or with a few people.
7. He tries to conceal his drinking.
8. He leans entirely upon alcohol as a crutch to sustain him.
9. He is unable to control when or how much he drinks.

Let it be emphasized that only 3% of American alcoholics are derelicts on skid road. The vast majority of alcoholics come from that segment of the population generally regarded as typically American. They are to be found among the professional groups, the managerial segment, the craftsmen, the merchants, the skilled and the unskilled workers as well as members of their families. Alcoholism ignores social, economic, and religious boundaries. It operates in virtually all varieties of environments.

Prevention of alcoholism is the ideal, but according to present knowledge total abstinence is the only certain preventive. Education, particularly through example, can achieve some degree of success in the program of prevention. A program directed toward moderation in drinking conceivably can have some general value, but it is of little value to those individuals who are highly susceptible to alcoholism.

Although programs of prevention have been relatively ineffective, progress is being made in the treatment of alcoholism. Medical, religious, social, and psychological means have been employed in the treatment of alcoholism.

Medical treatment in the 1930's was based upon the application of the conditioned response. Benzedrine sulfate was first administered to sensitize the individual to the injections of emetine which were to follow. Later the patient was given alcohol, which produced a distressing nausea. The treatment was continued for about a week, after which the alcohol produced such a revulsion in the patient that he could not even tolerate the smell of liquor. This method proved effective in more than half of the patients treated, but it represented such a severe insult to the body that relatively few practitioners use this method today.

Antabuse is used in much the same way. After a series of doses of Antabuse, a drink of alcohol produces apprehension, nervousness, and nausea. Antabuse can be taken daily in tablet form, but the insult effect can be considerable.

Perhaps the most promising advance in the medical treatment of alcoholism is the use of glutamine, an intermediate product in the synthesis of protein. This method has had more than ten years of trial, with encouraging results. A one gram capsule taken daily for three months has the effect of reducing tensions within the patient. This is a principle which differs from other medical treatment of alcoholism. Possible side effects are being studied before this method will be available for wide use.

Religion, through its appeal to a Higher Power, can aid the alcoholic. The feeling of acceptance, purpose, and meaning in life can be of assistance to the alcoholic in his attempt to help himself. Clergymen generally regard themselves as just one member of the team in the treatment of alcoholics. They usually refer alcoholics to treatment agencies.

Social agencies have an important role in the treatment of alcoholism. Working with the family and the subject, the social agencies can bring about the unity and cooperation essential to successful recovery from alcoholism.

Alcoholics Anonymous combines several approaches in its campaign for the treatment of alcoholism. It is an organization of men and women who share their experiences as alcoholics. It was founded in 1935 and now has more than 7000 groups or chapters and more than 200,000 members. Its purpose is to help others through the means of group therapy. There are no dues and no fees, and membership is entirely voluntarily. A chapter is organized somewhat informally by a group of recovered alcoholics. Any alcoholic may visit a chapter meeting and hear members relate their experiences in overcoming alcoholism. One member will serve as a sponsor for the new member and will assist in every way possible. The use of group psychology is the greatest contribution the organization makes though it works with physicians and in other ways is of value to the alcoholic.

The approach Alcoholics Anonymous uses in its treatment of alcoholism is indicated in the following twelve suggested steps:

1. We admitted we were powerless over alcohol—that our lives had become unmanageable.
2. Came to believe that a Power greater than ourselves could restore us to sanity.
3. Made a decision to turn our will and our lives over to the care of God as we understood Him.
4. Made a searching and fearless moral inventory of ourselves.
5. Admitted to God, to ourselves, and to another human being the exact nature of our wrongs.
6. We are entirely ready to have God remove all these defects of character.
7. Humbly asked Him to remove our shortcomings.
8. Made a list of all persons we had harmed and became willing to make amends to them all.
9. Made direct amends to such people wherever possible, except when to do so would injure them or others.
10. Continued to take personal inventory and, when we were wrong, promptly admitted it.
11. Sought through prayer and meditation to improve our conscious contact with God as we understood Him, praying only for knowledge of His will for us and the power to carry that out.
12. Having had a spiritual awakening as the result of these steps, we tried to carry this message to alcoholics and to practice these principles in all our affairs.*

---

*From Alcoholics Anonymous, New York, Works Publishing Co.

AlAnon Family Groups are composed of families of alcoholics joined together to understand the alcoholic member of their family and learn what they might contribute toward recovery. AlAteens recently was organized in Pasedena, Calif., for the purpose of understanding alcoholic parents. The formation of groups such as these point up the interest and concern in the problem of alcoholism and what might be done through the united efforts of laymen.

Problem drinkers. Problem drinkers represent a related but somewhat different group of about 4,500,000 persons in the United States. These have been variously classified, but three types or examples will be presented: cocktail set, aggressive drinkers, and dipsomaniacs.

Cocktail set. The cocktail set represents that group of social drinkers who have adopted regular cocktail parties as a necessary part of their mode of life. Many of these individuals are moderate drinkers, but alcoholism recruits many from these ranks. The cocktail break has replaced the coffee break in some offices and in some groups. Perhaps this is one price being paid for prosperity, but it may be symptomatic of social pathology.

Aggressive drinkers. Aggressive drinkers are usually week-end drinkers who imbibe freely and heavily to a point of extreme intoxication. Perhaps some of these individuals seek escape from nongratifying jobs or patterns of living. Others appear to use week-end drinking as a form of recreation—a decidedly vigorous type.

Dipsomaniac. The dipsomaniac is the sporadic drinker who, perhaps every six or seven months, indulges in a drinking orgy or spree lasting for a week or two. Between these sprees he is a teetotaler. During the drinking period he is not a social drinker but a solitary drinker. His drinking is of the most excessive form. An analysis of the dipsomaniac reveals that marked depression, moodiness, and physical and mental slowing down are the forerunners of the state which results in the spree. Finally intense depression, accompanied by marked feelings of inferiority, emotional tension, and a most painful mental state, drives the victim to find relief in the lift he gets from the effects of alcohol. The precipitating factor is not a conflict with society, but a tension within the individual. Although some of these individuals have marked cyclic manic depressive temperaments, many appear to be in the normal range of emotional development until the depressive symptoms appear. Whether glandular imbalance or altered over-all body chemistry is the physiological basis of the disorder has not been established. However, successful psychological treatment demonstrates that the disorder can be overcome. Alcoholics Anonymous has demonstrated the effectiveness of group psychotherapy. Medical treatment provides a second means for successful recovery by the use of stimulants during periods of extreme depression or physiological tension.

Society recognizes that these problem drinkers are sick people who are in need of medical care. Yet lack of knowledge has thwarted the willingness of society to do everything possible to restore these victims of disease to effective and enjoyable living. In 1962 the United States spent $11,628,260,000 on alcoholic beverages.* If 1% of that amount could be invested in research on the problems of alcoholism, certainly some progress could be made in this serious national health problem. At least it is reasonable to assume that the upward spiral of alcoholism could be checked.

Heredity in alcoholism. The role heredity plays in the life of an alcoholic is worthy of mention if for no other reason than that of evaluating the limited knowledge science possesses.

No phase of the alcohol problem is more permeated with misconceptions than the influence of heredity as a factor in alcoholism. Data reveal that the children of alcoholics are more likely to be imbibers of alcohol than the children of nonalcoholics. Yet a critical analysis of these data must distinguish between the influence of environment and the factor of heredity.

That children of inebriates so frequently become inebriates must be examined in the light of social conditioning. Reared in a home lacking in normal social restraint and adjustment, the youngster acquires attitudes toward the use of alcohol that may not be in harmony with the established mores of the social order. When a child lives in an environment in which alcohol is readily available, the probability of his being initiated into the use of alcohol is greater than when he lives in a home environment that does not include alcoholic beverages.

Since chronic alcoholism appears to be a maladjustment of a defective personality, one must look for the extent of inherited liability by examining the psychopathology of the alcoholic's inheritance. Nine independent studies of the family histories of the general run of inebriates show a hereditary liability factor in from 32% to 48% of the pedigrees. This includes all forms of psychosis in the inebriate's lineage. It does not establish a relationship between the psychosis and inebrity. Yet one justifiably can conclude that disposition toward alcoholism is not inherited, but apparently a constitutional makeup is inherited which lacks the integration to resist the social risks of alcoholism.

Independent studies of psychotic inebriates disclose that family histories of 62% to 80% of these individuals reveal a hereditary liability factor. In this group the factor of an inherently defective constitutional makeup is of unquestioned significance. However, not more than 10% of the alcoholic population are classed as alcoholic psychotic persons. Further, with this group the psychosis is actually the principal factor involved, and the inebriety is merely incidental.

Not all children of inebriates become inebriates. Many of them are teetotalers, certainly with no indication of a constitutional inferiority which finds support in alcohol. Above all it must be recognized that alcoholism as such is never transmitted from parents to offspring. Nor is there any evidence to support the widespread misconception that a taste or craving for alcohol is inherited.

---

*Drug Topics, New York, Topics Publishing Co., Inc., July 15, 1963.

If alcohol alters the germ plasm, thus the genetic potential of reproductive cells, no scientific evidence has been produced to support the conclusion. A person becomes unconscious when his blood has an alcohol concentration of 0.2%. He is dead when the concentration reaches 0.5%. In the laboratory an alcoholic concentration of 0.5% causes no demonstrable change in cells—including germ cells—by either dehydration, hydration, or irritation or by dissolving of cellular fats. Therefore obviously a person would be dead of alcoholic poisoning before the germ cells would be affected.

Length of life and alcoholism. Length of life appears to be affected by the action of alcohol. However, a valid definite conclusive statistical study of the influence of alcohol on longevity is made difficult by the vast number of variables existing in the life of each individual, many of which may have deterring effects upon long life. To isolate these factors or even to weigh them thus far has defied scientific investigation. It must be recognized that people who abstain from alcohol are usually temperate in other phases of living that are highly important to health promotion and life extension. Further, alcohol directly or indirectly influences the death of alcoholics that are due to accidents, suicide, venereal disease, nephritis, and pneumonia.

In the light of the experience of insurance companies and the special studies of biometrists, certain general conclusions may be stated on the relationship of alcohol to the length of life.

1. Total abstainers who have always been so, on the whole, are longer-lived than nonabstainers.
2. Light users of alcohol who take a single drink only occasionally are as long-lived as total abstainers.
3. Persons who drink moderately—two to four glasses (four to eight ounces) of whiskey (or equivalent) per day—have a higher mortality than the national average, partly due to the tendency of many in this group to exceed moderation in drinking.
4. Persons who drink occasionally to the point of intoxication or have a few protracted sprees yearly are distinctly shorter-lived than the average in their age category.
5. The problem drinkers have a decidedly short length of life as compared to the life expectancy for the nation as a whole.

Tobacco. During 1962 citizens of the United States spent $7,082,050,000 on tobacco products and smokers' accessories.* In recent years much has been said and written about the effects of tobacco smoking on human health. Much of the material has been of doubtful value because of the bias and emotional approach of individuals who tend to understate or overstate to serve their own purposes. Not a sales talk or a sermon, but an objective appraisal of valid data is the need for an evaluation of smoking in terms of health and health promotion.

---

*Drug Topics, New York, Topics Publishing Co., Inc., July 15, 1963.

Table 29. Death rates among smokers*

Category	Observed deaths	Expected deaths	Rate (base 100)
Never smoked	1644	1644	100
Smoked occasionally	646	595	109
Cigars only	925	761	122
Pipe only	774	694	112
Cigarettes only	4406	2623	168
Cigarettes and others	2910	2028	143

*From Hammond, E. Cuyler: The effects of smoking, Scientific American **207**:39, 1962.

Table 30. Relative death rate and daily cigarette consumption*

Category	Observed deaths	Expected deaths	Rate (base 100)
Never smoked	1644	1644	100
Fewer than 10 cigarettes per day	470	350	134
10-19 cigarettes per day	1833	1081	170
20-39 cigarettes per day	1063	541	196
40 or more cigarettes per day	263	118	225

*From Hammond, E. Cuyler: The effects of smoking, Scientific American **207**:39, 1962.

Smokers' death rates. A classic study of the possible relationship of smoking to death rate was conducted by E. Cuyler Hammond and Daniel Horn and reported by Dr. Hammond.* During the course of this study 7316 deaths occurred among subjects with a history of regular smoking. These deaths were divided according to primary cause as reported on death certificates. Only 4651 of these cigarette smokers would have died during the course of the study if their death rates had exactly matched those men of the same age who had never smoked. The difference of 2665 deaths (7316 minus 4651) can be considered "excess deaths" associated with the history of cigarette smoking. These results are presented in Table 29.

The lower death rate among cigar and pipe smokers is explained by their tendency not to inhale the smoke, whereas most cigarette smokers inhale though in varying degrees. The reason is that cigar and pipe tobacco give off an alkaloid smoke which is sharp and distressing and causes throat irritation. The method used in curing cigarette tobacco results in a neutral smoke which is not distressing.

Another analysis made by Hammond and Horn was the relation of daily cigarette consumption to the death rate. The results are shown in Table 30.

From the data in Table 30 one must conclude that the death rate for men who are heavy smokers of cigarettes (two packs or more per day) is about 2¼ times as high as among a comparable group of nonsmokers. From this our logical next step should be a consideration of what there is in tobacco smoke which is harmful to health and just what the effects of these substances are.

---

*Hammond, E. Cuyler: The effects of smoking, Scientific American **207**:39, 1962.

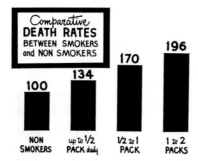

Fig. 46. Death rates from all causes, nonsmokers and smokers. Assessing the rate of non-smokers as 100, smokers have comparable rates of 134, 170, and 196 based upon their daily cigarette consumption. (From Hammond, E. C.: The effects of smoking, Scientific American **207**:39, 1962.)

Composition of tobacco smoke. The composition of tobacco smoke gives the key to the possible effects of smoking. In an anlysis of the composition of tobacco smoke, three basic factors must be recognized.

1. The composition of smoke varies not only in different plants, but also even in different parts of the same plant.
2. Products of combustion vary not only with the composition of the tobacco, but also with completeness of combustion.
3. Tolerance of the various products of tobacco combustion differs widely in different persons.

Besides the volatile alkaloid nicotine, tobacco smoke also contains the irritants ammonia, furfural, collidine, and benzpyrene, which are products of tobacco tar. Further, all cigarettes contain some hygroscopic agent for the maintenance of the proper moisture content of the tobacco. Glycerin is the most commonly used hygroscopic, and glycerin itself will give off acrolein, oxalic acid, and acetic acid, all of which are irritants. One major tobacco firm uses diethylene glycol as a hygroscopic which gives off only oxalic acid as an irritant.

Carbon monoxide in small amounts is also given off. It is characterized by its ability to displace oxygen in red blood corpuscles.

Action of nicotine. Nicotine and its action are the principal interests of the lay public in its consideration of the products in tobacco smoke. Nicotine is a rapidly acting poison. It frequently is used as an insecticide. One cigar or six cigarettes contain enough nicotine to kill two people if injected directly into the blood stream. Of course it is never used in that manner, nor does all of the nicotine from a cigarette enter the mouth of the smoker. The smoke of a cigarette contains only 14% to 33% of the nicotine contained in the tobacco, whereas the smoke of a cigar or pipe contains a higher percentage. The difference exists because the cigarette permits the nicotine to volatilize more easily. However, the shorter the cigarette, the greater will be the nicotine and tar content of the smoke reaching the smoker. The amount of nicotine absorbed by the body depends upon whether

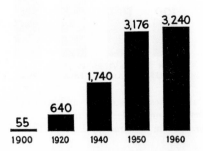

Fig. 47. Increase in cigarette consumption in the United States since 1900. Note correlation with increase in deaths from lung cancer. Figures represent millions of cigarettes. (From Hammond, E. C.: The effects of smoking, Scientific American **209**:39, 1962.)

Fig. 48. Change in death rate, 1930 to 1960. While the death rate from all causes declined 18%, the death rate from lung cancer increased 953%. (From Hammond, E. C.: The effects of smoking, Scientiflc American **207**:39, 1962.)

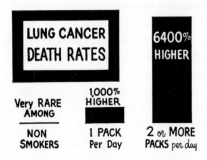

Fig. 49. Lung cancer death rates—nonsmokers and smokers. Almost nonexistent in non-smokers, cancer of the lungs takes an alarming toll among heavy smokers. (From Hammond, E. C.: The effects of smoking, Scientific American **207**:39, 1962.)

Table 31. Lung cancer among smokers and nonsmokers*

Classification	Number in group	Number with lung cancer	Per cent of group with lung cancer
Nonsmokers	32,560	2	0.006
Occasional smokers	11,720	4	0.03
Cigar smokers	14,477	4	0.027
Pipe smokers	12,121	6	0.049
Cigarette smokers	107,978	152	0.14

*From Hammond, E. Cuyler: The effects of smoking, Scientific American **207**:39, 1962.

smoke is inhaled and whether saliva is swallowed. Nicotine is a stimulant for some people and a narcotic for others.

Effect on respiration. The effect of smoking on respiration is predominantly the effect of smoke products on the lining of the respiratory tract. Irritants in tobacco tar are a greater threat to the smoker's health than is nicotine. Benzpyrene, furfural, and other components of tobacco tar injure the mucous membranes and account for the irritation of the tongue and throat, thus the smoker's cough. Conjunctivitis, irritation of the lining of the eyelids, is a frequent complaint of the smoker.

Deaths from lung cancer in the United States rose from 4000 in 1935 to 36,000 in 1960. From 1935 to 1960 the death rate from lung cancer among men increased 600%, and among women it increased 125%. In 1960, 86% of deaths from lung cancer were among men.

A recent study by E. Cuyler Hammond and Daniel Horn, staff members of the American Cancer Society, gives further indication of the possible relationship between cigarette smoking and lung cancer. Some 188,078 men between the ages of 50 and 69 years were followed over a period of two and one half years. During that time, 8105 of these men died. Of these, 168 had lung cancer. The distribution of these 168 by five classifications shows the extent of lung cancer in the various smoking and nonsmoking groups.

This longitudinal type of study has particular merit in revealing long-range effects of a given phenomenon. Follow-up of the surviving 179,973 men for several more years will provide highly important evidence of the relationship of smoking to lung cancer.* Present evidence indicates that a cigarette smoker exposes himself to the risk of cancer.

Since cancer of the lungs usually starts in the surface lining of the bronchiole tubes of the lungs, the cancer-producing agent (carcinogen) must be a substance or substances which can be inhaled into the bronchioles. No authority on the subject has contended that cigarette smoke is the only cause of cancer of the lungs. Asphalt road dust, exhaust from internal combustion engines, soot from coal and fuel oil furnaces, and industrial fumes have all been established as carcinogens. It must be recognized that men are more exposed to industrial and general atmos-

---

*Hammond, E. Cuyler: The effects of smoking, Scientific American **207**:39, 1962.

pheric carcinogens than are women, which may be an important factor in the higher incidence of cancer of the lungs among males. Present evidence indicates that occupational exposure, general air pollution, and excessive cigarette smoking are related to cancer of the lungs.

One factor which tends to cloud the cause-and-effect relationship of cigarette smoking and cancer of the lungs is the variation in susceptibility to cancer. Evidence indicates that people do vary in susceptibility to cancer. Yet all people are susceptible although science has not yet developed a test for relative susceptibility. This has led to the repeated question, "Why is it that, while some cigarette smokers develop lung cancer, others who smoke equally as much do not get lung cancer?" The answer is that they do get lung cancer.

Postmortem examinations of the lung tissue of heavy smokers who died without having diagnosed lung cancer indicate that all of these moderate and heavy smokers have lung cancer. These studies show that at first smoking inactivates respiratory cilia and then destroys the mucous cells. Next the basal cells of the lungs become cancerous, and basement membrane invasion begins. If these people had lived longer, their cancer would have been diagnosed.

There is no conclusive evidence that filters or king-sized cigarettes offer any special protection. There is little likelihood that the tobacco companies will ever produce tobacco without carcinogens because the temperature at which tobacco is burned produces a vast array of hydrocarbons.

Emphysema in smokers has become as great a concern among health scientists, as is cancer of the lungs. Virtually all reported cases of emphysema are among cigarette smokers.

Emphysema is a condition in which the delicate lining of the alveoli or air pockets of the lungs has broken down as a result of irritation. As a consequence the alveoli become vastly overextended. The lungs become larger and larger from the constant distention. The chest is hyperinflated and sometimes fixed in the inspiration position. Expiration of air is extremely difficult because of the chest and lung expansion and the inelasticity of the tissues. In the early stages of emphysema the person puffs excessively after light physical exertion. In time, climbing three or four steps will force the person to stop "to catch his breath."

Eventually emphysema will place an excessive load on the heart as a result of poor aeration of the blood. Emphysema sufferers become invalids for a period of about ten years before death overtakes them, often due to cardiovascular disease.

Practically all persons with emphysema are heavy smokers. The ingredients of tobacco tar appear to be the irritant producing the damage. Health scientists expect a spectacular increase in the incidence of emphysema in the United States during the next ten years.

The relationship of smoking to cancer of the lips is largely due to the irritation of heat at the mucocutaneous margin. Cigarettes or cigars smoked to the end will have the same effect as the old-fashioned clay pipe in the production of lip cancer.

It must be pointed out that not all cases of cancer of the lips and tongue are associated with tobacco smoking.

Effect on digestion. The effect on digestion is due to nicotine as well as to the irritants in the tobacco smoke.

In the stomach the action of nicotine allays the sensation of hunger by retarding the muscular action of the walls of the stomach. Fluoroscopic study of the effect of smoking shows that gastric motility is suspended for an hour or more, which accounts for the relief from hunger which smoking gives. Smoking reduces the desire for food, which frequently results in chronic malnutrition. The improvement in general health which is so frequently observed after a person quits smoking can be attributed largely to the beneficial effects of improved nutrition.

Irritation of the stomach associated with smoking appears to be due to the irritants of tobacco tars swallowed in the saliva. The resulting gastritis and associated gastric hyperacidity frequently cause symptoms which simulate gastric ulcers. However, no established proof or even valid evidence exists that smoking actually causes ulcers. It is known that, if ulcers exist, smoking aggravates the condition.

Effect on circulation. Empirical observation has long indicated that smokers have a higher incidence of cardiovascular disease and deaths than nonsmokers. Several limited studies have supported these observations. A recent well-conducted extensive study provides the most convincing evidence. In the April, 1962, issue of *The New England Journal of Medicine,* Joseph T. Doyle, Thomas R. Dawber, William B. Kannel, A. Sandra Heslin, and Harold A. Kahn reported on two studies of smoking in relation to the occurrence of coronary artery disease. These studies were conducted in Albany, New York, and Framingham, Massachusetts. Each subject in the study was given a thorough medical examination at the outset of this investigation. No symptoms of coronary artery disease were found in 4120 men at the start of the study. These men were re-examined from time to time over a number of years. Deaths from coronary artery disease as well as symptoms of this disease were found significantly more frequently among smokers than among nonsmokers. Men who smoked more than twenty cigarettes a day had a total death rate more than twice as high as among men who had never smoked. Exsmokers of cigarettes and also cigar and pipe smokers had coronary artery disease and death records similar to those of men who had never smoked.

Table 32. Deaths from coronary artery disease among smokers*

Category	Observed deaths	Expected deaths	Rate (base 100)
Never smoked	709	709	100
Fewer than 10 cigarettes per day	192	149	129
10-19 cigarettes per day	864	456	189
20-39 cigarettes per day	486	226	215
40 or more cigarettes per day	118	49	241

*From Hammond, E. Cuyler: The effects of smoking, Scientific American **207**:39, 1962.

The findings of these studies agree closely with other studies in the United States.

Data reported from the studies of E. Cuyler Hammond and Daniel Horn showed a high correlation between deaths from coronary artery disease and the smoker's daily cigarette consumption. The data from the study made by Hammond and Horn are of special interest and are presented in Table 32.

These data indicate the coronary artery disease death rate among heavy smokers to be almost two and one-half times as high as the rate among those who have never smoked. It must be concluded that heavy smokers will likely be indiscreet in other practices harmful to health, but the effect of smoking cannot sensibly be dismissed.

The effect of smoking on circulation is a dual effect upon heart and vessels through the effect on the nerves which control them. Smoking does not appear to damage the circulatory system by any direct action. Its effect arises from the action of nicotine on the nerves which govern the action of the heart and vessels. The endocrine system is affected, thus influencing circulation.

Smoking a cigarette causes increased constriction of the arteries, with a resulting rise in blood pressure from 10 to 20 mm. Hg. The effect is most pronounced in those individuals whose blood pressure is regularly above normal. Constriction of the small arteries of the extremities causes a pronounced drop in skin temperature of the hands and feet. The same vascular spasm accounts for the dizziness and suffocating chest pains experienced by some smokers. Surprisingly nicotine causes a constriction of the veins which not even the dilating effect of alcohol can counteract.

Buerger's disease (thromboangiitis obliterans) is a constriction or spasm of the larger arteries and veins of the extremities, with clots and subsequent gangrene as possible outcomes. Although the lower extremities are more frequently involved, the upper extremities may also be involved. Whether or just how smoking causes Buerger's disease has not been established. However, virtually all patients with Buerger's disease are smokers, and 90% of them obtain an arrest in the progress of

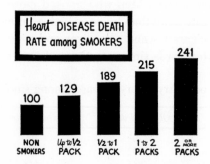

Fig. 50. Heart disease death rate—nonsmokers and smokers. Assessing the rate of nonsmokers as 100, smokers have comparable rates of 129, 189, 215, and 241 based upon their daily cigarette consumption. (From Hammond, E. C.: The effects of smoking, Scientific American **207:**39, 1962.)

the disease or experience improvement when smoking is stopped. Amputation because of gangrene is the end result when the disease is not arrested.

One cigarette accelerates the heart rate an average of ten beats per minute. Palpitation of the heart is about 50% more common in the smoker segment of our population than in the nonsmoker segment. Just what permanent harm to the heart is done by smoking is difficult to determine. Doubtless in many persons the effect is negligible. However, the person with a defective heart can ill afford to risk the possible hazards of smoking since the margin between his present heart condition and invalidism may well be bridged by the disturbing constituents of tobacco smoke.

Endocrine effects. Endocrine effects manifest themselves as a result of smoking only when chronic nicotine poisoning is present. Symptoms of chronic nicotine poisoning are tremor of the hands and increased reflex irritability. Some of the effect unquestionably is upon the thyroid gland. The blood picture of many excessive smokers with tremor resembles that of patients with exophthalmic goiter. Metabolism is abnormally high in about three fourths of these patients with tremor and falls, usually to normal range, when smoking is discontinued. In addition the iodine content of the blood tends to be high.

Longevity and smoking. The effect smoking has on longevity has long been a subject of much dispute. However, data from some studies are of value in appraising the possible effects of smoking on the length of life.

Studies of insurance companies and independent investigators have indicated that heavy smokers have a shorter life expectancy than nonsmokers. However, it must be acknowledged that excessive smokers are likely to live under great tension, which of itself is detrimental to longevity, and are apt to be intemperate in other practices. No doubt other hidden factors are incorporated in the classification of heavy smoker.

Investigations by Dr. Raymond Pearl of Johns Hopkins University on the question of smoking and longevity have generally been regarded as most reliable and valid. If one analyzes the result of Pearl's study of 1905 excessive smokers, 2814 moderate smokers, and 2094 nonsmokers, all American white males, it would appear that at 30 years of age for white males the nonsmoker had a life expectation of about 39 years, the moderate smoker about 36.5 years, and the excessive smoker about 29 years. A 30-year-old person who smokes a pack of cigarettes or more a day might calculate the minutes or hours of life he pays for the pack.

Motherhood and smoking. The question of motherhood and smoking is still in the category where conclusions are drawn on emotional bases, rather than on reasoned bases.

The phenomenon of expectant and nursing mothers smoking cigarettes is too recent for any extended studies or results. Perhaps not until the present crop of children under 15 years of age reaches late adulthood will a true picture of any effects be established definitely.

At present we must limit our analysis to the fact that nicotine can be identified in the blood stream of a smoker and in the milk of a nursing mother. Little doubt exists that the nicotine molecule can diffuse through the placental membrane to the fetus. The only question thus far unanswered is whether the nicotine affects the fetus adversely. To say that babies of smoking mothers are less healthy than babies of nonsmoking mothers may conceal such factors as basic biological endowment and general intemperance in living, as well as care of the child. Since the possibility exists that smoking may be detrimental to the well-being of her baby, discretion should motivate the expectant mother to give her child the benefit of the doubt and refrain from smoking during her pregnancy as well as during her nursing period.

Tobacco companies complain that much of the evidence on the harmful effects of smoking is statistical evidence. The answer is that science has long recognized statistical evidence as valid. Statistical evidence is used every day in scientific research and is generally accepted by the public. Who among us would advocate that an expectant mother consume thalidomide tablets during her pregnancy? Yet the evidence that thalidomide can produce developmental anomalies in the fetus is entirely statistical. Many of the possible effects of smoking first identified statistically subsequently have been verified by laboratory experimentation.

Why people smoke. Why people smoke is more than a mere academic question. It is one which delves into the motivation of human conduct.

Perhaps not in the entire history of mankind has a personal habit so rapidly engulfed a people as has the smoking habit in the United States during the past forty years. Of particular interest to the student of human behavior are the underlying factors which motivate the smoking habit.

The first trial in smoking is usually motivated by a desire for a new experience. Bombarded by clever, attractive, persistent, and psychologically effective advertising, the desire for a new experience is fanned to a kindling point. Desire may be precipitated by sheer curiosity, by group conformity, by group pressure, or even by revolt against social restraint.

Once the barrier has been broken, the individual does not find difficulty in trying a second cigarette, a third, and perhaps another. Handling the cigarette and having something in the mouth can have a somewhat soothing effect, and a cigarette becomes a means of relieving psychological tension.

Three tobacco addictants have been identified—nicotine, cotenine, and scopoletin. If a small amount of nicotine is injected at intervals into the skin of a habitual smoker, he will have no craving for a cigarette. Likewise, if one hundred adults, over a period of weeks, took tablets containing nontoxic amounts of nicotine, about ninety of them would develop habituation. If at the same time another one hundred adults took placebos, similar appearing tablets but without nicotine, only a few, through psychological effects, would tend to lean on the tablets.

Addictants produce a derangement of cellular metabolism. Once this sets in, the person experiences a certain uneasiness which he soon knows can be relieved by smoking another cigarette. This is commonly referred to as a craving for cigarettes and is the basic psychological change which must be considered in breaking the smoking habit. Psychological factors are more easily altered than the physiological factors.

Some people have stopped smoking by abruptly cutting off the practice. Some of these individuals were not addicts in the sense that there had been a cellular derangement. For these people it was not difficult to quit smoking. However, others have quit even though they were actual addicts, physiologically as well as psychologically. These people by intense motivation (e.g., fear or the attainment of a certain self-status), together with sheer determination, succeeded in giving up smoking. That these individuals suffered considerable distress bordering on torture is verified by many who have travelled this path. Few cigarette addicts could use this traumatic method in breaking their smoking practice.

A less stringent method can be employed by those smokers who are unable to use the crash approach to give up smoking. This method is designed to reduce the nicotine content of the body gradually until it reaches such a low level that the smoker can tolerate that level. Although there would be an advantage in beginning this practice when the individual is subjected to least tension in daily living, it can be effective if initiated at any time. For three weeks the individual smokes the customary number of cigarettes, but smokes less of each cigarette, so that during the third week less than half as much of each cigarette is used. Beginning with the fourth week, the individual smokes one less cigarette each day until the number reaches zero. During this time, he may experience some uneasiness which can be allayed by substitution such as gum, candy, coffee, running, taking a shower, or having a snack. A certain degree of personality integration is called for in any method, but this approach should be effective for any normal individual.

To replace liquor and tobacco the United States needs a new habit to provide relief from tension, fatigue, or sluggishness without the harmful effect of liquor and tobacco. Coffee, tea, and cola drinking serve as acceptable substitutes, but a better substitute is needed.

Marihuana. Marihuana is the Spanish or Mexican name for the drug known as cannabis. The drug is obtained from the dried flowering tops of the pistillate (female) plant, *Cannabis sativa.* This plant is also known as Indian hemp *(Cannabis indica)* and is grown quite extensively in various countries for the hemp fiber which is used in the manufacture of rope.

As solid and fluid extracts, Cannabis has been used occasionally in medical practice. Because of its variability in strength, its tendency to deteriorate, and great differences in individual susceptibility to its action, Cannabis seldom is employed in present-day medicine. Its use is to allay excitablity, relieve pain, and promote sleep. Any of its effects can be produced more safely and efficiently with other medicines.

The narcotic action of Cannabis is due to a bitter principle, cannabinol, which is in the resin.

Cannabis and its products are definitely of the Old World. Its use and its products thread the history and literature of Arabia and India, being mentioned again and again in the *Arabian Nights.*

In India and other eastern countries, a favorite form of this drug is hashish, a preserve or conserve made by cooking the flowering tops of Cannabis plants with sugar, spices, and aromatic herbs. It is then eaten with a spoon or other utensil. Another method of using the drug in these countries is to inhale the fumes from a bed of campfire coals on which have been placed the dried leaves and flowering tops of the plant.

In western countries, especially in the United States, it is used in the form of cigarettes, either alone or mixed with tobacco. The cigarettes are commonly called reefers, but occasionally other names are used, such as loco weed, joy weed, Indian boy, merry wonder, griffos, goof-butts, and a host of others.

Smoking of marihuana was introduced into the southwestern states by Mexican laborers. Since then marihuana smoking has spread to every state in the union. Most addicts in the United States are of high school and college age.

Action. The action of marihuana is unique. After a period of exhilaration in which the addict feels very important and everyone else seems to be insignificant, it produces comfort, indifference to outside influences, a dreamy state of mind, visual hallucinations, and an exaggeration of time and space so that a period of a few minutes seems a long time and short distances seem endless. A walk across a room seems like a long journey. The person may lose self-control and laugh and talk at random. His thoughts are irrational; he realizes it and laughs about it. If large amounts of cannabinal have been taken, general cerebral depression results in sleep or stupor. On awakening most people experience no hangover, and the whole experience is a pleasant one. This is the most pernicious and dangerous thing about marihuana and the prime reason for its wide use. A few individuals are made severely ill by the drug and have a fear of impending death. These do not become addicts.

Taken in sufficiently large quantities, marihuana produces an almost immediate lust, complete irresponsibility, and a tendency toward violence. Those addicted to Cannabis frequently develop a delirious rage during which they are temporarily, at least, irresponsible and likely to commit violent crimes. Its long-continued use leads gradually to physical emaciation as well as to mental degradation. Moral and esthetic values are lost. Many eventually become criminals.

The role of marihuana in crime is indicated by the report of the public prosecutor in New Orleans that of 450 prisoners he dealt with, 125 were marihuana addicts. His report reveals that slightly less than 50% of the murderers, about 20% of the larceny men, and about 18% of the robbery prisoners smoked marihuana habitually.

With mental decline complete mental disorder may result. Whereas psychosis due to marihuana addiction is more common in countries of the far east, marihuana psychosis is reported by our American hospitals for the mentally disordered.

Problem of control. The problem of control of marihuana is a challenge to the entire nation. American youth may be victimized by marihuana peddlers. In some cities petty gangsters, degenerates, and operators of resorts have been arrested for encouraging children of school age to smoke marihuana. Activities of marihuana peddlers are identical with those of other dope handlers. Generally the prospective customers are given one or more cigarettes until a craving for the drug develops. Then the price is raised to the highest figure that can possibly be obtained. Marihuana prices may range from a dollar each for cigarettes to fifteen cents for a full tobacco tin.

The very nature of the hemp plant makes its control difficult. It is hardy and can be grown successfully in every state in the union. It has been cultivated for commercial purposes in several states. Hemp seed is found in most mixtures of bird seed. Fibers of the plant are employed in rope making, and the oil is used in the process of mixing certain kinds of paints.

The problem of marihuana control became so great in the United States that Congress passed a law, effective in August, 1937, which is fully as rigid in regulating the production and distribution of marihuana as the Harrison Anti-narcotic Law is in regard to opium and morphine. The law provides that all producers, manufacturers, importers, dispensers, physicians, veterinarians, schools, and research workers handling marihuana must register and take out a tax stamp. All owners are responsible for either destroying the Cannabis on their property or registering under this act.

Although this act is patterned after the Harrison law, in some respects it is more stringent. It provides for a transfer tax of $100 per ounce or fraction thereof for persons not registered under the act and $1 per ounce or fraction thereof for duly registered persons. Each transfer requires payment of the tax. The effect has been to remove marhiuana completely from the legitimate market. The Boggs Act of 1951 and the Narcotic Control Act of 1956 have further strengthened the government's control over marihuana traffic as well as its control over other narcotics.

The basic problem is one of education to be carried on in the schools, churches, clubs, and various civic organizations. Youths especially should understand the effects of marihuana addiction and the methods of dope peddlers. This education could profitably also include the law enforcement officers.

Placing the hospitals* of the U. S. Public Health Service at the service of marihuana addicts provides these unfortunate persons with hope for recovery. Addicts without criminal offenses should be encouraged to submit voluntarily for treatment in sufficient time for a cure and then take their respective places in society. Such confinements to the narcotic farms should be confidential. Addicts with criminal offenses should be sentenced to the narcotic farms for cure and then returned to the proper penal institution for the remainder of the sentence.

---

*Lexington, Kentucky, and Fort Worth, Texas.

Perhaps marihuana lies as a dormant dragon which will raise its ugly head if an economic depression of even moderate proportions besets the nation. Yet even then it will be the youth of the nation who will be in greatest need of protection.

Caffeine, theophylline, and theobromine (xanthines). Caffeine, theophylline, and theobromine are drugs similar in chemical structure and action. Coffee contains caffeine and is obtained from the seeds of *Coffea arabica*. Tea, the leaves of *Thea sinensis*, contains caffeine and theophylline. Cocoa contains theobromine and is obtained from the seeds of *Theobroma cacao*. These three drugs are often referred to as the *xanthines*. Caffeine is a strong stimulant to the central nervous system, theophylline less strong, and theobromine relatively weak.

Caffeine first affects the cortex of the brain, particularly the sensory and psychic functions. With a therapeutic dose (150 to 250 mg. for an adult) thinking is cleared, and more sustained reasoning and improved association of thoughts result. Fatigue and drowsiness are reduced. Sensory reception and motor response are improved. Next the medulla oblongata is affected. Whereas the cord may be stimulated next in order, a greater than therapeutic dose is required to produce an effect. The actions in the circulatory system produce antagonistic effects. In consequence little effect on pulse rate or blood pressure is discernible from a therapeutic dose.

The average cup of coffee contains between 100 and 150 mg. of caffeine, which is a little less than a therapeutic dose. Coffee also contains resin which, combined with fat, will produce a gastrointestinal irritant, oleoresin. Thus the cream in coffee may contribute to gastric irritation, which is the principal objection to coffee from the standpoint of health. Tannin in tea may cause constipation. Individual susceptibility to caffeine varies considerably. Some people, highly sensitive to caffeine, may find one cup of coffee to be toxic. Children are generally more susceptible to xanthine effects than adults. In addition the displacing of milk in the dietary by coffee or tea is a valid objection. Cocoa, containing theobromine but not caffeine and made with milk, is nutritionally acceptable for children.

In some patients with cardiovascular and nervous disease, the intake of coffee is controlled or even forbidden. For normal people overindulgence may produce restlessness, disturbed sleep, and even cardiac irregularity. Habituation to the xanthine drugs is such a universal phenomenon in the United States that controlled mass studies of its effects are difficult. No reliable data exists that xanthine habituation, as we know it in the United States, has any effect upon the length of life or upon general health.

The amount of caffeine in a regular bottle of a cola drink is about half that in the usual cup of coffee. The caffeine used in cola drinks is obtained from tea. Since the effect of caffeine is not cumulative, the ordinary consumption of cola drinks should not be injurious to health or to life expectancy.

Aspirin (acetylsalicylic acid). Aspirin is an odorless white crystalline powder used extensively by the lay public to relieve fever (antipyretic action) and to reduce sensitivity to certain pains (analgesic action). Antipyretic action occurs chiefly by sweating, aided by excess water in the blood and cutaneous vasodilation. The effect on headache is not completely understood but is perhaps due to relief of intracranial pressure by mobilization of excess water. Tactile sensations and pain due to injury are not affected.

The usual 5-grain (0.3 gm.) aspirin tablet is normally harmless. Allergy to aspirin is usually limited to people with general allergic and asthmatic tendencies who are usually between 20 and 50 years of age. Addiction occurs only when chronic headache exists. Aspirin to relieve a temporary condition is justifiable, but a chronic headache indicates a basic disorder which should be brought to the immediate attention of a physician.

People in the United States consume over fifteen billion aspirin tablets a year, (42,000,000 per day) which is equivalent to about ninety tablets per capita per year. From 30 to 40 gm. (100 to 133 five-grain tablets) is usually fatal; although 10 gm. (33 five-grain tablets) sometimes proves to be fatal. Sweating, thirst, fast pulse, low blood pressure, deep breathing, delirium, and coma precede death.

Although aspirin irritates the mucous lining of the stomach in man and causes ulcers in experimental animals, no evidence exists that aspirin causes gastric ulcers in the human being. Free salicylic acid is a fairly good antiseptic, but if used in a mouthwash it appears to soften the enamel of the teeth.

As generally used, aspirin perhaps contributes to effectiveness and enjoyment of living although self-medication which masks serious basic deviations from the normal is an ever-present danger to individual and community health.

CHEMICAL POISONS

Whereas chemical poisons are principally industrial problems, two poison problems of a chemical nature are of immediate concern to the individual citizen. One of these, cosmetic poisoning, is declining in significance, but still represents a formidable health hazard to certain segments of the population. Carbon monoxide poisoning is a constant health hazard to a nation which relies so heavily upon illuminating gas for heating purposes and motor vehicles for transportation.

Cosmetic poisoning. For years the universal use of cosmetics has been a constant public health concern because of the poisonous effects of some cosmetic constituents. Poisonings have resulted from the effects of cosmetics both as irritants and as sensitizers. The direct irritating action of cosmetics has been tissue destruction, tissue burning, and generalized or local inflammation. For example, phenol on the bare skin, ammonium nitrate on abrasions, and eosin in lipstick have a direct irritating effect on the contacted tissues.

Economic competition, combined with the self-regulatory efforts of the pharmaceutical manufacturers, tended to drive irritating cosmetic poisons from the market, but the final blow was struck by the Federal Food, Drug, and Cosmetic Act of June 25, 1938. The primary function of the act was to protect the consuming public from health injury. For the next three years, a series of test cases indicated that the Food and Drug Administration had the means by which irritating poisons could be eliminated from commercially produced cosmetics. Since that time, irritants in cosmetics are virtually nonexistent.

However, specific sensitivity to cosmetics continues as a health problem and will probably always be a problem for certain individuals. In general, people who have a general tendency toward allergies are the ones who are sensitized by cosmetics. Whereas a dermatosis in one form or another is usually in the nature of a reaction, as in other allergies, reactivity to cosmetic constituents can result in disturbances of other tissues—indeed, can result in general constitutional disturbances.

Reports from various physicians, clinics, and investigators have revealed sensitivity to hair washes, hair rinses, ammoniacal bleaches, hair dyes, lipstick, medicated soaps, dental cleansers, mouthwashes, depilatories, perfumes, powders, deodorants, freckle removers, nail polishes, face creams, and cleansing creams. Localized reactions or generalized symptoms associated with the use of a particular cosmetic should arouse a suspicion of possible sensitivity. Planned elimination of the suspected offender may prove its guilt. In a doubtful case a physician should be consulted. Cosmetics may mar as well as make beauty. They may have a ful effect upon health.

Carbon monoxide poisoning. Carbon monoxide is a colorless, tasteless, and practically odorless gas which is slightly lighter than air. It arises from the incomplete combustion of coal, charcoal, and wood. It is present in natural illuminating gas and in the exhaust of gasoline motors. A carbon monoxide concentration in the air of 0.2% can be fatal to human beings. Air with 0.4% of carbon monoxide can be fatal to a human being in one hour. Because of his relatively large respiratory exchange, a child will be overcome by carbon monoxide much more quickly than an adult. Because it is easily overcome by carbon monoxide, the canary is used as a safety measure for human beings in certain occupations.

The harmful effects of carbon monoxide arise from oxygen starvation (anoxemia). Carbon monoxide has a greater affinity for the hemoglobin of the red corpuscles than does oxygen. In consequence oxyhemoglobin is displaced by carboxyhemoglobin.

Arterial blood normally contains 19.5 ml. of oxygen for each 100 ml. of blood. If less than 10% (1.95 ml. per 100 ml. of blood) of the oxygen in the blood stream has been displaced by carbon monoxide, the individual may not recognize any particular symptoms. However, a progressively higher concentration of carbon monoxide will produce progressively more severe symptoms.

1. From 10% to 20% displacement of oxygen in the blood by carbon monoxide will result in symptoms of headache, tightness over the forhead, burning sensation of the eyes, some dizziness, and a flushing of the face.
2. At 20% to 30% displacement the headache becomes severe, and throbbing in the head is felt.
3. When the concentration of carbon monoxide in the blood is from 30% to 50% of the normal oxygen content, new symptoms are apparent. Nausea,

vomiting, dimming of the vision, and increased respiratory rate precede fainting (syncope).

4. At the level of 50% to 70%, coma, convulsions, and depression of cardiac and respiratory functions are the forerunners of death, which occurs at about the 70% level. Although death is due to paralysis of respiration, no direct damage by carbon monoxide on nerve tissues occurs; the oxygen starvation causes function of the nerve cells to cease.

When a level of 50% is reached but death is prevented, damage to the brain or even apoplexy may occur. At a level of 30% death can result. Indeed, any poisoning of more than 10% may imperil the victim's life for a week. Glycosuria and other symptoms indicate physiological disturbances.

Everyday dangers of carbon monoxide poisoning arise from leaky home gas fixtures, leaky exhaust lines in motor cars, and running gasoline motors in closed garages. Every person should learn to recognize the early distinctive carbon monoxide poisoning symptoms of tightness over the forehead and smarting of the eyes. He should know that crawling to safety will mean less likelihood of fainting and and will permit him to take advantage of the lower carbon monoxide concentration near the floor.

Any person who suffers from carbon monoxide poisoning should have the services of a physician. Merely breathing normal air may not be enough to assure recovery. Carboxyhemoglobin is such a stable compound that the physician may find it necessary to use various means to dissociate the carbon monoxide from the hemoglobin. Carbon dioxide has been found to be most effective in promoting the breakdown of carboxyhemoglobin. Of course oxygen must be made available to the hemoglobin. Methylene blue is of doubtful value to break down carboxyhemoglobin although it is used occasionally. Novocain has been reported to be effective if used properly. However, few physicians are familiar with its proper use in carbon monoxide poisoning.

Mental, emotional, and social health

Part two

Mental, emotional, and
social health

Chapter 8

Normal mental and emotional health

MENTAL HEALTH

A high level of mental health is a goal that is achieved by understanding and application—not as the gift of inherited endowment or the product of hopeful wishing. Few people reach anywhere near 100% of their potentiality in mental health. Most normal individuals could improve their level of adjustment by a conscientious effort to understand what constitutes mental health and the means by which a higher level of adjustment may be attained. The modern mental hygiene movement recognizes the need for preventing and treating mental disorder, but places its primary emphasis upon the positive side—that of promoting a higher level of mental and emotional well-being for normal human beings. Modern mental hygiene has much to offer the normal individual by helping him to help himself in attaining a higher level of mental health.

Concisely stated, mental health is effective and enjoyable living. It is living a purposeful life of accepted accomplishment which gives consuming satisfaction and enjoyment with a minimum of friction and conflict either within the individual or between the individual and others about him. Not just accomplishment nor just enjoyment, but both of these together constitute the cofactor index of mental health.

Final appraisal of effectiveness and enjoyment is determined by the particular society in which one lives. Even within a general society, primary and secondary social groups will have divergent values of what constitutes accomplishment and which enjoyment is acceptable. This indicates that study and application are necessary for individual adjustment in the exceedingly complex society of present-day America.

Modern mental hygiene regards enjoyment as a more practical day-for-day realistic goal than happiness. The terms are relative, happiness being the highest form or state of positive emotions attainable by the normal individual but of relatively brief duration. Some mentally disordered patients exhibit a continual high state of happiness, but a normal individual does not tend to maintain prolonged happiness. Enjoyment is a feeling of buoyancy, elation, well-being, pleasure, agreeableness, satisfaction, and elevation. Happiness is a condition of supreme felicity and euphoria. Enjoyment is both a worthy and an attainable goal in one's quest and measure of mental health.

Normal mental health. That which is accepted as the usual by society is normal mental health. It is not the average, nor is it a definite entity. It is a range into which the greatest number of persons fit who are regarded as living within the acceptable bounds of social conduct. No two individuals in a group are exactly alike; yet all of the group may be regarded as normal if all fit into the general patterns of conduct and adjustment accepted by society.

It should be pointed out that merely being in the normal range is not an index of a desirable level of health. A person asleep may be almost perfectly adjusted to his environment and his needs. The desirable goal is a dynamic adjustment, one of constructive accomplishment and a resulting high level of enjoyment.

Effectiveness and enjoyment are relative, not absolute, factors. So too, mental health is relative, and within the normal range one finds various degrees of mental and emotional well-being. Some individuals live with a high degree of effectiveness. They have extensive plans and goals and experience success in their everyday living, with a minimum of friction and a maximum of enjoyment. They do not live perfectly. They experience failure, frustration, and disappointment, but to a minor degree. These are the people with an excellent level of mental health who freely and efficiently use their endowment in creating a world that provides personal satisfaction in harmony with environmental requirements. They rate A in mental health.

Individuals with a good level of mental health do not experience the high level of adjustment attained by members of the excellent group. This group attains a creditable quality of mental hygiene but below the attainment of the first group. Doubtless many of them are capable of achieving the top category through understanding and tangible application to improvement. This is perhaps the B group.

In the fair or C group is that vast majority of normal individuals who experience neither a great deal of friction and conflict nor much accomplishment or enjoyment. They live rather passive, uninteresting, uninspired lives. Many attain but half of their potential accomplishment in adjustment and a smaller portion of their share of enjoyment. It is in this group that most can be done to improve the level of mental health. Improvement can come through helping the individual acquire a more extensive and intensive understanding of mental health and its translation into a tangible program of improvement. Even an improvement of 10% would add greatly to the individual's living.

Adjustment in life is not an easy or a simple task. It is a task requiring constant application because, in effect, a person adjusts to four different worlds—the physical world, the social world, the religious world, and his own ideal world.

In pioneer days perhaps the greatest challenge to the individual was his adjustment to the *physical forces* in his existence. However, in modern America although physical forces still represent a factor of importance in human adjustment, technological advances have reduced the difficulty of adapting to the physical world. Further, man finds the physical world a highly consistent world. A child learns what to expect when he falls. It is always the same. He learns that heat and cold are consistent in their effects. The very consistency of the physical world makes one experience highly valuable in adjusting to a somewhat similar situation in the future.

No such consistency exists in the *social world*. The complex socioeconomic structure of modern America requires an extremely high level of human adaptability. Uncertainties and inconsistencies inherent in a highly developed competitive society lead to frequent frustration and even futility which are constant obstacles to mental health. The social matrix is one in which a vast maze of practices, mores, values, and standards exists, often with small but highly important shades of differences, all tending to make personal adjustment more difficult. A child must learn that what is acceptable behavior in the home may not be acceptable in school. The grownup is required to make different finely discriminating responses to two outwardly identical situations. Sensitivity to discrimination is acquired through the maturation of personality, which enables the individual to make effective adaptations with a maximum of effectiveness and a minimum of friction and conflict.

The most important factors in any person's enviroment are other people. An individual must make a specific adjustment to each person's personality. Yet the task is not an impossible one. Although people are all different, they are not so tremendously different. One can acquire the ability to adapt to individuals as one learns to evaluate what motivates human conduct in the normal channels of human relationships.

If in the metaphysical sense *religion* is regarded as one's response to the unknown in life, every person is challenged to make a religious adjustment. As an individual matures in other respects, he finds an expanding need for growth in his religious adjustment. With this need will sometimes arise a considerable lag in maturation, resulting in conflict and perhaps brief disturbance which motivates the individual to give proportionately more attention to this particular sphere of adjustment.

Somewhat interwoven with the religious in man's existence is his *idealistic world*. It is the level of life to which he aspires. Or perhaps, like the ship captain who never hopes to reach a star yet is guided by it, the individual sets his ideal as a goal toward which to strive but never reach. Often such an ideal motivates individuals to a higher realization of their abilities. However, too great a disparity between the island of the ideal and the mainland of reality may result in frustration and despair.

Uniqueness of personality. Personality is considered the distinctive psychophysiological organization of an individual that determines his unique adjustment to his environment. More than three billion people live on the surface of the earth; yet no two are exactly alike. Each person is unique, different from all others. Such uniqueness is readily explained by the following equation:

$$C \times E = I$$

in which C = constitutional endowment
E = environment
I = individuality

Environment is different for every individual. It exerts a constant unique effect upon the individual. The makeup of an individual's personality is determined by the interaction of his environment and his constitutional endowment, not by the addition of the environment to the constitution.

Even identical twins do not have identical constitutional endowments. The nutritive constituents going to make up protoplasmic materials will vary for the two embryos. From the nearly similar constitutional endowments of identical twins as the smallest margin of constitutional difference, we have various gradations of individuals extremely different in virtually all aspects of constitutional makeup.

Overt human conduct is expressed through the nervous system, which varies in its function, however slightly, from one individual to another. Of equal importance is the variation in the inner bodily environment affecting the nervous system. Advances in psychosomatic study have demonstrated the importance of normal and malfunctioning bodily processes in determining characteristics of personality. All aspects of the constitution have some degree of effect upon individuality. The body fluids, blood pressure, chronic infection, fatigue, and nutrition are factors of recognized importance.

Most normal people experience fluctuation in moods, usually of a cyclic nature, all undertsandable in terms of the variability in bodily function. Further, it is recognized that physiologically the threshold of excitability, of emotional responsiveness, varies from person to person in the normal range.

On the positive side normal people possess the constitutional requisites for good adjustment. The somatic approach to personality study aims by understanding to develop each individual to the highest potentialities of his basic endowment. A gardner does not expect to get a rose from a hyacinth bulb. The wise grower seeks to get the best possible hyacinth from the hyacinth bulb. Likewise, in a human being the aim is not to develop a replica of some other prominent personality. It is to develop in terms of each individual's endowment that quality of personality adjustment which will assure him of the highest level of accomplished living.

Endocrine glands and the constitution. Endocrine or ductless glands form a group of organs that produce substances called internal or endocrine secretions.

These secretions contain chemicals which, when taken into the blood stream and circulated freely through the body, have the power to rouse to action or to modify the action of some organ or organs distantly removed from the glands which secreted them.

Together with the nervous system, the endocrine system coordinates all bodily functions. Endocrine secretions function as an important environmental factor in the determination of the function of the nervous system. It must be recognized that the entire physique and not one system determines the somatic (bodily) basis of personality; yet the internal secretions have a relationship to body function which is of special significance in determining the basic emotional mold and responsiveness of the individual.

It is presumptive to speak of true endocrine types since all of the glands function in producing the particular constitution of any given individual. All of the endocrine glands are interrelated, the balance between them varying from individual to individual. Just as one instrument may be dominant and characterize an orchestra, one highly productive gland may reflect itself in a particular constitutional makeup in an individual.

It is a common observation that at puberty and the late climacteric, pronounced personality changes are exhibited. Less generally known is the fact that these landmarks in life are the focal points of pronounced endocrine changes, often with a complete rearrangement of the endocrine balance. An 18-year-old youth is different in personality and endocrine endowment than his 14-year-old brother. That his psychological pattern is equally different is easily understandable in terms of somatic and psychological interrelationships.

Precisely how the various internal secretions modify the individual's psychosomatic makeup is not completely understood. Constitutional endocrinology has revealed many of these endocrine functions, but many are still concealed.

Psychosomatic approach. The functional and organic approach to mental states in past decades has been replaced by the more scientific approach of considering the constitution and its function in terms of psychological reactions. The internal environment of the nervous system is given equal responsibility with a person's external environment in producing the basic personality of each individual. Deviations in personality must be considered in terms of somatic changes. Not just endocrine deviations, but all physiological deviations are capable of producing personality change. Likewise, the personality and mental health potential of any individual is conditioned by his physiological makeup. Personality is modifiable by internal physical factors as well as by external environmental factors. In the interaction of the constitution and the mentality lies the answer to personality factors which the psychosomatic approach can clarify.

Motivation of human conduct. Conduct exhibited outwardly tells the *what* of human behavior. Its most subtle implications lie in its emotional components. While conduct is normally both reasoned and emotional, the emotional manifestations usually give the best insight and indications of personality makeup. It is in the analysis of what gives rise to these emotional patterns that one discovers the focus of personality. It is the *how* and *why* of conduct.

Motivation is the intensification of behavior. Behind overt conduct lies a force or forces which give direction and intensification to conduct. That intensification finds its focus in the *self* and its awareness. The most important thing to each of us is our *self*. Its gratification motivates our basic conduct.

Physiological patterns. At birth the child possesses a myriad of physiological patterns, the result of inherited, developmental, and congenital factors. Behavior in confined to biological responses operating through these basic physiological patterns. These patterns assume the status of drives or tensions and give rise to emotional responses.

The newborn child soon exhibits patterns of hunger, thirst, pain, activity, rest, and comfort through which the self is expressed emotionally. A child in the early stages of infancy exhibits a limited range of emotional response, but the negative emotions of resentment, anger, and fear, although rather undifferentiated, are displayed with considerable intensity. If his hunger or thirst is not satisfied, the child exhibits negative emotions through crying and other conduct. If rest, activity, or comfort is disturbed, the child likewise exhibits anger or other negative emotions. However, the child exhibits little in the way of definite pleasant or positive emotions when these drives have been gratified. The emotional behavior of the newborn child thus appears to be the response of a frustration of the biological *self* mediated through basic physiological drives or patterns. These drives are important all through life as factors in the emotional responsiveness of the individual. Although they play relatively a lesser role in the behavior of later years, one readily recognizes a variation in his own emotional responses to hunger, thirst, pain, and other of the basic biological drives.

Universal socially conditioned patterns. Man is born a biological being, but he becomes a social being. Just when an awareness of a social self first occurs is difficult to determine. Perhaps it appears in the first few months of life. Oddly the concept of self seems to be centered not within ourselves but just in front of us, between the eyes. If one holds the point of his index finger about one inch in front of the bridge of his nose, he is pointing to the location of his self-feeling. It is odd that the concept of self should be outside the body, but it is there for all of us—for persons who are blind or have only one eye as well as for the rest of us.

Although at first the developing child appears to receive self-gratification entirely through the biological aspects of his needs and experience, he soon also appears to get self-gratification through certain socially conditioned motives, such as attention, affection, approval, praise, and security, which soon tend to bring forth positive emotions of pleasure, elation, and love. As we mature, applause, achievement, mastery, understanding, and superiority bring elation to the self and produce pleasant emotions.

Every normal person is self-interested and selfish. Every normal person wants attention, approval, affection, and praise. He seeks self-gratification and strives to avoid self-depreciation. Each person must learn to gratify his *self* through socially approved avenues. He must learn that he can get self-gratification and social approval by doing excellent work in school, not by throwing a stone through a school window.

By the same token, when the *self* is frustrated, provoked, or thwarted, negative emotions are aroused. Anger, resentment, hate, jealousy, envy, anxiety, and other negative emotions are only expressions of a disturbed self. Every normal person experiences negative emotions when his self concept has been disturbed. He needs to acquire the ability to substitute reasoned conduct for negative emotional responses.

Individually modified motives. Some individuals experience gratification from unusual activities or outlets hardly regarded as universal. Perhaps the seeking of a special privilege falls in this category or developing an unusual but worthless skill. The motivating factor is self-gratification, however bizarre the outward conduct may appear to be. So long as these activities do not interfere with the lives of other individuals, society usually tolerates these emotional outlets.

Development of the self. Life is a continuous process, not a series of sharply marked-off stages. Yet fairly distinctive periods in development can be recognized. Sharp cleavages between the periods do not exist. Actually one period or stage overlaps or dovetails into another.

Infancy and early childhood (birth to 5 years). This period has been variously called the *self-centered period,* egocentric period, autoerotic period, narcissistic period, and selfish period. Behavior is largely biological. The child is highly self-centered. He regards himself as the center of all the world about him. Even a 3-year-old child, without restraint, grasps for everything before him. He will play by himself 90% of the time even with a mate playing by his side. At the age of 5 years he still will play by himself 70% of the time.

To make a reasonable adjustment in the years to come, the child must learn to deny himself some things, to respect the interests and wishes of others. Perhaps the most effective conditioning in adjusting self-interest to social requirements occurs at this period.

Too much expression of the self at this stage in development may result in a selfish, ruthless, domineering type of personality in later years. Too much repression at this period may lead to excessive timidity, reticence, and withdrawal in later years. Or, when adolescence is attained, a revolt against restraint may express itself in belligerent asocial conduct. The solution lies in a compromise or middle course of not too much expression and not too much repression. The youngster must learn that most things are permissible when they are not injurious or harmful to others.

It should be pointed out that, whereas individuality is manifest before the age of 5 years, the personality mold has not been set for all time. Omissions in rearing the child to this age can be compensated for or corrected in subsequent years.

Yet serious failure in the socialization of the child during the first five formative years becomes progressively more difficult to overcome as the years go along.

Middle childhood (6 to 10 years). This period is rightly termed the *individualistic period.* The socializing effect of five years of association with human beings, particularly those of the same age, has reduced the intensity of self-interest. Yet while the youngster of this stage is not the highly egocentric person of the previous period, he has but a superficial interest in others. He is decidedly an individualist who prefers his own association in his various enterprises. He may acquire a friend, but it is just for a day. Next week it will be another. Attachments are transitory.

This is the time when a child should be given opportunities for developing some degree of self-reliance, dependability, regularity, industry, and responsibility, all assets in effective social adjustment and personality integration. Fortunate indeed is the youngster whose training at this period includes training in various skills. Whether the skills are in music, art, handicrafts, sports, or other areas of common interest, their greatest value lies in providing avenues for social expression and acceptance in the years ahead.

Highly essential at this stage of life is the development of a high level of self-regard or feeling of worthiness, based upon reasonable success and accomplishment and an expressed appreciation by others. The youngsters should have something to live up to rather than something to live down. It provides the nucleus for the development of a positive type of personality.

Later childhood (11 to 15 years). Known as the *gang* or *homophilic period,* this stage displays a redirection of expression of the self. Self-interest is now divided with loyalty to a group of the same sex. At times the primary expression of loyalty is to the group, self-interest being relegated to a secondary role. No demonstrated biological basis exists to account for the grouping and segregation of the sexes. A possible explanation lies in the wide divergence of interests manifest at this stage. At 12 years of age girls are physiologically and socially almost two years in advance of boys and have more mature and more extensive interests. Although these boys and girls have some interests in common, members of each sex tend to acquire a multitude of distinctive primary interests.

Direction of this gregarious tendency into wholesome channels will help the youngsters to attain concepts and constructive experiences in cooperation and group action, attributes necessary throughout life in the United States.

A passive interest in the opposite sex rules out any great interest in "punch-and-wafer" sociability, but social relations as by-products of everyday activities are of sufficient value to be important in personality development. Corecreation provides wholesome social experience for the youngster.

Whereas the sex grouping apparent at this stage tends to decline as a primary characteristic in adult years, a tendency toward group segregation of the sexes continues throughout life. Common male interests still keep the mature man interested in masculine groups. Likewise, although a woman's primary expression may be directed to her husband and family, she still will seek the groups and group activity of her own sex.

Youth (16 to 20 years). Adolescence is often termed the period of *heterosexuality* because of the manifest interest in the opposite sex. This interest, although at first rather generalized, with maturity tends to become focused on a type in the opposite sex and usually finally centers on one individual.

To many observers adolescence is considered a sort of pathological state in which deviation and abnormality are the rule rather than the exception. While some special aspects of adjustment are most pronounced at this period of life, the youth period is best described as a transition period between childhood and adulthood. In this period the individual at times exhibits the consistency of maturity and at other times the inconsistency of immaturity. If more maladjustments and crises occur during this period than at any previous time, it is usually because unresolved problems which have been mounting merely crystallize at this time with the individual's newly displayed self-assertion.

Adolescence is more than a biological change. It involves mental, social, and other changes in the individual's makeup. It is not a sudden overnight reversal, but a gradual transition, varying from individual to individual in time of onset and rate of change.

Youth is a period of transition from the dependence of childhood to the independence of adulthood. It is a period of emancipation in which the youngster wishes to be recognized as an independent individual in his own right. Self-assertion, determination, and independence of action disturb the parents who still think of their youthful son or daughter as a child.

Sometimes this drive for emancipation is carried to the extreme of outright revolt against parents, teachers, and even society itself. It results in the "angry young men and young women" who appear to get a certain questionable type of attention and recognition. They seem to get a certain inner gratification from challenging everything that exists. Some of them may become openly antisocial. Tragically they often pay for these early forays by being unaccepted throughout their lives. They find difficulty in developing friendships. They find their choice of a possible marriage partner decidedly limited. Even marriage turns out badly because of their belligerent temperament.

Youth with this tendency should take a painstaking inventory of themselves, immediately initiate action to dissolve this belligerence in their makeup, and proceed on a new philosophy that life is not one continuous warfare. It is a matter of give and take, live and let live, and adjustment and adaptation to many people, factors, and problems. We live in an imperfect world of imperfect people, and the ability to appreciate people in spite of their imperfections must be developed by all who would live effectively and enjoyably in a complex society of unique personalities.

Life moves into progressive complexity for the adolescent. He moves swiftly into a more complex adult world, without an adult's experience. However, an 18-

year-old youth is usually natively as intelligent as he will ever be. His intellect enables him to solve a myriad of problems, sometimes with complete success, other times only partially, sometimes with satisfaction, and still other times with disturbance.

Youth is a highly sensitive and idealistic period—imaginative, enthusiastic, and flexible. This idealism is frequently a factor in failure and disturbance. Yet no competent counselor would advise an adolescent to lower his ideals except when too great a disparity exists between reality and the ideal.

For a high level of adjustment now and in the future, the mental health needs of the adolescent can be summarized briefly: (1) status within his social group, (2) group membership and active participation, (3) maturing standard of values, (4) major purpose in life, (5) enjoyment through success, (6) positive motivation in self-regard, and (7) self-recognition in growth.

Religious conflicts of youth occur when the simple religion of childhood is inadequate to meet the needs of the more mature person. The need for religious growth and maturity indicates the solution.

Young adulthood (21 to 35 years). In this period the ultimate goal of the self is a place in the sun, but the immediate goal is to get a foot on the first rung of the ladder. The self is directed toward the establishment of a certain degree of advantage and security, social as well as economic. Although the emotional mold is quite well established by the age of 20 years, the self expresses itself through new-found motivations, with variations in the characteristic emotional patterns.

Failure to attain reasonable social and economic status and security by the age of 30 years is often a portent of maladjustment ahead. It does not necessarily mean mental disorder, criminality, or other extreme states. It usually means that the individual never seems to be able to catch up to the civilization in which he finds himself. He is on the borderline of normality, never quite able to catch up with the demands of life. He is mute evidence of the need for the development early in life of self-regard, self-reliance, and objectivity.

Middle adulthood (35 to 60 years). During this period the self is directed toward a status of worldly importance. It is a period of aggressive offense, striving for the goal of a top place in the sun. Vocational, social, familial, religious, and all other relationships tend to be pointed toward this self-realization. Frustrations, failures, and disappointments may increase aggressiveness, which is expressed at times in asocial conduct, or the goals may be modified and self-gratification found in lesser stations or in a compromise with ideals. Fortunate is the individual who learns to attain effectiveness and enjoyment in life, as things are, instead of bewailing because things are not precisely as he would want them to be.

Later adulthood (60—). At this stage in life the self usually has attained some status from which it does not want to decline. The self assumes a defensive position to retain whatever place in the sun it may have. To preserve the *status quo* gives security and stability to the ego. Change produces uncertainty and the need for readjustment, both of which tend to become more disturbing and more difficult with advancing years. Clashes of interest between individuals in this age period and those in the middle-adult period can be expected in the dynamic competitive American scene.

Attributes of a well-adjusted personality. Personality requisites for adjusting to the present-day, complex, rugged, none-too-generous world are not measured in superficial rules of social etiquette or in unattainable idealistic standards. Personality attributes must be measured in terms of the fiber or timber of the individual's makeup which enables him to meet the rigors of adjustment with reasonable effectiveness. Although attributes must be considered separately, it is the unity of the total personality which is the true index of integration. Distinguishing qualities of an individual must be taken as a whole in a final appraisal of personality.

Philosophy of life. What is the ultimate purpose of this life? This question was asked of the members of a college-entering class. Only 28% had a crystallized concept of any ultimate purpose in life. Of the members of the graduating class four years later, 82% had a crystallized philosophy of life.

Through the ages man has sought an all-purpose catalytic life goal. Property, money, wealth, power, knowledge, prestige, superiority in some category, economic security—all have been the ultimate life purpose of members of the human species. Some persons, realizing these materialistic goals are but clay that will ultimately collapse, have used these goals as a means to a further final goal, that of service to their fellow men.

Over 2000 years ago, a wise man asked, "If I am not for myself, who will be; but if I am for myself alone, what am I?" He recognized his tendency to be self-interested and his need to promote that self-interest. Yet he recognized that self-interest could be only a means to a higher end. That end is service to others—in regular vocational pursuits, in avocations, without sacrifice, with sacrifice, in the common channels, and in unusual situations. A life goal of *service* is one that survives all circumstances. No one can take from an individual the gratification of a life of service, a life for the betterment of humanity. To be an asset to your fellow men does not require movieland heroics and complete self-denial. Effectiveness in planned living, which includes self-growth and maintenance, as well as service to others is the pattern. Fortunate is he whose life's vocation makes an outstanding and highly important contribution to society. More fortunate is he who gets sincere enjoyment through his service. His sole complaint is that life is too short.

Immediate goals. A distant life's goal of service must be implemented by intermediate realistic goals that gives definiteness and direction to the ultimate goal. Immediate objectives must be those that will challenge the individual to develop his greatest potentialities. These goals must be realistic in terms of attainment and worth if effectiveness and enjoyment in living are to be attained.

Often a person sets a worthwhile goal which he works toward and finally reaches, only to have the goal vanish when he reaches it. He finds the glitter and attractiveness gone, the goal a disappointment. If he considers his own growth in the journey to the goal, he will discover that, whereas that goal once loomed high above him, in the meantime he has matured to a position equal to or above the standard of the goal. He needs but to locate a new goal and chart a course to it.

Confidence which is justifiable. Early in life each of us becomes aware that others about us are like ourselves. We soon become aware that not only are they larger than we are, but they are also more capable. Our own inadequacies and incapacity are accentuated during the subsequent years. A 3-year-old child begins to understand why he is not permitted to handle certain objects. Later in school his mistakes and errors are marked out in red pencil. It is little wonder that every normal individual possesses a feeling of inferiority.

This feeling of inferiority persists as a backdrop to all of an individual's activities. Individuals with a high level of mental health adjust to the feeling of inferiority and do not strive to eliminate it totally. Each one recognizes his imperfections, his shortcomings. He needs to give more emphasis to his assets and less to his liabilities. He recognizes that failures and embarrassment are the lot of all, but that rarely does a single failure or embarrassment greatly affect one's life. Whereas perfection may be the ideal, imperfection is the substance of universal human conduct. Accepting imperfection as need for improvement, not for apology, can make a feeling of inferiority a positive factor rather than a liability. As in any other maturation process, improvement in adjustment to an inferiority feeling is a gradual day-by-day adjustment to specific aspects of inferiority.

Courage, particularly to face new situations. New situations hold a certain fascination that is mingled with apprehension. Most normal people recall anticipating a new situation with fear and dread. After the situation passed uneventfully, the individual was at a loss to account for his fears. Analysis usually reveals the common fear of the unfamiliar—one of the first fears acquired. This is pyramided by imagination, conditioned by a feeling of inferiority that visualizes all the mishaps and disasters that might result. Perhaps fear of failure is our greatest obstacle to success.

Likely, no normal person ever completely overcomes his apprehension of a new situation, but the tension can be reduced by the attempt to substitute reasoned conduct for emotional reaction. If he reviews his past performances, he will recall that intensive planning and preparation have usually assured success in any undertaking. In addition a certain degree of anxiety can be highly beneficial since the resulting effect of epinephrine from the adrenal glands, together with the function of the autonomic neuron system, puts the individual at his most effective level physically and mentally.

Self-reliance. At birth one is completely dependent upon others. With maturation the contribution of others decreases as the individual's own contribution increases. In the complex socioeconomic matrix in the United States perhaps no one is completely independent of all others. Economic and social interdependence characterizes life in the United States. Yet within that framework each individual must attain a high level of the ability to rely upon his own resources in adapting to that particular environmental complex in which he lives.

Self-discipline. Perhaps no one is perfectly self-disciplined, but most normal individuals would live more effectively and enjoyably if they developed the practice of doing necessary things in the order of their importance and necessity, not in terms of likes and dislikes. A high level of self-discipline is essential to a high level of mental health.

Stamina under stress. The ability to mobilize one's resources and work with sustained tenacity in a trying situation or crisis often determines the difference between average and superior accomplishments. Some people of ordinary ability attain a high degree of effectiveness in life because of a highly developed determination to meet a challenge or situation successfully. Doing so in many situations of lesser importance has a maturation value in the development of one's ability to mobilize one's resources and to sustain effort.

Adaptability. Life is not static; it is dynamic, and effective living requires constant adaptation. Well-adjusted young people are adapting constantly, with a minimum of friction and often without an awareness of significant change. In later years adaptability tends to become more difficult. Occasionally one observes open resistance and even hostility to inevitable change, an indication of poor adjustment.

Stability. Perhaps poise is best represented in the degree of stability one possesses. The ideal type of stability is that which allows for flexibility in adjustment in each particular type of situation. A personality which is invariable, however stable, is usually an uninteresting one, perhaps because it is too predictable. Yet while such consistency is usually associated with effectiveness and enjoyment in living, it represents personality of a rigid form as contrasted with the ideal of integration with flexibility. Resolution of purpose and action, conditioned by a sensitivity to change, is essential to high adjustability.

Orderliness. Orderly association or unity is a key attribute of a high degree of mental health. The unity in a well-adjusted personality creates an individuality which identifies the person in the minds of others. Such an identification of oneness is difficult in maladjusted persons. Whether unity in personality can best be evaluated in terms of its effect on others or in descriptive terms is difficult to determine. Either evaluation would give an end result of a unified individuality.

Objectivity. Important as self-interest is in human behavior, good adjustment requires that self-interest be held in restraint and at times even relegated to a secondary role. This ability to restrain the self and deal outside of self-interest is essential to the attainment of a high-level adjustment. What is commonly referred to as broadmindedness is in effect objectivity characterized by impartiality which deals with the external world in terms of conditions as they are, not as the self may wish them to be.

A person, extremely objective in one situation, may be extremely subjective in another situation. Many parents, otherwise reasonably objective, are highly subjective when their own children are the concern. Objectivity requires constant self-discipline.

Concept of humor. Doubtless no such thing as a sense of humor exists, but people do vary in their ability to conceive the humorous in life. A concept of humor is largely acquired through the influence of other individuals, particularly parents. Basic to an appreciation of the humorous is a well-integrated personality. Precisely what humor is has not been entirely understood. At times a feeling of superiority, at times of frustration, at times of the unexpected, and at times of the incompatible will all be basic to the arousal of humor.

Regardless of its genesis, humor serves as an excellent buffer in the otherwise extremely serious drama of life. It lightens tension and gives a stimulus both to effectiveness and to enjoyment in living.

Interests in others. Life is social, and society is mental. Human associations are bound together by thoughts expressed between individuals. Basic to effectiveness in social adjustment is a sincere interest in others. Perhaps all normal people are interested in their friends, in other people. However, it is usually a passive interest, even a lazy interest. Or, if it is more than passive, the interest is not expressed openly or effectively. An active interest, sincerely expressed, is the requirement.

Self-interest is usually the principal obstacle to an interest in others, thus to social adjustment. Yet self-interest can be turned into a social asset by gaining self-gratification through service to others. Altercentricity, self-gratification through projection of self-interest to the welfare of others, is the nucleus of a socially successful personality. Perhaps because it gives status to the ego of others, this projection of the self produces more than sheer social acceptance. It produces a certain degree of social attractiveness which lifts the individual out of the uninspiring category of the commonplace.

A wholesome vital interest in others demands a discriminating appreciation of their accomplishments, interests, skills, experiences, plans, ambitions, and personal qualities. It requires an appreciation of the fine qualities of an individual despite his imperfections. A definite comprehension and appreciation of each associate's individuality will provide the focus for projecting one's interest to them. It reduces one's own self-consciousness and supplies the means for creating a favorable ego status for others.

Whereas a man receives greater gratification from an appreciation of his accomplishments than from attention to him as a person, a woman appears to receive greatest gratification from a personal interest in her as a personality. Whether this difference is a socially conditioned response is difficult to determine. Nevertheless a socially successful individual recognizes the distinction in the response of men and women.

No person is socially perfect, but perhaps no one is as poorly adjusted socially as he thinks he is. Every person experiences some degree of social inadequacy and failure. No persons succeeds in being liked by everyone who is acquainted with him. Yet an analysis of past success and failure, combined with definite preparation for future experiences, should produce significant improvement in any person's social adjustment.

Personality disintegration. Disintegration of personality is characterized by a loss of the usual reasoned conduct and the substitution of emotional behavior arising from a feeling of inadequacy and futility. Life purposes appear to be lost or valueless. The situation becomes overwhelming. The individual is unable to mobilize his resources. He feels more and more inadequate and distressed.

Disintegration appears in various degrees of intensity. Normal people experience some degree of disintegration at times, usually as a result of fatigue. In the vernacular, "They go to pieces," but the disturbances are infrequent and are short in duration. A situation which seems to be overwhelming and insurmountable is reduced in stature by a night's sleep. In the more severe form, disintegration may be either a predisposing or a precipitating factor in suicide. Complete personality disintegration is displayed in the various psychoses.

Causes of disintegration. Fatigue, pain, disease, speed of present-day life, personal disaster (loss of job), family disaster (death), and distractions, such as exaggerated fears and obsessions, are the principal causes of personality disintegration.

Building a well-integrated personality by adjusting to the specific situations of day-to-day living is the preventive for serious disintegration and the assurance of wholesome living.

Some suggestions for promoting mental health. There are many practices and attitudes that an individual can adopt or follow in the promotion of good mental health.

1. Sound physical well-being makes easier the development of wholesome mental and emotional health. Poor physical health and unhappiness usually travel together.

2. Achieve a temperate realization of life's satisfactions. Adjustment must be made between the ideal and the attainable, between the demands of personal gratification and society's requirements, and between convictions held and practices followed.

3. Recognition of reality as the state of affairs with which one must deal is fundamental to mental health. When the situation cannot be changed, energy is expended more profitably by making the best of what is rather than by bewailing what is not.

4. Each individual can discover, especially through his own past experience, some things he does better than other things. Usually greater satisfaction comes from achievement within one's own range of ability than from failing attempts at unattainable goals.

5. Comparison and competition can engender vicious practices. The worth

of any mode of living can be found more happily apart from the determination to beat someone else. Strive to do things well rather than to beat someone else at it.

6. Daydreams about the future are not harmful if they result in planned action. Normal people enjoy the luxury of moderate daydreaming. Excessive daydreaming, as an escape mechanism, indicates unwholesome adjustment.

7. Few, if any, situations constitute hopeless handicaps. It is always possible to find someone, no better equipped, working out a satisfactory solution.

8. Some people enjoy sympathy so much that they try to deserve commiseration. Ailments are magnified, difficulties exaggerated, and minor troubles inflated because of the satisfaction of having other people seem sympathetic. Well-adjusted people do not enjoy their misery.

9. Some people are handicapped by the false belief that they have peculiarities and problems which other normal people do not have. However, human nature and experience is such that few personal characteristics and problems exist which are not the lot of thousands of other persons.

10. Mistakes and failures are occasions for learning, not for deceit and lamentation.

11. Disagreeable tasks and situations are made worse by attempts to ignore them or put them off. Done promptly and with dispatch, as a mere matter of course, they consume much less energy.

12. An avocation, side-line interest, or hobby is not a necessity, but it may be an excellent vehicle for promoting mental health.

13. The most important thing in any person's environment is other people, and perhaps their most important influence is their attitudes.

14. Sensitiveness to criticism is not an indication of good adjustment. Strive to reduce egocentricity and develop objectivity as a means to better mental health.

15. Perhaps 90% of normal life is commonplace and drudgery. The most satisfactory life attitudes include a place for difficult, tiresome, and unheroic activities. Success in doing the dull commonplace things of existence is usually a matter of habbit.

16. Every life has its tragedies. How one reacts to life's severest trials is conditioned by past growth in adjustment.

17. The emotional maturity which enables one to face the world, sufficient for whatever may happen, to make the best of it, independent of any particular help, is usually the result of successfully assuming this self-reliance in many specific situations over a period of years.

18. Acquire a rational view of your own qualifications. Every person has shortcomings or liabilities, but he also has his assets which should be given a preferred position in his self-appraisal.

19. Be yourself. Do not try to deceive others. Sincerity is essential to the most wholesome adjustment.
20. Have definiteness and plan for an orderly living. Adjustment requires that an individual must choose and plan, not drift.
21. Develop reasonable efficiency. Do things well as a matter of course and take pride in your ability. Skills contribute to enjoyment in living, and the world pays off on excellence.
22. The truest single test of mental balance is the ability to see yourself as others see you, to have insight.

MENTAL DISORDER

Those individuals with a disordered mentality *(dementia)* must be differentiated from those with a deficient mentality *(amentia)*. They represent an extremely important problem in the promotion of personal and community health. Mentally disordered persons are ill persons who should be given the same consideration and care provided for other citizens who are ill. Both prevention and care in mental illness should be the concern of all citizens.

The study, prevention, treatment, and cure of mental disorders are the province of the psychiatrist. Yet every community can benefit by having informed citizens who understand the nature of mental disorder and who are aware of the early indications of mental disturbance. Many tragedies could have been prevented if some layman had recognized a developing mental disorder for what it was and had been instrumental in having the disordered person referred to a psychiatrist. The layman is not expected to be an expert on mental disorders. His role is that of an informed and understanding citizen.

Psychosis is the scientific term for mental disorder or illness. Insanity is a legal term. A person is not insane unless a court of law has decreed that he is mentally irresponsible.

Mental disorder must be regarded as relative or a matter of degree. Normal individuals may exhibit certain of the characteristics of the disorders, but to a minor degree. Normal does not mean perfection. Doubtless every normal person has slight personality deviations but of such a minor nature that they are accepted as within the normal range. Recognition of deviations from the normal requires an understanding of the various types of mental disorders and their distinguishing characteristics.

Classification of disorders. The classification of mental disorders undergoes constant revision in response to changing concepts of mental disorder and to new discoveries in the research field. Mental disorders may be classed very simply by such general terms as psychosis, neurosis, and personality disorder, or they may be classed by an elaborate system based upon causes of disorder.

A psychosis basically is a disturbance of ideas. The individual has delusions, illusions, or hallucinations or otherwise is derailed in his idea of reality. Neurosis basically is a disturbance of the emotions. The individual reacts emotionally

Table 33. Classification of mental disorders

Classification	Equivalent terms
Disorders caused by or associated with disturbance of brain tissue function	
Acute brain disorders	
Chronic brain disorders	Organic psychoses
Disorders of psychogenic orgin or without clearly	
defined physical cause or structural brain change	
Psychotic disorders	Functional psychoses
Psychoneurotic disorders	Psychoneuroses
Psychophysiologic disorders	Organ neuroses
Personality disorders	
Transient situational	Character disorders

out of all proportion to a situation or has an emotional mold which deviates from the normal pattern. Personality disorder is more a crippling or deformity of personality than a disorder. The individual may be a "bit queer," or at the other pole he may be extremely complex and even contradictory in personality makeup.

Psychosis. Psychosis or major illness indicates mental illness so serious as to make the person socially incompetent and irresponsible. It may be an acute or a chronic condition. It may express itself anywhere between the two extremes of complete withdrawal and violent mania. Individuals with this degree of disorder are usually institutionalized.

Neurosis. Neurosis or minor mental illness indicates a condition outside of the normal range of behavior but not frankly disordered. Individuals in this category usually exhibit indications of instability and personality deficiency. They are just outside of the normal range. The fashionable nervous breakdown is an example of personality inadequacy in the realm of neurosis. A neurotic condition may be of short duration or may continue to the time of death. Perhaps 15% of this group are institutionalized, but the rest remain free in society, some in seclusion as removed from the midstream of life as are those who are institutionalized.

Personality disorder. Personality disorder designates a condition in which the individual lacks the poise to maintain his emotional balance because of a deficiency or disturbance in his emotional makeup. People of this type are generally free in the community and, although they are not psychotic or neurotic, display personality liabilities which set them off as people possessed, not quite achieved, a little queer, somewhat incongruous, or a bit touched. Some of these individuals are highly endowed in one characteristic and poorly endowed in another. This lack of balance is quite characteristic of them. Some possess contradictory qualities in a complex make-up. They may possess a high level of native intellect, yet lack emotional poise. They lack the insight characteristic of a well-adjusted personality. They possess a crippled or deformed personality rather than a disordered personality.

Standard professional nomenclature recognizes two basic classifications of mental disorder, based on cause of disease.

It is important to recognize that a distinction is made between mental disorders arising from damage to brain tissue and disorders which arise as a result of faulty thought patterns. Doubtless in all mental disorders there is a physical disturbance as well as a psychological disturbance. This psychosomatic interpretation of mental illness is widely accepted by both medical practitioners and mental hygienists. Mental health and physical health are inseparable aspects of general personal health. Promotion of health should recognize this basic principle.

Treatment of mental disorders. For centuries the only treatment for mental disorders was the psychological approach based upon the hypothesis that the person suffered from certain incorrect thought patterns which could be corrected by providing a more simple or understandable environment for the patient. Some medication was used, but merely as temporary sedatives. However, with the recognition of the relationship between the physiological and the psychological functions of the human being, the psychosomatic approach was emphasized. As a result experimentation on the physiological basis of mental disorder has been bearing fruit and gives promise of being the first definite breakthrough in the scientist's quest for an understanding of mental disorder and its treatment.

Several effective drugs are being used, of which *lysergic acid diethylamide* (L.S.D.) is a classical example. Experiments have shown that in large doses it induces a dreamlike state in which the patient has bizarre hallucinations. He may feel completely removed from reality. He may experience a dreamworld of fantastic colors. The condition produced by the drug resembles one form of psychosis, schizophrenia, in which the patient tends to be withdrawn from reality. The resemblance is so pronounced that the state produced by the drug is referred to as artificial schizophrenia.

Interestingly L.S.D. which produces these symptoms artificially is used to treat mental disorders in psychotic patients. Administered in small doses, the effect of the drug is the reverse of what it is when the drug is given in large amounts. In small doses L.S.D. provides an emotional release for the patient by breaking down memory blocks and otherwise reviving normal thought patterns. Combined with psychotherapy, L.S.D. can clear up some mild forms of emotional disturbance as well as help to overcome more severe forms of mental disorder.

Medical therapy combined with psychotherapy has begun to have a tangible effect in lowering the population in our institutions for mental patients. Between 1956 and 1957 for the first time in the history of the United States, there was a decline in the number of patients in our 496 hospitals for the mentally disordered.

If this trend can be continued, not only will the cost of caring for mental patients be decreased, but also the general contribution to the health and welfare of the nation will be incalculable. The obvious need is for more research in the field of mental disorder.

Table 34. Patients in hospitals for mental disease

Year	No. of patients	Rate per 100,000
1958	619,508	361.4
1959	616,384	353.1
1960	609,795	342.0

The layman and mental disorder. It is not the responsibility of laymen to diagnose mental disorder. However, the informed layman can recognize personality deviations which fall outside the normal range. Diagnosis, treatment, and care of mentally disordered persons are the province of the medical profession. As in other illness the earlier a person with a developing psychosis is brought to the attention of a physician, the greater is the likelihood of successful treatment and full recovery. If the medical profession is to see these persons with a mental disorder in the early stages, informed laymen must be able to recognize certain personality disturbances as being indicative of possible mental disorder and make every effort to ensure the individual the services of a physician.

APPRAISAL OF MENTAL HYGIENE

The field of mental hygiene is not something mystical and foreboding. Although there are many aspects not yet understood in the field, a considerable body of knowledge exists which the interested individual can use in his efforts to attain a better-adjusted personality. He may never rid himself completely of the "mental measles" or "emotional chickenpox" that most normal people have. Yet through knowledge and its application he can build up and maintain a higher level of mental health, which is represented in more effective and more enjoyable living. That same knowledge and its application can contribute to the promotion of community mental health. It is not in concealing knowledge of mental health but in making knowledge available that the practice of personal and community mental hygiene can be constructively effective.

Chapter 9

Preparation for
family living

Marriage is the most intimate partnership in society. Success in marriage is
one of the glorious achievements of mankind. Whoever achieves this crowning
glory fulfills the mission of a successful life. Success in marriage is too demanding and too important to be left to mere chance. The evidence is truly convincing that the goddess of chance grants small odds to the man and woman entering
into life's greatest venture without adequate preparation. Fundamental to the
attainment of success in marriage is a sound understanding of and preparation for
the undertaking. Success further demands that the partners continue to work at
the task of making an effective marriage. Marriage is a way of life, not a by-product. If its demands are high, its rewards are even higher. Marriage can give to
life a meaning, a fullness, a completeness, and a fruitfulness which gratify the
normal desire for a worthy life. It is an ennobling enterprise in which the individual finds personal gratification and the community finds stability. Marriage is
the keystone of our social structure in the United States.

Every normal boy and girl looks forward to marriage with mingled apprehension and anticipation. The apprehension stems partially from the concern one has
for a new experience, but essentially from fear of the tragedy which marriage
can be. The anticipation rises from the knowledge that marriage can be the avenue
to a joyous and fruitful life. Youth possesses the means for happiness in marriage
but not the wisdom or experience to utilize these attributes to the fullest degree.
If marriage today is more complex and demanding than it was in pioneer days, we
possess greater knowledge and resources for meeting that increased complexity.

MARRIAGE IN MODERN AMERICA

One need not be a social scientist to recognize that modern America presents
a social structure which differs from that of any other in recorded history. It differs

markedly from the social matrix of past generations in the United States. Women of today occupy a different station in the economic, political, and community life than their sisters did before them. The highly competitive economic world of today takes the man away from the home and makes greater demands of him than was true of his pioneer forefathers. The fast tempo of modern life and the extreme mobility of the population are factors which have a profound effect upon the institution of marriage. Today each of us has a multitude of acquaintances but relatively few friends. The impersonal nature of society today reduces the extent to which social pressure affects personal relationships and responsibilities. Yet mobility doubtless has been of importance in the promotion of marriage in the last two decades. Mobility provides greater opportunities in the selection of a mate, but it also results in greater demands in terms of maturation of personality and knowledge of factors demanded by marriage. Certainly data on marriage reveal there exists today as great an opportunity for marriage as in past generations.

Likelihood of marriage. Reports by the U.S. Bureau of the Census reveal that 92% of all men and women have been married by the age of 45 years. This exceeds the experience of previous generations. Today 50% of all girls and 18% of all boys have married by the time they are 20 years of age. More than 80% of our women and 66% of our men have married by the time they are 25 years of age. If the completely nonmarriageable persons, such as the seriously defective, are

Table 35. Males and females in the United States census

Year	Males	Per cent	Females	Per cent	Total	Females per 1000 males
1890	32,237,101	51.2	30,710,613	48.8	62,947,714	953
1900	38,816,448	51.1	37,178,127	48.9	75,994,575	957
1910	47,332,277	51.5	44,639,989	48.5	91,972,266	942
1920	53,900,431	51.0	51,810,189	49.0	105,710,620	961
1930	62,137,080	50.6	60,637,966	49.4	122,775,046	976
1940	66,061,592	50.2	65,607,683	49.8	131,669,275	992
1950	74,833,239	49.7	75,864,122	50.3	150,697,361	1014
1960	88,331,000	49.3	90,992,000	50.7	179,323,000	1030

Table 36. Males and females in the United States, 1960 census by certain age groups

Age group	Males	Females	Females per 1000 males
15-19 years	6,634,000	6,586,000	991
20-24 years	5,272,000	5,528,000	1042
25-29 years	5,333,000	5,336,000	1000
30-34 years	5,846,000	6,103,000	1044
35-39 years	6,080,000	6,402,000	1053

Table 37. Marriages and divorces in the United States, 1890 to 1962

Year	Marriages	Rate per 1000 population	Divorces	Rate per 1000 population
1890	530,937	8.4	31,735	0.5
1900	709,000	9.3	55,751	0.7
1910	948,166	10.3	83,045	0.9
1920	1,274,476	12.0	170,505	1.6
1930	1,126,856	11.3	191,591	1.6
1940	1,565,015	12.1	264,000	2.0
1950	1,667,231	11.1	385,114	2.6
1958	1,451,000	8.4	380,000	2.2
1959	1,494,000	8.5	396,000	2.2
1962	1,600,000	8.5	410,000	2.2

Table 38. Median age for first marriage in the United States, 1890 to 1961

Year	Age of groom	Age of bride
1890	26.1	22.0
1910	25.1	21.6
1930	24.3	21.3
1949	22.7	20.3
1961	22.8	20.3

eliminated in our calculations, it is apparent that almost everyone has an opportunity to marry. Even though females now outnumber males, these marriage data should convince the girl of college age that female aggressiveness in mate-seeking is not necessary. She can make herself available without making herself obvious.

Although the marriage rate fluctuates, U. S. Bureau of the Census reports on marriage and divorce reveal a tendency for a recent general decline in numbers and rates for both marriage and divorce.

The median age for marriage has declined during the past half century, as revealed by the reports of the 1950 Mid-Century White House Conference on Children and Youth.

It is recognized that the median tells very little about the extremes, but in this instance the trend in the median reflects the general trend toward earlier marriages.

In 1961 in first marriages the average age of the bride was 20.3 years and that of the groom was 22.8 years. In remarriages the average age of the bride was 35.4 years and that of the groom was 39.7 years. Early marriages continue to be the trend in the United States.

In 1960 the United States had 41,500,000 adult married women and 21,327,000 adult women not married. These latter can be divided into 3 groups: (1) 11,-822,000 never married, (2) 8,047,000 widows, and (3) 1,458,000 divorcees. Consciously or unconsciously many women resist marriage. Fear of marriage itself, fear of having certain personal deficiencies, real or imaginary, revealed, and refusal to exchange their present satisfying status of independence for the shared status in marriage account for the resistance to marriage. These women may or may not be interested in sex and men.

Many women interested in having a husband do not find one. They remain interested in men, sex, and marriage though their likelihood of marriage declines with the advance in years. At 30 years of age a woman's chances of marriage are one in two, at 40 years of age, one in five, at 50 years of age, one in sixteen, and at 60 years of age, one in sixty-two. However, many unmarried women live more enjoyable, more productive, and more enriched lives than many married women.

In the United States one out of every ten families is headed by a woman. Widows and divorcees constitute a considerable portion of this group, but many unmarried women support their elderly parents and in effect are the head of the family.

In 1960 the United States also had 41,500,000 married men but 3,696,000 fewer unmarried men than unmarried adult women. The 17,631,000 unmarried men are divided into three categories: (1) 14,331,000 adult bachelors, (2) 2,272,000 widowers, and (3) 1,028,000 divorced men. Many men do not marry because of poor health. Others do not marry because of their vocations, such as one requiring extensive travel. Many prefer the independent role of bachelor rather than the responsibilities of marriage. In the later years of life many of these feel a void in their lives and experience the realization that their lives have lacked the productivity they might have achieved through marriage.

Individual's need for marriage. Society has an obvious stake in marriage and the family because the family is the keystone of our whole social structure. No society has survived which was not based on the family as the living unit. Family responsibility and marriage are inseparable in a stable society. In its experiment with a familyless society, Russia quickly learned that having the state care for and assume responsibility for children led to chaos. In a state where the parents do not assume responsibility for progeny, society crumbles from the lack of social cohesiveness which the family tie provides. Russia quickly abandoned its attempt to create a society *sans* the family. For its own survival society must encourage and regulate the institution of marriage and parental responsibility.

Beyond the interest of society in marriage one must recognize that marriage satisfies normal personal needs.

Need for status. The need for status is an impelling purpose in marriage. In the American society to be married is normal. In the marriage role the individual experiences the gratification which comes from acceptance by associates. Marriage represents a landmark in the accomplishments and progress of successful living.

Need for a feeling of worthiness. The need for a feeling of worthiness is met by marriage, first by the approval of the marriage partner and, second, by the approbation of relatives and friends. To be held in sufficiently high esteem to be accepted for the role of marriage tends to elevate the individual's self-regard or self-reverence. It gives the person something more to live up to.

Emotional security. Emotional security growing out of the normal need for love is to be found in marriage. Love gives to the self the ultimate in gratification as expressed in exhilarating positive emotions. Marriage can provide the highest form of emotional gratification. Although all of us remain individualistic, marriage can submerge that individualism in a joint expression of interdependence which provides a satisfying inner security.

Sexual expression. Sexual expression is a natural physiological, psychological, and social need of all normal young people. The moral code in the United States requires that sexual drives be expressed only in the married state. The American sex edict has a firm, scientific, and rational basis. Man is sexual by nature, and the subjective end of sex is erotic pleasure. Yet the sexual apparatus of a man and woman is naturally and essentially reproductive. In its normal operation and full expression, it is creative of human life and is the natural means for the preservation of the human species. Marriage fulfills the natural need for sexual expression and procreation.

Companionship. Companionship is sought by every normal young man and young woman. Companionship can be found in many avenues of life, but its highest expression is to be found in marriage. The close intimate relationship of marriage with its mutuality of interests and achievements engenders a feeling of companionship which satisfies even the most intensive longing for association with other fellow beings. Love and companionship are not identical. Companionship encompasses the sharing of the common experiences of existence. It provides the confidence and security to be found in a dependable partnership. It permits the exchange of viewpoints, appreciations, and aspirations. The normal individual does not seek an alter-ego, but feels the need for a confidant. This need is perhaps greater in the complex somewhat impersonal society of today than it was in times past.

Conflict with other purposes. At times the pursuits and requirements of marriage will conflict with other obligations and aspirations. Marriage may conflict with personal individualized interests, with business and civic demands, with personal ambitions, and even with obligations to relatives. Conflicts are inherent in the complexity of modern living, and marriage, imperfect as it is, can be no exception. Preparation for marriage must include the maturity esssential for solving the conflicts which are normally encountered in marriage.

MATURATION FOR MARRIAGE

Marriage is for adults. The level of maturity of personality required for successful marriage is as demanding as that for any other experience or avenue of life. An individual may be adequate for successful adaptation to single life and be grossly inadequate for the needs of marriage adjustment. The poorly adjusted single person is ill prepared for marriage.

Personality integration of a level sufficient to enable one to meet the demands of marriage is the result of successfully meeting the multitude of situations which life presents. The self-reliance sufficient for marriage is the product of a process of maturation. The egocentricity of early childhood is inadequate for marriage; yet individuals who are as self-centered as a 3-year-old child enter marriage. To remain at the emotional level of a 12-year-old child, when attachment to the gang represents the individual's primary loyalty, does not qualify one for the role of marriage, in which loyalty to the mate is primary. Adolescent instability is not adequate for marriage. Although marriage does not demand perfection, it does demand that level of maturity in which the individual can maintain his or her individuality and yet submerge individuality to the common interest of the partnership.

The mature state. Self-esteem, tempered by humility, is characteristic of mature adjustment. A rational view of one's own qualifications, with insight adequate to see one's true self, is essential. An objective view of the realities of life is an attribute of a mature personality. Sincerity, stability, and a facility for readjusting to the disappointments and disturbances of life will provide triple insurance for successful marriage.

Perhaps the one quality which most needs to be cultivated, if one is to be mature for marriage, is the ability to appreciate people in spite of their imperfections. Many a person goes through life judging other people by their poorest qualities, but in turn expecting to be judged by his own best qualities. A person who goes through life acquiring a liking for people despite their shortcomings is developing an attribute of infinite value in marriage. We are imperfect people in an imperfect world. To approach marriage in the knowledge that ones mate is imperfect but is admirable nonetheless is a more realistic approach than that of expecting perfection.

Elements of human love. A certain degree of maturation must be attained in terms of the love which is both the core and the elixir of marriage. The intimate personal relationships of marriage encompass a combination of complex factors which a person must be competent to comprehend and express. Love is a highly involved expression of self which demands a reciprocal interrelationship for its fulfillment. Herbert Spencer contended that the love of man and woman for each other is composed of the following nine elements:

1. Physical sex impulses
2. Feeling for beauty
3. Affection
4. Admiration
5. Desire for approbation
6. Self-esteem
7. Proprietary feeling
8. Extended liberty of action from the absence of personal barriers
9. Exaltation of the sympathies*

---

*From Spencer, Herbert: Principles of psychology.

There is little doubt that love has the element of selfishness or egocentricity in it. Yet in its highest form love is a type of altercentricity in which the individual obtains self-gratification by mutual expression with a mate. In men love has a strong element of possessiveness. In women love basically gratifies their desire for attention. Both of these factors are expressions of egocentricity. Mature love is a reciprocal relationship in which the man and woman complement each other in a mutual gratification of personal worthiness.

Mature love is cultivated. Infatuation is a superficial romantic attraction, frequently no more than another example of the fictitious "falling in love at first sight." A man and woman at first sight may experience a strong attraction based primarily upon physical attractiveness or awareness. It can well be the genesis of a mature love relationship, but it must be seasoned through further comradeship and the experience of tribulations and gratifications which everyday living will provide.

Dr. Paul Popenoe lists five factors of a well-rounded attitude toward love.

1. Biological impulse leading to sex attraction
2. Tenderness and affection
3. Comradeship
4. A developing desire for children
5. A desire for economic independence°

Typical of a maturing love is a new perspective of values and worthiness. Factors which once seemed extremely important become inconsequential, and in their place new values, standards, goals, and interest arise which symbolize the upward spiral of seasoned love. Certainly love need not destroy individuality. It can contribute measurably to its greater development. In contributing to the joint love personality, each of the individual personalities is enriched.

DATING

Unfortunately for many young Americans love-making has assumed the status of a recreation. Many Europeans conclude that Americans are promiscuous because our young people so freely date, kiss, and engage in physical intimacies. Dating properly should be regarded as a preparation or conditioning for the development of mature love. Dating presents a paradox in that, whereas, emotional responsiveness must be cultivated, moral standards must be preserved. Yet the two aspects are compatible if a margin of control is maintained. Dating a person whom one respects and who returns that respect will be adequate assurance of control.

Dating practices are undergoing gradual change on a nationwide basis. Yet provincialism in dating does exist. Although it still is customary for the man to initiate the action necessary for dating, customs and practices are developing which make acceptable certain overtures on the part of the woman. This is laudable even though it is recognized that basically the male is the aggressor in mat-

°From Popenoe, Paul: Marriage before and after, New York, 1953, Wilfred Funk, Inc.

ters of social relationships and the female the more receptive participant. A better selection of mates would result if women had the initial choice, instead of men. Even where it is considered improper for the woman to propose a date, women nevertheless tend to enter more and more into the planning for the date. Some men choose not to date. Women rarely by personal preference choose not to date. Women can arrange to make themselves available for requests for dates. Some forethought and planning may be necessary to provide the essential availability.

Among a considerable segment of college students, a "good night peck" is considered to be the accepted parting exchange even on the first date. An embrace with the kiss seems to be reserved for subsequent dates. "Necking" seems to be accepted for persons going steady or keeping company. However, "being pinned" in many cases does not mean going steady in the usual sense. It may merely be a form of social security which assures one of dates, especially for important events. Petting is acceptable during an engagement, and sexual intercourse is reserved for marriage. Each young man and young woman must appraise standards of conduct in terms of all factors involved, not merely in terms of the popular concepts dictated by persons who regard dating as merely a vicarious thrill.

Occasionally a girl finds herself with an escort who chooses to take unjustified liberties. Every girl should recognize that her chastity is in the custody of her escort. When she finds herself coping with physical force, her best defense is perhaps an appeal to her escort's chivalry, particularly to whether his mother would approve of his conduct. She will need to assume the initiative the first moment her escort fails to heed her insistence that he restrain himself. Her words of appeal to his own self-esteem and that of his sisters and parents are her best defense. She cannot hope to match the physical prowess of her escort.

Dating is a necessary prelude to engagement and eventual marriage. There is no single magic formula. The trials and tribulations of dating doubtless contribute to the individual's maturation and preparation for marriage. To review dating experiences and from this analysis discover possibilities for making dates more successful should be fruitful to a young person in terms of improved dating. Not to profit by experience is to fail to mature in this important adventure.

College students commonly make the mistake of assuming that being pinned or engaged is a permanent arrangement. A pinning or an engagement is a temporary thing. It is marriage that should be for keeps. If more pinnings and engagements were broken, many unfortunate marriages which terminate in divorce would be prevented. One or both members of a pinned or engaged couple may recognize that their relationship is not soundly based and that a strong likelihood exists that marriage will be a stormy voyage. Yet because of a mistaken idea that they have committed themselves to an insoluble relationship, neither has the fortitude or integrity to terminate the pinning or engagement. In the social structure in the United States an engagement is a temporary or trial relationship, and marriage is the permanent union.

SELECTING A MATE

The selection of a mate is a process, not a lottery. It requires the use of reason as well as of the emotions. It demands insight and vision to appreciate the present qualities of an individual in terms projected into the future. After all, a person who is fascinating as a short-termed acquaintance may be imposible as a long-time companion. It is better to discover this before the fact rather than afterward.

Each individual has a distinctive problem in the selection of a mate which he must assume responsibility for solving. He is a wise person who profits by the experience of others, and, although general experience must be applied to a specific situation, the young man or young woman can profit from a knowledge of the experience of the general married population. By analyzing the data revealed by studies of marriages, youth of today can find a guide to the difficult problem of selecting a mate. Application lies with the young man or young woman though the services of a marriage counselor can be of marked assistance.

Marriage success runs in families, and so does marriage failure and divorce. Children with a close relationship, but not an inseparable attachment, with their parents have excellent prospects for successful marriage. Marriage partners need not be alike in temperament. Their temperaments can be supplemental and thus meet the needs of marriage. Antagonistic temperaments are not conducive to companionable marriage.

A tendency exists to mate on the basis of socioeconomic status, general background, educational level, residential locality, and religious backgrounds. Most college men marry below their educational station, and about half of the college women marry educational equals. Women prefer an intellectually superior man, and men prefer to marry down on the intellectual scale. Studies reveal that the preferred situation is that in which the man and woman are of about the same educational background; although if the man has a higher educational attainment, the situation is almost equally as good. Economic background is not as significant as formerly except when the girl is required to adjust to a lower standard of living. This she does not do too well. However, girls usually adjust effectively to a higher standard of living.

Age differences are not significant either way for young people if the age difference is not more than about four years. As much as eight or ten years would be a factor. If the wife is ten years older, the childbearing period will be short. If the husband is ten years older, a long widowhood is likely, because on the average, a wife outlives her husband by eight years.

About 20% of the marriages in the United States are remarriages. Census data reveal that a divorced man is a 50% higher marriage risk than one who has not been divorced. Women who are divorced are more than a 50% higher marriage risk than women who have not been divorced. Actually divorce rates increase with the number of marriages. People who are marrying for the third time have a higher prospect of divorce than those who are marrying for a second time, and for these in turn the risk is higher than for those who are marrying for the first time.

A marriage associated with a church has a high probability of success. Marriages between Protestants and Catholics are less likely to succeed than marriages within each faith. The divorce rate among Protestant-Catholic marriages is about four times as high as within the Catholic faith and twice as high as within the Protestant fold. Interfaith marriages are frowned upon by both Catholic and Protestant church authorities. About 4% of Jewish marriages are interfaith, and these are usually between a Jewish man and a gentile woman. Here again interfaith marriages are frowned upon by religious authorities.

In all of these comments certain factors can be recognized which are of special importance in marriage success. These factors basically are expressions of the qualities which make up the marriage partners. Certain background factors are important, and certain personality attributes are significant.

Background factors. Man has long sought the ingredients of successful marriage, but only in more recent years has a truly scientific approach been made to determine the factors in the background of a person who is successful in marriage. The research of Dr. Lewis M. Terman and associates indicates that ten factors in the background of a person are indicative of a high degree of success in marriage.

1. Superior happiness of parents
2. Childhood happiness
3. Lack of conflict with mother
4. Home discipline that was firm, not harsh
5. Strong attachment to mother
6. Strong attachment to father
7. Lack of conflict with father
8. Parental frankness about matters of sex
9. Infrequency and mildness of childhood punishment
10. Premarital attitude toward sex that was free from disgust or aversion*

From this study it is apparent that relationships in the early home life of an individual are of special importance in preparing him for the eventual needs of marriage.

The work of Dr. Paul Popenoe and Donna Wicks and Dr. Ernest W. Burgess and Dr. Leonard S. Cottrell, Jr., further supports Terman's findings by revealing that when an individual had the background combination of a joyous childhood in a home possessed of much happiness, the marriage prognosis was highly favorable. Well-adjusted well-mated parents set a marriage pattern for their children which in turn carries over into the marriages of the next generation. Being reared in a wholesome home atmosphere means the opportunity to practice the type of adjustment marriage will require. A person with this background has an advantage in marriage. A person without this background will have to put forth extra effort in making marriage a success.

Personality factors. Adjustment to the usual demands of life requires a certain degree of personality integration. It requires a certain timber or fiber in one's

---

*From Terman, Lewis, M., et al.: Psychological factors in marital happiness, New York, 1938, McGraw-Hill Book Co., Inc.

makeup to adjust to the problems and demands of everyday living. Marriage makes demands of the personality beyond the requirements of the usual life adjustments. A person not able to adapt reasonably effectively to the demands of the everyday world is ill fitted for the trials marriage will present. Marriage is a union of two personalities, each an individual in his or her own right. Each will retain that individuality but will be required to make some adjustment to the joint relationship or marriage personality. Marriage demands a stability of self-status because, although it can elevate the self-feeling to its highest pinnacle, it can also have a deflationary effect upon the ego. The individual whose demands for self-gratification can be met realistically in the nonglamorous activities of everyday living doubtless has attained the level of personality integration necessary for successful marriage. With this first essential the individual will grow during marriage and improve in ability to meet the challenges of married living.

No one is perfectly prepared for the venture of marriage, but many people possess extremely high qualifications. From this top level of capability on down the ladder are to be found various degrees of adequacy, sufficient for successful marriage. Below those who are adequate but not highly endowed are the marginal individuals whose possibility of success is extremely doubtful. At the bottom of the ladder are the unmarriageable who could not possibly make a success of marriage.

Several social scientists have developed rating instruments in an attempt to appraise an individual's personality qualifications or fitness for marriage. These devices are not infallible, nor are they precise, but they are of value in pointing up specific traits which are extremely important in marriage adjustment. They thus are instruments for obtaining information. With analysis and interpretation of the information an individual can obtain considerable insight into the degree of his marriageability. This is particularly true if the information is supplemented by counseling. The Burgess-Cottrell Marriage Prediction Scale, the Rosewell Johnson Temperament Test, and the Clifford Adams lists of traits have been used effectively for several years.

A study of interest to college students was conducted by Dr. Reuben Hill, who asked a group of students to rate several factors in order of importance in the selection of a mate. The relative importance of these factors as rated by the students is significant.

1. Dependable character
2. Emotional stability and maturity
3. Pleasing disposition
4. Mutual love and attraction
5. Good health
6. Desire for home and children
7. Refinement
8. Neatness
9. Ambition and industriousness
10. Good cook and housekeeper
11. Chastity
12. Education and general intelligence
13. Sociability
14. Similar religious backgrounds
15. Good looks
16. Similar educational backgrounds
17. Favorable social status or rating
18. Good financial prospects
19. Similar political backgrounds*

---

*From Hill, Reuben: Campus values in mate selection, J. Home Economics 37:557, 1945.

The fact that dependable character and emotional stability and maturity were rated as most important indicates that students recognize the basic qualities essential for the long journey of matrimony. Such attributes of personality as sincerity, stability, dependability, self-reliance, self-discipline, adaptability, orderliness, congeniality, sociability, and interest in people are symbols of qualification for marriage.

Of interest is a survey by C. L. Anderson of 1100 men students and 700 women students in four colleges in three different states, in which these students rated the qualities they most valued in members of the opposite sex. The order of rank represents such fine differences that two and even three qualities would be statistically of the same rank. Yet the lists are of interest.

QUALITY VALUED BY COLLEGE MEN IN WOMEN	QUALITY VALUED BY COLLEGE WOMEN IN MEN
1. Congeniality	1. Congeniality
2. Feminity	2. Intelligence
3. Physical attractiveness	3. Friendliness
4. Neatness	4. Sincerity
5. Sincerity	5. Dependability
6. Cheerfulness	6. Education
7. Friendliness	7. Vocational ability
8. Fairness	8. Masculinity
9. Intelligence	9. Neatness
10. Tolerance	10. Physical attractiveness
11. Education	11. Tact
12. Humor	12. Good morals
13. Tact	13. Humor
14. Modesty	14. Honesty
15. Honesty	15. Good manners

Doubtless there is no single index for predicting compatibility, but people possessing well-integrated personalities are likely to adjust to almost any marriage situation.

Undesirable traits. Certain personality characteristics manifest themselves as indications of inadequacy for marriage, especially when these characteristics are so extreme as to be readily discernible. Although every person has minor imperfections or shortcomings, some people have such pronounced shortcomings that these are their distinguishing characteristics. These traits are symptoms of a lack of personality integration and maturity. While these individuals may not always be maladjusted, they lack the degree of adjustment required in marriage. Unfavorable characteristics may appear in several forms and in varying degrees of severity.

Egotism or conceit	Hypersensitivity
Selfishness	Excessive restlessness
Tendency to domineer	Unrestrained impulsiveness
Aggressions	Uncontrolled anger outbursts
Arrogance	Hysterical tendencies
Emotional instability	Chronic tenseness and anxiety

Inability to relax	Tactlessness
Hypochondriacal tendencies	Constant craving for excitement
Pronounced depressions	Exhibitionism
Antagonisms and hostility	Boisterousness
Suspiciousness	Sex aversion
Dishonesty	Exaggerated interest in sex

Obviously no one individual will display all of these characteristics, but several of these traits may appear in an individual as a poor marriage risk. An overly sensitive individual who reads into situations things that are not present and who is easily offended is poorly equipped for the rigors of marriage.

ENGAGEMENT

Engagement is a bridge between two families, the one the individual has belonged to in the past and the one the individual will belong to in the future. It is a preface to marriage in which the partners have opportunities for adjustment to each other and to problems of mutual concern. In our society in which trial marriage is not accepted, the engagement provides a test of considerable value in determining compatibility and likelihood of marriage success. However, an engagement based entirely upon entertainment relationships is not realistic enough for preparation for marriage. Participation in the commonplace activities of everyday existence will develop a more realistic insight into the possibilities of future adjustment than will the tinsel and bells of perpetual entertainment.

Evidence indicates that elopment results in a high rate of unsuccessful marriages. Short engagements also result in low success in marriage. However, elopement and short engagement usually are a reflection of the impulsive nature of the people involved. Hence personal instability rather than time of engagement is the disintegrating factor. Conceivably a short engagement could be adequate and result in a highly successful marriage.

Too long an engagement can have adverse effects, particularly if the long unmarried state produces disturbing conflicts. Premarital sexual intercourse is more frequent among persons with long engagements. In addition if engagement is the means and marriage the end, a degree of impatience and dissatisfaction may develop.

An acceptable standard is an engagement of not less than six months or more than eighteen months. This time schedule will both allow for a true relationship and prevent an unwise marriage. It will permit the development of the type of relationship in which both partners feel they have known each other all of their lifetime. No element of strangeness will be felt in the relationship. There will be agreement on most questions. The few disagreements will be resolved. Such a relationship requires that each individual be willing to make concessions, to compromise, to permit the partner to save face—to retain status—and to develop a feeling of mutual need and trust. The greatest obstacle to such an adjustment is egocentricity of a type which seeks a dominant position in the relationship. Some small uncertainty and doubt may find its way into the finest relationship, but a well-developed feeling of mutual trust will dispel these doubts and uncertainties.

With increased affection comes increased intimacy, even to the point of personal confessions. Perhaps there is a vicarious thrill in making such confessions, but, unless they are important to the approaching marriage, they would be better unrevealed. These matters might profitably be discussed with a marriage counselor. Counselor service is desirable in case of differences and conflicts when either or both of the participants are unable to resolve the difficulty. The marriage counselor helps people to help themselves in solving problems relating to marriage. Many people have been highly successful in marriage without the services of a counselor, but many individuals have found counseling service invaluable.

MARITAL MATURITY

Marriage is not a transient episode. There is a certain finality about marriage which demands a certain maturity of the persons entering into it. Many authorities on marriage contend that "when to marry," in terms of maturity, is more important than certain personality traits. It is recognized that both partners will mature in marriage, but a certain level of maturation should have been attained before the wedding date if the marriage is to have a reasonble chance to succeed. No set formula applies, but a combination of factors which indicate maturity can serve as an index or guide. Emotional, social, moral, vocational, and physical maturation are required for marriage.

Emotional maturity. If there were one requirement for marriage more important than all others, it would be emotional maturity. A person with the ability to adjust effectively to frustration, to control both positive and negative emotions, and to find desirable self-gratification in the everyday world is well prepared for the adjustments of marriage. Consistency, stability, and adaptability indicate a high level of emotional maturity. The ability to substitute reasoning for the negative emotions and to obtain emotional gratification through the normal avenues accepted by our society is essential to marriage. Self-reliance, self-discipline, pride without hypersensitivity, and an ability to laugh at oneself are further indications of emotional maturity. Every individual suffers some disintegration or emotional disturbance, but a quick recovery is typical of a well-adjusted emotionally mature individual.

Perfection is not required for marriage, nor will it ever exist. But marriage is not for the highly egocentric, overly sensitive, selfish, overly dependent, inconsiderate, unrealistic, and highly emotional type of individual. Such an individual cannot give to marriage what such a union requires or receive from it what marriage has to offer.

Social maturity. No person feels totally adequate socially. Yet most people adjust better socially then they think they do. Marriage entails certain social demands and obligations. To have had a diversity of social experiences in early life is indeed fortunate. Such experiences tend to reduce one's uneasiness in the presence of strangers and tend to increase one's ability to adapt to various social situations. Social success, to a considerable degree, depends upon an individual's interest in people. Social maturity is represented in one's interest in meeting and knowing people and in one's desire to participate in wholesome social functions. Social adjustment is not limited to the "punch-and-wafer" type of social function but includes those civic, extravocational, neighborhood, church, and other enterprises involving group participation. The person who actually fears such participation, who shuns such activities, or who is disinterested is handicapped for marriage because wholesome family living includes a place for association with other individuals and groups. A person matures socially through participation in social enterprises. The catalyst is an interest in other people.

Moral maturity. Morality implies conformity to a code of conduct decreed by society for its preservation and advancement. Maturity from the moral standpoint includes a concept of right. A mature person will abide by the code of conduct set up by society though provisions of the code may interfere with his own desires or wishes. Maturity is expressed in personal sacrifice for the common good. Maturity includes a willingness to accept responsibility for one's acts. It is expressed in one's acceptance of the individual rights granted by society as a personal privilege and not as license to do whatever one may prefer. Moral maturity is characterized by one's ability to accept and discharge one's obligations as a citizen, a member of a social group, a member of a family, a friend, and a marriage partner.

The individual who evades personal responsibilities and the requirements of society is morally immature. Such an individual is a poor marriage prospect. The individual who breaches rules of society is not mature morally. The individual who uses devious ways of circumventing social requirements lacks the moral qualities essential for marriage. Success in marriage demands moral fiber in both participants.

Vocational maturity. A person must learn to work, and the earlier in life one assumes responsibility for tasks and learns to accomplish things, the better prepared he will be for the adult world of work. Marriage imposes the obligation of earning sufficient income to maintain a household. Occupation interest and the ability to measure up to the work demands of an occupation are primary requisites. Reliability, consistency, perserverance, and the ability to accept monotonous tasks cheerfully are indicative of the vocational maturity essential for occupational success. The person without work experience is hardly prepared for the role of marriage. This applies to both partners.

Physical maturity. An adult or nearly adult level of physical maturation would be assumed as a requirement for marriage. Biological maturity and physical development sufficient for the needs of adult life represent the level of physical maturity one should have for marriage. This does not imply that the individual must have attained complete physical maturity by the day of marriage. An individual may continue to mature physically until the age of 30 years. Hence some degree of physical maturation occurs in most marriages. However, the person who has not attained about 90% of his physical maturation might do well to postpone marriage until a more mature level is reached.

Age of marriage. The present tendency toward earlier marriage is accompanied by an increasing divorce rate although the earlier marriage age is not the only cause of the increased divorce rate. Perhaps chronological age masks the maturity of the individual; hence, there is some objection to considering chronological age as an isolated factor. However, "At what age should one marry?" is a frequent question.

Studies indicate that if a girl is under 18 years of age at the time of her wedding, the chance of marriage success is rather poor. From 18 years of age up to 30 years of age there appears to be an increase in a woman's ability to adjust to marriage. Thus marriage in the third decade of life appears to be most appropriate from the standpoint of adjustment to marriage. Economic, educational, and family considerations would also favor this time of marriage.

Considerable risk is involved in a marriage in which a male is under 22 years of age. Likewise marriage after a male has passed the age of 30 years involves considerable risk. From the standpoint of most likely success, marriage when the man is between 23 and 30 years of age is the ideal.

It must be recognized that exceptions to these general patterns will exist. A young couple on a farm may have a much less difficult time than a young couple living in a highly complex industrial metropolis. Yet marriage success or failure is not the exclusive province of either rural or urban residents.

Military service and marriage. For a man who plans to make a career of military service, marriage presents the usual problems, with a few variations included. Frequent moving will mean that the couple will have no established residence, the children will have no home town, and housing and related factors will be frequent problems. However, there can be compensations in terms of relative economic security, diversity of experiences, and travel opportunities. Although it is true that there is a high divorce rate among wartime marriages, peacetime marriages of career military men are generally as successful as marriages in the civilian segment of our population.

For a young man going into military service for two or three years, marriage presents a different problem. When he is told that absence makes the heart grow fonder, he wonders if it means fonder of someone else. He knows that propinquity is extremely important in matters of love. If he does not marry before going into the service, he may have some concern about marriage after his military service terminates.

Marriage in which the couple is separated by military service does present some advantages. It provides the man with a strong home tie and provides a certain degree of established security for the wife. The interrelationship can provide both with a personal gratification which results in desirable emotional experiences. A personal satisfaction results from keeping intact a marriage in which they are separated by hundreds of miles.

Disadvantages of separation due to military service can strain the marriage relationship. Loneliness, children, sexual tensions, and financial problems are but a few of the obstacles which may have to be overcome when the husband and wife are separated by military service. All of these problems can be resolved, but, before embarking upon marriage which will involve separation by service in the Armed forces, a couple must appraise their ability to make adjustments in terms of the problems which will arise. Perhaps the sacrifices of waiting until the man has returned from service are less demanding than the dangers of separation in marriage.

Marriage in college. With the increasing tendency of couples to enter marriage with plans for both to work, there has been an increasing tendency for students to marry while still in college. Some arrange to have the wife work in order to finance the education of the husband, but these plans are sometimes disrupted by childbirth. In those situations in which the husband supports a family and attends school, the double assignment jeopardizes both enterprises.

Marriage in college may mean additional complexities not normally present in marriage. Yet people adequately qualified make a success of marriage while attending college. However, marriage during college is not for unqualified or even marginal individuals. A person who could not make a success of marriage under usual circumstances would be ill prepared to meet the difficulties which will arise in a marriage during college days.

MARRIAGE AS A WAY OF LIFE

Adjustment in marriage is relative. No one adjusts perfectly, but many people attain an extremely high level of adaptation. However, not even a high degree of adjustment is necessary for a marriage to be classed as successful. Moderately effective adaptation can mean a satisfactory marriage. Success in marriage is an accomplishment not all persons are capable of achieving. It requires both personal ability in adjustment and a conscientious application of that ability. Success in marriage can give special meaning to one's life, extending beyond vocational or other success.

As in all other human pursuits marriage consists of a series of problems which must be solved. Many of these problems are represented by the ordinary day-to-day needs and situations which demand a solution, but the most important problems are those of a personal or intimate nature. They involve matters of personal conflict, of self-status, and of personal frustration. For their solution these matters of deepest concern require a combination of personality integration and an understanding of human conduct. They require a combination of self-reliance and confidence. With application marriage partners develop their ability to deal with the problems which arise. The resulting maturation enables them to fit into the marriage pattern with increased effectiveness and increased gratification.

Roles of husband and wife. Marriage is not a fifty-fifty proposition in all respects. The intense competition of modern industrial United States places such demands upon a man that his vocation may assume the primary role in terms of both his time and his interest. To a wife the marriage and home normally constitute her primary interest. Her outside interests are secondary to her role as wife and homemaker. As a consequence a wife frequently contributes more than half of what goes into the marriage itself. This is not to minimize the importance of the husband's income and its significance in marriage. It points to a factor wives often fail to understand when they complain that their husbands are so interested in business that they have less time for their home life than they have for business. A wife should expect to adapt her life to fit her husband's life as determined by the demands of his occupation. Top-rung vocational success is not attained on a daily nine to five o'clock schedule.

It is recognized that some husbands devote virtually no time to their home life, with a resulting marriage failure. If a wife is contributing 90% of the time and effort that goes into a marriage, it cannot be termed a successful marriage because marriage is a partnership, not a solo enterprise. When the wife's contribution is considerably less than half of what she should contribute, the marriage is doomed to failure unless the husband is an exceptional male who is in a position to compensate for his wife's deficiencies. The best assurance in marriage is for both partners to accept the role of contributing all they logically can to the partnership. Companionship is a necessary component of marriage. The husband's appreciation of his wife's domestic role and her appreciation of his contribution are fortifying factors.

Working wife. For both economic and psychological reasons a considerable proportion of American wives are gainfully employed outside of the home. The principal purpose is to secure necessary additional family income.

In the United States in 1961, 36.8% of all females 14 years of age and over were in the labor force. About 44.4% of all single women were employed, 34% of married women were working, and 39% of widows and divorcees were employed. Thus it is apparent that there is almost as large a proportion of married women working as there are unmarried women who work.

Many women successfully accept the dual role of housewife and wage earner.

Table 39. Proportion of wives working in relation to husband's income in the United States, 1952

Husband's salary ($)	Per cent of wives working
Under 1000	24
1000 to 1999	28
2000 to 2999	29
3000 to 3999	27
4000 to 4999	24
5000 to 5999	20
6000 to 6999	15
10,000 and over	13

Money is the major area of problems for married couples, and in many instances the supplementary family income provided by the wife is the difference between a successful or an unsuccessful marriage. A wife who works can be a successful homemaker. Her role as a wage earner requires certain adjustments in the home. Usually the husband does more in the home, and perhaps there is less leisure.

Working wives per se are not a cause of juvenile delinquency. Many working mothers have done a magnificent job of rearing their youngsters. Unqualified wives could not do an acceptable job of rearing children if they had twenty-six hours in the day. There is a valid objection to wives working while their children are small, but, once the children are old enough to care for themselves, the mother could properly go back to work.

Outside work can have a psychological value for a wife, particularly for a mother whose children are grown. She obtains a feeling of productivity when she works. The resulting self-gratification contributes to a high level of mental health. Obviously every working wife can obtain mental health value from the productivity and social contacts of her work.

Society has serious reservations about the wife who is voluntarily childless in order to work. There are serious objections to a mother who works in order to obtain extravagant luxuries, even though the children may not be neglected. Society has a stake in the children and weighs the assets and liabilities of working wives in terms of success in marriage, particularly as measured by the circumstances of the children.

Marriage economics. Money is one of the major problems of modern marriage. There are various creature needs and requirements which must be met, but rarely will there be enough income to fulfill all purposes. It is necessary to harmonize demands with resources. In the management of finances newlyweds find it wise to be highly conservative. Loan sharks prosper on nonconservative young couples, who soon find themselves saddled with harassing financial commitments which threaten to destroy their marriage.

A finance management plan is needed which includes income, most important needs, fixed expenses such as rent, installment payments, church pledges, insurance and taxes, and variable expenses such as food, clothing, household costs, medical care, personal needs, and recreation. Agreement on family spending is as psychologically beneficial as it is economically sound. By whom and how finances are handled can be worked out to the satisfaction of both partners if recognition is given to the usual roles of wife and husband in family spending. In the typical household the wife spends more than three fourths of what is spent for consumable goods. The husband enters into the purchases of major items, such as the home, automobile, television set, and insurance. Different ideas on what must come first are certain to arise, but these differences are more easily resolved when a finance management plan is being followed. Often the differences are based on social values rather than on economic factors.

Parenthood. Between 1940 and 1960 family size was showing an increase.

National statistics reveal that in 1960 as compared with 1940 there was an increase of 82% in third births, 54% in fourth births, and 30% in fifth births. Additional members in the family means that the family resources must be divided among more individuals. Yet it is in the rearing of the family that supreme personal gratification is attained in marriage. Parenthood is the crowning glory of marriage, but parenthood carries with it demands and sacrifices. Highly qualified parents meet the demands of parenthood without great difficulty. Children help parents to mature.

Parenthood enriches a successful marriage, but it is not a cure for unsuccessful marriage. Children can place a further strain between parents who already are not too well adjusted. Conflicts, jealousies, and misunderstandings can develop which were not present before the child came into the family. It takes preparation to be successful husbands and wives. It takes further preparation to be successful parents.

WIDOWHOOD

Most marriages are terminated by death, and the longer life expectation of the female is reflected in the statistics on widowhood. On the average in the United States a wife outlives her husband by eight years. The United States census for 1960 revealed 8,047,000 widowed women and 2,272,000 widowed men. About 550,000 women are widowed each year. More than 90,000 of these are under 45 years of age. Adjustment to widowhood can be as challenging a problem as adjustment to marriage. It is more difficult in the sense that there is little opportunity for preparation because the role is suddenly cast upon one. Those individuals who have been successful in meeting the problems and demands of life over the years usually possess the personality integration necessary for adjustment to widowhood.

DIVORCE

Divorce is a legal action which represents a social pathology of greater significance than is generally recognized. Divorce represents a failure in human adjustment which affects more than the two individuals directly involved. In many cases it has a greater impact upon other people than upon the two individuals being divorced. The composite effect of divorce is to leave a blight upon society itself.

The present divorce rate indicates that 19.6% of all marriages result in divorce. Approximately two thirds of divorced couples are childless, and about one fifth have one child. In the marriage cycle the highest incidence of divorce is in the third year, and a sharp drop in the divorce rate occurs after the seventh year of marriage.

Pathway to divorce. Although events leading to divorce follow various paths, certain changes within one or both of the partners are usually present. First, one of the partners experiences a loss of identity in the previously joint relationship.

Table 40. Causes of divorce (United States census, 1950)

Official cause	Per cent
Cruelty	50
Desertion	38
Neglect to provide	8
Adultery	4
Drunkenness	2
Other causes	3

Rapport ends, and each functions as an isolated personality. When marriage serves no purpose in terms of the individual's worthiness, a loss of self-esteem results. When marriage no longer provides self-gratification, there is a tendency to build a wall around oneself, and frequently the partner does likewise. If at this critical stage instead of each defying the other to get over the wall, either of the partners is willing and able to abandon the role of isolation, the final break leading to legal action may be prevented.

Loss of self-status is an underlying factor in divorce. As long as an individual can retain his self-esteem, there is little likelihood of turning to divorce for the solution of a pending problem. The problem becomes a crisis when the individuals lose their self-status or self-reverence.

Cause of divorce. United States census data on divorce reveal very little change from year to year in the causes of divorce as stated in court records. However, the official cause may conceal the true cause, which may be financial problems, jealousy, or general dissatisfaction with the marriage relationship.

Properly considered, divorce means a failure in human adjustment by one or both of the marriage partners. Although some individuals are incapable of success in marriage, many divorces can be prevented if the individuals concerned attempt to understand the problem they have and strive to work out an acceptable solution. Financial difficulties prove to be the Achilles' heel in many marriages. Adjustment to finances can be worked out as well as adjustment to other factors, such as in-laws, friends, social life, sex, children, and habits. Such an approach requires considerable effort but is worth all that it requires. Assistance of a qualified counselor can be of real value. Divorce is usually an escape, not a solution.

PREPARING FOR MARRIAGE

A positive approach to the question of divorce is the improvement of marriage. Just as one must be informed in other spheres of human activity, so too one should be informed on marriage. Sufficient research and clinical experience are available to serve as a basis for an understanding of the essentials of both premarital and marital adjustments. In the past obtaining this information was left to mere chance. Young people learned through observation and through the counsel of parents. These resources are still available, but more than these sources

Fig. 51. Family living class. An informal atmosphere which encourages all students to participate is particularly effective in the study of marriage.

Fig. 52. Premarriage counseling. A competent counselor can be of assistance to persons who are planning marriage. (Photograph by Hosmer.)

are needed. Fortunately the functional education of today includes a place in the curriculum for the study of marriage. Education has no greater opportunity to serve society than in preparing students for their future careers as husbands, wives, and parents.

Formal classroom study of marriage is directed to the basic problems. No course could deal with all of the specific problems each member of the class will encounter. However, such study can prepare the student to deal more effectively with these problems when they do arise. The student's understanding of the fundamentals of marriage gives him a base from which to operate. He also knows sources of knowledge, how to approach marriage problems, and the value of counseling services. Knowledge of marriage does not guarantee success, but it adds to one's assets for marriage and reduces one's liabilities. Above all it creates an objective point of view toward the problems of marriage, which is extremely important in assuring marriage success.

SEX EDUCATION

An important phase of one's preparation is an understanding of sex and reproduction. Marriage is more than just a matter of sex and reproduction; yet the sexual aspect of marriage is a highly significant phase of the marriage relationship. Many marriages, otherwise highly successful, have floundered on the shoals of sexual incompatibility. With few exceptions this incompatibility stemmed from a lack of understanding of this most personal of all human relationships.

Sex is the emotional response generated by the association of male and female, growing out of their distinctive functional, biological, and social differences. This emotional response is experienced even in ordinary social relationships of men and women, but its greatest intensity is associated with the reproductive function. Reproduction is the biological process involved in the generation of offspring.

Maturation and heterosexuality. An understanding of the biological basis of sex and reproduction is essential to a grasp of this extremely important aspect of man's endowment. The physiological basis of differences between male and female provides an insight into the distinctive sex characteristics of the two sexes.

Until the age of 10 years there is little difference physiologically between the girl and the boy. At this age the anterior pituitary gland, located beneath the brain, secretes a gonad-stimulating hormone. The daily output of this hormone increases until a mature amount is secreted. For girls living in the temperate zone this stage is generally reached during the age of 14 years although it may occur at an earlier or later age and be within the normal range. When the output of the hormone reaches the mature level, the ovaries are stimulated to maturity, the function of the reproductive system attains a mature level, and the menstrual cycle is initiated.

Maturation of the ovaries in the girl results in the secretion of female sex hormones *(estrogens)* in relatively large amounts, producing the bodily reactions and secondary sex characteristics of the biologically mature woman. She may experience some unusual reactions and perhaps a resulting conflict, with some tendency toward social withdrawal or negativism. She should understand that her transition is a natural biological phenomenon with associated social adjustment that is normal for women. This is the menarche or menarchial age.

In the boy the output of the pituitary hormone does not reach the mature level until about a year later than in the girl. In the boy the testes are stimulated to maturity, and in addition to producing sperms the testes produce male sex hormones *(androgens)* which give rise to the typical bodily reactions and secondary sex characteristics of the biologically mature man. Although no landmark of maturity, such as menses, occurs in the male, this coming of biological age is properly designated in the male as viripotence or the age of viripotence. As with girls some boys experience some psychological conflict, expressed usually through negativism, but like the girl the boy usually adjusts to the situation in a few months although effective counselling will hasten the adjustment.

It must be recognized that masculinity and femininity are relative terms. Every normal male will produce female sex hormones *(estrogens)*, but in relatively lesser amounts than the male sex hormones. The normal female produces male sex hormones *(androgens)*, though in lesser amounts than estrogens. Thus varying degrees of biological masculinity and femininity are recognized.

In addition to these biological changes a psychological change occurs. It manifests itself in an attraction to the opposite sex. The attraction at first tends to be generalized and becomes more selective or specific with further maturation. Because of this attraction for the opposite sex, this stage is usually referred to as the heterosexual period or adolescence.

The sex force tends to be more intense in the male than in the female. The principal explanation lies in the accumulation of androgens in the testes, which tends to sensitize the responsiveness of the reproductive system. However, although the sex drive may be stronger in the male, the social order in the United States not only accepts this assertiveness, but actually promotes the sexual aggressiveness of the male. Whereas this pattern exists in varying forms in most countries of the world, in some primitive societies the female is the aggressor in affairs of love.

A basic difference between man and woman in their response to the opposite sex exists. To the male the female is most strongly attractive biologically. The anatomy of the female has an erotic attraction for the male. Although the social attractiveness of a woman has more and more appeal as a man matures, the physical attractiveness of a woman continues to be a factor of importance. Obviously social conditioning plays a role in the form of sexual restraint or expression the male exhibits.

Among the young married women in the United States a greater variety of sex responsiveness is exhibited than among the young unmarried men. About 10% of the unmarried young women resemble men in the force of their sex responsiveness. If a particular biological endowment distinguishes these women from others, scientists have thus far failed to discover the distinctive factor. These women are not sexually excited by the anatomy of the male, but the social attractiveness and attention of the male produces a high degree of erotic responsiveness.

Approximately another 50% of the unmarried young women in the United States will have what might be classified as the typical sex responsiveness of the female. It is a generalized response and is not centered in the genitals nor is it strongly biological. She finds pleasure in the social attractiveness of the members of the opposite sex. The attention of a man is the spark that she requires for an erotic response which is not too intense but unmistakably pleasurable. Some women in this category question that they are sexually normal because they do not experience near ecstasy in the embrace of a man. "A man loves a woman, but a woman loves love" perhaps describes the phenomenon. The typical young woman is capable of attaining the highest level of erotic responsiveness, but frequently not until after successful sexual experience in the marriage relationship.

About 40% of the unmarried young women in the United States are sexually unawakened or are unresponsive. They feel no great exhilaration in their association with the opposite sex. They enjoy the sociability of their relationship with men but perhaps largely in terms of social status. Most but not all of this group will be at least partially awakened sexually after the inception of sexual intercourse in marriage. Some 15% of the married women in the United States appear to be unawakened sexually, have never experienced sexual gratification even of a minor form. Their deficiency is not a physiological one but primarily a psychological or social problem.

In the male and in the sexually awakened female, sex represents an exhilarating and invigorating force within the dynamic personality makeup of the individual.

Sex conflict. Especially for the unmarried young man, the desire for the opposite sex becomes an extremely powerful urge with a consuming resultant tension. Hunger for food and desire for love are two of the strongest drives he experiences. To add to his problem he recognizes that legally and morally he has no right to satisfy his sex urge. Society decrees that this powerful tension must be held in restraint until marriage. He thus often regards himself as abnormal since he so strongly desires that which society forbids. Yet his is but the experience of every normal unmarried young man in the United States. In him is centered a conflict between a strong biological force and an established social edict. The conflict may vary in degree from slightly disturbing to impelling.

It cannot be denied that the sexual drive or impulse in the human species is at times imperious and aggressive. Because this sexual drive is a strong force, it has always been and doubtless always will be subject to social control. Society is compelled to impose this control for its own welfare and survival. It would be informative to review mankind's attempts to resolve this sex problem.

Premarital sexual intercourse. No one familiar with the social order in the United States would contend that premarital sexual intercourse is nonexistent. Yet it is not so common as some alarmists maintain. The extensiveness varies with different social groups, being considerably less among college students and college graduates than among people of noncollege groups.

Before an appraisal is made of premarital intercourse in the light of modern society, certain misconceptions, shared particularly by some young men, might profitably be explored in terms of scientific knowledge. These misconceptions and the answers to these false impressions can be stated briefly.

1. "Engaging in sexual relations is an indication of manliness; only a weakling will not indulge." Self-restraint and compliance with the ethics of society require more stability and a more mature personality than does self-indulgence. The capacity for reproduction is not the final criterion of social manliness.

2. "Everybody does it." To project self-responsibility an individual often resorts to rationalization of this type. Although he knows that he is exaggerating, mere statement gives him some solace—although decidedly a small degree.

3. "Sexual experience before marriage is necessary for successful sexual relations in marriage." A vast number of married partners have attained a high level of sexual adjustment without premarital experience. Often sexual relations before marriage damage and even destroy any chance of happy sexual adjustment after marriage.

4. "Sexual intercourse is a necessary outlet for the expenditure of energy." A multitude of wholesome outlets are available for every young person, in which he can attain both effectiveness and enjoyment in living through accomplishment.

5. "Nocturnal emissions, or wet dreams, are not natural and are unhealthy." Nocturnal emissions are the result of normal function and have no known effect on normal sex function. Some young men have an emission once a week and others every second, third, or fourth week. It is merely a matter of expelling an excess of a product of the body. It is a normal complement of good health.

Some of the consequences of premarital sexual relations indicate the risks involved, which both the man and woman must face: (1) social ostracism, (2) feelings of guilt, fear, and worry, (3) dissatisfaction and disillusionment, (4) conception and illegitimate parenthood, (5) disrupted educational and life plans, and (6) venereal infection.

The double standard of sex morality in the United States has tended to fuse toward a single standard, but the girl still bears the major stigma of sexual relations outside of marriage bonds. The fact that it is the female who bears the child will perhaps always tend to make her the primary focus of the attention of society in its appraisal of illegitimacy. Yet society does not absolve the male.

He is held accountable for his conduct. He has an undeniable responsibility and obligation enforced by the social order. Although some transgressors escape with impunity, the danger is too great for any normal young woman and young man to risk.

To the young man who may be tempted in premarital sex relations, some positive action on the part of the individual can be effective in meeting society's standards.

1. Dating only a young woman of a type or level who would be an acceptable marriage mate. This does not imply that he intends to marry the person dated. It merely indicates the desirability of selecting associates he holds in high respect and esteem.

2. Avoiding bodily intimacies, however innocent and minor at the outset, because of the likelihood of further exploration fanned by biological responsiveness and youthful curiosity. Toying with temptation may be exciting, but the piper's price can be a preamble to disaster.

3. Avoiding the practice of going to isolated and secluded places on dates.

4. Avoiding the use of alcohol. Even a small amount of alcohol may reduce inhibitions below the threshold of restraint. Both alcohol and sexual responsiveness tend to have a narcotic effect. Alcohol, bodily intimacy, and seclusion are the triad of illicit relations.

Control of the sex drive poses a real challenge for the young woman whose sexual responsiveness is as intense as that of the typical young man. She finds that she must grant herself considerable reserve to retain her self-possession. She is aware that even small liberties may lead to uncontrolled erotic excitement.

For the girl with the typical female generalized sexual responsiveness, three problems merit consideration. The first is her innate curiosity about sex and sexual experience. Any normal young lady will be curious about sex, and the emotional power of curiosity has motivated many young women to engage in premarital intercourse. Curiosity is a normal human characteristic, but its control is a personal problem of conditioned restraint.

A second problem arises from the attentions of the married man "whose wife does not understand him and who is planning a divorce." The flattery of an older man's attention, coupled with the experience of the mature hunter, makes the inexperienced young woman an easy prey if she is foolish enough to accept the initial attention of the married man.

A third question which, upon occasion, plagues some girls is whether it is necessary to submit sexually to assure herself of a husband. Doubtless for some married women this has been the course of events, but the odds are too great for any girl to be deceived by whispered rumor of necessity. A girl can make herself attractive and available to worthwhile young men without stepping outside the bonds of socially accepted standards of conduct. Although she is biologically attractive to the man, the young lady becomes progressively more socially attractive as she cultivates a wholesome intense interest in his abilities, achievements, and ambitions. His respect for her begins to approach the level of affection as he appreciates her interest in him as an accomplished individual. Sincerity of interest will reflect itself in the relation between the two. A woman a man tends to place on a pedestal is not one he is likely to subject to immorality.

Most girls who submit to premarital sexual relations do not do so because of intense sexual desire. They do so to attain a certain status, that of being especially important to their partner because of the role they fulfill. Some girls purposely resort to the use of alcohol in order to blame intoxication for their conduct. They actually do not convince anyone, not even themselves. No status is higher than that of self-respect.

For the sexually unawakened young woman who has a neutral attitude toward sex or who doubts her sexual normality, perhaps to let sleeping dogs lie is the course of action. She should engage in everyday social activities she finds highly enjoyable even though her association with the opposite sex does not provide the romantic exhilaration she believes every other girl experiences. However, with engagement and then the considerate intimacies of marriage, her sexual respon- siveness can rise gradually to the highest level. The psychological will activate the physiological.

Self-stimulation or gratification. As a solution to the sex conflict, masturbation is not regarded as acceptable by the social order in the United States. In today's culture an individual matures sexually years before he is capable of establishing a home and, according to social standards, give expression to his sexual impulses and desires. Therefore, for his own good and the good of society, he is expected to conform to the conventions within the culture. This means the sex drive should be controlled if it is to become a positive force in the development of the per- sonality. One should remember that any great drive or power must be controlled or its creative force fails to be a constructive one. Scientists have provided answers to misconceptions surrounding the question of self-stimulation. Studies of the problem of masturbation reveal some interesting conclusions.

1. No loss of energy results. In the male, seminal fluid is produced at a uni- form rate independent of frequency of emissions. In the female no emission occurs.

2. Studies reveal neither a physiological nor an anatomical disturbance; hence no physical harm occurs.

3. Psychologists agree that the serious question is that of feeling guilty or ashamed. If this occurs, the individual's religious and other views should be resolved if integration is to be attained and worry dispelled.

4. Intelligence is not affected. No one has demonstrated that masturbation causes feeble-mindedness. Nor has anyone demonstrated that intelligence is affected by masturbation for any person at any level.

5. Neither sterility nor infertility results. The capacity to produce functional sperms and ova is affected by various physiological factors but not by masturbation.

6. There can be no physiological effect on future offspring.
7. Self-stimulation which continues into adulthood is not a normal sex pattern. It is not likely to be the cause of emotional difficulty but is more likely to be a sign of an emotional problem which should be discussed with a counselor or physician who can provide necessary professional advice.
8. Appearance is not altered by masturbation. Pimples (acne) are caused by organisms *(Staphylococcus albus)* abetted by certain physiological conditions such as occur in some individuals during the period of adolescence. Further, no one can detect by appearance whether a person has engaged in masturbation any more than one can detect by appearance whether a person has engaged in sexual intercourse.

Recognizing the logical desirability and the need for self-control, many individuals seek to stop the practice of self-stimulation. Such individuals should formulate a realistic program directed to an attainable goal. Such a program should emphasize wholesome everyday association with members of the opposite sex. Such associations tend to replace phantasy with reality. The projection of drives and urges into socially acceptable outlets can prove to be profitable. Keeping occupied, avoiding solitude, and avoiding sleeping late are all helpful. Building up one's self-esteem through cleanliness and neatness can be helpful. Perfection may not be attained but some lesser degree of success can be worthwhile.

Many people have been successful in controlling the practice of self-stimulation and have gone on to normal sex relations in marriage. They have attained the ideal goal of self-control in matters of sex.

Continence or self-restraint. Complete sexual restraint is achieved by perhaps half of the unmarried young women in the United States. A much smaller proportion of unmarried men attain the goal. No evidence exists that continence is either harmful or healthful physiologically. Perhaps a resultant feeling of self-reliance or self-mastery may produce a healthful psychological effect which in itself can be sufficient reward. As an ideal, sexual continence has much to commend it.

A male who practices continence will experience nocturnal emissions (wet dreams) about every two, three, or four weeks. These are normal physiological responses to an accumulation of semen and are not harmful either physiologically or psychologically.

Sexual adjustment in marriage. Adjustment to sex is merely one aspect of the over-all problem of personal adjustment, but sexual adjustment in marriage is something more than a matter of blind chance. It entails the complementary adjustment of two well-adjusted personalities. While male and female are complementary and each makes a distinctive contribution to the marriage relationship, each retains his or her individuality. Neither completely sublimates the self to the love relationship. Self-interest remains. Yet normal egocentricity can be retained in successful marriage by the proper projection of the self into the marriage partnership. The husband can retain his feeling of possessiveness, of strong biological attraction, with a supporting social responsiveness. The wife can satisfy her desire for the adoration of her mate. However, for erotic harmony consideration of each other must be a major motive. A man and woman approaching marriage with mutual consideration as a dominant motive have a prerequisite for sexual adjustment. It is especially important that the man in marriage give every consideration to the erotic gratification of his wife. Although sexual harmony is the joint task of both partners, the primary responsibility rests with the husband.

Not too many years ago a wife in the United States played a passive role in sex relations. Sexual relations served the dual purpose of reproduction and the gratification of the husband. A wife was truly in the service of her husband. Modern American marriage recognizes mutual gratification as a requirement of sexual experience.

Consideration of his wife should begin with the wedding night. The wife needs understanding affection and tenderness, not uncontrolled passion. The experience of the wedding night may well condition the erotic responsiveness of the wife throughout her marriage. Refraining from sexual relations on the wedding night would certainly be indicated if the bride is tired, frightened, tense, or otherwise disturbed. Such consideration will be rewarded manyfold in the years ahead. Not until both partners are responsive should sexual relations be approached.

Sexual intercourse represents the most intimate of all human relationships. In consequence months of patience, restraint, and experimentation may be necessary to attain the highest level of erotic harmony. Much of the necessity for the long period often needed for adjustment results from the differing timetables of the husband and wife. The husband's curve of sexual responsiveness is abrupt. The wife's timetable and curve are slow and gradual. In consequence the love-play must extend over a considerable period of time if both partners are to attain erotic readiness. In some cases more than two hours are required by the wife for reaching a state of readiness. The enlightened husband who gives this factor its proper consideration will be adequately rewarded by a gratified and affectionate wife. The unenlightened husband may have a frigid disillusioned wife.

Defloration (removal of the hymen) is of some concern to the prospective bride, but it need not be. The hymen or maidenhead is a partial ring of membrane across the lower border of the vaginal orifice. Its absence or presence is no index of virginity. It may never have been present. Or it may have been torn during intercourse and may have rehealed. The likelihood is extremely remote that the hymen can be damaged accidentally.

With proper consideration by the groom the hymen will not be torn. In the sexually aroused bride the resulting relaxation or dilatation of the vaginal tract will prevent any injury during sexual relations. The hymen will be stretched moderately, but no injury or pain will result. It should be a pleasurable experience, not a painful one.

Although it may be some weeks or months before the bride attains an orgasm, her sexual experience nevertheless can be enjoyable and satisfying. Complete sexual harmony may take months to cultivate.

An orgasm is a nervous reaction, perhaps the most pleasant sensation the human body experiences. In the male it results in an emission of fluid semen. The female has no such emission though the nervous reaction doubtless is similar to that experienced by the male.

Following the orgasm a pleasurable afterglow results and is followed by a feeling of passive comfort even to the extent of drowsiness. Just as the female requires a longer time to attain the peak of responsiveness, her afterglow is likewise considerably longer that that of the male.

Sexual maladjustment. Youthful ignorance of natural function, feelings of sin and guilt, fears, morbid introspection, and feelings of wrongdoing and unworthiness all contribute to sexual maladjustment. It requires no great insight to recognize that the problem is a psychological one. Its solution requires understanding and patience. It demands that the individual must understand his situation and what needs to be done because in his ability to help himself lies the key to readjustment. It must be based upon the realization that attraction to the opposite sex is in the plan of nature, a function to be guided, not shunned. It requires a realization that what is pleasurable is not necessarily immoral, that sex of itself is not destructive or immoral. Sex is a force for the exhilaration of life and the perpetuation of mankind.

Readjustment will be gradual, not miraculously abrupt. Wholesome acceptance of one's erotic functions will be attained through a continuous positive program of wholesome acceptance of sex as one phase of normal social relations. Complete success is not always attained, but some degree of positive improvement should contribute to the effectiveness and enjoyment of life. Adjustment to the sexual aspect of life is merely one aspect of general personality adjustment.

The male reproductive system. The reproductive and excretory systems of the male have a common passageway, the urethra; yet their functions are completely different.

Until about one month before birth the gonads (testes) remain in the abdominal cavity where they develop. About this time in development the testes descend through the inguinal canals into the pouch or scrotum. Occasionally the testes fail to descend, a condition known as cryptorcism. The obstetrician attending the birth routinely examines a newborn child and corrects any such condition immediately. If the condition cannot be corrected immediately, surgery is often performed years later.

When the testes remain in the abdominal cavity, a high temperature, $100°$ F., prevents the testes from attaining mature function. Failure to produce sperms and sufficient androgens results in sterility and delayed masculine maturation. The lower temperature of the scrotum, $90°$ to $94°$ F., appears to be optimum for the production of sperms and androgens.

Whereas the anterior pituitary gland actively secretes a gonad-stimulating hormone (interstitial tissue-stimulating hormone) at the age of 10 years, as has been stated, not until about the age of 15 or 16 years is a sufficient amount produced

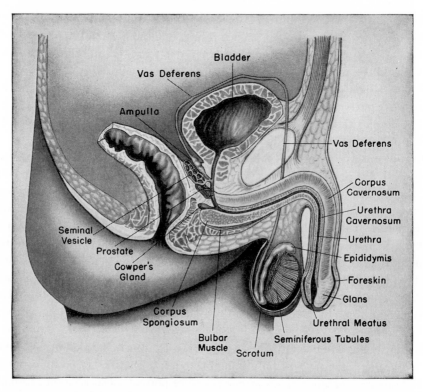

Fig. 53. Cross section of the male reproductive system.

to stimulate the gonads to mature function. At this time functional sperms begin to be produced, as well as the androgens, testosterone and androsterone.

In most men the left testis is the larger and hangs lower. In some men the testes are about equal in size; in some the right is the larger. All are normal conditions. Actually only one testis is essential for fertility.

In size the average mature testis is about 1½ × 1¼ × 1 inch. It has the general shape of an elongated plum.

Structurally the testis is composed of approximately 500 coiled seminiferous tubules and a single comma-shaped epididymis. The tubules are coiled and closely packed, but, stretched out, each is about a foot or more in length. Thus over 500 feet of fine tubules are present in a testis. It is in the walls of the tubules that germinal issue is located—tissue which produces the sperms. Between the tubules the interstitial tissue produces testosterone and androsterone. The epididymis is about 1½ inches long, but stretched out it is over 5 feet in length. It serves merely as a storage receptacle.

Sperms begin to be produced by cell division at the outer margin of the walls of the tubule. As the cell proceeds toward the lumen of the tube, it undergoes two divisions, resulting in four mature sperms from the original one produced by the first cell division. In a healthy young male around the age of 29 years, sperms are produced at the highest rate of about 100,000,000 a week. A sperm is the smallest cell in the body and is composed of a head, which is the nucleus, a body, and a tail. Its over-all length is about 1/500 of an inch. The head is about 1/6000 of an inch broad.

A small amount of fluid is produced by the tubules, thus providing the moisture necessary for the life of the sperms. The sperms collect in the epididymis where they are stored. While in the epididymis, the sperms exhibit very little motility, but they are living cells and undergo further maturation.

The androgens produced by the interstitial tissue are essential to the vitality of the sperms. They are also responsible for secondary male sex characteristics.

Each epididymis continues as a long slender tube, the vas deferens, which passes up through the inguinal canal. Each over 10 inches long, these two tubes arch behind the bladder and join the urethra at a point just beneath the bladder. The urethra extends from the bladder to the end of the penis and is the passageway through which both urine and semen are discharged from the body.

Two seminal vesicles, located beneath the bladder, are pouches about 2 inches long. They produce a cloudy fluid which is added to the discharge during an emission.

Just beneath the vesicles and behind the urethra, a single chestnut-shaped organ, the prostate gland, secretes a clear fluid with a fishlike odor. Prostatic fluid is added to the semen during emission. This fluid stimulates the granules in the body of the sperm, causing the whipping action of the tail and thus producing motility. In later life the prostatic output declines markedly, and the gland may enlarge and cause a constriction of the urethra. Surgery and hormone therapy have been used successfully in treating the condition.

The external organ of copulation, the penis, sometimes is referred to as a blood muscle. A shaft, or body of the penis, is composed of cavernous spaces, a urethra cavernosum surrounding the urethra and two corpora cavernosa on the sides. When the penis is flaccid, the cavernous spaces are collapsed and empty. During

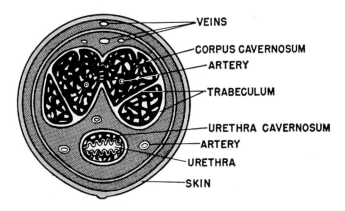

Fig. 54. Schematic transverse section of the shaft of the penis.

sexual excitement the outgoing flow of blood is reduced by a constriction of the veins. The excess blood empties into the cavernous spaces, producing an erection of the organ. The mechanism is controlled by nerve fibers arising in the lumbar region of the spinal cord. In some cases the penis is bowed during erection, but the condition has no significance.

The head portion or glans is sexually the most sensitive tissue in the male. It contains a high number of touch receptors. A fold of skin which may cover or be drawn back from the glans is the foreskin. For the most healthful condition the foreskin should be relaxed enough to be drawn back of the glans. This allows for the bathing of the oily deposit, smegma, produced by glands just back of the glans.

In the male the urethra is a ¼-inch tube about 11 inches long. Made acid by urine, it is alkalized by a secretion from the two Cowper's glands located in the pelvic cavity. The structure of the inner surface of the urethra tends to cause the urine to be voided in a twisting stream.

In the pelvic cavity a continuation of the urethra cavernosum expands to become the corpus spongiosum which is partially surrounded by a bulbar muscle. During an orgasm stimulation of motor nerves causes a highly pleasurable contraction of the bulbar muscle which in turn exerts pressure on the spongiosum. The partial vacuum created draws fluid from the epididymis in each testis. As the mass passes the seminal vesicles and prostate, seminal and prostatic fluids are added. Semen leaves the urethra in a series of four or five spurting emissions. A discharge of 3 ml. (about 1 teaspoonful) of the cloudy semen with a fishlike odor will contain about 200,000,000 sperms.

Following the emission the penis tends to return to the customary flaccid condition. The erectile sensitivity is markedly reduced, and a consequent erection is not likely for some time. However, an emission is usually satisfying for some time to come.

Sterility in the male. One of every nine married couples in the United States is involuntarily childless. Whereas sterility—the inability to produce offspring—is less frequent in the male than in the female, the ratio is but two to three. Usually the sterile male is normal in appearance. No outward signs are apparent. Various causes of sterility in the male have been recognized.

1. Closure of the genital tract is perhaps the most frequent cause of sterility. Infection, e.g., gonorrhea, migrating to the testes may produce lesions in the tubes. Scar tissue which forms in the healing process may close off the tubes. Although sperms will still be produced, they cannot be emitted. Sperms are merely dissolved by body fluids. Infection of the genital tract during mumps in an adolescent can be prevented by chemotherapy.

2. Deficient sperms are produced by about 2% of the men in the United States. Only by intensive microscopic analysis can a deficiency of sperms be detected. No successful treatment for the condition exists.

3. Deficiency of androgens as a cause of sterility in some cases can be treated successfully.
4. Deficiency in prostatic fluid results in sperms with inadequate motility. Although usually a condition of later years, prostatic deficiency does occur at all ages in manhood.
5. Pronounced diabetes may render a man sterile.
6. Marked thyroxin deficiency can contribute to sterility.

Some men possess a low degree of fertility (infertility), but they are not totally sterile. On occasion they are able to conceive. Permitting sperms a long time to mature in the epididymis may be helpful. An improvement in general health is also helpful in some persons.

Surgical sterilization. Surgical sterilization of the male is known as a vasectomy. The vas deferens on both sides is tied off or ligated. The ligature requires an incision through the skin and subcutaneous tissue external to the inguinal canals. Entry into the abdominal cavity is unnecessary. Sperms continue to be produced, but will be dissolved and absorbed into the body tissue. Sexual responsiveness will not be altered. The emission during an orgasm will contain only seminal and prostatic fluid, no sperms. In a year's time at the place of the ligature the inner surface of the wall of the vas will become fused.

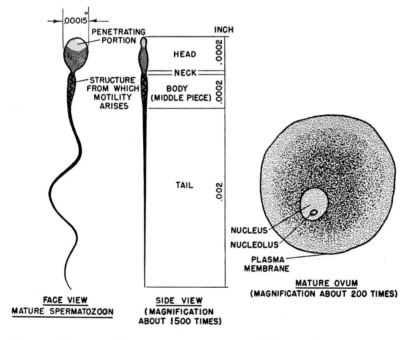

Fig. 55. Diagram of a typical functional spermatozoon and functional ovum. On the spermatozoon note the whiplike tail or flagellum. In the ovum note the granular-like structure of the cytoplasm, which is heavy and granular near the center and clear near the periphery. (From Anderson, C. L.: Physical and emotional aspects of marriage, St. Louis, 1953, The C. V. Mosby Co.)

The female reproductive system. In the female the reproductive and excretory systems are completely separate though closely related in anatomical position.

The external genital structures (vulva) are the major and minor folds, the clitoris at the superior margin, and the vaginal orifice at the inferior margin. On a small scale the clitoris is homologous with the penis. It possesses a glans, shaft, and cavernosa. It is the most sensitive portion of the genital system and is capable of erection.

A canal, the *vagina*, is the passageway of the system to the exterior of the body. At the orifice a hymen may form a partial dam across the opening. The vagina forms an upward angle of about 40 degrees. The depth of the anterior surface is about 4 inches, and that of the posterior surface is about 1 inch greater. Normally the channel is decidedly acid. Two small *Bartholin glands* empty an oily lubricant into the vaginal tract. The glands secrete actively during sexual arousal but may secrete excessively at other times due to pressure or other stimulation.

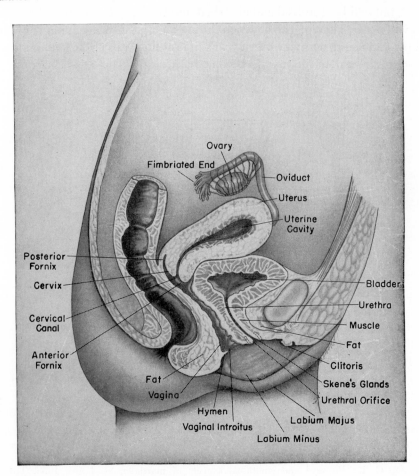

Fig. 56. Cross section of the female reproductive system.

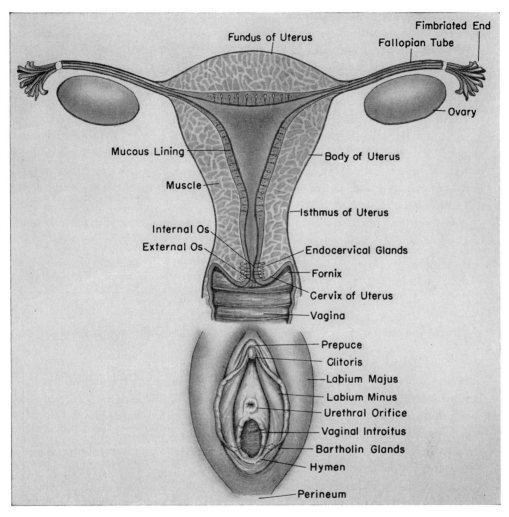

Fig. 57. Schematic diagram of the female external genital structures and front-view section of the internal genital structures.

The *uterus* (womb) is the shape of an inverted pear. It is about 3 inches long, 2 inches wide, and 1 inch in thickness. It is thick-walled, and the ligaments which hold it in place permit some movement of the organ.

Right and left uterine tubes or *oviducts* grow out of the upper portion of the body of the uterus. These tubes, called fallopian tubes, are about 3 inches long. The distal end of the tube is open and is called the fimbriated end.

Beneath each oviduct is an *ovary*, about the size and shape of an almond nut. A mature ovary is about 1½ × ¾ × ½ inch in size and is covered by a transparent membrane. The cortex of the ovary possesses germinal tissue which produces the ova or germ cells of the female. In the newborn infant the smooth pale cortex of an ovary may contain 50,000 immature ova, but by puberty perhaps less than

15,000 still remain. The ovarian cortex of a middle-aged woman is usually roughened and dark in color.

When at about 14 years of age the girl's output of gonadotropin (follicle-stimulating hormone) is sufficient to produce maturity of the ovaries, the menstrual cycle is initiated. However, she will not be fertile for several months. Apparently several menstrual cycles are required to complete the maturation of the reproductive system. The second menses may be two or three months after the first. Subsequent intervals may be irregular. Marked regularity is the exception even in women between 20 and 40 years of age. The variation in the cycle may be between 15 and 50 days. Medical science has much to offer in correcting irregularities of menstruation. In any case of doubtful function the woman should consult a physician.

The menstrual cycle without fertilization. A simple diagrammatic presentation of a representative 28-day cycle reveals five distinct phases.

Days	4	8	3	8	5	4
Phase	A	B	C	D	E	A
	Menstruation	Follicle development	Ovulation	Corpus luteum activity	Corpus luteum atrophy	Menstruation

Phase A—menstruation; phase B—follicle development. As a result of stimulation by the follicle-stimulating hormone (FSH), a fluid-filled sac (follicle) begins to develop around one of the ova in either the left or right ovary. The developing follicle produces a hormone, estrone, which circulates about the body in the blood stream. The general function of this hormone is that of preparing the reproductive system for the development of an embryo.

Specific effects include the following:

1. In the uterus a formation of an extensive network of capillaries completely filled with blood
2. Increase in sensitivity of the uterus
3. Thickening of the mucous lining of the entire genital tract
4. Stimulation of the ducts of the breasts

Phase C—ovulation. During this phase the follicle ruptures, and the ovum is liberated from the cortex of the ovary. Although it is true that the time of ovulation may exhibit considerable variation, present evidence indicates the most likely time is as indicated in the diagram. A few women can detect the rupturing of the follicle by a sharp pain (mittelschmerz) in the region of the ovary, followed by quick relief from the pain. Recently developed tests make detection of ovulation quite definite.

The ovaries do not necessarily alternate in the release of ova. Biopsies show that in most women one ovary is the more prolific. Actually only one ovary is necessary for fertility. During her lifetime the average woman liberates about 400 ova. After the age of 40 years quite frequently the menstrual cycle occurs without the liberation of an ovum (anovulation).

For a short period of time the ovum is in the abdominal cavity, outside of the genital tract. A combination of fluid movement and pressure difference moves the ovum toward the open end of the oviduct. Time required for the journey is perhaps one or two hours. The ovum lodges in the upper one third of the oviduct where it receives moisture and nourishment by diffusion from the mucous lining of the oviduct. The ovum lives in the oviduct perhaps as long as three days. If it is not fertilized, it dies and is dissolved by the surrounding fluid.

Phase D—corpus luteum activity. In the cortex of the ovary rupture of the follicle leaves a depression in which a mass of yellow cells appear. This yellow mass is called the *corpus luteum* (yellow body). It is stimulated by a second anterior pituitary gonadotropin, luteinizing hormone (L.H.), and produces a hormone, *progesterone*. The general function of progesterone is to stabilize the genital tract. Its specific effects include the following:

1. Stabilizing the supplementary vascular supply of the uterus
2. Decreasing the sensitivity and contractility of the uterine musculature

Phase E—corpus luteum atrophy. The corpus luteum recedes if the ovum is not fertilized, and thus no imbedding of an embryo in the uterine lining occurs. The corpus luteum begins to dry up, and the output of progesterone declines rapidly. With this decline the genital preparation becomes unstable. Finally the entire preparation tends to disintegrate, and menses begin again.

The menstrual cycle with fertilization. No deviation from the previous cycle occurs until phase C, ovulation. If the individual has sexual intercourse during or just before the two or three days the ovum remains functional in the upper one third of the oviduct, conception or fertilization may occur. During intercourse some of the semen is deposited in the vagina, but some of it is emitted into the entrance of the uterus. The acidity of the vagina immobilizes those sperms coming in contact with acid, but many of those at the uterine entrance start their journey immediately. An orgasm of the woman produces a suction action of the uterus and thus facilitates the movement of sperms up the uterus. Although an orgasm in the female may be helpful, it is not essential for conception. Sperms have a difficult long (6 inches) journey ahead. They swim in all directions, tending to go against any current present. The journey takes perhaps from two to six hours. Many sperms perish, and only the most hardy survive. In their wanderings some sperms go up one oviduct and others go up the other duct. It appears to be mere chance rather than any attraction mechanism.

When one sperm impregnates (fertilizes) the ovum, a chemical fertilization membrane forms around the ovum and repels all other sperms. The moment the sperm enters the ovum is the most important moment in each of our lives. The tiny ovum (1/100 inch in diameter) and the much smaller sperm unite to form a single cell, the *zygote*. The zygote remains in the oviduct and goes through a series of divisions until finally a tiny mass of cells (blastula) is formed. In about ten days the blastula descends and imbeds itself in the mucous lining of the uterus. The imbedding is termed *implantation.*

This implantation changes the hormone picture because it causes a new hormone to be produced which stimulates the anterior pituitary gland to secrete large amounts of luteinizing hormone. As a result the corpus luteum does not dry up but secretes progesterone until about four months later when the placenta secretes the hormone progesterone which takes over the function of stabilizing the genital system.

Signs of pregnancy are the following:
1. Cessation of menses. Not proof, but an indication of pregnancy, absence of menses is usually the first definite landmark.
2. Enlargement and firmness of the uterus.
3. Morning nausea. The placenta produces a new hormone which in some individuals stimulates the vomiting center in the brain. Usually the condition clears up without treatment, but drugs can be used to relieve it.
4. Brown discoloration of the nipples and pigmentation of the sagittal line on the skin of the abdomen.
5. Changes in the breasts.
6. Certain subjective signs occasionally are present—emotional changes, capricious appetite, and aversions for certain foods.

The Friedman test for pregnancy is highly reliable. It is based on the principle that the urine of a pregnant woman contains a hormone normally not present, which causes a definite change in the ovaries of lower animals. Usually pregnancy tests are not effective until the pregnancy is of at least six weeks' duration.

In order of appearance the symptoms of pregnancy may be indicated in three phases or trimesters: The symptoms of the first three months are cessation of menses, firmness of uterus, morning nausea, and changes in the breasts; those of the second three months are enlargement of the uterus, movement of the fetus, and perhaps uterine contractions; those of the third phase are fetal movement, ability to feel the fetus, and heart sounds.

Prenatal care. Modern science has eliminated most of the dangers and inconveniences of childbearing. Proper prenatal care is the basic essential of safe and sure childbirth. Proper prenatal care, based upon understanding, is not a difficult course for an expectant mother.

A thorough initial examination by a physician with regular follow-up consultations as scheduled by the physician is a prime requirement. Moderate activity and adequate rest and sleep are essential. An adequate quantitative and qualitative diet prescribed by the obstetrician will protect the health of the mother and assure the best possible development of her child. Overweight of the mother can be as serious a problem as an inadequate diet.

The many advantages of hospital delivery have made it an almost universally accepted practice in the United States. Whereas very little equipment and services may be necessary for some deliveries, there is added assurance in having available

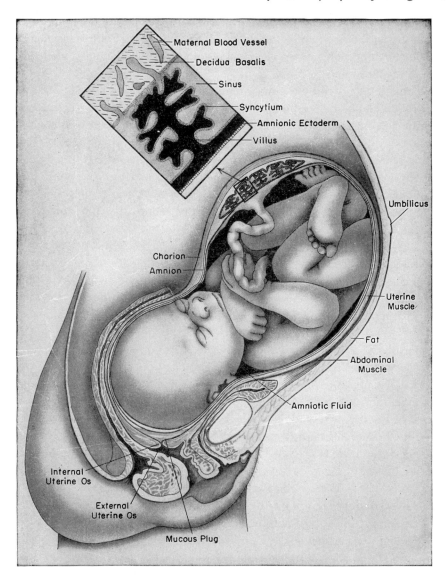

Maternal Blood Vessel
Decidua Basalis
Sinus
Syncytium
Amnionic Ectoderm
Villus
Umbilicus
Chorion
Amnion
Uterine Muscle
Fat
Abdominal Muscle
Amniotic Fluid
Internal Uterine Os
External Uterine Os
Mucous Plug

Fig. 58. Fetus at term and magnified section of the placenta. In the placenta the maternal blood circulates in the large spaces or sinuses which receive blood from the vessels of the uterine wall. The sinuses are lined by highly permeable tissue (syncytium) which separates the fetal blood stream and the maternal blood stream.

all equipment and services necessary for difficult delivery or for emergencies. Postnatal care of a high level can also be provided.

Sterility in the female. A recently married woman may be sterile for a year or two. Then without medical aid she becomes fertile. Perhaps sexual experience has had the effect of toning up the reproductive system. Sterility beyond two years should be brought to the attention of a physician.

A woman may be sterile with one man but fertile with another if she forms antagonistic antibodies against the semen of one and not against the semen of the other. The high protein content of semen accounts for the likelihood of the formation of antibodies.

Incompatibility of the husband's seminal fluid can cause sterility. However, compatibility can be determined by a test in which a drop of semen and a smear of uterine secretion are layered. If the sperms become immotile, incompatibility exists.

Some of the more common causes of sterility may be mentioned briefly:

1. Closing of the oviducts, usually as the result of infection, can cause sterility. Gonorrheal infection of the oviducts can result in scar tissue, which causes adhesion of the tube walls. Rheumatic fever and tuberculosis may cause a closure of the oviducts. A chronic catarrhal condition of the tubes may result in congestion which in effect is a closure of the tubes.
2. Endocrine imbalance or inadequacy, more frequently than recognized, is a cause of sterility. Inadequate estrone means insufficient uterine preparation; inadequate progesterone results in an unstable uterine preparation. Either condition may cause sterility, but both conditions are amenable to endocrine treatment.
3. Displaced uterus, more frequently the cause of low fertility, may be the cause of sterility. Uterine ligaments, stretched during childbearing, permitting the uterus to tilt, may account for the inability of some women to have more than one child. A malposition of the uterus is correctable.
4. Poor quality ova, sometimes due to general poor health, is a cause of sterility. Sometimes improvement in general health corrects the condition, but generally medical science has little to offer in answer to this biological inadequacy.
5. Untreated diabetes mellitus may cause sterility.
6. Thyroxin deficiency, with the resulting low basal metabolic rate, can be a cause of sterility. The administration of thyroxin may be successful in correcting sterility due to a low production of thyroxin.

Surgical sterilization. Surgical sterilization of the female is known as salpingectomy. It may be necessary if a pregnancy would be dangerous, but in addition to the medical aspect certain moral aspects must be considered. Sterilization may consist of cauterization of the proximal or uterine opening of the oviducts by inserting the cauterizing instrument into the uterine cavity. More often sterilization consists in opening the abdominal wall and tying off the two oviducts at the proximal ends. Ovulation continues as usual, but sperms cannot reach the ovum. The ova will be dissolved and absorbed. Since endocrine function is not altered, menses continue as usual. Sexual responsiveness is not altered. Adhesion of the oviduct walls occurs after the oviducts have been tied for a year or two. Thus, even if the ligatures are removed, sterility may remain.

The menopause. The menopause is a cessation of menstruation. It is the end result of the climacteric or change of life. The change occurs usually between the ages of 42 and 48 years. In some women the change may be abrupt, but it usually extends over a period of about five years and is uneventful.

The climacteric in the female is produced by the inability of the ovaries to continue the usual output of estrogens. This deficiency in turn results in overactivity of pituitary output which may overstimulate other glands. In consequence the endocrine changes may result in marked physiological and psychological effects, such as hot flashes, dizziness, night sweats, insomnia, fever and chills, altered blood pressure, irritability, depression, hyperemotionalism, weepiness, discontent, and sometimes frank psychosis. Adequate endocrine therapy can allay the symptoms and aid nature in making a gradual transition to the new level of life. Associates may aid the individual by practicing patience and understanding.

The climacteric in the male is due to a decline in androgen output, which affects the entire endocrine balance. Its onset is usually after the age of 50 years, but it may occur earlier. The transition usually takes about two years, but may be more abrupt or extended. Symptoms are similar to those in the female. The man recognizes some changes in himself and feels below par in general physical and mental capacity. His ability to concentrate and apply himself effectively seems to be below his customary performance. In time he levels off and is as accomplished as formerly. In most men the change is uneventful.

GENERAL CONSIDERATION OF SEX AND REPRODUCTION

Adjustment to the sex aspect of one's life is merely one phase of the general problem of human adjustment. Admittedly one of the most difficult aspects of adjustment, sex has been fitted successfully into the everyday living of millions of people and has enabled them to live more effectively and enjoyably. In the quest for wholesome sex adjustment chance favors the informed person. Sexual knowledge in the hands of a person whose general life adjustment is of a high order should logically result in a wholesome sex life.

Reproduction serves to perpetuate the human species. It is perhaps the greatest wonder of the universe. With the blessings of parenthood comes corresponding responsibilities. Unfortunately many individuals capable of being mothers and fathers seem to be incapable of being parents. The social aspects of reproduction are man's responsibility. Nature grants the biological favor without the social favor. Each human being must strive to merit the gifts of nature if the human species is to persevere—and improve.

Planning for health protection

Chapter 10

Prevention of disease

Historical background. Mankind has struggled constantly either directly or indirectly against disease. His efforts have not always been directed understandingly because there was little scientific information available until the nineteenth century. Until this late period, incantations, prayers, and magic were the main approaches to control, and an attitude of resignation was prevalent. An aggressive approach toward prevention of disease was not possible until the basic facts of disease were discovered.

Hygiene and sanitation have been practiced in limited ways since the beginning of history. Ancient civilized races had a partial appreciation of sanitation if the elaborate wells and irrigation systems of the early Egyptians and the closed water carriage sewers, aqueducts, and baths of the Romans are accepted as evidence. The Hebrews developed and practiced an excellent system of personal hygiene which became a part of their religion.

During the Dark Ages this knowledge and these practices were lost, and sanitation almost ceased to exist. Filth and pestilence were everywhere, and the death rate was enormous. Closed sewers were abandoned and neglected, or at least no new structures of this nature were built, and no substitute was made for them in the development of cities. Excavations in some of the old walled cities of Europe reveal that newer street levels are often five or six feet higher than the original levels because of the accumulation of dirt and filth. The moats surrounding walled towns and castles became stagnant sewers. Streets became the depository for waste of all kinds

Naturally disease and pestilence would flourish under such conditions, but even after the reawakening of sanitation high death rates and epidemics prevailed. The great sanitary revival of the nineteenth century began with the discovery of bacteria and the demonstration of their role in communicable disease by Pasteur (1822 to 1895), Koch (1843 to 1910), and others. With the knowledge growing out of these epochal discoveries it was possible to plan a new attack and to control environment and communicable disease to an extent hitherto unknown. Since these discoveries there has been a steady decline in deaths due to bacteria and other pathogens. Unfortunately there has been a lag between the discovery of new methods and techniques and their application in reducing the ills that afflict mankind. This lag is due in large part to a failure to disseminate scientific information to those who would profit by it. Education has not kept pace with scientific advances.

Universal distribution of disease. Disease is a common phenomenon in all forms of life. It varies with species, races, geographic location, climate, and mode of living. Complete eradication of disease, although not theoretically impossible, is not probable in the near future. Men will need to accomplish great strides in sanitation, in hygiene, in education, in improvement of racial stocks through application of eugenic principles, and control of zoonosis before any such hope can be entertained seriously.

Currently man is subject to a variety of diseases that are present all the time, with marked seasonal increases in certain months. These are referred to as endemic diseases. At times there occurs a large number of diseases far in excess of the usual expectancy. The name epidemic is applied to such an occurrence. In some instances, assuming a world-wide character, a disease may sweep in severe form over a large segment of the habitable world, as occurred during the outbreak of influenza in 1918 to 1919. Such a manifestation is called a pandemic.

The advances made by scientific medicine in combating the prevalence and force of smallpox, bubonic plague, typhoid, syphilis, cholera, yellow fever, malaria, and poliomyelitis are tokens of promise that should hearten mankind in its struggle for existence.

Whereas the outlook is most promising with respect to the communicable diseases, the continued high death rate from the noncommunicable diseases of middle life presents serious problems to public health workers. The answer to the problem of diseases of middle life is not wholly clear, to say nothing of the diseases of the aged, but the fact that an understanding of personal and community hygiene is necessary to help people to live more wholesomely seems clearly indicated.

The struggle against health hazards and disease continues even though in certain areas communicable disease has been drastically reduced. New hazards, many man-made, and new pathogens appear. Some of the current and future health hazards that must be solved include chronic disease, air and water pollution, food additives (processed and unnatural), pesticides, radiation and radiological wastes, and accidents.

Health and disease. The concept that health is freedom from disease is incomplete. Health is a means of helping people reach their attainable goals. Health is a state of well-being or balanced functioning. Health equilibrium teeters on the fulcrum of environment with disease agents on one end of the teeter, attempting to unbalance the forces of the host that resists at the opposite end. This places the fulcrum (environment) in a strategic position.

Health is a very relative concept. It probably is misleading to assume that disease may have a single cause. A multiplicity of causes are always needed to produce that alteration of tissues creating maladjustment. The cause of disease can no longer be thought of as a single entity. Most illness is a basic imbalance in man's physiological adaptation to multiple physical and emotional stresses (multiple causation or multiple factors). This emphasizes the fact that what we call health is essentially a struggle between various factors that exist below the horizon.

Conversely disease may be characterized as the alteration of living cells in tissues that endangers survival in their environment. Three factors are suggested by this definition: environment, survival, and structure.

In the past gross factors of disease have been classified and described. These have been the foci of much investigation. We now know that surprising effects are likely to result from even minute disturbances of inner relationships. Extensive studies on trace elements, radiations, air pollution, food additives, and other factors indicate how delicate is the balance between health and disease.

Today germs are not our principal enemy. A large part of human disease is chemical rather than bacterial in origin. The trouble may be either excess or deficiency. The body cells can recover to an amazing degree from these chemical upsets. Continued excess or deficiency brings heavy burdens and tragedies; their prevention is a significant part of current medical practice. The working hypothesis is that all disease is chemical and, when enough is known, chemically correctible. Fundamental research related to the life processes is an essential element in disease-oriented research. This fact focuses attention upon body chemistry and physiology.

The modern world is characterized by rapid change, occurring at such speed that man's adaptive powers have difficulty or are incapable of adjusting to new conditions without harmful effects. Some of these maladjustments are apparent, and others are unnoticed and unpredictable. Some may be acute, whereas others may have long-range effects.

The end product of an efficient complex society is modification of environment and way of life. This results in unpredictable responses of man to the environment. These changes and responses are reflected in the new pattern of diseases occasioned by ubiquitous microorganisms in the environment and even in our bodies heretofore considered essentially harmless. These organisms become pathogens only when general body resistance has been lowered by disturbances in individual physiology (body chemistry) or social conditions (stress and strain).

Epidemiological evidence indicates that evolutionary adaptive processes play a decisive role in resistance to disease. This leads to the possibility that natural forces are more effective than medical procedures in the long run.

This changes the old concept that infectious disease is caused only by highly virulent pathogens which have been largely controlled by medical techniques, immunization, chemiotherapy, and antibiotics. Infectious diseases have become less destructive, and epidemics in America have nearly disappeared. The changing genetic structure of the population and the ways of life have altered the physiology of the body (chemistry) and have affected the spread of pathogens and our resistance to them. *This is another way of saying that disease now must be thought of as the result of the total biological and sociological conditions of our environment.* Biological risks reside in man's changes in his intimate social environment, his personal habits, and his pattern of behavior.

In a general sense disease is the opposite of health. It is a harmful departure from normal. Disease is usually associated with misery, whereas health is associated with abundant zestful living. Disease is not a static condition but a changing one. It is the result of malfunction which produces change. These changes may take place rapidly or slowly, producing mild reactions or severe results ending in death.

Disease may be classified in various ways. It is often described in various terms which characterize its course. An *acute disease* is characterized by sudden onset and is usually not of a prolonged duration, perhaps days or a few weeks. Many children's diseases such as chickenpox, whooping cough, scarlet fever, or measles are acute diseases. A condition which develops slowly and runs a long course is described as a *chronic disease.* Often symptoms are not apparent for some time, and then they may be indefinite and general. The course of these diseases is long and persistent. As contrasted to children's diseases, the chronic diseases usually attack middle-aged persons. Some diseases in this group are cancer, diabetes, some forms of heart and kidney malfunction, and leprosy. Tuberculosis is a chronic disease which attacks persons in all age groups. Its highest incidence is among members in the group from 25 to 44 years of age. The mortality rate is highest among persons in the older age groups.

Workers in industry are exposed to various hazards associated with their occupation or trade. When a disease is peculiar to an industry or the industry predisposes to it, the condition is called an *occupational disease.* Examples of occupational diseases are lead poisoning, arsenic poisoning, radium poisoning, fish poisoning (Alaska), silicosis, and caisson disease.

Often symptoms appear for which no structural change can be demonstrated. These are called *functional diseases.* Faulty operation of the nervous system may be functional. A tissue or an organ which is defective or undergoing pathological change is referred to as showing *organic disease.* Some forms of heart disease are functional; others are organic. Bright's disease, cancer, diabetes, and cirrhosis are organic diseases. Such diseases are noncommunicable.

A disease which can be communicated from one person to another or from other animals to man is classified as a *communicable disease*. Obviously such diseases must be infectious in nature; i.e., they are due to the invasion of parasites under such conditions as will permit them to cause harm to the host.

Reduction in death rate. During the twentieth century the application of the laws of sanitation, the development and utilization of the science of microbiology, and the advances in scientific medicine have produced a marked decline in the death rate. The decrease in the general mortality rate that has taken place in the first half of the present century is largely due to the decrease in infant mortality, where the saving of life has been tremendous. Accompanying this reduction has been a change in the type of disease that produces death. If the same death rates prevailed in 1960 as were in effect in 1940, approximately 235,000 more deaths would have occurred than actually did occur.

In 1900 the leading causes of death were pneumonia, tuberculosis, diarrhea and enteritis, heart disease, nephritis, diseases of early infancy and congenital malformations, accidents, apoplexy, and cancer. At the present time the leading causes of death are diseases of the heart, cancer, intracranial lesions, accidents, diseases of early infancy, pneumonia and influenza, general arteriosclerosis, diabetes mellitus, congenital malformations, and cirrhosis of the liver. Further analysis indicates that, while many communicable diseases have come under control, chronic organic diseases are on the increase.

There has been a striking shift in the death rate from acute respiratory infections to chronic diseases. Sixty years ago 94% of all mortality resulted from acute infectious diseases, whereas at present about 75% of all deaths are produced by the chronic diseases. This is not merely a picture of the deaths of old people; about 50% of the persons who die from chronic diseases are under 45 years of age and more than 70% are under 55 years of age.

Many factors have contributed to this change. Discussion of these will bear upon an exposition of the basic principles involved in preventive measures.

Salient factors in control of communicable diseases. There are many popular misconceptions regarding the contracting of infection and the transmission and control of communicable diseases. One false notion is that a strong vigorous body protects an individual from infections. Nothing could be farther from the truth. The introduction of virulent pathogenic microorganisms into the body of a susceptible individual usually results in disease no matter what his strength or size. The most effective means of control and prevention of communicable disease is concerted community action in utilizing modern available scientific techniques.

The well-informed member of a community will have confidence in right action and will show his recognition of the obligation he owes as a good citizen to society to use all protective measures for himself and his family and to insist that other members of society do likewise. The good citizen will not remain unprotected and dangerous to his fellows when proved and protective aids are available. Thus cooperation and mutual assistance are very important in the control of environmental factors.

The salient factors of importance for all persons to understand if they are to cooperate intelligently in the control and prevention of communicable diseases may be listed in five groups: (1) the causative agent and its nature, (2) reservoirs of disease, (3) exit of organisms from the body, (4) ways and means of disease transference, and (5) blocking routes of transmission.

THE CAUSATIVE AGENT AND ITS NATURE

Through the pages of history diseases have been attributed to many different causes. Even today some people believe that God punishes man by inflicting disease upon him, and some hold that evil thoughts can cause disease. In civilized countries, however, these are a small minority of the populace. From time to time over the years, philosophers, physicians, and scientists have suspected that minute organisms, too small to be seen by the unaided eye, might be the cause of disease, but, until the discoveries of Pasteur and Koch led to the demonstration of the germ theory of disease, doubt about the matter remained.

These microorganisms were probably seen for the first time in the latter part of the seventeenth century when Anton van Leeuwenhoek, the indefatigable Dutch microscopist, observed, drew, and described bacteria and protozoa. He sent his findings to the Royal Society of London in 1673. Among other things he said, "I saw with wonder that my material contained many tiny animals which moved about in the most amusing fashion. The largest of these showed the liveliest and most active motions." This report was confirmed by Robert Hooke (1635 to 1703); yet this important discovery did not bear fruit for nearly a century.

The real science of bacteriology and the relation between bacteria and disease were the result of the investigations of Louis Pasteur (1822 to 1895). Pasteur's investigations kindled an interest in the relation of microorganisms to disease. He demonstrated conclusively that microorganisms were related to infectious disease in insects and plants through his studies on the pébrine sickness of silkworms, which he proved to be caused by a protozoan parasite.

Thus the real science of bacteriology began with Pasteur. He gave the world the germ theory of disease. Briefly his magnificient contributions include the following: (1) the role of microorganisms in putrefaction, fermentation, and decay; (2) the discovery of a treatment for anthrax; and (3) the discovery of a treatment for rabies. The latter has been the greatest publicized, probably through the establishment of Pasteur institutes for the treatment of rabies. The implications of these contributions to humanity have been so far-reaching that it is difficult to visualize or appreciate them.

In 1881 Robert Koch (1843 to 1910), a German investigator, published his fundamental researches on pathogenic bacteria which established bacteriology as an independent biological science. Among the more important of Koch's many contributions was the discovery of several pathogenic microorganisms, including the anthrax bacillus, the cholera vibrio, and the tubercle bacillus. Koch's development of solid culture media made possible a more accurate study of microorganisms through the ability to grow them in pure culture. This device made it possible to establish the specific agent of disease with much greater certainty. Heretofore the process had been based upon a rather unscientific procedure.

Koch's postulates were designed to provide the evidence necessary to prove that an organism was the causative agent of a disease. A brief statement of these postulates is as follows:

1. A specific organism must be associated with all cases of a specific disease, and a reasonable pathological relationship to the disease, its symptoms, and lesions must be established.
2. This organism must be obtained from the body of the patient and grown in pure culture.
3. When the pure culture is introduced in the body of a susceptible human being or animal, it must reproduce the disease.
4. The organism must be recovered from the experimental subject, identified, and grown in pure culture.

The subsequent contributions of Loeffler, Roux, Bordet, Ehrlich, Kitasato, Metchnikoff, and others established bacteriology as a science, and this long-hidden secret of nature began to be unraveled.

The more recent knowledge of the causative agents of disease includes many microorganisms other than bacteria. Some of these are true fungi, protozoa, rickettsia, and viruses or ultramicroscopic forms. The study of microorganisms has now been termed microbiology, a more inclusive term than bacteriology.

Nonpathogenic organisms. Many of the microorganisms that abound in nature are very useful in the human economy; only a small number produce disease in man. Among the beneficial actions of bacteria are the transformation of chemical elements such as nitrogen, carbon, and sulfur from unusable combinations to forms that plants and animals can use. The ability of certain types of bacteria to modify the composition of the soil and the character of crops is of great importance to the farmer. The importance of bacteria in making atmospheric nitrogen available to plants is important in man's survival. Moreover, bacteria make possible certain vital processes in the production of dairy and food products. Butter and cheese have a characteristic aroma and flavor due to the action of bacteria and true fungi, and certain industrial processes, such as tanning, retting of flax, production of sauerkraut, production of butanol and butyric acid, manufacture of ethyl alcohol, and curing of tea, require the presence of microorganisms. Other organisms not only attack and kill living organisms (antibiotic action), but also destroy and disintegrate dead bodies.

Pathogenic microorganisms. Pathogenic (disease-producing) microorganisms may be classified according to their form, living habits, cultural characteristics, and other criteria.

Bacteria. Of the various microorganisms the bacteria are the most numerous and cause the greatest number of diseases affecting man. They are small unicellular plants; their size is indicated in microns (a micron is 1/25,000 of an inch or

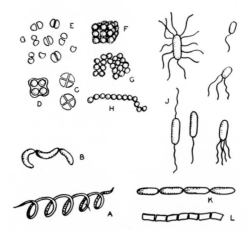

Fig. 59. Types of bacteria. **A,** Spirillum; **B,** vibrio of Asiatic cholera; **C** and **D,** tetracocci, **E,** diplococci; **F,** sarcinii; **G,** staphylococci; **H,** streptococci; **J,** different forms of bacilli with flagella; **K** and **L,** types of bacilli with rounded and square ends.

1/1,000,000 of a meter). Bacteria vary somewhat in size from the *Hemophilus influenzae,* which is approximately 0.2 × 1.5 microns, to the larger forms, such as the anthrax bacillus which is about 1.2 × 5 microns.

Bacteria produce their effects by their enormous numbers. They reproduce themselves about every thirty minutes. If their propagation were uninterrupted for twenty-four hours, one bacterium would multiply to 281,500,000 bacteria; if this rate were continued for three days, their total weight would reach approximately 148,356,000 pounds. This immense number can be appreciated when the volume and weight of an individual bacterium is considered. The volume of one bacterium has been estimated to be about 0.000,000,000,390 cubic millimeter, and the weight about 0.000,000,000,417 milligram. When organisms can grow with such rapidity, it is obvious that something usually happens to the process, or a person harboring them would be overwhelmed by the very mass itself. There are forces in the body that combat this growth. These will be described later.

Bacteria were classified according to their morphology or shape early in the development of the science of bacteriology. Later bacteria and their behavior were studied on the basis of biological, physical, and chemical concepts, which resulted in a modern classification based on what they do rather than on how they look. Probably only a few of the bacteria in existence have been isolated and identified. New ones are constantly being added to the list. About one hundred of those known at the present time are pathogenic to man.

Some of the diseases produced by pathogenic bacteria are tuberculosis, scarlet fever, diphtheria, bacillary dysentery, cerebrospinal meningitis, pneumonia, whooping cough, tetanus, plague, Asiatic cholera, anthrax, glanders, Malta fever, typhoid, gonorrhea, and gangrene.

Pathogenic bacteria in their normal growth processes affect the body in different ways. The body reacts to these processes, and this reaction constitutes, in many cases, the signs and symptoms of the disease. As other living things do, bacteria need food; this they secure as they invade the tissues and take from the cells, tissues, and fluids the materials they need for growth. This action in itself is injurious to man. Tuberculosis is an example. Moreover, as a normal part of their life processes, certain bacteria secrete soluble poisons which are absorbed by the lymph and blood streams and transported widely throughout the body where they do damage to the most highly organized cells and tissues. Diphtheria and scarlet fever are good examples of the damage done by soluble poisons. Some bacteria give off poisons only as they die and their cell bodies disintegrate. As this occurs, the poisons are absorbed into the blood and lymph streams and carried to cells and tissues. Typhoid fever is an example of this type of action. Other bacteria in their reaction with body tissues initiate clogging, clotting, agglutination, and precipitation.

Upon entrance into the body some bacteria stimulate a counterreaction in the tissues which has the effect of overcoming the injury of the invading enemy or of eliminating the enemy from the body or, in other cases, of walling off a protected area from its action. This reaction has been termed inflammation, which is a generalized reaction and is manifested by fever, heat, redness, and swelling.

The type of virulence of the invading organisms often characterizes the resulting inflammation. The symptoms and names of various diseases of the tissues are indicated by the suffix *itis,* which literally means inflammation. Thus designations commonly used include tonsillitis, bronchitis, laryngitis, appendicitis, and colitis.

Spirochetes. Another group of microorganisms producing disease are the spirochetes. These have been difficult to classify; they are smaller than bacteria and differ in form, but many of their properties relate them to bacteria rather than to protozoa. In form and characteristics they may be described as long, slender, motile, flexible organisms which twist corkscrewlike on their axis, divide transversely, and move forward and backward. The causative agent of syphilis, the *Treponema pallidum,* is a member of this group.

Rickettsia. The rickettsia are much smaller than bacteria (0.3×0.5 of a micron), require an insect host, and live as an intercellular parasite. This would characterize them as protozoa rather than as bacteria, but they are classified as a separate group. About forty of these organisms have been identified, but of these only a few are pathogenic in man. Rocky Mountain spotted fever, typhus fever, scrub typhus, tsutsugamushi, Q fever, and trench fever are well known examples of disease produced by organisms of this group.

Viruses. Viruses are ultramicroscopic in size, so small that they will pass through a Pasteur porcelain filter since they are less than 0.004 micron. The poliomyelitis virus, one of the smallest, is about 25 millimicrons in size (nearly 1 million to 1 inch). Their small size, poor staining qualities, and low refractive power have made this group difficult to study. With the development of the electron microscope, which permits the viewing of an object as small as one one millionth of a millimeter, our knowledge has increased.

About 160 viruses have been isolated, but as yet little is known about them. Some known facts include the following. They are made up of two parts, a nucleus composed of nucleic acid and a protein membrane or coat. When inside a cell, the virus is very active, disrupting the metabolism of the cell and releasing many new viruses which ultimately destroy it. Thus the viruses are released and other body cells are penetrated. Outside the cell the virus appears inert and lifeless.

The virus occupies an important role in communicable disease, the control of which has shifted from bacteria-caused infections to virus-caused infections. It is reliably estimated that two thirds of the illnesses occurring in family groups are respiratory. Possibly as much as 94% of these are caused by viruses. So far very little is known on how to prevent or treat virus diseases. Medicines including antibiotics are ineffective against them. The main reliance is upon immunity—natural or acquired by vaccines. This has occasioned intensive research into virus diseases. How viruses function is unsolved.

The list of diseases caused by these organisms is increasing rapidly and now includes about fifty different infectious human diseases. Poliomyelitis, common cold, influenza, rabies, mumps, encephalitis, yellow fever, hepatitis, herpes zoster, mononucleosis, red eyes, sore throat, aching joints, croup, acute bronchitis, pneumonia in infants, nonbacterial meningitis, summer rash, diarrhea, acute respiratory infections, and mild paralysis are examples.

Viruses present a problem in their wide proliferation and their ability to produce new strains which are not affected by existing vaccines.

Bacteriophage (bacterium eater) is a virus which is a parasite of bacteria. No evidence exists that bacteriophage cause disease in the human or that bacteriophage can be used to combat bacteria pathogenic to man.

Fungi. The fungi or yeasts and molds produce many diseases of the skin. Among the more common examples are ringworm or the so-called athlete's foot infection, tinea cruris.

Protozoa. Protozoa, the lowest group in the animal kingdom, are simple one-celled organisms. Many widespread tropical diseases are produced by this group. Examples are malaria, amebic dysentery, and African sleeping sickness.

Metazoa. The metazoa, the next class in the animal kingdom, are many-celled and include tapeworms, intestinal roundworms, the trichinae, the filariae, flukes, and leeches. Many tropical diseases are caused by this group. In the United States hookworm infection present in the South and trichinosis caused by eating infected raw or incompletely cooked pork are well known.

RESERVOIRS OF DISEASE

Man and other animals are the two great sources of communicable diseases. Usually the diseases that affect man do not attack other animals. Malaria, mumps, measles, scarlet fever, infantile paralysis, smallpox, syphilis, typhoid fever, and typhus fever are peculiar to man although some of these may be produced experimentally in other animals.

The term *zoonosis* has recently been applied to diseases naturally transmitted between vertebrate animals and man. In the past these diseases have not been thought to play an important role in the communicable diseases affecting man. Currently a much larger role and more importance is accorded them. The number of diseases in this category is increasing as research is directed toward the nature of man and his environment. Lack of accurate reporting and even of recognition of these diseases make estimates of cases nearly impossible. It is generally accepted that they are on the increase. In the United States domestic animals are the greatest source of danger to man. Salmonella infection is widespread in man and animals. Various types of human salmonellosis, all characterized by diarrhea, are recognized. Other groups of diseases causing concern are leptospirosis and some viral encephalitides (psittacosis, Q fever, and arthropod-borne encephalitides).

Other diseases in this group include anthrax from cattle and sheep, glanders from horses, rabies from dogs, cats, and foxes, undulant fever from goats, swine, and cattle, foot-and-mouth disease from cattle, Rocky Mountain spotted fever from rodents, tetanus from horses, tularemia from rodents, and trichinosis. Recently it has been established that malaria may be transmitted from monkeys to man. Many of these diseases occur infrequently in man and usually only sporadically.

Although urban dwellers may not come in contact with farm animals, cats, dogs, birds, and other pets are reservoirs for some of the diseases of this group.

An understanding of the conditions under which microorganisms grow and multiply will indicate the reasons why man is so largely his own source of disease. Most pathogens do not live long outside of the body, and very few multiply outside of it. A few types can live outside the body in suitable media such as milk; examples of this group are the organisms responsible for diphtheria, scarlet fever, septic sore throat, and typhoid fever. In order for pathogenic organisms to grow and multiply, there must be available proper food —some organisms are highly selective in this matter—proper conditions of alkalinity or acidity (pH), proper moisture, proper temperature, and, in some instances, darkness.

It is apparent that these conditions are seldom met outside of the human body. Organisms are so selective in their food supply that they grow only in certain tissues of the body. For example, the diphtheria bacillus grows best on the mucous membrane of the throat and nasal passages; the *Micrococcus meningitidis* (meningococcus), on the coverings of the brain and spinal cord; the *Salmonella typhi* (typhoid bacillus), on the membrane of the small intestine and in the blood; and the pneumococcus, in the lungs. On the other hand, some organisms attack with avidity almost any tissue; thus the *Mycobacterium tuberculosis* (tubercle bacillus) and the *Treponema pallidum* of syphilis attack almost any tissue of the body.

It is a misconception that pathogenic microorganisms could not possibly multiply in the soil or decaying vegetable matter. Actually few organisms can resist for long periods of time the destructive forces they encounter outside the body. An example of this is the *Clostridium tetani* whose normal habitat is the intestines of the horse. However, it will exist for a long period of time in the soil and, if injected into the blood stream of a human being, will cause tetanus or lockjaw. These resistant forms are called spores. In unusual conditions organisms that can multiply outside the human body are the ones causing syphilis, gonorrhea, pneumonia, influenza, tuberculosis, meningitis, smallpox, and whooping cough.

It is clear and irrefutable that man acts as a reservoir of disease and, in this respect, is his own worst enemy. Since the germ theory of disease established the fact that man was the source of many of his diseases, the sanitarian could now direct his efforts to block the environmental pathways by which man spread disease to other men. The contamination of water and food supplies by persons with disease is now a social problem as well as a sanitary problem; control of such disease is dependent upon the cooperation of man with man. Not only must individuals cooperate with others, but, if the cooperation is to be intelligent, they must also be well informed in these matters. Therefore much of the hope for the prevention and control of disease rests upon education.

As an illustration of the success from intelligent cooperation, the diseases of typhoid fever, cholera, yellow fever, malaria, and bubonic plague may be cited. These diseases, conveyed from person to person through various media and insects, have been controlled largely through sanitary procedures. In the cases mentioned it was not necessary to secure the consent of the individual. The passage of laws and the appropriation of money were sufficient to provide water treatment plants, sewage treatment and disposal plants, drainage of swamps, pasteurization of milk, and milk codes. These services aimed at the control of the environment poduced a sharp decline in the death rate in those diseases that are spread from man to man by water, food, milk, insects, and soil pollution.

The control of diseases that are spread through social contact and for which immunization materials are available has been less successful because in these instances the consent of the individual is required. This is even more difficult in those diseases conveyed over this route for which there is no specific immunization. Too often the individual is uninformed, frequently he is uncooperative, and each generation must be educated to its responsibilities in the matter. If the same resuts are to be reached that have accrued from the sanitary control of environment, constant education must be maintained to ensure enlightment and cooperation.

EXIT OF ORGANISMS FROM THE BODY

Diseases may be classified according to the way in which the causative agent leaves the body. It is important to understand this since it indicates a means of

Table 41. Classification of common communicable diseases (according to discharges)

Nose and throat discharge group	Fecal and urinary discharge group	Blood transfer group	Suppurative process group
Cerebrospinal meningitis	Amebic dysentery	African sleeping sickness	Anthrax
Chickenpox	Bacillary dysentery	Malaria	Erysipelas
Diphtheria	Cholera	Plague	Gonorrhea
Influenza	Hookworm	Rocky Mountain fever	Septicemia
Measles	Paratyphoid	Yellow fever	Scarlet fever
Pneumonia	Poliomyelitis		Small pox
Poliomyelitis	Typhoid fever		Syphilis
Scarlet fever	Viral hepatitis		
Small pox			
Tuberculosis			
Whooping cough			

control over the spread of disease from person to person. There are four groups to be considered.

The nose and throat discharge group. Diseases of this group are prevalent in temperate zones although they are found elsewhere. These are usually acute diseases that from time to time assume epidemic and pandemic proportions. They are explosive in nature. The organisms are spread directly from person to person by direct contact. Some of the diseases in this group are pneumonia, measles, whooping cough, scarlet fever, mumps, tonsillitis, the common cold, influenza, tuberculosis, septic sore throat, chickenpox, diphtheria, cerebrospinal meningitis, and smallpox.

Common cold. The common cold (coryza) is worthy of special mention because of its high incidence, its importance, and the many popular misconceptions relating to it.

Surveys in the United States reveal that males average two colds a year and females average three colds a year. Colds are less prevalent during the summer months, and a cold during the summer does not last longer than those during the winter. People who complain of a cold the year around are likely suffering from chronic sinusitis. Colds account for about 50% of all absences from work and for twenty times as much lost time as accidents. Children lose an average of about four days a school year because of colds.

A cold is believed to be caused by a virus. Evidence indicates that several strains of virus may cause a cold. However, apparently the same virus can cause different constitutional effects in different individuals. The incubation period varies from twenty-four to forty-eight hours. The infection is communicable during the last few hours of the incubation period and for about three days after the onset of symptoms. Without treatment of any kind symptoms last about seven days. Rest in bed may shorten this period a day or even two days. An immunity of three months' duration usually results.

Actually the cold is an allergic response to the virus or its products. As in other allergies the foreign substance causes irritated cells lining the respiratory tract to release excessive amounts of histamine, a capillary poisoning. The resulting dilation of the capillaries and the increased permeability of their membranes result in the symptoms of the cold. Antihistamines for the cold, as antihistamines for any allergy, are chemical substances which combine with histamines and thus neutralize them. Antihistamines for a cold can do no more than reduce symptoms of a cold. They cannot prevent or cure a cold. Because of their possible toxic effect, antihistamines should be taken only upon the prescription of a physician.

The common cold is rarely the direct cause of death although it may be a forerunner of such serious diseases as pneumonia, bronchitis, laryngitis, and other respiratory ailments.

Many of the popular notions on the prevention and treatment of a cold, under the scrutiny of science, have been found to be misconceptions.

1. Sodium bicarbonate neither prevents, treats, nor cures a cold, and it does not relieve symptoms.
2. Citrus fruit, presumably to alkalinize the body, has no effect on a cold. Actually the body is not less alkaline during a cold.
3. Administration of vitamin A, if there is definite vitamin deficiency, improves the defenses of the body but does not prevent a cold.
4. Laxatives do not prevent or relieve a cold.
5. Aspirin may give some relief from distress or pain but will have no effect on the infection.
6. Antibiotics and sulfa compounds have no known effect on a cold but do affect sequelae.
7. Vapor sprays or ultraviolet light have a doubtful effect on preventing the spread of a cold.

A typical epidemic of colds occurs on a college campus at the beginning of each term. The crowding of registration permits the few students with infection to communicate it to others. Two days later the first contingent has the beginning of a cold. Two days later a second contingent joins the chain until two-thirds of the student body and faculty are eventually infected. During an epidemic of colds certain practices may be of value in avoiding a cold: (1) wear moderate clothes, (2) avoid getting wet, (3) avoid excessive fatigue, (4) avoid crowds, (5) wash hands frequently with soap, (6) blow the nose gently through both nostrils, (7) use disposable tissues and burn them, and (8) do not use common drinking and eating utensils. Obviously strict adherence to these practices may be to no avail.

The fecal and urinary discharge group. Diseases of this group are spread from person to person by indirect contact, usually through milk, water, food, and soil. Included in this group are typhoid fever, paratyphoid fever A and B, amebic dysentery, bacillary dysentery, cholera, viral hepatitis, and hookworm. The number of diseases from this group prevalent in a community is a reliable index of the community's cleanliness and housekeeping. Adequate protection of water supplies, of sewage disposal, of swimming and bathing facilities, of producing and marketing food and milk supplies, together with control of insects and rodents, can practically eliminate this group of diseases. Sanitary science has markedly reduced the incidence of these disorders and has made an outstanding contribution to the reduction of the number of deaths from diseases. This reduction has far exceeded any expectation of fifty years ago.

The blood transfer group. Diseases in this group can be brought under control largely through the application of sanitary techniques to insects and rodents. Usually an intermediate host is essential for the transmisson of diseases in this group. In this process of biological transmission the life cycle of the agent occurs partly in the insect and partly in man. The diseases concerned in this group are found principally in tropical countries. Of those diseases occurring in the United States malaria organisms are transmitted from person to person by the female Anopheles mosquito, yellow fever organisms are transmitted by the Aedes mosquito, plague is transmitted from rodents to man by the flea, epidemic typhus is transmitted by the human louse, Rocky Mountain spotted fever is transmitted from squirrels, rabbits, prairie dogs, and woodchucks to man by ticks, and tularemia is usually transmitted to persons handling infected rabbits. Infection is transmitted among animals by ticks, lice, flies, and fleas.

Not all diseases that insects convey to man require a biological cycle of transmission. An insect carrying infectious material on its legs or body parts may crawl over food that is subsequently eaten by man or, in crawling on the skin, may deposit infectious material which may gain entrance to the body through abrasions that are present. This is a mechanical transmission. There has been no part of the life cycle of the causative agent in the insect.

The suppurative process group. Some diseases affecting the skin spread rather directly from person to person through lesions and pustules with suppurative discharges of pus. Some of the diseases in this group are syphilis, erysipelas, smallpox, scarlet fever, septicemia, and anthrax.

Vehicles of travel. There are seven main routes over which microorganisms are conveyed from person to person. These are social contact, air, water, milk, food, insects, and ground pollution. The social contact route accounts for about 70% of the cases of communicable disease; the nose and throat and the suppurative discharge groups of diseases are conveyed in this manner. The urinary and fecal discharge group is conveyed mainly by water, milk, food, and soil. Milk may transfer septic sore throat, diphtheria, scarlet fever, and typhoid fever. Insects convey the blood transfer group. The air may convey some of the nose and throat group.

WAYS AND MEANS OF TRANSFER OF DISEASE

In the preceding pages of this chapter the discussion has presented the more general aspects of disease control. In the discussion of the ways and means of the transference of causative agents from person to person, we are dealing with

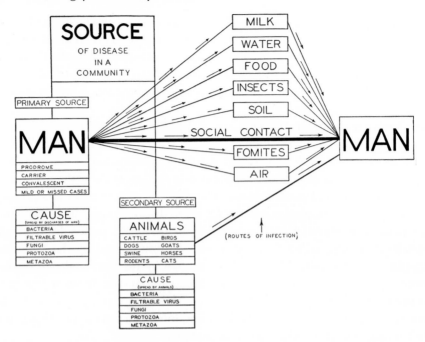

Fig. 60.   Routes over which diseases travel. In the prevention of the spread of infectious disease, one of man's most effective means is to block routes over which the pathogenic organisms travel.

mechanisms and types of individuals, an appreciation of which is necessary for intelligent cooperation by the individual in community control of disease.

With the recognition of man as the main reservoir of infection, the following questions arise: How is disease transferred from person to person? Where does it come from? and Why does one person in a group contract the disease and not another? Further questions that naturally arise are: What was the route of travel followed? How many others were infected from the same source? and What was the source? Our present knowledge permits the answering of these questions with a great deal of definiteness.

Before exact knowledge was available on the ways and means of disease transfer, man hit upon devices which were only accidentally effective. Maritime quarantine is an illustration. Originally it was instituted in the belief that infection was spread from port to port by the ship itself; hence quarantine required a forty-day period of anchoring outside the port of call before landing was permitted (quaranta is a Latin word meaning forty). This was effective because the period was long enough to allow most diseases to run their course. Segregation of lepers was a similar fortuitous device. A recognition of its effectiveness required that lepers carry bells to warn of their coming so that others might avoid close contact. In leprosy a long contact period is necessary in order to convey the disease; therefore this method was effective. As people gathered into cities and formed close aggregations, the intimate association of individuals made easy the transfer of disease from person to person. The school, street car, office, theater, tenement, apartment, and factory are modern arrangements that facilitate transfer of infection.

The importance of personal hygiene under such conditions can be readily appreciated. Good hygiene demands that the hands and fingers should not touch objects that others have handled, but this can be followed only in part. Certainly it is important and possible to keep the fingers and objects out of the mouth and not to use a common drinking cup, toothbrush, washcloth, or towel. The common use of personal articles should be discouraged.

Casual observation will show how often these simple rules are violated. The introduction into the mouth of fingers, pencils, thread, gummed labels, envelopes, erasers, the laying of the toothbrush on fouled surfaces such as the washbowl, and the cleaning of the silver in restaurants with a handkerchief are not uncommon practices. The fingers of waiters often are on the food; water glasses are handled by their rims; and silver is handled by the blade, the tine, and the bowl.

The ways and means of transference of agents of disease from person to person is by direct contact, indirect contact, and by intermediate host.

Direct contact. Direct contact is the most common means of infection transference and accounts for approximately 80% of all cases of communicable disease. This mechanism is often referred to as *droplet infection* or *social contact*. In this process fresh infectious material is transferred through kissing, shaking hands, sneezing, and coughing or by using towels, cups, and other objects shortly after others have made personal use of them.

Three conditions are necessary for direct contact to operate: (1) the distance traveled must be short, (2) the material transferred must be fresh, and (3) the elapsed time interval must be short. Since agents of infection as a rule do not travel far, the chance of infection being transferred diminishes inversely as the cube of the distance traveled.

In the respiratory group of diseases the infective agents leave the body through discharges from the nose and throat, enter the body through the nose and mouth, and are spread mainly by direct contact. These diseases reach their greatest prevalence in the fall and winter months and often attain epidemic proportions. A partial explanation of this is found in the low temperatures and unpleasant atmospheric conditions of the winter months which induce greater congestion because of the longer time spent indoors. In addition to close contact the artificial heating of rooms with the attendant high temperatures, low humidity, and drafts are doubtless factors. Moreover, the amount of activity is reduced, and sunlight is diminished. Although these will not induce infection, they may enhance the opportunity for bacterial invasion.

Diseases involving lesions of the mucous tissue or the skin may also be spread by direct contact. Syphilis and gonorrhea are usually spread in this manner.

Indirect contact. The ways and means of indirect contact infection are just the opposite from those of direct contact transference. The distance traveled is great, the infectious material may be old, and the elapsed time may be long. The routes traveled are usually water, food, soil, and many inanimate objects.

The transference of any one of the diseases in the fecal and urinary discharge group affords an example of the way this process works. For example, the personnel of a logging operation on high ground in the winter which utilizes surface privies results in the deposit of fecal material on the snow or frozen ground. It may stay there for weeks. In the spring when the snow or ground thaws, the excreta, which may contain the *Salmonella typhosa* (typhoid bacillus) from a carrier in the camp, are transported to a stream in the surface runoff. If this water is used for drinking purposes, there is a possibility that the consumer may contract typhoid fever. Under this condition the distance traveled by the infectious material may be great, the material may be weeks old, and the elapsed time may be long.

Some of the respiratory diseases can be spread by indirect contact by means of handkerchiefs, utensils, and other intermediate products, called *fomites,* but the usual method is by direct contact.

Intermediate host. The blood transfer group of diseases are spread through an intermediate host or *vector;* this involves a blood-sucking insect or other arthropod that requires mammalian blood for its development. The infectious agent floating freely in the blood stream of the human being gains entrance into the insect as it draws blood from the human being. After entering the insect, the organism undergoes part of its normal life cycle. Later the insect, in feeding again on a human being, injects the sporozoite or young parasite into the blood stream of the new victim where it now undergoes its life cycle, and the conveyed disease develops if the individual is susceptible.

There is no other way that these diseases are transferred under normal conditions. A specific type of insect is needed and a proper time interval is essential. The Anopheles mosquito is necessary for the transfer of malaria, the *Aedes aegypti* mosquito for yellow fever, and the tsetse fly for African sleeping sickness.

BLOCKING ROUTES OF TRANSMISSION

There are many well-established methods for blocking the various routes of disease transmission. Fortunately the inability of the pathogenic organisms to adapt themselves to a wide range of environmental conditions offers much hope in the restriction of their spread and propagation. Their range of activity is restricted to a limited environment. In the body of a human being as they grow and multiply, they encounter unfavorable influences because they do harm to the body, which reacts against them. Once they leave, their existence depends upon reaching another host. Their powers of travel are limited. They cannot fly or climb and hence must depend upon vehicles of transportation which are very restricted. Conditions outside the body are normally so severe that the pathogen must reach another human being quickly. Some adverse conditions they encounter outside the body are sunlight, dryness, and lack of suitable food supply. Upon reaching a new host they must find a portal of entry. In addition the new host may not be susceptible and hence not a suitable medium for multiplication. Public health departments have developed routines and methods of procedure that apply to the control of any communicable disease.

General method of blocking. Of primary and paramount importance is an early and accurate diagnosis of the disease. The path of transmission can be blocked only if the nature of the disturbance is accurately known. The diagnosis of a disease should be reported to the health department as soon as possible for purposes of establishing routes of travel and for analyzing, mapping, and charting the contact picture. Isolation and quarantine should be set up if they are indicated. Concurrent disinfection is a standard procedure. All persons coming into contact with the patient should be under observation during the period of incubation. Whenever effective prophylactic (preventive) measures are available, they should be instituted. Finally, and of great importance, an educational campaign is essential to inform the community of how the infection spreads and how the public may cooperate in control measures.

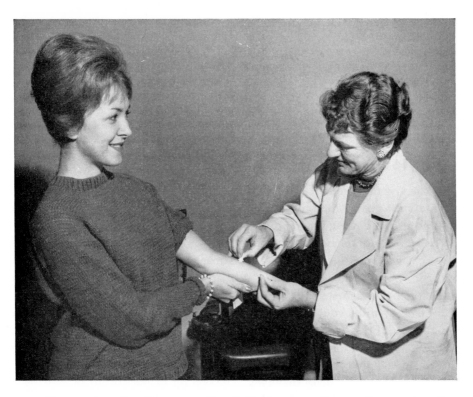

Fig. 61. Tine test for tuberculosis. A simple reliable skin test with a small pronged applicator which is discarded after each individual test. A reading taken within two days will indicate whether the subject has had a tuberculous infection. A subsequent chest x-ray will determine whether a person with a positive reaction to the skin test has infection at present. (Courtesy Oregon State Board of Health.)

Fig. 62. Chest x-ray plates following a positive skin test. The one-two procedure of skin test plus chest x-ray provides a highly reliable means for the detection of tuberculosis. The chest x-ray also is helpful in the detection of other diseases. (Courtesy Oregon State Board of Health.)

STANDARDIZED CONTROLS

To these general routine procedures, standardized controls for specific infections are instituted by the physician. In addition public health officials have various methods and devices at their disposal.

Control of water route. Sanitary methods may be initiated as necessary for water control through treatment plants, stream pollution control, sewage collection, and sewage treatment. This is usually an early part of community long-range planning rather than an emergency program.

Control of milk route. Milk as a medium of transfer may be controlled through herd testing for tuberculosis and brucellosis, inspection and supervision of dairies, pasteurization of milk, medical inspection of employees, rating of dairy plants, scoring of milk, establishment of milk codes, and passage of ordinances.

Control of insect-borne diseases. The control of the spread of diseases by insects depends upon the combined efforts of medical science, entomology, and sanitary science, for a knowledge of the disease, the parasite, and the insect is necessary if adequate preventive measures are to be undertaken. It may be impossible to eliminate all of the insect hosts, but a substantial reduction in numbers will result in a decrease in disease spread. Control measures consist of the destruction of breeding places by draining and filling of swamps, by removing stagnant waters, by oiling waters, by spraying with larvacides, by properly constructing wells, springs, and cisterns, and by eliminating casual water.

Control of food route. Control of the food route is difficult and requires constant and strict supervision of both production and distribution. The public health approach has undergone constant change and revision but always in the direction of more rigid and sustained inspection and sanitary safeguards over the growing, production, distribution, and preparation of food. This is especially true with respect to food consumed raw. Lettuce, cabbage, carrots, celery, and many other vegetables that are grown under intensive truck garden culture require stringent sanitary supervision to assure that the foods reach the consumer in a safe condition for consumption. Sea foods must receive the same kind of stringent supervision.

One of the great health hazards is the dirty unsanitary restaurant; therefore all restaurants must receive careful supervision. At one time emphasis was placed on the medical examination of food handlers, but this procedure is administratively unworkable. Attention is now focused upon cleanliness in the preparation of food, of utensils, dishes, and cutlery, of workers' personal hygiene, hands, and clothing, of food-handling techniques, and of food storage. The practice of making sanitary ratings of restaurants and publishing such scores in the monthly reports of the public health departments is of greatest value when an informed public understands and is governed by the ratings.

Control of soil pollution. Soil contaminated by human discharges is an age-old problem that requires persistent and unrelenting attention. City dwellers frequently have a false sense of security in the effectiveness of the sanitary methods employed by their own community. Overflow of the Ohio and Missouri Rivers with its aftermath of disease and pestilence has demonstrated how readily many communities may be subjected to primitive conditions. Because some communities are lax in the disposal of human waste, they maintain a constant menace to themselves as well as to their neighbors.

In many sections of our country the continuous contamination of the soil, clothing, food, and feet still exists. The proper disposal of human discharges is an essential for the health of all persons.

Control of air route. A half century ago it was believed that the air was the important route for the transmission of disease. In modern times this concept has been changed, and the primary attention is focused on direct contact. In the last decade, however, the air route of transmission of infectious material and particulate matter in air has again assumed importance. Evidence now indicates that air may transmit respiratory diseases, especially under indoor conditions.

The effect of polluted air is expressed in the following three ways:
1. Acute manifestations such as the extreme air pollution that occurred in the Meuse Valley in Belgium, in 1930, in Donora, Pennsylvania, in 1948,

and in London, England, in 1952 and 1956. During one week in London 4000 to 5000 more people died than would have normally. Fortunately such occurrences are rare.

2. The accumulated effect of breathing polluted air over a long period is not understood and difficult to document. There is a growing feeling that this does have a detrimental effect on health. Urbanization and concentration of industry appear to be related to the higher death rate of city dwellers in such diseases as arteriosclerosis and other heart diseases and cancer of the stomach, esophagus, and lung.

3. Smog may or may not prove to cause long-range health damage, but it unquestionably is undesirable since it causes acute and temporary inflammation of the eyes and detrimental psychological effects.

Air pollution can cause death among aged and infirm persons and serious illness to the general population.

There are three principal ways in which infections may be spead by aerial contamination: droplets, droplet nuclei, and dust. *Droplets* are rather large collections of moisture expelled from the mouth and nose by sneezing or coughing and are usually transferred by propulsion through the air directly into the eye, mouth, or open wounds. This is more correctly classified as direct contact or social contact. These droplets do not travel far, and they soon settle to the floor. *Droplet nuclei* are minute residues from the evaporation of droplets and may be inhaled into the body. These are very light and may float in the air for a long period of time, especially in enclosed areas. *Dust* is contaminated by droplets and droplet nuclei. which settle down and become a part of the dust. Most authorities consider droplet nuclei and dust a part of air-borne transmission. Which of these is the more important is not known; their importance probably varies with different age groups, seasons of the year, environmental factors, and diseases.

Control of the air route may be helped slightly by mechanical ventilation, ultraviolet irradiation, disinfectant vapors, and dust suppression. Dust may be suppressed by oiling floors and other objects. While bacteria in the air are reduced, insufficient evidence is available to conclude that oiling prevents disease. In operating rooms, contagious wards, and pediatric wards, ventilation, ultraviolet light, and glycol vapors appear to be of possible value in the reduction of air-borne infections.

The general and indiscriminate use of ultraviolet irradiation and glycol vapors in schools, barracks, industry, stores, and places where the public congregates is not warranted on evidence available at the present time.

The further control of air-borne infection must await scientific studies that will show that the techniques used actually reduce the spread of infection, under what environmental conditions they are effective, and that the procedure is not harmful to the individual.

It must be concluded that air decontamination is of some value, that continued study is needed, and that any advance that can be made in controlling the spread of disease of the upper respiratory tract is a significant contribution to public health.

Control of social contact route. As indicated previously this route of travel has not been so well controlled as the other routes because an enlightened and cooperative citizenry is necessary for effective measures. A reduction in the death rate among respiratory diseases which are conveyed largely over this route depends upon the widespread utilization of standardized controls, intelligent cooperation with the physician and public health personnel, and the practice of personal and community hygiene.

THE DISEASE CYCLE

Most communicable diseases follow a characteristic pattern of development. Six stages or periods are typical. These are called incubation, prodrome, fastigium, defervescence, convalescence, and defection periods. The length of these periods varies from disease to disease.

Incubation period. After an infectious agent gains entrance to the body of a susceptible person, it must multiply in order to produce disease. Enormous numbers are necessary to cause disease. This increase occurs during the incubation period. No symptoms of disease are apparent in the person acting as the host to the invaders. The disease is usually not communicable during the incubation period although measles and chickenpox apparently are transmitted during the last three days of the incubation period.

Prodromal period. As the pathogenic agent increases in number, the body reacts to the invader usually in a somewhat general manner marked by the characteristic symptoms of the common cold—nasal discharge, watery eyes, headache, mild fever, irritability, general aches, restlessness, perhaps a cough, and digestive disturbance. At this stage the signs and symptoms are not clear enough to diag-

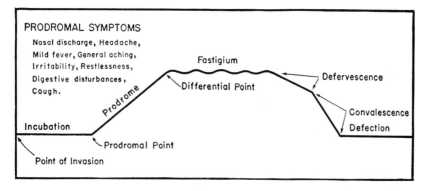

Fig. 63. Course of an infectious respiratory disease. All respiratory infections follow the course depicted by this graph. In school, the prodromal and convalescent periods pose the greatest problems in disease control because the infected person may be well enough to be up and around and thus expose others. (From Anderson, C. L.: School health practice, St. Louis, 1956, The C. V. Mosby Co.)

nose the disease, but the condition is now highly communicable. The prodrome lasts from one to two days. Since the victim often believes he "just has a cold," he may continue his usual routine and expose a considerable number of people.

Fastigium. Near the end of the prodrome the invaders have reached sufficiently large numbers to produce the characteristic differential signs of the disease in question. Now the diagnosis can be made. The disease is at its height and is communicable, but as a rule the patient is ill enough to be in bed so that contacts are few and the danger of spread at this stage is reduced.

Defervescence. During the height of the disease the body defenses either begin to defeat the invading pathogens or succumb to them. In the recovery period symptoms decline, and the patient begins to feel better. The disease remains but is declining in severity. In most cases the improvement of the patient proceeds uneventfully; in others the patient suffers a weakening of the body defenses, which permits the invaders to get a fresh start or permits another pathogen to cause disease. Thus a *relapse* is said to have occurred. The rapidity of return of the disturbing symptoms is explained by the fact that the body still contains large numbers of virulent agents which, as multiplication resumes, soon reach symptomatic proportions.

Convalescence. In the typical case, following the disappearance of symptoms of acute disease, a period of recuperation is necessary to regain normal strength and vitality. During this convalescence the patient may still harbor virulent organisms, and the disease may be transmitted to other individuals.

Defection period. As the forces that combat the invading organisms gain ascendancy, the number of pathogens is reduced, and, as the individual recovers, they are eliminated entirely from the body. The time interval of the defection period varies. Some persons never succeed in entirely eliminating the infection; the symptoms may disappear and health is apparently restored, but the agents remain. Such persons are known as *carriers*. Not all diseases have a defection period. A notable exception is tuberculosis. Recovery from this disease does not imply that the tubercle bacilli are completely eliminated from the body, but rather that the organisms are walled off into structures, called tubercles, where they may remain quiescent for long periods of time.

TYPES OF INDIVIDUALS WHO SPREAD DISEASE

Four types of individuals important in the spread of disease are the carrier, the prodromal patient, the patient with a mild or missed case, and the convalescent.

Carriers. A person who harbors pathogenic organisms and is discharging them from the body while apparently healthy himself is called a carrier. Several different types of carriers exist; their names are self-explanatory: active carriers, intermittent carriers, intestinal and urinary carriers, blood and tissue carriers, oral carriers, and many others. Some carriers exist without a previous history of the disease. Carriers are common after an occurence of typhoid fever, dysentery, diphtheria, cholera, influenza, and cerebrospinal meningitis. The carrier is probably the main reservoir of infection, bridging the gap between epidemics and seasonal prevalences.

Recognition of the carrier has produced new methods of disease control, but the control and cure of the carrier is a very difficult task. The discovery of a carrier may involve long laboratory procedures, both costly and time consuming; intermittent carriers may be inactive and escape detection at the time of examination. Many carriers are unaware of their condition. Even after detection, elimination of the pathogenic organisms may be impossible. If cure is impossible, then efforts at control are needed. Since they have not committed a usually recognized crime, carriers cannot be incarcerated except in conspicuous cases. It is possible to place limitations on their activities and occupations; they can be supervised and instructed in how to be less dangerous to others through sanitary isolation and sound personal hygiene. Permissible occupations are painting, mechanics, banking, tailoring, and similar work; but baking, cooking, serving food, and barbering are occupations that should be denied to carriers.

Patients with mild and missed cases. A number of atypical cases of disease are not diagnosed clinically. Disease varies from mild attacks to those severe enough to cause death. Influenza, diphtheria, yellow fever, scarlet fever, typhoid fever, dengue fever, measles, and many other diseases may occur in so mild a form that they pass unrecognized. Because these persons are up and walking around, they usually are referred to as ambulatory patients.

The great difficulty in controlling persons with mild or unrecognized disease is apparent. Although mild, the disease may be transferred to other persons in whom it may assume a virulent form. Often the disease may reach its height and cause severe reactions for only a few hours. In either case symptoms are not pronounced, often a physician never sees the patient, and the disease passes unrecognized.

Prodromal patients. During the prodrome the person is not yet feeling the full effects of the infection and so may appear in public and mingle with others at a time when he is able to communicate the disease that is developing within him. Since the diagnosis cannot be made at this time, he may ascribe his headache to something he ate, his general malaise to a bad night's sleep, and his general discomfort to the weather.

The prodrome is a very important factor since the virulence of the organism is known to be high at this time. Most contacts are made during this period. Recognition of this fact is of extreme importance in controlling epidemics.

Convalescents. The convalescent is a factor in the dissemination of disease but is probably not so important as the other three types. The organisms are not as virulent, probably because of the effect of the resistive forces of the body upon them, but the patient can still communicate the disease and is likely to receive visitors.

EFFECTIVENESS OF ISOLATION AND QUARANTINE

Segregation of the reservoir or probable reservoir of infection has been an effective, although not perfect, means of preventing the spread of disease. *Isolation* is the segregation of an infected person (or animal) until all danger of conveying infection has passed. Variability in the duration of the communicable state complicates the problem of control. Isolation can be highly effective when laboratory methods can be used to determine the absence or presence of the infectious agent. Examination of sputum for the tubercle bacillus, nose and throat smears for the detection of the diphtheria bacillus, and the testing of fecal and urinary discharges for the presence of typhoid and dysentery organisms make isolation highly effective in these diseases. When no laboratory tests are available, arbitrary periods of time must be used. No provision for individual variation can be made. The longer the period of isolation, the greater will be the injustice to those patients whose communicability period is unusually short. An arbitrary isolation period can be satisfactory for such diseases as measles and chickenpox for which no convalescent carriers exist, but will be unsatisfactory in diseases, such as scarlet fever, for which convalescent carriers are possible. Carriers are not marked by an X on the forehead.

Detention of susceptible persons who have been exposed to infectious disease is termed *quarantine*. These "contacts" are detained for the maximum incubation period, calculated from the time of exposure. When laboratory findings can be used, quarantine can be less stringent and yet more effective.

The limitation of isolation and quarantine procedures arises from the difficulties inherent in the prodromal and convalescent stages of persons with active cases, from persons with missed and hidden cases, and from unrecognized carriers. Imperfect though isolation and quarantine may be, they still are effective weapons of disease control.

DEFENSE AGAINST DISEASE

The phenomena of sickness, death, and recovery are known to all. Many other interesting items in connection with disease have been observed: the variability in the severity of the same disease between individuals and from year to year and recurrence or nonrecurrence. These events must be understood as the interaction between the body and the invading causative agent is studied.

Disease develops as a result of the inimical effects produced on the body by pathogenic microorganisms, and symptoms are indications of the reaction of the body toward the pathogen. The battle for survival between the body defenses and the causative agent is not a simple matter. Many factors which vary from individual to individual are concerned: susceptibility, resistance, physiological states, and environmental conditions.

The ability of the individual to resist pathogenic agents is a mechanism through which individuals survive infectious diseases. If it were not for the defenses of the host, the invasion of pathogens doubtless would result in death.

Even in epidemics not all persons contract disease, and under ordinary conditions only a few members of a group fall prey to infection. Three factors determine the occurrence of disease in individuals: the number of invading organisms, their virulence, and the resistance of the host. This may be represented by the following equation in which N is the number of organisms, V their virulence, and R the resistance of the body:

$$D = \frac{NV}{R}$$

If any of these factors are varied, the course of the disease will be affected. It is questionable that if one pathogen were introduced into the body it would produce disease. Usually substantial numbers are present at one time. It is obvious that large numbers have a better chance of survival in the body, and, of course, with the rapidity of multiplication they reach enormous numbers more rapidly than do smaller groups. The virulence of organisms differs from time to time. For instance, influenza seems more severe some years than other years.

In order to grow and multiply, organisms attack body tissues to obtain food. If a proper food supply cannot be obtained, the organisms and their effect are short-lived and uneventful. Other factors already mentioned, such as alkalinity, temperature, moisture, and darkness, are important if the organisms are to flourish.

General resistance. The human body possesses a number of factors which act as barriers or defenses against all organisms pathogenic to man. These mechanisms are nonspecific in their action, attacking all foreign organisms with varying degrees of effectiveness. Usually these mechanisms are sufficient to cause the destruction of the invader.

Besides serving as a mechanical barrier, the human skin is moderately acid, which is an unfavorable medium for most pathogens. Some pathogens invade the hair follicles with resulting infection, and some fungi may cause skin infection such as the common ringworm type. The hookworm has the rare ability to burrow through the human skin and gain entrance to the body. Despite these exceptions the skin must be considered an almost impregnable defense against infection.

Mucous secretions of the respiratory tract intercept pathogens which the microscopic hairlike cilia of the mucous cells sweep outwardly. Other defenses are the hydrochloric acid of the stomach and the high alkalinity of the intestines. Salinity of the tears protects the eyes and eyelids against infection. Of special protective value is the fever mechanism. An elevation in temperature is the body's response to the disturbing effects of the invading parasites. Since most pathogens are inactivated at temperatures slightly higher than the normal for the human body, a fever makes easier the body's task of destroying the organisms.

Phagocytosis. The process of enveloping, dissolving, and absorbing microorganisms is termed phagocytosis and is an important first-line defense of the body. Phagocytes are either free-moving (leukocytes), such as certain of the white blood cells, or fixed (endothelial cells), such as certain of the cells of the liver, lymph nodes, and spleen. Phagocytes are not always able to overcome the pathogen, and, when they fail, infection may be the end result if other body defenses are not adequate. The ability of phagocytes to overcome a second invasion by a particular organism may be greatly increased as a result of the production by the tissues of a substance, *opsonin*. This substance, which is specific for a particular organism, prepares the organism for the engulfing and dissolving action of the phagocytes.

Interference with body defenses. Various physiological and environmental factors may affect resistance adversely. Some incidental conditions or factors that may indirectly affect general resistance are organic disease, injury, malnutrition, chronic infection, exposure to heat or cold, extended fatigue, alcohol, and some drugs. In general the effect is to alter the responsiveness of the body processes to infectious agents. Since these factors tend to predispose an individual to infection, sound health practice would place special emphasis on the avoidance of such conditions or factors. When preventive efforts are not totally successful, immediate measures should be taken to correct conditions and initiate counteraction.

Immunity. Immunity is complete resistance to a particular infectious disease and is due to the presence of certain chemicals (antibodies) in the tissues. These antibodies may neutralize toxins, may agglutinate, or may precipitate organisms.

Natural immunity. It is a common observation that some animal species have an inherent or natural immunity to a disease to which another species is susceptible. If smallpox, typhoid fever, and other infectious diseases occur in a family, domestic animals are never affected. Similarly, when dogs suffer from distemper, human beings are not affected. Organisms that produce disease in plants do not produce disease in animals. Pathogenic microorganisms that cause disease in warm-blooded animals are not pathogenic to cold-blooded animals. Similarly most microorganisms that infect birds do not produce disease in mammals. These are examples of natural immunity. In general it may be said that natural immunity is operative in species, races, and individuals. Age, sex, and inheritance also influence resistance to disease.

Negroes appear to be relatively resistant to hookworm infection; Jewish people have a low death rate from tuberculosis, whereas the Indians have a high fatality rate. Between the ages of 15 and 30 years women are more susceptible to tuberculosis than men and succumb about twice as frequently as men. Many childhood diseases are not contracted by adults. Some families appear to have complete resistance to pneumonia, whereas other families appear to be highly susceptible.

Acquired immunity. The fact that some diseases are only contracted once, whereas in other instances second attacks are common, is well known. When the body becomes resistant or nonsusceptible to second attacks, an acquired immunity is said to exist. A similar resistance may be acquired by inoculating a person with an antigenic substance or through the utilization of an antiserum produced outside the body of the patient. When acquired immunity exists, defensive substances are found in the body that destroy the pathogen or toxin which occasioned the production of defensive substances. These antagonistic substances are called antibodies. Apparently they are produced by lymphoid tissue and are present in all cells. Their presence in the blood can be demonstrated most easily. Two types of acquired immunity are recognized.

Active immunity. Active immunity exists when an individual has been stimulated to produce his own antibodies either through an attack of a disease or by inoculation with an antigenic substance. An antigen is a substance, usually protein, which when introduced into the body will cause a reaction, resulting in the formation of antagonistic substances which counteract the antigen producing them.

After a time the antibodies may disappear from the blood stream. The capacity to reproduce them rapidly, in case of a second invasion of the organisms originally occasioning their production, is not lost. Thus resistance may again be developed to the particular organism involved. This immunity may persist for a long period of time.

The length of time that active immunity lasts varies with different diseases and can extend for a very short time or can be lifelong. Second attacks are common in influenza, pneumonia, gonorrhea, and malaria, are frequent in syphilis, erysipelas, tetanus, and dengue fever, are rare in measles, mumps, scarlet fever, smallpox, chickenpox, and poliomyelitis, and are unknown in yellow fever and plague.

The duration of immunity depends upon the organism causing the attack and the individual differences of the persons attacked. That some people have second attacks of a disease whereas others do not is a common observation. Biologics used to produce active immunity vary with the antigen used as well as with the disease. Individual differences are also operative.

Passive immunity. When antibodies have been produced in one body and subsequently injected into another individual, a passive immunity is developed. In this case the duration of the immunity is short; the borrowed protective substances tend to disappear as the blood is renewed. Since the antibodies have been borrowed from an immunized person or animal, they will counteract the specific type of substance occasioning their production. Since the patient's body tissues have not been stimulated to produce them, the antibodies act as a cure, but do not convey a lasting immunity.

Perhaps the classical example of passive immunity is the *infantile immunity* of the first six months of life. At the placenta, antibodies from the mother's blood stream diffuse into the blood stream of the fetus. Since the child's tissues are not themselves stimulated to form antibodies, the length of the immunity lasts only while the mother's antibodies survive in the child.

Immunity in action. The science of immunology has had its greatest development during the twentieth century. Basic to this science is the understanding of resistance, susceptibility, natural and acquired immunity, and antigen and antibody activity.

The commercial production of antigens and antibodies on a large scale, under strict supervision, and with a high standard of purity has made possible the widespread application of biological therapy and immunization. These products have been given the name *biologics*.

There are two main types of biologics: vaccines (antigens) and antisera (antibodies).

Vaccines. These are antigens and are used to produce an active immunity. This active immunity is produced in different ways, dependent upon the type of antigen and the manner in which the antibody produces its result. In general they may be divided into the following groups: attenuated or modified living viruses (smallpox and rabies); virulent living organisms; dead bacteria (typhoid vaccine); products of bacteria, toxins, and modified toxins (toxoid); and mixtures of toxins and antitoxins.

In practice, between the ages of 3 and 6 months, the child is immunized against diphtheria, pertussis, and tetanus by the use of a multiple biologic possessing all three antigens. Vaccination against smallpox by the age of 6 months is also recommended. Early immunization protects the child for the first few years of life when these diseases are most likely to be fatal. In addition the immunity tends to be of longer duration.

Antisera. These contain immune antagonistic substances or antibodies. They are used in passive immunization and as a cure. These products may be divided into three classes, dependent upon the antigen stimulating their production; toxins produce antitoxic sera, bacterial antigens (endotoxin type) produce antibacterial sera, and convalescent sera may be either antitoxic or antibacterial.

Convalescent serum is recovered from a human being instead of from a lower-animal. The use of this class of serum is not widespread, with the exception of its use in measles, because it must be taken from patients who have recovered from a disease. These cases may not occur in large numbers, the amount of serum taken from the patient cannot be great, and the consent of the patient must be obtained. These sera act in the same manner and produce the same result as those produced by lower animals.

Convalescent serum has been used widely in the treatment of measles. Normal blood serum of adults who have had measles may be used. With the widespread collection of whole blood during World War II and subsequently gamma globulin, a by-product of the production of serum albumin, became available for distribution through state boards of health by the American Red Cross. Gamma globulin is used the same as convalescent serum.

Specific prevention. Many new biologics continue to appear; some are valuable, whereas others are not. Whether a product is worthwhile depends upon its effectiveness, safety, and ease of administration. It usually takes some time to apply these criteria. Biologics that have met these requirements are available

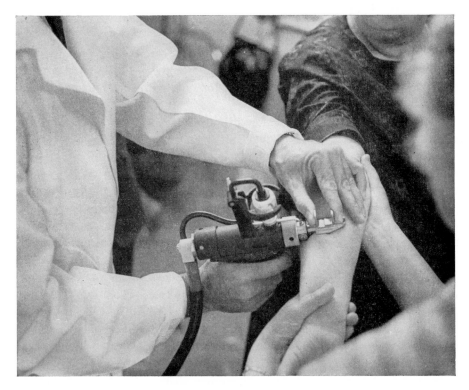

Fig. 64. Jet spray method of immunization against influenza. Quick, effective, and relatively painless, this method of administering a vaccine is becoming more widely used when innoculation is necessary. (Courtesy Oregon State Board of Health.)

for protection by active immunization in the following diseases: smallpox, diphtheria, scarlet fever, whooping cough, tetanus, typhoid fever, rabies, Rocky Mountain spotted fever, yellow fever, typhus, influenza, poliomyelitis, measles, and some types of pneumococcic pneumonia. Others that are in the experimental stage include active immunization for other types of pneumococcic pneumonia and meningococcic meningitis.

Biologics for passive immunization are available for use in scarlet fever, tetanus, diphtheria, measles, mumps, whooping cough, and chickenpox. Some are more effective than others. The opportunity for control of communicable disease by this method is not so great as by active immunization.

INFECTIONS OF THE GENITAL SYSTEM

Several harmless microorganisms are normally found on the external genitals, particularly in the female. The vulva may harbor baccilli, cocci, spirochetes, sarcina, yeasts, and other forms. These organisms generally are harmless.

Few organisms are found in the vagina. The acidity of the vaginal canal creates a poor medium for microorganisms.

The uterus, oviducts, and ovaries as well as the testes and vasa deferentia are normally free of microorganisms.

Syphilis (lues). Because its symptoms resemble those of a vast number of diseases, syphilis is called the great imitator. Many prevailing popular misconceptions indicate that there is still a need for public understanding of the true nature of syphilis.

Syphilis is specific for man. It now exists in every country of the world. Although the incidence is lower in the United States than in Europe or Asia, it nevertheless is a major disease problem here. In 1945 a report* by the U. S. Public Health Service revealed that in the examination of 531,236 selective service men between January 1, 1943, and May 31, 1943, for the representative age of 28 years, 3% of the single white men and 18.2% of the single Negroes were syphilitic. The incidence among women is generally about two thirds that among men. The highest incidence in both sexes is among persons in the age group between 16 and 30 years. Although syphilis occurs among persons in all social strata, there is a disproportionately high incidence among persons in groups with low moral standards. A. U. S. Public Health Service report† for 1958 reveals a total of 115,173 cases of syphilis reported to official health agencies.

Treponema pallidum (Spirochaeta pallida) is the causative agent in syphilis and was discovered by F. Schaudin in 1905. It is a slender corkscrew-shaped organism with from eight to twenty-four regular spirals. An extremely delicate organism, it is destroyed by heat, cold, drying, soap and water, and weak disinfectants and cannot live in free air.

In its early stages syphilis is highly communicable. Syphilis is transmitted from the chancre or lesion of the primary stage and from the moist lesions of the secondary stage. Perhaps 90% of all cases of syphilis are acquired through sexual intercourse. Less than 5% of all cases are classed as accidental. Damp towels, common drinking utensils, and accidental surgical inoculation are possible means of accidental transmission. Syphilitic lesions of the mouth account for a number of cases acquired through kissing. Prenatal syphilis accounts for about 4% of the known cases. If the mother's infection is recent, the fetus will acquire the organism through the placenta between the fifth and ninth month of development. However, early treatment of the mother prevents fetal infection. If the mother's syphilis is of more than five years' duration, the fetus is not likely to be infected.

All people are susceptible to syphilis. One attack does not produce immunity although second attacks are rare.

The incubation period of syphilis is usually about twenty one days, with a range between ten and forty days.

---

*Venereal disease information, published by the U. S. Public Health Service, Washington, D. C., October, 1945.
†Report by Venereal Disease Division, U. S. Public Health Service, Washington, D. C., 1958, vol. 7, no. 54.

The *primary stage* is characterized by a syphilitic sore, the chancre, which appears at the point of invasion. Thus it may appear on the genitals or at extragenital locations. Nothing in the appearance of the syphilitic chancre distinguishes it from other sores. Only through finding the spirochetes in the lesion by the use of a dark-field microscope can it be pronounced a syphilitic chancre. The chancre will usually clear uneventfully whether or not it is treated.

The *secondary stage* appears about forty five days after the chancre heals. It runs a chronic course between six weeks and six months in duration. It is a highly communicable stage. Symptoms include skin eruptions, mucous patches in the mouth (not canker sores), mild fever, unusual aches and pains, sore throat, and disturbed vision. Recovery from these symptoms can be spontaneous.

The *tertiary stage* may show no outward manifestations for years. It may involve any system, organ, or tissue in the body. Organs most frequently involved are the heart, arteries, brain, skin, and bones. A hard tumor (gumma) with a soft gummy center usually forms.

About 3% of all known persons with syphilis develop general paresis (dementia paralytica) or syphilitic psychosis. A smaller percentage acquire tabes dorsalis (locomotor ataxia) due to syphilitic involvement of the spinal cord that results in incoordination of the legs and other disturbances.

The precise death rate from syphilis is hard to determine. Officially it does not rank in the first ten causes of death; yet many deaths that are listed as due to some other cause are technically due to syphilis. However, if early treatment were available to all patients, deaths from syphilis would approach zero. Development of effective forms of treatment for syphilis, early detection of all cases, and making treatment available to all would reduce the incidence of syphilis to the role of a minor health problem. To assume that such a program would completely eliminate syphilis in the United States is unduly optimistic. It may approach the theoretical goal of extinction and thus protect the citizenry generally, thereby elevating the national standard of health.

Gonorrhea. The great sterilizer, gonorrhea, is specific for man. It involves the mucous tissues, particularly of the genital tract. Not often fatal, it is nevertheless a serious menace to health.

Chinese writings of thirty centuries ago reveal that gonorrhea existed then. The Bible (Lev. XV) refers to the affliction. In 1646 Boston had a serious epidemic. Not until 1790, however, was gonorrhea distinguished from syphilis.

Epidemiologists estimate at least two cases of gonorrhea for every case of syphilis, which places the estimation at more than 500,000 cases of gonorrhea in the United States in any one year. About one third of that number are reported each year to official health agencies. The highest incidence occurs among persons in the 16-year to 30-year age group. Males have an incidence about double that of females. Like syphilis, gonorrhea is most prevalent in groups with low moral standards.

The causative agent was discovered by A. L. S. Neisser in 1879, and the disease is sometimes called neisserian infection. *Neisseria gonorrhoeae* is a paired oval-shaped organism found in large numbers in the cells of pus from involved mucous tissue. The organism is killed quite easily by drying, heat, and weak disinfectants. In the moisture of the human body it may live for years. In pus outside of the body it may survive an hour.

Practically all cases in adults are acquired through sexual congress. Whereas the organism is easy to detect in the urethra of the male, it is difficult to isolate from the deeper structures of the female genital organs.

Accidental infection of young girls occurs occasionally from articles containing pus from an active condition. Contaminated toilet seats, towels, and clothing serve as means of transmission. Fortunately most accidental infections are simple external infections which can be cleared up quickly. About one half of these cases are actually infection from coccus organisms other than the gonococcus and thus are not gonorrhea.

Accidental infection of the conjunctiva of the eyelids can occur in adults or children. A towel with fresh pus may carry the organism to the eye. Dangers in the indiscriminate use of common or public towels are apparent.

All people are susceptible to gonorrhea. One attack does not produce immunity although a transient increased resistance to subsequent infection may occur.

The incubation period is usually from three to seven days, although it may be as short as one day or as long as two weeks. The first recognized symptom is usually a yellowish-green discharge from the involved mucous tissue. The pus has a distinctive odor. In the male the urethra becomes inflamed, and urination becomes painful. Complications in the male may involve the deeper genital structures. In the female the vulva, urethra, or vagina may be involved. From the vagina the deeper genital structures may become infected. The female often has no particularly great pain associated with the infection. Chronic gonorrhea in the female is quite common.

Ophthalmia neonatorum, inflammation of the eyelid lining of newborn infants, is often due to gonorrheal infection contracted from a gonorrheal mother during delivery. Blindness can result. Prophylactic treatment by a drop of silver nitrate (1.5%) in each eye of every newborn child is required by all fifty states. Penicillin treatment of the mother two or three weeks before delivery would protect the child equally effectively and clear up the mother's infection. Penicillin in the eyes of newborn infants has been used successfully in place of silver nitrate.

Successful treatment of gonorrhea had tended to produce a laxity in the battle

Table 42. Reported cases of gonorrhea and syphilis in United States in 1951, 1955, and 1958

Disease	*1951*	*1955*	*1958*
Gonorrhea	254,057	244,279	241,792
Syphilis	174,924	123,004	115,173

against the disease. Like syphilis, it will not be totally eradicated by treatment. Carelessness and indifference to syphilis and gonorrhea constitute a danger to the health of the public.

Reports of the U. S. National Office of Vital Statistics indicate a gradual decline in the number of reported cases of gonorrhea and syphilis in the United States during the past several years; yet these diseases constitute a menace to the nation. Epidemiologists usually estimate the actual existing number of cases of gonorrhea and syphilis to be more than twice the number reported. This would mean approximately one half million cases of gonorrhea and one quarter million cases of syphilis. The danger from these diseases still lurks in the land, and they still take a monumental toll in anguish, pain, degeneration, and death. To use modern treatment if one is infected is a wise course to follow, but the wiser course is to follow a mode of living which will not expose one to these infections.

Chancroid. Least serious of the venereal infections is chancroid or soft chancre. *Hemophilus ducreyi,* a streptobacillus (chainlike arrangement of rods), is the causative agent. A delicate organism, it is easily destroyed by temperature change and weak disinfectants. It lives but a short time outside the human body. The incubation period is from three to six days.

An inflammatory disease, chancroid appears as small painful ulcers which resemble the chancre of syphilis but are much softer. Beginning as a pustule on the genitals, an ulcer soon appears and pus is discharged.

Many cases clear up without treatment with no apparent complications.

Lymphogranuloma venereum. The least known of this group of diseases is one that is caused by a virus and involves the lymph system. Incubation varies, being about six weeks in most cases. In the female ulcers appear at the entrance to the vagina, and globular masses may develop. The rectum may also become involved. In the male an ulcer appears just behind the glans of the penis. Inguinal lymph nodes may show involvement and be extremely tender. Mild conditions heal spontaneously, but the sulfa compounds are highly effective in the treatment of all these patients.

FADS, FALLACIES, AND QUACKERY

People with ills, real or imagined, are usually susceptible to promised cures, especially if they are quick and painless. Health as a commodity is so highly prized that it is easily exploited. Surveys have shown that over 75% of all advertising makes an appeal to health.

The widespread acceptance of the importance of health has not made people aware of the facts about how health may be achieved and maintained. The custom in ancient Babylonia of displaying the sick in the public square so that passersby who had recovered from similar symptoms might prescribe treatment that had been effective in their cure is understandable. With the modern knowledge that is available, it is not so understandable that people who have recovered from illness are so ready to diagnose the ills of others and suggest medications. But still more confounding is ready acceptance of such service by many.

In addition to this there is much self-diagnosis and treatment. The latter is exploited through advertising of patent medicines, one-shot treatments, and fads. In addition quacks, charlatans, and various healers flourish. Although laws have been passed to control false advertising, the licensing of practitioners, and the adulteration of various products consumed, the public nevertheless spends enormous amounts for quack services and adulterated goods annually.

The diagnosis and treatment of disease is a complicated matter requiring the services of the best talent available. The knowledge and services available in this area are so great that it takes years of education to learn to apply them to the best advantage. The body of scientific knowledge is so great that specialists in various areas have developed. Therefore the selection of a practitioner to treat one's ills is important.

Advertising in the newspaper, in magazines, on radio, and on television bombards the public with material and claims that are difficult to evaluate. Many times scientific facts are exploited but only part of the story is told; as a result only part of the truth is told and imagined benefits are suggested. The ill effects of the unscientific use of advertised products are seldom mentioned.

There are several things to keep in mind when one uses services and products in the health field.

1. Usually there are no quick easy cures.
2. The maintenance of health is a continuous process. No one product, be it food or exercise device, will produce the desired result. There is no easy way; authorities may give useful advice, but you must give of your own efforts if desired goals are to be achieved.
3. The selection of a health adviser should be made before an emergency occurs. If the most reliable and adequate professional services available are to be obtained, the education, experience, and standing in the community of the practitioner should be thoroughly investigated.
4. Use health products only on professional advice and purchase only those products certified as acceptable by national associations such as the American Medical Association or the American Dental Association.
5. Fads, nostrums, and quacks should be avoided.

DEGENERATIVE DISEASES

This is a general term which has been applied to conditions resulting in the breakdown of the heart, arteries, and kidneys. The term usually indicates a noninflammatory condition and is associated with aging. These diseases have increased greatly during this century. This is partly because a great number of persons are living to an age when these diseases begin to express themselves and partly because of a lack of knowledge of how to diagnose, treat, and prevent these conditions. As life expectancy continues to increase, it can be confidently expected

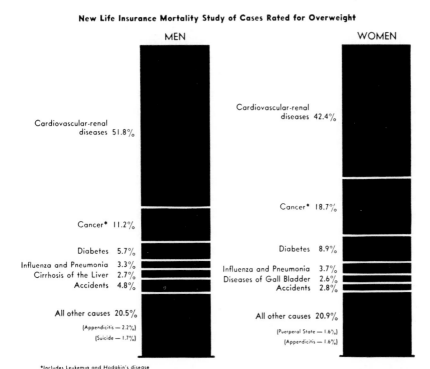

Experience of Metropolitan Life Insurance Company Substandard Ordinary Issues, 1925-1934, traced to 1950

Fig. 65. Overweight and mortality. Preliminary analysis indicates that in both sexes the mortality is excessively high from all the degenerative diseases of the heart, arteries, and kidneys, from diabetes, and from diseases of the liver and gallbladder. Deaths from childbearing also exceeded the expected number. Death rates from cardiovascular-renal conditions were relatively highest at ages under 45 years. Of the major diseases, diabetes showed relatively the greatest excess mortality—more than three times the expected number in each sex. The death rate from cirrhosis of the liver among men was more than twice the normal. (Courtesy Metropolitan Life Insurance Co.)

that degenerative diseases will become progressively important. As previously indicated, this problem has aspects other than medical and public health. Sociological and economic problems also arise. It is not in the province of this book to treat these aspects except to call attention to them and to point out that the problem of care may become a public health problem rather than one of welfare.

Arteriosclerosis. This is a chronic disturbance of the vascular walls, characterized by deposits of fats and other substances, reduction in the size of the lumen, and inelasticity of the walls. The cause of this condition is not well understood. Very little scientific evidence is available. There is general agreement that increased intra-arterial pressure and hypertension, metabolic disturbances, increased concentration of fats in the blood, and diabetes contribute to arteriosclerosis. Nervous stresses and strains may have an effect on the genesis of arteriosclerosis. Treatment is difficult, prolonged, and often ineffective.

Atherosclerosis. This disease is probably the number-one killer of middle-aged and aged persons in the United States. The crux of the problem in arteriosclerosis is atherosclerosis. Within limits the disease is preventable and curable.

Basically it is a metabolic disease. A decisive note is played by alterations in the cholesterol-lipid-lipoprotein metabolism. Without these alterations atherosclerosis, at least in middle-aged persons, would seldom occur, regardless of the functional state of the cardiovascular system.

The American diet is high in calories, lipids, cholesterol (estimates indicate that 40% of the total calories are in the form of fats), and salt. Such a diet is detrimental to the cardiovascular system and furnishes the prerequisite for atherosclerosis. On the other hand, commonly, our diets are inadequate in minerals, amino acids, essential fatty acids, and specific vitamins.

The problem is not that simple, however, and factors other than diet are operative. Among these are sedentary habits, a sex differential in coronary atherosclerosis (middle-aged men being more susceptible than middle-aged women), genetics, fatigue, tension, stress, diabetes mellitus, renal diseases, hypothyroidism, and hypertension.

The last few years have seen much progress in the understanding of this disease, and there now is much hope that effective prophylaxis and therapeutic measures will be developed.

Hypertension. High blood pressure or other cardiovascular tension is perhaps the greatest cause of death in the United States today. It is a disease of middle and old age, affects women more often than men, but is more serious to the latter. Unfortunately there is a paucity of information concerning this condition. An inherited factor is recognized. Successful treatment of arteriosclerosis and hypertension is dependent upon early recognition. After the symptoms have become well developed, treatment is still far from satisfactory. Prevention seems based on a regimen of life which eliminates smoking, a diet with a minimum of milk, eggs, and animal fats, avoidance of obesity, and a reduction of nervous strain.

Heart disease. Statistically speaking, deaths from this disease have increased tremendously during the twentieth century. There are many types of cardiovascular disease produced by different causes and under different conditions. Until the various types of these diseases and the conditions that cause them are known, control and prevention will be handicapped.

Undoubtedly some of the increase in the incidence of heart disease is due to more accurate diagnosis and to a gradually aging population. This, however, is only a part of the picture. Heart disease occurring in people under 45 years of age is usually due to heart infection, often rheumatic fever or other infection.

Any disease producing infectious toxemia may damage the heart. Diphtheria, scarlet fever, bacterial endocarditis, tuberculosis, meningitis, and gonococcus infection are examples of diseases which may result in heart damage.

Coronary disease causes much crippling and many sudden deaths. Its sudden

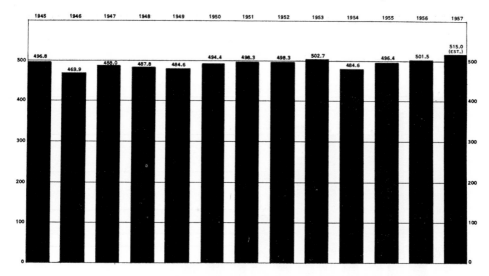

Fig. 66. Crude death rates for diseases of the heart and circulation for the years 1945 to 1957 have remained rather constant. (Courtesy National Health Education Committee.)

and dramatic action has caused much fear. This disease and hypertension are two major causes of heart disease. It occurs usually after 40 years of age, is more common in the white race than in the Negro race, and attacks males more often than females. It is essentially an arterial disease that results in calcification of the walls of the coronary vessels and consequent reduction in the size of the lumen. Since the coronary vessels supply blood to the muscles of the heart, the seriousness of coronary obstruction is apparent. The cause of the condition is atherosclerosis, and there is no specific preventive therapy. It may be sex-linked because of the large proportion of males suffering from the disease. Diabetes mellitus and hypertension aggravate the condition. Thus it is important that diabetes be discovered early.

Thyroid disorders may affect the heart deleteriously; hence this condition should be diagnosed early and corrected. Anemia may affect the heart adversely, and, if organic heart disease is present, the anemia should be prevented or corrected immediately. Tuberculosis of the outer lining of the heart (pericardium) occurs in a limited number of persons. Since many infections of the heart are caused by coccus organisms, it is encouraging that the sulfa compounds are effective in many instances in controlling these infections.

Rheumatic fever. Inflammation of the joints is an implied disorder in this disease, but it is not the main feature, for it is mainly a disease that involves the heart, often causing permanent damage. Its largest incidence is in children and young people. The causative agent is unknown, but some facts have been established.

1. Streptococcal infections in the upper respiratory tract are usually the exciting cause and are followed in about four weeks by an attack of rheu-

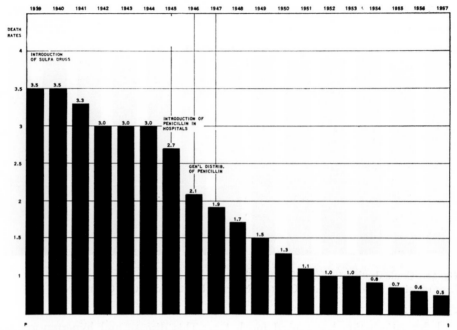

Fig. 67. The decline in deaths due to rheumatic fever has been dramatic. Death rates per 100,000 estimated midyear population; data from U. S. National Office of Vital Statistics. (Courtesy National Health Education Committee.)

matic fever. Children with sore throats should be treated by a physician, and thus rheumatic fever could be prevented.

2. Patients should be protected against colds that are conveyed to them by others. Colds may cause a reactivation of rheumatic processes.

3. Patients may be aided by living in tropical and semitropical countries during the winter months.

4. The sulfa compounds and penicillin give promise of protection in the treatment of the original infection and in the prevention of recurring activation of rheumatic fever in a susceptible child.

Climate affects the incidence of this disease, colder climates being unfavorable. There is a familial tendency toward the disease, and socioeconomic status has a marked effect.

Nephritis. This is a general term applied to many diseases of the kidneys. Two types are common, acute and chronic nephritis. Acute nephritis often occurs in children and young adults, usually as a complication from some acute infection. The kidneys are damaged by the toxins of the infective agent. Symptoms of nephritis in many instances are not so frank as those of the disease that occasioned the damage. Recovery results in nearly all patients, but the kidneys often do not return to normal. Thus the disease becomes chronic, which may lead to death at about 40 years of age.

Chronic nephritis results either from acute nephritis, arteriosclerosis of the blood vessels of the kidney, or high blood pressure which affects the kidneys. This disturbs the function of the kidney, and body wastes are not removed, resulting eventually in the body's becoming poisoned. Often fluids are retained in the tissues and edema develops. These end results do not occur for some time and often extend over a period of years. The length of life can be extended if the condition is discovered early and a proper routine is followed.

CHRONIC DISEASES

Diabetes mellitus. This disease has been increasing in importance. In 1900 it was the twenty-seventh disease on the list of causes of death; today it is eighth. About 50,000 new cases of this disease occur each year, three fifths of them among females. This disease is caused principally by malfunction of certain endocrine glands in the pancreas (islands of Langerhans), which produce a substance called insulin. Recent evidence indicates that the pituitary gland is also involved, as are probably the liver and adrenals.

A predisposition to a deficiency of the islands of Langerhans appears to be an inherited factor. When diabetes mellitus occurs in succeeding generations in the same family, the onset is in the early decades of life. At the present time eugenic considerations regarding selective marriage as a means of reducing diabetes do not appear to be too encouraging. Potential diabetic patients may often be recognized by studying the family history.

Prevention of diabetes is not easy even when conditions are known. Overeating and lack of exercise should be avoided. Early detection is important.

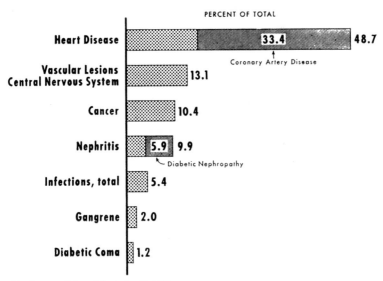

PERCENT OF TOTAL

Heart Disease — 33.4 | 48.7
Coronary Artery Disease

Vascular Lesions Central Nervous System — 13.1

Cancer — 10.4

Nephritis — 5.9 | 9.9
Diabetic Nephropathy

Infections, total — 5.4

Gangrene — 2.0

Diabetic Coma — 1.2

*Deaths reported through September 11, 1956.

Fig. 68. Selected causes of death among diabetic patients. Data based on experience of the Joslin Clinic, Boston, Mass., 1950 to 1956. (Courtesy Metropolitan Life Insurance Co.)

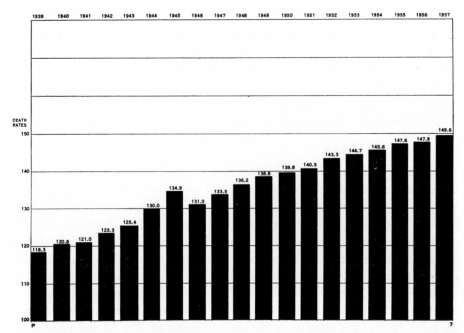

Fig. 69. Steady increase in the number of deaths due to cancer. Death rates per 100,000 estimated midyear population; data from the U. S. National Office of Vital Statistics. (Courtesy National Health Education Committee.)

---

7 DANGER SIGNALS OF CANCER

Everyone Should Know

1. Any sore that does not heal.

2. A lump or thickening, in the breast or elsewhere.

3. Unusual bleeding or discharge.

4. Any change in a wart or mole.

5. Persistent indigestion or difficulty in swallowing.

6. Persistent hoarseness or cough.

7. Any change in normal bowel habits.

(Courtesy American Cancer Society)

Fig. 70. Time to see your physician. These are nature's warnings which should be brought to the attention of a physician at once. Such promptness may save a life—your life.

Cancer. This disease usually occurs after 40 years of age. The older the person, the greater is the likelihood of cancer. It is one of the major unsolved medical and sociological problems of the present. Cancer ranks second in the causes of mortality, with definitely more male deaths than female.

Cellular growth in the body usually proceeds in an orderly fashion. In cancer, cell growth in localized areas becomes rapid and disorganized. The growth and increase of cells serve no useful purpose. If the condition is unchecked, extension of the growth area may take place. Spread may be through extension into adjacent spaces or by the cells being transported to other portions of the body where new foci of growth are started. In the latter case the blood and lymph are usually the vehicles of transmission.

The cause of cancer is not known. It is not communicable, and a single injury does not cause it. Such meager evidence makes prevention difficult. Repeated chronic irritations, either thermal, chemical, or mechanical, appear to predispose an area to cancer. Thus chronic irritations should be avoided. Prevention of spread depends on early detection and treatment of precancerous and cancerous lesions.

While the condition is localized, the chance for cure is good. Two means of treatment are available—surgery and irradiation by roentgen rays, radium, or isotopes. Current trends in the reduction of cancer in females is encouraging, especially in some types of cancer. This reduction is only a beginning. Widespread educational campaigns, encouragement of early medical advice, and the extension of cancer detection clinics, hospitals, and other facilities to handle the increased number of patients presenting themselves are necessary. Research must be continued and expanded.

THE PERIODIC MEDICAL EXAMINATION

Most gains in the future in life expectancy must be made in the saving of life after 40 years of age or in a concerted attack upon the chronic and degenerative diseases. These diseases have three things in common.

1. Their development is usually slow and insidious, with symptoms so benign that damage is often irreparable before frank symptoms manifest themselves.
2. The maximum period of incidence occurs after 40 years of age.
3. Early detection offers the best chance of control because, at present, cure in many cases is not encouraging.

The basis of control of the diseases of middle and later life is the periodic medical examination. The idea of systematic regular stocktaking or an inventory of one's health assets and liabilities appears logical and intelligent. The periodic health examination is of value at all ages, but, from 30 years on, periodic examinations by physicians skilled in proper techniques or in a clinic where specialists and extensive diagnostic aids are available will pay dividends in long, effective, and enjoyable living.

As indicated, usually frank symptoms of the degenerative diseases do not appear until considerable damage has been done. It is often possible to detect the beginning of these diseases many years in advance of their open expression. Early detection often permits the removal of the cause, or through advice and counsel the development can be materially slowed or arrested. The chance of cure is much greater in the early stages of the disease. If people would exercise the same intelligent approach and protective measures that are accepted in the control of communicable diseases, undoubtedly a marked decline in the mortality from these conditions would result.

Health examinations are excellent opportunities for health instruction, improvement of health habits, and correction of faulty practices. They should not only prolong life, but also increase the pleasure and productivity of life. As the individual grows older, his capacity for work decreases, his vitality lessens, and his reserves become weaker. It is important that the individual recognize this. During the examination these matters may be made clear by the physician.

The assurance that one is in good condition is psychologically and physically stimulating. Much strain, tension, and worry are often removed. Thus the examination is more that the discovery of disease. It has a positive educational value.

The periodic medical examination is a valuable preclinical service; it reveals unsuspected disease, unearths tendencies toward disease, and discloses present health status. Armed with this information, the physicians are in a position to evaluate, prescribe for, and educate the patient. This is the essence of preventive medicine: prevention rather than cure, avoid unfavorable conditions by early discovery, and obstruct the development of a disease condition. It is our most effective weapon in this area at the present time.

Chapter 11

State and
local health services

The state is responsible for the health of its people. Each state has its own laws; hence there is a varied pattern of public health organization at the state level. Most states have similarities of organization, including a separate department of public health, a full-time medical health officer in charge, and a state board of health which determines general policies, establishes the state sanitary code, and approves the budget. At the state level both official and voluntary agencies operate in the promotion of health.

The principal state voluntary health agencies act as agents of the national voluntary organizations serving special health interests. The state organization supervises and coordinates the work of the voluntary agency in the state and in the local communities. State voluntary health agencies usually have a professional staff of organizers, executives, and other specialists. A state agency is ordinarily the nucleus around which community branches function. It provides the leadership in the organization of a health program, fund raising, health education, and general promotion. Usually a portion of the funds raised in a drive by a state agency is returned to the community branch of the state organization.

Services furnished at the state level and available to communities, whether as grants-in-aid or through clinics or other means, usually originate from the state headquarters.

STATE HEALTH SERVICES
Health responsibilities of the state

Public health is primarily a function of the state. From the founding of the nation, the responsibility for protecting the health of the people has been recognized as an inherent right and duty of the state. This responsibility was pointedly stated more than a century ago by Lemuel Shattuck:

> It is the duty of the state to extend over the people its guardian care, that those who cannot or will not protect themselves, may nevertheless be protected; and that those who can and desire to do it may have the means of doing it more easily. This right and authority should be exercised by wise laws, wisely administered; and when this is neglected they should be held answerable for the consequences of this neglect.*

Health authority is vested in the police power of the state and is recognized by the federal government and the courts. The police power is the power of the people, vested in the government, to pass such laws and take such action as is necessary to promote the health, safety, morals, and general welfare of society. It is founded on the principle of the greatest good for the greatest number. The police power grants the state almost unlimited authority to legislate in health or any other matters relating to the general welfare. Only two limitations are imposed upon the state's police power. (1) A statute may not be contrary to the provisions of the Federal Constitution. For example, the state may not pass laws contrary to the Fourteenth Amendment to the Constitution: "No state shall deprive any person of life, liberty, or property without due process of law." (2) Any act or performance under the provisions of the police power must be *reasonable*.

Diversity of state health agencies

Whereas a state health department is the principal state health agency, in every state an amazing number of state agencies will be found to be engaged in promoting health. Usually the agency is concerned with one specific health problem, and in most instances health is not the primary function of the agency.

The titles of several of these state agencies that participate in health activities indicate the nature of their health service.

Department of Welfare, Social Security, Emergency Relief, General Assistance, etc.
Department of Agriculture
Department of Labor, Labor and Industry, Labor and Immigration, etc.
Department of Education, Public Instruction, etc.
Special boards, commissions, or independent offices established specifically for the activity indicated (Tuberculosis Board or Commission, Cancer Commission, Workmen's Compensation Commission or Bureau, Industrial Accident Board, Dairy and Food Commission, Hotel Commission, Livestock Sanitary Board, Water Resources Board, Commission for the Blind, Crippled Children's Commission, Mental Disease Commission or Department, State Toxicologist, State Veterinarian, etc.)
Board of Control, Board of Affairs, Department of State Institutions, etc.
Independent State Hospital, Independent State Laboratory
Department of Conservation
State University or College
Department of Mines and Minerals
Department of Engineering, Department of Public Utilities
State Experiment Station

---

*From Shattuck, Lemuel: Report of a general plan for the promotion of public and personal health, Boston, 1850, Dutton and Wentworth, State Printers.

Independent Licensing and Examining Boards
Department of Motor Vehicles, Department of Public Safety
Department of Civil Service and Registration, Department of Registration and Educa-
tion*

The state health department

Each of the fifty states has an executive department or agency which administers the public health activities for the state. In most states these departments
have been created by action of the state legislature. In four instances the state
constitution has created the state department of health and has detailed the
functions of the agency.

The Massachusetts State Board of Health, established in 1869, was the first
state health board. Yet even in Massachusetts organized local health agencies
had been in existence for almost a century prior to 1869. Some variation in organization was inevitable as subsequent state health agencies were established,
but the most general plan is that in which health authority is vested in a board
which appoints a full-time executive who administers the functions of the department.

An extremely satisfactory setup has been that in which a board of about nine
members is chosen by the governor of the state. Board members serve without
pay but are reimbursed for expenses incurred by meeting attendance and other
duties. Appointment for six years with staggered terms has been a satisfactory
arrangement. Regular meetings are held at least four times a year. Properly the
board should be composed of representative citizens. The board should cooperate
with all professions but should not be dominated by any one profession. A group
of representative citizens who reflect the needs and wishes of all the people is the
prescription for a state board of health, not a staff of health experts. Sometimes
nonofficial consulting committees of specialists in a field are appointed to advise
the board. Expert services are provided by the professional staff, not by the
board.

Powers of the state board of health. A state board of health has extensive
powers for health promotion. Yet essentially the state health agency furnishes
indirect health services to individual citizens. However, the scope of the powers
and functions of the board indicates the importance of state health promotion,
indirect though it may be. Seven of the recognized powers of the board are code-
making, quasijudicial powers, administration, investigation, supervision and consultation, education, and coordination with other agencies. For clarification some
of these functions merit further elaboration.

Code-making power. The code-making power of the board is a quasilegisla-
tive one. Legislation enacted by the legislature laying down general health laws
usually delegates to the state board of health the power to make rules and regu-

---

*From Mountin, J. W., and Flook, Evelyn: Guide to Health Organization in the United States,
Washington, D. C., 1951, U. S. Government Printing Office, pp. 42, 43.

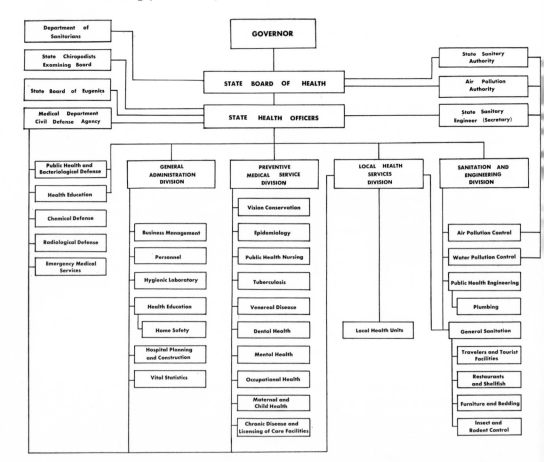

Fig. 71. Health services in a moderate-sized state. The diagram reveals that more limited services and a less complex organization exist in a state with a population of moderate size. Even states with a small population can afford an adequate state health department as an investment in the health of all of its citizens. (Courtesy Oregon State Board of Health.)

lations to carry out the provisions of the law. In consequence boards have adopted sanitary codes which have the effect of law. In practice the provisions of the sanitary code are recommended to the board by its professional staff. Courts have upheld the power of the board to enact rules and regulations but have ruled that the board cannot go outside of health matters nor can it delegate its power to another agency.

Quasijudicial powers. The quasijudicial powers are inherent in the power of the board to summon before it persons alleged to have violated state health regulations. If necessary, the board may summon witnesses. Hearings may be preliminary to granting or revoking a license. Of course, since the courts are the final arbiters of judicial matters, the individual concerned has the right to contest the action of the board by filing an appeal in court.

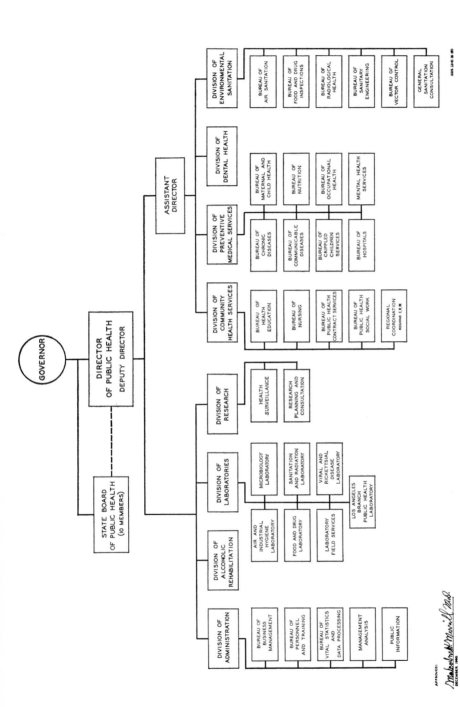

Fig. 72. Health services in a large state. This diagram illustrates the magnitude of services and organization of the official state health agency of the state with a large population. (Courtesy State of California, Department of Public Health, December, 1960.)

Administrative functions. The administrative functions of the state board of health are delegated to a staff of full-time professional specialists. The chief administrative officer is the state health commissioner although other designations than commissioner are used. He is usually appointed by the governor upon recommendation of the state board of health. Appointment for a term of six years is typical although appointment may be for an indefinite term. The state health commissioner usually has a medical degree and, in addition, training and experience in public health work. His principal functions can be enumerated briefly: (1) general administration, (2) recommendation of health legislation, rules, and regulations for consideration by the board, (3) appointment of personnel, (4) supervision of the bureaus, (5) preparation of the budget, (6) enforcement of health regulations, and (7) contact with other official agencies, with nonofficial organizations, and with the general public.

Although the administrative organization of the principal health agency varies somewhat from state to state, the usual administrative arrangement follows the scalar principle of the functional units in steps as in a scale. At the top of the pyramid is the commissioner, the primary units are divisions, and the divisions are divided into sections (or bureaus). A director is in charge of each division. The director is responsible for the professional and other personnel working in his division. Each division represents a specific function or area of health service. Sections will have a head as administrator.

Vital statistics section. The vital statistics section may well be called the health statistics recording unit of the state. In almost every state his agency collects reports of births, sicknesses, marriages, and deaths. The reports may be routed through the county clerks, but the state vital statistics section is the permanent custodian of these official records. The state board of health decrees which diseases are reportable. To facilitate reporting, standard forms for reporting births, marriages, divorces, diseases, and deaths are furnished by the state.

Local health administration division. The local health administration division functions in the coordination of state and local health efforts. It also supervises grants to local health departments and exercises general supervision over local health units.

Epidemiology section. The epidemiology section is responsible for the control of communicable diseases, generally including venereal diseases. Rules and regulations governing disease control are adopted by the board upon the recommendation of this division. Actual administration of these regulations is largely a local function although the state section carries on special epidemiological investigations. During a severe epidemic the state section may advise local officials or even assume control. The services of the state health laboratory are always available in the administration of the activities of communicable disease control.

Sanitation and engineering division. The sanitation and engineering division has extensive responsibilities. Municipalities construct and maintain their own water works and sewage disposal plants, but the law provides that plans for these plants or for alterations must be approved by the state sanitation and engineering division. Actually the division provides municipalities with advisory services and checks the operation of municipal water and sewage plants. Sanitary supervision of public swimming pools, public resorts and tourist camps, highways, public buildings, restaurants, and even milk supplies are responsibilities of the state sanitation and engineering division.

Laboratory section. The laboratory section is often designated the state health laboratory. This agency, through its laboratory facilities, provides services for diagnostic, confirmation, and release purposes. It examines water and milk samples as well as smears, blood, and other specimens submitted by competent persons. Usually all of these services are given without charge. Some state health laboratories furnish biologics and pharmaceuticals (e.g., silver nitrate) without charge to physicians. Some state laboratories have their own facilities for producing biologics.

Maternal and child health section. The maternal and child health section in some states is called the section of nursing. Public health nurses are registered nurses who have had additional training in public health. In the field of maternal and child health they serve essentially as health counselors. Although most of the staff of the maternal and child health section are nurses, other personnel frequently include physicians, dentists, health educators, dietitians, and social workers. Activities cover a broad field of health promotion.

Health education by means of pamphlets, demonstrations, exhibits, lectures, and films	Organization of volunteer health services
	Supervision of midwives
	School health nursing services
Maternity consultation clinics	Cooperation with local health agencies
Dental clinics	Well-child clinics
Nutrition classes	Immunization clinics
Health conferences and demonstrations	

Health education section. The health education section has responsibility for one of the most difficult and most important services in modern public health promotion. Centered around a state health library, the section functions in cooperation with both official and voluntary agencies. Periodic bulletins, films, leaflets, posters, news items, demonstrations, lectures, and other instructional devices are the products of the health education section.

Dental health section. The dental health section promotes dental health through demonstrations, lectures, clinics, and other health education measures. The division does not provide dental services to individual citizens but strives to interest the citizen in his own dental health problem.

Mental health section. The mental health section is a relatively recent unit of the state department of health. Its major emphasis is upon the mental health of normal individuals although it is concerned also with the prevention of mental disorder. A recent development is the operation of child guidance clinics. Its staff of phychiatrists, psychologists, health educators, and social workers strives to acquaint the general public with the possibilities and needs in mental health promotion. Through cooperation with other agencies, mental health knowledge and consulting service are brought within the reach of the general public.

Occupational health section. The occupational health section is occasionally found in some agency other than the state department of health. Some industrial processes are hazardous to workers. Not only occupational injuries, but also occupational diseases are the concern of the occupational health section. State health rules and regulations governing dangerous conditions in industry have the force of law. Occupational diseases must be reported in some states. Hazards must be corrected. In addition to this regulating responsibility the section conducts research in problems of health in industry and provides a consultation service for industries seeking solutions to health hazards peculiar to their operations.

Other state health sections and divisions. Other state health sections and divisions will be found in certain states. However, in these divisions, as in those discussed, the service to the individual citizen is an indirect one. Actually various patterns of administrative organization are to be found. Oregon, an average-sized state of average per capita wealth, has a different state health organization than California, a state with a large population. Historical development, special needs, and expediency determine the setup of the state department of health.

In many states too many administrative subdivisions result in inefficiency and confusion. At times additional sections have been created merely to give rank to some staff member. In some states functions other than health have been assigned to the state health department. Registration of embalmers and of podiatrists is important to the citizens of the state but is hardly the function of the state board of health.

LOCAL HEALTH SERVICES

Varied community health agencies. The organizations in a community that contribute to and promote health are many and varied. It is difficult to have a far-reaching well-balanced health program in any community without a well-organized health department adequately financed and staffed, working with other agencies in the community. Beyond the organizations themselves, which work to prevent disease and to promote wholesome living conditions, there are also other local groups concerned with the customs, the habits, and the daily life activities of people as they bear upon the welfare and health of the community as a whole. In both these lines of social effort, public approval and support are essential.

If the community is interested and informed, the cooperation of physicians, dentists, other professional groups, and the public will provide ordinances and laws and will mobilize financial and personal resources in backing the program.

If the community is interested, there will be facilities for wholesome play and recreation, opportunities for music and dramatics, art projects in various forms, various activities in adult education, and wholesome social life generally.

There are many groups in a community interested in some phase of public health. Besides the official health department, schools, recreation groups, civic

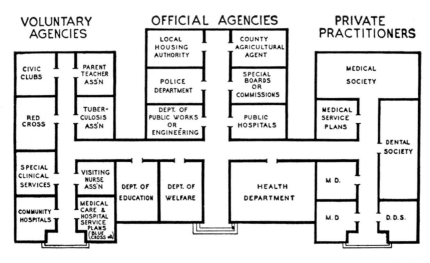

Fig. 73. Levels of health organization. The ground floor of the health structure—local official and voluntary agencies and private practitioners. (Courtesy U. S. Public Health Service.)

and welfare organizations, various voluntary groups, professional organizations of physicians, dentists, and nurses, as well as others, make important contributions to community public health. To avoid waste and duplication, to avoid misunderstanding, to provide a health forum, and to mobilize the community's health resources, a central council may be organized.

The health council. At the local level health councils have been effective in coordinating the health work of the various agencies concerned. Health councils can do community health planning, provide a means of mutual assistance, and integrate efforts for a well-rounded attack upon community health problems. Through their membership health councils may collect valuable data, organize programs, and provide for concerted efforts in such things as surveying local health needs and resources, pooling the experiences of the various agencies, and attempting to plan ways to meet unfavorable situations and thus reduce waste, duplication, and friction. Communities should investigate the possibilities of establishing a health council.

Various types of councils exist. Among these are health councils that represent official and voluntary agencies, chamber of commerce health councils at both national and local levels, neighborhood health committees, block leader plan of the Civil Defense organization, and public health committees at municipal and county levels.

It is expected that leadership will come from the health department, but professional groups, social agencies, voluntary agencies, schools, churches, women's clubs, parent-teacher associations, and civic clubs have a definite interest in health. Programs may be initiated and directed under different auspices—health department, public schools, jointly by school and health department, and sometimes by

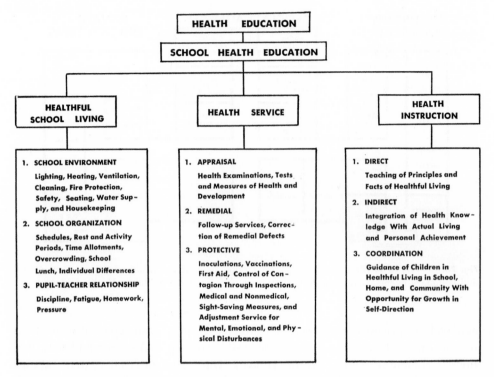

Fig. 74. School health program. In the modern American school, health is something more than a mere academic subject. The promotion of the child's present health, as well as an awareness of his future health needs, is a concern of the school. (Courtesy L. J. Sparks, Willamette University, Salem, Ore.)

voluntary agencies. Community health education is fundamental to a successful community health program. Every agency or group engaged in health work must educate the public to the services offered and the need for these services. Community of effort in health education yields the most effective results.

School health program. The public schools assume a responsibility for the health of the child while he is in school as well as an obligation in solving many of the health problems of the community.

Public schools make a very definite and real contribution to community health, not only through their own responsibilities to the children, but also through their cooperation with health authorities and other organizations in the community. The combined approach of the home, school, and community to problem solving produces fruitful results.

The school has six definite responsibilities that operate in three areas: (1) health promotion, (2) health protection, and (3) assistance in the prevention and alleviation of physical defects and sickness when discovered. These include provision for the healthful school environment, a health guidance program, the care of an emergency health condition, the teaching of scientific health information, the development of sound health habits and attitudes, and the adaptation of the school program to the exceptional child.*

Scope of school health program. The scope of the school health program has been stated† to include six policies. The first is to provide for healthful school living through standards for safety and sanitation, adequate food service, maintenance of teachers' health, and promotion of mental and emotional health of teachers and pupils. The second is to provide health instruction in the entire curriculum, especially in courses designed for the elementary, junior, and senior high schools, and through school participation in community health education. The third aims to provide services for health protection and improvement through first aid for emergencies, prevention and control of communicable disease, and health appraisal, guidance, and assistance. The fourth emphasizes the hygienic aspects of physical education and seeks to adapt programs to individual needs, to secure adequate activity programs, and to develop health safeguards in athletics. The fifth designates the education and care of handicapped persons through identification of the need, adjustment of programs, adjustment of individuals, special classes, and properly prepared teachers. The sixth denotes the needed qualifications of health education personnel.

Organizations promoting health through recreation. Recreational opportunities are offered by a large number of agencies. They vary markedly as to type; some serve their members only and others the entire community. Some offer only one type of activity; others offer a wide scope. Some exist for private gain and are known as commercial recreation; others are private or municipal ones which serve and aim primarily for the enrichment of life. Recreation may be the total interest of the agency, or it may be incidental to other activity.

Agencies existing for recreation may be classified as follows: official agencies which are maintained at federal, state, and local levels; private agencies which are maintained exclusively for the membership of the club, membership usually being on a selective basis; semipublic agencies usually supported by a private fund but not exclusive and not necessarily affording an opportunity for recreation solely on a membership basis; and commercial recreational agencies catering to a public demand for leisure time activity.

Most recreation, to be effective, must take place more or less regularly; hence, facilities must be located centrally and be readily accessible to the population served. Facilities provided by state and federal agencies usually take care of only sporadic recreation and cater primarily to tourists or the development of some natural recreational asset.

---

*American Association of School Administrators: Health in Schools, Twentieth Year Book, Washington, D. C., 1951, National Education Association, pp. 12-13.
†Suggested School Health Policies, A Charter for School Health, A Report by the National Committee on School Health Policies. Prepared by the National Committee on School Health Policies of the National Conference for Cooperation in Health Education and published by the National Education Association and the American Medical Association, Washington, D. C., and Chicago, 1956,

Recreation at the local level is highly diversified and offers a variety of activity. This is to be expected, for here the everyday life needs of the people must be met. The park board, recreation commission, and school recreation department are usually the official community agencies providing recreation programs. These agencies, as indicated, provide a wide variety of outlets. Other official agencies in the community that have recreational significance are the public library, museum, and art gallery.

Playgrounds and indoor recreational activities are the same whether under the auspices of the park board, recreation commission, or the school system. The park department usually controls large tracts of land which are ideal for games and sports, picnicking, rowing and canoeing, water sports, hiking, horseback riding, golf, tennis, archery, baseball, and other games. Band concerts, zoos, aquariums, botanical gardens, pageants, and outdoor theater activity are often found in well-developed park recreational programs.

The development of recreation agencies. The recreation department is a recent development; its sole purpose is to develop recreation for the people. Usually it is operated as a commission and tends to coordinate and utilize all civic facilities. It has a wide application of service, and its program is usually extensive and varied.

The public schools, in addition to providing the in-school physical education and recreation program for the students, often conducts a community recreation program for adults. Activities in public schools center around playgrounds, athletic fields, and indoor recreational centers. In many cities the only indoor recreational facilities available are found in the public schools.

Private recreation agencies include industries, churches, civic and fraternal organizations, and clubs of one type or another. Semipublic agencies include the Young Men's Christian Association, Young Women's Christian Association, settlement houses, Boy Scouts of America, Girl Scouts of the U. S. A., Camp Fire Girls, Young Men's Hebrew Association, Young Women's Hebrew Association, and others. A recent development has been youth hostels which stimulate tours and extended trips. Overnight facilities are organized and supervised by this organization.

Various commercial agencies exist for recreational purposes. Large sums of money are involved in these programs. The primary motive back of the commercial agency is profit for the owner. Much of this is entertainment rather than recreation. Amusements of various kinds, including motion pictures, radio, theaters, night clubs, and dance halls, are examples. In addition to these, professional prize fighting, horse racing, dog racing, as well as bicycle, motorcycle, and automobile racing, are examples of sports developed primarily as entertainment for spectators.

Commercial recreation has provided a definite service in certain areas when municipal development of facilities has been inadequate. These include swimming pools, bathing beaches, tennis courts, golf courses, roller and ice skating rinks, bowling alleys, billiard parlors, and winter sports areas.

There is an urgent need for cooperative planning in recreation. Perhaps all of the services and agencies mentioned are necessary. There is need, however, for coordination, for control, and for development of a well-balanced program. In some instances there is perhaps too much emphasis on commercial recreation and professional sports which contribute to passive spectator entertainment rather than to active participation recreation.

Health contribution of civic and welfare organizations. There are many civic and welfare organizations which have charters for stated purposes, such as social, civic, fraternal, recreational, educational, professional, religious, etc. A partial list of some of these organizations shows their magnitude and comprehensiveness.

Church	Young Women's Christian Association
Salvation Army	American Farm Bureau
Service clubs (Rotary, etc.)	Granges
Fraternal organizations	Blue Cross Hospital Insurance Plan
Women's clubs	4-H Clubs
Parent-Teacher Associations	American Red Cross
Boy Scouts of America	Chambers of commerce
Girl Scouts of the U.S.A.	Labor unions
Woman's Christian Temperance Union	Safety councils
Young Men's Christian Association	Rural health councils
American Legion	

There are at least 10,000 organizations of this type that use some of their funds and efforts on health programs of different kinds. In many cases the programs of these groups are entered into without the advice and counsel of a professional staff and often with little regard to the general health program of the community. It is to be expected that often duplication of effort results. The health program of these organizations is of two types—service for the membership of the organization and community-wide service.

The work of these organizations could be much more effective if the counsel and advice of the official agencies in the community were sought. Since many of these agencies operate at national, state, and local levels, supervision and counsel by the national organization would be helpful.

These organizations at a local level tend to provide help where it is needed. Their programs are difficult to distinguish from welfare activities in many cases. The entire gamut of public health activities is covered in some form or another by these various organizations. The campaigns of various service and fraternal organizations for the Crippled Children's Society are outstanding, and a laudable contribution is made in this area. Medical and dental clinics, public health nursing services, child care centers, day nurseries, hot lunches for schools, camps, vaccination programs, and purchases of mechanical aids for the handicapped are rather common projects.

The worth of this work to the community is not only in the contribution to health and welfare directly, but also indirectly in a health education program that informs a large number of people of the factors involved in health and welfare. Thus indirectly the health, physical, and moral tones of the community are often raised.

With a constantly informed public there is a tendency to mobilize the personnel and facilities of the community to meet the needs more quickly and more intelligently. When sustained programs have been maintained, problems have often arisen which necessitated professional advice. Hence over the years sustained projects have become better organized, have less lost motion, utilize professional advice, and result in cooperation with other groups and pooling of resources, experience, and funds.

There is much misdirected effort, duplication of projects, and waste of money; yet, on the other hand, much is accomplished. These programs and processes are quite in keeping with our American way of life. Through experience, consultation, and advice they constitute another medium for disseminating health information to the general public. This in turn results in a public that is ready and willing to participate and contribute to a sound, well-developed, directed, and organized health and welfare program.

These groups are often interested in health and welfare legislation although this is not a primary concern of these organizations; yet they provide an informed, intelligent, and usually influential group that has given considerable aid in getting health and welfare legislation passed by endorsement of legislative acts, by petitions, by contacts with legislators, and by other means.

As projects get underway and become established and accepted by the community, they should be assumed by the official agency. Whereas rural areas are served by several organizations, community groups should extend their services to surrounding rural areas. Rural health councils have been successful in coordinating and mobilizing forces for the betterment of health in rural areas.

General community health services. The explosive population growth and the continued concentration of people, production, and services in metropolitan areas are creating health problems of increasing magnitude and complexity. Some of the community environmental health problems include air pollution, water pollution, radiological hazards, occupational hazards, and community sanitation problems. At present the most urgent community problems are polluted water and air, open refuse dumps, substandard housing, overflowing septic tanks, and "urban sprawl." In addition other difficulties—social, moral, economic, and political—are engendered.

Community hygiene in the United States assumes that, although individuals have responsibility for their own health and well-being, the community has a vested interest in the health of its citizens. Community life itself imposes hazards upon the individual which the individual alone is unable to meet. The health and well-being of any community depends upon both individual and community action. Communities have the authority and the responsibility to provide certain health facilities and services for their citizens.

Public water supply. Furnishing water fit to drink is an accepted responsibility of an American community although many citizens regard water as a commodity and its sale as not a proper function of government. Yet almost all cities in the United States operate municipal water plants to furnish necessary water for household, industrial, and other purposes.

The ultimate source of water is rain. As it falls to the earth, that which re-mains in lakes, rivers, and streams or in shallow wells and springs is classed as surface water. Some of it percolates through the soil for some distance and is classed as ground water. In the usual terrain, a supply with a water table deeper than 25 feet and not available for vegetative growth is classed as a ground water supply. Cities usually plan on a water supply which will yield 100 gallons per capita per day. Some industrial communities base their plans on 150 gallons per capita per day. About 46% of the cities in the United States use ground water as the city supply. Cities under 50,000 usually seek such a water supply, and health authorities favor a ground water supply. Yet industry usually favors surface water. The reasons are apparent when one considers the merits and demerits of ground water and surface water.

Ground water	Surface water
Merits	Merits
1. Free from color	1. Abundant
2. Free from turbidity-suspended particles	2. Low mineral content
	Demerits
3. Free from pollution	1. Usually polluted
4. Free from contamination	2. Usually contaminated
5. Cool (48° to 51° F.)	3. Turbid
Demerits	4. Highly colored
1. Inadequate amounts	
2. Highly mineralized	

Ground water. As a municipal supply, ground water is usually safe. Low capital outlay as well as low operating cost makes ground water an extremely cheap commodity. Test wells will outline the amount of ground water that can be obtained for city use. Drillers locate water-bearing gravel beds of at least a yard in depth. A gravel bed is actually a natural reservoir for water. Usually gravel beds at different levels are located. If water is obtained from two or more different levels, the community is better assured of an uninterrupted flow of water.

Deep wells are usually drilled and are spaced 100 to 1000 feet apart. They are usually cased with tightly fitting pipes which vary from 6 to 24 inches in diameter. At the bottom of the pipe a brass strainer permits the water to filter in from the gravel bed. Electrically operated centrifugal turbine pumps are used to raise the water into a receiving tank. From here another pump may force the water into the storage or pressure tank. Usually a building houses the pumps and other equipment.

There is nothing mysterious about the sand that purifies water. Sand grains serve as particles to which bacteria may attach and secrete a sticky covering. As some bacteria form a sticky covering over sand grains, those bacteria which follow stick in this biological film. Thus, as water percolates into the ground,

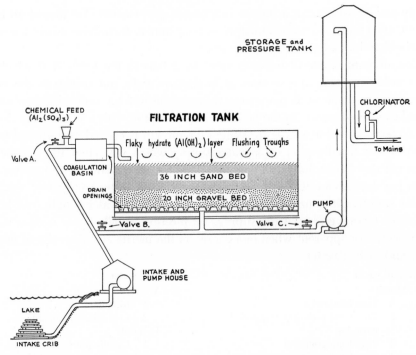

Fig. 75. Schematic diagram of a water purification plant. The rapid sand filtration method uses an artificial chemical precipitate to intercept bacteria. During operation, valves **A** and **C** remain open and valve **B** is closed. To clean away the hydrate layer, valves **A** and **C** are closed and valve **B** is opened, thus reversing the direction of flow. The hydrate floats into troughs and is run off, and the whole cleaning process requires but an hour's time.

these sticky films filter out bacteria. However, ground water may be contaminated from impurities in the underground stream, from leakage along the sides of the well casing, or from seepage of surface water at the top of the well because of inadequate surface protection.

Well water is usually clear enough for effective chlorination although chlorination of ground water is not always necessary. Usually cities with ground water not needing chlorination will have a chlorination unit standing by in case of an emergency. Water samples for bacterial analysis are taken at least once a month.

The bacteriologist does not seek specific pathogens in a water sample. He plates 1 ml. of the sample, diluted 1:1000 with distilled water, and incubates (37° C.) the plate for forty-eight hours. He then examines the plate for colonies of *Escherichia coli*, nonpathogenic organisms found in the human colon. The inference is that if *Escherichia coli* are present in water, human discharges are getting into the water, and the danger exists that pathogens from the same source will eventually get into the supply.

Surface water. Surface water usually requires treatment, and over 20% of the population in the United States drink water that has passed through a filtration plant.

The rapid sand filtration plant is an American development, although the European slow sand filtration plant is still used by a few American cities. The rapid sand method uses an artificially formed chemical layer to intercept bacteria, whereas the slow sand method depends upon a film formed by bacteria. In either method, if the water is turbid and contains considerable sediment, a preliminary settling tank or chamber is used to hold the water for a period of time to permit the sediment to settle to the bottom of the chamber. This settling chamber precedes the filtration bed.

In rapid sand filtration the water from the settling chamber flows through a mixing chamber where a coagulant is introduced into the stream. Aluminum sulfate, $Al_2(SO_4)_3$, is frequently used as the coagulant although other chemicals are used. As the aluminum sulfate comes in contact with the calcium carbonate in the water, an insoluble flaky hydrate, $Al(OH)_3$, is formed. As the water flows into the filtration tank, this flaky hydrate begins to settle down and carries suspended particles with it.

The filtration bed is composed of a 36-inch sand bed upon a 20-inch gravel bed. On top of the sand of the filtration bed the aluminum hydrate and organic matter form a gelatinous mass. As the water percolates through this tough gelatinous layer, much suspended matter, including 95% of the bacteria, is removed. A filtration tank the size of an ordinary classroom of 24×30 feet can filter 2,000,000 gallons per day. This is forty times the output of an equal sized tank used in the slow sand filtration method.

After a time the upper layer of the filter bed becomes clogged, and the water flow and filtering are retarded. Then the flow of water is reversed and is forced back up through the gravel and sand bed. The sand particles become suspended in the water, the grains of sand dance about and rub against each other, and thus clean and scour one another. The gelatinous mass and the organic matter collected on top of the sand rise to the water surface and are carried away by overflow troughs. This method is time saving, requiring but an hour of one person's time.

After filtration, decontamination is advisable, and chlorination is the usual method. If chlorine is to be effective, the water must be clear. By electrolytic decomposition of chlorine salts, commercial firms produce gaseous chlorine which is sold in sealed tanks. A specially designed valvular device automatically admits a controlled amount of chloride gas into a small auxiliary stream of water. In water chlorine forms hypochlorous acid which precipitates proteins of bacteria. This highly chlorinated small stream enters the principal water main where a chlorine concentration between 0.2 and 0.3 ppm will destroy all pathogenic organisms. At this concentration the chlorine cannot be detected by either smell or taste. In some emergencies a chlorine concentration of 0.5 ppm will be maintained. At this concentration water consumers can detect the chlorine.

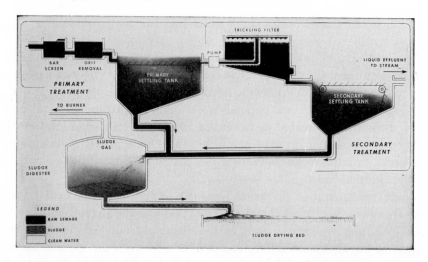

Fig. 76. Diagram of sewage treatment plant. A bar screen and a grit chamber remove materials in suspension. The primary settling tank permits organic matters to settle out, and the sludge is passed on to the sludge digester for decomposition. Trickling filters permit oxidation of putrescible matters to stable compounds. The secondary settling tank completes the oxidation of the wastes and permits the final clear effluent to flow to a final place of disposal such as a river or lake. Dried sludge from the drying bed is used as a fertilizer. (Courtesy Oregon State Board of Health.)

However, even at higher concentrations chlorine causes no known physiological effects.

Sewage disposal. All liquid wastes from dwelling establishments are classed as sewage. Domestic sewage is that from dwelling establishments, and industrial sewage consists of the various liquid wastes that commercial firms produce. Obviously there is no uniformity in the composition of sewage. If sewage were one thing, we doubtless would have a chemical formula for it.

Communities throughout the nation have accepted responsibility for removing sewage by constructing sewerage systems which remove all liquid wastes from the home, street cleanings, surface drainage, and other sources. However, with the rapid expansion in population and industrialization in the United States, merely disposing of sewage has not been enough. Sewage must undergo treatment to remove both bacteria and matters in suspension and solution before it is permitted to flow into natural waters. Because of untreated sewage, many of our streams are merely open sewers. Sewage may harbor organisms which cause typhoid fever, paratyphoid fever, cholera, dysentery, and hookworm. In addition raw sewage may be damaging to agricultural, industrial, and recreational interests adjacent to a polluted stream.

Many enlightened communities have recognized the necessity for sewage treatment and have constructed sewage treatment plants. However, the seriousness of stream pollution and the procrastination of many communities have forced federal and state governments to compel communities to treat sewage before dumping it into natural waters. The U. S. Public Health Service is responsible

Fig. 77. Modern sewage disposal plant for a community of less than 5000 people. Note the two open clarifiers or settling tanks, and to the left, the two sludge digestion tanks. Only primary treatment is carried out here. (Courtesy Oregon State Board of Health.)

for the control of interstate stream pollution, where as the state health department or other agency is responsible within the state.

Sewage treatment. The treatment of sewage makes use of those processes by which the decomposable organic matter is removed or oxidized, and the pathogenic bacteria are removed or killed. Although complete purification of sewage is possible, such complete treatment is rarely necessary. The extent of the treatment depends upon the local situation. In general the effluent from a sewage treatment plant should not create a nuisance or cause conditions offensive to the community it serves or to other people. In addition the treatment must be sufficiently effective to prevent sewage from contaminating natural waters, destroying marine life, injuring livestock, or decreasing property values along the river or other disposal terminal.

Different methods of sewage treatment are used, but the most typical municipal sewage treatment involves the series of processes which follow:

I. Primary treatment (to remove suspended particles)
    A. Screening—Removes floating objects, e.g., sticks
    B. Sedimentation—Settles and decomposes suspended particles
        1. Grit chambers—Slow down velocity of flow and permit sand and other suspended solids to settle to the bottom. Two chambers, used alternately, provide opportunity for cleaning out accumulated grit from bottom of chamber.
        2. Tank treatment—The typical sedimentation tank permits organic matter to settle but leaves the digestion of sludge to later treat-

ment. An Imhoff tank permits organic matter in suspension to settle to the bottom where anaerobic bacteria can decompose it. By
separating settling from bacterial activity the one action does not
interfere with the other. In some plants a coagulant (alum, ferric
chloride, etc.) is added which speeds settling. Accumulated sludge
may have to be pumped from the bottom of the tank.

II. Secondary treatment (oxidation of organic matter)
  A. Filtration—Permits aerobic bacteria to oxidize putrescible matters to
      stable compounds
    1. Trickling sand filter—Consists of a bed of crushed stone, gravel, or
        similar materials, with underdrains. Sewage is sprayed on top of
        the bed from nozzles or perforated pipes that rotate just above the
        stone bed. Dosing and resting periods are alternated. Accumulat-
        ing organisms oxidize wastes to stabilize nitrates. Reduced action
        in winter will be balanced by higher oxygen content of the cold
        water.

III. Final treatment (disposal of effluents)
     Treatment should reduce suspended particles and biological oxygen de-
     mand sufficiently so that the receiving stream will assimilate the effluent.
     The nature of the receiving water should indicate the condition of the
     effluent. If the stream is not used for drinking or fishing or other recrea-
     tion purpose, the effluent need not be of high quality. If the stream serves
     as a municipal water supply, the effluent from the sewage treatment plant
     should be clear and almost devoid of bacteria.
  A. Dilution—When an ocean, a large lake, or a large stream is the receiv-
      ing body, no further treatment of the sewage effluent may be neces-
      sary, especially if the lake or stream is not the source of a public
      water supply.
  B. Decontamination—As a supplement to normal treatment, it is often
      necessary to chlorinate sewage effluent, especially during the summer
      months when dissolved oxygen and water level are both low. From
      10 to 20 ppm of chlorine is added, which will provide a chlorine resid-
      ual above 0.2 ppm.

IV. Sludge treatment and disposal
  A. Digestion—Sludge digestion is necessary to produce a stabilized un-
      objectionable final form. A specially constructed tank permits anaero-
      bic bacteria to reduce the sewage solids by 50%. The digestion process
      is basically the completion of both the nitrogen cycle and the car-
      bon cycle.
  B. Disposal—Digested wet sludge is layered about 1 foot thick over a
      6-inch layer of sand supported by gravel. Liquids filter through the
      bed to drain tile. During the summer, sludge dries sufficiently in two
      weeks to permit the sludge cake to be removed and used as a fertilizer.

Garbage and refuse disposal. An accumulation of garbage and rubbish is a menace to public health, utilizes valuable space, causes nuisances, creates fire hazards, and produces unsightly conditions. This is generally recognized, and municipal governments have assumed responsibility for the collection and disposal of garbage and other wastes. It is largely municipal housekeeping.

Disposal of garbage and refuse depends somewhat upon local factors and the location of a community. Some coastal towns carry garbage out to sea and dump it. Inland cities dispose of garbage by reduction, hog feeding, incineration, open burning, sanitary fills, dumps, or converting to sewage.

Reduction consists in cooking garbage in large steam kettles to recover grease and cattle food products. Many reduction plants are being abandoned because of odor and high operating cost.

Hog feeding as a garbage disposal method is frowned upon by health officials because of the spread of trichinosis, unsanitary feeding lots, insect and vermin breeding areas, and foul odors.

Incineration in adequate plants with competent operators is a method of garbage and refuse disposal highly recommended by health authorities.

Sanitary fills and dumps are subject to many objectionable conditions unless they are properly planned and supervised. Too often fills and dumps act as breeding places for rats, mice, and insects.

Converting garbage to sewage by grinding it before discharging it into the sewerage system is a successful method of disposal. Municipal sewage disposal plants are able to handle this additional load without jeopardizing the operation of the plant. In addition to the numerous cities in which garbage is converted to sewage, over 250,000 household grinders are in operation in the United States. Jasper, Indiana, makes it possible for all city householders to have a grinder unit. This plan has interesting possibilities and may make the garbage can obsolete.

Hospitals. The hospital, which in the past has been considered an institution of last resort, in modern thinking is a place of first resort and for emergencies. The old conception of the hospital has affected its location in various areas. In many cases it has resulted in a large portion of the population being unserved or at a considerable distance from the hospital.

Within a generation tremendous changes have taken place in the hospital. The changes have ranged from hospitals with a few beds to accommodate emergency patients (many operations were performed in the home, and little or no nursing service, except that provided by the patient's family, was available) to the modern hospital with equipment, facilities, and services to make possible the application of new advancements in medicine and surgery. In addition the hospital has been accepted by the public as a necessary adjunct to good medical service. In 1951, one out of every nine Americans was admitted to the hospital; in 1961 the ratio was one to eight. Hospital admissions in 1961 were 23,375,000 persons, an increase of 405,000 over 1960.

The advances in surgery, the development of the laboratory and modern hospital equipment including the x-ray machine, surgeries, laboratories, heliotherapy, and hydrotherapy, the inclusion and scientific training of technicians including nurses, laboratory workers, physical therapists, occupational therapists, and social workers all indicate advances in hospital care, treatment, and usage. This is evidence of a demand and realization by the public for the necessity for these expanded services. With the extension of the services so that more and more of the population is served and with the increase in the number of beds in tax-maintained hospitals and in privately owned hospitals, the cost of medical care has increased (actually medical care costs have not risen so fast or so high as other consumer costs), not only because of the amount of hospitalization utilized, but also because of the cost of hospital care itself. Realistically the increase in the cost of hospitalization is overbalanced by the increased services available and provided. The number of days that a patient stays in a hospital has been markedly lowered and thus the over-all costs of many illnesses and surgical treatments have been reduced. This also reduces the need for additional beds because of an increase in the turnover of patients. Every indication points toward the fact that hospital costs will continue to increase.

Hospitals provide four principal types of service: general, mental, tuberculosis, and long-term care which includes special nursing homes. The shortages and needs for hospitals are distributed unevenly, both geographically and service-wise. Inhabitants of small cities have been at a disadvantage with respect to hospitalization. The volume of construction has been much smaller in low-income

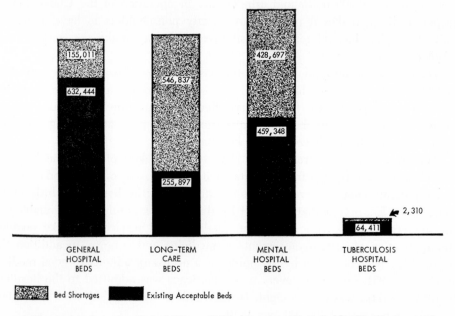

Fig. 78. Hospital beds in the United States, 1955. (Courtesy U. S. Public Health Service.)

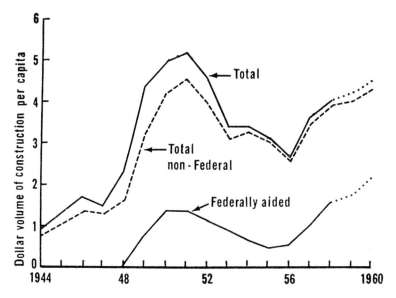

Fig. 79. Chart shows the value of all hospital construction in the United States and its territories, at constant prices, from 1944 to 1960. Hospital construction has increased markedly since 1956 but is still inadequate because of obsolescence and an expanding population. (Courtesy U. S. Public Health Service.)

regions. This is being partially corrected through a program of federal assistance for hospital construction so that every county or community in the United States will have adequate hospital facilities.

In 1962 the total additional need for acceptable beds was 1,132,855 beds or 45% over those available. The largest increase in hospital beds since 1955 is in facilities for long-term care, with an increase from 45,000 to 255,897 acceptable beds and 546,837 additional ones needed. Acceptable beds in tuberculosis hospitals had decreased from 86,000 to 64,411 with 2,310 additional needed. This illustrates the great progress in the control of tuberculosis and the rapid increase of the degenerative diseases.

About one third of the cost of all hospital construction is met through the Hill-Burton program and nearly all this is in low-income areas. The Hill-Burton program has benefited teaching hospitals, improved design of hospitals and related health facilities, initiated new and better hospital licensure laws, increased the minimum standards of hospital operation and maintenance, and directed attention to related health facilities. The cost of all projects approved for federal assistance was in excess of $3,500,000,000. Sixty-eight per cent of all approved applications were for general hospitals. There has been a tremendous increase in hospital plans between 1946 and 1962. Large as this increase appears to be, an expanding population and mounting obsolescence have held this gain to less than 0.5 bed per 1000 of the population for acceptable facilities.

During the postwar era there has been substantial new hospital construction.

Yet in 1962 there were 1,412,000 acceptable beds and 332,648 nonacceptable beds with 1,132,855 additional needed. Federal hospitals that render service to civilians but do not provide community-wide service to the general public have a capacity of 126,000 beds in veterans' hospitals and about 8000 beds operated by the U. S. Public Health Service for merchant seamen and others. The U. S. Public Health Service now maintains hospitals for Indians.

Increasing attention is being given to related health facilities, in addition to hospitals, to provide communities with well-rounded comprehensive health services. Modern health care requires many facilities unthought of thirty years ago. These include facilities for prevention, treatment, diagnosis, extended care, and rehabilitation.

Increasing service to ambulatory patients is being provided by hospitals, clinics, and public health centers. These centers sponsor specialized service to psychiatric, heart, tuberculosis, cancer, and dental patients. States are beginning to bring general basic hospital services to the patient in his own community through the establishment of regional clinics and provision of diagnostic and treatment centers in general hospitals. Here again the problem is to render service in the small community.

The hospital is the hub around which many services in the community center. In addition to the usual care for acute and long-term illness under direct medical care, the community itself must provide additional facilities, such as nursing homes, convalescent homes, and diagnostic and treatment centers. In these facilities, skilled care not requiring hospital resources can be provided under medical supervision.

City health department. The establishment and maintenance of a health department has long been a recognized health service of local government. In 1798 Baltimore, Maryland, established the first-full time city health department in the United States. In 1952, 281 cities had full-time health departments. In 1911 Yakima County, Washington, organized the first full-time county health department. In 1952 of the 3070 counties in the United States, 1688 counties had full-time health service; some counties incorporated the service as part of a health district comprising two or more counties, and the remainder established their own county health department.

Many small communities still maintain part-time health officers, a practice to which there are many objections.

1. The person usually is not trained for the work. A competent physician is not necessarily trained in public health.
2. The position is a side line which is given incidental attention.
3. Difficulties arise when the health officer must impose isolation and quarantine regulations on his private clientele.
4. Other physicians contend that the health officer uses his official position to promote his private practice.
5. The position is frequently a political plum.

6. The salary is too low to attract the most capable persons.
7. Extra duties are too numerous to be handled adequately in a part-time schedule.

Full-time city health departments consist of a director, a sanitarian, public health nurses, and a clerk. Large cities may have additional personnel, such as assistant director, epidemiologist, statistician, and laboratory technician. The city council or commission usually serves as the board of health. Most cities under 20,000 population contend that they cannot afford to maintain a full-time health department, but such cities are usually interested in supporting a county unit or a district unit of two or more counties.

Health and disease are no respecters of city boundaries, and modern transportation and communication have made the city and surrounding rural area one community. It is only natural that county health departments should develop. Stimulated by grants from the Rockefeller Foundation and the U. S. Public Health Service, county health service has grown encouragingly since 1911.

Because the local health department is closest to the people, it is the most important of all health agencies. It is the one unit which gives a direct health service to the ordinary person in his everyday living. Every citizen should have the benefit of such service in the protection and promotion of his health. Yet there are more than 45,000,000 people in the United States for whom this service is not available.

Legal aspects of local health. The state delegates much of its powers to local governmental units to exercise within their own territorial limits. Legislatures grant home rule charters to cities, giving the cities self-rule in various fields including the power to create a health department. In addition county health departments are created in conformity with statutes passed by the state legislature. This power of the legislature to delegate health authority to local governmental subdivisions has been recognized by the courts.

A county health department usually has no jurisdiction over cities within the county which have full-time health departments although state laws may make other provisions. In recent years city and county health agencies have combined into a single county health unit.

Local health rules and regulations must be consistent with state laws, and within the territory embraced by the health department local health rules and regulations have the force of state regulations. Local regulations may impose higher standards than the state regulations, but they cannot be lower than state standards. Thus a local regulation can require a longer isolation period for a particular disease than does the state, but the local period of time cannot be less than that provided by state regulations. Many local health boards adopt the model sanitary code developed by the U. S. Public Health Service. Local health authority can extend beyond the corporate limits of the county or city only by specific state law conferring such extraterritorial jurisdiction.

Through the police power delegated to it by the state, a local board of health may pass regulations controlling or governing existing and anticipated health problems. Communicable disease control measures, sanitation of public milk supplies, water pollution, food handling, insect breeding areas, improper sewage disposal, and other health matters can be anticipated, and regulations can be enacted. However, many unhealthful conditions or practices cannot be anticipated and must be dealt with as a nuisance.

Nuisances. Anything is considered a nuisance which injures, annoys, damages, or otherwise causes inconvenience. It recognizes the maxim: So use your own as not to injure others. A number of nuisances by their nature are of health significance, but many nuisances, e.g., rubbish, untidy back yards, and noises, are of doubtful health significance.

Three classes of nuisances are recognized. (1) A public nuisance affects a considerable number of people by violating a public right, e.g., pollution of a public water supply. (2) A private nuisance affects only one person or family, e.g., an open sewer drain spilling onto another's property. (3) A mixed nuisance affects both an individual and a considerable number of persons, e.g., a factory creating obnoxious odors and smoke.

In the absence of a regulation covering an existing condition, the board of health may cite a person to appear before it to answer to the charge of maintaining a nuisance. Certain principles of responsibility apply to the matter of a nuisance.

1. Motive is not a consideration.
2. Time is not a consideration.
3. Possession of license to conduct a business does not excuse a nuisance.
4. Negligence is not an excuse.
5. Lack of financial means to correct the condition is not a valid excuse.
6. Municipalities are not responsible for a nuisance in connection with a governmental function but are responsible in connection with a proprietary function, e.g., piggery.
7. A nuisance is a basis for revocation of a license.

Three remedies are available for dealing with existing nuisances.

1. Summary abatement is necessary when immediate action is imperative because the condition constitutes an emergency impelling danger to human health or welfare. Before any action is taken, notice should be given to the person responsible for the condition to permit him to correct the nuisance. If this person fails to take the necessary action, summary abatement is in order. A health official or a private citizen must proceed with caution in taking direct action to correct a nuisance because he personally is liable for his acts. His actions should be *reasonable*. To snare a dog suspected of rabies and impound him would be a reasonable course, but to shoot the dog may be regarded by a court as unreasonable if the owner should sue the health official for the death of the dog.
2. Suit in equity to abate a nuisance is filed in the court of jurisdiction and

asks that an injunction be issued restraining the responsible party from continuing the condition. Public nuisances are usually abated in this manner when other means have failed. A group of citizens themselves may initiate action, but usually citizens request their health officials to initiate action.

3. Suit for damages may be filed in court asking financial compensation for the damage done to the plaintiff. If the suit is won and the court awards damages, a new cause of action can be presented as long as the nuisance continues.

Obviously the prevention of nuisances by wise legislation is the sensible approach. Tactful and diplomatic officials can correct many conditions through cooperation and understanding. A public health official who must rely repeatedly upon his ultimate authority is not the most competent person professionally.

County health department. Because of the growth of the full-time county health department in the past quarter century, a special consideration of its functions is in order. Basically its organization and function are analogous to those of the city health department, with some variations inherent in the governmental and territorial nature of the county.

County board of health. The typical county board of health is composed of nine nonpaid representative citizens appointed by the county board of supervisors or commissioners. If one member of the board of supervisors also serves on the health board, the supervisors will be kept informed of the activities of the board. Members of the board of health frequently serve staggered terms of six years. The board of health meets four times a year regularly and at other times as necessary. Board members are usually granted travel and other expenses incident to meeting attendance. The board of health establishes general health policies, adopts a sanitary code, passes special regulations, approves the budget, elects the director of the health program, and, upon recommendation of the director, appoints members of the health staff. The board may hold hearings on health conditions. Frequently the staff director serves as secretary of the board.

Finances. For the support of the county health department, finances are usually derived from three sources. The Social Security Act provided the U. S. Public Health Service with funds for subsidizing county health units. Originally the U. S. Public Health Service, through the state health department, granted aid on a matching basis for the establishment of a county health unit. To be eligible for a federal grant, the county health unit must be staffed by adequately trained full-time professional personnel. The reduced funds of the U. S. Public Health Service has necessitated a reduction in the amount of the grants from this source. Some states supplement the federal grant so that a county or district health unit is within the reach of all counties. With a minimum (in practice, the standard) of $2.50 per capita per annum adequate health service should be available to all if federal and state grants are available to the county or district.

The staff and functions. Full-time professional personnel actually carry out the

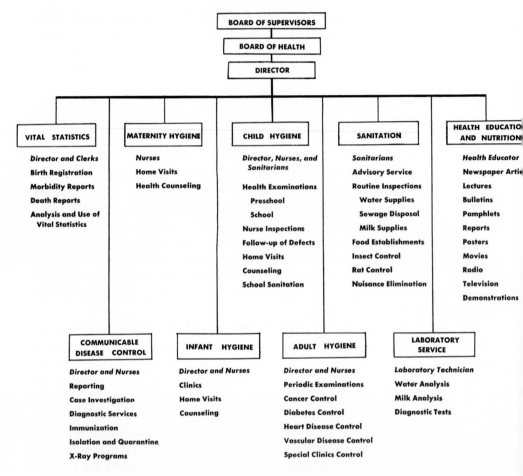

Fig. 80. Organization and services of a county health department. It will be noted that treatment of diseases is not an official function of the health department. Health promotion and protection are the responsibilities of the department.

health program for the people of the county. Any recommendation for the number of staff personnel is subject to modification to fit the territorial factors and population distribution of any specific county. A typical staff consists of the following members:

One health director	per	50,000	people
One public health nurse	per	6,000	people
One public health sanitarian	per	15,000	people
One public health educator	per	50,000	people
One laboratory technician	per	20,000	people
One sanitary engineer	per	60,000	people
One public health dentist	per	100,000	people
One clerk	per	20,000	people

A recent trend is the addition of an administrative assistant to relieve the director of many routine administrative and budgetary responsibilities. Thus more time is available to the director for medical supervision and service. It is estimated that the number of persons served by the director would increase from 50,000 to 75,000.

To translate this staff distribution into a practical county situation, a population of about 50,000 should be prescribed. If necessary, two or more counties should unite into a district health unit to approximate a total population of 50,-000. On this basis a staff and budget could be suggested, recognizing many variables in different situations which would require modifications in both staff and budget.

Health functions fall into certain basic categories: (1) vital statistics, (2) control of communicable diseases, (3) promotion of maternal, infant, child, and adult health, (4) environmental sanitation, (5) public health laboratory service, (6) health education, and (7) chronic disease program.

Vital statistics. Bookkeeping in public health is more important than in business. The figures in public health bookkeeping are those of births, illnesses, marriages, and deaths. Vital statistics or public health statistics consist in the application of statistical methods to the vital facts of human existence. To the health staff these data indicate the health needs of the county, the strengths and weaknesses of the health program, and the future emphasis in the department's activities. Health data are obtained by registration and enumeration.

Registration of certain facts is required by law. A physician must report every case he has of the communicable diseases which the health regulations list as reportable. However, to make reporting simple, health departments have a simple form on which the physician can quickly record the necessary data and mail without postage to the department. This franking privilege is made possible through the integration of local, state, and federal health efforts in the control of disease. Birth and death records are received from the county clerk.

Enumeration of health data is usually for a special purpose. Dental examinations, health examinations, milk samples, water samples, and special surveys are sources of data of significance.

Table 43. Health department budget for county of 50,000 population

Personnel	Salary ($)	Expense ($)	Total
1 director	14,500	1,500	
8 nurses	48,000	7,200	
2 laboratory technicians	11,000		
2 sanitarians	10,800	2,400	
1 health educator-nutritionist	5,400	1,000	
2 clerks	7,200		
Office		10,000	
Laboratory		3,000	
Miscellaneous		3,000	
	96,900	28,100	$125,000

Health data are a means to an end, not an end in themselves. Properly utilized in a statistical way, they paint a health picture not only of today but of health in progress. Certain rates are of particular importance.

1. Birth rate is the ratio of the number of live births per 1000 of the population. Thus:

$$\frac{\text{Number of live births}}{\text{Population}} \times 1000 = \text{Birth rate}$$

2. General death rate is the ratio of the number of deaths per 1000 of the population. Thus:

$$\frac{\text{Number of deaths}}{\text{Population}} \times 1000 = \text{Death rate}$$

3. Infant mortality rate is the ratio of the number of deaths under one year per 1000 live births. Thus:

$$\frac{\text{Number of deaths under one year}}{\text{Number of live births}} \times 1000 = \text{Infant mortality rate}$$

The infant mortality rate is the best single index of community environmental sanitation.

4. Maternal mortality rate is the ratio of the number of deaths of mothers due to childbirth per 1000 live births. Thus:

$$\frac{\text{Number of deaths of mothers (due to childbirth)}}{\text{Number of live births}} \times 10,000 = \text{Maternal mortality rate}$$

5. Specific death rate is the ratio of the number of deaths for a specific cause (or age group) per 100,000 population. Thus:

$$\frac{\text{Number of deaths (specific cause)}}{\text{Population}} \times 100,000 = \text{Specific death rate}$$

6. Fatality rate is the ratio of the number of deaths due to a specific cause to the number of cases. It is always expressed as a per cent. Thus:

$$\frac{\text{Number of deaths due to a specific cause}}{\text{Number of cases of the cause}} = \text{Fatality rate (\%)}$$

Control of communicable diseases. To prevent the spread of communicable diseases requires constant vigilance and a comprehensive well-planned program which includes certain general measures: (1) immunization, (2) public health instruction, (3) control of carriers, (4) sanitation, and (5) protection of water supplies.

Control measures concentrate on the infected individual and his environment: (1) recognition of disease, (2) prompt reporting of cases, (3) isolation procedures, (4) quarantine, (5) concurrent disinfection, and (6) terminal disinfection.

All communicable diseases are included in this program.

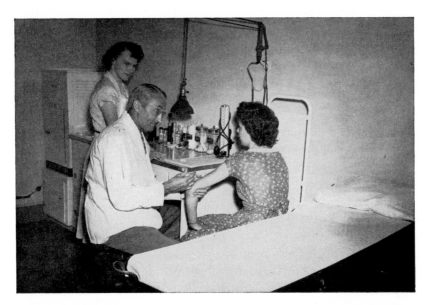

Fig. 81. Communicable disease control. Immunization is one of the important activities in communicable disease control of the local health department. (Courtesy Oregon State Board of Health.)

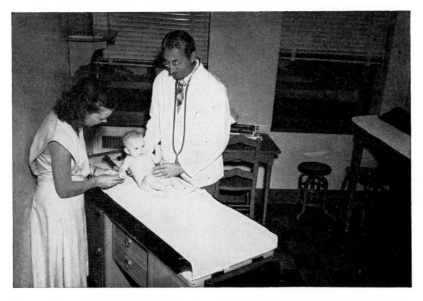

Fig. 82. Well-baby clinic. The present-day local health department is interested in the child who is well, as well as in the child who is ill. (Courtesy Oregon State Board of Health.)

Promotion of maternal health. Public health nurses are essentially family health counselors. Some health units use that designation rather than nurse. As a family health counselor, the nurse does no bedside nursing except in an emergency or as a demonstration for the instruction of some member of the family. Yet the public health nurse is the key figure in the maternity, infant, and child health program. She is the principal factor in the typical maternity health program which includes both direct and indirect means of health promotion.

Direct means of health promotion for expectant mothers are as follows:

1. Promotion of the expectant mother's health through early medical examination, prevention and correction of impairments, proper rest, moderate exercise, proper nutrition, sunshine, avoidance of extreme fatigue, avoidance of poisons, and avoidance of infection
2. Adequate delivery facilities, hospital or home
3. Obstetrical services
4. Postnatal care

Indirect means consist of the following:

1. Public education
2. Laws governing employment
3. Medical insurance with maternity benefits
4. Improvement of socioeconomic conditions

Promotion of infant and child health. In cooperation with all agencies which contribute to child health, the public health nurse counsels parents in matters relating to the health of their children. Her functions may be summarized as follows:

1. Encourage parents to have children examined at regular intervals.
2. Assist parents in understanding the health conditions and needs of their children.
3. Help secure necessary medical diagnosis and treatment for the sick. The health department does not provide medical treatment but strives to bring together medical service and the person needing medical service.
4. Teach home nursing techniques to members of the family and supervise these attendants.
5. Assist the family to carry out necessary sanitary and other essential measures.
6. Help to improve social conditions that affect health.
7. Influence the community to develop health facilities.

Promotion of adult health. With the extension of the expectation of life, new health problems have appeared. The aging process predisposes to certain chronic organic disorders, some of which are preventable and most of which are amenable to treatment. Overweight, heart conditions, vascular disturbances, kidney disorders, metabolic disorders, diabetes, and arthritis are among the important afflictions of middle and late adulthood. A constructive public health program can do much to prevent these conditions by (1) health education that emphasizes a slow pace, avoiding infection, clearing up all infection immediately, avoiding extreme fatigue, proper diet, proper rest, and frequent check-ups, (2) annual thorough health examination, and (3) correction of all remediable disorders.

Environmental sanitation. The sanitarian is not concerned with sanitation conditions in private homes except in an advisory or consulting capacity. He gives advice on sanitation when asked by a householder; through general health education he encourages home sanitation measures. His primary concern is the sanitation of public places, supplies, and conditions. This includes public water supplies, sewage disposal, milk and milk products, food processing and serving, public buildings, industrial establishments, swimming pools, bathing beaches, insect control, and nuisances.

Public health laboratory service. Many county health units rely on a state laboratory for their laboratory needs, but practice indicates many advantages in having a local laboratory, which offers convenience of location and reduced time for transportation to the laboratory. Epidemiologists, nurses, sanitarians, and water plant attendants submit specimens for examination, analysis, and appraisal. Examinations are made as a diagnostic aid to practicing physicians. Effective control of communicable diseases, of public milk supplies, and of public water supplies is greatly dependent upon laboratory services. The laboratory provides all containers and materials necessary for the collection of specimens. If biological products are supplied, the laboratory keeps these in stock and assumes responsibility for dispensing them.

Fig. 83. Laboratory services. Blood tests, bacteria identifications, sputum examinations, and water and milk analyses are among the services performed in the public health laboratory. (Courtesy Oregon State Board of Health.)

Health education service. Any effective modern health program must be based upon sound health education which modifies the living practices of the people in keeping with modern health principles. Effective public health education must (1) get the public to *accept* a practice or program, (2) arouse a *desire* in people to benefit by it, and (3) obtain *participation* by the people.

All persons, agencies, and devices which can contribute to health education should be enlisted, but the usual means are health councils, civic groups, schools, newspapers, booklets, radio, exhibits, motion pictures, demonstrations, forums, speakers, and meetings. The principal obstacles to effective public health education are public apathy, commercial advertising (particularly radio and television), cultists, superficial health examinations, and professional incompetence.

Health education is a continuous job in which all members of the county health staff participate. It is a task which requires the enlistment of all available community educational resources.

Appraisal of local health services. Communities with full-time health departments have experienced a significant decline in communicable diseases, preventable defects, disabilities, infant deaths, child deaths, and maternal deaths. Citizens of these communities have enjoyed a higher level of health, a greater life expectancy, and a guardianship over their living conditions which assured every citizen an opportunity for the most wholesome living possible in modern times.

Every citizen has the right to the highest possible level of health his endowment affords. Changing concepts and approaches in health are of little import unless they become available to all of the citizenry. Full-time local health departments provide a direct health service to every citizen in the United States. They are an investment in more effective and enjoyable living. In addition they yield economic returns in reduced illness, reduced wage losses, reduced invalidism and dependency, reduced medical costs, increased earning power, and an extended productive span of life.

Chapter 12

National and international
health services

The social philosophy in the United States places primary responsibility for personal health upon the individual himself. Yet it recognizes that in the complex society of today no one is totally self-sufficient in attaining and maintaining a high level of health. To supplement individual efforts in health protection and promotion, health organizations have been established on international, national, state, and local levels. On each of these levels voluntary agencies are those which are financed by private contributions. Official agencies are those which are governmental and are supported by tax funds.

VOLUNTARY HEALTH AGENCIES

The public health movement in the United States owes a debt of gratitude to voluntary health organizations. The health pioneering, the dissemination of health information, the promotion of projects to the point at which they have been assumed by official agencies, the subsidization of projects, and the sponsoring of legislation and research by these agencies have contributed immeasurably to the advancement and development of public health in the United States. Although the promotion of health is obviously a governmental function, the American democratic process has left much in health work to the initiative of the individual and to private organizations.

Our American way of life and our unique development in America made the establishment of the voluntary health agency inevitable. A free society of citizens with initiative and a realistic vision of their needs has favored the establishment of nongovernmental agencies to secure what government does not provide. Social institutions and social phenomena do not spring up overnight. They grow out of needs and urges and develop through pressures created by groups of people attempting to solve problems. Discoveries, ideas, attitudes, motives, and opportunities of the nineteenth century made possible the sound health programs that are in existence at the present time. It has been emphasized previously that progress in public health is dependent not only upon scientific knowledge, but also upon the dissemination of this information to the people.

The program of the voluntary health agency is usually highly specialized and limited to one health interest or problem. In general, as stated by S. M. Gunn and P. S. Platt, voluntary health agencies are concerned with three types of problems: (1) treatment of specific diseases, such as tuberculosis, poliomyelitis, venereal disease, and cancer; (2) the safeguarding of certain organs and structures, such as eyes, ears, heart, teeth, and the muscle and skeletal systems; and (3) problems which affect the health and welfare of special groups, with interest centered in maternal and child hygiene, mental hygiene, and adult health.

There are three types of voluntary health agencies: professional health organizations, promotional health organizations, and health foundations.

Professional health organizations. A professional society or association is composed of persons with a common background who have pursued prescribed and systematic studies and training, who are able to meet standards of certification, who seek to serve particular purposes in society, and who are able to uphold high professional ideals. There are several of special interest.

American Medical Association. The American Medical Association was established in May, 1847. The purpose in organizing the Association was stated as follows in the constitution:

> . . . for cultivating and advancing medical knowledge; for elevating the standard of medical education; for promoting the usefulness, honor, and interest of the medical profession; for enlightening and directing public opinion in regard to the duties, responsibilities and requirements of medical men; for exciting and encouraging emulation and concert of action in the profession; and for facilitating and fostering friendly intercourse between those engaged in it.

At the present time its constitution says that "the object of the Association is to promote the science and art of medicine and the betterment of public health."

The organization was founded for and has served primarily the interest of private medical practitioners. Yet much of the activity of the Association has been planned to serve and protect the public interest and to give the best possible medical service to the people.

Actually the Association consists of a federation of state societies which in turn are made up of county medical societies; hence it is an association of state societies rather than of individuals.

In addition to raising the standards of medical education, the Association has insisted upon high requirements for the licensing of medical practitioners. It is constantly giving much time and thought to improving the quality of medical service and keeping the members informed of advancements in medicine. The Association, through its checking and classification of hospitals as approved or not approved, has contributed greatly to the improvement of hospital service.

Publications of the Association include the *Journal of the American Medical Association,* which is a weekly publication, perhaps the leading journal of its kind in the world. The *American Medical Directory* is published every two years. As a guide for physicians and medical students, the *Quarterly Cumulative Index Medicus* lists by author, title, and subject matter the material published in approximately 1300 medical periodicals throughout the world. *Today's Health* (formerly *Hygeia*) is the health education publication of the Association. It is concerned primarily with personal and community health.

American Dental Association. The American Dental Association was established about 1860. Previously there had been another association, but this had broken up over matters of policy and practice. Although the Association was organized to advance personal and professional interests, it has, since its inception, been interested in raising the quality of dental education, elevating standards of dental practice, and keeping dental practitioners acquainted with new techniques and pactices. The welfare of the patient has been an important consideration. Much of the Association's time, in the beginning, was spent in fighting the evils of certain commercial concerns which held patents on machines and processes necessary for the practice of the dental art.

The organization of the American Dental Association is much the same as the American Medical Association. In the beginning it was an organization of individual practitioners, but it later became an association of state societies. It publishes the *Journal of the American Dental Association* and a yearly index of periodical dental literature.

American Public Health Association. The American Public Health Association came into being in September, 1872. It rapidly broadened its scope of interest from sanitary improvement to the development of a broad public health program growing out of an appreciation of the role of hygiene in social progress and human welfare.

Its constitution states the objectives of the organization as follows:

> . . . with the design to secure concerted effort and establish some adequate plans in the cultivation of hygienic knowledge, and to procure more effective application of sanitary principles and laws. . . . The objects of this Association shall be the advancement of sanitary science and the promotion of organizations and measures for the practical application of public hygiene.

The Association is organized into thirteen sections which indicate the scope of work and the variety of interest. These sections are laboratory, health officers, statistics, engineering, industrial hygiene, food and nutrition, maternal and child health, public health education, public health nursing, epidemiology, school health, dental health, and medical care.

The Association has developed standards which have been widely adopted and accepted on methods for the examination of dairy products, water, and sewage, the design and operation of swimming pools, diagnostic procedures and reagents, the appraisal of local health work, a model health code for cities, the standardization of public health training, and many more. It conducts surveys both at the request of other organizations and in connection with the work of its committees. It issues a monthly publication, the *Journal of Public Health*.

National League for Nursing. The National League for Nursing was formed in 1952 when the following three national nursing organizations and four national committees combined their programs and resources: the National League of Nursing Education (founded 1893), the National Organization for Public Health Nursing (1912), the Association of Collegiate Schools of Nursing (1933), the Joint Committee on Practical Nurses and Auxiliary Workers in Nursing Services (1945), the Joint Committee on Careers in Nursing (1948), the National Committee for the Improvement of Nursing Services (1949), and the National Nursing Accrediting Service (1949).

The National League for Nursing consists of two divisions: the Division of Nursing Services (made up of the Department of Hospital Nursing and the Department of Public Health Nursing) and the Division of Nursing Education (made up of the Department of Diploma and Associate Degree Programs and the Department of Baccalaureate and Higher Degree Programs). The aim of the organization is "that the nursing needs of the people may be met."

The Department of Public Health Nursing continues the practices and objectives of the former National Organization for Public Health Nursing. These objectives are the following:

> . . . to stimulate responsibility for the health of the community by establishing and extending public health nursing; to bring about cooperation among nurses, physicians and all others interested in public health; to develop standards of public health nursing; to maintain a central bureau of information and assistance in such service; and to publish periodicals and bulletins.

Membership includes both public health nurses and friends of public health nursing. Thus it has professional and nonprofessional members.

The official magazine of the National League for Nursing is *Nursing Outlook*. It also sponsors *Nursing Research*.

American Association for Health, Physical Education, and Recreation. The American Association for Health, Physical Education, and Recreation had its beginning in 1885 as the American Association for the Advancement of Physical Education. In 1937 the present Association became a department of the National Education Association. It has unique opportunities for developing the positive aspects of health. Several active sections of the association bear directly upon health, such as school physicians, school nursing, health teaching, nutrition education, therapeutics, dental health, mental health, and recreation. The association operates by setting up desirable programs that may become operative in local communities. The professions of health education and physical education have serious deficiencies that are partly inherent in most teaching, such as partial training of personnel and failure to maintain high professional standards in education, in selection of students, in certification, and in appointments. The development of a professional viewpoint has been slow, and morale has been low. The *Journal* of the American Association for Health, Physical Education, and Recreation is the official monthly publication. The *Research Quarterly* is published four times a year.

Promotional health organizations. Humanitarianism has had an impress upon the development of public health, as well as upon the development of public welfare and charities, the change of attitude toward mentally deficient persons, the study of tenements and slums, and the development of responsibility by industry for the welfare of its workers. It has produced a profound change in the social attitude not only toward life, but also toward the control of disease. Governmental agencies were slow in the late nineteenth and early twentieth centuries to translate into action many of these developments. The formation of voluntary agencies for the implementing of these ideas and for the alleviation of these conditions was a result of the response of our social attitude in the twentieth century toward life.

National Tuberculosis Association. The National Tuberculosis Association was

Fig. 84. Voluntary health agency in action. Directly or indirectly, voluntary health agencies affect the lives of every citizen in the United States. (Courtesy Oregon Tuberculosis Association.)

founded in 1904. At that time twenty-three associations were already in existence at state and local levels. It was the first voluntary agency of the educational, promotional type. Its approach has consisted of educating, pioneering, demonstrating, and research.

From the first it has emphasized the economic and social causes as they affect the development of tuberculosis. From the very beginning education has been the cornerstone of the program of the Association. Stress has been placed on the fact that it is not only necessary to extend knowledge through scientific research, but also to disseminate it widely through educating the public, the health and medical practitioners, and the patient. Only in this manner can knowledge be an effective tool and achieve its full potentialities.

The objects of the Association are set forth in Article II of the Constitution, which reads as follows:

> The objects of the Association shall be: (a) the study of tuberculosis in all its forms and relations; (b) treatment and prevention of tuberculosis; (c) the encouragement of the prevention and scientific treatment of tuberculosis; (d) to stimulate, unify and standardize the work of the various tuberculosis associations throughout the country; (e) to cooperate with medical societies and with other nonofficial and official organizations interested in tuberculosis and related health problems; (f) to promote international relations in connection with the study and control of tuberculosis and related diseases.

It was early realized that any effective campaign to combat tuberculosis must be initiated and operated at the local level; hence the national Association organized groups at the local level to provide effective machinery for the promotion of its program.

From the beginning the Association has been well financed, and possibly at the present time, because of the Christmas seals campaign, more people contribute and participate in this program than in any other philanthropic project.

The Association has conducted an extensive research program in the statistical, rehabilitation, microbiological diagnosis, and therapeutic phases of tuberculosis. As would be expected, the health education program of the Association is very extensive and extremely well developed, including programs not only for tuberculosis education, but also for the entire range of public health and school health education. All phases of public health—nutrition, housing, industrial hygiene, and sanitation—have a bearing on tuberculosis; hence if the problem is to be dealt with adequately, all features that contribute and bear upon tuberculosis should receive emphasis.

The Association publishes the *American Review of Tuberculosis and Pulmonary Diseases,* the official journal of the American Trudeau Society, the medical section of the NTA; *Tuberculosis Abstracts* for physicians; and the *Bulletin,* for public health workers, school personnel, and others interested in the program against tuberculosis. In addition it publishes a wide variety of popularly written leaflets and pamphlets on various phases of health education that affect tuberculosis.

National Foundation. The National Foundation (for Infantile Paralysis) is one of the latest promotional agencies, having been organized in 1938. Its rise has been spectacular and dramatic. This association was popularized and given a tremendous impetus by the efforts of the late President Franklin D. Roosevelt, who had been stricken by this disease. In the beginning it was financed largely through the March of Dimes Program and the celebration of the President's birthday with balls and parties. Its growth has been noteworthy. By 1955, 3100 chapters had been established, reaching into every county and territory in the United States. Several state chapters are in existence, and in most of the states administrative branches of the National Foundation have been established.

The purposes of the National Foundation at its founding were the following:

1. To direct, unify, stimulate, coordinate, and further the knowledge of, and the work being done on, any and all phases of infantile paralysis, including study and research into the cause, nature, and methods of prevention of the disease, and the prevention of harmful aftereffects of the disease.

2. To arrange for, and to direct, unify, stimulate, coordinate, and further the work being done on the treatment, in lawfully established institutions conducted by others, of persons afflicted with infantile paralysis and/or suffering from its aftereffects.

3. To make voluntary contributions or grants of money from funds of the corporation at any time, and from time to time, to individuals who are disabled or handicapped in whole or in part as a result of infantile paralysis or to lawfully established agencies for the benefit of such persons or for the purpose of prevention, diagnosis, treatment, alleviation, or aftertreatment of infantile paralysis.

In 1958 the name of the organization was shortened to the National Foundation, and its objectives were expanded to become . . . "an organized force for medical research, patient care and professional education, flexible enough to meet new health problems as they arise." The expanded new program includes investigation into arthritis, birth defects (congenital malformations), virus diseases, and disorders of the central nervous system as well as poliomyelitis.

The function of the chapters, which are in a sense branch offices of the parent organization, is "to give direct medical assistance to those afflicted with infantile paralysis," and to raise funds to maintain national and local activities. A large proportion of the funds raised locally remain in the community for expenditure.

Funds from the National Foundation aided in demonstrating the effectiveness of the Salk vaccine through participation in the 1954 Poliomyelitis Vaccine Field Trial. Undoubtedly this project advanced markedly the widespread use and acceptance of this scientific discovery, perhaps the shortest elapsed time between discovery and widespread application on record.

American Social Hygiene Association. The American Social Hygiene Association was preceded by several other organizations. Dr. Prince A. Morrow organized the American Society of Sanitary and Moral Prophylaxis in 1905. This was the first systematic medical approach toward social hygiene. The membership of the society was composed of representatives of the medical profession and the laity, including women. In general this has been continued. Health education has played an important role in the program of the society. During the years immediately following 1905, the causative agent of syphilis and prophylactic measures for the disease were discovered.

In 1914 various national groups amalgamated into the American Social Hygiene Association, the present national organization. Objectives of this society are stated as follows in Article II of the Association's Constitution:

> The purposes of this Association shall be to acquire and diffuse knowledge of the established principles and practices and of any new methods, which promote or give assurance of promoting, social health; to advocate the highest standards of private and public morality; to suppress commercialized vice; to organize the defense of the community by every available means, educational, sanitary, or legislative, against the diseases of vice; the conduct on request inquires into the present condition of prostitution and the venereal diseases in American towns and cities; and to secure mutual acquaintance and sympathy and cooperation among the local societies for these or similar purposes.

The influence of three schools of thought can be seen in the development of the various organizations which entered the American Social Hygiene Association and were instrumental in laying the background and foundation for the present association.

The first group was concerned with moral issues, the evils of commercial prostitution, and white slavery. Another group was interested in attacking the problems of syphilis and gonorrhea, which was primarily a medical approach. The third group was interested in bringing the knowledge of sex and social hygiene into the open where it could be made available to the public, especially to the younger people.

The official publication is the *Journal of Social Hygiene.*

American Cancer Society, Inc. The American Cancer Society, Inc., was formed in 1913. The objective of the Society was "to disseminate knowledge concerning the symptoms, diagnosis, treatment, and prevention of cancer; to investigate the conditions under which cancer is found; and to compile statistics in regard thereto." Medical groups were the prime movers in the establishment of this organization, but its work has been carried on in large part by laymen.

An early educational campaign was adopted to acquaint the public with the basic facts regarding the control of cancer and its cure—that early cancer is curable, that early diagnosis is extremely important, and that prompt scientific treatment is the only way of obtaining a cure. The prime object of the educational campaign was to overcome fear. An impersonal approach is necessary. Accurate information and the dissipation of rumors and speculation are important; confidence must be established.

The Society has stimulated further interest in cancer in schools of medicine, fostered research, stimulated health departments to increased interest in the program, helped to organize a National Advisory Cancer Council, and influenced, through its legislative program, the passing of the National Cancer Act and the creation of the National Cancer Institute as a part of the U. S. Public Health Service.

The Women's Field Army, an auxiliary group, enlists the active participation of laymen in a program of health education. This group includes over 200,000 enlisted voluntary workers. The cancer program is supervised and controlled by the local medical profession in each county. The relation between the community and the national organization is cooperative. The main income of the organization is from endowments, contributions, and dues. Many states have state cancer societies which are a part of the national organization.

The official publication is *CA—A Bulletin of Cancer Progress.*

American Red Cross. The American Red Cross does not fit into any of the three patterns of health organizations. It has quasigovernmental status, being incorporated under a charter granted by Congress. Its president is the President of the United States. The organization was established in 1881. Its operation is in accordance with the terms of the Geneva Treaty of 1864, which was formally ratified by the United States in 1882. Because of its charter, the Red Cross renders a wartime service but also works for relief in any extensive calamity (disaster relief).

In peace time the Red Cross has been closely identified with public health surveys and has established health centers, sponsored health demonstration projects, and furnished public health nursing service for otherwise unserved rural areas. Its training programs in first aid, water safety, home nursing, accident prevention, and nutrition have definite and far-reaching public health significance.

The Red Cross works closely with governmental and private organizations at all levels—national, state, and local. Local chapters are often organized on a county basis, but are closely supervised by the national organization, which establishes policy and must approve all new local projects.

Health foundations. Many foundations are active in public health work. Only a few will be considered here. Some have wide comprehensive programs, whereas others are highly specific in their activities.

Rockefeller Foundation. The Rockefeller Foundation was chartered in 1913 under the laws of the state of New York with the purpose of "promoting the well-being of mankind throughout the world."

The charter of the Rockefeller Foundation in part states:

It shall be within the purposes of said corporation to use as means to that end research, publications, the establishment and maintenance of charitable, benevolent, religious, missionary, and public education activities, agencies, and institutions, and the aid of any such activities, agencies, and institutions already established and any other means and agencies which from time to time shall seem expedient to its members or trustees.

The foundation consists of five divisions: (1) International Health, (2) Medical Sciences, (3) Natural Sciences, (4) Social Sciences, and (5) Humanities.

The International Health Division is an operating agency with its own laboratories and scientific staffs. Three phases of work have been attempted: first, the control of specific diseases, such as yellow fever, influenza, and tuberculosis; second, aids to departments of health; and third, demonstrations, aid to selected schools, public health education, and the granting of postgraduate fellowships in public health. The research laboratories have made many important contributions in the treatment of yellow fever, typhus, influenza, and malaria.

The other four divisions are nonoperating agencies. They support university, laboratory, and other research groups. They also provide fellowships for postdoctoral work. A wide range of activity is sponsored through various grants and appropriations.

Milbank Memorial Fund. The Milbank Memorial Fund was established in 1905 with the objective "to improve the physical, mental, and moral condition of humanity and generally to advance charitable and benevolent objects."

Its activities are primarily in preventive medicine. Its objectives are attained by the establishment of grants and fellowships, and as an agency its contributions are to the fields of social welfare, medicine, public health, research, and education. It sponsors research and studies in these fields and related activities, such as population trends. It has done much exploratory work, has sponsored demonstrations and projects, and recently has been interested in measurements of various aspects of public health. The activities of the Fund have included an interest in school lunches, mental hygiene, food research, dental studies, defective vision, prenatal and postnatal instruction, and public health demonstrations. Annual conferences are sponsored by the Fund for the discussion of important public health problems and studies.

Commonwealth Fund. The Commonwealth Fund was established in 1918 with the stated objective: "To do something for the welfare of mankind." Its activities have included education, health, medical education and research, and mental hygiene. Large portions of its funds have been expended in the fields of physical and mental well-being. It has attempted to further public health practices and procedures through research and good teaching in medical schools, by the extension of public health services to rural communities, by providing and improving hospital facilities, by standardizing hospital services in rural communities, and by strengthening community facilities for mental health services in this country and in Great Britain.

W. K. Kellogg Foundation. The W. K. Kellogg Foundation was established in 1930. Its object was "the promotion of the health, education, and the welfare of mankind, but principally of children and youth, directly or indirectly, without regard to sex, race, creed, or nationality." The nineteen points listed in the Children's Charter of the White House Conference on Child Health and Protection in 1930 have been accepted as goals.

The Foundation operates through a program of application of knowledge to situations. It is a functional problem-solving approach rather than research or relief. The program begins in the home in an attempt to teach people to help themselves. Programs have been organized on a community-wide basis, in which grants have been made to various counties for the establishment of county health departments. In addition to this, health education programs have been fostered in the public schools, which link school and community together in public health projects.

Cooperation and coordination of voluntary agencies. The voluntary agencies, including promotional, professional, foundation, and civic and welfare organizations, have made tremendous contributions to the health and welfare of the American people. Certain strengths and weaknesses can be observed in these organizations. The freedom of choice, of selection, and of program is one of their strongest characteristics. This carries with it a flexibility to meet changing conditions.

There is much dissipation of effort because too many agencies are interested in similar problems. The very specialization of these agencies contributes to this and makes it possible. The effectiveness of these agencies has suffered because of a lack of integration and coordination between the different groups. Some unity of action between voluntary health agencies seems to be indicated.

Voluntary health agencies pioneer in a specific health field, often to demonstrate what can be done. When that health field is taken over by an official agency, the need for the voluntary agency may no longer exist. Few voluntary agencies have thus far been dissolved.

Difficulties in cooperation. In 1921 the National Health Council came into being. This organization consists of about fifty voluntary national groups interested in health betterment, with the U. S. Public Health Service as an advisory member. In the beginning this council was rather well financed and staffed with well-qualified personnel. Its contribution to date has not been great. Four or five years after its establishment, it became rather ineffective and many of its projects were abandoned. It did not produce national leadership for the voluntary agencies, and attempts at coordination between the various agencies were not effective. It has continued that way until recently when some revitalization has occurred through the organization of National Health Forums, the inauguration of Community Health Week, the creation of functioning committees, and the publication of such journals as *Signs of the Health Times, Health Career's Guidebook*, and others. There has been a marked growth and expansion of activities.

This organization has great potential for integration, cooperation, and unification of health programs.

OFFICIAL NATIONAL HEALTH SERVICES

All health authorities and other informed citizens agree that the federal government should promote the health of the public. Yet if we look for specific federal authority to promote public health, we will seek in vain.

Our Federal Constitution is a grant of power to the federal government by the states. The Tenth Amendment states that the powers not delegated to the United States by the Constitution, nor prohibited by it to the states, are reserved to the states, respectively, or to the people. Control over the health of the people was a recognized function of the states before the national Constitution was

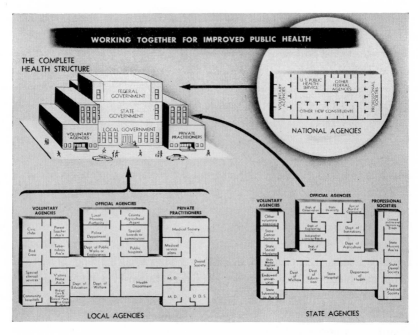

Fig. 85. Levels of health organization of official and voluntary health agencies at local, state, and national levels. (Courtesy U. S. Public Health Service.)

adopted, and no mention of health is made in the Constitution. States never gave up their health function and remain the legal repository of health promotion.

Federal authority to promote health is derived from the broad general clauses of the Constitution: (1) regulation of interstate commerce, (2) taxing power, (3) appropriate money for the general welfare, (4) create agencies for the general welfare, (5) postal power, (6) patent office, (7) treaty-making power, and (8) war power.

Other than the many independent governmental agencies, every executive department of the federal government has one or more branches directly or indirectly concerned with public health. With the exception of perhaps a half dozen branches, the health work is subordinated to the general purpose of the agency. Coordination of these scattered and often overlapping activities has resisted the most determined efforts of legislators and health specialists alike.

The principal federal health agency is the U. S. Public Health Service, but many other federal agencies are involved in health work.

In addition to the U. S. Public Health Service some fifty-five other departments, bureaus, and agencies are engaged in health work, according to an investigation by J. W. Mountin and Evelyn Flook. In most cases there is little interrelationship between these groups. Among these are the sanitary and health service of the various national parks and the health activities of the Women's Bureau located in the Department of Labor. The Department of Agriculture has activities relating to general sanitation, especially of food and dairy products. These include the study of the sanitation of dairies and dairy products, the production of meat and meat products, and the administration of laws relating to the production of food and drugs. The Consular Service of the State Department also engages in public health activities through the submission of public health reports from other countries. Bills of health to all vessels bound for ports in the United States are issued by the consular service.

U. S. Public Health Service. The U. S. Public Health Service responsibilities fall into three main categories: research, medical and hospital services, and public health practice. The U. S. Public Health Service was established in 1902 and was an outgrowth of the Marine Hospital Service which dates back to 1798. In 1917 physical and mental examinations of all aliens entering the United States were required. A national leprosarium at Carville, Louisiana, was established in that year. In 1929 a program of mental hygiene and the medical care of federal prisoners and narcotic addicts became responsibilities of the U. S. Public Health Service.

Duties of the service were materially increased by the Social Security Act of 1935, Under this Act, all grants-in-aid to states, to strengthen state and local health departments, were administered by the U. S. Public Health Service.

In 1937 the National Cancer Act was passed, and the Venereal Disease Control act followed in 1938. In 1939 the U. S. Public Health Service was moved from the Treasury Department to the Federal Security Agency. Some other health agencies of other departments were also affected. The Public Health Law enacted in 1944 was an important milestone in development of the Public Health Service, resulting in expansion, reorganization and consolidation of the service and a revision of laws relating to public health. Upon the establishment of the Department of Health, Education, and Welfare in 1953, it became a part of that Department.

There has been a definite tendency to place all federal health service and funds under the jurisdiction of the U. S. Public Health Service. Many of the direct appropriations for health in the federal government are expended through the U. S. Public Health Service, which in turn allocates funds and services to the various local subdivisions of the states. The present-day tendency is for centralization rather than decentralization, as it has been for the past several years.

Administration. Administration of the U. S. Public Health Service is the responsibility of the Surgeon General who is the chief administrative officer. He is appointed by the President, with the consent of Congress. The Surgeon General shares the planning, coordination, and administration of Service activities with the Deputy Surgeon General, the Assistant Surgeon General, the Executive Officer, and the chiefs of the three operating bureaus. His appointment is for four years.

The officers of the U. S. Public Health Service are commissioned the same as are those in the military services. The regular corps of commissioned officers is

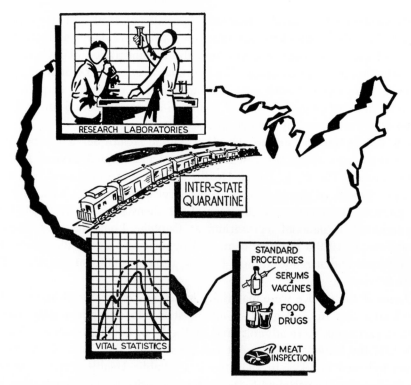

Fig. 86. Interstate health protection. The health services of the federal government function directly for the protection of interstate health. (Courtesy U. S. Public Health Service.)

made up of physicians, dentists, sanitary engineers, public health nurses, and specialists in the field of chemistry, entomology, and zoology. Civilian employees serve in many capacities.

The U. S. Public Health Service employs about 32,000 people engaged in 300 different occupations in over 600 locations. About 10,000 are at the National Institutes of Health, Bethesda, Maryland.

The Public Health Service provides medical and hospital care through hospitals, clinics, and health centers in 250 locations on land and sea in the United States and foreign countries. These facilities number 65 hospitals, 25 outpatient clinics, and 42 Indian and Alaskan Native Health Centers.

In 1963 the U. S. Public Health Service had a budget of $1,581,540,000. Some of the items in the budget indicate the activities of the Service.

Hospital and medical facilities (Hill-Burton)	226,156,000
National Institutes of Health	912,108,000
Indian health activities	64,965,000
Medical services	121,320,000
Chronic diseases	50,920,000
Communicable diseases	30,600,000
Environmental health activities	166,826,000
Health research facilities	115,419,000

National Health Advisory Council. The National Health Advisory Council, consisting of fourteen members, acts in an advisory capacity. The membership of the Council is made up of ten appointees by the Surgeon General who serve for a term of four years, the director of the National Institutes of Health, and a representative from the Army, the Navy and the Bureau of Animal Industry.

Various other advisory groups include the National Advisory Cancer Council, the Advisory Board for the Control of Biological Products, and the Federal Advisory Board of Hospitalization.

The major functions of the U. S. Public Health Service are organized into four departments: the Office of the Surgeon General, the National Institutes of Health, the Bureau of Medical Services, and the Bureau of State Services. The National Library of Medicine is also a part of the Public Health Service.

Office of the Surgeon General. The Office of the Surgeon General is composed of the Division of Public Health Methods, the Division of Finance, the Division of Personnel, and the Division of Administrative Services. This office is staffed by about 470 employees.

National Institutes of Health. The National Institutes of Health, the focal point for national support of biomedical research, is the center of research activities in the Service. It is located on a 300-acre tract at Bethesda, Maryland, a suburb of Washington, D. C. It is composed of nine institutes. In order of their establishment they are: Cancer, Heart, Microbiology, Dental Research, Mental Health, Neurological Diseases and Blindness, Arthritis and Metabolic Diseases, Allergy and Infectious Diseases (successor to Microbiology), General Medical Sciences, and Child Health and Human Development. In addition there are a Clinical Center, Division of Biologics Standards, Division of Research Services, Division of Research Grants, and Division of Research Facilities and Resources.

The research function of the U. S. Public Health Service has expanded rapidly since 1946. It is one of the most hopeful signs in the field of public health. Recent enactments and appropriations for scientific research give hope that this work will be extended further.

The National Institutes of Health makes its facilities available to various scientists and public health authorities. It makes grants-in-aid to universities, hospitals, and laboratories for research and other projects that are recommended by the National Advisory Council.

The beneficial results from major medical research have been remarkable. Some are dramatic, and others, while not so dramatic, are nevertheless effective in the reduction of pain, sickness, and death. Among the more notable recent accomplishments are the discovery and development of the following: (1) poliomyelitis vaccines which are 90% effective in preventing paralytic forms of poliomyelitis, (2) tranquilizers and other drugs including psychic energizers for the treatment of mental illness, which have greatly increased the number of patients released from mental hospitals, (3) antihypertensive drugs that reduce the number of deaths from hypertension, (4) anticoagulants used in the treat-

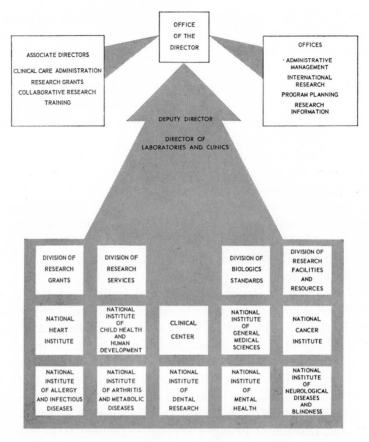

Fig. 87. Organization and services of the National Institutes of Health. (Courtesy U. S. Public Health Service.)

ment of heart disease and stroke, (5) a diagnostic test for rheumatoid arthritis which can be performed in about twenty minutes, (6) oral antidiabetic drugs which for some patients eliminate the need for the administration of insulin by injection, (7) accurate diagnostic test for phenylketonuria, (8) proof that malaria can be transmitted from the monkey to man, (9) a simple effective emergency treatment for burn shock, and (10) partial cracking of the genetic code.

It is reliably estimated that 2,000,000 lives have been saved since 1944 as a result of medical research. The foregoing are recent developments. It should be noted that medical research has been responsible for the trend from communicable diseases as the main cause of death at the beginning of the century to the chronic organic degenerative diseases as the present time. Between 1937 and 1957 the death rate has been reduced 15%, and 24 years have been added to the life expectancy since 1900.

In 1963 the U. S. Public Health Service spent $912,108,000 on medical research in the National Institutes of Health and in grants to universities, research centers, and training programs.

The total expenditure for biomedical research in 1961 was in excess of one billion dollars. Of this amount the federal government financed 57%, industry 29%, and others 14%. The total amount as an isolated statistic seems enormous, but it shrinks considerably when compared with the amounts spent in 1962 for the following: (1) confections, $2,663,850,000; (2) tobacco products, $7,082,050,000; (3) alcoholic beverages, $11,628,260,000; (4) foreign travel, $2,936,000,000.

When the benefits to the individual, society, and the nation of the amounts spent for luxuries are contrasted with the benefits of the amounts spent for medi-

Fig. 88. Under guidance of medical officers of the U. S. Public Health Service, quarantine patient is removed by launch from an incoming ship. (Courtesy U. S. Public Health Service.)

Fig. 89. Inspecting sanitary facilities aboard planes. (Courtesy U. S. Public Health Service.)

cal research, it would appear that greater expenditures for medical research are warranted.

Bureau of Medical Services. The Bureau of Medical Services administers all medical services of the federal government. These include all medical activities of the U. S. Public Health Service in which direct service is rendered. Its divisions are Foreign Quarantine, Hospital Facilities, Hospitals, Indian Health Services, Dental Resources, and Nursing Resources. The Bureau assigns personnel from the U. S. Public Health Service to prisons under the Justice Department, to the Coast Guard under the Treasury Department, to the Maritime Administration under the Commerce Department, to the Bureau of Employees Compensation under the Labor Department, to the Foreign Service under the State Department, and to the Office of Vocational Rehabilitation in the Department of Health, Education, and Welfare.

Bureau of State Services. The Bureau of State Services includes the Division of General Health Services, the Division of Special Health Services, the Division of Sanitary Engineering Services, the Division of International Health, the Division of Dental Public Health, the Communicable Diseases Center, and the Public Health Service Regional Organization.

The Division of General Health Services handles the grants-in-aid from the federal government to the various state and local health services. This Division provides staff services for the development of new programs, conducts studies into the adequacy of present methods of meeting current needs, and gives technical assistance in solving problems in public health administration.

The National Office of Vital Statistics compiles, analyzes, and publishes national reports on births, deaths, fetal deaths, marriages, divorces, and occurrence of notifiable diseases.

The Division of Special Health Services directs programs toward special health problems of particular population groups. Among these are diabetes, heart disease, tuberculosis, venereal disease, and occupational health. Other major activities are consulting service in the fields of occupational medicine, engineering, nursing, toxicology, biochemistry, sickness absenteeism, and others.

The future. The growth of the U. S. Public Health Service during the past twenty years has been tremendous. The recent development of a research program has wide implications and is perhaps one of the most fruitful fields in which the federal government can engage. Since many projects in research require large sums of money and special expensive laboratory equipment, the federal government is an ideal agency for this purpose. The results of the research are usually applicable throughout the entire nation.

The program of grants-in-aid to states and local communities in certain areas is a worthwhile service. It can be confidently expected that the contribution and impress of the U. S. Public Health Service are going to be considerably greater in the future. Although the program of the U. S. Public Health Service is essentially an indirect service to the individual citizen, it is nevertheless an indispensable service, particularly as a supplement to state and local health services.

Cooperation of the U. S. Public Health Service with other agencies. Many public medical services sponsored by various federal agencies have subsequently come under the administration of the U. S. Public Health Service, some of these are the Farm Security Administration (medical care for farm families), the Farm Security Administration and War Food Administration (medical care for migratory workers), the Department of Justice (medical care for federal prisoners), the Department of the Interior (medical care for the Indians), and the Federal Employees Compensation Commission (review of compensation claims).

To reduce absenteeism several departments established an emergency medical service and health care for their employees. Data as well as administrative and counsel services are furnished by the U. S. Public Health Service to any such groups at the request of any federal department or agency. Under the Federal Housing Authority, health and medical services to resident workers in the War Housing Projects were administered by the U. S. Public Health Service.

Other medical services. Medical service is provided for members of the Armed Forces. In addition several hospitals (St. Elizabeth's Hospital and Freedman's Hospital in Washington, D. C.) are operated. The Public Health Department of the District of Columbia is operated by the federal government. Medical care for construction workers on projects such as the Tennessee Valley Authority and similar projects is sponsored federally.

Medical care for veterans. At the present time the medical care of veterans is an enormous task. This is not a new procedure, but it has been enlarged and increased after each succeeding war. The Veterans' Administration offers complete care including hospitalization and outpatient treatment for service-connected conditions. Hospitalization also has been provided for nonservice-connected disability but not outpatient treatment.

Vocational rehabilitation. Medical service is provided also through federal grants-in-aid, administered by the Office of Vocational Rehabilitation. This includes vocational counselling, vocational training, prosthetic appliances, and placement services for the physically handicapped. In 1943 the service was further increased to include vocational rehabilitation of all disabled persons, including blind persons and emotionally and mentally handicapped persons, and to provide any service necessary to fit disabled people for remunerative occupations. This service operates on both federal and state levels.

Medical service for disabled persons includes medical examination and any type of medical or allied service which will reduce the individual's disability as a handicap to employment. Medical, surgical, and psychiatric service, physical and occupational therapy, hospitalization, dentistry, drugs and supplies, prosthetic appliances, convalescent and nursing home service, etc.—all these are provided if they will increase employability.

OFFICIAL INTERNATIONAL HEALTH ORGANIZATIONS

Health activities on an international scale are of importance to the national health of the United States. Health and disease are no respectors of international boundaries, and nations have long recognized the need for cooperation and united effort in health protection and promotion. On professional health matters nations have had little difficulty in working out agreements and programs of mutual benefit. Harmony has characterized the function of all international health organizations.

International congresses on hygiene and epidemiology have been held at irregular intervals since 1852 when the first such congress met in Brussels. From these meetings the *International Office of Public Hygiene* was created by agreement between forty nations on December 9, 1907. Until the birth of the League of Nations, the Office of Public Hygiene served as the international exchange for health knowledge and cooperation.

League of Nations Health Section. In 1923 a Health Section was formed in the Secretariat of the League of Nations to exchange health information, control pandemics, standardize laboratory products and procedures, conduct research, and cooperate in solving common health problems.

World Health Organization. At the International Health Conference held in the United States in 1946, representatives of sixty-seven governments signed the constitution of the World Health Organization (WHO). On April 7, 1948, the necessary twenty-sixth country officially confirmed its signature to complete the ratification of the constitution and give official life to the World Health Organization. It is an integral part of the United Nations.

In 1964 more than one hundred nations were members of WHO. Headquarters are maintained at Geneva, Switzerland, with six regional organizations, each representing a major geographical area of the world (Table 44).

WHO is administered by the Director General of the Secretariat. A high quality, capable permanent staff is maintained. The permanent staff is augmented on a temporary basis by highly skilled scientists in special fields as the need arises in the solution of health problems in any part of the world.

WHO operates on an annual budget of approximately $15,000,000 contributed by assessments levied upon the various members, according to a formula, with a limitation that no nation shall pay more than 33⅓% of the total assessment.

Table 44

Region	Regional office
South East Asia	New Delhi
Eastern Mediterranean	Alexandria
The Americas (Pan-American Sanitary Bureau)	Washington, D. C.
Western Pacific	Manila
Africa	Brazzaville
Europe	Copenhagen

STRUCTURE OF THE HEADQUARTERS SECRETARIAT

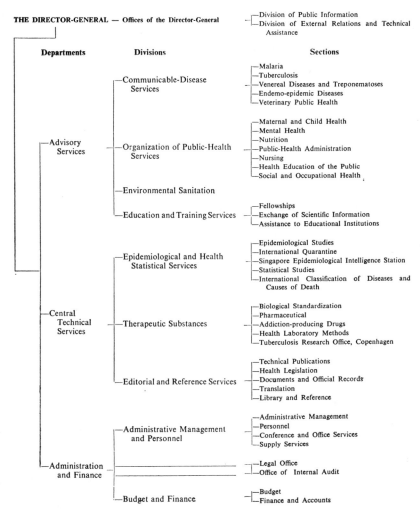

Fig. 90. (From *The work of WHO,* published by the Division of Public Information, World Health Organization, Palais des Nations, Geneva, Switzerland, 1955.)

WHO extends its efforts to virtually all health matters that are of universal concern and importance. Its own technical experts initiate and conduct programs independently of other organizations, but much of its work is done in collaboration with other agencies of the United Nations. It serves as a clearing house for health information and technical services.

All nations can turn to WHO for practical help in their health problems. Upon request its advisory service provides consultants, teachers, or demonstration teams, usually utilizing and working in cooperation with national public health administrations and local groups assigned to the job by their own health authorities.

WHO takes part in the United Nations Expanded Programme of Technical Assistance for economic development of underdeveloped countries. WHO cooperates closely with other agencies, among which are the United Nations Children's Fund, the United Nations Specialized Agencies, especially the Food and Agriculture organization, the United Nations Educational, Scientific and Cultural Organization, the Technical Assistance Board, and the International Labor Organization.

The technical services of WHO include fact finding, the administration of international regulations passed by the Health Assembly, an international warning system (spread of disease), international sanitary regulations, standardization into international units of many drugs, an international pharmacopoeia, and many more.

The general organization of WHO indicates the extensiveness of its services. The *WHO Chronical* is published monthly.

FUTURE CONSERVATION OF HUMAN RESOURCES

The possibilities for accomplishment are almost unlimited for both official and voluntary agencies at the national level. Many of the voluntary agencies are approaching the accomplishment of their original purpose. The federal agencies as yet have only scratched the surfaces of the contributions that they might make. The social philosophy of the United States will determine the role that the federal agencies will take as contrasted to private, individual, and voluntary services. In what future areas the federal government will operate and under what conditions are difficult to predict.

A plan for the medical care of the American people has been widely discussed during the past two decades. The last depression and World War II as well as the evolution of the federal government in increased social service have affected the philosophy and thinking of many people. Whether a nationwide medical care program will emerge remains to be seen. There is little question but that the government must assume control and responsibility in various health areas that have to do distinctly with federal functions. Research, the control of biological products, the Pure Food and Drug Act, and health problems that develop from interstate commerce are widely accepted as definite functions of the federal government. Whereas doubts exist regarding the socialization of medical care, there is wide approval for the continued efforts of government to conserve the precious human resources of the nation.

Early efforts at conservation. The conservation of the human resources of the nation has been the subject of much study over a long period of time. Some of the important milestones are of interest. In 1909 President Theodore Roosevelt appointed a group to study the Conservation of National Resources. A Sub-Committee on National Health made recommendations relating to the improvement of preventive medicine.

In 1909 the first White House Conference on Child Health and Protection was held. Due to the stimulus of this conference the Children's Bureau of the Department of Labor was organized. These conferences have been continued at ten-year intervals. The 1930 White House Conference produced over thirty volumes, perhaps the most comprehensive treatment of current child health and protection ever published. This conference also produced the *Children's Charter.* Similar conferences have been held and include the White House Conference on Children in a Democracy, 1940, the Mid-Century White House Conference on Children and Youth, 1950, and the Golden Anniversary Conference on Children and Youth, 1960. This last Conference was broader in scope than any of the previous ones. More than seven thousand participants were in session for one week.

Conservation through medical care. In 1932 the Committee on the Cost of Medical Care, after a five-year study, made its report and recommendations. The report showed the uneven distribution of medical care as to both the community and the individual. The report pointed out that there was no national plan for the medical care of indigent persons or federal funds for care of the sick poor. Among the recommendations were the promotion of public health facilities on a nationwide basis and governmental control of measures concerning medical, nursing, and hospital care of indigent persons. A majority report recommended some system of governmental sickness insurance and group practice in community hospitals.

In 1935 the Committee on Economic Security, in reporting to President Franklin D. Roosevelt, recommended the establishment of a National Health Program. This Committee called attention to the failure to apply scientific knowledge in preventive medicine and health promotion. Out of this grew the Social Security Act of 1935.

This Social Security Act markedly increased public health services and the opportunity to initiate constructive public health programs. The general title of the act states its purpose, as follows:

> To provide for the general welfare by establishing a system of Federal old-age benefits, and by enabling the several States to make more adequate provision for aged persons, blind persons, dependent and crippled children, maternal and child welfare, public health and the administration of their unemployment-compensation laws; to establish a Social Security Board; to raise revenue; for other purposes.

In 1935 and 1936 the National Health Survey was conducted by the U. S. Public Health Service. The extent of illness in the United States, with its relationship to economic and social forces, was shown on a greater scale than by any other known survey. This survey confirmed many of the findings made by the Committee on the Cost of Medical Care.

In 1938 President Franklin D. Roosevelt appointed the Interdepartmental Committee to Coordinate Health and Welfare Activities. Its major purpose was to consider a national health program. It advised expanding public health services including the existing Federal-State Cooperative Program, increasing full-time county health units, and attacking special public problems such as "the eradication of tuberculosis, venereal diseases, malaria, and certain occupational hazards, the lowering of mortality from pneumonia and cancer, the reduction of morbidity in the case of mental disorders."

The Committee held it to be desirable to expand the present Federal-State Cooperative Program for Maternal and Child Health Services specifically along the lines of "maternity care and care of new-born infants, medical care of the children, and services for crippled children."

Federal grants-in-aid for needed hospital and similar facilities and some assistance in operating costs for a limited period of time were recommended. General, tuberculosis, and mental hospitals were included, and provision for outpatient service was advised. In addition the Committee proposed federal grants-in-aid to states for medical care for the medically needy, for a more general program of medical care, and for federal action toward the development of a program of disability compensation.

In 1944 the American Public Health Association issued an official statement on medical care as it relates to a national health program.*

This report is the most comprehensive statement of a national health plan that has been made. A student of the problem should study the full report carefully; here it is necessary only to sketch the main points very briefly. At the outset are listed the insufficient and inadequate medical care of a large portion of the population, the extensive deficiencies in physical facilities, the shortages in quantity and quality of personnel, the lack of public health departments in many communities, and the need for expansion of research. The report sets as its object medical care for the entire population to provide all essential preventive, diagnostic, and curative services. It proposes to finance the plan by social insurance supplemented by general taxation or by general taxation alone; it recommends a single agency to administer the plan at all levels—federal, state, and local. It suggests that public health departments assume major responsibilities under the plan, that construction programs be directed by the U. S. Public Health Service, and that coordination of all official health agencies be secured. Finally there are set forth plans for training of personnel, development of research, and expansion of services, especially to rural areas.

In 1945 the Report on Local Health Units for the Nation by the Sub-Committee on Local Health Units of the Committee on Administrative Practice of the American Public Health Association was published. Recognizing the need of supplying full-time health services at the community level to all people in the nation, it suggested a new administrative mechanism for obtaining this goal, as follows:

> Employing the same set of guides for each state—complete coverage with basic minimum full-time service; units of jurisdiction of populations large enough (50,000 or more) to support and justify staffs of full-time professionally trained persons; at the cost of approximately $1 per capita.†

---

*Medical care in National Health Program, Am. J. Pub. Health 34:1252, 1944.
†From Local health units for the nation, published by the Commonwealth Fund, New York, 1945, p. iii.

Such a plan would establish about 1200 units of local jurisdiction employing the principle of local cooperation, which would pool community resources and thus achieve economy and efficiency. This does not change the control of the primary services of public health, but continues them as a function of the local units of government. The support comes from tax resources of the local unit except in cases in which it must be supplemented by state and federal funds. Units will continue to have supplemental supervisory, consultative, coordinative, standardizing, and research service by the state board of health, which in turn receives a like service from the federal health agencies.

The National Advisory Committee on Local Health Departments was created by the National Health Council in 1959 to again study and make a report on current needs and weaknesses of local health units. After a fifteen-year interval, reappraisal is indicated.

In general this plan has been approved by the American Medical Association, the American Public Health Association, and the State and Provincial Health Authorities of North America, as indicated by the following resolutions.

Approval of the American Medical Association was stated as follows:

> WHEREAS, a major inadequacy in the civilian health protection in war as in peace time exists consequent upon the failure of many states and of not less than half the counties in the states to provide even minimum necessary sanitary and other preventive services for health by full-time professionally trained medical and auxiliary personnel on a merit system basis, supported by adequate tax funds from local and state, and, where necessary, from federal sources: therefore be it
> RESOLVED, that the Trustees of the American Medical Association be urged to use all appropriate resources and influences of the Association to the end that at the earliest possible date complete coverage of the nation's area and population by local, county, district or regional full-time modern health services be achieved.*

Approval by the American Public Health Association was as follows:

> WHEREAS, the immediate emergencies of wartime and the continuing necessities of a nation at peace require health protection for all within our boundaries, and
> WHEREAS, the most effective state and national health services can be provided only when all communities have accepted the responsibility of applying the science and art of preventive medicine as a permanent function of local civil government, therefore be it
> RESOLVED, that collaboration with other professional, official and voluntary organizations be sought to obtain total coverage of the nation by local health units at the earliest practicable date.†

Approval by the State and Provincial Health Authorities of North America was as follows:

> WHEREAS, the outstanding deficiency in public health administration throughout the North American Continent is the lack of over-all coverage by legally constituted local health organizations, and
> WHEREAS, expansion in the field of public health demands that every segment of the population should receive the benefit of full-time public health protection, and

---

*American Medical Association, House of Delegates, June 10, 1942.
†American Public Health Association, Governing Council, October 29, 1942.

WHEREAS, studies have been made by the Committee on Administrative Practice of the American Public Health Association for the purpose of evolving a plan for complete public health services, and said Committee has reached agreements with the State Health Officers as to the desirable pattern for full-time public health units in 39 states, representing over 85 per cent of the population of the United States; therefore

BE IT RESOLVED, that the Conference of State and Provincial Health Authorities of North America urge the implementation of such a program throughout the Continent of North America.[*]

Health insurance. The effort to ensure against sickness has evolved from a social movement which has been established for a century and a half. The necessity for its development was brought about, first, by the Industrial Revolution with its great benefits and terrific hazards which aroused in mankind a definite urge for security of the individual, and, second, through the development and elaboration of medical science from which have come great good and profit to mankind. To make the most efficient use of the many benefits which medical science has to offer, organization and machinery must be developed.

From these two developments during the past two decades, health insurance has become firmly established. This movement which may now be regarded as a part of our social philosophy involves all health interests, including private, government, labor, and industrial management. Insurance is a device to substitute average costs for variable costs. In this instance it is a device to spread the cost of medical service among a larger number of persons because of the cost and unpredictability of sickness to the individual. Different names are used for this device—organization for payment, prepayment, or pooled payment. In the achievement of its purpose many problems arise out of the medical service made available to large groups; these involve professional and public education, preventive services, and the quality of care. It is the application of the service that has been difficult. The principle of health insurance has been accepted widely.

Most of the plans for health insurance so far developed in the United States have been voluntary; that is, the individual has the privilege of enrolling or not, as he pleases, or, after enrolling, he may cancel his membership at any time. Most of the recently proposed federal legislation concerning health insurance embraces some form of voluntary enrollment. Two types of plans are in existence at the present time. These two types may be illustrated by the Blue Cross Hospital plan and the plan which comes under the auspices of medical societies. Many of the pioneer plans were concerned largely with hospital benefits. At present coverages have been broadened to include hospital, surgery, and sickness benefits.

Under the Blue Cross type of plan may be listed the various hospital service plans which are sponsored by the hospitals themselves, usually with the approval of the Hospital Service Plan Commission of the American Hospital Association. This is usually a nonprofit corporation whose director serves without pay, and

---

[*]State and Provincial Health Authorities of North America, Conference, March 22, 1944.

the voting control is vested largely with the representatives of the hospital and the medical profession.

The plans of medical societies follow in many ways the Blue Cross plan. Usually a nonprofit corporation is formed, with the voting control in the hands of representatives of medical professions.

Under both plans contracts are entered into with groups of employed persons who pay regular fees, usually by means of payroll deductions. Often dependents of the employees are included in the benefits. Usually there is at the time of sickness free choice of hospital from among those of the participating group. The medical society plans offer freedom of choice of a physician from among those participating in the program. The Blue Cross plan also offers freedom of choice of physicians. Both plans are usually supervised by the various state insurance departments.

Other groups that work or are rendering service in this area are industrial and labor unions, medical cooperatives, physician-owned prepayment group clinics, commercial accident and health insurance, Farm Security Administration, and miscellaneous types which are sponsored by religious groups, fraternal organizations, and so on.

The numbers of civilians enrolled in these plans are about equally divided between the Blue Cross and private insurance companies. In 1961, more than 136,000,000 persons or 75% of the population were protected by some form of voluntary health insurance. In addition many others are protected through the Armed Services, penal institutions, sanitariums, college health services, liability insurance, workmen's compensation, Veterans' Administration, Federal Social Security, and other types of protection.

There are five types of health insurance: hospital expense, surgical expense, regular medical expense, major medical expense (catastrophic), and loss-of-income policies. At the end of 1961 persons protected by the various plans were as follows:

Hospital expense	136,500,000
Surgical expense	127,000,000
Regular medical expense	94,000,000
Loss-of-income	43,000,000
Major medical expense	34,000,000

The fastest growing group in 1961 was major medical expense, with a 24% gain over 1960. Other rapidly growing types of voluntary health insurance provided protection against medical expense for hospital, physicians' fees, drugs, and other costs. The coverage of persons in the group over 65 years of age from 1952 to 1961 increased from 26% to 53%. The rate of increase of those over 65 years of age is greater than those under 65 years of age. In 1961 voluntary insuring groups paid to insured persons 6.4 billion dollars, a 12% increase over 1960.

It is difficult to fit health insurance on a nationwide basis into all our communities because of our social philosophy. Nationalization of public health, however, is receiving intensive study at the present time. The many aspects of the problem and the diversity existing in the nation present serious difficulties. Some of these difficulties arise because the population is decidedly heterogeneous rather than homogeneous. In addition the expansiveness of the country and the wide variations in economic status, type of industry, tradition, and culture from section to section add to the difficulty. Under these conditions any national health plan would have to be very flexible. Such a project presents nearly insurmountable obstacles. To many people a nationwide scheme would encroach upon local self-government and personal freedom. Our dilemma is that as a people we want security and the best social conditions obtainable but are undecided on how much personal freedom we are willing to sacrifice for these benefits.

The answer to these and many more perplexing questions must be determined before we can have a national health program and security without the sacrifice of individual freedom.

The economics of health and disease. There are at least three economic aspects of health and disease: (1) the cost of medical service, (2) the loss of earning capacity to the patient, and (3) the loss of productive labor to industry and society.

More than 21 billion dollars was spent in 1961 on medical care cost or about 6% of the amount spent for all personal needs. This represents 6.8 billion dollars more than 1956 and 11.7 billion dollars more than in 1951. In addition acute illnesses and injuries resulted in 250.3 million lost days by workers in 1960. The loss in productivity from this cause is staggering.

Many things have happened that have increased the cost of medical care. With each advance in scientific medicine and allied fields, the quality of medical service is enhanced. The discovery and subsequent utilization of roentgen rays, radium therapy, insulin, sulfa drugs, the antibiotics (penicillin, streptomycin, Aureomycin, Chloromycetin, and Terramycin), cortisone and ACTH, and many more fortify medical practice with powerful weapons of attack and prevention. But for both patient and physician there is an increase in cost. In addition advances in surgical techniques, surgical equipment, and various mechanical aids have added to the cost. Accompanying these developments has been an increase in the cost of medical education. Today the minimum education above the public school level required for medical practitioners is eight years. As the level of adequacy of medical service has risen, the cost has also increased.

Most of the thinking relative to the cost of medical care is based upon our own individual conception of adequate medical care and does not take into consideration the advances that have been made in this area. Such a premise can only be as valid as our experience with the best in modern practice in the various sections of the country at different economic levels. Many of us think in terms of the medical care of twenty and twenty-five years ago, with little thought or appreciation of the added contributory factors, such as new procedures made possible by essential equipment, buildings, and personnel. The newer knowledge which is constantly being added in this area demands extended educational preparation for the various groups engaged in the healing art, including physicians, nurses, and pharmacists as well as more facilities and equipment. It is important to note that with the necessary added cost of the expanded service the amount that the physician gets out of the dollar for the cost of medical care is now about twenty-three cents, whereas in 1938 it was thirty-one cents.

The conception of adequate medical care changes from era to era. There has developed in this country a social consciousness which demands the right to health and freedom from preventable disease. Thus the increasing cost of medical care is due in part to advances in scientific research, to an awakened and enlightened social consciousness, to the ability of medicine to render much more adequate service, and to a desire on the part of the people to receive such service.

The cost of medical care to the nation is a staggering sum. Surveys have been made from time to time in this area. There is a definite consistency in the findings from period to period. At present about 21 billion dollars are spent annually for personal health services or an average of $116 a person. Medical and hospital insurance pay for about 8% of the medical care portion; individual private payments account for about 70%; taxes pay for about 20%; whereas private charity pays less than 2%.

The public is spending a larger portion of its income for medical services than it did in 1938—an increase from 4% to 6.2%. This compares with 6.1% for recreation and 5.3% for tobacco and alcoholic beverages. The return to the public is much greater, however, because of the advances in medical and public health science since that time. The increased length of life and the comparative freedom from communicable disease are the results of health progress aided by a higher standard of living including better food, better housing, and better sanitation. The cost of medical care to the individual might even be considered to have lowered. Such things as the virtual control of pneumonia, which was formerly a costly long treatment in a hospital, the reduction of time spent in hospitals for many types of surgery, for maternity care, and for other sicknesses, the impact of the Salk and Sabin vaccines on the reduction of poliomyelitis, and many more have reduced the medical bill and, far more important, have relieved people with various illnesses of the consequent suffering, the long nonproductive period, and the expense of a long illness.

The 21 billion dollars spent annually for personal health service is a vast sum of money. There is no general agreement as to whether this amount is enough to secure the best health for all the people. There are no accepted standards by which this can be judged. The question of how much of the national production or of the family income we wish to spend for health services is unanswered. There is evidence that tax funds are being spent in greater and greater amounts for this purpose. The question of how far tax moneys and government funds should be used is discussed widely.

The problem warrants serious study. Whether services and vast additional amounts of money are necessary must be determined scientifically and unemotionally. How the money will be raised, how it will be spent, and under what auspices are aspects that need careful intensive critical study. It certainly can be accepted that it must be administered and expended in such a manner that the tenets of democracy, the freedom of the individual, and the freedom of initiative will not be endangered.

Nationalization of health. During the last few years increasing attention has been directed toward a national health program. Public health organizations as well as health insurance received intensive study occasioned largely by the depression of 1929. Several studies have been made showing the need for adequate medical, nursing, and hospital care for all people in every community. One of the first studies on a wide scale was made during the last half of the 1920's; twenty-eight reports were published. In 1934 President Roosevelt appointed a Committee on Economic Security to make recommendations for a program "against misfortunes which cannot be wholly eliminated in this man-made world of ours." One of the problems investigated was the economics of medical care. In 1935 the Social Security Act was passed. In 1935 and 1936 the U. S. Public Health Service conducted a National Health Survey. This was the most extensive survey of sickness ever undertaken. It included a house-to-house canvass of over 700,000 households in urban communities in eighteen states and 37,000 households in rural areas in six states.

The need for continuing information of this kind was apparent. In 1956 Congress authorized the U. S. Public Health Service to make continuing national surveys and special studies on the current amount, distribution, and effects of illness and disability. This act established the U. S. National Health Survey. Periodic reports by this agency are extremely valuable in evaluating progress and in planning future public health programs.

Progress and agreement. The social philosophy of the nation toward public health in the United States has been developing very rapidly. There is a definite demand for these services for all people. There is an increasing development of health programs at the national level, and federal agencies and bureaus are becoming more articulate in what should be done to transfer this influence to the state and local levels. This development has progressed without much resistance because of the grants-in-aid or subsidies to the state and local groups. It is apparent that much study, legislation, and advancement toward a national health program has taken place. Certain aspects of the problems have been recognized and attempts have been made to rectify them.

Bibliography

Chapter 1. The student and his health

American Association for Health, Physical Education, and Recreation: A forward look in college health education, Washington, D. C., 1956, The Association.

Bachman, W. W., and associates: Health resources in the United States: personnel, facilities and services, Washington, D. C., 1952, The Brookings Institution.

Bass, A. D., and Moe, G. K.: Congenital heart disease, Washington, D. C., 1960, American Association for the Advancement of Science.

Bland, J. H.: Arthritis, New York, 1960, The Macmillan Co.

Brams, W. A.: Managing your coronary, ed. 2, Philadelphia, 1956, J. B. Lippincott Co.

Clark, R. L.: The book of health, Princeton, N. J., 1962, D. Van Nostrand Co., Inc.

Cook, J.: Remedies and rackets, New York, 1958, W. W. Norton & Co., Inc.

Diehl, H. S.: Textbook of healthful living, ed. 6, New York, 1960, McGraw-Hill Book Co., Inc.

Dublin, L. I.: The facts of life from birth to death, New York, 1951, The MacMillan Co.

Dubos, R.: Mirage of health, New York, 1959, Harper & Row, Publishers.

Eichenlaub, J. E.: College health, New York, 1962, The Macmillan Co.

Gallup, G., and Hill, E.: The secrets of long life, New York, 1960, Random House, Inc.

Galton, L.: Exercise helps you live longer, Science Digest **40**:30, 1959.

Hoehling, A. A.: The great epidemics, Boston, 1961, Little, Brown & Co.

Johns, E. B., Sutton, W. C., and Webster, E. E.: Health for effective living, ed. 3, New York, 1962, McGraw-Hill Book Co., Inc.

Johnson, W. R.: Health concepts for college students, New York, 1962, The Ronald Press Co.

Jordan, S. M.: Health and happiness, New York, 1962, Devin-Adair Co.

Lang, Gladys E.: Old age in America, New York, 1961, H. W. Wilson Co.

Luisada, L. L.: Cardiovascular functions, New York, 1962, McGraw-Hill Book Co., Inc.

Maxcy, K. F. (editor): Rosenau, M. J.: Preventive medicine and public health, ed. 8, New York, 1956, Appleton-Century-Crofts, Inc.

National Vital Statistics Division: Vital statistics of the United States, Washington, D. C. (annual), U. S. Government Printing Office.

Paul, B. D., and Miller, W. B.: Health, culture and community, New York, 1955, Russell Sage Foundation.

Pinckney, E. R.: You can prevent illness, Philadelphia, 1960, J. B. Lippincott Co.

Roth, A.: The teen-age years, Garden City, New York, 1960, Doubleday & Co., Inc.

Shock, N. W.: Aging: some social and biological aspects, New York, 1960, American Association for the Advancement of Science.

Sigerist, H. E.: Landmarks in the history of hygiene, London, 1956, Oxford University Press.

Society of Actuaries: Build and blood pressure study, vol. 1, Chicago, 1959, The Society.

Standish, S., Bennet, B., White, Kathleen, and Powers, L. E.: Why patients see doctors, Seattle, 1955, University of Washington Press.

Stearn, A. E., and Stearn, Esther W.: College

hygiene for total health, Philadelphia, 1961, J. B. Lippincott Co.

Schifferes, J. J.: Essentials of healthier living, New York, 1960, John Wiley & Sons, Inc.

Stankovich, P. J.: Awake to a new way of life, New York, 1963, Vantage Press, Inc.

Turner, C. E.: Personal and community health, ed. 12, St. Louis, 1963, The C. V. Mosby Co.

Chapter 2. Inherited basis of health

Abnormal chromosomes, Science News Letter, 79: Jan. 28, 1961.

Ashley Montagu, M. F.: Human heredity, New York, 1959, World Publishing Co.

Bearn, A. G., and German, J. L.: Chromosomes and disease, Scientific American 205:66-89, Nov., 1961.

Boyd, W. C.: Genetics and the races of man, Boston, 1958 (paper-back ed.), Boston University Press.

Boyer, S. H.: Papers on human genetics, Englewood Cliffs, N. J., 1963, Prentice-Hall, Inc.

Butterworth, T., and Strean, L. P.: Clinical genodermatology, Baltimore, 1962, Williams & Wilkins Co.

Colin, E. C.: Elements of genetics, New York, 1956, McGraw-Hill Book Co., Inc.

Crow, J. F.: Genetics notes, ed. 4, Minneapolis, 1960, Burgess Publishing Co.

Dublin, L. I., and Marks, H. H.: The inheritance of longevity. Proceedings of the Association of Life Insurance Medical Directors, New York, 1941, Life Insurance Association of America, vol. 28, p. 41.

Dunn, L. C. (editor): Genetics in the twentieth century, New York, 1951, The Macmillan Co.

Dunn, L. C., and Dobzhansky, T.: Heredity, race and society, ed. 2, New York, 1952, The New America Library of World Literature, Inc.

Gardner, E. J.: Principles of genetics, New York, 1960, John Wiley & Sons, Inc.

Gardner, L. I.: Molecular genetics and human disease, Springfield, Ill., 1960, Charles C Thomas, Publishers.

Gates, R. R.: Human genetics (2 vol.), New York, 1946, The Macmillan Co.

Harrison, G.: Genetical variations in human populations, New York, 1961, Pergamon Press.

Hill, J. B., and Hill, Helen D.: Genetics and human heredity, New York, 1955, McGraw-Hill Book Co., Inc.

Huntington, E.: Mainsprings of civilization, New York, 1945, John Wiley & Sons, Inc.

Kalow, Werner: Pharmacogenetics—heredity and response to drugs, Philadelphia, 1952, W. B. Saunders Co.

McKusick, Victor: Medical genetics 1958-60, St. Louis, 1961, The C. V. Mosby Co.

Merrell, D. J.: Evolution and genetics, New York, 1962, Holt, Rinehart & Winston, Inc.

Neel, J. V., and Shull, W. J.: Human heredity, Chicago, 1954, University of Chicago Press.

Pearl, R. P., and Pearl, Ruth D.: The ancestry of the long-lived, Baltimore, 1934, John Hopkins Press.

Peters, J. A. (editor): Classic papers in genetics, Englewood Cliffs, N. J., 1959, Prentice-Hall, Inc.

Rasmuson, Marianne: Genetics on the population level, Stockholm, 1961, Bonnier's Scandinavian University Books.

Rivers, T. M.: Birth defects to be research target, Journal of Home Economics 52: Jan., 1960.

Roberts, J. A. F.: An introduction to medical genetics, ed. 21, London, 1959, Oxford University Press.

Rowley, J. D.: Review of recent studies of chromosomes in mongolism, American Journal of Mental Deficiency 66: Jan., 1962.

Scheinfeld, A.: Basic facts of human heredity, New York, 1961, Affiliated Publishers, Inc.

Scheinfeld, A.: Why you are you, New York, 1959, Abelard-Schuman, Ltd.

Scheinfeld, A.: The human heredity handbook, Philadelphia, 1956, J. B. Lippincott Co.

Sheldon, W. H., Stevens, S. S., and Tucker, W. B.: The varieties of human physique, New York, 1940, Harper & Brothers.

Sinnott, E. W., Dunn, L. C., and Dobzhansky, T.: Principles of genetics, ed. 5, New York, 1958, McGraw-Hill Book Co., Inc.

Snyder, L. H.: The principles of heredity, ed. 5, Boston, 1957, D. C. Heath & Co.

Stern, C.: Principles of human genetics, San Francisco, 1960, W. H. Freeman & Co.

Sutton, Harry: Genes, enzymes and inherited diseases, New York, 1961, Holt, Rinehart & Winston, Inc.

Waddington, C. H.: New patterns in genetics and development, New York, 1962, Columbia University Press.

Wallace, B., and Dobzhansky, T.: Radiation, genes and man, New York, 1959, **Henry Holt & Co., Inc.**

Williams, R. J.: Free and unequal, Austin, 1953, University of Texas Press.

Williams, R. J.: Key to health: your heredity, Science Digest 53: April, 1963.

Winchester, A. M.: Genetics, a survey of the principles of heredity, ed. 2, Boston, 1958, Houghton Mifflin Co.

Chapter 3. Daily personal health care

American Dental Association, Council on Dental Health: Floridation in the prevention of dental caries, ed. 3, Chicago, 1953, The Association.

Andrews, G. C.: Diseases of the skin, ed. 4, Philadelphia, 1954, W. B. Saunders Co.

Behrman, H. T.: Scalp in health and disease, St. Louis, 1952, The C. V. Mosby Co.

Blatz, H. (editor): Radiation hygiene handbook, New York, 1959, McGraw-Hill Book Co., Inc.

Canfield, N.: Hearing: a hankbook for laymen, Garden City, N. Y., 1959, Doubleday & Co., Inc.

Claus, W. C.: Radiation biology and medicine, Reading, Mass., 1958, Addison-Welsey Publishing Co., Inc.

Cole, H. N.: The skin in health and disease, Chicago, 1948, American Medical Association.

Davis, H. (editor): Hearing and deafness: a guide for laymen, New York, 1960, Holt, Rinehart & Winston, Inc.

Goldsmith, N. R.: You and your skin, Springfield, Ill., 1953, Charles C Thomas, Publisher.

Illuminating Engineering Society: Recommended practice of home lighting, New York, 1947, The Society.

Illuminating Engineering Society: Standard practice for school lighting, New York, 1948, The Society.

Lindsay, J. R.: The yearbook of ear, nose and throat, Chicago, 1961-1962, Yearbook Medical Publishers, Inc.

Montagna, W.: The structure and function of the skin, New York, 1956, Academic Press, Inc.

Moulton, F. R.: Dental caries and fluorine, Washington, D. C., 1946, American Association for the Advancement of Science.

Muhler, J. C., and Hine, M. K. (editors): Fluorine and dental health, Bloomington, Ind., 1959, University of Indiana Press.

National Academy of Sciences-National Research Council: The biological effects of atomic radiation, a report to the public, Washington, D. C., 1956, The Academy.

Ogg, Elizabeth: Save your sight, New York, 1954, Public Affairs Press.

Rothman, S.: Physiology and biochemistry of the skin, Chicago, 1954, University of Chicago Press.

Rothman, Stephen: The human integument—normal and abnormal, Washington, D. C., 1959, American Association for the Advancement of Science.

Shaw, J. H. (editor): Fluoridation as a public health measure, Washington, D. C., 1954, American Association for the Advancement of Science.

Smelser, G. K.: The structure of the eye, New York, 1961, International Congress of Anatomists.

Sutton, R. L., and Sutton, R. L., Jr.: Diseases of the skin, ed. 11, St. Louis, 1956, The C. V. Mosby Co.

Torrington Manufacturing Company: How to have comfort from moving air, Torrington, Conn., 1950, Torrington Manufacturing Co.

United States Atomic Energy Commission: Radiation safety and major activities of the atomic energy program, Washington, D. C., 1957, U. S. Government Printing Office.

Vail, D. T.: The truth about your eyes, ed. 2, New York, 1959, Farrar, Straus, & Cudahy, Inc.

World Health Organization: Air pollution, New York, 1961, Columbia University Press.

Yaffe, C. D., and Jones, H. H.: Noise and hearing, Pub. no. 850, Washington, D. C., 1961, U. S. Public Health Service.

Yahraes, H.: Your teeth: how to save them, New York, 1956, Public Affairs Press.

Chapter 4. Nutrition in health

Bogert, L. Jean: Nutrition and physical fitness, ed. 7, Philadelphia, 1960, W. B. Saunders Co.

Brock, J. F.: Recent advances in human nutrition, Boston, 1961, Little Brown & Co.

Brozek, J. F.: Conference on the role of body measurements and human nutrition, Detroit, 1956, Wayne University Press.

Byrd, O. E.: Nutrition sourcebook, Stanford, 1955, Stanford University Press.

Cannon, P. R.: The importance of proteins in resistance to disease, J.A.M.A. **128**:360, 1945.

Chaney, M. S., and Ahlborn, M.: Nutrition, ed. 6, Boston, 1960, Houghton Mifflin Co.

Cooper, F. L., Barber, E., and Mitchell, H.:

Nutrition in health and disease, ed. 13, Philadelphia, 1958, J. B. Lippincott Co.

Davidson, L.: Human nutrition and dietetics, Baltimore, 1959, Williams & Wilkins Co.

Goodhart, R. S.: Nutrition for you, New York, 1958, Dutton & Co.

Keys, A., and Keys, Margaret: Eat well and stay well, New York, 1959, Doubleday & Co., Inc.

Leverton, Ruth M.: Food becomes you, Ames, 1960, Iowa State University Press.

Lecht, S. H. (editor): Therapeutic exercise, ed. 2, New Haven, Conn., 1961, Physical Medicine Library.

Maddox, Gaynor: Vitamin Pills are not a food substitute, Today's Health 39: Nov., 1961.

Martin, E. A.: Nutrition in action, New York, 1963, Holt, Rinehart & Winston, Inc.

McCollum, E. V.: A history of nutrition, Boston, 1957, Houghton Mifflin Co.

McDermott, Irene E., Trilling, Mabel B., and Nicholas, Florence W.: Food for better living, ed. 3, Philadelphia, 1960, J. B. Lippincott Co.

McHenry, E. W.: Foods without fads, Philadelphia, 1960, J. B. Lippincott Co.

Page, L., and Phipard, E. F.: Essentials of an adequate diet, Home Economics Research Reports, Washington, D. C., 1957, U. S. Government Printing Office.

Sherman, H. C., and Lanford, Caroline S.: Essentials of nutrition, ed. 4, New York, 1957, The Macmillan Co.

Stevenson, Gladys T., and Miller, Cora: Introduction to foods and nutrition, New York, 1960, John Wiley & Sons, Inc.

Tonkin, R. D.: The story of peptic ulcer, Philadelphia, 1957, W. B. Saunders Co.

von Haller, Albert: The vitamin hunters, Philadelphia, 1962, Chilton Co.

Watt, Bernice K., and Stiebeling, Hazel K.: Food, yearbook of the U. S. Department of Agriculture, Washington, D. C., 1959, U. S. Government Printing Office.

White, Ruth B.: You and your food, Englewood Cliffs, N. J., 1961, Prentice-Hall, Inc.

Wohl, M. G., and Goodhart, R. S.: Modern nutrition in health and disease, Philadelphia, 1960, Lea & Febiger.

Young, J. R.: Experimental inquiry into the principles of nutrition and the digestive system, Urbana, 1959, University of Illinois Press.

Ziegler, P. T.: The meat we eat, Danville, Ill., 1962, The Interstate Printers and Publishers.

Chapter 5. Exercise, fatigue, and rest

Athletic Institute: Exercise and fitness, Chicago, 1960, The Institute.

Bookwalter, K. W., and Bookwalter, C. W.: Fitness for secondary school youth, Washington, 1956, American Association for Health, Physical Education, and Recreation.

Brightbill, C. K.: Man and leisure, Englewood Cliffs, N. J., 1961, Prentice-Hall, Inc.

Bucher, Charles A.: Foundations of physical education, ed. 3, St. Louis, 1960, The C. V. Mosby Co.

Consolazio, Frank C., Johnson, Robert E., and Pecora, Louis J.: Physiological Measurements of metabolic functions of man, New York, 1963, McGraw-Hill Book Co., Inc.

Davis, E. C., and Logan, G. A.: Biophysical values of muscular activity, Dubuque, Iowa, 1961, William C. Brown Co.

Drury, Blanche J.: Posture and figure control through physical education, Palo Alto, Calif., 1961, National Press Publications.

Hilliard, Marion: Women and fatigue, New York, 1961, Doubleday & Co., Inc.

Johnson, Warren R.: Science and medicine of exercise and sports, New York, 1960, Harper & Row, Publishers.

Jokl, Ernst: The clinical physiology of fitness and rehabilitation, Springfield, Ill., 1958, Charles C Thomas, Publisher.

Kleitman, N: Sleep and Wakefulness, Chicago, 1962, University of Chicago Press.

Karpovich, Peter V.: Physiology of muscular activity, ed. 5, Philadelphia, 1959, W. B. Saunders Co.

Kraus, Hans, and Raab, Wilhelm: Hypokinetic disease, Springfield, Ill., 1961, Charles C Thomas, Publisher.

Langley, L. L., and Cheraskin, E.: The physiology of man, ed. 2, New York, 1958, McGraw-Hill Book Co., Inc.

Larson, L. A.: Health and fitness in the modern world, Chicago, 1961, Athletic Institute.

Licht, S. H.: Therapeutic exercise, New Haven, Conn., 1958, Yale University Press.

Lowman, Charles Leroy, and Young, Carl Haven: Postural fitness, Philadelphia, 1960, Lea & Febiger.

Miller, Benjamin F., and Miller, Zelma: Good health, Philadelphia, 1960, W. B. Saunders Co.

Morehouse, L. E.: Physiology of exercise, St. Louis, 1959, The C. V. Mosby Co.

President's Council on Fitness and Youth: Fitness of American youth, first, second, and third reports, Washington, D. C., 1957, 1958, and 1959, Youth Physical Fitness,

Parts One and Two, 1961, Physical Fitness Elements in Recreation, 1962, U. S. Government Printing Office.

Steinhaus, A. H.: Toward an understanding of health and physical education, Dubuque, Iowa, 1963, W. C. Brown Co.

Tuttle, W. W., and Schottelius, B. A.: Textbook of physiology, ed. 14, St. Louis, 1961, The C. V. Mosby Co.

Walke, N. S., Droscher, N., and Volpe, M. D.: Health and fitness, Dubuque, Iowa, 1962, W. C. Brown Co.

Willgoose, Carl E.: Evaluation in health education and physical education, New York, 1961, McGraw-Hill Book Co., Inc.

Chapter 6. Safety for health promotion

American Public Health Association: Accident prevention, New York, 1961, The Blakiston Division-McGraw-Hill Book Co., Inc.

American Red Cross: Numerous pamphlets, Washington, D. C., American Red Cross National Headquarters.

Automobile Manufacturers' Association: Automobile facts and figures (published annually), Detroit, The Association.

Brody, Leon, and Stack, Herbert J.: Highway safety and driver education, New York, 1954, Prentice-Hall, Inc.

California Department of Fish and Game: Home and hunter safety, Sacramento, 1955, The Department.

Center for Safety Education: Man and the motor car, ed. 6, Englewood, N. J., 1959, Prentice-Hall, Inc.

Florio, A. E., and Stafford, G. T.: Safety education, ed. 2, New York, 1962, McGraw-Hill Book Co., Inc.

Halsey, M. L.: Accident prevention, New York, 1961, McGraw-Hill Book Co., Inc.

National Board of Fire Underwriters: Numerous pamphlets, New York, The Board.

National Bureau of Standards: Safety for the household (circular 463), Washington, D. C., 1948, U. S. Government Printing Office.

National Committee on Safety Education: Numerous pamphlets, Washington, D. C., National Education Association.

National Safety Council: Accident facts, Chicago, annual edition, The Council.

National Safety Council: Numerous pamphlets, Chicago, The Council.

National Rifle Association: Numerous pamphlets on hunter safety, Washington, D. C., The Association.

Smith, Julian W.: Shooting hunting, Washington, D. C., 1960, American Association for Health, Physical Education, and Recreation.

Stack, H. J., and Elkow, J. D.: Education for safe living, ed. 3, New York, 1957, Prentice-Hall, Inc.

Chapter 7. Substances harmful to health

Alcoholics Anonymous Publications, New York, Works Publishing Co.

American Medical Association: Manual on Alcoholism, Chicago, 1956, The Association.

Anslinger, H. J., and Anslinger, W. P.: The traffic in narcotics, New York, 1953, Funk & Wagnalls Co.

Beckman, Harry: Drugs, their nature, action and use, New York, 1958,

Brookes, V. J., and Jacobs, M. B.: Poisons, ed. 2, Princeton, N. J., 1958, D. Van Nostrand Co., Inc.

Burns, Harold: Drugs, medicines and man, New York, 1962, Charles Scribner's Sons.

Chafetz, M. E., and Demone, H. W., Jr.: Alcoholism and society, New York, 1962, Oxford University Press.

Dack, G. M.: Food poisoning, ed. 2, Chicago, 1955, University of Chicago Press.

D'Alongo, C. A.: The drinking problem and its control, Houston, Texas, 1959, The Gulf Publishing Co.

Dreisbach, R. H.: Handbook of poisoning: diagnosis and treatment, ed. 2, Los Altos, Calif., 1959, Lange Medical Publications.

Green, H.: Science looks at smoking, New York, 1957, Coward-McCann, Inc.

Hammond, E. Cuyler: Smoking in relation to heart disease, American Journal of Public Health **50**: March, 1960.

Hammond, E. Cuyler: The effects of smoking, Scientific American **207**: July, 1962.

Hammond, E. Cuyler, and Garfinkel, Lawrence: Smoking habits of men and women, Journal of National Cancer Institute **27**: August, 1961.

Himwick, H. E.: Alcoholism, Washington, D. C., 1958, American Association for the Advancement of Science.

Hock, P. H., and Zubin, J.: Problems of addiction and habituation, New York, 1958, Grune & Stratton, Inc.

Isbell, H.: What to know about drug addiction, Public Health Pub. no. 94, Washington, D. C., 1951, U. S. Government Printing Office.

Jellinek, E. M.: The disease concept of alcoholism, New Haven, Conn., 1960, Yale University Press.

King, A.: The cigarette habit: a scientific cure, Garden City, New York, 1959, Doubleday & Co., Inc.

Maurer, D. W., and Dogel, V. H.: Narcotics and narcotic addiction, ed. 2, Springfield, Ill., 1963, Charles C Thomas, Publisher.

McCord, W., and McCord, Joan: Origins of alcoholism, Stanford, 1960, Stanford University Press.

Merrill, F. T.: Marihuana, the new dangerous drug, Washington Opium Research Committee, Foreign Policy Association, Inc., 1938.

Monroe, Margaret Ellen: Alcohol education for the layman, New Brunswick, N. J., 1959, Rutgers University Press.

Ochsner, A.: Smoking and health, Minneapolis, 1959, Julian Messner, Inc.

Pearl R.: Alcohol and longevity, New York, 1926, Alfred A. Knopf, Inc.

Rea, F. B.: Alcoholism, its psychology and cure, New York, 1956, Philosophical Library, Inc.

Rutgers University: Alcohol, science and society, Quarterly Journal of Studies on Alcohol, New Brunswick, N. J., 1945, Rutgers University Press.

Rutgers University: Journal of Studies on Alcohol, Supplements:
Alcohol and crime
Alcohol and industrial efficiency
Alcohol beverages as a food and their relation to nutrition
Alcohol beverages, health, and length of life
Alcohol, heredity, and germ damage
Facts on cirrhosis of the liver
Facts on delirium tremens
Government and the alcohol problem
How alcohol beverages affect behavior
How alcohol beverages affect the body
Moderate and excessive users of alcoholic beverages
Production and properties of alcoholic beverages
The problems of alcohol
What happens to alcohol in the body

Saltman, Jules: Emphysema, New York, 1962, Public Affairs Press.

Seltzer, C. C.: Masculinity and smoking, Science 130:Nov., 1959.

Strauss, R., and Bacon, S.D.: Drinking in college, New Haven, Conn., 1953, Yale University Press.

Tyler, H. R.: Botulinus toxin: effect on the central nervous system of man, Science 139: Mar., 1963.

United States Bureau of Narcotics: Regulation no. 1 relating to importation, manufacture, production of marihuana, Washington, D. C., 1938, U. S. Government Printing Office.

United States Internal Revenue Service: Statistics relating to the alcohol and tobacco industries, 1952 to 1953, Washington, D. C., 1954, The Service.

Vogel, V. H., and Vogel, Virginia: Facts about drug addiction, Chicago, 1960, Science Research Associates, Inc.

Williams, R. J.: Alcoholism: the nutritional approach, Austin, 1959, University of Texas Press.

Yahraes, H.: Alcoholism is a sickness, New York, 1946, Public Affairs Press.

Chapter 8. Normal mental and emotional health

Abrahamsen, D.: The road to emotional maturity, Englewood Cliffs, N. J., 1958, Prentice-Hall, Inc.

Anderson, Camilla M.: Beyond Freud: a creative approach to mental health, New York, 1957, Harper & Brothers.

Beers, C. W.: A mind that found itself, New York, 1948, Doubleday & Co., Inc.

Bernard, H. W.: Mental hygiene for classroom teachers, New York, 1961, McGraw-Hill Book Co., Inc.

Blaine, G. B.: Emotional problems of the student, New York, 1961, Appleton-Century-Crofts, Inc.

Carroll, H. A.: Mental hygiene, ed. 3, Englewood Cliffs, N.J., 1956, Prentice-Hall, Inc.

Crow, L. D., and Crow, Alice: Adolescent development and adjustment, New York, 1956, McGraw-Hill Book Co., Inc.

Dach, Elizabeth M.: Your community and mental health, New York, 1958, Public Affairs Press.

Dalton, R. H.: Personality and social interaction, Boston, 1961, D. C. Heath & Co.

Dicks, R. L.: Toward health and wholesomeness, New York, 1960, The Macmillan Co.

Duvall, Evelyn M.: Art and skill of getting along with people, Englewood Cliffs, N. J., 1961, Prentice-Hall, Inc.

Farnsworth, D. L.: Mental health in college and university, Cambridge, Mass., 1957, Harvard University Press.

Fink, D. H.: Release from tension, ed. 2, New York, 1953, Simon and Schuster, Inc.

Frank, L. K., Harrison, R., Hellersberg, Elizabeth F., and others: Personality development in adolescent girls, Urbana, Ill., 1953, University of Illinois Press.

Glasser, James R.: Mental health or mental illness, New York, 1961, Harper & Row, Publishers.

Hountras, Peter T., Jr.: Mental hygiene: a text of readings, Columbus, Ohio, 1961, Charles E. Merrill Books, Inc.

Kaplan, L.: Mental health and human relations in education, New York, 1959, Harper & Brothers.

Katz, B., and Lehner, G. F. L.: Mental hygiene in modern living, New York, 1953, The Ronald Press Co.

Kennedy, J. A.: Relax and live, Englewood Cliffs, N. J., 1953, Prentice-Hall, Inc.

Klein, D. B.: Mental hygiene; A survey of personality disorders and mental health, New York, 1956, Holt, Rinehart & Winston, Inc.

Lang, Gladys E.: Mental health, New York, 1958, The H. W. Wilson Co.

Layman, Emma: Mental health through physical education and recreation, Minneapolis, 1955, Burgess Publishing Co.

Lehner, G. F.: Explorations in personal adjustment, ed. 2, Englewood Cliffs, N. J., 1957, Prentice-Hall, Inc.

McKown, Robin: Pioneers in mental health, New York, 1961, Dodd, Mead & Co.

Ridenour, Nina: Mental health in the United States, Cambridge, Mass., 1961, Harvard University Press.

Schindler, J. A.: How to live 365 days a year, Englewood Cliffs, N. J., 1957, Prentice-Hall, Inc.

Sontag, L. W.: Mental growth and personality development, Yellow Springs, Ohio, 1958, Antioch Press.

Stevenson, G. S.: Mental health planning for social action, New York, 1956, McGraw-Hill Book Co., Inc.

Strang, Ruth M.: The adolescent views himself, New York, 1957, McGraw-Hill Book Co., Inc.

Strecker, E. A.: Discovering ourselves, ed. 3, New York, 1958, The Macmillan Co.

Tebbel, J. W.: The magic of balanced living; a man's key to health, well-being, and peace of mind, New York, 1956, Harper & Brothers.

Thorman, George: Toward mental health, New York, Public Affairs Pamphlets.

Chapter 9. Preparation for family living

Abrahamsen, D.: The road to emotional maturity, Englewood Cliffs, N. J., 1958, Prentice-Hall, Inc.

Anderson, C. L.: Physical and emotional aspects of marriage, St. Louis, 1953, The C. V. Mosby Co.

Baber, R. E.: Marriage and the family, ed. 2, New York, 1953, McGraw-Hill Book Co., Inc.

Baruch, Dorothy: New ways in sex education, New York, 1959, McGraw-Hill Book Co., Inc.

Blood, R. O.: Marriage, New York, 1962, Free Press of Glencoe.

Bossard, J. H. S., and Boll, Eleanor Stoker: One marriage, two faiths, New York, 1957, The Ronald Press Co.

Bossard, J. H. S., and Boll, Eleanor Stoker: Why marriages go wrong, New York, 1958, The Ronald Press Co.

Bowman, H. A.: Marriage for moderns, ed. 4, New York, 1960, McGraw-Hill Book Co., Inc.

Burgess, E. W., and Locke, H. J.: The family, from institution to companionship, ed. 2, New York, 1960, American Book Co.

Burgess, E. W., and others: Courtship, engagement and marriage, Philadelphia, 1954, J. B. Lippincott Co.

Burgess, E. W., Wallin, P., and Schultz, G.: Engagement and marriage, Philadelphia, 1954, J. B. Lippincott Co.

Byrd, O. E.: Family life sourcebook, Stanford, 1956, Stanford University Press.

Cavan, Ruth: American marriage, a way of life, New York, 1960, Thomas Y. Crowell Co.

Cavan, Ruth: Marriage and family in the modern world, New York, 1960, Thomas Y. Crowell Co.

Duvall, Evelyn R.: Family development, ed. 2, Philadelphia, 1962, J. B. Lippincott Co.

Duvall, Evelyn R., and Hill, R.: Being married, New York, 1960, Association Press.

Duvall, Evelyn M., and Duvall, S. M. (editors): Sex ways, New York, 1961, Association Press.

Duvall, Evelyn M., and Hill, R.: When you marry, rev. ed., Boston, 1962, D. C. Heath & Co.

Duvall, Evelyn M., and Johnson, Joy Duvall:

The art of dating, New York, 1960, Association Press.

Eckert, R. G.: Sex attitudes in the home, New York, 1956, Association Press.

Ehrmann, W. W.: Premarital dating behavior, New York, 1959, Holt, Rinehart & Winston, Inc.

Fishbein, M., and Kennedy, R.: Modern marriage and family living, London, 1957, Oxford University Press.

Force, Elizabeth S.: Teaching and family life education, New York, 1962, Columbia University Press.

Frank, L. K.: Conduct of sex, New York, 1961, William Morrow & Co.

Jacobsen, P. H.: American marriage and divorce, New York, 1959, Holt, Rinehart & Winston, Inc.

Kinsey, A. C., et al.: Sexual behavior in the human female, Philadelphia, 1953, W. B. Saunders Co.

Kinsey, A. C., et al.: Sexual behavior in the human male, Philadelphia, 1948, W. B. Saunders Co.

Landis, J. T., and Landis, Mary G.: Building a successful marriage, ed. 3, Englewood Cliffs, N. J., 1958, Prentice-Hall, Inc.

Landis, J. T., and Landis, Mary G.: Personal adjustment, marriage and family living, ed. 2, Englewood Cliffs, N. J., 1957, Prentice-Hall, Inc.

Landis, P. H.: Making the most of marriage, New York, 1957, The Macmillan Co.

Lee, A. M., and Lee, Elizabeth B.: Marriage and the family, New York, 1961, Barnes & Noble, Inc.

Le Masters, E. E.: Modern courtship and marriage, New York, 1957, The Macmillan Co.

Lewin, S. A., and Gilmore, J.: Sex without fear, rev. ed., New York, 1962, Medical Research Press.

Lewinsohn, Richard: A history of sexual customs, New York, 1959, Harper & Row, Publishers.

Merrill, F. E.: Courtship and marriage, rev. ed., New York, 1959, Holt, Rinehart & Winston, Inc.

Mills, C. A.: Climatic effects on growth and development, American Anthropologist, p. 297, 1942.

Mitchell, R. M., and Klein, T.: Nine months to go, Philadelphia, 1960, J. B. Lippincott Co.

Moore, E. R.: The case against birth control, New York, 1944, The Century Co.

Mudd, Emily Hartshorne, and Krich, A.: Man and wife, New York, 1957, W. W. Norton & Co., Inc.

National Education Association: Sex education, sixteenth yearbook, Washington, D. C., 1944, The Association.

Parker, Elizabeth: The seven ages of woman, Baltimore, 1960, Johns Hopkins University Press.

Pike, J. A.: If you marry outside your faith, rev. ed., New York, 1962, Harper & Brothers.

Stone, A., and Stone, Hannah M.: A marriage manual, ed. 2, New York, 1952, Simon & Schuster, Inc.

Sullenger, T. E.: Neglected areas in family living, Boston, 1960, Christopher Publishing House.

Truxal, A. G., and Merrill, F. E.: Marriage and the family, Englewood Cliffs, N. J., 1953, Prentice-Hall, Inc.

Winch, R. F.: Mate-selection, New York, 1958, Harper & Row, Publishers.

Winch, R. F., and McGinnis, R.: Selected studies in marriage and the family, ed. 2, New York, 1962, Holt, Rinehart & Winston, Inc.

Young, L. R.: Out of wedlock, New York, 1954, McGraw-Hill Book Co., Inc.

Chapter 10. Prevention of disease

American Public Health Association: The control of communicable diseases in man, ed. 9, New York, 1960, The Association.

Anderson, G. W., and Arnstein, M. G.: Communicable disease control, ed. 4, New York, 1962, The Macmillan Co.

Dubos, René J.: Bacterial and mycotic infections of man, ed. 3, Philadelphia, 1958, J. B. Lippincott Co.

Elkin, I. I.: A course in epidemiology, New York, 1961, Pergamon Press.

Frobisher, Martin, Jr.: Fundamentals of bacteriology, ed. 7, Philadelphia, 1963, W. B. Saunders Co.

Hilleboe, Herman E., and Larimore, Granville W.: Preventive medicine, Philadelphia, 1959, W. B. Saunders Co.

Hoehling, A. A.: The great epidemics, Boston, 1961, Little, Brown & Co.

May, Jacques M.: The ecology of human disease, New York, 1959, M. D. Publications, Inc.

Rivers, Thomas M., and Horsfall, Frank L.: Viral and rickettsial infections of man, ed. 3, Philadelphia, 1959, J. B. Lippincott Co.

Rosen, George: A history of public health, New York, 1958, M. D. Publications, Inc.

Smith, David T., and Conant, Norman F.: Zinsser's Bacteriology, ed. 12, New York, 1960, Appleton-Century-Crofts, Inc.

Top, Franklin H.: Communicable diseases, ed. 4, St. Louis, 1960, The C. V. Mosby Co.

United States Department of Agriculture: Animal diseases, Washington, D. C., 1956, U. S. Government Printing Office.

Wells, W. F.: Air-borne contagion and hygiene, Cambridge, Mass., 1955, Harvard University Press.

Chapter 11. State and local health services

American Public Health Association: Guide to a community health study, New York, 1960, The Association.

Anderson, C. L.: School health practice, ed. 3, St. Louis, 1964, The C. V. Mosby Co.

Anderson, G. W., and Arnstein, M. G.: Communicable disease control, ed. 4, New York, 1962, The Macmillan Co.

Babbitt, Harold E.: Sewage and sewage treatment, ed. 8, New York, 1958, John Wiley & Sons, Inc.

Babbitt, Harold E., and Doland, James J.: Water supply engineering, ed. 5, New York, 1955, McGraw-Hill Book Co., Inc.

Carnley, P. B., and Bigman, S. K.: Acquaintance with municipal government health services in a low-income urban population, American Journal of Public Health **52:** Nov., 1962.

Cassedy, J. H.: Charles V. Chapin and the public health movement, Cambridge, Mass., 1962, Harvard University Press.

Earle, H.: Medical societies—how medical care is guaranteed to all, Today's Health **40:** Jan., 1962.

Ehlers, V. M., and Steel, E. W.: Municipal and rural sanitation, ed. 5, New York, 1958, McGraw-Hill Book Co., Inc.

Hanlon, John J.: Principles of public health administration, ed. 3, St. Louis, 1960, The C. V. Mosby Co.

Hardenbergh, William A.: Water supply and purification, ed. 3, Scranton, Pa., 1952, International Textbook Co.

Hobson, William: The theory and practice of public health, New York, 1961, Oxford University Press.

Hopkins, E. S., and Schulze, W. H.: Practice of sanitation, ed. 3, Baltimore, 1958, Williams & Wilkins Co.

Margolius, Sidney: A consumer's guide to health insurance plans, New York, 1962, Public Affairs Committee.

Mustard, Harry S., and Stebbins, Ernest L.: Introduction to public health, ed. 4, New York, 1959, The Macmillan Co.

Pirrie, D., and Dalzell-Ward, A. J.: A textbook of health education, London, 1962, Tavistock Publications.

Smillie, Wilson G., and Kilbourne, Edwin D.: Preventive medicine and public health, ed. 3, New York, 1963, The Macmillan Co.

Smillie, Wilson G., and Porterfield, John D.: Administration of health services, ed. 4, New York, 1959, The Macmillan Co.

Smolensky, Jack, and Haar, F. B.: Principles of community health, Philadelphia, 1961, W. B. Saunders Co.

Spiegelman, Mortimer: Ensuring medical care for the aged, Homewood, Ill., 1960, Richard D. Irwin, Inc.

Steel, Ernest W.: Water supply and sewerage, ed. 4, New York, 1960, McGraw-Hill Book Co., Inc.

Turner, C. E.: Personal and community health, ed. 12, St. Louis, 1963, The C. V. Mosby Co.

Wallace, H. M.: Health services for mothers and children, Philadelphia, 1962, W. B. Saunders Co.

Wasserman, Clara S.: Health organizations of the United States and Canada, Ithaca, New York, 1961, Cornell University Press.

Chapter 12. National and international health services

American Public Health Association: Medical care in a national health program, American Journal of Public Health, Dec., 1944.

Calder, Ritchie: Ten steps forward, Geneva, Switzerland, 1959, WHO's Division of Public Health Information.

Hanlon, J. J.: Principles of public health administration, ed. 3, St. Louis, 1960, The C. V. Mosby Co.

Health Insurance Institute: Source book of health insurance data, New York, yearly, Health Insurance Institute.

Mustard, Harry S., and Stebbins, Ernest L.: Introduction to public health, ed. 4, New York, 1959, The Macmillan Co.

Smillie, W. G., and Kilbourne, Edwin D.: Preventive medicine and public health, ed. 3, New York, 1963, The Macmillan Co.

United States Public Health Service: The Public Health Service today, Washington, D. C., 1955, U. S. Government Printing Office.

Wasserman, Clara S., and Wasserman, Paul: Health organizations of the United States and Canada: national, regional and state, Ann Arbor, Mich, 1961, Edwards Brothers, Inc.

Williams, R. C.: The United States Public Health Service, Washington, D. C., 1951, Commissioned Officers Association of the United States Public Health Service.

World Health Organization: Modern living, World Health, Journal of the World Health Organization, Nov., 1962, Columbia University Press.

Films and film sources

FILMS

Chapter 1. The student and his health

Arteriosclerosis, 13½ min., American Heart Association

Be Your Age, 11½ min., Metropolitan Life Insurance Co.

Challenge: Science Against Cancer, 35 min., International Film Bureau, Inc.

Choose to Live, 11 min., United World Films

Circulation, 16 min., United World Films

Common Heart Disorders and Their Causes, 17 min., McGraw-Hill Book Co., Inc.

Doctor Examines Your Heart, 10 min., Bray Studios

Guard Your Heart, 27 min., Bray Studios

Heart Disease—Its Major Causes, 11 min., Encyclopaedia Britannica Films

Heart—How It Works, 11 min., McGraw-Hill Book Co., Inc.

Heart to Heart, 10 min., American Heart Association

Hemo the Magnificent, 59 min., Association Films

Miracle Money (Quackery), 22 min., Teaching Film Custodians

New Frontiers of Medicine, 17 min., McGraw-Hill Book Co., Inc.

Once Too Often, 25 min., United World Films

Progress on Trial, 17 min., Teaching Film Custodians

Stop Rheumatic Fever, 12½ min., American Heart Association

The Doctor Speaks His Mind, 22 min., American Cancer Society

They Grow Up So Fast, 27 min., American Association for Health, Physical Education, and Recreation

Together for Health, 22 min., Michigan Department of Health

Chapter 2. Inherited basis of health

Heredity, 11 min., Encyclopaedia Britannica Films

Heredity and Environment, 10 min., Coronet Films

Heredity and Family Environment, 9 min., McGraw-Hill Book Co., Inc.

Heredity in Animals, 10 min., United World Films

Heredity and Prenatal Development, 21 min., McGraw-Hill Book Co., Inc.

Human Heredity, 20 min., E. C. Brown Trust

Medical Genetics, No. 1, 28 min., Johns Hopkins University

Medical Genetics, No. 2, 28 min., Johns Hopkins University

Science and Superstition, 10 min., Coronet Films

Chapter 3. Daily personal health care

Anatomy—The Human Skin, 10 min., Bray Studios

Body Care and Grooming, 20 min., McGraw-Hill Book Co., Inc.

Come Clean, 8 min., American Dental Association

Control of Body Temperature, 11 min., Encyclopaedia Britannica Films

Easy on the Eyes, 15 min., National Safety Council

Eyes and Their Care, 11 min., Encyclopaedia Britannica Films, Inc.

Eyes for Tomorrow, 22 min., National Society for Prevention of Blindness

How the Ear Functions, 11 min., Knowledge Builders

How the Eye Functions, 15 min., Knowledge Builders

How to Be Well Groomed, 10 min., Coronet Films

How You See It, 10 min., Jam Handy Organization

How We Hear, 10 min., Bray Pictures Corp.

Human Skin, 12 min., Bray Studios

Johnny's New Vision, 16¼ min., National Society for the Prevention of Blindness

Life Begins Again, 15 min., Western Electric Co.

Magic Lens, 20 min., Movies, U. S. A.

Matter of Choice, 27½ min., American Dental Association

More Than Meets the Eye, 26 min., American Optometric Association

Nose, Throat and Ears, 11 min., McGraw-Hill Book Co., Inc.

Right to Hear, 31 min., State University of Iowa

The Human Hair, 11 min., Bray Studios

The Sun: Friend or Enemy, 5 min., Information Films

Tooths and Consequences, 10 min., American Dental Association

What Do We Know About Teeth? 14½ min., American Dental Association

Wonderland of Vision, 20 min., Better Vision Institute, Inc.

World of Sound, 10½ min., Teaching Film Custodians, Inc.

Your Ears, 10 min., Young America Films, Inc.

Chapter 4. Nutrition in health

A Guide to Good Eating, 10 min., National Dairy Council

Food, 15 min., Young America Films, Inc.

Fraud Fighters, 17 min., McGraw-Hill Book Co., Inc.

Losing to Win, 10 min., Association Films, Inc.

Meats With Approval, 17 min., United World Films

Obesity, 12 min., Encyclopaedia Britannica Films

Proof of the Pudding, 10 min., Metropolitan Life Insurance Co.

Something You Didn't Eat, 9 min., U. S. Department of Agriculture

Strange Hunger, 35 min., American Society of Baking Engineers

Understanding Vitamins, 14 min., Encyclopaedia Britannica Films, Inc.

Weight Reduction Through Diet, 20 min., National Dairy Council and Association Films, Inc.

Chapter 5. Exercise, fatigue, and rest

Exercise and Health, 10 min., Coronet Films

Good Sportsmanship, 10 min., Coronet Films

Improving Your Posture, 10 min., Coronet Films

Our Feet, 11 min., Bray Studios

Posture and Exercise, 11 min., Encyclopaedia Britannica Films, Inc.

Proper Steps, 9 min., Flory Films

Rest and Health, 10 min., Coronet Films

The Muscular System, 11 min., Educational Film Department, United World Films, Inc.

They Grow Up So Fast, 27 min., American Association for Health, Physical Education, and Recreation

Chapter 6. Safety for health promotion

Anatomy of an Accident, 26½ min., Association Films, Inc.

Anyone at All (Safety), 22 min., Encyclopaedia Britannica Films

Auto U.S.A. 27½ min., National Commission on Safety, N.E.A.

Danger Is Your Companion, 27 min., American Red Cross

It Didn't Have to Happen, 13 min., International Film Bureau, Inc.

One to a Customer, 11 min., Aetna Casualty and Surety Co.

Outboard Outings, 19 min., National Commission on Safety, N.E.A.

Safe as You Make It, 10 min., National Safety Council

Safe Driving Series, three films, 11 min. each, Coronet Films

Stop Them Before They Start, 14 min., Aetna Casualty and Surety Co.

Take Time to Live, 12 min., National Safety Council

That They May Live, 28 min., University of Toronto

To Live Tomorrow, 13½ min., U. S. Federal Civil Defense

Traffic With the Devil, 20 min., National Safety Council

You Can Take It With You, 13 min., National Safety Council

What's Your Driving Eye-Q? 13 min., National Commission on Safety, N.E.A.

Chapter 7. Substances harmful to health

Alcohol and the Human Body, 15 min., Encyclopaedia Britannica Films

Alcoholism, 22 min., Encyclopaedia Britannica Films

Allergies, 12 min., Encyclopaedia Britannica Films

Any Boy—U.S.A., 20 min., Women's Christian Temperance Union

Drug Addiction, 22 min., Encyclopaedia Britannica Films

Fraud Fighters, 17 min., McGraw-Hill Book Co., Inc.

High Temperature Short Time Pasteurization, 21 min., United World Films

I Am an Alcoholic, 18 min., McGraw-Hill Book Co., Inc.

Meats With Approval, 17 min., United World Films

Problem Drinkers, 19 min., McGraw-Hill Book Co., Inc.

Should You Drink? 21 min., Mc-Graw Hill Book Co., Inc.

Tobacco and the Human Body, 15 Min., Encyclopaedia Britannica Films

To Smoke or Not to Smoke, 20 min., American Cancer Society, Inc.

Triumph Without Drums (Pure Food and Drug Act), 10 min., Teaching Film Custodians

What's Under the Label? (Pure Foods and Drugs), 11 min., National Film Board of Canada

Chapter 8. Normal mental and emotional health

Adventure in Maturity, 22 min., International Film Bureau

Age of Turmoil, 20 min., National Association for Mental Health, Inc.

Angry Boy, 33 min., International Film Bureau, Inc.

Control Your Emotions, 13½ min., Coronet Films

Developing Friendships, 10 min., Coronet Films

Emotional Health, 20 min., McGraw-Hill Book Co., Inc.

Endocrine Glands, 11 min., Encyclopaedia Britannica Films

Farewell to Childhood, 23 min., International Film Bureau, Inc.

Feelings of Depression, 30 min., McGraw-Hill Book Co., Inc.

Feeling of Hostility, 27 min., McGraw-Hill Book Co., Inc.

Feeling of Rejection, 23 min., McGraw-Hill Book Co., Inc.

Making Life Adjustments, 20 min., McGraw-Hill Book Co., Inc.

Mental Health, 12 min., Encyclopaedia Britannica Films

Out of True, 41 min., International Film Bureau

Overcoming Worry, 10 min., Coronet Films

Preface to Life, 29 min., United World Films, Government Films Department

Roots of Happiness, 24 min., International Film Bureau

Shades of Gray, 62 min., DuArt Film Laboratories

The Meaning of Adolescence, 16 min., National Association for Mental Health, Inc.

The Lonely Night, 62 min., International Film Bureau, Inc.

What's on Your Mind? 10 min., National Film Board of Canada

You and Your Attitudes, 10 min., American Film Center

You are not Alone, 33 min., Association Films, Inc.

Youth and the Law, 36 min., National Association for Mental Health, Inc.

Chapter 9. Preparation for family living

A Family Affair, 31 min., International Film Bureau, Inc.

A Normal Birth, 15 min., Medical Arts Productions

Choosing Your Marriage Partner, 13 min., Coronet Films

Courtship to Courthouse, 15 min., McGraw-Hill Book Co., Inc.

Early Marriage, 20 min., E. C. Brown Trust

Family Life, 10 min., Coronet Films

Growing Girls, 13 min., Encyclopaedia Britannica Films

How Do You Know It's Love? 13½ min., Coronet Films

Human Reproduction, 20 min., McGraw-Hill Book Co., Inc.

It Takes All Kinds, 20 min., McGraw-Hill Book Co., Inc.

Know Your Baby, 10 min., Sterling Films

Marriage and Divorce, 15 min., McGraw-Hill Book Co., Inc.

Marriage Is a Partnership, 16 min., Coronet Films

Marriage Today, 22 min., McGraw-Hill Book Co., Inc.

Meaning of Engagement, 13 min., Coronet Films

Preface to Life, 30 min., U. S. Public Health Service

Social-Sex Attitudes in Adolescence, 22 min., McGraw-Hill Book Co., Inc.

Story of Menstruation, 10 min., Association Films

This Charming Couple, 19 min., McGraw-Hill Book Co., Inc.

When Should I Marry? 19 min., National Association for Mental Health, Inc.

Who's Boss, 16 min., McGraw-Hill Book Co., Inc.

Chapter 10. Prevention of disease

Arteriosclerosis, 13½ min., American Heart Association

Accent on Use, 20 min., National Foundation for Infantile Paralysis

Behind the Shadows, 15 min., National Tuberculosis Association

Body Defense Against Disease, 11 min., Encyclopaedia Britannica Films

Body Fights Bacteria, 15 min., McGraw-Hill Book Co., Inc.

Challenge: Science Against Cancer, 33 min., International Film Bureau

Common Cold, 11 min., Encyclopaedia Britannica Films

Common Heart Disorders and Their Causes, 17 min., McGraw-Hill Book Co., Inc.

Fight Syphilis, 10 min., U. S. Public Health Service

Health Is a Victory, 12 min., American Social Hygiene Association

Heart Disease—Its Major Cause, 11 min., Encyclopaedia Britannica Films

Immunization, 11 min., Encyclopaedia Britannica Films

Invisible Armour, 20 min., National Film Board of Canada

Lease on Life, 20 min., National Tuberculosis Association

Let's Have Fewer Colds, 10 min., Coronet Films

Miracle of Living, 39 min., United World Films

Miracle Money (Quackery), 22 min., Teaching Film Custodians

Newsreel (Poliomyelitis), 10 min., National Foundation for Infantile Paralysis

Our Job to Know, 18 min., American Social Hygiene Association

Poliomyelitis—Diagnosis and Management, 60 min., British Information Service

Sneezes and Sniffles, 10 min., McGraw-Hill Book Co., Inc.

Stop Rheumatic Fever, 12½ min., American Heart Association

Story of Dr. Jenner, 10 min., Teaching Film Custodians

Story of Louis Pasteur, 17 min., Teaching Film Custodians

Taming the Crippler (Poliomyelitis'), 16 min., McGraw-Hill Book Co., Inc.

The Doctor Speaks His Mind, 22 min., American Cancer Society

Time Out, 25 min., National Tuberculosis Association

Tuberculosis, 11 min., Encyclopaedia Britannica Films

Working for Better Public Health Through Recognition of Feeling, 25 min., Community Disease Service

You Can Help, 10 min., National Tuberculosis Association

You, Time and Cancer, 16 min., American Cancer Society

Chapter 11. State and local health services

A Community Problem (Garbage Disposal), 13 min., Caterpillar Tractor Co.

Another Light (Community Hospital), 15 min., Bailey Films

City Water Supply, 10 min., Encyclopaedia Britannica Films

Community Health and You, 19 min., McGraw-Hill Book Co., Inc.

Community Health in Action, 22 min., International Film Bureau, Inc.

Community Health Is Up to You, 18 min., McGraw-Hill Book Co., Inc.

High Temperature Short Time Pasteurization, 21 min., United World Films

Laboratory Control of Milk, 9 min., United World Films

Let's Look at Water, 21 min., National Film Board of Canada

Report to the People (Public Health), 13 min., Dairy Council of St. Louis

Rural Health, 17 min., National Film Board of Canada

School Health in Action, 25 min., Samuel P. Orleans and Associates

So Much for So Little (Public Health), 11 min., United World Films

Tale of the Twin Cities (Sewage Disposal), 20 min., University of Minnesota

Together for Health, 22 min., Michigan Department of Health

Working Together for Health, 22 min., Michigan Department of Health

Water Supply, 11 min., Academy Films

Your Health Department, 20 min., National Motion Picture Co.

Your Health Department in Action, 20 min., Samuel P. Orleans and Associates

Chapter 12. International and national health services

At Our House, 9 min., Columbia University

Battle for Bread (United Nations), 23 min., McGraw-Hill Book Co., Inc.

Common Concern (International Health), 10 min., National Film Board of Canada

House of Mercy (Hospitals), 15 min., McGraw-Hill Book Co., Inc.

Journey Into Medicine, 36 min., United World Films

Men of Medicine, 20 min., McGraw-Hill Book Co., Inc.

New Frontiers of Medicine, 17 min., McGraw-Hill Book Co., Inc.

The World Is Rich, 43 min., United Nations

This Is Their Story, 23 min., United Nations

Triumph Without Drums, 10 min., Teaching Film Custodians

FILM SOURCES

Academy Films, Box 3088, Hollywood, Calif.

Alcoholics Anonymous, General Board, P.O. Box 459, New York 17, N. Y.

American Association for Health, Physical Education, and Recreation, 1201 Sixteenth St., N.W., Washington 6, D. C.

American Cancer Society, 521 West 57th St., New York, N. Y.

American Dental Association, 222 East Superior St., Chicago 11, Ill.

American Film Center, P. O. Box 363, San Jose 3, Calif.

American Foot Care Institute, 1775 Broadway, New York 19, N. Y.

American Heart Association, 44 East 23rd St., New York 10, N. Y.

Amercan Leprosy Missions, 4 Garber Square, Ridgewood, N. J.

American Medical Association, Bureau of Health Education, 535 North Dearborn St., Chicago 10, Ill.

American Optometric Association, 4030 Choteau Ave., St. Louis 10, Mo.

American Petroleum Institute, 50 West 50th St., New York, N. Y.

American Red Cross, 1730 E St., N.W., Washington, D. C.

American Social Health Association, 1790 Broadway, New York 19, N. Y.

American Society of Bakery Engineers, De-partment of Visual Education, 208 Third Ave., S.E., Minneapolis, Minn.

Association Films, Inc., 351 Turk St., San Francisco, Calif.

Avis Films, 932 North LaBrea, Hollywood 38, Calif.

Bailey Films, Inc., 6509 DeLongpre Ave., Hollywood 28, Calif.

Better Vision Institute, Inc., 630 Fifth Ave., New York, N. Y.

Brandon Films, Inc., Western Cinema Guild, 290 Seventh Ave., San Francisco 18, Calif.

Bray Pictures Corp., 729 Seventh Ave., New York 19, N. Y.

British Information Service, 30 Rockefeller Plaza, New York, N. Y.

E. C. Brown Trust, 220 S. W. Alder St., Portland 4, Ore.

Castle, 7356 Melrose Ave., Hollywood 46, Calif.

Caterpillar Tractor Company, Peoria, Ill.

Churchill-Wexler Film Productions, 81 North Seward St., Los Angeles 38, Calif.

Columbia University Press, Center for Mass Communication, 1125 Amsterdam Ave., New York 27, N. Y.

Community Disease Center, Chamblee, Ga.

Contemporary Films, Alvin J. Gordon, 1859 Powell St., San Francisco 11, Calif.

Coronet Films, Coronet Building, Chicago, Ill.

Dairy Council of St. Louis, 4030 Choteau Ave., St. Louis, Mo.

Sid Davis Productions, 3826 Cochran Ave., Los Angeles 56, Calif.

DuArt Film Laboratories, 245 West 55th St., New York 19, N. Y.

Eastman Films, Eastman Kodak Co., Informational Films Division, 343 State St., Rochester 4, N. Y.

Educator's Progress Service, Randolph, Wis.

Eli Lilly, Public Relations Department, Indianapolis, Ind.

Encyclopaedia Britannica Films, Inc., Wilmette, Ill.

Farm Film Foundation, 1731 Eye St., N.W., Washington 6, D. C.

Film Publishers, 25 Broad St., New York 4, N. Y.

Flory Films, 303 East 71st St., New York 19, N. Y.

Gateway Productions, Inc., 1859 Powell St., San Francisco 11, Calif.

General Motors Corp., 3044 W. Grand Blvd., Detroit 2, Mich.

General Picture Production, 621 6th Ave., Des Moines 9, Iowa

Harmon Division of Visual Experiment, 140 Nassau St., New York 38, N. Y.

Information Foundation, 420 Lexington Ave., New York 17, N. Y.

Institute of Inter-American Affairs, 499 Pennsylvania Ave., N.W., Washington 25, D. C.

International Film Bureau, Suite 308-316, 57 East Jackson Blvd., Chicago 4, Ill.

Jam Handy Organization, 2821 East Grand Blvd., Detroit 11, Mich.

Johns Hopkins University School of Medicine, 800 Second Ave., New York 17, N. Y.

Johnson and Johnson, Promotion Department, New Brunswick, N. J.

Kimberly-Clark Corp., Neenah, Wis.

Knowledge Builders, Visual Education Center Building, Lowell and Cherry Lane, Floral Park, N. Y.

March of Time, McGraw-Hill Book Co., Text Film Department, 330 West 42nd St., New York 18, N. Y.

McGeary-Smith Laboratories, 1905 Fairview Ave., N.E., Washington 2, D. C.

McGraw-Hill Book Co., Inc., Text Film Department, 330 West 42nd St., New York 18, N. Y.

Medical Motion Pictures, Committee on Medical Motion Pictures, American Medical Association, 535 North Dearborn St., Chicago 10, Ill.

Michigan Department of Health, Visual Education Service, Lansing, Mich.

Medical Arts Productions, P. O. Box 4042, Stockton, Calif.

Modern Talking Picture Service, Inc., 3 E. 54th St., New York 22, N. Y.

Movies, U. S. A., Inc., 729 Seventh Ave., New York 19, N. Y.

National Association for Mental Health, Inc., 10 Columbus Circle, New York 19, N. Y.

National Dairy Council, 111 North Canal St., Chicago 6, Ill.

National Film Board of Canada, 1270 Avenue of the Americas, New York 20, N. Y.

National Foundation, 800 2nd Ave., New York 17, N. Y.

National Motion Picture Company, West Main St., Mooresville, Ind.

National Safety Council, 425 North Michigan Ave., Chicago 11, Ill.

National Society for the Prevention of Blindness, 1790 Broadway, New York 19, N. Y.

National Tuberculosis Association, 1790 Broadway, New York 19, N. Y.

Personal Products, Education Department, Milltown, N. J.

Portafilms, 418 North Glendale Ave., Glendale 6, Calif.

Rarig Motion Picture Co., 5514 University Way, Seattle 5, Wash.

Samuel P. Orleans and Associates, Knoxville, Tenn.

Seminar Films, Inc., 347 Madison Ave., New York 17, N. Y.

Smith, Kline & French Laboratories, 1530 Spring Garden St., Philadelphia 1, Pa.

Social Science Films, 4030 Chouteau Ave., St. Louis 10, Mo.

State University of Iowa, Iowa City, Ia.

Sterling Television Co., Sterling Films, 205 East 43rd St., New York 17, N. Y.

Teaching Film Custodians, Inc., 25 West 43rd St., New York 18, N. Y.

United States Bureau of Mines, 4800 Forbes St., Pittsburgh 13, Pa.

United States Department of Agriculture, Motion Picture Service, Office of Information, Washington 25, D. C.

United States Department of Health, Education, and Welfare, Washington 25, D. C.

United States Federal Civil Defense, Motion Picture Service, Washington 25, D. C.

United States Public Health Service, Communicable Disease Center, 605 Volunteer Building, Atlanta 3, Ga.

United Nations, Film Division, Room 1003, 1600 Broadway, New York 19, N. Y.

United World Films, Inc., Educational Film Department and Government Films Department, 1445 Park Ave., New York 29, N. Y., or 605 West Washington Blvd., Chicago 6, Ill., or 7356 Melrose Ave., Hollywood 46, Calif.

University of Michigan, Ann Arbor, Mich.

University of Minnesota, Minneapolis, Minn.

Visual Training Institute, 40 East 49th St., New York, N. Y.

Warren's Motion Pictures, Box 107, Dayton, Ohio

Western Electric Co., Motion Picture Bureau, 195 Broadway, New York 7, N. Y.

Woman's Christian Temperance Union, 1730 Chicago Ave., Evanston, Ill.

Young America Films, Inc., 18 East 41st St., New York 17, N. Y.

Index

A

Abnormalities, chromosomal, 77
Abscess, gum, 127
Absorption, 142
Accident-prone persons, 205, 209
Accidents, 190
  age, 195
  attitudes, 197
  cost, 195
  farm, 202
  fatal, 194
  health, 192
  home, 198
  human factor, 196
  motor vehicle, 206
  occupational, 204
Acid, acetic, 241
  acetylsalicylic, 252
  amino, 142, 143, 153
  ascorbic, 157
  carbonic, 179
  fatty, 143
  lactic, 179
  oxalic, 241
  uric, 225
Acne, 106, 307
Acrolein, 241
Act, Food, Drug, and Cosmetics, 253
  Harrison Anti-Narcotic, 230, 251
  Hill-Burton, 391
  National Cancer, 415
  Social Security, 425
  Venereal Disease Control, 415
Action, muscular, 175
Acuity, visual, 135
Adaptability, 271
Addict, marihuana, 250
  morphine, 229
Addiction, drug, 228
Adjustment, sexual, 307
Adolescence, 267

Adult health promotion, 400
Adulthood, later, 268
  middle, 268
  young, 268
Aedes aegypti, 342
African sleeping sickness, 334
Afterglow, 309
Age, chronological, 84
  group, 195
  marriage, 294
  menarchial, 302
  mental, 84
  physiological, 101
Agencies, community health, 376
  official health, 369
  recreation, 380
  state health, 370
  voluntary health, 70, 369
Agent, causative, 330
Ages, Dark, 325
Aging, normal, 30
  pathological, 32
Air conditioning, 114
AlAnon, 237
Alcohol, 231, 239
  circulation, 233
  digestion, 232
  ethyl, 331
  malnutrition, 233
Alcoholics Anonymous, 236
Alcoholism, 234
  heredity, 238
  length of life, 239
  problem drinkers, 237
Alkaline reserve, 176
Allergy, food, 226
  inheritance, 91
Aluminum sulfate, 385
Alveoli, 175
Amblyopia, 136
Amentia, 275

American Association for Health, Physical
  Education, and Recreation, 406
American Cancer Society, 410
American Council on Education, 18
American Dental Association, 405
American Medical Association, 404
American Medical Directory, 405
American Public Health Association, 405
American Red Cross, 411
American Review of Tuberculosis, 408
American Social Hygiene Association, 409
Ammonia, 241
Ammonium nitrate, 253
Anabolism, 174
Analogous paired chromosomes, 74
Anaphylaxis, 91
Androgens, 302, 310
Androsterone, 310
Anemia, 161
  congenital, 80
  pernicious, 82
Anesthesia, 230
Aneurysm, 45
Angina pectoris, 47
Angstrom unit, 109
Anomalies, developmental, 99
Anovulation, 317
Anoxemia, 254
Antabuse, 235
Anthrax, 330, 332
Antibiotics, 44, 67
Antibodies, 43, 352
Antigen, 353, 354
Antiseptic, 231
Antisera, 352, 354
Antitoxin, 354
Appendicitis, 92
Appraisal, local health services, 402
Arteriosclerosis, 45, 361
Aspirin, 252
Astigmatism, 90, 136
Astringent, 103, 231
Atheroma, 45
Atherosclerosis, 45, 362
Athlete's foot, 107
Atopy, 91
Atropine, 136
Attitudes, safety, 197
Autointoxication, 225

B

Bacteria, 331, 525
Bacteriology, 330
Bacteriophage, 334
Baldness, 104
Bantus, 45
Barbiturates, 230
Basal metabolism, 143
Bathing, 102
Baths, cleansing, 102
  contrast, 102
  sedative, 103
  stimulating, 103

Beeton, M., 79
Benzedrine sulfate, 235
Benzpyrene, 241
Beriberi, 233
Biologics, 354
Blackheads, 105
Blastula, 317
Blepharitis, 137
Blindness, 130
  color, 89
Blue Cross Hospital Plan, 428
Boils, 107
Bordet, J., 331
Botulism, 227
Brain wave, 88
Breath, unpleasant, 128
Britton, R. H., 131
Brunn, 76
Buerger's disease, 246
Build, body, 41
Bureau of Agricultural Economics, 202
Bureau of Medical Services, 420
Bureau of State Services, 420
Burgess, Ernest W., 288

C

CA—A Bulletin of Cancer Progress, 411
Caffeine, 252
Calciferol, 158
Calcium, 160
Caloric expenditure, 147
Calorie, 141
  values, 151
Canal, inguinal, 309
Cancer, 51, 367
Canker, 128
Cannabinol, 249
Cannabis sativa, 249
Carbohydrate, 141
Carbon dioxide, 255
  monoxide, 115, 241, 254
Carboxyhemoglobin, 254
Carcinogens, 93, 243
Care, postnatal, 319
  prenatal, 318
Caries, dental, 126
Carotene, 156
Carrier, 348
Case, mild and missed, patients with, 349
Catabolism, 174
Cataract, 136
Cauterization, 320
Cavernosum, 311
Cavity, 126
Chancre, 356
Chancroid, 359
Changes, sensory, 31
Charter, Children's, 412, 425
Chemistry, body, 176
Chemotherapy, 67, 292
Chickenpox, 328, 337, 347, 355
Child health promotion, 400

Childhood, 265
  later, 266
  middle, 266
Chlorination, 384, 385
Chlorophyll, 140
Chromosome, 72
  sex, 75, 89
Circulation, 101, 233, 245
Cirrhosis, liver, 232, 328
City health department, 392
Cleanliness, 102
Cleft palate, 99
Climacteric, 321
Clitoris, 314
Clostridium botulinum, 227
  tetani, 336
Clothing, 104
Clubbed feet, 99
  hands, 99
Cocoa, 252
Coffea arabica, 252
Cola, 252
Cold, common, 334, 337
  sores, 106
Collidine, 241
Color blindness, 89
Commissioner, state health, 374
Commonwealth Fund, 412
Communicable disease control, 398
Conduct, motivation, 263
Conduction, nerve, 233
Conflict, sex, 303
Constitution and physical endowment, 262
Contact, direct, 341
  indirect, 341
  social, 341
Contacts, 350
Continence, 307
Contraception, 96
Convalescence, 348
Convalescent, 349
Corns, 106
Corpus luteum, 316, 317
Correns, C., 76
Cost, medical care, 425, 430
Cottrell, Leonard S., 288
Council, health, 377
County health department, 395
    board, 395
      finances, 395
      functions, 395
Courage, 270
Cramp, 184
Cream, cold, 103
  vanishing, 103
Creatin, 225
Creatinin, 225
Crest load and metabolism, 174
Cretinism, 99
Cryptorchism, 309
Crypts, tonsil, 128, 224

Cycle, disease, 347
  menstrual, 316, 317
  sleep, 181

D

Dandruff, 105
Dating, 285
Dawber, T. R., 245
Daydreams, 274
Deafness, conduction, 129
  perceptive, 130
Death(s), accidental, 191
  causes, 59, 61
  postponing, 63
  reduction rate, 329
Defection, 348
Defects, congenital, 43, 99
  highway, 208
Defervescence, 348
Deficiency, mental, 84
Defloration, 308
Dementia, 275
  paralytica, 357
Dental caries, 126
Deodorant, 103
Deoxyribose nucleic acid, 73
Department, county health, 395
  Health, Education, and Welfare, 415
  local health, 69, 392, 393
  state health, 371
Depilatories, 103
Dermatologist, 105, 107
Dermatosis, 254
Detritus, 102
Development, follicle, 316
de Vries, H. H., 76
Diabetes insipidus, 93
  mellitus, 53, 92, 324, 363
Diathesis, 77, 93
Diet, balanced, 167
Diethylene glycol, 241
Digestion, 142, 232, 245,
  and health, 166
Dipsomaniac, 237
Director, health, 393, 396
Disease, acute, 328
  arteriosclerosis, 45, 361
  atherosclerosis, 45, 362
  blood vessels, 43
  Buerger's, 246
  chronic, 51, 328, 365
  communicable, 329
  control, 329
  defense, 350
  degenerative, 42, 360
  functional, 328
  heart, 43, 328, 362
  hypertension, 362
  insect-borne, 342, 344
  nephritis, 328, 364
  occupational, 328
  organic, 328

Disease—cont'd
  pernicious anemia, 82
  prevention, 36, 325
  reservoir, 334
  spread, 339
  transference, 339
  venereal, 356
Disinfectant, 231
Disjunction, 78
Dislocation, congenital, 99
Disorders, cardiovascular, 48, 83
  developmental, 98
  mental, 87, 275, 276, 277
  mouth, 126
  nonhereditary, 98
  personality, 276
  skin, 105
  vision, 136
Disposal, garbage and refuse, 389
Divorce, 298
  cause, 299
  pathway, 298
Dominance, incomplete, 75
  irregular, 88, 90
Dominant inheritance, 75
Doyle, J. T., 245
Dreams, 183
Drinker, problem, 237
Driver, drinking, 206
  drunken, 206
  education, 212
  training, 212
Droplet nuclei, 346
Droplets, 346
Drugs, 228, 230
  addiction, 228
Dublin, L. I., 80
Durnin, J.V.G.A., 147
Dyspepsia, 92
Dysrhythmia, 88

E

Economics of health and disease, 430
Eczema, 105
Edema, 51
Education, driver, 212
  general, 17, 18
  safety, 210
  sex, 301
Egyptians, 325
Ehrlich, P., 331
Electrocardiogram, 175
Electroencephalogram, 88
Electroencephalograph, 88
Emissions, nocturnal, 307
Emotions, negative, 264
  positive, 264
Emphysema, 244
Encephalitis, 335
Endemic diseases, 326
Endocarditis, 44, 224
Endocrines, 176, 247

Energy, 140
  kinetic, 140
  needs, 140
  potential, 140
Enforcement, safety, 208
Engagement, 291
Engineering, safety, 210
Enzymes, 223
Epidemic, 325, 326, 338
Epididymis, 310
Epilepsy, 88
Erythroblastosis fetalis, 80
Escherichia coli, 384
Estrogens, 302
Estrone, 316
Eugenics, 95
  negative, 95
  positive, 97
Examinations, dental, 121
  immigrants, 95
  periodic health, 367
Exercise, 171
  effects, 173
    doubtful, 177
  general considerations, 187
Expectancy, life, 37, 38
Expenditure, caloric, 147

F

Facilities, hospital, 69, 389
Fads, 359
Fallacies, 359
Falls, 199
Farsightedness, 90, 130
Fastigium, 348
Fatalities, home, 198
  pedestrian, 206
Fatigue, 179, 180
  acute, 179
  chronic, 180
  physiological, 179
  visual, 131
Fats, 142
Faults, skin, 106
Fear, 270
Feeblemindedness, 85
Feet, clubbed, 99
  painful, 180
Fertile, 316
Fertility, 316
Fertilization, 316, 317
Films and film sources, 443
Filtration, rapid sand, 385
Firearms, 220
Fitness, 171, 173
  interpretation, 172
  physical, 172
  President's Citizens' Advisory Committee,
    171
Flexibility, 176
Flook, Evelyn, 371, 414

Fluid, prostatic, 311
  seminal, 311
Fluorine treatment, 122
Follicle, 316
Fomites, 342
Food, 140
  additives, 326
  organic, 141
  values, 151
Food and Drug Administration, 253
Foot-candle, 134
Foreskin, 312
Four Broad Food Groups, 164
Friedreich's ataxia, 88
Function, endocrine, 32
Functions, state health, 369, 371
Fungi, 334
Furfural, 241
Furuncles, 107

G

Galton, Sir Francis, 95
Gametic purity, 76
Garbage, collection, 389
  disposal, 389
Gastritis, 232
Genes, 73
Genetics, 72
Geriatrics, 30
Germ theory, 330, 336
Gerontology, 30
Giantism, 99
Gingivitis, 128
Gland, anterior pituitary, 301, 309
  apocrine, 101
  Bartholin, 314
  Cowper's, 312
  prostate, 311
  sebaceous, 105
  thyroid, 144, 162, 247
Glanders, 332
Glans, 312
Glare, 135
Glaucoma, 90, 136
Glucose, 140, 141
Glutamine, 235
Glycerin, 241
Glycerol, 143
Glycogen, 140, 142
Glycosuria, 92, 255
Goals, immediate, 269
  ultimate, 269
Goiter, 162
  exophthalmic, 247
Gonadotropin, 301, 316
Gonads, 309
Gonorrhea, 337, 357
Groups of diseases, blood transfer, 337, 339
  fecal and urinary, 337, 338
  nose and throat, 337
  suppurative process, 337, 339

H

Hair, gray, 31, 104
Hammond, E. Cuyler, 240, 243, 245
Harelip, 99
Health, 15
  adult, 400
  agencies, 369, 370, 376, 381
  community, 67, 381, 382
  council, 377
  dental, 375
  education, 19, 375
  emotional, 20
  foundations, 411
  indices, 24
  infant and child, 375, 400
  insurance, 428
  interrelationship, 67
  levels, 26
  maternal, 375, 400
  mental, 20, 259, 273, 375
  modern, 22
  normal, 22, 260
  occupational, 376
  oral, 121
  personal, 67
  promotion, 20, 29
  protection, 21
  public, 369
  resources, 68
  school, 376
  services, 378, 403
  social, 20
Hearing, 128
  defective, 129
  impairments, 129
Heart, athlete's, 175
  rheumatic fever, 43
Heat prostration, 110
Hebrews, 325
Heliotherapy, 67
Hemolysins, 225
Hemophilus ducreyi, 359
  influenza, 332
Hemp, Indian, 249
Hepatitis, viral, 337, 338
Heredity, 33, 71, 238
Hermaphroditism, 99
Herpes simplex, 106
Heslin, A. Sandra, 245
Heterosexuality, 267, 301
Heterozygous inheritance, 74
Hill, Reuben, 289
Holmes, J. S., 80
Holmes, Oliver Wendell, 96
Homatropine, 136
Homophilic period, 266
Homozygous inheritance, 74
Hooke, Robert, 330
Hormone, follicle-stimulating, 316
  gonadotropin, 316
  gonad-stimulating, 309
  interstitial tissue-stimulating, 309

Horn, Daniel, 240
Hospitals, 389
  beds, 390
  U. S. Public Health Service, 420, 421
Humidity, 111
  excessive, 112
  relative, 111
Humor, 272
Huntington's chorea, 88
Hydrotherapy, 67
Hygiene, community, 67, 326
  dental, 121
  mental, 20, 259
  oral, 36
  personal, 20, 67, 325, 341
  physical, 171
  social, 20, 171, 257
Hygrometer, 111
Hygroscopic, 241
Hymen, 314
Hyperglycemia, 92
Hypermetropic vision, 90
Hyperopia, 90, 136
Hypersensitivity, 91
Hypertension, 47, 362
Hypnotic medication, 230
Hypnotoxin, 181
Hypochondriasis, 63, 179

I

Idiocy, mongoloid, 78
Illumination, 134
Immunity, 178, 352, 353
  acquired, 352
  active, 353
  infantile, 353
  natural, 352
  passive, 353
Immunology, 353
Impairments, 57
Impetigo contagiosa, 107
Implantation, 318
Impregnate, 317
Incubation, 347
  period, 347, 356
Infancy, 265
Infection, 329
  droplet, 341
  focal, 224
  neisserian, 358
  venereal, 359
  Vincent's, 127
Inferiority, 270
Infertility, 313
Inflammation, 44, 102, 333
Influenza, 65, 329, 336
Inheritance, 35, 40, 72, 80
  allergy, 91
  appendicitis, 92
  astigmatism, 90
  cancer, 93

Inheritance—cont'd
  cardiovascular disorders, 83
  cataract, 90
  color blindness, 89
  diabetes insipidus, 93
    mellitus, 92
  epilepsy, 88
  eye defects, 89
  gastric ulcer, 91
  glaucoma, 90
  Huntington's chorea, 88
  hyperopia, 90
  intelligence, 84
  longevity, 80
  manic depressive psychosis, 88
  multiple gene, 85
  myopia, 90
  neuropathologies, 88
  pernicious anemia, 82
  predisposition, 77, 87
  ptosis, 90
  Rh factor, 80
  sex-linked, 89
Injuries, 181
  birth, 84
Insulin, 92
Insurance, health, 428
  hospital, 69, 428
  medical, 69
Intelligence, 84
  quotient, 84
Intercourse, premarital, 291, 303, 304
  sexual, 308
Intermediate host, 342
International Health Division of U. S. Public
  Health Service, 420
International Office of Public Hygiene, 422
Iodine, 162
Iron, 161
Islets of Langerhans, 92
Isolation, 350

J

Journal of the American Dental Association,
  405
Journal of the American Medical Associa-
  tion, 405
Journal of Health, Physical Education, and
  Recreation, 406
Journal of Public Health, 406
Journal of Social Hygiene, 410

K

Kahn, H. A., 245
Kannel, W. B., 245
Kellogg Foundation, 412
Kitasato, S., 331
Klinefelter's syndrome, 78
Koch, Robert, 326, 330, 331
Kulp, J. L., 120

L

Lactobacillus acidophilus, 126
Laws, Mendel's, 76
    sterilization, 96
    Workmen's Compensation, 204
League of Nations Health Section, 422
Learning, levels, 16
Leeuwenhoek, Anton, 330
Legal aspects of local health, 393
Legislation, motor vehicle, 208
Leprosarium, 415
Leukocytes, 351
Leviticus, 357
Life expectancy, 37, 38, 54
        extension, 53
    length, 239
Ligaments, uterine, 320
Locomotor ataxia, 357
Loeffler, F. A. J., 331
Longevity, 79
Lotions, hair, 105
    hand, 103
Love, 284
Lues, 356
Lymphogranuloma venereum, 359
Lysergic acid diethylamide, 277

M

Macules, 107
Maidenhead, 314
Maladjustment, sexual, 309
Malaria, 334, 337, 353
Malnutrition, 233
Malocclusion, 128
Marihuana, 249, 251
    action, 250
    control, 251
Marks, H. H., 80
Marriage, 279
    age, 294
    in college, 295
    companionship, 283
    conflict, 283
    consanquineous, 97
    economics, 297
    emotional maturity, 292
    factors, 288, 289
    husband-wife relationship, 295
    likelihood, 280
    marriageability, 289
    mate selection, 287
    and military service, 294
    in modern America, 279
    need for, 282
    preparation for, 299
    sexual adjustment, 307
        expression, 283
        intercourse, 308
    social maturity, 292
    tables, 281
    vocational maturity, 293
    working wife, 296

Masturbation, 306
Maternal health promotion, 400
    impressions, 99
Maturation, 301
Maturity, 292, 302
    emotional, 292
    marital, 292
    moral, 293
    physical, 293
    social, 292
    vocational, 293
Measles, 129, 337, 347, 353, 354
Medication, 106, 131
Melanin, 108
Membrane, fertilization, 317
    periodontal, 127
Menarche, 302
Mendel, Gregor Johann, 76
Menopause, 320
Menses, 318, 320
Menstruation, 316, 320
Metabolism, 174, 232
    basal, 143
        rate, 101, 145
Metazoa, 334
Metchnikoff, E., 331
Methylene blue, 255
Micron, 310, 331, 333
Microorganisms, 331
Microscope, electron, 66
Midgetism, 99
Milbank Memorial Fund, 412
Mild or missed cases, patients with, 349
Minerals, 160
    source, 160
Mittelschmerz, 316
Molds, 334
Moles, 106
Mongolian idiocy, 78
Morgan, Karl Z., 120
Morphine, 229
Morrow, P. A., 409
Motherhood, 247
Motivation, 263
Motives, modified, 265
Mountin, J. W., 371, 414
Movement, air, 113
Mumps, 334
Muscle, bulbar, 312
Mutations, gene, 93
Myocarditis, 44
Myopia, 90, 136

N

Narcosis, 228
Narcotics, 233, 249
National Foundation (for Infantile Paralysis), 408
National Health Advisory Council, 417
National Health Council, 413
National Health Survey, 425, 432
National Institutes of Health, 417

National League for Nursing, 406
National Office of Vital Statistics, 420
National Safety Council, 190, 191, 193, 194
National Tuberculosis Association, 407
Nationalization of health, 432
Nausea, morning, 318
Neisser, A. L., 357
Neisseria gonorrheae, 358
Neoplasms, 93
Nephritis, 50, 329, 364
Neuropathologies, 88
Neurosis, 276
Niacin, 159
Nicotine, 241
Nodes, inguinal lymph, 357
Nondisjunction, 77
Nuisance, 394
    remedies, 394
Nursing Outlook, 406
Nursing Research, 406
Nutrition, 36, 139, 140
    community, 169
    dental, 121
    eye, 134
    skin, 101

O

Obesity, 145
Objectivity, 271
Obstetrician, 309
Obstruction, visual, 208
Occupation, 41
Oculist, 131
Office of Vocational Rehabilitation, 421
Oiliness, excessive, 105
Ointment, sulphur, 107
Oleoresin, 252
Ophthalmia neonatorum, 358
Ophthalmologist, 131
Optician, 131
Optometrist, 131
Orderliness, 271
Organism, nonpathogenic, 331
    pathogenic, 331
Organizations, civic, 381
    welfare, 381
Orgasm, 309, 312, 317
Orthodontia, 128
Ostracism, social, 304
Outboard Motor Club of America, 217
Ovary, 315
Overexertion, 173
Oviduct, 315
Ovulation, 316, 317
Ovum, 74, 315, 316, 317
Oxyhemoglobin, 254

P

Pancreas, 92
Pandemic, 326
Papaver, somniferum, 229
Parenthood, 297

Paresis, general, 357
Passmore, R., 147
Pasteur, Louis, 326, 330
Patterns, conditioned, 264
    emotional, 263
    physiological, 264
Pearl, Raymond, 80, 247
Pearson, K., 79
Pedigree, 85
Pellagra, 233
Penis, 311
Periocarditis, 44
Period, convalescence, 348
    defection, 348
    defervescence, 348
    fastigium, 348
    incubation, 347
    prodromal, 347, 349
Pernicious anemia, 82
Personality, 262
    disintegration, 273
    disorder, 276
    uniqueness, 262
    well-adjusted, 269
Pertussis, 354
Phagocytosis, 351
Phenylalanine, 86
Phenylketonuria, 85
Philosophy, 269
Phosphorus, 161
Photosynthesis, 140
Pillemer, Louis, 30
Pills, sleeping, 230
Pink eye, 137
Pituitary gland, 92, 144, 301, 309, 318
Podiatrist, 376
Poisons, 223
    action, 223
    bacterial, 224
    carbon monoxide, 254
    chemical, 253
    classification, 224
    cosmetic, 253
    food, 225
    metabolic, 224
    ptomaine, 227
    sensitivity, 223
    soluble, 333
Police power, 370
Poliomyelitis, 334, 337
Polish, nail, 104
Pollution, air, 114
    soil, 345
    stream, 344
Polydipsiac, 234
Popenoe, Paul, 285, 288
Postulates, Koch's, 331
Posture, 185
Powers, code-making, 371
    quasijudicial, 372
    of state board of health, 371
Practices, safety, 197

Predisposition, inherited, 77, 87
Pregnancy, 318
Preservative, alcohol used as, 231
Prevention, farm accidents, 203
    fire, 213
    home accidents, 199
    motor vehicle accidents, 208
    occupational accidents, 204
Prime of life, 34
Professional health organizations, 404
Progesterone, 317
Program, evaluation of safety, 220
    school health, 378
    Standard Highway Safety, 208
Properdin, 30
Prostration, heat, 110
Protein, 142, 226
    deficiency, 155
    requirement, 153
Protoplasm, 72
Protozoa, 334
Psittacosis, 335
Psychosis, 82, 276
    alcoholic, 238
    Huntington's chorea, 88
    manic depressive, 88
    schizophrenia, 87
    syphilitic, 357
Psychosomatic approach, 263
Psychrometer, 111
Ptomaine, 227
Ptosis, 90
Putrefaction, 227
Pyorrhea, 127

Q

Q fever, 335
Quackery, 359
Quarantine, 340, 350
Quarterly Cumulative Index Medicus, 405

R

Rabies, 335
Race and longevity, 40
Radiation, infrared, 109
    ultraviolet, 107
Radioactive particles, 118
Radioisotopes, 52, 367
Radium, 52, 367
Rate, birth, 398
    death, 59, 398
    fatality, 398
    infant mortality, 398
    maternal death, 398
    metabolic, 101
    specific death, 398
Rauwolfia serpentina, 48
Rays, infrared, 109
    ultraviolet, 107
Recessive inheritance, 75
Recreation, 188, 379
    agencies, 380

Recreational—cont'd
    commercial, 189
    community, 188
    facilities, 189
    leadership, 189
Registration, health data, 397
Regulation needs, nutritional, 155
Relapse, 348
Relaxation, 36, 168, 181
Reproduction, 301
    female system, 314
    male system, 309
Research Quarterly, 407
Reservoir, disease, 334
Resistance, 351
Respiration, 243
Rest, 36, 180
    inadequate, 180
Rh incompatibility, 80
Rheumatic fever, 43, 363
Riboflavin, 159
Rickets, 67, 159
Rickettsia, 333
Right Food List, 164
Ringworm, 107
Rockefeller Foundation, 411
Rocky Mountain spotted fever, 333
Roentgen unit, 119
Romans, 325
Roosevelt, F. D., 425
Roosevelt, T., 424
Round shoulders, 186
Routes of transmission, 345
    air, 343
    blocking, 342
    food, 345
    general, 343
    insect-borne, 344
    milk, 344
    social, 347
    soil pollution, 345
    standardized control, 344
    water, 344
Roux, P. E., 331
Royal Observatory, 111
Royal Society of London, 330

S

Safety, 190
    attitudes, 197
    boat, 217
    councils, 192
    farm, 202
    fire, 213
    home, 198
    hunting and fishing, 219
    knowledge, 196
    motor vehicle, 205
    occupational, 204
    practice, 197
    recreational, 215
    skill, 197

Safety—cont'd
  traffic, 208
  water, 215
Salk vaccine, 409
Salpingectomy, 320
Sanguination, 82
Sanitary code, 372
Sanitation, 325, 374, 401
  environmental, 401
Sarcoptes scabiei, 107
Scabies, 107
Scalp, 104
Schaudin, F., 356
Schizophrenia, 87
School health program, 378
Science, health, 65
Scrotum, 309
Scurvy, 67, 158
Secretion, lacrimal, 134
  uterine, 320
Sedative, 230
Self, 264, 265
  -development, 265
  -discipline, 271
  -interest, 272
  -reliance, 270
Semen, 312
Septicemia, 339
Serum, convalescent, 354
Service, college health, 68
  dental, 69
  health education, 402
  laboratory, 401
  medical, 68
Sewage disposal, 386
  treatment, 387
Sewers, 325
Sex, 40
  adjustment, 307
  conflict, 303
  double standard, 304
  education, 301
  experience, 304
  maladjustment, 309
Sex-linked inheritance, 89
Shattuck, Lemuel, 370
Shock therapy, 87
Silver nitrate, 358
Sinusitis, 180, 337
Skill, safety, 197
Skin, 100
  and atmosphere, 110
  preparations, 106
  ultraviolet radiation, 107
Sleep, 181
  cycle, 181
  need, 181
  promotion, 184
Smallpox, 326, 337, 354
Smegma, 312
Smokers' death rates, 240

Smoking, 239
  habit, 248
  tobacco, 239
Sodium thiosulphate, 107
Sore, canker, 128
  cold, 106
Span of life, 37
Specialists, safety, 205
Sperm, 310
Spina bifida, 99
Spirochetes, 333
Spongiosum, 312
Stability, 26, 37, 271
Stage, syphilis, primary, 357
  secondary, 357
  tertiary, 357
Stamina, 271
Staphylococcus albus, 106, 307
State health department, 371
  administration, 374
  dental health, 375
  epidemiology, 374
  health education, 375
  laboratory, 375
  maternal and child health, 375
  mental health, 375
  occupational health, 376
  powers, 371
  sanitation and engineering, 374
  vital statistics, 374
Status, civil, 42
Sterility, 312, 319
Sterilization, 96
  laws, 96
  surgical, 95, 313, 320
Stimulants, effect, 223
Streptococcus hemolyticus, 43
  viridans, 43
Styes, 137
Suffocation, mechanical, 199
Sulfur, 107
Sunburn, 108
Sunlight, 109
Sunshine unit (SU), 119
Sunstroke, 110
Supply, public water, 382
Surgeon General, 415, 417
Survey, farm safety, 203
  home safety, 199
Syndrome, Klinefelter's, 78
  Turner's, 79
Syphilis, 99, 333, 356
System, circulatory, 32
  digestive, 31
  female reproductive, 314
  male reproductive, 309
  neuron, 31
  respiratory, 31

T

Tabes dorsalis, 357
Talcum, 103

Tartar, 127
Teeth, brushing, 121
Temperament, 41
Temperature, 110
Tension, emotional, 180
Terman, Lewis M., 288
Test, basal metabolism, 143
    Friedman, 318
    intelligence, 84
Testis, 310
Testosterone, 310
Tetanus, 184, 332
Thea sinenis, 252
Theobromine, 252
Theophylline, 252
Therapy, biological, 354
    endocrine, 84, 87, 230, 320
    shock, 87
    thyroxin, 84
Thermotherapy, 67
Thiamin, 157
Throat, septic, 129
Thromboangiitis obliterans, 246
Thyroid gland, 92, 101, 144, 150
Thyroxin, 101, 144, 145, 150
Tissue, connective, 31
Tobacco, 239
    composition, 241
Today's Health, 405
Toothbrushing, 121
Toxemia, 180
Toxin, 33, 224, 225, 354
Toxoids, 354
Trachoma, 138
Training, driver, 212
Treatment, sewage, 387
        final, 388
        primary, 387
        secondary, 388
        sludge, 388
Treaty, Geneva, 411
Tree, vascular, 42
Trench mouth, 127
Treponema, pallidum, 127, 333, 356
Trichinosis, 334
Triethylene glycol, 109
Trimesters, 318
Tschermak, E., 76
Tsutsugamushi, 333
Tube, eustachian, 129
    fallopian, 315
Tuberculosis, 180, 331, 337
Tuberculosis Abstracts, 408
Tubules, seminiferous, 310
Tularemia, 335
Turner's syndrome, 79
Twins, identical, 262
Typhoid fever, 67, 333, 336, 337, 338
Typhus fever, 333
    scrub, 333
Tyrosine, 86, 108

U

Ulcer, duodenal, 92
    gastric, 91, 232
    genital, 359
Ultraviolet, 107
Underweight, 150
Undulant fever, 335
U. S. Public Health Service, 415
        budget, 416
        Bureau of Medical Services, 420
        Bureau of State Services, 420
        personnel, 416
Urea, 225
Uremia, 225
Urethra, 311
Uterine ligaments, 320
Uterus, 315

V

Vaccine, 354
Vagina, 314
Values, mental health, 177
van Leeuwenhoek, Anton, 330
Vapors, germicidal, 109
Vas deferens, 311
Vasectomy, 313
Vector, 342
Vehicles of travel, 339
Venom, 223
Ventilation standards, 113
        window-gravity, 114
Veterans Administration, 421
Viral hepatitis, 337, 338
Viripotence, 302
Virus, 333
Visceroptosis, 186
Vision, 130
    conservation, 131
    speed, 135
Vital statistics, 374, 397
Vitamins, 156
    deficiency, 156
    needs, 156
    source, 157, 158, 159
Vocational rehabilitation, 421
von Tschermak, E., 76
Vulva, 314

W

Warts, 106
Wastes, metabolic, 224
Water, 162
    filtration, 385
    ground, 383
    metabolic, 162
    pollution, 326, 383
    supply, 382
    surface, 383, 384
    treatment, 384
Weight, 145
    determination, 145
    fluctuations, 148

White House Conference, 412, 424
Whooping cough, 336, 337
Wicks, Donna, 288
Widowhood, 282, 298
World Health Organization (WHO), 422

X

Xanthines, 252
Xerophthalmia, 67, 134, 157

Y

Yakima County, Washington, 392
Yeast, 231, 334
Yellow fever, 326, 337, 339
Youth, 267

Z

Zoonosis, 326, 335
Zygote, 98, 317